Linux Programming by Example

Arnold Robbins

PRENTICE HALL
Professional Technical Reference
Upper Saddle River, NJ 07458
www.phptr.com

PRENTICE
HALL
PTR

© 2004 Pearson Education, Inc.

Publishing as Prentice Hall Professional Technical Reference

Upper Saddle River, New Jersey 07458

Prentice Hall PTR offers discounts on this book when ordered in quantity for bulk purchases or special sales. For more information, please contact: U.S. Corporate and Government Sales, 1-800-382-3419, corpsales@pearsontechgroup.com. For sales outside of the United States, please contact: International Sales, 1-317-581-3793, international@pearsontechgroup.com.

Printed in the United States of America

ISBN 0-13-142964-7

Text printed on recycled paper

First printing

Pearson Education LTD.
Pearson Education Australia PTY, Limited
Pearson Education Singapore, Pte. Ltd.
Pearson Education North Asia Ltd.
Pearson Education Canada, Ltd.
Pearson Educación de Mexico, S.A. de C.V.
Pearson Education—Japan
Pearson Education Malaysia, Ptd. Ltd.

To my wife Miriam,
and my children,
Chana, Rivka, Nachum, and Malka.

Contents

Preface

O ne of the best ways to learn about programming is to read well-written programs. This book teaches the fundamental Linux system call APIs—those
that form the core of any significant program—by presenting code from production
programs that you use every day.

By looking at concrete programs, you can not only see how to use the Linux APIs,
but you also can examine the real-world issues (performance, portability, robustness)
that arise in writing software.

While the book's title is *Linux Programming by Example*, everything we cover, unless
otherwise noted, applies to modern Unix systems as well. In general we use "Linux"
to mean the Linux kernel, and "GNU/Linux" to mean the total system (kernel, libraries, tools). Also, we often say "Linux" when we mean all of Linux, GNU/Linux
and Unix; if something is specific to one system or the other, we mention it explicitly.

Audience

This book is intended for the person who understands programming and is familiar
with the basics of C, at least on the level of *The C Programming Language* by Kernighan
and Ritchie. (Java programmers wishing to read this book should understand C pointers,
since C code makes heavy use of them.) The examples use both the 1990 version of
Standard C and Original C.

In particular, you should be familiar with all C operators, control-flow structures,
variable and pointer declarations and use, the string management functions, the use of
`exit()`, and the `<stdio.h>` suite of functions for file input/output.

You should understand the basic concepts of *standard input*, *standard output*, and
standard error and the fact that all C programs receive an array of character strings
representing invocation options and arguments. You should also be familiar with the
fundamental command-line tools, such as `cd`, `cp`, `date`, `ln`, `ls`, `man` (and `info` if you

have it), `rmdir`, and `rm`, the use of long and short command-line options, environment variables, and I/O redirection, including pipes.

We assume that you want to write programs that work not just under GNU/Linux but across the range of Unix systems. To that end, we mark each interface as to its availability (GLIBC systems only, or defined by POSIX, and so on), and portability advice is included as an integral part of the text.

The programming taught here may be at a lower level than you're used to; that's OK. The system calls are the fundamental building blocks for higher operations and are thus low-level by nature. This in turn dictates our use of C: The APIs were designed for use from C, and code that interfaces them to higher-level languages, such as C++ and Java, will necessarily be lower level in nature, and most likely, written in C. It may help to remember that "low level" doesn't mean "bad," it just means "more challenging."

What You Will Learn

This book focuses on the basic APIs that form the core of Linux programming:

- Memory management
- File input/output
- File metadata
- Processes and signals
- Users and groups
- Programming support (sorting, argument parsing, and so on)
- Internationalization
- Debugging

We have purposely kept the list of topics short. We believe that it is intimidating to try to learn "all there is to know" from a single book. Most readers prefer smaller, more focused books, and the best Unix books are all written that way.

So, instead of a single giant tome, we plan several volumes: one on Interprocess Communication (IPC) and networking, and another on software development and code portability. We also have an eye toward possible additional volumes in a *Linux*

Programming by Example series that will cover topics such as thread programming and GUI programming.

The APIs we cover include both system calls and library functions. Indeed, at the C level, both appear as simple function calls. A *system call* is a direct request for system services, such as reading or writing a file or creating a process. A *library function*, on the other hand, runs at the user level, possibly never requesting any services from the operating system. System calls are documented in section 2 of the reference manual (viewable online with the `man` command), and library functions are documented in section 3.

Our goal is to teach you the use of the Linux APIs by example: in particular, through the use, wherever possible, of both original Unix source code and the GNU utilities. Unfortunately, there aren't as many self-contained examples as we thought there'd be. Thus, we have written numerous small demonstration programs as well. We stress programming principles: especially those aspects of GNU programming, such as "no arbitrary limits," that make the GNU utilities into exceptional programs.

The choice of everyday programs to study is deliberate. If you've been using GNU/Linux for any length of time, you already understand what programs such as `ls` and `cp` do; it then becomes easy to dive straight into *how* the programs work, without having to spend a lot of time learning *what* they do.

Occasionally, we present both higher-level and lower-level ways of doing things. Usually the higher-level standard interface is implemented in terms of the lower-level interface or construct. We hope that such views of what's "under the hood" will help you understand how things work; for all the code you write, you should always use the higher-level, standard interface.

Similarly, we sometimes introduce functions that provide certain functionality and then recommend (with a provided reason) that these functions be avoided! The primary reason for this approach is so that you'll be able to recognize these functions when you see them and thus understand the code using them. A well-rounded knowledge of a topic requires understanding not just what you can do, but what you should and should not do.

Finally, each chapter concludes with exercises. Some involve modifying or writing code. Others are more in the category of "thought experiments" or "why do you think …" We recommend that you do all of them—they will help cement your understanding of the material.

Small Is Beautiful: Unix Programs

Hoare's law:
"Inside every large program is a small program
struggling to get out."
—C.A.R. Hoare—

Initially, we planned to teach the Linux API by using the code from the GNU utilities. However, the modern versions of even simple command-line programs (like mv and cp) are large and many-featured. This is particularly true of the GNU variants of the standard utilities, which allow long and short options, do everything required by POSIX, and often have additional, seemingly unrelated options as well (like output highlighting).

It then becomes reasonable to ask, "Given such a large and confusing forest, how can we focus on the one or two important trees?" In other words, if we present the current full-featured program, will it be possible to see the underlying core operation of the program?

That is when *Hoare's law*[1] inspired us to look to the original Unix programs for example code. The original V7 Unix utilities are small and straightforward, making it easy to see what's going on and to understand how the system calls are used. (V7 was released around 1979; it is the common ancestor of all modern Unix systems, including GNU/Linux and the BSD systems.)

For many years, Unix source code was protected by copyrights and trade secret license agreements, making it difficult to use for study and impossible to publish. This is still true of all commercial Unix source code. However, in 2002, Caldera (currently operating as SCO) made the original Unix code (through V7 and 32V Unix) available under an Open Source style license (see Appendix B, "Caldera Ancient UNIX License," page 655). This makes it possible for us to include the code from the early Unix system in this book.

Standards

Throughout the book we refer to several different formal standards. A *standard* is a document describing how something works. Formal standards exist for many things, for example, the shape, placement, and meaning of the holes in the electrical outlet in

---

[1] This famous statement was made at *The International Workshop on Efficient Production of Large Programs* in Jablonna, Poland, August 10–14, 1970.

your wall are defined by a formal standard so that all the power cords in your country work in all the outlets.

So, too, formal standards for computing systems define how they are supposed to work; this enables developers and users to know what to expect from their software and enables them to complain to their vendor when software doesn't work.

Of interest to us here are:

1. *ISO/IEC International Standard 9899: Programming Languages — C, 1990.* The first formal standard for the C programming language.

2. *ISO/IEC International Standard 9899: Programming Languages — C, Second edition, 1999.* The second (and current) formal standard for the C programming language.

3. *ISO/IEC International Standard 14882: Programming Languages — C++, 1998.* The first formal standard for the C++ programming language.

4. *ISO/IEC International Standard 14882: Programming Languages — C++, 2003.* The second (and current) formal standard for the C++ programming language.

5. *IEEE Standard 1003.1–2001: Standard for Information Technology — Portable Operating System Interface (POSIX®).* The current version of the POSIX standard; describes the behavior expected of Unix and Unix-like systems. This edition covers both the system call and library interface, as seen by the C/C++ programmer, and the shell and utilities interface, seen by the user. It consists of several volumes:

   • *Base Definitions.* The definitions of terms, facilities, and header files.

   • *Base Definitions — Rationale.* Explanations and rationale for the choice of facilities that both are and are not included in the standard.

   • *System Interfaces.* The system calls and library functions. POSIX terms them all "functions."

   • *Shell and Utilities.* The shell language and utilities available for use with shell programs and interactively.

Although language standards aren't exciting reading, you may wish to consider purchasing a copy of the C standard: It provides the final definition of the language. Copies can be purchased from ANSI[2] and from ISO.[3] (The PDF version of the C standard is quite affordable.)

The POSIX standard can be ordered from The Open Group.[4] By working through their publications catalog to the items listed under "CAE Specifications," you can find individual pages for each part of the standard (named "C031" through "C034"). Each one's page provides free access to the online HTML version of the particular volume.

The POSIX standard is intended for implementation on both Unix and Unix-like systems, as well as non-Unix systems. Thus, the base functionality it provides is a subset of what Unix systems have. However, the POSIX standard also defines optional *extensions*—additional functionality, for example, for threads or real-time support. Of most importance to us is the *X/Open System Interface* (XSI) extension, which describes facilities from historical Unix systems.

Throughout the book, we mark each API as to its availability: ISO C, POSIX, XSI, GLIBC only, or nonstandard but commonly available.

Features and Power: GNU Programs

Restricting ourselves to just the original Unix code would have made an interesting history book, but it would not have been very useful in the 21st century. Modern programs do not have the same constraints (memory, CPU power, disk space, and speed) that the early Unix systems did. Furthermore, they need to operate in a multilingual world—ASCII and American English aren't enough.

More importantly, one of the primary freedoms expressly promoted by the Free Software Foundation and the GNU Project[5] is the "freedom to study." GNU programs are intended to provide a large corpus of well-written programs that journeyman programmers can use as a source from which to learn.

---

[2] http://www.ansi.org

[3] http://www.iso.ch

[4] http://www.opengroup.org

[5] http://www.gnu.org

By using GNU programs, we want to meet both goals: show you well-written, modern code from which you will learn how to write good code and how to use the APIs well.

We believe that GNU software is better because it is free (in the sense of "freedom," not "free beer"). But it's also recognized that GNU software is often *technically* better than the corresponding Unix counterparts, and we devote space in Section 1.4, "Why GNU Programs Are Better," page 14, to explaining why.

A number of the GNU code examples come from gawk (GNU awk). The main reason is that it's a program with which we're very familiar, and therefore it was easy to pick examples from it. We don't otherwise make any special claims about it.

Summary of Chapters

Driving a car is a holistic process that involves multiple simultaneous tasks. In many ways, Linux programming is similar, requiring understanding of multiple aspects of the API, such as file I/O, file metadata, directories, storage of time information, and so on.

The first part of the book looks at enough of these individual items to enable studying the first significant program, the V7 ls. Then we complete the discussion of files and users by looking at file hierarchies and the way filesystems work and are used.

Chapter 1, "Introduction," page 3,
> describes the Unix and Linux file and process models, looks at the differences between Original C and 1990 Standard C, and provides an overview of the principles that make GNU programs generally better than standard Unix programs.

Chapter 2, "Arguments, Options, and the Environment," page 23,
> describes how a C program accesses and processes command-line arguments and options and explains how to work with the environment.

Chapter 3, "User-Level Memory Management," page 51,
> provides an overview of the different kinds of memory in use and available in a running process. User-level memory management is central to every nontrivial application, so it's important to understand it early on.

Chapter 4, "Files and File I/O," page 83,
>   discusses basic file I/O, showing how to create and use files. This understanding is important for everything else that follows.

Chapter 5, "Directories and File Metadata," page 117,
>   describes how directories, hard links, and symbolic links work. It then describes file metadata, such as owners, permissions, and so on, as well as covering how to work with directories.

Chapter 6, "General Library Interfaces — Part 1," page 165,
>   looks at the first set of general programming interfaces that we need so that we can make effective use of a file's metadata.

Chapter 7, "Putting It All Together: `ls`*," page 207,*
>   ties together everything seen so far by looking at the V7 `ls` program.

Chapter 8, "Filesystems and Directory Walks," page 227,
>   describes how filesystems are mounted and unmounted and how a program can tell what is mounted on the system. It also describes how a program can easily "walk" an entire file hierarchy, taking appropriate action for each object it encounters.

The second part of the book deals with process creation and management, interprocess communication with pipes and signals, user and group IDs, and additional general programming interfaces. Next, the book first describes internationalization with GNU `gettext` and then several advanced APIs.

Chapter 9, "Process Management and Pipes," page 283,
>   looks at process creation, program execution, IPC with pipes, and file descriptor management, including nonblocking I/O.

Chapter 10, "Signals," page 347,
>   discusses signals, a simplistic form of interprocess communication. Signals also play an important role in a parent process's management of its children.

Chapter 11, "Permissions and User and Group ID Numbers," page 403,
>   looks at how processes and files are identified, how permission checking works, and how the setuid and setgid mechanisms work.

Chapter 12, "General Library Interfaces — Part 2," page 427,
> looks at the rest of the general APIs; many of these are more specialized than the first general set of APIs.

Chapter 13, "Internationalization and Localization," page 485,
> explains how to enable your programs to work in multiple languages, with almost no pain.

Chapter 14, "Extended Interfaces," page 529,
> describes several extended versions of interfaces covered in previous chapters, as well as covering file locking in full detail.

We round the book off with a chapter on debugging, since (almost) no one gets things right the first time, and we suggest a final project to cement your knowledge of the APIs covered in this book.

Chapter 15, "Debugging," page 567,
> describes the basics of the GDB debugger, transmits as much of our programming experience in this area as possible, and looks at several useful tools for doing different kinds of debugging.

Chapter 16, "A Project That Ties Everything Together," page 641,
> presents a significant programming project that makes use of just about everything covered in the book.

Several appendices cover topics of interest, including the licenses for the source code used in this book.

Appendix A, "Teach Yourself Programming in Ten Years," page 649,
> invokes the famous saying, "Rome wasn't built in a day." So too, Linux/Unix expertise and understanding only come with time and practice. To that end, we have included this essay by Peter Norvig which we highly recommend.

Appendix B, "Caldera Ancient UNIX License," page 655,
> covers the Unix source code used in this book.

Appendix C, "GNU General Public License," page 657,
> covers the GNU source code used in this book.

Typographical Conventions

Like all books on computer-related topics, we use certain typographical conventions to convey information. *Definitions* or first uses of terms appear in italics, like the word "Definitions" at the beginning of this sentence. Italics are also used for *emphasis*, for citations of other works, and for commentary in examples. Variable items such as arguments or filenames, appear `like this`. Occasionally, we use a bold font when a point needs to be made **strongly**.

Things that exist on a computer are in a constant-width font, such as filenames (`foo.c`) and command names (`ls`, `grep`). Short snippets that you type are additionally enclosed in single quotes: '`ls -l *.c`'.

`$` and `>` are the Bourne shell primary and secondary prompts and are used to display interactive examples. **User input** appears in a different font from regular `computer output` in examples. Examples look like this:

```
$ ls -l                      Look at files. Option is digit 1, not letter l
foo
bar
baz
```

We prefer the Bourne shell and its variants (`ksh93`, Bash) over the C shell; thus, all our examples show only the Bourne shell. Be aware that quoting and line-continuation rules are different in the C shell; if you use it, you're on your own![6]

When referring to functions in programs, we append an empty pair of parentheses to the function's name: `printf()`, `strcpy()`. When referring to a manual page (accessible with the `man` command), we follow the standard Unix convention of writing the command or function name in italics and the section in parentheses after it, in regular type: *awk*(1), *printf*(3).

Where to Get Unix and GNU Source Code

You may wish to have copies of the programs we use in this book for your own experimentation and review. All the source code is available over the Internet, and your GNU/Linux distribution contains the source code for the GNU utilities.

---

[6] See the *csh*(1) and *tcsh*(1) manpages and the book *Using csh & tcsh*, by Paul DuBois, O'Reilly & Associates, Sebastopol, CA, USA, 1995. ISBN: 1-56592-132-1.

Unix Code

Archives of various "ancient" versions of Unix are maintained by The UNIX Heritage Society (TUHS), `http://www.tuhs.org`.

Of most interest is that it is possible to browse the archive of old Unix source code on the Web. Start with `http://minnie.tuhs.org/UnixTree/`. All the example code in this book is from the Seventh Edition Research UNIX System, also known as "V7."

The TUHS site is physically located in Australia, although there are mirrors of the archive around the world—see `http://www.tuhs.org/archive_sites.html`. This page also indicates that the archive is available for mirroring with `rsync`. (See `http://rsync.samba.org/` if you don't have `rsync`: It's standard on GNU/Linux systems.)

You will need about 2–3 gigabytes of disk to copy the entire archive. To copy the archive, create an empty directory, and in it, run the following commands:

```
mkdir Applications 4BSD PDP-11 PDP-11/Trees VAX Other

rsync -avz minnie.tuhs.org::UA_Root .
rsync -avz minnie.tuhs.org::UA_Applications Applications
rsync -avz minnie.tuhs.org::UA_4BSD 4BSD
rsync -avz minnie.tuhs.org::UA_PDP11 PDP-11
rsync -avz minnie.tuhs.org::UA_PDP11_Trees PDP-11/Trees
rsync -avz minnie.tuhs.org::UA_VAX VAX
rsync -avz minnie.tuhs.org::UA_Other Other
```

You may wish to omit copying the `Trees` directory, which contains extractions of several versions of Unix, and occupies around 700 megabytes of disk.

You may also wish to consult the TUHS mailing list to see if anyone near you can provide copies of the archive on CD-ROM, to avoid transferring so much data over the Internet.

The folks at Southern Storm Software, Pty. Ltd., in Australia, have "modernized" a portion of the V7 user-level code so that it can be compiled and run on current systems, most notably GNU/Linux. This code can be downloaded from their web site.[7]

It's interesting to note that V7 code does not contain any copyright or permission notices in it. The authors wrote the code primarily for themselves and their research, leaving the permission issues to AT&T's corporate licensing department.

---

[7] `http://www.southern-storm.com.au/v7upgrade.html`

GNU Code

If you're using GNU/Linux, then your distribution will have come with source code, presumably in whatever packaging format it uses (Red Hat RPM files, Debian DEB files, Slackware .tar.gz files, etc.). Many of the examples in the book are from the GNU Coreutils, version 5.0. Find the appropriate CD-ROM for your GNU/Linux distribution, and use the appropriate tool to extract the code. Or follow the instructions in the next few paragraphs to retrieve the code.

If you prefer to retrieve the files yourself from the GNU ftp site, you will find them at ftp://ftp.gnu.org/gnu/coreutils/coreutils-5.0.tar.gz.

You can use the wget utility to retrieve the file:

```
$ wget ftp://ftp.gnu.org/gnu/coreutils/coreutils-5.0.tar.gz       Retrieve the distribution
... lots of output here as file is retrieved ...
```

Alternatively, you can use good old-fashioned ftp to retrieve the file:

```
$ ftp ftp.gnu.org                                    Connect to GNU ftp site
Connected to ftp.gnu.org (199.232.41.7).
220 GNU FTP server ready.
Name (ftp.gnu.org:arnold): anonymous                 Use anonymous ftp
331 Please specify the password.
Password:                                            Password does not echo on screen
230-If you have any problems with the GNU software or its downloading,
230-please refer your questions to <gnu@gnu.org>.
...                                                  Lots of verbiage deleted
230 Login successful. Have fun.
Remote system type is UNIX.
Using binary mode to transfer files.
ftp> cd /gnu/coreutils                               Change to Coreutils directory
250 Directory successfully changed.
ftp> bin
200 Switching to Binary mode.
ftp> hash                                            Print # signs as progress indicators
Hash mark printing on (1024 bytes/hash mark).
ftp> get coreutils-5.0.tar.gz                        Retrieve file
local: coreutils-5.0.tar.gz remote: coreutils-5.0.tar.gz
227 Entering Passive Mode (199,232,41,7,86,107)
150 Opening BINARY mode data connection for coreutils-5.0.tar.gz (6020616 bytes)
###########################################################################
###########################################################################
...
226 File send OK.
6020616 bytes received in 2.03e+03 secs (2.9 Kbytes/sec)
ftp> quit                                            Log off
221 Goodbye.
```

Once you have the file, extract it as follows:

```
$ gzip -dc < coreutils-5.0.tar.gz | tar -xvpf -
... lots of output here as files are extracted ...
```
Extract files

Systems using GNU `tar` may use this incantation:

```
$ tar -xvpzf coreutils-5.0.tar.gz
... lots of output here as files are extracted ...
```
Extract files

In compliance with the GNU General Public License, here is the Copyright information for all GNU programs quoted in this book. All the programs are "free software; you can redistribute it and/or modify it under the terms of the GNU General Public License as published by the Free Software Foundation; either version 2 of the License, or (at your option) any later version." See Appendix C, "GNU General Public License," page 657, for the text of the GNU General Public License.

Coreutils 5.0 File	Copyright dates
lib/safe-read.c	Copyright © 1993–1994, 1998, 2002
lib/safe-write.c	Copyright © 2002
lib/utime.c	Copyright © 1998, 2001–2002
lib/xreadlink.c	Copyright © 2001
src/du.c	Copyright © 1988–1991, 1995–2003
src/env.c	Copyright © 1986, 1991–2003
src/install.c	Copyright © 1989–1991, 1995–2002
src/link.c	Copyright © 2001–2002
src/ls.c	Copyright © 1985, 1988, 1990, 1991, 1995–2003
src/pathchk.c	Copyright © 1991–2003
src/sort.c	Copyright © 1988, 1991–2002
src/sys2.h	Copyright © 1997–2003
src/wc.c	Copyright © 1985, 1991, 1995–2002

Gawk 3.0.6 File	Copyright dates
eval.c	Copyright © 1986, 1988, 1989, 1991–2000

Gawk 3.1.3 File	Copyright dates
`awk.h`	Copyright © 1986, 1988, 1989, 1991–2003
`builtin.c`	Copyright © 1986, 1988, 1989, 1991–2003
`eval.c`	Copyright © 1986, 1988, 1989, 1991–2003
`io.c`	Copyright © 1986, 1988, 1989, 1991–2003
`main.c`	Copyright © 1986, 1988, 1989, 1991–2003
`posix/gawkmisc.c`	Copyright © 1986, 1988, 1989, 1991–1998, 2001–2003
Gawk 3.1.4 File	**Copyright dates**
`builtin.c`	Copyright © 1986, 1988, 1989, 1991–2004
GLIBC 2.3.2 File	**Copyright dates**
`locale/locale.h`	Copyright © 1991, 1992, 1995–2002
`posix/unistd.h`	Copyright © 1991–2003
`time/sys/time.h`	Copyright © 1991–1994, 1996–2003
Make 3.80 File	**Copyright dates**
`read.c`	Copyright © 1988–1997, 2002

Where to Get the Example Programs Used in This Book

The example programs used in this book can be found at `http://authors.phptr.com/robbins`.

About the Cover

> "This is the weapon of a Jedi Knight ..., an elegant weapon for
> a more civilized age. For over a thousand generations the Jedi
> Knights were the guardians of peace and justice in the Old
> Republic. Before the dark times, before the Empire."
> **—Obi-Wan Kenobi—**

You may be wondering why we chose to put a light saber on the cover and to use it throughout the book's interior. What does it represent, and how does it relate to Linux programming?

In the hands of a Jedi Knight, a light saber is both a powerful weapon and a thing of beauty. Its use demonstrates the power, knowledge, control of the Force, and arduous training of the Jedi who wields it.

The elegance of the light saber mirrors the elegance of the original Unix API design. There, too, the studied, precise use of the APIs and the Software Tools and GNU design principles lead to today's powerful, flexible, capable GNU/Linux system. This system demonstrates the knowledge and understanding of the programmers who wrote all its components.

And, of course, light sabers are just way cool!

Acknowledgments

Writing a book is lots of work, and doing it well requires help from many people. Dr. Brian W. Kernighan, Dr. Doug McIlroy, Peter Memishian, and Peter van der Linden reviewed the initial book proposal. David J. Agans, Fred Fish, Don Marti, Jim Meyering, Peter Norvig, and Julian Seward provided reprint permission for various items quoted throughout the book. Thanks to Geoff Collyer, Ulrich Drepper, Yosef Gold, Dr. C.A.R. (Tony) Hoare, Dr. Manny Lehman, Jim Meyering, Dr. Dennis M. Ritchie, Julian Seward, Henry Spencer, and Dr. Wladyslaw M. Turski, who provided much useful general information. Thanks also to the other members of the GNITS gang: Karl Berry, Akim DeMaille, Ulrich Drepper, Greg McGary, Jim Meyering, François Pinard, and Tom Tromey, who all provided helpful feedback about good programming practice. Karl Berry, Alper Ersoy, and Dr. Nelson H.F. Beebe provided valuable technical help with the Texinfo and DocBook/XML toolchains.

Good technical reviewers not only make sure that an author gets his facts right, they also ensure that he thinks carefully about his presentation. Dr. Nelson H.F. Beebe, Geoff Collyer, Russ Cox, Ulrich Drepper, Randy Lechlitner, Dr. Brian W. Kernighan, Peter Memishian, Jim Meyering, Chet Ramey, and Louis Taber acted as technical reviewers for the entire book. Dr. Michael Brennan provided helpful comments on Chapter 15. Both the prose and many of the example programs benefited from their reviews. I hereby thank all of them. As most authors usually say here, "Any remaining errors are mine."

I would especially like to thank Mark Taub of Pearson Education for initiating this project, for his enthusiasm for the series, and for his help and advice as the book moved through its various stages. Anthony Gemmellaro did a phenomenal job of realizing my concept for the cover, and Gail Cocker's interior design is beautiful. Faye Gemmellaro made the production process enjoyable, instead of a chore. Dmitry Kirsanov and Alina Kirsanova did the figures, page layout, and indexing; they were a pleasure to work with.

Finally, my deepest gratitude and love to my wife, Miriam, for her support and encouragement during the book's writing.

Arnold Robbins
Nof Ayalon
ISRAEL

Part

Files and Users

Chapter 1

Introduction

In this chapter

If there is one phrase that summarizes the primary GNU/Linux (and therefore Unix) concepts, it's "files and processes." In this chapter we review the Linux file and process models. These are important to understand because the system calls are almost all concerned with modifying some attribute or part of the state of a file or a process.

Next, because we'll be examining code in both styles, we briefly review the major difference between 1990 Standard C and Original C. Finally, we discuss at some length what makes GNU programs "better," programming principles that we'll see in use in the code.

This chapter contains a number of intentional simplifications. The full details are covered as we progress through the book. If you're already a Linux wizard, please forgive us.

1.1 The Linux/Unix File Model

One of the driving goals in the original Unix design was *simplicity*. Simple concepts are easy to learn and use. When the concepts are translated into simple APIs, simple programs are then easy to design, write, and get correct. In addition, simple code is often smaller and more efficient than more complicated designs.

The quest for simplicity was driven by two factors. From a technical point of view, the original PDP-11 minicomputers on which Unix was developed had a small address space: 64 Kilobytes total on the smaller systems, 64K code and 64K of data on the large ones. These restrictions applied not just to regular programs (so-called *user level* code), but to the operating system itself (*kernel level* code). Thus, not only "Small Is Beautiful" aesthetically, but "Small Is Beautiful" because there was no other choice!

The second factor was a negative reaction to contemporary commercial operating systems, which were needlessly complicated, with obtuse command languages, multiple kinds of file I/O, and little generality or symmetry. (Steve Johnson once remarked that "Using TSO is like trying to kick a dead whale down a beach." TSO is one of the obtuse mainframe time-sharing systems just described.)

1.1.1 Files and Permissions

The Unix file model is as simple as it gets: A file is a linear stream of bytes. Period. The operating system imposes no preordained structure on files: no fixed or varying record sizes, no indexed files, nothing. The interpretation of file contents is entirely up to the application. (This isn't quite true, as we'll see shortly, but it's close enough for a start.)

Once you have a file, you can do three things with the file's data: read them, write them, or execute them.

Unix was designed for time-sharing minicomputers; this implies a multiuser environment from the get-go. Once there are multiple users, it must be possible to specify a file's permissions: Perhaps user `jane` is user `fred`'s boss, and `jane` doesn't want `fred` to read the latest performance evaluations.

For file permission purposes, users are classified into three distinct categories: *user*: the owner of a file; *group*: the group of users associated with this file (discussed shortly); and *other*: anybody else. For each of these categories, *every* file has separate read, write, and execute permission bits associated with it, yielding a total of nine permission bits. This shows up in the first field of the output of '`ls -l`':

```
$ ls -l progex.texi
-rw-r--r--    1 arnold    devel         5614 Feb 24 18:02 progex.texi
```

Here, `arnold` and `devel` are the owner and group of `progex.texi`, and `-rw-r--r--` are the file type and permissions. The first character is a dash for regular file, a `d` for directories, or one of a small set of other characters for other kinds of files that aren't important at the moment. Each subsequent group of three characters represents read, write, and execute permission for the owner, group, and "other," respectively.

In this example, `progex.texi` is readable and writable by the owner, and readable by the group and other. The dashes indicate absent permissions, thus the file is not executable by anyone, nor is it writable by the group or other.

The owner and group of a file are stored as numeric values known as the *user ID* (UID) and *group ID* (GID); standard library functions that we present later in the book make it possible to print the values as human-readable names.

A file's owner can change the permission by using the `chmod` (change mode) command. (As such, file permissions are sometimes referred to as the "file mode.") A file's group can be changed with the `chgrp` (change group) and `chown` (change owner) commands.[1]

---

[1] Some systems allow regular users to change the ownership on their files to someone else, thus "giving them away." The details are standardized by POSIX but are a bit messy. Typical GNU/Linux configurations do not allow it.

Group permissions were intended to support cooperative work: Although one person in a group or department may own a particular file, perhaps everyone in that group needs to be able to modify it. (Consider a collaborative marketing paper or data from a survey.)

When the system goes to check a file access (usually upon opening a file), if the UID of the process matches that of the file, the owner permissions apply. If those permissions deny the operation (say, a write to a file with `-r--rw-rw-` permissions), the operation fails; Unix and Linux do not proceed to test the group and other permissions.[2] The same is true if the UID is different but the GID matches; if the group permissions deny the operation, it fails.

Unix and Linux support the notion of a *superuser*: a user with special privileges. This user is known as `root` and has the UID of 0. `root` is allowed to do **anything**; all bets are off, all doors are open, all drawers unlocked.[3] (This can have significant security implications, which we touch on throughout the book but do not cover exhaustively.) Thus, even if a file is mode `----------`, `root` can still read and write the file. (One exception is that the file can't be executed. But as `root` can add execute permission, the restriction doesn't prevent anything.)

The user/group/other, read/write/execute permissions model is simple, yet flexible enough to cover most situations. Other, more powerful but more complicated, models exist and are implemented on different systems, but none of them are well enough standardized and broadly enough implemented to be worth discussing in a general-purpose text like this one.

1.1.2 Directories and Filenames

Once you have a file, you need someplace to keep it. This is the purpose of the *directory* (known as a "folder" on Windows and Apple Macintosh systems). A directory is a special kind of file, which associates filenames with particular collections of file metadata, known as *inodes*. Directories are special because they can only be updated by the operating system, by the system calls described in Chapter 4, "Files and File I/O,"

---

[2] The owner can always change the permission, of course. Most users don't disable write permission for themselves.

[3] There are some rare exceptions to this rule, all of which are beyond the scope of this book.

page 83. They are also special in that the operating system dictates the format of directory entries.

Filenames may contain any valid 8-bit byte except the / (forward slash) character and ASCII NUL, the character whose bits are all zero. Early Unix systems limited filenames to 14 bytes; modern systems allow individual filenames to be up to 255 bytes.

The inode contains all the information about a file except its name: the type, owner, group, permissions, size, modification and access times. It also stores the locations on disk of the blocks containing the file's data. All of these are data *about* the file, not the file's data itself, thus the term *metadata*.

Directory permissions have a slightly different meaning from those for file permissions. Read permission means the ability to search the directory; that is, to look through it to see what files it contains. Write permission is the ability to create *and remove* files in the directory. Execute permission is the ability to go through a directory when opening or otherwise accessing a contained file or subdirectory.

> NOTE If you have write permission on a directory, you can remove files in that directory, even if they don't belong to you! When used interactively, the rm command notices this, and asks you for confirmation in such a case.
>
> The /tmp directory has write permission for everyone, but your files in /tmp are quite safe because /tmp usually has the so-called sticky bit set on it:
>
> ```
> $ ls -ld /tmp
> drwxrwxrwt   11 root     root         4096 May 15 17:11 /tmp
> ```
>
> Note the t is the last position of the first field. On most directories this position has an x in it. With the sticky bit set, only you, as the file's owner, or root may remove your files. (We discuss this in more detail in Section 11.5.2, "Directories and the Sticky Bit," page 414.)

1.1.3 Executable Files

Remember we said that the operating system doesn't impose a structure on files? Well, we've already seen that that was a white lie when it comes to directories. It's also the case for binary executable files. To run a program, the kernel has to know what part of a file represents instructions (code) and what part represents data. This leads to the notion of an *object file format*, which is the definition for how these things are laid out within a file on disk.

Although the kernel will only run a file laid out in the proper format, it is up to user-level utilities to create these files. The compiler for a programming language (such as Ada, Fortran, C, or C++) creates object files, and then a linker or loader (usually named `ld`) binds the object files with library routines to create the final executable. Note that even if a file has all the right bits in all the right places, the kernel won't run it if the appropriate execute permission bit isn't turned on (or at least one execute bit for `root`).

Because the compiler, assembler, and loader are user-level tools, it's (relatively) easy to change object file formats as needs develop over time; it's only necessary to "teach" the kernel about the new format and then it can be used. The part that loads executables is relatively small and this isn't an impossible task. Thus, Unix file formats have evolved over time. The original format was known as `a.out` (Assembler OUTput). The next format, still used on some commercial systems, is known as COFF (Common Object File Format), and the current, most widely used format is ELF (Extensible Linking Format). Modern GNU/Linux systems use ELF.

The kernel recognizes that an executable file contains binary object code by looking at the first few bytes of the file for special *magic numbers*. These are sequences of two or four bytes that the kernel recognizes as being special. For backwards compatibility, modern Unix systems recognize multiple formats. ELF files begin with the four characters `"\177ELF"`.

Besides binary executables, the kernel also supports executable *scripts*. Such a file also begins with a magic number: in this case, the two regular characters `#!`. A script is a program executed by an interpreter, such as the shell, `awk`, Perl, Python, or Tcl. The `#!` line provides the full path to the interpreter and, optionally, one single argument:

```
#! /bin/awk -f

BEGIN { print "hello, world" }
```

Let's assume the above contents are in a file named `hello.awk` and that the file is executable. When you type '`hello.awk`', the kernel runs the program as if you had typed '`/bin/awk -f hello.awk`'. Any additional command-line arguments are also passed on to the program. In this case, `awk` runs the program and prints the universally known `hello, world` message.

The `#!` mechanism is an elegant way of hiding the distinction between binary executables and script executables. If `hello.awk` is renamed to just `hello`, the user typing 'hello' can't tell (and indeed shouldn't have to know) that hello isn't a binary executable program.

1.1.4 Devices

One of Unix's most notable innovations was the unification of file I/O and device I/O.[4] Devices appear as files in the filesystem, regular permissions apply to their access, and the same I/O system calls are used for opening, reading, writing, and closing them. All of the "magic" to make devices look like files is hidden in the kernel. This is just another aspect of the driving simplicity principle in action: We might phrase it as *no special cases for user code.*

Two devices appear frequently in everyday use, particularly at the shell level: /dev/null and /dev/tty.

/dev/null is the "bit bucket." All data sent to /dev/null is discarded by the operating system, and attempts to read from it always return end-of-file (EOF) immediately.

/dev/tty is the process's current controlling terminal—the one to which it listens when a user types the interrupt character (typically CTRL-C) or performs job control (CTRL-Z).

GNU/Linux systems, and many modern Unix systems, supply /dev/stdin, /dev/stdout, and /dev/stderr devices, which provide a way to name the open files each process inherits upon startup.

Other devices represent real hardware, such as tape and disk drives, CD-ROM drives, and serial ports. There are also software devices, such as pseudo-ttys, that are used for networking logins and windowing systems. /dev/console represents the system console, a particular hardware device on minicomputers. On modern computers, /dev/console is the screen and keyboard, but it could be a serial port.

Unfortunately, device-naming conventions are not standardized, and each operating system has different names for tapes, disks, and so on. (Fortunately, that's not an issue for what we cover in this book.) Devices have either a b or c in the first character of 'ls -l' output:

---

[4] This feature first appeared in Multics, but Multics was never widely used.

```
$ ls -l /dev/tty /dev/hda
brw-rw----   1 root      disk       3,    0 Aug 31 02:31 /dev/hda
crw-rw-rw-   1 root      root       5,    0 Feb 26 08:44 /dev/tty
```

The initial b represents block devices, and a c represents character devices. Device files are discussed further in Section 5.4, "Obtaining Information about Files," page 139.

1.2 The Linux/Unix Process Model

A process is a running program.[5] Processes have the following attributes:

- A unique process identifier (the PID)
- A parent process (with an associated identifier, the PPID)
- Permission identifiers (UID, GID, groupset, and so on)
- An address space, separate from those of all other processes
- A program running in that address space
- A current working directory ('.')
- A current root directory (/; changing this is an advanced topic)
- A set of open files, directories, or both
- A permissions-to-deny mask for use in creating new files
- A set of strings representing the environment
- A scheduling priority (an advanced topic)
- Settings for signal disposition (an advanced topic)
- A controlling terminal (also an advanced topic)

When the main() function begins execution, all of these things have already been put in place for the running program. System calls are available to query and change each of the above items; covering them is the purpose of this book.

New processes are always created by an existing process. The existing process is termed the *parent*, and the new process is termed the *child*. Upon booting, the kernel handcrafts the first, primordial process, which runs the program /sbin/init; it has process ID

---

[5] Processes can be suspended, in which case they are not "running"; however, neither are they terminated. In any case, in the early stages of the climb up the learning curve, it pays not to be too pedantic.

`1` and serves several administrative functions. All other processes are descendants of `init`. (`init`'s parent is the kernel, often listed as process ID `0`.)

The child-to-parent relationship is one-to-one; each process has only one parent, and thus it's easy to find out the PID of the parent. The parent-to-child relationship is one-to-many; any given process can create a potentially unlimited number of children. Thus, there is no easy way for a process to find out the PIDs of all its children. (In practice, it's not necessary, anyway.) A parent process can arrange to be notified when a child process terminates ("dies"), and it can also explicitly wait for such an event.

Each process's address space (memory) is separate from that of every other. Unless two processes have made explicit arrangement to share memory, one process cannot affect the address space of another. This is important; it provides a basic level of security and system reliability. (For efficiency, the system arranges to share the read-only executable code of the same program among all the processes running that program. This is transparent to the user and to the running program.)

The current working directory is the one to which relative pathnames (those that don't start with a `/`) are relative. This is the directory you are "in" whenever you issue a '`cd someplace`' command to the shell.

By convention, all programs start out with three files already open: standard input, standard output, and standard error. These are where input comes from, output goes to, and error messages go to, respectively. In the course of this book, we will see how these are put in place. A parent process can open additional files and have them already available for a child process; the child will have to know they're there, either by way of some convention or by a command-line argument or environment variable.

The *environment* is a set of strings, each of the form '`name=value`'. Functions exist for querying and setting environment variables, and child processes inherit the environment of their parents. Typical environment variables are things like PATH and HOME in the shell. Many programs look for the existence and value of specific environment variables in order to control their behavior.

It is important to understand that a single process may execute multiple programs during its lifetime. Unless explicitly changed, *all* of the other system-maintained attributes (current directory, open files, PID, etc.) remain the same. The separation of "starting a new process" from "choosing which program to run" is a key Unix innovation.

It makes many operations simple and straightforward. Other operating systems that combine the two operations are less general and more complicated to use.

1.2.1 Pipes: Hooking Processes Together

You've undoubtedly used the pipe construct ('|') in the shell to connect two or more running programs. A pipe acts like a file: One process writes to it using the normal write operation, and the other process reads from it using the read operation. The processes don't (usually) know that their input/output is a pipe and not a regular file.

Just as the kernel hides the "magic" for devices, making them act like regular files, so too the kernel does the work for pipes, arranging to pause the pipe's writer when the pipe fills up and to pause the reader when no data is waiting to be read.

The file I/O paradigm with pipes thus acts as a key mechanism for connecting running programs; no temporary files are needed. Again, generality and simplicity at work: no special cases for user code.

1.3 Standard C vs. Original C

For many years, the de facto definition of C was found in the first edition of the book *The C Programming Language*, by Brian Kernighan and Dennis Ritchie. This book described C as it existed for Unix and on the systems to which the Bell Labs developers had ported it. Throughout this book, we refer to it as "Original C," although it's also common for it to be referred to as "K&R C," after the book's two authors. (Dennis Ritchie designed and implemented C.)

The 1990 ISO Standard for C formalized the language's definition, including the functions in the C library (such as `printf()` and `fopen()`). The C standards committee did an admirable job of standardizing existing practice and avoided inventing new features, with one notable exception (and a few minor ones). The most visible change in the language was the use of *function prototypes*, borrowed from C++.

Standard C, C++, and the Java programming language use function prototypes for function declarations and definitions. A prototype describes not only the function's return value but also the number and type of its arguments. With prototypes, a compiler can do complete type checking at the point of a function call:

```
extern int myfunc(struct my_struct *a,          Declaration
                  struct my_struct *b,
                  double c, int d);

int myfunc(struct my_struct *a,                 Definition
           struct my_struct *b,
           double c, int d)
{
    ...
}

...
struct my_struct s, t;
int j;

...
/* Function call, somewhere else: */
j = my_func(& s, & t, 3.1415, 42);
```

This function call is fine. But consider an erroneous call:

```
j = my_func(-1, -2, 0);                         Wrong number and types of arguments
```

The compiler can immediately diagnose this call as being invalid. However, in Original C, functions are declared without the argument list being specified:

```
extern int myfunc();                            Returns int, arguments unknown
```

Furthermore, function definitions list the parameter names in the function header, and then declare the parameters before the function body. Parameters of type int don't have to be declared, and if a function returns int, that doesn't have to be declared either:

```
myfunc(a, b, c, d)                              Return type is int
struct my_struct *a, *b;
double c;                                       Note, no declaration of parameter d
{
    ...
}
```

Consider again the same erroneous function call: 'j = my_func(-1, -2, 0);'. In Original C, the compiler has no way of knowing that you've (accidentally, we assume) passed the wrong arguments to my_func(). Such erroneous calls generally lead to hard-to-find runtime problems (such as segmentation faults, whereby the program dies), and the Unix lint program was created to deal with these kinds of things.

So, although function prototypes were a radical departure from existing practice, their additional type checking was deemed too important to be without, and they were added to the language with little opposition.

In 1990 Standard C, code written in the original style, for both declarations and definitions, is valid. This makes it possible to continue to compile millions of lines of existing code with a standard-conforming compiler. New code, obviously, should be written with prototypes because of the improved possibilities for compile-time error checking.

1999 Standard C continues to allow original style declarations and definitions. However, the "implicit `int`" rule was removed; functions must have a return type, and all parameters must be declared.

Furthermore, when a program called a function that had not been formally declared, Original C would create an implicit declaration for the function, giving it a return type of `int`. 1990 Standard C did the same, additionally noting that it had no information about the parameters. 1999 Standard C no longer provides this "auto-declare" feature.

Other notable additions in Standard C are the `const` keyword, also from C++, and the `volatile` keyword, which the committee invented. For the code you'll see in this book, understanding the different function declaration and definition syntaxes is the most important thing.

For V7 code using original style definitions, we have added comments showing the equivalent prototype. Otherwise, we have left the code alone, preferring to show it exactly as it was originally written and as you'll see it if you download the code yourself.

Although 1999 C adds some additional keywords and features beyond the 1990 version, we have chosen to stick to the 1990 dialect, since C99 compilers are not yet commonplace. Practically speaking, this doesn't matter: C89 code should compile and run without change when a C99 compiler is used, and the new C99 features don't affect our discussion or use of the fundamental Linux/Unix APIs.

1.4 Why GNU Programs Are Better

What is it that makes a GNU program a GNU program?[6] What makes GNU software "better" than other (free or non-free) software? The most obvious difference is the GNU General Public License (GPL), which describes the distribution terms for GNU software. But this is usually not the reason you hear people saying "Get the GNU version of `xyz`,

---

[6] This section is adapted from an article by the author that appeared in Issue 16 of *Linux Journal*. (See `http://www.linuxjournal.com/article.php?sid=1135`.) Reprinted and adapted by permission.

it's much better." GNU software is generally more robust, and performs better, than standard Unix versions. In this section we look at some of the reasons why, and at the document that describes the principles of GNU software design.

The *GNU Coding Standards* describes how to write software for the GNU project. It covers a range of topics. You can read the *GNU Coding Standards* online at `http://www.gnu.org/prep/standards.html`. See the online version for pointers to the source files in other formats.

In this section, we describe only those parts of the *GNU Coding Standards* that relate to program design and implementation.

1.4.1 Program Design

Chapter 3 of the *GNU Coding Standards* provides general advice about program design. The four main issues are compatibility (with standards and Unix), the language to write in, reliance on nonstandard features of other programs (in a word, "none"), and the meaning of "portability."

Compatibility with Standard C and POSIX, and to a lesser extent, with Berkeley Unix is an important goal. But it's not an overriding one. The general idea is to provide all necessary functionality, with command-line switches to provide a strict ISO or POSIX mode.

C is the preferred language for writing GNU software since it is the most commonly available language. In the Unix world, Standard C is now common, but if you can easily support Original C, you should do so. Although the coding standards prefer C over C++, C++ is now commonplace too. One widely used GNU package written in C++ is `groff` (GNU `troff`). With GCC supporting C++, it has been our experience that installing `groff` is not difficult.

The standards state that portability is a bit of a red herring. GNU utilities are ultimately intended to run on the GNU kernel with the GNU C Library.[7] But since the kernel isn't finished yet and users are using GNU tools on non-GNU systems, portability is desirable, just not paramount. The standard recommends using Autoconf for achieving portability among different Unix systems.

---

[7] This statement refers to the HURD kernel, which is still under development (as of early 2004). GCC and GNU C Library (GLIBC) development take place mostly on Linux-based systems today.

1.4.2 Program Behavior

Chapter 4 of the *GNU Coding Standards* provides general advice about program behavior. We will return to look at one of its sections in detail, below. The chapter focuses on program design, formatting error messages, writing libraries (by making them reentrant), and standards for the command-line interface.

Error message formatting is important since several tools, notably Emacs, use the error messages to help you go straight to the point in the source file or data file at which an error occurred.

GNU utilities should use a function named `getopt_long()` for processing the command line. This function provides command-line option parsing for both traditional Unix-style options ('`gawk -F: ...`') and GNU-style long options ('`gawk --field-separator=: ...`'). All programs should provide `--help` and `--version` options, and when a long name is used in one program, it should be used the same way in other GNU programs. To this end, there is a rather exhaustive list of long options used by current GNU programs.

As a simple yet obvious example, `--verbose` is spelled exactly the same way in *all* GNU programs. Contrast this to `-v`, `-V`, `-d`, etc., in many Unix programs. Most of Chapter 2, "Arguments, Options, and the Environment," page 23, is devoted to the mechanics of argument and option parsing.

1.4.3 C Code Programming

The most substantive part of the *GNU Coding Standards* is Chapter 5, which describes how to write C code, covering things like formatting the code, correct use of comments, using C cleanly, naming your functions and variables, and declaring, or not declaring, standard system functions that you wish to use.

Code formatting is a religious issue; many people have different styles that they prefer. We personally don't like the FSF's style, and if you look at `gawk`, which we maintain, you'll see it's formatted in standard K&R style (the code layout style used in both editions of the Kernighan and Ritchie book). But this is the only variation in `gawk` from this part of the coding standards.

Nevertheless, even though we don't like the FSF's style, we feel that when modifying some other program, sticking to the coding style already used is of the utmost importance. Having a consistent coding style is more important than which coding style you pick. The *GNU Coding Standards* also makes this point. (Sometimes, there is no detectable consistent coding style, in which case the program is probably overdue for a trip through either GNU `indent` or Unix's `cb`.)

What we find important about the chapter on C coding is that the advice is good for *any* C coding, not just if you happen to be working on a GNU program. So, if you're just learning C or even if you've been working in C (or C++) for a while, we recommend this chapter to you since it encapsulates many years of experience.

1.4.4 Things That Make a GNU Program Better

We now examine the section titled *Writing Robust Programs* in Chapter 4, *Program Behavior for All Programs*, of the *GNU Coding Standards*. This section provides the principles of software design that make GNU programs better than their Unix counterparts. We quote selected parts of the chapter, with some examples of cases in which these principles have paid off.

> Avoid arbitrary limits on the length or number of *any* data structure, including file names, lines, files, and symbols, by allocating all data structures dynamically. In most Unix utilities, "long lines are silently truncated." This is not acceptable in a GNU utility.

This rule is perhaps the single most important rule in GNU software design—*no arbitrary limits*. All GNU utilities should be able to manage arbitrary amounts of data.

While this requirement perhaps makes it harder for the programmer, it makes things much better for the user. At one point, we had a `gawk` user who regularly ran an `awk` program on more than 650,000 files (no, that's not a typo) to gather statistics. `gawk` would grow to over 192 megabytes of data space, and the program ran for around seven CPU hours. He would not have been able to run his program using another `awk` implementation.[8]

> Utilities reading files should not drop NUL characters, or any other nonprinting characters *including those with codes above 0177*. The only sensible exceptions would be utilities specifically intended for interface to certain types of terminals or printers that can't handle those characters.

---

8 This situation occurred circa 1993; the truism is even more obvious today, as users process gigabytes of log files with `gawk`.

It is also well known that Emacs can edit any arbitrary file, including files containing binary data!

> Whenever possible, try to make programs work properly with sequences of bytes that represent multibyte characters, using encodings such as UTF-8 and others.[9] Check every system call for an error return, unless you know you wish to ignore errors. Include the system error text (from `perror` or equivalent) in *every* error message resulting from a failing system call, as well as the name of the file if any and the name of the utility. Just "cannot open foo.c" or "stat failed" is not sufficient.

Checking every system call provides robustness. This is another case in which life is harder for the programmer but better for the user. An error message detailing what exactly went wrong makes finding and solving any problems much easier.[10]

Finally, we quote from Chapter 1 of the *GNU Coding Standards*, which discusses how to write your program differently from the way a Unix program may have been written.

> For example, Unix utilities were generally optimized to minimize memory use; if you go for speed instead, your program will be very different. You could keep the entire input file in core and scan it there instead of using stdio. Use a smarter algorithm discovered more recently than the Unix program. Eliminate use of temporary files. Do it in one pass instead of two (we did this in the assembler).

> Or, on the contrary, emphasize simplicity instead of speed. For some applications, the speed of today's computers makes simpler algorithms adequate.

> Or go for generality. For example, Unix programs often have static tables or fixed-size strings, which make for arbitrary limits; use dynamic allocation instead. Make sure your program handles NULs and other funny characters in the input files. Add a programming language for extensibility and write part of the program in that language.

---

[9] Section 13.4, "Can You Spell That for Me, Please?", page 521, provides an overview of multibyte characters and encodings.

[10] The mechanics of checking for and reporting errors are discussed in Section 4.3, "Determining What Went Wrong," page 86.

> Or turn some parts of the program into independently usable libraries. Or use a simple garbage collector instead of tracking precisely when to free memory, or use a new GNU facility such as obstacks.

An excellent example of the difference an algorithm can make is GNU `diff`. One of our system's early incarnations was an AT&T 3B1: a system with a MC68010 processor, a whopping two megabytes of memory and 80 megabytes of disk. We did (and do) lots of editing on the manual for `gawk`, a file that is almost 28,000 lines long (although at the time, it was only in the 10,000-lines range). We used to use '`diff -c`' quite frequently to look at our changes. On this slow system, switching to GNU `diff` made a stunning difference in the amount of time it took for the context diff to appear. The difference is almost entirely due to the better algorithm that GNU `diff` uses.

The final paragraph mentions the idea of structuring a program as an independently usable library, with a command-line wrapper or other interface around it. One example of this is GDB, the GNU debugger, which is partially implemented as a command-line tool on top of a debugging library. (The separation of the GDB core functionality from the command interface is an ongoing development project.) This implementation makes it possible to write a graphical debugging interface on top of the basic debugging functionality.

1.4.5 Parting Thoughts about the "GNU Coding Standards"

The *GNU Coding Standards* is a worthwhile document to read if you wish to develop new GNU software, enhance existing GNU software, or just learn how to be a better programmer. The principles and techniques it espouses are what make GNU software the preferred choice of the Unix community.

1.5 Portability Revisited

Portability is something of a holy grail; always sought after, but not always obtainable, and certainly not easily. There are several aspects to writing portable code. The *GNU Coding Standards* discusses many of them. But there are others as well. Keep portability in mind at both higher and lower levels as you develop. We recommend these practices:

Code to standards.

> Although it can be challenging, it pays to be familiar with the formal standards for the language you're using. In particular, pay attention to the 1990 and 1999

ISO standards for C and the 2003 standard for C++ since most Linux programming is done in one of those two languages.

Also, the POSIX standard for library and system call interfaces, while large, has broad industry support. Writing to POSIX greatly improves the chances of successfully moving your code to other systems besides GNU/Linux. This standard is quite readable; it distills decades of experience and good practice.

Pick the best interface for the job.

If a standard interface does what you need, use it in your code. Use Autoconf to detect an unavailable interface, and supply a replacement version of it for deficient systems. (For example, some older systems lack the `memmove()` function, which is fairly easy to code by hand or to pull from the GLIBC library.)

Isolate portability problems behind new interfaces.

Sometimes, you may need to do operating-system-specific tasks that apply on some systems but not on others. (For example, on some systems, each program has to expand command-line wildcards instead of the shell doing it.) Create a new interface that does nothing on systems that don't need it but does the correct thing on systems that do.

Use Autoconf for configuration.

Avoid `#ifdef` if possible. If not, bury it in low-level library code. Use Autoconf to do the checking for the tests to be performed with `#ifdef`.

1.6 Suggested Reading

1. *The C Programming Language*, 2nd edition, by Brian W. Kernighan and Dennis M. Ritchie. Prentice-Hall, Englewood Cliffs, New Jersey, USA, 1989. ISBN: 0-13-110370-9.

   This is the "bible" for C, covering the 1990 version of Standard C. It is a rather dense book, with lots of information packed into a startlingly small number of pages. You may need to read it through more than once; doing so is well worth the trouble.

2. *C, A Reference Manual*, 5th edition, by Samuel P. Harbison III and Guy L. Steele, Jr. Prentice-Hall, Upper Saddle River, New Jersey, USA, 2002. ISBN: 0-13-089592-X.

This book is also a classic. It covers Original C as well as the 1990 and 1999 standards. Because it is current, it makes a valuable companion to *The C Programming Language*. It covers many important items, such as internationalization-related types and library functions, that aren't in the Kernighan and Ritchie book.

3. *Notes on Programming in C*, by Rob Pike, February 21, 1989. Available on the Web from many sites. Perhaps the most widely cited location is `http://www.lysator.liu.se/c/pikestyle.html`. (Many other useful articles are available from one level up: `http://www.lysator.liu.se/c/`.)

   Rob Pike worked for many years at the Bell Labs research center where C and Unix were invented and did pioneering development there. His notes distill many years of experience into a "philosophy of clarity in programming" that is well worth reading.

4. The various links at `http://www.chris-lott.org/resources/cstyle/`. This site includes Rob Pike's notes and several articles by Henry Spencer. Of particular note is the *Recommended C Style and Coding Standards*, originally written at the Bell Labs Indian Hill site.

1.7 Summary

- "Files and processes" summarizes the Linux/Unix worldview. The treatment of files as byte streams and devices as files, and the use of standard input, output, and error, simplify program design and unify the data access model. The permissions model is simple, yet flexible, applying to both files and directories.

- Processes are running programs that have user and group identifiers associated with them for permission checking, as well as other attributes such as open files and a current working directory.

- The most visible difference between Standard C and Original C is the use of function prototypes for stricter type checking. A good C programmer should be able to read Original-style code, since many existing programs use it. New code should be written using prototypes.

- The *GNU Coding Standards* describe how to write GNU programs. They provide numerous valuable techniques and guiding principles for producing robust, usable software. The "no arbitrary limits" principle is perhaps the single most important of these. This document is required reading for serious programmers.

• Making programs portable is a significant challenge. Guidelines and tools help, but ultimately experience is needed too.

Exercises

1. Read and comment on the article "The GNU Project",[11] by Richard M. Stallman, originally written in August of 1998.

---

[11] http://www.gnu.org/gnu/thegnuproject.html

Chapter 2

Arguments,
Options,
and
the Environment

In this chapter

C ommand-line option and argument interpretation is usually the first task of any program. This chapter examines how C (and C++) programs access their command-line arguments, describes standard routines for parsing options, and takes a look at the environment.

2.1 Option and Argument Conventions

The word *arguments* has two meanings. The more technical definition is "all the 'words' on the command line." For example:

```
$ ls main.c opts.c process.c
```

Here, the user typed four "words." All four words are made available to the program as its arguments.

The second definition is more informal: Arguments are all the words on the command line *except* the command name. By default, Unix shells separate arguments from each other with *whitespace* (spaces or TAB characters). Quoting allows arguments to include whitespace:

```
$ echo here are lots    of spaces
here are lots of spaces                              The shell "eats" the spaces
$ echo "here are lots    of spaces"
here are lots    of spaces                           Spaces are preserved
```

Quoting is transparent to the running program; echo never sees the double-quote characters. (Double and single quotes are different in the shell; a discussion of the rules is beyond the scope of this book, which focuses on C programming.)

Arguments can be further classified as *options* or *operands*. In the previous two examples all the arguments were operands: files for ls and raw text for echo.

Options are special arguments that each program interprets. Options change a program's behavior, or they provide information to the program. By ancient convention, (almost) universally adhered to, options start with a dash (a.k.a. hyphen, minus sign) and consist of a single letter. *Option arguments* are information needed by an option, as opposed to regular operand arguments. For example, the fgrep program's -f option means "use the contents of the following file as a list of strings to search for." See Figure 2.1.

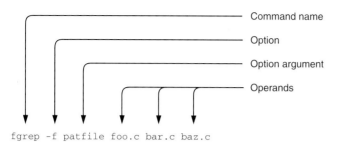

```
fgrep -f patfile foo.c bar.c baz.c
```

FIGURE 2.1
Command-line components

Thus, `patfile` is not a data file to search, but rather it's for use by `fgrep` in defining the list of strings to search for.

2.1.1 POSIX Conventions

The POSIX standard describes a number of conventions that standard-conforming programs adhere to. Nothing requires that your programs adhere to these standards, but it's a good idea for them to do so: Linux and Unix users the world over understand and use these conventions, and if your program doesn't follow them, your users will be unhappy. (Or you won't have any users!) Furthermore, the functions we discuss later in this chapter relieve you of the burden of manually adhering to these conventions for each program you write. Here they are, paraphrased from the standard:

1. Program names should have no less than two and no more than nine characters.

2. Program names should consist of only lowercase letters and digits.

3. Option names should be single alphanumeric characters. Multidigit options should not be allowed. For vendors implementing the POSIX utilities, the `-W` option is reserved for vendor-specific options.

4. All options should begin with a '-' character.

5. For options that don't require option arguments, it should be possible to group multiple options after a single '-' character. (For example, '`foo -a -b -c`' and '`foo -abc`' should be treated the same way.)

6. When an option does require an option argument, the argument should be separated from the option by a space (for example, '`fgrep -f patfile`').

The standard, however, does allow for historical practice, whereby sometimes the option and the operand could be in the same string: 'fgrep -fpatfile'. In practice, the getopt() and getopt_long() functions interpret '-fpatfile' as '-f patfile', not as '-f -p -a -t ...'.

7. Option arguments should not be optional.

    This means that when a program documents an option as requiring an option argument, that option's argument must always be present or else the program will fail. GNU getopt() does provide for optional option arguments since they're occasionally useful.

8. If an option takes an argument that may have multiple values, the program should receive that argument as a single string, with values separated by commas or whitespace.

    For example, suppose a hypothetical program myprog requires a list of users for its -u option. Then, it should be invoked in one of these two ways:

    ```
    myprog -u "arnold,joe,jane"        Separate with commas
    myprog -u "arnold joe jane"        Separate with whitespace
    ```

    In such a case, you're on your own for splitting out and processing each value (that is, there is no standard routine), but doing so manually is usually straightforward.

9. Options should come first on the command line, before operands. Unix versions of getopt() enforce this convention. GNU getopt() does not by default, although you can tell it to.

10. The special argument '--' indicates the end of all options. Any subsequent arguments on the command line are treated as operands, even if they begin with a dash.

11. The order in which options are given should not matter. However, for mutually exclusive options, when one option overrides the setting of another, then (so to speak) the last one wins. If an option that has arguments is repeated, the program should process the arguments in order. For example, 'myprog -u arnold -u jane' is the same as 'myprog -u "arnold,jane"'. (You have to enforce this yourself; getopt() doesn't help you.)

12. It is OK for the order of operands to matter to a program. Each program should document such things.

13.   Programs that read or write named files should treat the single argument '-' as meaning standard input or standard output, as is appropriate for the program.

Note that many standard programs don't follow all of the above conventions. The primary reason is historical compatibility; many such programs predate the codifying of these conventions.

2.1.2 GNU Long Options

As we saw in Section 1.4.2, "Program Behavior," page 16, GNU programs are encouraged to use long options of the form `--help`, `--verbose`, and so on. Such options, since they start with '`--`', do not conflict with the POSIX conventions. They also can be easier to remember, and they provide the opportunity for consistency across all GNU utilities. (For example, `--help` is the same everywhere, as compared with `-h` for "help," `-i` for "information," and so on.) GNU long options have their own conventions, implemented by the `getopt_long()` function:

1.   For programs implementing POSIX utilities, every short (single-letter) option should also have a long option.

2.   Additional GNU-specific long options need not have a corresponding short option, but we recommend that they do.

3.   Long options can be abbreviated to the shortest string that remains unique. For example, if there are two options `--verbose` and `--verbatim`, the shortest possible abbreviations are `--verbo` and `--verba`.

4.   Option arguments are separated from long options either by whitespace or by an = sign. For example, `--sourcefile=/some/file` or `--sourcefile /some/file`.

5.   Options and arguments may be interspersed with operands on the command line; `getopt_long()` will rearrange things so that all options are processed and then all operands are available sequentially. (This behavior can be suppressed.)

6.   Option arguments can be optional. For such options, the argument is deemed to be present if it's in the same string as the option. This works only for short options. For example, if `-x` is such an option, given '`foo -xYANKEES -y`', the argument to `-x` is '`YANKEES`'. For '`foo -x -y`', there is no argument to `-x`.

7. Programs can choose to allow long options to begin with a single dash. (This is common with many X Window programs.)

Much of this will become clearer when we examine `getopt_long()` later in the chapter.

The *GNU Coding Standards* devotes considerable space to listing all the long and short options used by GNU programs. If you're writing a program that accepts long options, see if option names already in use might make sense for you to use as well.

2.2 Basic Command-Line Processing

A C program accesses its command-line arguments through its parameters, `argc` and `argv`. The `argc` parameter is an integer, indicating the number of arguments there are, including the command name. There are two common ways to declare `main()`, varying in how `argv` is declared:

```
int main(int argc, char *argv[])          int main(int argc, char **argv)
{                                          {
    . . .                                      . . .
}                                          }
```

Practically speaking, there's no difference between the two declarations, although the first is conceptually clearer: `argv` is an array of pointers to characters. The second is more commonly used: `argv` is a pointer to a pointer. Also, the second definition is technically more correct, and it is what we use. Figure 2.2 depicts this situation.

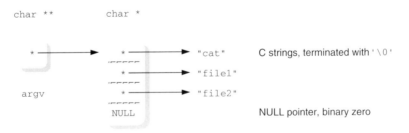

FIGURE 2.2
Memory for `argv`

By convention, `argv[0]` is the program's name. (For details, see Section 9.1.4.3, "Program Names and `argv[0]`," page 297.) Subsequent entries are the command line arguments. The final entry in the `argv` array is a `NULL` pointer.

argc indicates how many arguments there are; since C is zero-based, it is always true that 'argv[argc] == NULL'. Because of this, particularly in Unix code, you will see different ways of checking for the end of arguments, such as looping until a counter is greater than or equal to argc, or until 'argv[i] == 0' or while '*argv != NULL' and so on. These are all equivalent.

2.2.1 The V7 echo Program

Perhaps the simplest example of command-line processing is the V7 echo program, which prints its arguments to standard output, separated by spaces and terminated with a newline. If the first argument is -n, then the trailing newline is omitted. (This is used for prompting from shell scripts.) Here's the code:[1]

```
1   #include <stdio.h>
2
3   main(argc, argv)                          int main(int argc, char **argv)
4   int argc;
5   char *argv[];
6   {
7       register int i, nflg;
8
9       nflg = 0;
10      if(argc > 1 && argv[1][0] == '-' && argv[1][1] == 'n') {
11          nflg++;
12          argc--;
13          argv++;
14      }
15      for(i=1; i<argc; i++) {
16          fputs(argv[i], stdout);
17          if (i < argc-1)
18              putchar(' ');
19      }
20      if(nflg == 0)
21          putchar('\n');
22      exit(0);
23  }
```

Only 23 lines! There are two points of interest. First, decrementing argc and simultaneously incrementing argv (lines 12 and 13) are common ways of skipping initial arguments. Second, the check for -n (line 10) is simplistic. -no-newline-at-the-end also works. (Compile it and try it!)

---

[1] See /usr/src/cmd/echo.c in the V7 distribution.

Manual option parsing is common in V7 code because the `getopt()` function hadn't been invented yet.

Finally, here and in other places throughout the book, we see use of the `register` keyword. At one time, this keyword provided a hint to the compiler that the given variables should be placed in CPU registers, if possible. Use of this keyword is obsolete; modern compilers all base register assignment on analysis of the source code, ignoring the `register` keyword. We've chosen to leave code using it alone, but you should be aware that it has no real use anymore.[2]

2.3 Option Parsing: `getopt()` and `getopt_long()`

Circa 1980, for System III, the Unix Support Group within AT&T noted that each Unix program used ad hoc techniques for parsing arguments. To make things easier for users and developers, they developed most of the conventions we listed earlier. (The statement in the System III *intro*(1) manpage is considerably less formal than what's in the POSIX standard, though.)

The Unix Support Group also developed the `getopt()` function, along with several external variables, to make it easy to write code that follows the standard conventions. The GNU `getopt_long()` function supplies a compatible version of `getopt()`, as well as making it easy to parse long options of the form described earlier.

2.3.1 Single-Letter Options

The `getopt()` function is declared as follows:

```
#include <unistd.h>                                            POSIX

int getopt(int argc, char *const argv[], const char *optstring);

extern char *optarg;
extern int optind, opterr, optopt;
```

The arguments `argc` and `argv` are normally passed straight from those of `main()`. `optstring` is a string of option letters. If any letter in the string is followed by a colon, then that option is expected to have an argument.

---

[2] When we asked Jim Meyering, the Coreutils maintainer, about instances of `register` in the GNU Coreutils, he gave us an interesting response. He removes them when modifying code, but otherwise leaves them alone to make it easier to integrate changes submitted against existing versions.

To use `getopt()`, call it repeatedly from a `while` loop until it returns -1. Each time that it finds a valid option letter, it returns that letter. If the option takes an argument, `optarg` is set to point to it. Consider a program that accepts a -a option that doesn't take an argument and a -b argument that does:

```
int oc;                 /* option character */
char *b_opt_arg;

while ((oc = getopt(argc, argv, "ab:")) != -1) {
    switch (oc) {
    case 'a':
        /* handle -a, set a flag, whatever */
        break;
    case 'b':
        /* handle -b, get arg value from optarg */
        b_opt_arg = optarg;
        break;
    case ':':
        ...         /* error handling, see text */
    case '?':
    default:
        ...         /* error handling, see text */
    }
}
```

As it works, `getopt()` sets several variables that control error handling.

`char *optarg`

The argument for an option, if the option accepts one.

`int optind`

The current index in `argv`. When the `while` loop has finished, remaining operands are found in `argv[optind]` through `argv[argc-1]`. (Remember that 'argv[argc] == NULL'.)

`int opterr`

When this variable is nonzero (which it is by default), `getopt()` prints its own error messages for invalid options and for missing option arguments.

`int optopt`

When an invalid option character is found, `getopt()` returns either a '?' or a ':' (see below), and `optopt` contains the invalid character that was found.

People being human, it is inevitable that programs will be invoked incorrectly, either with an invalid option or with a missing option argument. In the normal case, `getopt()`

prints its own messages for these cases and returns the `'?'` character. However, you can change its behavior in two ways.

First, by setting `opterr` to `0` before invoking `getopt()`, you can force `getopt()` to remain silent when it finds a problem.

Second, if the *first* character in the `optstring` argument is a colon, then `getopt()` is silent *and* it returns a different character depending upon the error, as follows:

Invalid option

> `getopt()` returns a `'?'` and `optopt` contains the invalid option character. (This is the normal behavior.)

Missing option argument

> `getopt()` returns a `':'`. If the first character of `optstring` is not a colon, then `getopt()` returns a `'?'`, making this case indistinguishable from the invalid option case.

Thus, making the first character of `optstring` a colon is a good idea since it allows you to distinguish between "invalid option" and "missing option argument." The cost is that using the colon also silences `getopt()`, forcing you to supply your own error messages. Here is the previous example, this time with error message handling:

```
int oc;              /* option character */
char *b_opt_arg;

while ((oc = getopt(argc, argv, ":ab:")) != -1) {
    switch (oc) {
    case 'a':
        /* handle -a, set a flag, whatever */
        break;
    case 'b':
        /* handle -b, get arg value from optarg */
        b_opt_arg = optarg;
        break;
    case ':':
        /* missing option argument */
        fprintf(stderr, "%s: option `-%c' requires an argument\n",
                argv[0], optopt);
        break;
    case '?':
    default:
        /* invalid option */
        fprintf(stderr, "%s: option `-%c' is invalid: ignored\n",
                argv[0], optopt);
        break;
    }
}
```

A word about flag or option variable-naming conventions: Much Unix code uses names of the form `xflg` for any given option letter *x* (for example, `nflg` in the V7 echo; `xflag` is also common). This may be great for the program's author, who happens to know what the *x* option does without having to check the documentation. But it's unkind to someone else trying to read the code who doesn't know the meaning of all the option letters by heart. It is much better to use names that convey the option's meaning, such as `no_newline` for echo's -n option.

2.3.2 GNU `getopt()` and Option Ordering

The standard `getopt()` function stops looking for options as soon as it encounters a command-line argument that doesn't start with a '-'. GNU `getopt()` is different: It scans the entire command line looking for options. As it goes along, it *permutes* (rearranges) the elements of `argv`, so that when it's done, all the options have been moved to the front and code that proceeds to examine `argv[optind]` through `argv[argc-1]` works correctly. In all cases, the special argument '--' terminates option scanning.

You can change the default behavior by using a special first character in `optstring`, as follows:

`optstring[0] == '+'`

> GNU `getopt()` behaves like standard `getopt()`; it returns options in the order in which they are found, stopping at the first nonoption argument. This will also be true if `POSIXLY_CORRECT` exists in the environment.

`optstring[0] == '-'`

> GNU `getopt()` returns *every* command-line argument, whether or not it represents an argument. In this case, for each such argument, the function returns the integer 1 and sets `optarg` to point to the string.

As for standard `getopt()`, if the first character of `optstring` is a ':', then GNU `getopt()` distinguishes between "invalid option" and "missing option argument" by returning '?' or ':', respectively. The ':' in `optstring` can be the second character if the first character is '+' or '-'.

Finally, if an option letter in `optstring` is followed by *two* colon characters, then that option is allowed to have an optional option argument. (Say that three times fast!) Such an argument is deemed to be present if it's in the same `argv` element as the option, and absent otherwise. In the case that it's absent, GNU `getopt()` returns the option letter and sets `optarg` to `NULL`. For example, given—

```
while ((c = getopt(argc, argv, "ab::")) != 1)
    ...
```

—for `-bYANKEES`, the return value is `'b'`, and `optarg` points to `"YANKEES"`, while for `-b` or '`-b YANKEES`', the return value is still `'b'` but `optarg` is set to `NULL`. In the latter case, `"YANKEES"` is a separate command-line argument.

2.3.3 Long Options

The `getopt_long()` function handles the parsing of long options of the form described earlier. An additional routine, `getopt_long_only()` works identically, but it is used for programs where *all* options are long and options begin with a single '`-`' character. Otherwise, both work just like the simpler GNU `getopt()` function. (For brevity, whenever we say "`getopt_long()`," it's as if we'd said "`getopt_long()` and `getopt_long_only()`.") Here are the declarations, from the GNU/Linux *getopt*(3) manpage:

```
#include <getopt.h>                                          GLIBC

int getopt_long(int argc, char *const argv[],
        const char *optstring,
        const struct option *longopts, int *longindex);

int getopt_long_only(int argc, char *const argv[],
        const char *optstring,
        const struct option *longopts, int *longindex);
```

The first three arguments are the same as for `getopt()`. The next option is a pointer to an array of `struct option`, which we refer to as the *long options table* and which is described shortly. The `longindex` parameter, if not set to `NULL`, points to a variable which is filled in with the index in `longopts` of the long option that was found. This is useful for error diagnostics, for example.

2.3.3.1 Long Options Table

Long options are described with an array of `struct option` structures. The `struct option` is declared in `<getopt.h>`; it looks like this:

```
struct option {
    const char *name;
    int has_arg;
    int *flag;
    int val;
};
```

The elements in the structure are as follows:

`const char *name`

This is the name of the option, *without* any leading dashes, for example, `"help"` or `"verbose"`.

`int has_arg`

This describes whether the long option has an argument, and if so, what kind of argument. The value must be one of those presented in Table 2.1.

The symbolic constants are macros for the numeric values given in the table. While the numeric values work, the symbolic constants are considerably easier to read, and you should use them instead of the corresponding numbers in any code that you write.

`int *flag`

If this pointer is NULL, then `getopt_long()` returns the value in the `val` field of the structure. If it's not NULL, the variable it points to is filled in with the value in `val` and `getopt_long()` returns 0. If the `flag` isn't NULL but the long option is never seen, then the pointed-to variable is not changed.

`int val`

This is the value to return if the long option is seen or to load into `*flag` if `flag` is not NULL. Typically, if `flag` is not NULL, then `val` is a true/false value, such as 1 or 0. On the other hand, if `flag` is NULL, then `val` is usually a character constant. If the long option corresponds to a short one, the character constant should be the same one that appears in the `optstring` argument for this option. (All of this will become clearer shortly when we see some examples.)

Each long option has a single entry with the values appropriately filled in. The last element in the array should have zeros for all the values. The array need not be sorted; `getopt_long()` does a linear search. However, sorting it by long name may make it easier for a programmer to read.

TABLE 2.1
Values for `has_arg`

Symbolic constant	Numeric value	Meaning
no_argument	0	The option does not take an argument.
required_argument	1	The option requires an argument.
optional_argument	2	The option's argument is optional.

The use of `flag` and `val` seems confusing at first encounter. Let's step back for a moment and examine why it works the way it does. Most of the time, option processing consists of setting different flag variables when different option letters are seen, like so:

```
while ((c = getopt(argc, argv, ":af:hv")) != -1) {
    switch (c) {
    case 'a':
        do_all = 1;
        break;
    case 'f':
        myfile = optarg;
        break;
    case 'h':
        do_help = 1;
        break;
    case 'v':
        do_verbose = 1;
        break;
    ...                    Error handling code here
    }
}
```

When `flag` is not `NULL`, `getopt_long()` *sets the variable for you*. This reduces the three cases in the previous `switch` to one case. Here is an example long options table and the code to go with it:

```
int do_all, do_help, do_verbose;    /* flag variables */
char *myfile;

struct option longopts[] = {
    { "all",     no_argument,       & do_all,     1   },
    { "file",    required_argument, NULL,         'f' },
    { "help",    no_argument,       & do_help,    1   },
    { "verbose", no_argument,       & do_verbose, 1   },
    { 0, 0, 0, 0 }
};
...
```

```
while ((c = getopt_long(argc, argv, ":f:", longopts, NULL)) != -1) {
    switch (c) {
    case 'f':
        myfile = optarg;
        break;
    case 0:
        /* getopt_long() set a variable, just keep going */
        break;
    ...                        Error handling code here
    }
}
```

Notice that the value passed for the `optstring` argument no longer contains `'a'`, `'h'`, or `'v'`. This means that the corresponding short options are not accepted. To allow both long and short options, you would have to restore the corresponding `cases` from the first example to the `switch`.

Practically speaking, you should write your programs such that each short option also has a corresponding long option. In this case, it's easiest to have `flag` be `NULL` and `val` be the corresponding single letter.

2.3.3.2 Long Options, POSIX Style

The POSIX standard reserves the `-W` option for vendor-specific features. Thus, by definition, `-W` isn't portable across different systems.

If `W` appears in the `optstring` argument followed by a semicolon (note: *not* a colon), then `getopt_long()` treats `-Wlongopt` the same as `--longopt`. Thus, in the previous example, change the call to be:

```
while ((c = getopt_long(argc, argv, ":f:W;", longopts, NULL)) != -1) {
```

With this change, `-Wall` is the same as `--all` and `-Wfile=myfile` is the same as `--file=myfile`. The use of a semicolon makes it possible for a program to use `-W` as a regular option, if desired. (For example, GCC uses it as a regular option, whereas `gawk` uses it for POSIX conformance.)

2.3.3.3 `getopt_long()` Return Value Summary

As should be clear by now, `getopt_long()` provides a flexible mechanism for option parsing. Table 2.2 summarizes the possible return values and their meaning.

TABLE 2.2
`getopt_long()` return values

Return code	Meaning
0	`getopt_long()` set a flag as found in the long option table.
1	`optarg` points at a plain command-line argument.
`'?'`	Invalid option.
`':'`	Missing option argument.
`'x'`	Option character `'x'`.
−1	End of options.

Finally, we enhance the previous example code, showing the full `switch` statement:

```
int do_all, do_help, do_verbose;    /* flag variables */
char *myfile, *user;                /* input file, user name */

struct option longopts[] = {
    { "all",     no_argument,       & do_all,       1    },
    { "file",    required_argument, NULL,           'f'  },
    { "help",    no_argument,       & do_help,      1    },
    { "verbose", no_argument,       & do_verbose,   1    },
    { "user"   , optional_argument, NULL,           'u'  },
    { 0, 0, 0, 0 }
};
...
while ((c = getopt_long(argc, argv, ":ahvf:u::W;", longopts, NULL)) != -1) {
    switch (c) {
    case 'a':
        do_all = 1;
        break;
    case 'f':
        myfile = optarg;
        break;
    case 'h':
        do_help = 1;
        break;
    case 'u':
        if (optarg != NULL)
            user = optarg;
        else
            user = "root";
        break;
    case 'v':
        do_verbose = 1;
        break;
    case 0:     /* getopt_long() set a variable, just keep going */
        break;
```

```
#if 0
    case 1:
        /*
         * Use this case if getopt_long() should go through all
         * arguments.  If so, add a leading '-' character to optstring.
         * Actual code, if any, goes here.
         */
        break;
#endif
    case ':':    /* missing option argument */
        fprintf(stderr, "%s: option `-%c' requires an argument\n",
                argv[0], optopt);
        break;
    case '?':
    default:     /* invalid option */
        fprintf(stderr, "%s: option `-%c' is invalid: ignored\n",
                argv[0], optopt);
        break;
    }
}
```

In your programs, you may wish to have comments for each option letter explaining what each one does. However, if you've used descriptive variable names for each option letter, comments are not as necessary. (Compare `do_verbose` to `vflg`.)

2.3.3.4 GNU `getopt()` or `getopt_long()` in User Programs

You may wish to use GNU `getopt()` or `getopt_long()` in your own programs and have them run on non-Linux systems. That's OK; just copy the source files from a GNU program or from the GNU C Library (GLIBC) CVS archive.[3] The source files are `getopt.h`, `getopt.c`, and `getopt1.c`. They are licensed under the GNU Lesser General Public License, which allows library functions to be included even in proprietary programs. You should include a copy of the file COPYING.LIB with your program, along with the files `getopt.h`, `getopt.c`, and `getopt1.c`.

Include the source files in your distribution, and compile them along with any other source files. In your source code that calls `getopt_long()`, use '#include <getopt.h>', not '#include "getopt.h"'. Then, when compiling, add `-I.` to the C compiler's command line. That way, the local copy of the header file will be found first.

---

[3] See http://sources.redhat.com.

You may be wondering, "Gee, I already use GNU/Linux. Why should I include `getopt_long()` in my executable, making it bigger, if the routine is already in the C library?" That's a good question. However, there's nothing to worry about. The source code is set up so that if it's compiled on a system that uses GLIBC, the compiled files will not contain any code! Here's the proof, on our system:

```
$ uname -a                              Show system name and type
Linux example 2.4.18-14 #1 Wed Sep 4 13:35:50 EDT 2002 i686 i686 i386 GNU/Linux
$ ls -l getopt.o getopt1.o              Show file sizes
-rw-r--r--    1 arnold    devel         9836 Mar 24 13:55 getopt.o
-rw-r--r--    1 arnold    devel         10324 Mar 24 13:55 getopt1.o
$ size getopt.o getopt1.o               Show sizes included in executable
   text    data     bss     dec     hex filename
      0       0       0       0       0 getopt.o
      0       0       0       0       0 getopt1.o
```

The `size` command prints the sizes of the various parts of a binary object or executable file. We explain the output in Section 3.1, "Linux/Unix Address Space," page 52. What's important to understand right now is that, despite the nonzero sizes of the files themselves, they don't contribute anything to the final executable. (We think this is pretty neat.)

2.4 The Environment

The *environment* is a set of '`name=value`' pairs for each program. These pairs are termed *environment variables*. Each `name` consists of one to any number of alphanumeric characters or underscores ('_'), but the name may not start with a digit. (This rule is enforced by the shell; the C API can put anything it wants to into the environment, at the likely cost of confusing subsequent programs.)

Environment variables are often used to control program behavior. For example, if `POSIXLY_CORRECT` exists in the environment, many GNU programs disable extensions or historical behavior that isn't compatible with the POSIX standard.

You can decide (and should document) the environment variables that your program will use to control its behavior. For example, you may wish to use an environment variable for debugging options instead of a command-line argument. The advantage of using environment variables is that users can set them in their startup file and not have to remember to always supply a particular set of command-line options.

Of course, the disadvantage to using environment variables is that they can *silently* change a program's behavior. Jim Meyering, the maintainer of the Coreutils, put it this way:

> It makes it easy for the user to customize how the program works without changing how the program is invoked. That can be both a blessing and a curse. If you write a script that depends on your having a certain environment variable set, but then have someone else use that same script, it may well fail (or worse, silently produce invalid results) if that other person doesn't have the same environment settings.

2.4.1 Environment Management Functions

Several functions let you retrieve the values of environment variables, change their values, or remove them. Here are the declarations:

```
#include <stdlib.h>

char *getenv(const char *name);                    ISO C: Retrieve environment variable
int setenv(const char *name, const char *value,    POSIX: Set environment variable
          int overwrite);
int putenv(char *string);                          XSI: Set environment variable, uses string
void unsetenv(const char *name);                   POSIX: Remove environment variable
int clearenv(void);                                Common: Clear entire environment
```

The getenv() function is the one you will use 99 percent of the time. The argument is the environment variable name to look up, such as "HOME" or "PATH". If the variable exists, getenv() returns a pointer to the character string value. If not, it returns NULL. For example:

```
char *pathval;

/* Look for PATH; if not present, supply a default value */
if ((pathval = getenv("PATH")) == NULL)
    pathval = "/bin:/usr/bin:/usr/ucb";
```

Occasionally, environment variables exist, but with empty values. In this case, the return value will be non-NULL, but the first character pointed to will be the zero byte, which is the C string terminator, '\0'. Your code should be careful to check that the return value pointed to is not NULL. Even if it isn't NULL, also check that the string is not empty if you intend to use its value for something. In any case, don't just blindly use the returned value.

To change an environment variable or to add a new one to the environment, use `setenv()`:

```
if (setenv("PATH", "/bin:/usr/bin:/usr/ucb", 1) != 0) {
    /* handle failure */
}
```

It's possible that a variable already exists in the environment. If the third argument is true (nonzero), then the supplied value overwrites the previous one. Otherwise, it doesn't. The return value is -1 if there was no memory for the new variable, and 0 otherwise. `setenv()` makes private copies of both the variable name and the new value for storing in the environment.

A simpler alternative to `setenv()` is `putenv()`, which takes a single `"name=value"` string and places it in the environment:

```
if (putenv("PATH=/bin:/usr/bin:/usr/ucb") != 0) {
    /* handle failure */
}
```

`putenv()` blindly replaces any previous value for the same variable. Also, and perhaps more importantly, the string passed to `putenv()` is placed *directly* into the environment. This means that if your code later modifies this string (for example, if it was an array, not a string constant), the environment is modified also. This in turn means that you should *not* use a local variable as the parameter for `putenv()`. For all these reasons `setenv()` is preferred.

> NOTE The GNU `putenv()` has an additional (documented) quirk to its behavior. If the argument string is a name, then without an = character, the named variable is *removed*. The GNU env program, which we look at later in this chapter, relies on this behavior.

The `unsetenv()` function removes a variable from the environment:

```
unsetenv("PATH");
```

Finally, the `clearenv()` function clears the environment entirely:

```
if (clearenv() != 0) {
    /* handle failure */
}
```

This function is not standardized by POSIX, although it's available in GNU/Linux and several commercial Unix variants. You should use it if your application must be very security conscious and you want it to build its own environment entirely from scratch. If `clearenv()` is not available, the GNU/Linux *clearenv*(3) manpage recommends using '`environ = NULL;`' to accomplish the task.

2.4.2 The Entire Environment: `environ`

The correct way to deal with the environment is through the functions described in the previous section. However, it's worth a look at how things are managed "under the hood."

The external variable `environ` provides access to the environment in the same way that `argv` provides access to the command-line arguments. You must declare the variable yourself. Although standardized by POSIX, `environ` is purposely not declared by any standardized header file. (This seems to evolve from historical practice.) Here is the declaration:

```
extern char **environ;    /* Look Ma, no header file! */              POSIX
```

Like `argv`, the final element in `environ` is `NULL`. There is no "environment count" variable that corresponds to `argc`, however. This simple program prints out the entire environment:

```
/* ch02-printenv.c --- Print out the environment. */

#include <stdio.h>

extern char **environ;

int main(int argc, char **argv)
{
    int i;

    if (environ != NULL)
        for (i = 0; environ[i] != NULL; i++)
            printf("%s\n", environ[i]);

    return 0;
}
```

Although it's unlikely to happen, this program makes sure that `environ` isn't `NULL` before attempting to use it.

Variables are kept in the environment in random order. Although some Unix shells keep the environment sorted by variable name, there is no formal requirement that this be so, and many shells don't keep them sorted.

As something of a quirk of the implementation, you can access the environment by declaring a *third* parameter to `main()`:

```
int main(int argc, char **argv, char **envp)
{
    ...
}
```

You can then use `envp` as you would have used `environ`. Although you may see this occasionally in old code, we don't recommend its use; `environ` is the official, standard, portable way to access the entire environment, should you need to do so.

2.4.3 GNU env

To round off the chapter, here is the GNU version of the `env` command. This command adds variables to the environment for the duration of one command. It can also be used to clear the environment for that command or to remove specific environment variables. The program serves double-duty for us, since it demonstrates both `getopt_long()` and several of the functions discussed in this section. Here is how the program is invoked:

```
$ env --help
Usage: env [OPTION]... [-] [NAME=VALUE]... [COMMAND [ARG]...]
Set each NAME to VALUE in the environment and run COMMAND.

  -i, --ignore-environment   start with an empty environment
  -u, --unset=NAME           remove variable from the environment
      --help      display this help and exit
      --version   output version information and exit

A mere - implies -i.  If no COMMAND, print the resulting environment.

Report bugs to <bug-coreutils@gnu.org>.
```

Here are some sample invocations:

```
$ env - myprog arg1                        Clear environment, run program with args

$ env - PATH=/bin:/usr/bin myprog arg1      Clear environment, add PATH, run program

$ env -u IFS PATH=/bin:/usr/bin myprog arg1  Unset IFS, add PATH, run program
```

The code begins with a standard GNU copyright statement and explanatory comment. We have omitted both for brevity. (The copyright statement is discussed in Appendix C, "GNU General Public License," page 657. The `--help` output shown previously is enough to understand how the program works.) Following the copyright and comments are header includes and declarations. The 'N_("string")' macro invocation (line 93) is for use in internationalization and localization of the software, topics covered in Chapter 13, "Internationalization and Localization," page 485. For now, you can treat it as if it were the contained string constant.

```
 80   #include <config.h>
 81   #include <stdio.h>
 82   #include <getopt.h>
 83   #include <sys/types.h>
 84   #include <getopt.h>
 85
 86   #include "system.h"
 87   #include "error.h"
 88   #include "closeout.h"
 89
 90   /* The official name of this program (e.g., no `g' prefix).  */
 91   #define PROGRAM_NAME "env"
 92
 93   #define AUTHORS N_ ("Richard Mlynarik and David MacKenzie")
 94
 95   int putenv ();
 96
 97   extern char **environ;
 98
 99   /* The name by which this program was run. */
100   char *program_name;
101
102   static struct option const longopts[] =
103   {
104     {"ignore-environment", no_argument, NULL, 'i'},
105     {"unset", required_argument, NULL, 'u'},
106     {GETOPT_HELP_OPTION_DECL},
107     {GETOPT_VERSION_OPTION_DECL},
108     {NULL, 0, NULL, 0}
109   };
```

The GNU Coreutils contain a large number of programs, many of which perform the same common tasks (for example, argument parsing). To make maintenance easier, many common idioms are defined as macros. GETOPT_HELP_OPTION_DECL and GETOPT_VERSION_OPTION (lines 106 and 107) are two such. We examine their definitions shortly. The first function, usage(), prints the usage information and exits. The _("string") macro (line 115, and used throughout the program) is also for internationalization, and for now you should also treat it as if it were the contained string constant.

```
111  void
112  usage (int status)
113  {
114    if (status != 0)
115      fprintf (stderr, _("Try `%s --help' for more information.\n"),
116               program_name);
117    else
118      {
119        printf (_("\
120  Usage: %s [OPTION]... [-] [NAME=VALUE]... [COMMAND [ARG]...]\n"),
121               program_name);
122        fputs (_("\
123  Set each NAME to VALUE in the environment and run COMMAND.\n\
124  \n\
125    -i, --ignore-environment   start with an empty environment\n\
126    -u, --unset=NAME           remove variable from the environment\n\
127  "), stdout);
128        fputs (HELP_OPTION_DESCRIPTION, stdout);
129        fputs (VERSION_OPTION_DESCRIPTION, stdout);
130        fputs (_("\
131  \n\
132  A mere - implies -i.  If no COMMAND, print the resulting environment.\n\
133  "), stdout);
134        printf (_("\nReport bugs to <%s>.\n"), PACKAGE_BUGREPORT);
135      }
136    exit (status);
137  }
```

The first part of `main()` declares variables and sets up the internationalization. The functions `setlocale()`, `bindtextdomain()`, and `textdomain()` (lines 147–149) are all discussed in Chapter 13, "Internationalization and Localization," page 485. Note that this program does use the `envp` argument to `main()` (line 140). It is the only one of the Coreutils programs to do so. Finally, the call to `atexit()` on line 151 (see Section 9.1.5.3, "Exiting Functions," page 302) registers a Coreutils library function that flushes all pending output and closes `stdout`, reporting a message if there were problems. The next bit processes the command-line arguments, using `getopt_long()`.

```
139  int
140  main (register int argc, register char **argv, char **envp)
141  {
142    char *dummy_environ[1];
143    int optc;
144    int ignore_environment = 0;
145
146    program_name = argv[0];
147    setlocale (LC_ALL, "");
148    bindtextdomain (PACKAGE, LOCALEDIR);
149    textdomain (PACKAGE);
150
151    atexit (close_stdout);
```

```
152
153    while ((optc = getopt_long (argc, argv, "+iu:", longopts, NULL)) != -1)
154      {
155        switch (optc)
156          {
157          case 0:
158            break;
159          case 'i':
160            ignore_environment = 1;
161            break;
162          case 'u':
163            break;
164          case_GETOPT_HELP_CHAR;
165          case_GETOPT_VERSION_CHAR (PROGRAM_NAME, AUTHORS);
166          default:
167            usage (2);
168          }
169      }
170
171    if (optind != argc && !strcmp (argv[optind], "-"))
172      ignore_environment = 1;
```

Here are the macros, from `src/sys2.h` in the Coreutils distribution, that define
the declarations we saw earlier and the 'case_GETOPT_xxx' macros used above (lines
164–165):

```
/* Factor out some of the common --help and --version processing code.  */

/* These enum values cannot possibly conflict with the option values
   ordinarily used by commands, including CHAR_MAX + 1, etc.  Avoid
   CHAR_MIN - 1, as it may equal -1, the getopt end-of-options value.  */
enum
{
  GETOPT_HELP_CHAR = (CHAR_MIN - 2),
  GETOPT_VERSION_CHAR = (CHAR_MIN - 3)
};

#define GETOPT_HELP_OPTION_DECL \
  "help", no_argument, 0, GETOPT_HELP_CHAR
#define GETOPT_VERSION_OPTION_DECL \
  "version", no_argument, 0, GETOPT_VERSION_CHAR

#define case_GETOPT_HELP_CHAR                      \
  case GETOPT_HELP_CHAR:                           \
    usage (EXIT_SUCCESS);                          \
    break;

#define case_GETOPT_VERSION_CHAR(Program_name, Authors)              \
  case GETOPT_VERSION_CHAR:                                          \
    version_etc (stdout, Program_name, PACKAGE, VERSION, Authors);   \
    exit (EXIT_SUCCESS);                                             \
    break;
```

The upshot of this code is that `--help` prints the usage message and `--version` prints version information. Both exit successfully. ("Success" and "failure" exit statuses are described in Section 9.1.5.1, "Defining Process Exit Status," page 300.) Given that the Coreutils have dozens of utilities, it makes sense to factor out and standardize as much repetitive code as possible.

Returning to `env.c`:

```
174     environ = dummy_environ;
175     environ[0] = NULL;
176
177     if (!ignore_environment)
178       for (; *envp; envp++)
179         putenv (*envp);
180
181     optind = 0;                       /* Force GNU getopt to re-initialize. */
182     while ((optc = getopt_long (argc, argv, "+iu:", longopts, NULL)) != -1)
183       if (optc == 'u')
184         putenv (optarg);              /* Requires GNU putenv. */
185
186     if (optind != argc && !strcmp (argv[optind], "-"))      Skip options
187       ++optind;
188
189     while (optind < argc && strchr (argv[optind], '='))     Set environment variables
190       putenv (argv[optind++]);
191
192     /* If no program is specified, print the environment and exit. */
193     if (optind == argc)
194       {
195         while (*environ)
196           puts (*environ++);
197         exit (EXIT_SUCCESS);
198       }
```

Lines 174–179 copy the existing environment into a fresh copy of the environment. The global variable `environ` is set to point to an empty local array. The `envp` parameter maintains access to the original environment.

Lines 181–184 remove any environment variables as requested by the `-u` option. The program does this by rescanning the command line and removing names listed there. Environment variable removal relies on the GNU `putenv()` behavior discussed earlier: that when called with a plain variable name, `putenv()` removes the environment variable.

After any options, new or replacement environment variables are supplied on the command line. Lines 189–190 continue scanning the command line, looking for environment variable settings of the form '*name=value*'.

Upon reaching line 192, if nothing is left on the command line, env is supposed to print the new environment, and exit. It does so (lines 195–197).

If arguments are left, they represent a command name to run and arguments to pass to that new command. This is done with the execvp() system call (line 200), which *replaces* the current program with the new one. (This call is discussed in Section 9.1.4, "Starting New Programs: The exec() Family," page 293; don't worry about the details for now.) If this call returns to the current program, it *failed*. In such a case, env prints an error message and exits.

```
200    execvp (argv[optind], &argv[optind]);
201
202    {
203      int exit_status = (errno == ENOENT ? 127 : 126);
204      error (0, errno, "%s", argv[optind]);
205      exit (exit_status);
206    }
207  }
```

The exit status values, 126 and 127 (determined on line 203), conform to POSIX. 127 means the program that execvp() attempted to run didn't exist. (ENOENT means the file doesn't have an entry in the directory.) 126 means that the file exists, but something else went wrong.

2.5 Summary

- C programs access their command-line arguments through the parameters argc and argv. The getopt() function provides a standard way for consistent parsing of options and their arguments. The GNU version of getopt() provides some extensions, and getopt_long() and getopt_long_only() make it possible to easily parse long-style options.

- The environment is a set of '*name=value*' pairs that each program inherits from its parent. Programs can, at their author's whim, use environment variables to change their behavior, in addition to any command-line arguments. Standard routines (getenv(), setenv(), putenv(), and unsetenv()) exist for retrieving environment variable values, changing them, or removing them. If necessary, the entire environment is available through the external variable environ or through the char **envp third argument to main(). The latter technique is discouraged.

Exercises

1. Assume a program accepts options -a, -b, and -c, and that -b requires an argument. Write the manual argument parsing code for this program, without using getopt() or getopt_long(). Accept -- to end option processing. Make sure that -ac works, as do -bYANKEES, -b YANKEES, and -abYANKEES. Test your program.

2. Implement getopt(). For the first version, don't worry about the case in which 'optstring[0] == ':''. You may also ignore opterr.

3. Add code for 'optstring[0] == ':'' and opterr to your version of getopt().

4. Print and read the GNU getopt.h, getopt.c and getopt1.c files.

5. Write a program that declares both environ and envp and compares their values.

6. Parsing command line arguments and options is a wheel that many people can't refrain from reinventing. Besides getopt() and getopt_long(), you may wish to examine different argument-parsing packages, such as:

   • The *Plan 9 From Bell Labs arg*(2) argument-parsing library,[4]
   • Argp,[5]
   • Argv,[6]
   • Autoopts,[7]
   • GNU Gengetopt,[8]
   • Opt,[9]
   • Popt.[10] See also the *popt*(3) manpage on a GNU/Linux system.

7. Extra credit: Why can't a C compiler completely ignore the register keyword? Hint: What operation *cannot* be applied to a register variable?

---

[4] http://plan9.bell-labs.com/magic/man2html/2/arg

[5] http://www.gnu.org/manual/glibc/html_node/Argp.html

[6] http://256.com/sources/argv

[7] http://autogen.sourceforge.net/autoopts.html

[8] ftp://ftp.gnu.org/gnu/gengetopt/

[9] http://nis-www.lanl.gov/~jt/Software/opt/opt-3.19.tar.gz

[10] http://freshmeat.net/projects/popt/?topic_id=809

Chapter 3

User-Level Memory Management

In this chapter

ithout memory for storing data, it's impossible for a program to get any work done. (Or rather, it's impossible to get any *useful* work done.) Real-world programs can't afford to rely on fixed-size buffers or arrays of data structures. They have to be able to handle inputs of varying sizes, from small to large. This in turn leads to the use of *dynamically allocated memory*—memory allocated at runtime instead of at compile time. This is how the GNU "no arbitrary limits" principle is put into action.

Because dynamically allocated memory is such a basic building block for real-world programs, we cover it early, before looking at everything else there is to do. Our discussion focuses exclusively on the user-level view of the process and its memory; it has nothing to do with CPU architecture.

3.1 Linux/Unix Address Space

For a working definition, we've said that a *process* is a running program. This means that the operating system has loaded the executable file for the program into memory, has arranged for it to have access to its command-line arguments and environment variables, and has started it running. A process has five conceptually different areas of memory allocated to it:

Code

Often referred to as the *text segment*, this is the area in which the executable instructions reside. Linux and Unix arrange things so that multiple running instances of the same program share their code if possible; only one copy of the instructions for the same program resides in memory at any time. (This is transparent to the running programs.) The portion of the executable file containing the text segment is the *text section*.

Initialized data

Statically allocated and global data that are initialized with nonzero values live in the *data segment*. Each process running the same program has its own data segment. The portion of the executable file containing the data segment is the *data section*.

Zero-initialized data

Global and statically allocated data that are initialized to zero by default are kept in what is colloquially called the *BSS* area of the process.[1] Each process running the same program has its own BSS area. When running, the BSS data are placed in the data segment. In the executable file, they are stored in the *BSS section*.

The format of a Linux/Unix executable is such that only variables that are initialized to a nonzero value occupy space in the executable's disk file. Thus, a large array declared 'static char somebuf[2048];', which is automatically zero-filled, does not take up 2 KB worth of disk space. (Some compilers have options that let you place zero-initialized data into the data segment.)

Heap

The *heap* is where dynamic memory (obtained by malloc() and friends) comes from. As memory is allocated on the heap, the process's address space grows, as you can see by watching a running program with the ps command.

Although it is possible to give memory back to the system and shrink a process's address space, this is almost never done. (We distinguish between releasing no-longer-needed dynamic memory and shrinking the address space; this is discussed in more detail later in this chapter.)

It is typical for the heap to "grow upward." This means that successive items that are added to the heap are added at addresses that are numerically greater than previous items. It is also typical for the heap to start immediately after the BSS area of the data segment.

Stack

The *stack segment* is where local variables are allocated. Local variables are all variables declared inside the opening left brace of a function body (or other left brace) that aren't defined as static.

On most architectures, function parameters are also placed on the stack, as well as "invisible" bookkeeping information generated by the compiler, such as room for a function return value and storage for the return address representing the return from a function to its caller. (Some architectures do all this with registers.)

---

[1] BSS is an acronym for "Block Started by Symbol," a mnemonic from the IBM 7094 assembler.

It is the use of a stack for function parameters and return values that makes it convenient to write *recursive* functions (functions that call themselves).

Variables stored on the stack "disappear" when the function containing them returns; the space on the stack is reused for subsequent function calls.

On most modern architectures, the stack "grows downward," meaning that items deeper in the call chain are at numerically lower addresses.

When a program is running, the initialized data, BSS, and heap areas are usually placed into a single contiguous area: the data segment. The stack segment and code segment are separate from the data segment and from each other. This is illustrated in Figure 3.1.

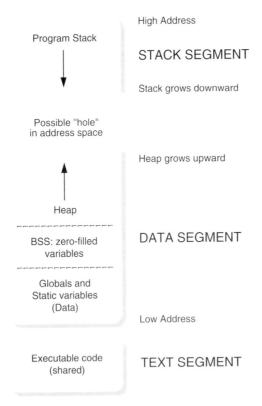

FIGURE 3.1
Linux/Unix process address space

Although it's theoretically possible for the stack and heap to grow into each other, the operating system prevents that event, and any program that tries to make it happen is asking for trouble. This is particularly true on modern systems, on which process address spaces are large and the gap between the top of the stack and the end of the heap is a big one. The different memory areas can have different hardware memory protection assigned to them. For example, the text segment might be marked "execute only," whereas the data and stack segments would have execute permission disabled. This practice can prevent certain kinds of security attacks. The details, of course, are hardware and operating-system specific and likely to change over time. Of note is that both Standard C and C++ allow `const` items to be placed in read-only memory. The relationship among the different segments is summarized in Table 3.1.

TABLE 3.1
Executable program segments and their locations

Program memory	Address space segment	Executable file section
Code	Text	Text
Initialized data	Data	Data
BSS	Data	BSS
Heap	Data	
Stack	Stack	

The `size` program prints out the size in bytes of each of the text, data, and BSS sections, along with the total size in decimal and hexadecimal. (The `ch03-memaddr.c` program is shown later in this chapter; see Section 3.2.5, "Address Space Examination," page 78.)

```
$ cc -O ch03-memaddr.c -o ch03-memaddr          Compile the program
$ ls -l ch03-memaddr                            Show total size
-rwxr-xr-x    1 arnold    devel        12320 Nov 24 16:45 ch03-memaddr
$ size ch03-memaddr                             Show component sizes
   text    data    bss     dec    hex filename
   1458     276      8    1742    6ce ch03-memaddr
$ strip ch03-memaddr                            Remove symbols
$ ls -l ch03-memaddr                            Show total size again
-rwxr-xr-x    1 arnold    devel         3480 Nov 24 16:45 ch03-memaddr
$ size ch03-memaddr                             Component sizes haven't changed
   text    data    bss     dec    hex filename
   1458     276      8    1742    6ce ch03-memaddr
```

The total size of what gets loaded into memory is only 1742 bytes, in a file that is 12,320 bytes long. Most of that space is occupied by the *symbols*, a list of the program's variables and function names. (The symbols are not loaded into memory when the program runs.) The `strip` program removes the symbols from the object file. This can save significant disk space for a large program, at the cost of making it impossible to debug a core dump[2] should one occur. (On modern systems this isn't worth the trouble; don't use `strip`.) Even after removing the symbols, the file is still larger than what gets loaded into memory since the object file format maintains additional data about the program, such as what shared libraries it may use, if any.[3]

Finally, we'll mention that *threads* represent multiple threads of execution within a *single* address space. Typically, each thread has its own stack, and a way to get *thread local* data, that is, dynamically allocated data for private use by the thread. We don't otherwise cover threads in this book, since they are an advanced topic.

3.2 Memory Allocation

Four library functions form the basis for dynamic memory management from C. We describe them first, followed by descriptions of the two system calls upon which these library functions are built. The C library functions in turn are usually used to implement other library functions that allocate memory and the C++ `new` and `delete` operators.

Finally, we discuss a function that you will see used frequently, but which we don't recommend.

3.2.1 Library Calls: `malloc()`, `calloc()`, `realloc()`, `free()`

Dynamic memory is allocated by either the `malloc()` or `calloc()` functions. These functions return pointers to the allocated memory. Once you have a block of memory

---

2 A *core dump* is the memory image of a running process created when the process terminates unexpectedly. It may be used later for debugging. Unix systems named the file `core`, and GNU/Linux systems use `core.pid`, where *pid* is the process ID of the process that died.

3 The description here is a deliberate simplification. Running programs occupy much more space than the `size` program indicates, since shared libraries are included in the address space. Also, the data segment will grow as a program allocates memory.

of a certain initial size, you can change its size with the `realloc()` function. Dynamic memory is released with the `free()` function.

Debugging the use of dynamic memory is an important topic in its own right. We discuss tools for this purpose in Section 15.5.2, "Memory Allocation Debuggers," page 612.

3.2.1.1 Examining C Language Details

Here are the function declarations from the GNU/Linux *malloc*(3) manpage:

```
#include <stdlib.h>                                                  ISO C

void *calloc(size_t nmemb, size_t size);     Allocate and zero fill
void *malloc(size_t size);                   Allocate raw memory
void free(void *ptr);                        Release memory
void *realloc(void *ptr, size_t size);       Change size of existing allocation
```

The allocation functions all return type `void *`. This is a *typeless* or *generic pointer*; all you can do with such a pointer is cast it to a different type and assign it to a typed pointer. Examples are coming up.

The type `size_t` is an unsigned integral type that represents amounts of memory. It is used for dynamic memory allocation, and we see many uses of it throughout the book. On most modern systems, `size_t` is `unsigned long`, but it's better to use `size_t` explicitly than to use a plain `unsigned` integral type.

The `ptrdiff_t` type is used for address calculations in pointer arithmetic, such as calculating where in an array a pointer may be pointing:

```
#define MAXBUF ...
char *p;
char buf[MAXBUF];
ptrdiff_t where;

p = buf;
while (some condition) {
    ...
    p += something ;
    ...
    where = p - buf;     /* what index are we at? */
}
```

The `<stdlib.h>` header file declares many of the standard C library routines and types (such as `size_t`), and it also defines the preprocessor constant `NULL`, which represents the "null" or invalid pointer. (This is a zero value, such as 0 or '`((void *) 0)`'.

The C++ idiom is to use 0 explicitly; in C, however, NULL is preferred, and we find it to be much more readable for C code.)

3.2.1.2 Initially Allocating Memory: `malloc()`

Memory is allocated initially with `malloc()`. The value passed in is the total number of bytes requested. The return value is a pointer to the newly allocated memory or NULL if memory could not be allocated. In the latter event, errno will be set to indicate the error. (errno is a special variable that system calls and library functions set to indicate what went wrong. It's described in Section 4.3, "Determining What Went Wrong," page 86.) For example, suppose we wish to allocate a variable number of some structure. The code looks something like this:

```
struct coord {                          /* 3D coordinates */
    int x, y, z;
} *coordinates;
unsigned int count;                     /* how many we need */
size_t amount;                          /* total amount of memory */

/* ... determine count somehow... */
amount = count * sizeof(struct coord);  /* how many bytes to allocate */

coordinates = (struct coord *) malloc(amount);  /* get the space */
if (coordinates == NULL) {
    /* report error, recover or give up */
}
/* ... use coordinates ... */
```

The steps shown here are quite boilerplate. The order is as follows:

1. Declare a pointer of the proper type to point to the allocated memory.

2. Calculate the size *in bytes* of the memory to be allocated. This involves multiplying a count of objects needed by the size of the individual object. This size in turn is retrieved from the C sizeof operator, which exists for this purpose (among others). Thus, while the size of a particular struct may vary across compilers and architectures, sizeof always returns the correct value and the source code remains correct and portable.

    When allocating arrays for character strings or other data of type char, it is not necessary to multiply by sizeof(char), since by definition this is always 1. But it won't hurt anything either.

3. Allocate the storage by calling `malloc()`, assigning the function's return value to the pointer variable. It is good practice to cast the return value of `malloc()`

to that of the variable being assigned to. In C it's not required (although the compiler may generate a warning). We strongly recommend *always* casting the return value.

Note that in C++, assignment of a pointer value of one type to a pointer of another type does requires a cast, whatever the context. For dynamic memory management, C++ programs should use `new` and `delete`, to avoid type problems, and not `malloc()` and `free()`.

4.   Check the return value. *Never* assume that memory allocation will succeed. If the allocation fails, `malloc()` returns `NULL`. If you use the value without checking, it is likely that your program will immediately die from a *segmentation violation* (or *segfault*), which is an attempt to use memory not in your address space.

If you check the return value, you can at least print a diagnostic message and terminate gracefully. Or you can attempt some other method of recovery.

Once we've allocated memory and set `coordinates` to point to it, we can then treat `coordinates` as if it were an array, although it's really a pointer:

```
int cur_x, cur_y, cur_z;
size_t an_index;
an_index = something;
cur_x = coordinates[an_index].x;
cur_y = coordinates[an_index].y;
cur_z = coordinates[an_index].z;
```

The compiler generates correct code for indexing through the pointer to retrieve the members of the structure at `coordinates[an_index]`.

> NOTE The memory returned by `malloc()` is *not* initialized. It can contain any random garbage. You should immediately initialize the memory with valid data or at least with zeros. To do the latter, use `memset()` (discussed in Section 12.2, "Low-Level Memory: The `memXXX()` Functions," page 432):
>
> ```
> memset(coordinates, '\0', amount);
> ```
>
> Another option is to use `calloc()`, described shortly.

Geoff Collyer recommends the following technique for allocating memory:

```
some_type *pointer;

pointer = malloc(count * sizeof(*pointer));
```

This approach guarantees that the `malloc()` will allocate the correct amount of memory without your having to consult the declaration of `pointer`. If `pointer`'s type later changes, the `sizeof` operator automatically ensures that the count of bytes to allocate stays correct. (Geoff's technique omits the cast that we just discussed. Having the cast there also ensures a diagnostic if `pointer`'s type changes and the call to `malloc()` isn't updated.)

3.2.1.3 Releasing Memory: `free()`

When you're done using the memory, you "give it back" by using the `free()` function. The single argument is a pointer previously obtained from one of the other allocation routines. It is safe (although useless) to pass a null pointer to `free()`:

```
free(coordinates);
coordinates = NULL;      /* not required, but a good idea */
```

Once `free(coordinates)` is called, the memory pointed to by `coordinates` is *off limits*. It now "belongs" to the allocation subroutines, and they are free to manage it as they see fit. They can change the contents of the memory or even release it from the process's address space! There are thus several common errors to watch out for with `free()`:

Accessing freed memory

> If unchanged, `coordinates` continues to point at memory that no longer belongs to the application. This is called a *dangling pointer*. In many systems, you can get away with continuing to access this memory, at least until the next time more memory is allocated or freed. In many others though, such access won't work.

> In sum, accessing freed memory is a bad idea: It's not portable or reliable, and the *GNU Coding Standards* disallows it. For this reason, it's a good idea to immediately set the program's pointer variable to NULL. If you then accidentally attempt to access freed memory, your program will immediately fail with a segmentation fault (before you've released it to the world, we hope).

Freeing the same pointer twice

> This causes "undefined behavior." Once the memory has been handed back to the allocation routines, they may merge the freed block with other free storage under management. Freeing something that's already been freed is likely to lead to confusion or crashes at best, and so-called double frees have been known to lead to security problems.

Passing a pointer not obtained from `malloc()`, `calloc()`, *or* `realloc()`

This seems obvious, but it's important nonetheless. Even passing in a pointer to somewhere in the middle of dynamically allocated memory is bad:

```
free(coordinates + 10);         /* Release all but first 10 elements. */
```

This call won't work, and it's likely to lead to disastrous consequences, such as a crash. (This is because many `malloc()` implementations keep "bookkeeping" information *in front of* the returned data. When `free()` goes to use that information, it will find invalid data there. Other implementations have the bookkeeping information at the end of the allocated chunk; the same issues apply.)

Buffer overruns and underruns

Accessing memory outside an allocated chunk also leads to undefined behavior, again because this is likely to be bookkeeping information or possibly memory that's not even in the address space. Writing into such memory is much worse, since it's likely to destroy the bookkeeping data.

Failure to free memory

Any dynamic memory that's not needed should be released. In particular, memory that is allocated inside loops or recursive or deeply nested function calls should be carefully managed and released. Failure to take care leads to *memory leaks*, whereby the process's memory can grow without bounds; eventually, the process dies from lack of memory.

This situation can be particularly pernicious if memory is allocated per input record or as some other function of the input: The memory leak won't be noticed when run on small inputs but can suddenly become obvious (and embarrassing) when run on large ones. This error is even worse for systems that must run continuously, such as telephone switching systems. A memory leak that crashes such a system can lead to significant monetary or other damage.

Even if the program never dies for lack of memory, constantly growing programs suffer in performance, because the operating system has to manage keeping in-use data in physical memory. In the worst case, this can lead to behavior known as *thrashing*, whereby the operating system is so busy moving the contents of the address space into and out of physical memory that no real work gets done.

While it's possible for `free()` to hand released memory back to the system and shrink the process address space, this is almost never done. Instead, the released memory is kept available for allocation by the next call to `malloc()`, `calloc()`, or `realloc()`.

Given that released memory continues to reside in the process's address space, it may pay to zero it out before releasing it. Security-sensitive programs may choose to do this, for example.

See Section 15.5.2, "Memory Allocation Debuggers," page 612, for discussion of a number of useful dynamic-memory debugging tools.

3.2.1.4 Changing Size: `realloc()`

Dynamic memory has a significant advantage over statically declared arrays, which is that it's possible to use exactly as much memory as you need, and no more. It's not necessary to declare a global, `static`, or automatic array of some fixed size and hope that it's (a) big enough and (b) not too big. Instead, you can allocate exactly as much as you need, no more and no less.

Additionally, it's possible to change the size of a dynamically allocated memory area. Although it's possible to shrink a block of memory, more typically, the block is grown. Changing the size is handled with `realloc()`. Continuing with the `coordinates` example, typical code goes like this:

```
int new_count;
size_t new_amount;
struct coord *newcoords;

/* set new_count, for example: */
new_count = count * 2;              /* double the storage */
new_amount = new_count * sizeof(struct coord);

newcoords = (struct coord *) realloc(coordinates, new_amount);
if (newcoords == NULL) {
    /* report error, recover or give up */
}

coordinates = newcoords;
/* continue using coordinates ... */
```

As with `malloc()`, the steps are boilerplate in nature and are similar in concept:

1. Compute the new size to allocate, in bytes.

2. Call `realloc()` with the original pointer obtained from `malloc()` (or from `calloc()` or an earlier call to `realloc()`) and the new size.

3. Cast and assign the return value of `realloc()`. More discussion of this shortly.

4. As for `malloc()`, *check* the return value to make sure it's not `NULL`. Any memory allocation routine can fail.

When growing a block of memory, `realloc()` often allocates a new block of the right size, copies the data from the old block into the new one, and returns a pointer to the new one.

When shrinking a block of data, `realloc()` can often just update the internal bookkeeping information and return the same pointer. This saves having to copy the original data. However, if this happens, *don't assume you can still use the memory beyond the new size!*

In either case, you can assume that if `realloc()` doesn't return `NULL`, the old data has been copied for you into the new memory. Furthermore, the old pointer is no longer valid, as if you had called `free()` with it, and you should not use it. This is true of all pointers into that block of data, not just the particular one used to call `free()`.

You may have noticed that our example code used a separate variable to point to the changed storage block. It would be possible (but a bad idea) to use the same initial variable, like so:

```
coordinates = realloc(coordinates, new_amount);
```

This is a bad idea for the following reason. When `realloc()` returns `NULL`, the original pointer is still valid; it's safe to continue using that memory. However, if you reuse the same variable and `realloc()` returns `NULL`, you've now *lost* the pointer to the original memory. That memory can no longer be used. More important, that memory can no longer be freed! This creates a memory leak, which is to be avoided.

There are some special cases for the Standard C version of `realloc()`: When the `ptr` argument is `NULL`, `realloc()` acts like `malloc()` and allocates a fresh block of storage. When the `size` argument is `0`, `realloc()` acts like `free()` and *releases* the memory that `ptr` points to. Because (a) this can be confusing and (b) older systems don't implement this feature, we recommend using `malloc()` when you mean `malloc()` and `free()` when you mean `free()`.

Here is another, fairly subtle, "gotcha."[4] Consider a routine that maintains a static pointer to some dynamically allocated data, which the routine occasionally has to grow. It may also maintain automatic (that is, local) pointers into this data. (For brevity, we omit error checking code. In production code, don't do that.) For example:

```
void manage_table(void)
{
    static struct table *table;
    struct table *cur, *p;
    int i;
    size_t count;

    ...
    table = (struct table *) malloc(count * sizeof(struct table));
    /* fill table */
    cur = & table[i];        /* point at i'th item */
    ...
    cur->i = j;              /* use pointer */
    ...
    if (some condition) {    /* need to grow table */
        count += count/2;
        p = (struct table *) realloc(table, count * sizeof(struct table));
        table = p;
    }

    cur->i = j;              /* PROBLEM 1: update table element */

    other_routine();         /* PROBLEM 2: see text */
    cur->j = k;              /* PROBLEM 2: see text */
    ...
}
```

This looks straightforward; manage_table() allocates the data, uses it, changes the size, and so on. But there are some problems that don't jump off the page (or the screen) when you are looking at this code.

In the line marked 'PROBLEM 1', the cur pointer is used to update a table element. However, cur was assigned on the basis of the *initial* value of table. If *some condition* was true and realloc() returned a different block of memory, cur now points into the original, freed memory! Whenever table changes, any pointers into the memory need to be updated too. What's missing here is the statement 'cur = & table[i];' after table is reassigned following the call to realloc().

---

[4] It is derived from real-life experience with gawk.

The two lines marked 'PROBLEM 2' are even more subtle. In particular, suppose other_routine() makes a *recursive* call to manage_table(). The table variable could be changed again, completely invisibly! Upon return from other_routine(), the value of cur could once again be invalid.

One might think (as we did) that the only solution is to be aware of this and supply a suitably commented reassignment to cur after the function call. However, Brian Kernighan kindly set us straight. If we use indexing, the pointer maintenance issue doesn't even arise:

```
table = (struct table *) malloc(count * sizeof(struct table));
/* fill table */
...
table[i].i = j;          /* Update a member of the i'th element */
...
if (some condition) {   /* need to grow table */
    count += count/2;
    p = (struct table *) realloc(table, count * sizeof(struct table));
    table = p;
}

table[i].i = j;          /* PROBLEM 1 goes away */
other_routine();         /* Recursively calls us, modifies table */
table[i].j = k;          /* PROBLEM 2 goes away also */
```

Using indexing doesn't solve the problem if you have a *global* copy of the original pointer to the allocated data; in that case, you still have to worry about updating your global structures after calling realloc().

> NOTE   As with malloc(), when you grow a piece of memory, the newly allocated memory returned from realloc() is not zero-filled. You must clear it yourself with memset() if that's necessary, since realloc() only allocates the fresh memory; it doesn't do anything else.

3.2.1.5 Allocating and Zero-filling: calloc()

The calloc() function is a straightforward wrapper around malloc(). Its primary advantage is that it zeros the dynamically allocated memory. It also performs the size calculation for you by taking as parameters the number of items and the size of each:

```
coordinates = (struct coord *) calloc(count, sizeof(struct coord));
```

Conceptually, at least, the calloc() code is fairly simple. Here is one possible implementation:

```
void *calloc(size_t nmemb, size_t size)
{
    void *p;
    size_t total;

    total = nmemb * size;              Compute size
    p = malloc(total);                 Allocate the memory

    if (p != NULL)                     If it worked ...
        memset(p, '\0', total);        Fill it with zeros

    return p;                          Return value is NULL or pointer
}
```

Many experienced programmers prefer to use `calloc()` since then there's never any question about the contents of the newly allocated memory.

Also, if you know you'll need zero-filled memory, you should use `calloc()`, because it's possible that the memory `malloc()` returns is already zero-filled. Although you, the programmer, can't know this, `calloc()` can know about it and avoid the call to `memset()`.

3.2.1.6 Summarizing from the GNU Coding Standards

To summarize, here is what the *GNU Coding Standards* has to say about using the memory allocation routines:

> Check every call to `malloc` or `realloc` to see if it returned zero. Check `realloc` even if you are making the block smaller; in a system that rounds block sizes to a power of 2, `realloc` may get a different block if you ask for less space.

> In Unix, `realloc` can destroy the storage block if it returns zero. GNU `realloc` does not have this bug: If it fails, the original block is unchanged. Feel free to assume the bug is fixed. If you wish to run your program on Unix, and wish to avoid lossage in this case, you can use the GNU `malloc`.

> You must expect `free` to alter the contents of the block that was freed. Anything you want to fetch from the block, you must fetch before calling `free`.

In three short paragraphs, Richard Stallman has distilled the important principles for doing dynamic memory management with `malloc()`. It is the use of dynamic memory and the "no arbitrary limits" principle that makes GNU programs so robust and more capable than their Unix counterparts.

We do wish to point out that the C standard requires `realloc()` to *not* destroy the original block if it returns `NULL`.

3.2.1.7 Using Private Allocators

The `malloc()` suite is a general-purpose memory allocator. It has to be able to handle requests for arbitrarily large or small amounts of memory and do all the book-keeping when different chunks of allocated memory are released. If your program does considerable dynamic memory allocation, you may thus find that it spends a large proportion of its time in the `malloc()` functions.

One thing you can do is write a *private allocator*—a set of functions or macros that allocates large chunks of memory from `malloc()` and then parcels out small chunks one at a time. This technique is particularly useful if you allocate many individual instances of the same relatively small structure.

For example, GNU `awk` (gawk) uses this technique. From the file `awk.h` in the gawk distribution (edited slightly to fit the page):

```
#define getnode(n)     if (nextfree) n = nextfree, nextfree = nextfree->nextp;\
                       else n = more_nodes()

#define freenode(n)    ((n)->flags = 0, (n)->exec_count = 0,\
                       (n)->nextp = nextfree, nextfree = (n))
```

The `nextfree` variable points to a linked list of `NODE` structures. The `getnode()` macro pulls the first structure off the list if one is there. Otherwise, it calls `more_nodes()` to allocate a new list of free `NODE`s. The `freenode()` macro releases a `NODE` by putting it at the head of the list.

> NOTE When first writing your application, do it the simple way: use `malloc()` and `free()` directly. *If and only if* profiling your program shows you that it's spending a significant amount of time in the memory-allocation functions should you consider writing a private allocator.

3.2.1.8 Example: Reading Arbitrarily Long Lines

Since this is, after all, *Linux Programming by Example*, it's time for a real-life example. The following code is the `readline()` function from GNU Make 3.80

(`ftp://ftp.gnu.org/gnu/make/make-3.80.tar.gz`). It can be found in the file `read.c`.

Following the "no arbitrary limits" principle, lines in a `Makefile` can be of any length. Thus, this routine's primary job is to read lines of any length and make sure that they fit into the buffer being used.

A secondary job is to deal with continuation lines. As in C, lines that end with a backslash logically continue to the next line. The strategy used is to maintain a buffer. As many lines as will fit in the buffer are kept there, with pointers keeping track of the start of the buffer, the current line, and the next line. Here is the structure:

```
struct ebuffer
  {
    char *buffer;       /* Start of the current line in the buffer.  */
    char *bufnext;      /* Start of the next line in the buffer.  */
    char *bufstart;     /* Start of the entire buffer.  */
    unsigned int size;  /* Malloc'd size of buffer. */
    FILE *fp;           /* File, or NULL if this is an internal buffer.  */
    struct floc floc;   /* Info on the file in fp (if any).  */
  };
```

The `size` field tracks the size of the entire buffer, and `fp` is the `FILE` pointer for the input file. The `floc` structure isn't of interest for studying the routine.

The function returns the number of lines in the buffer. (The line numbers here are relative to the start of the function, not the source file.)

```
 1  static long
 2  readline (ebuf)                              static long readline(struct ebuffer *ebuf)
 3        struct ebuffer *ebuf;
 4  {
 5    char *p;
 6    char *end;
 7    char *start;
 8    long nlines = 0;
 9
10    /* The behaviors between string and stream buffers are different enough to
11       warrant different functions.  Do the Right Thing.  */
12
13    if (!ebuf->fp)
14      return readstring (ebuf);
15
16    /* When reading from a file, we always start over at the beginning of the
17       buffer for each new line.  */
18
19    p = start = ebuf->bufstart;
20    end = p + ebuf->size;
21    *p = '\0';
```

We start by noticing that GNU Make is written in K&R C for maximal portability. The initial part declares variables, and if the input is coming from a string (such as from the expansion of a macro), the code hands things off to a different function, `readstring()` (lines 13 and 14). The test '`!ebuf->fp`' (line 13) is a shorter (and less clear, in our opinion) test for a null pointer; it's the same as '`ebuf->fp == NULL`'.

Lines 19–21 initialize the pointers, and insert a NUL byte, which is the C string terminator character, at the end of the buffer. The function then starts a loop (lines 23–95), which runs as long as there is more input.

```
23    while (fgets (p, end - p, ebuf->fp) != 0)
24      {
25        char *p2;
26        unsigned long len;
27        int backslash;
28
29        len = strlen (p);
30        if (len == 0)
31          {
32            /* This only happens when the first thing on the line is a '\0'.
33               It is a pretty hopeless case, but (wonder of wonders) Athena
34               lossage strikes again!  (xmkmf puts NULs in its makefiles.)
35               There is nothing really to be done; we synthesize a newline so
36               the following line doesn't appear to be part of this line.  */
37            error (&ebuf->floc,
38                  _("warning: NUL character seen; rest of line ignored"));
39            p[0] = '\n';
40            len = 1;
41          }
```

The `fgets()` function (line 23) takes a pointer to a buffer, a count of bytes to read, and a `FILE *` variable for the file to read from. It reads one less than the count so that it can terminate the buffer with '`\0`'. This function is good since it allows you to avoid buffer overflows. It stops upon encountering a newline or end-of-file, and if the newline is there, it's placed in the buffer. It returns NULL on failure or the (pointer) value of the first argument on success.

In this case, the arguments are a pointer to the free area of the buffer, the amount of room left in the buffer, and the FILE pointer to read from.

The comment on lines 32–36 is self-explanatory; if a zero byte is encountered, the program prints an error message and pretends it was an empty line. After compensating for the NUL byte (lines 30–41), the code continues.

```
43          /* Jump past the text we just read.  */
44          p += len;
45
46          /* If the last char isn't a newline, the whole line didn't fit into the
47             buffer.  Get some more buffer and try again.  */
48          if (p[-1] != '\n')
49            goto more_buffer;
50
51          /* We got a newline, so add one to the count of lines.  */
52          ++nlines;
```

Lines 43–52 increment the pointer into the buffer past the data just read. The code then checks whether the last character read was a newline. The construct p[-1] (line 48) looks at the character *in front of* p, just as p[0] is the current character and p[1] is the next. This looks strange at first, but if you translate it into terms of pointer math, *(p-1), it makes more sense, and the indexing form is possibly easier to read.

If the last character was not a newline, this means that we've run out of space, and the code goes off (with goto) to get more (line 49). Otherwise, the line count is incremented.

```
54  #if !defined(WINDOWS32) && !defined(__MSDOS__)
55          /* Check to see if the line was really ended with CRLF; if so ignore
56             the CR.  */
57          if ((p - start) > 1 && p[-2] == '\r')
58            {
59              --p;
60              p[-1] = '\n';
61            }
62  #endif
```

Lines 54–62 deal with input lines that follow the Microsoft convention of ending with a Carriage Return-Line Feed (CR-LF) combination, and not just a Line Feed (or newline), which is the Linux/Unix convention. Note that the #ifdef *excludes* the code on Microsoft systems; apparently the <stdio.h> library on those systems handles this conversion automatically. This is also true of other non-Unix systems that support Standard C.

```
64          backslash = 0;
65          for (p2 = p - 2; p2 >= start; --p2)
66            {
67              if (*p2 != '\\')
68                break;
69              backslash = !backslash;
70            }
71
```

```
72            if (!backslash)
73              {
74                p[-1] = '\0';
75                break;
76              }
77
78            /* It was a backslash/newline combo.  If we have more space, read
79               another line.  */
80            if (end - p >= 80)
81              continue;
82
83            /* We need more space at the end of our buffer, so realloc it.
84               Make sure to preserve the current offset of p.  */
85          more_buffer:
86            {
87              unsigned long off = p - start;
88              ebuf->size *= 2;
89              start = ebuf->buffer = ebuf->bufstart = (char *) xrealloc (start,
90                                                       ebuf->size);
91              p = start + off;
92              end = start + ebuf->size;
93              *p = '\0';
94            }
95          }
```

So far we've dealt with the mechanics of getting at least one complete line into the buffer. The next chunk handles the case of a continuation line. It has to make sure, though, that the final backslash isn't part of multiple backslashes at the end of the line. It tracks whether the total number of such backslashes is odd or even by toggling the `backslash` variable from 0 to 1 and back. (Lines 64–70.)

If the number is even, the test '! backslash' (line 72) will be true. In this case, the final newline is replaced with a NUL byte, and the code leaves the loop.

On the other hand, if the number is odd, then the line contained an even number of backslash pairs (representing escaped backslashes, \\ as in C), and a final backslash-newline combination.[5] In this case, if at least 80 free bytes are left in the buffer, the program `continues` around the loop to read another line (lines 78–81). (The use of the magic number 80 isn't great; it would have been better to define and use a symbolic constant.)

---

[5] This code has the scent of practical experience about it: It wouldn't be surprising to learn that earlier versions simply checked for a final backslash before the newline, until someone complained that it didn't work when there were multiple backslashes at the end of the line.

Upon reaching line 83, the program needs more space in the buffer. Here's where the dynamic memory management comes into play. Note the comment about preserving p (lines 83–84); we discussed this earlier in terms of reinitializing pointers into dynamic memory. end is also reset. Line 89 resizes the memory.

Note that here the function being called is `xrealloc()`. Many GNU programs use "wrapper" functions around `malloc()` and `realloc()` that automatically print an error message and exit if the standard routines return NULL. Such a wrapper might look like this:

```
extern const char *myname;     /* set in main() */

void *xrealloc(void *ptr, size_t amount)
{
    void *p = realloc(ptr, amount);

    if (p == NULL) {
        fprintf(stderr, "%s: out of memory!\n", myname);
        exit(1);
    }
}
```

Thus, if `xrealloc()` returns, it's guaranteed to return a valid pointer. (This strategy complies with the "check every call for errors" principle while avoiding the code clutter that comes with doing so using the standard routines directly.) In addition, this allows valid use of the construct '`ptr = xrealloc(ptr, new_size)`', which we otherwise warned against earlier.

Note that it is not always appropriate to use such a wrapper. If you wish to handle errors yourself, you shouldn't use it. On the other hand, if running out of memory is always a fatal error, then such a wrapper is quite handy.

```
97    if (ferror (ebuf->fp))
98      pfatal_with_name (ebuf->floc.filenm);
99
100   /* If we found some lines, return how many.
101      If we didn't, but we did find _something_, that indicates we read the last
102      line of a file with no final newline; return 1.
103      If we read nothing, we're at EOF; return -1.  */
104
105   return nlines ? nlines : p == ebuf->bufstart ? -1 : 1;
106 }
```

Finally, the `readline()` routine checks for I/O errors, and then returns a descriptive return value. The function `pfatal_with_name()` (line 98) doesn't return.

3.2.1.9 GLIBC Only: Reading Entire Lines: `getline()` and `getdelim()`

Now that you've seen how to read an arbitrary-length line, you can breathe a sigh of relief that you don't have to write such a function for yourself. GLIBC provides two functions to do this for you:

```
#define _GNU_SOURCE 1                                           GLIBC
#include <stdio.h>
#include <sys/types.h>             /* for ssize_t */

ssize_t getline(char **lineptr, size_t *n, FILE *stream);
ssize_t getdelim(char **lineptr, size_t *n, int delim, FILE *stream);
```

Defining the constant `_GNU_SOURCE` brings in the declaration of the `getline()` and `getdelim()` functions. Otherwise, they're implicitly declared as returning `int`. `<sys/types.h>` is needed so you can declare a variable of type `ssize_t` to hold the return value. (An `ssize_t` is a "signed `size_t`." It's meant for the same use as a `size_t`, but for places where you need to be able to hold negative values as well.)

Both functions manage dynamic storage for you, ensuring that the buffer containing an input line is always big enough to hold the input line. They differ in that `getline()` reads until a newline character, and `getdelim()` uses a user-provided delimiter character. The common arguments are as follows:

`char **lineptr`

A pointer to a `char *` pointer to hold the address of a dynamically allocated buffer. It should be initialized to NULL if you want `getline()` to do all the work. Otherwise, it should point to storage previously obtained from `malloc()`.

`size_t *n`

An indication of the size of the buffer. If you allocated your own buffer, `*n` should contain the buffer's size. Both functions update `*n` to the new buffer size if they change it.

`FILE *stream`

The location from which to get input characters.

The functions return `-1` upon end-of-file or error. The strings hold the terminating newline or delimiter (if there was one), as well as a terminating zero byte. Using `getline()` is easy, as shown in `ch03-getline.c`:

```
/* ch03-getline.c --- demonstrate getline(). */

#define _GNU_SOURCE 1
#include <stdio.h>
#include <sys/types.h>

/* main --- read a line and echo it back out until EOF. */

int main(void)
{
    char *line = NULL;
    size_t size = 0;
    ssize_t ret;

    while ((ret = getline(& line, & size, stdin)) != -1)
        printf("(%lu) %s", size, line);

    return 0;
}
```

Here it is in action, showing the size of the buffer. The third input and output lines are purposely long, to force `getline()` to grow the buffer; thus, they wrap around:

```
$ ch03-getline                                          Run the program
this is a line
(120) this is a line
And another line.
(120) And another line.
A lllllllllllllllllooooooooooooooooooooooooooooonnnnnnnnnnnnnnnnnnggg
gggggggg    llliiiiiiiiiiiiiiiiiiinnnnnnnnnnnnnnnnnnneeeeeeeeee
(240) A lllllllllllllllloooooooooooooooooooooooooooooonnnnnnnnnnnnnnnnng
nnngggggggggggg    lllliiiiiiiiiiiiiiiiiiiinnnnnnnnnnnnnnnnnnnneeeeeeeeee
```

3.2.2 String Copying: `strdup()`

One extremely common operation is to allocate storage for a copy of a string. It's so common that many programs provide a simple function for it instead of using inline code, and often that function is named `strdup()`:

```
#include <string.h>

/* strdup --- malloc() storage for a copy of string and copy it */

char *strdup(const char *str)
{
    size_t len;
    char *copy;

    len = strlen(str) + 1;    /* include room for terminating '\0' */
    copy = malloc(len);

    if (copy != NULL)
        strcpy(copy, str);

    return copy;              /* returns NULL if error */
}
```

With the 2001 POSIX standard, programmers the world over can breathe a little easier: This function is now part of POSIX as an XSI extension:

```
#include <string.h>                                          XSI

char *strdup(const char *str);          Duplicate str
```

The return value is NULL if there was an error or a pointer to dynamically allocated storage holding a copy of str. The returned value should be freed with free() when it's no longer needed.

3.2.3 System Calls: brk() and sbrk()

The four routines we've covered (malloc(), calloc(), realloc(), and free()) are the standard, portable functions to use for dynamic memory management.

On Unix systems, the standard functions are implemented on top of two additional, very primitive routines, which directly change the size of a process's address space. We present them here to help you understand how GNU/Linux and Unix work ("under the hood" again); it is highly unlikely that you will ever need to use these functions in a regular program. They are declared as follows:

```
#include <unistd.h>                                          Common
#include <malloc.h>      /* Necessary for GLIBC 2 systems */

int brk(void *end_data_segment);
void *sbrk(ptrdiff_t increment);
```

The `brk()` system call actually changes the process's address space. The address is a pointer representing the end of the data segment (really the heap area, as shown earlier in Figure 3.1). Its argument is an absolute logical address representing the new end of the address space. It returns `0` on success or `-1` on failure.

The `sbrk()` function is easier to use; its argument is the increment in bytes by which to change the address space. By calling it with an increment of `0`, you can determine where the address space currently ends. Thus, to increase your address space by 32 bytes, use code like this:

```
char *p = (char *) sbrk(0);      /* get current end of address space */
if (brk(p + 32) < 0) {
    /* handle error */
}
/* else, change worked */
```

Practically speaking, you would not use `brk()` directly. Instead, you would use `sbrk()` exclusively to grow (or even shrink) the address space. (We show how to do this shortly, in Section 3.2.5, "Address Space Examination," page 78.)

Even more practically, you should *never* use these routines. A program using them can't then use `malloc()` also, and this is a big problem, since many parts of the standard library rely on being able to use `malloc()`. Using `brk()` or `sbrk()` is thus likely to lead to hard-to-find program crashes.

But it's worth knowing about the low-level mechanics, and indeed, the `malloc()` suite of routines is implemented with `sbrk()` and `brk()`.

3.2.4 Lazy Programmer Calls: `alloca()`

"Danger, Will Robinson! Danger!"
—The Robot—

There is one additional memory allocation function that you should know about. We discuss it *only* so that you'll understand it when you see it, but you should *not* use it in new programs! This function is named `alloca()`; it's declared as follows:

```
/* Header on GNU/Linux, possibly not all Unix systems */        Common
#include <alloca.h>

void *alloca(size_t size);
```

The `alloca()` function allocates `size` bytes from the *stack*. What's nice about this is that the allocated storage disappears when the function returns. There's no need to explicitly free it because it goes away automatically, just as local variables do.

At first glance, `alloca()` seems like a programming panacea; memory can be allocated that doesn't have to be managed at all. Like the Dark Side of the Force, this is indeed seductive. And it is similarly to be avoided, for the following reasons:

- The function is nonstandard; it is not included in any formal standard, either ISO C or POSIX.

- The function is not portable. Although it exists on many Unix systems and GNU/Linux, it doesn't exist on non-Unix systems. This is a problem, since it's often important for code to be multiplatform, above and beyond just Linux and Unix.

- On some systems, `alloca()` can't even be implemented. All the world is not an Intel x86 processor, nor is all the world GCC.

- Quoting the manpage (emphasis added): "The `alloca` function is machine and compiler dependent. *On many systems its implementation is buggy.* Its use is discouraged."

- Quoting the manpage again: "On many systems `alloca` cannot be used inside the list of arguments of a function call, because the stack space reserved by `alloca` would appear on the stack in the middle of the space for the function arguments."

- It encourages sloppy coding. Careful and correct memory management isn't hard; you just to have to think about what you're doing and plan ahead.

GCC generally uses a built-in version of the function that operates by using inline code. As a result, there are other consequences of `alloca()`. Quoting again from the manpage:

> The fact that the code is inlined means that it is impossible to take the address of this function, or to change its behavior by linking with a different library.

> The inlined code often consists of a single instruction adjusting the stack pointer, and does not check for stack overflow. Thus, there is no `NULL` error return.

The manual page doesn't go quite far enough in describing the problem with GCC's built-in `alloca()`. If there's a stack overflow, the return value is *garbage*. And you have no way to tell! This flaw makes GCC's `alloca()` impossible to use in robust code.

All of this should convince you to stay away from `alloca()` for any new code that you may write. If you're going to have to write portable code using `malloc()` and `free()` anyway, there's no reason to also write code using `alloca()`.

3.2.5 Address Space Examination

The following program, `ch03-memaddr.c`, summarizes everything we've seen about the address space. It does many things that you should not do in practice, such as call `alloca()` or use `brk()` and `sbrk()` directly:

```
 1   /*
 2    * ch03-memaddr.c --- Show address of code, data and stack sections,
 3    *                    as well as BSS and dynamic memory.
 4    */
 5
 6   #include <stdio.h>
 7   #include <malloc.h>     /* for definition of ptrdiff_t on GLIBC */
 8   #include <unistd.h>
 9   #include <alloca.h>     /* for demonstration only */
10
11   extern void afunc(void);    /* a function for showing stack growth */
12
13   int bss_var;               /* auto init to 0, should be in BSS */
14   int data_var = 42;         /* init to nonzero, should be data */
15
16   int
17   main(int argc, char **argv) /* arguments aren't used */
18   {
19       char *p, *b, *nb;
20
21       printf("Text Locations:\n");
22       printf("\tAddress of main: %p\n", main);
23       printf("\tAddress of afunc: %p\n", afunc);
24
25       printf("Stack Locations:\n");
26       afunc();
27
28       p = (char *) alloca(32);
29       if (p != NULL) {
30           printf("\tStart of alloca()'ed array: %p\n", p);
31           printf("\tEnd of alloca()'ed array: %p\n", p + 31);
32       }
33
```

```
34          printf("Data Locations:\n");
35          printf("\tAddress of data_var: %p\n", & data_var);
36
37          printf("BSS Locations:\n");
38          printf("\tAddress of bss_var: %p\n", & bss_var);
39
40          b = sbrk((ptrdiff_t) 32);    /* grow address space */
41          nb = sbrk((ptrdiff_t) 0);
42          printf("Heap Locations:\n");
43          printf("\tInitial end of heap: %p\n", b);
44          printf("\tNew end of heap: %p\n", nb);
45
46          b = sbrk((ptrdiff_t) -16);   /* shrink it */
47          nb = sbrk((ptrdiff_t) 0);
48          printf("\tFinal end of heap: %p\n", nb);
49      }
50
51  void
52  afunc(void)
53  {
54          static int level = 0;        /* recursion level */
55          auto int stack_var;          /* automatic variable, on stack */
56
57          if (++level == 3)            /* avoid infinite recursion */
58              return;
59
60          printf("\tStack level %d: address of stack_var: %p\n",
61                  level, & stack_var);
62          afunc();                     /* recursive call */
63      }
```

This program prints the locations of the two functions `main()` and `afunc()` (lines 22–23). It then shows how the stack grows downward, letting `afunc()` (lines 51–63) print the address of successive instantiations of its local variable `stack_var`. (`stack_var` is purposely declared `auto`, to emphasize that it's on the stack.) It then shows the location of memory allocated by `alloca()` (lines 28–32). Finally it prints the locations of data and BSS variables (lines 34–38), and then of memory allocated directly through `sbrk()` (lines 40–48). Here are the results when the program is run on an Intel GNU/Linux system:

```
$ ch03-memaddr
Text Locations:
    Address of main: 0x804838c
    Address of afunc: 0x80484a8
Stack Locations:
    Stack level 1: address of stack_var: 0xbffff864
    Stack level 2: address of stack_var: 0xbffff844      Stack grows downward
    Start of alloca()'ed array: 0xbffff860
    End of alloca()'ed array: 0xbffff87f                 Addresses are on the stack
```

```
Data Locations:
    Address of data_var: 0x80496b8
BSS Locations:
    Address of bss_var: 0x80497c4              BSS is above data variables
Heap Locations:
    Initial end of heap: 0x80497c8            Heap is immediately above BSS
    New end of heap: 0x80497e8                And grows upward
    Final end of heap: 0x80497d8              Address spaces can shrink
```

3.3 Summary

• Every Linux (and Unix) program has different memory areas. They are stored in separate parts of the executable program's disk file. Some of the sections are loaded into the same part of memory when the program is run. All running copies of the same program share the executable code (the text segment). The `size` program shows the sizes of the different areas for relocatable object files and fully linked executable files.

• The address space of a running program may have holes in it, and the size of the address space can change as memory is allocated and released. On modern systems, address `0` is not part of the address space, so don't attempt to dereference `NULL` pointers.

• At the C level, memory is allocated or reallocated with one of `malloc()`, `calloc()`, or `realloc()`. Memory is freed with `free()`. (Although `realloc()` can do everything, using it that way isn't recommended). It is unusual for freed memory to be removed from the address space; instead, it is reused for later allocations.

• Extreme care must be taken to

  • Free only memory received from the allocation routines,

  • Free such memory once and only once,

  • Free unused memory, and

  • Not "leak" any dynamically allocated memory.

• POSIX provides the `strdup()` function as a convenience, and GLIBC provides `getline()` and `getdelim()` for reading arbitrary-length lines.

- The low-level system call interface functions, `brk()` and `sbrk()`, provide direct but primitive access to memory allocation and deallocation. Unless you are writing your own storage allocator, you should not use them.

- The `alloca()` function for allocating memory on the stack exists, but is not recommended. Like being able to recognize poison ivy, you should know it only so that you'll know to avoid it.

Exercises

1. Starting with the structure—

   ```
   struct line {
       size_t buflen;
       char *buf;
       FILE *fp;
   };
   ```

   —write your own `readline()` function that will read an any-length line. Don't worry about backslash continuation lines. Instead of using `fgets()` to read lines, use `getc()` to read characters one at a time.

2. Does your function preserve the terminating newline? Explain why or why not.

3. How does your function handle lines that end in CR-LF?

4. How do you initialize the structure? With a separate routine? With a documented requirement for specific values in the structure?

5. How do you indicate end-of-file? How do you indicate that an I/O error has occurred? For errors, should your function print an error message? Explain why or why not.

6. Write a program that uses your function to test it, and another program to generate input data to the first program. Test your function.

7. Rewrite your function to use `fgets()` and test it. Is the new code more complex or less complex? How does its performance compare to the `getc()` version?

8. Study the V7 *end*(3) manpage (`/usr/man/man3/end.3` in the V7 distribution). Does it shed any light on how '`sbrk(0)`' might work?

9. Enhance `ch03-memaddr.c` to print out the location of the arguments and the environment. In which part of the address space do they reside?

## Chapter 4

Files
and
File I/O

In this chapter

T his chapter describes basic file operations: opening and creating files, reading and writing them, moving around in them, and closing them. Along the way it presents the standard mechanisms for detecting and reporting errors. The chapter ends off by describing how to set a file's length and force file data and metadata to disk.

4.1 Introducing the Linux/Unix I/O Model

The Linux/Unix API model for I/O is straightforward. It can be summed up in four words: open, read, write, close. In fact, those are the names of the system calls: `open()`, `read()`, `write()`, `close()`. Here are their declarations:

```
#include <sys/types.h>                            POSIX
#include <sys/stat.h>         /* for mode_t */
#include <fcntl.h>            /* for flags for open() */
#include <unistd.h>           /* for ssize_t */

int open(const char *pathname, int flags, mode_t mode);
ssize_t read(int fd, void *buf, size_t count);
ssize_t write(int fd, const void *buf, size_t count);
int close(int fd);
```

In the next and subsequent sections, we illustrate the model by writing a *very* simple version of `cat`. It's so simple that it doesn't even have options; all it does is concatenate the contents of the named files to standard output. It does do minimal error reporting. Once it's written, we compare it to the V7 `cat`.

We present the program top-down, starting with the command line. In succeeding sections, we present error reporting and then get down to brass tacks, showing how to do actual file I/O.

4.2 Presenting a Basic Program Structure

Our version of `cat` follows a structure that is generally useful. The first part starts with an explanatory comment, header includes, declarations, and the `main()` function:

```
1   /*
2    * ch04-cat.c --- Demonstrate open(), read(), write(), close(),
3    *                errno and strerror().
4    */
5
6   #include <stdio.h>       /* for fprintf(), stderr, BUFSIZ */
7   #include <errno.h>       /* declare errno */
8   #include <fcntl.h>       /* for flags for open() */
9   #include <string.h>      /* declare strerror() */
```

```
10  #include <unistd.h>      /* for ssize_t */
11  #include <sys/types.h>
12  #include <sys/stat.h>   /* for mode_t */
13
14  char *myname;
15  int process(char *file);
16
17  /* main --- loop over file arguments */
18
19  int
20  main(int argc, char **argv)
21  {
22      int i;
23      int errs = 0;
24
25      myname = argv[0];
26
27      if (argc == 1)
28          errs = process("-");
29      else
30          for (i = 1; i < argc; i++)
31              errs += process(argv[i]);
32
33      return (errs != 0);
34  }
```
   ... continued later in the chapter ...

The `myname` variable (line 14) is used later for error messages; `main()` sets it to the program name (`argv[0]`) as its first action (line 25). Then `main()` loops over the arguments. For each argument, it calls a function named `process()` to do the work.

When given the filename - (a single dash, or minus sign), Unix `cat` reads standard input instead of trying to open a file named -. In addition, with no arguments, `cat` reads standard input. `ch04-cat` implements both of these behaviors. The check for '`argc == 1`' (line 27) is true when there are no filename arguments; in this case, `main()` passes "`-`" to `process()`. Otherwise, `main()` loops over all the arguments, treating them as files to be processed. If one of them happens to be "`-`", the program then processes standard input.

If `process()` returns a nonzero value, it means that something went wrong. Errors are added up in the `errs` variable (lines 28 and 31). When `main()` ends, it returns 0 if there were no errors, and 1 if there were (line 33). This is a fairly standard convention, whose meaning is discussed in more detail in Section 9.1.5.1, "Defining Process Exit Status," page 300.

The structure presented in `main()` is quite generic: `process()` could do anything we want to the file. For example (ignoring the special use of `"-"`), `process()` could just as easily remove files as concatenate them!

Before looking at the `process()` function, we have to describe how system call errors are represented and then how I/O is done. The `process()` function itself is presented in Section 4.4.3, "Reading and Writing," page 96.

4.3 Determining What Went Wrong

"If anything can go wrong, it will."
—**Murphy's Law**—

"Be prepared."
—**The Boy Scouts**—

Errors can occur anytime. Disks can fill up, users can enter invalid data, the server on a network from which a file is being read can crash, the network can die, and so on. It is important to *always* check every operation for success or failure.

The basic Linux system calls almost universally return -1 on error, and 0 or a positive value on success. This lets you know that the operation has succeeded or failed:

```
int result;

result = some_system_call(param1, param2);
if (result < 0) {
    /* error occurred, do something */
}
else
    /* all ok, proceed */
```

Knowing that an error occurred isn't enough. It's necessary to know *what* error occurred. For that, each process has a predefined variable named `errno`. Whenever a system call fails, `errno` is set to one of a set of predefined error values. `errno` and the predefined values are declared in the `<errno.h>` header file:

```
#include <errno.h>                                    ISO C

extern int errno;
```

`errno` itself may be a macro that *acts like* an `int` variable; it need not be a real integer. In particular, in threaded environments, each thread will have its own private version of `errno`. Practically speaking, though, for all the system calls and functions in this book, you can treat `errno` like a simple `int`.

4.3.1 Values for `errno`

The 2001 POSIX standard defines a large number of possible values for `errno`. Many of these are related to networking, IPC, or other specialized tasks. The manpage for each system call describes the possible `errno` values that can occur; thus, you can write code to check for particular errors and handle them specially if need be. The possible values are defined by symbolic constants. Table 4.1 lists the constants provided by GLIBC.

TABLE 4.1
GLIBC values for `errno`

Name	Meaning
E2BIG	Argument list too long.
EACCES	Permission denied.
EADDRINUSE	Address in use.
EADDRNOTAVAIL	Address not available.
EAFNOSUPPORT	Address family not supported.
EAGAIN	Resource unavailable, try again (may be the same value as EWOULDBLOCK).
EALREADY	Connection already in progress.
EBADF	Bad file descriptor.
EBADMSG	Bad message.
EBUSY	Device or resource busy.
ECANCELED	Operation canceled.
ECHILD	No child processes.
ECONNABORTED	Connection aborted.
ECONNREFUSED	Connection refused.
ECONNRESET	Connection reset.
EDEADLK	Resource deadlock would occur.
EDESTADDRREQ	Destination address required.
EDOM	Mathematics argument out of domain of function.
EDQUOT	Reserved.
EEXIST	File exists.

TABLE 4.1 *(Continued)*

Name	Meaning
EFAULT	Bad address.
EFBIG	File too large.
EHOSTUNREACH	Host is unreachable.
EIDRM	Identifier removed.
EILSEQ	Illegal byte sequence.
EINPROGRESS	Operation in progress.
EINTR	Interrupted function.
EINVAL	Invalid argument.
EIO	I/O error.
EISCONN	Socket is connected.
EISDIR	Is a directory.
ELOOP	Too many levels of symbolic links.
EMFILE	Too many open files.
EMLINK	Too many links.
EMSGSIZE	Message too large.
EMULTIHOP	Reserved.
ENAMETOOLONG	Filename too long.
ENETDOWN	Network is down.
ENETRESET	Connection aborted by network.
ENETUNREACH	Network unreachable.
ENFILE	Too many files open in system.
ENOBUFS	No buffer space available.
ENODEV	No such device.
ENOENT	No such file or directory.
ENOEXEC	Executable file format error.
ENOLCK	No locks available.
ENOLINK	Reserved.
ENOMEM	Not enough space.

TABLE 4.1 *(Continued)*

Name	Meaning
ENOMSG	No message of the desired type.
ENOPROTOOPT	Protocol not available.
ENOSPC	No space left on device.
ENOSYS	Function not supported.
ENOTCONN	The socket is not connected.
ENOTDIR	Not a directory.
ENOTEMPTY	Directory not empty.
ENOTSOCK	Not a socket.
ENOTSUP	Not supported.
ENOTTY	Inappropriate I/O control operation.
ENXIO	No such device or address.
EOPNOTSUPP	Operation not supported on socket.
EOVERFLOW	Value too large to be stored in data type.
EPERM	Operation not permitted.
EPIPE	Broken pipe.
EPROTO	Protocol error.
EPROTONOSUPPORT	Protocol not supported.
EPROTOTYPE	Protocol wrong type for socket.
ERANGE	Result too large.
EROFS	Read-only file system.
ESPIPE	Invalid seek.
ESRCH	No such process.
ESTALE	Reserved.
ETIMEDOUT	Connection timed out.
ETXTBSY	Text file busy.
EWOULDBLOCK	Operation would block (may be the same value as EAGAIN).
EXDEV	Cross-device link.

Many systems provide other error values as well, and older systems may not have all the errors just listed. You should check your local *intro*(2) and *errno*(2) manpages for the full story.

> NOTE errno should be examined *only* after an error has occurred and before further system calls are made. Its initial value is 0. However, nothing changes errno between errors, meaning that a successful system call does *not* reset it to 0. You can, of course, manually set it to 0 initially or whenever you like, but this is rarely done.

Initially, we use errno only for error reporting. There are two useful functions for error reporting. The first is perror():

```
#include <stdio.h>                                           ISO C

void perror(const char *s);
```

The perror() function prints a program-supplied string, followed by a colon, and then a string describing the value of errno:

```
if (some_system_call(param1, param2) < 0) {
    perror("system call failed");
    return 1;
}
```

We prefer the strerror() function, which takes an error value parameter and returns a pointer to a string describing the error:

```
#include <string.h>                                          ISO C

char *strerror(int errnum);
```

strerror() provides maximum flexibility in error reporting, since fprintf() makes it possible to print the error in any way we like:

```
if (some_system_call(param1, param2) < 0) {
    fprintf(stderr, "%s: %d, %d: some_system_call failed: %s\n",
            argv[0], param1, param2, strerror(errno));
    return 1;
}
```

You will see many examples of both functions throughout the book.

4.3.2 Error Message Style

C provides several special macros for use in error reporting. The most widely used are __FILE__ and __LINE__, which expand to the name of the source file and the current line number in that file. These have been available in C since its beginning. C99 defines an additional predefined identifier, `__func__`, which represents the name of the current function as a character string. The macros are used like this:

```
if (some_system_call(param1, param2) < 0) {
    fprintf(stderr, "%s: %s (%s %d): some_system_call(%d, %d) failed: %s\n",
        argv[0], __func__, __FILE__, __LINE__,
    param1, param2, strerror(errno));
    return 1;
}
```

Here, the error message includes not only the program's name but also the function name, source file name, and line number. The full list of identifiers useful for diagnostics is provided in Table 4.2.

TABLE 4.2
C99 diagnostic identifiers

Identifier	C version	Meaning
`__DATE__`	C89	Date of compilation in the form `"Mmm nn yyyy"`.
`__FILE__`	Original	Source-file name in the form `"program.c"`.
`__LINE__`	Original	Source-file line number in the form `42`.
`__TIME__`	C89	Time of compilation in the form `"hh:mm:ss"`.
`__func__`	C99	Name of current function, as if declared `const char __func__[] = "name"`.

The use of `__FILE__` and `__LINE__` was quite popular in the early days of Unix, when most people had source code and could find the error and fix it. As Unix systems became more commercial, use of these identifiers gradually diminished, since knowing the source code location isn't of much help to someone who only has a binary executable.

Today, although GNU/Linux systems come with source code, said source code often isn't installed by default. Thus, using these identifiers for error messages doesn't seem to provide much additional value. The *GNU Coding Standards* don't even mention them.

4.4 Doing Input and Output

All I/O in Linux is accomplished through *file descriptors*. This section introduces file descriptors, describes how to obtain and release them, and explains how to do I/O with them.

4.4.1 Understanding File Descriptors

A *file descriptor* is an integer value. Valid file descriptors start at 0 and go up to some system-defined limit. These integers are in fact simple indexes into each process's table of open files. (This table is maintained inside the operating system; it is not accessible to a running program.) On most modern systems, the size of the table is large. The command 'ulimit -n' prints the value:

```
$ ulimit -n
1024
```

From C, the maximum number of open files is returned by the getdtablesize() (get descriptor table size) function:

```
#include <unistd.h>                                              Common

int getdtablesize(void);
```

This small program prints the result of the function:

```
/* ch04-maxfds.c --- Demonstrate getdtablesize(). */

#include <stdio.h>            /* for fprintf(), stderr, BUFSIZ */
#include <unistd.h>           /* for ssize_t */

int
main(int argc, char **argv)
{
    printf("max fds: %d\n", getdtablesize());
    exit(0);
}
```

When compiled and run, not surprisingly the program prints the same value as printed by ulimit:

```
$ ch04-maxfds
max fds: 1024
```

File descriptors are held in normal int variables; it is typical to see declarations of the form 'int fd' for use with I/O system calls. There is no predefined type for file descriptors.

In the usual case, every program starts running with three file descriptors already opened for it. These are standard input, standard output, and standard error, on file descriptors 0, 1, and 2, respectively. (If not otherwise redirected, each one is connected to your keyboard and screen.)

Obvious Manifest Constants. An Oxymoron?

When working with file-descriptor-based system calls and the standard input, output and error, it is common practice to use the integer constants 0, 1, and 2 directly in code. In the overwhelming majority of cases, such *manifest constants* are a bad idea. You never know what the meaning is of some random integer constant and whether the same constant used elsewhere is related to it or not. To this end, the POSIX standard requires the definition of the following *symbolic constants* in <unistd.h>:

STDIN_FILENO   The "file number" for standard input: 0.

STDOUT_FILENO   The file number for standard output: 1.

STDERR_FILENO   The file number for standard error: 2.

However, in our humble opinion, using these macros is overkill. First, it's *painful* to type 12 or 13 characters instead of just 1. Second, the use of 0, 1, and 2 is *so* standard and *so* well known that there's really no grounds for confusion as to the meaning of these particular manifest constants.

On the other hand, use of these constants leaves no doubt as to what was intended. Consider this statement:

```
int fd = 0;
```

Is fd being initialized to refer to standard input, or is the programmer being careful to initialize his variables to a reasonable value? You can't tell.

One approach (as recommended by Geoff Collyer) is to use the following enum definition:

```
enum { Stdin, Stdout, Stderr };
```

These constants can then be used in place of 0, 1, and 2. They are both readable and easier to type.

4.4.2 Opening and Closing Files

New file descriptors are obtained (among other sources) from the open() system call. This system call opens a file for reading or writing and returns a new file descriptor for subsequent operations on the file. We saw the declaration earlier:

```
#include <sys/types.h>                                    POSIX
#include <sys/stat.h>
#include <fcntl.h>
#include <unistd.h>

int open(const char *pathname, int flags, mode_t mode);
```

The three arguments are as follows:

`const char *pathname`

> A C string, representing the name of the file to open.

`int flags`

> The bitwise-OR of one or more of the constants defined in `<fcntl.h>`. We describe them shortly.

`mode_t mode`

> The permissions mode of a file being created. This is discussed later in the chapter, see Section 4.6, "Creating Files," page 106. When opening an existing file, omit this parameter.[1]

The return value from `open()` is either the new file descriptor or –1 to indicate an error, in which case `errno` will be set. For simple I/O, the `flags` argument should be one of the values in Table 4.3.

TABLE 4.3
Flag values for `open()`

Symbolic constant	Value	Meaning
O_RDONLY	0	Open file only for reading; writes will fail.
O_WRONLY	1	Open file only for writing; reads will fail.
O_RDWR	2	Open file for reading and writing.

We will see example code shortly. Additional values for `flags` are described in Section 4.6, "Creating Files," page 106. Much early Unix code didn't use the symbolic values. Instead, the numeric value was used. Today this is considered bad practice, but we present the values so that you'll recognize their meanings if you see them.

The `close()` system call closes a file: The entry for it in the system's file descriptor table is marked as unused, and no further operations may be done with that file descriptor. The declaration is

```
#include <unistd.h>                                              POSIX

int close(int fd);
```

---

[1] `open()` is one of the few variadic system calls.

The return value is 0 on success, -1 on error. There isn't much you can do if an error does occur, other than report it. Errors closing files are unusual, but not unheard of, particularly for files being accessed over a network. Thus, it's good practice to check the return value, particularly for files opened for writing.

If you choose to ignore the return value, specifically cast it to void, to signify that you don't care about the result:

```
(void) close(fd);         /* throw away return value */
```

The flip side of this advice is that too many casts to void tend to the clutter the code. For example, despite the "always check the return value" principle, it's exceedingly rare to see code that checks the return value of printf() or bothers to cast it to void. As with many aspects of C programming, experience and judgment should be applied here too.

As mentioned, the number of open files, while large, is limited, and you should always close files when you're done with them. If you don't, you will eventually run out of file descriptors, a situation that leads to a lack of robustness on the part of your program.

The system closes all open files when a process exits, but—except for 0, 1, and 2—it's bad form to rely on this.

When open() returns a new file descriptor, it always returns the lowest unused integer value. *Always.* Thus, if file descriptors 0–6 are open and the program closes file descriptor 5, then the next call to open() returns 5, not 7. This behavior is important; we see later in the book how it's used to cleanly implement many important Unix features, such as I/O redirection and piping.

4.4.2.1 Mapping FILE * Variables to File Descriptors

The Standard I/O library functions and FILE * variables from <stdio.h>, such as stdin, stdout, and stderr, are built on top of the file-descriptor-based system calls.

Occasionally, it's useful to directly access the file descriptor associated with a <stdio.h> file pointer if you need to do something not defined by the ISO C standard. The fileno() function returns the underlying file descriptor:

```
#include <stdio.h>                                              POSIX

int fileno(FILE *stream);
```

We will see an example later, in Section 4.4.4, "Example: Unix cat," page 99.

4.4.2.2 Closing All Open Files

Open files are inherited by child processes from their parent processes. They are, in effect, *shared*. In particular, the position in the file is shared. We leave the details for discussion later, in Section 9.1.1.2, "File Descriptor Sharing," page 286.

Since programs can inherit open files, you may occasionally see programs that close all their files in order to start out with a "clean slate." In particular, code like this is typical:

```
int i;

/* leave 0, 1, and 2 alone */
for (i = 3; i < getdtablesize(); i++)
    (void) close(i);
```

Assume that the result of `getdtablesize()` is 1024. This code works, but it makes (1024 − 3) * 2 = 2042 system calls. 1020 of them are needless, since the return value from `getdtablesize()` doesn't change. Here is a better way to write this code:

```
int i, fds;

for (i = 3, fds = getdtablesize(); i < fds; i++)
    (void) close(i);
```

Such an optimization does not affect the readability of the code, and it can make a difference, particularly on slow systems. In general, it's worth looking for cases in which loops compute the same result repeatedly, to see if such a computation can't be pulled out of the loop. In all such cases, though, be sure that you (a) preserve the code's correctness and (b) preserve its readability!

4.4.3 Reading and Writing

I/O is accomplished with the `read()` and `write()` system calls, respectively:

```
#include <sys/types.h>                                          POSIX
#include <sys/stat.h>
#include <fcntl.h>
#include <unistd.h>

ssize_t read(int fd, void *buf, size_t count);
ssize_t write(int fd, const void *buf, size_t count);
```

Each function is about as simple as can be. The arguments are the file descriptor for the open file, a pointer to a buffer to read data into or to write data from, and the number of bytes to read or write.

The return value is the number of bytes actually read or written. (This number can be smaller than the requested amount: For a read operation this happens when fewer than count bytes are left in the file, and for a write operation it happens if a disk fills up or some other error occurs.) The return value is -1 if an error occurred, in which case errno indicates the error. When read() returns 0, it means that end-of-file has been reached.

We can now show the rest of the code for ch04-cat. The process() routine uses 0 if the input filename is "-", for standard input (lines 50 and 51). Otherwise, it opens the given file:

```
36  /*
37   * process --- do something with the file, in this case,
38   *             send it to stdout (fd 1).
39   *             Returns 0 if all OK, 1 otherwise.
40   */
41
42  int
43  process(char *file)
44  {
45      int fd;
46      ssize_t rcount, wcount;
47      char buffer[BUFSIZ];
48      int errors = 0;
49
50      if (strcmp(file, "-") == 0)
51          fd = 0;
52      else if ((fd = open(file, O_RDONLY)) < 0) {
53          fprintf(stderr, "%s: %s: cannot open for reading: %s\n",
54                  myname, file, strerror(errno));
55          return 1;
56      }
```

The buffer buffer (line 47) is of size BUFSIZ; this constant is defined by <stdio.h> to be the "optimal" block size for I/O. Although the value for BUFSIZ varies across systems, code that uses this constant is clean and portable.

The core of the routine is the following loop, which repeatedly reads data until either end-of-file or an error is encountered:

```
58          while ((rcount = read(fd, buffer, sizeof buffer)) > 0) {
59              wcount = write(1, buffer, rcount);
60              if (wcount != rcount) {
61                  fprintf(stderr, "%s: %s: write error: %s\n",
62                      myname, file, strerror(errno));
63                  errors++;
64                  break;
65              }
66          }
```

The rcount and wcount variables (line 45) are of type ssize_t, "signed size_t," which allows them to hold negative values. Note that the count value passed to write() is the return value from read() (line 59). While we want to read fixed-size BUFSIZ chunks, it is unlikely that the file itself is a multiple of BUFSIZ bytes big. When the final, smaller, chunk of bytes is read from the file, the return value indicates how many bytes of buffer received new data. Only those bytes should be copied to standard output, not the entire buffer.

The test 'wcount != rcount' on line 60 is the correct way to check for write errors; if some, but not all, of the data were written, then wcount will be positive but smaller than rcount.

Finally, process() checks for read errors (lines 68–72) and then attempts to close the file. In the (unlikely) event that close() fails (line 75), it prints an error message. Avoiding the close of standard input isn't strictly necessary in this program, but it's a good habit to develop for writing larger programs, in case other code elsewhere wants to do something with it or if a child program will inherit it. The last statement (line 82) returns 1 if there were errors, 0 otherwise.

```
68      if (rcount < 0) {
69          fprintf(stderr, "%s: %s: read error: %s\n",
70              myname, file, strerror(errno));
71          errors++;
72      }
73
74      if (fd != 0) {
75          if (close(fd) < 0) {
76              fprintf(stderr, "%s: %s: close error: %s\n",
77                  myname, file, strerror(errno));
78              errors++;
79          }
80      }
81
82      return (errors != 0);
83  }
```

`ch04-cat` checks every system call for errors. While this is tedious, it provides robustness (or at least clarity): When something goes wrong, `ch04-cat` prints an error message that is as specific as possible. The combination of `errno` and `strerror()` makes this easy to do. That's it for `ch04-cat`, only 88 lines of code!

To sum up, there are several points to understand about Unix I/O:

I/O is uninterpreted.
> The I/O system calls merely move bytes around. They do no interpretation of the data; all interpretation is up to the user-level program. This makes reading and writing binary structures just as easy as reading and writing lines of text (easier, really, although using binary data introduces portability problems).

I/O is flexible.
> You can read or write as many bytes at a time as you like. You can even read and write data one byte at a time, although doing so for large amounts of data is more expensive that doing so in large chunks.

I/O is simple.
> The three-valued return (negative for error, zero for end-of-file, positive for a count) makes programming straightforward and obvious.

I/O can be partial.
> Both `read()` and `write()` can transfer fewer bytes than requested. Application code (that is, *your* code) must always be aware of this.

4.4.4 Example: Unix `cat`

As promised, here is the V7 version of `cat`.[2] It begins by checking for options. The V7 `cat` accepts a single option, `-u`, for doing unbuffered output.

The basic design is similar to the one shown above; it loops over the files named by the command-line arguments and reads each file, one character at a time, sending the characters to standard output. Unlike our version, it uses the `<stdio.h>` facilities. In many ways code using the Standard I/O library is easier to read and write, since all buffering issues are hidden by the library.

---

[2] See `/usr/src/cmd/cat.c` in the V7 distribution. The program compiles without change under GNU/Linux.

```
 1   /*
 2    * Concatenate files.
 3    */
 4
 5   #include <stdio.h>
 6   #include <sys/types.h>
 7   #include <sys/stat.h>
 8
 9   char    stdbuf[BUFSIZ];
10
11   main(argc, argv)                              int main(int argc, char **argv)
12   char **argv;
13   {
14       int fflg = 0;
15       register FILE *fi;
16       register c;
17       int dev, ino = -1;
18       struct stat statb;
19
20       setbuf(stdout, stdbuf);
21       for( ; argc>1 && argv[1][0]=='-'; argc--,argv++) {
22           switch(argv[1][1]) {                Process options
23           case 0:
24               break;
25           case 'u':
26               setbuf(stdout, (char *)NULL);
27               continue;
28           }
29           break;
30       }
31       fstat(fileno(stdout), &statb);           Lines 31–36 explained in Chapter 5
32       statb.st_mode &= S_IFMT;
33       if (statb.st_mode!=S_IFCHR && statb.st_mode!=S_IFBLK) {
34           dev = statb.st_dev;
35           ino = statb.st_ino;
36       }
37       if (argc < 2) {
38           argc = 2;
39           fflg++;
40       }
41       while (--argc > 0) {                     Loop over files
42           if (fflg || (*++argv)[0]=='-' && (*argv)[1]=='\0')
43               fi = stdin;
44           else {
45               if ((fi = fopen(*argv, "r")) == NULL) {
46                   fprintf(stderr, "cat: can't open %s\n", *argv);
47                   continue;
48               }
49           }
```

```
50              fstat(fileno(fi), &statb);            Lines 50–56 explained in Chapter 5
51              if (statb.st_dev==dev && statb.st_ino==ino) {
52                  fprintf(stderr, "cat: input %s is output\n",
53                      fflg?"-": *argv);
54                  fclose(fi);
55                  continue;
56              }
57              while ((c = getc(fi)) != EOF)          Copy file contents to stdout
58                  putchar(c);
59              if (fi!=stdin)
60                  fclose(fi);
61          }
62      return(0);
63  }
```

Of note is that the program always exits successfully (line 62); it could have been written to note errors and indicate them in main()'s return value. (The mechanics of process exiting and the meaning of different exit status values are discussed in Section 9.1.5.1, "Defining Process Exit Status," page 300.)

The code dealing with the struct stat and the fstat() function (lines 31–36 and 50–56) is undoubtedly opaque, since we haven't yet covered these functions, and won't until the next chapter. (But do note the use of fileno() on line 50 to get at the underlying file descriptor associated with the FILE * variables.) The idea behind the code is to make sure that no input file is the same as the output file. This is intended to prevent infinite file growth, in case of a command like this:

```
$ cat myfile >> myfile                    Append one copy of myfile onto itself?
```

And indeed, the check works:

```
$ echo hi > myfile                        Create a file
$ v7cat myfile >> myfile                  Attempt to append it onto itself
cat: input myfile is output
```

If you try this with ch04-cat, it will keep running, and myfile will keep growing until you interrupt it. The GNU version of cat does perform the check. Note that something like the following is beyond cat's control:

```
$ v7cat < myfile > myfile
cat: input - is output
$ ls -l myfile
-rw-r--r--    1 arnold   devel           0 Mar 24 14:17 myfile
```

In this case, it's too late because *the shell* truncated myfile (with the > operator) before cat ever gets a chance to examine the file!

In Section 5.4.4.2, "The V7 cat Revisited," page 150, we explain the struct stat code.

4.5 Random Access: Moving Around within a File

So far, we have discussed *sequential* I/O, whereby data are read or written beginning at the front of the file and continuing until the end. Often, this is all a program needs to do. However, it is possible to do *random access* I/O; that is, read data from an arbitrary position in the file, without having to read everything before that position first.

The *offset* of a file descriptor is the position within an open file at which the next read or write will occur. A program sets the offset with the `lseek()` system call:

```
#include <sys/types.h>     /* for off_t */                        POSIX
#include <unistd.h>        /* declares lseek() and whence values */

off_t lseek(int fd, off_t offset, int whence);
```

The type `off_t` (offset type) is a signed integer type representing byte positions (offsets from the beginning) within a file. On 32-bit systems, the type is usually a `long`. However, many modern systems allow very large files, in which case `off_t` may be a more unusual type, such as a C99 `int64_t` or some other *extended* type. `lseek()` takes three arguments, as follows:

`int fd`

   The file descriptor for the open file.

`off_t offset`

   A position to which to move. The interpretation of this value depends on the `whence` parameter. `offset` can be positive or negative: Negative values move toward the front of the file; positive values move toward the end of the file.

`int whence`

   Describes the location in the file to which `offset` is relative. See Table 4.4.

TABLE 4.4
whence **values for** `lseek()`

Symbolic constant	Value	Meaning
`SEEK_SET`	0	`offset` is absolute, that is, relative to the beginning of the file.
`SEEK_CUR`	1	`offset` is relative to the current position in the file.
`SEEK_END`	2	`offset` is relative to the end of the file.

Much old code uses the numeric values shown in Table 4.4. However, any new code you write should use the symbolic values, whose meanings are clearer.

The meaning of the values and their effects upon file position are shown in Figure 4.1. Assuming that the file has 3000 bytes and that the current offset is 2000 before each call to lseek(), the new position after each call is as shown:

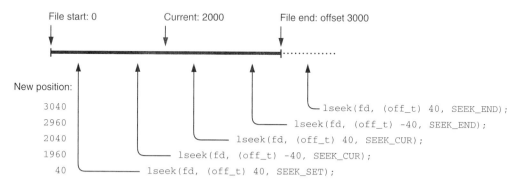

FIGURE 4.1
Offsets for lseek()

Negative offsets relative to the beginning of the file are meaningless; they fail with an "invalid argument" error.

The return value is the new position in the file. Thus, to find out where in the file you are, use

```
off_t curpos;
...
curpos = lseek(fd, (off_t) 0, SEEK_CUR);
```

The l in lseek() stands for long. lseek() was introduced in V7 Unix when file sizes were extended; V6 had a simple seek() system call. As a result, much old documentation (and code) treats the offset parameter as if it had type long, and instead of a cast to off_t, it's not unusual to see an L suffix on constant offset values:

```
curpos = lseek(fd, 0L, SEEK_CUR);
```

On systems with a Standard C compiler, where lseek() is declared with a prototype, such old code continues to work since the compiler automatically promotes the 0L from long to off_t if they are different types.

One interesting and important aspect of lseek() is that it is possible to seek beyond the end of a file. Any data that are subsequently written at that point go into the file, but with a "gap" or "hole" between the data at the previous end of the file and the new data. Data in the gap read as if they are all zeros.

The following program demonstrates the creation of holes. It writes three instances of a `struct` at the beginning, middle, and far end of a file. The offsets chosen (lines 16–18, the third element of each structure) are arbitrary but big enough to demonstrate the point:

```
1   /* ch04-holes.c --- Demonstrate lseek() and holes in files. */
2
3   #include <stdio.h>        /* for fprintf(), stderr, BUFSIZ */
4   #include <errno.h>        /* declare errno */
5   #include <fcntl.h>        /* for flags for open() */
6   #include <string.h>       /* declare strerror() */
7   #include <unistd.h>       /* for ssize_t */
8   #include <sys/types.h>    /* for off_t, etc. */
9   #include <sys/stat.h>     /* for mode_t */
10
11  struct person {
12      char name[10];        /* first name */
13      char id[10];          /* ID number */
14      off_t pos;            /* position in file, for demonstration */
15  } people[] = {
16      { "arnold", "123456789", 0 },
17      { "miriam", "987654321", 10240 },
18      { "joe",    "192837465", 81920 },
19  };
20
21  int
22  main(int argc, char **argv)
23  {
24      int fd;
25      int i, j;
26
27      if (argc < 2) {
28          fprintf(stderr, "usage: %s file\n", argv[0]);
29          return 1;
30      }
31
32      fd = open(argv[1], O_RDWR|O_CREAT|O_TRUNC, 0666);
33      if (fd < 0) {
34          fprintf(stderr, "%s: %s: cannot open for read/write: %s\n",
35                  argv[0], argv[1], strerror(errno));
36          return 1;
37      }
38
39      j = sizeof(people) / sizeof(people[0]);    /* count of elements */
```

Lines 27–30 make sure that the program was invoked properly. Lines 32–37 open the named file and verify that the open succeeded.

The calculation on line 39 of j, the array element count, uses a lovely, portable trick: The number of elements is the size of the entire array divided by the size of the first element. The beauty of this idiom is that it's always right: No matter how many elements you add to or remove from such an array, the compiler will figure it out. It also doesn't require a terminating *sentinel* element; that is, one in which all the fields are set to zero, NULL, or some such.

The work is done by a loop (lines 41–55), which seeks to the byte offset given in each structure (line 42) and then writes the structure out (line 49):

```
41      for (i = 0; i < j; i++) {
42          if (lseek(fd, people[i].pos, SEEK_SET) < 0) {
43              fprintf(stderr, "%s: %s: seek error: %s\n",
44                  argv[0], argv[1], strerror(errno));
45              (void) close(fd);
46              return 1;
47          }
48
49          if (write(fd, &people[i], sizeof(people[i])) != sizeof(people[i])) {
50              fprintf(stderr, "%s: %s: write error: %s\n",
51                  argv[0], argv[1], strerror(errno));
52              (void) close(fd);
53              return 1;
54          }
55      }
56
57      /* all ok here */
58      (void) close(fd);
59      return 0;
60  }
```

Here are the results when the program is run:

```
$ ch04-holes peoplelist                Run the program
$ ls -ls peoplelist                    Show size and blocks used
  16 -rw-r--r--    1 arnold    devel     81944 Mar 23 17:43 peoplelist
$ echo 81944 / 4096 | bc -l            Show blocks if no holes
20.00585937500000000000
```

We happen to know that each disk block in the file uses 4096 bytes. (How we know that is discussed in Section 5.4.2, "Retrieving File Information," page 141. For now, take it as a given.) The final bc command indicates that a file of size 81,944 bytes needs 21 disk blocks. However, the -s option to ls, which tells us how many blocks a file really uses, shows that the file uses only 16 blocks![3] The missing blocks in the file are the holes. This is illustrated in Figure 4.2.

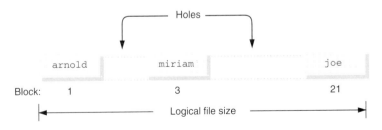

FIGURE 4.2
Holes in a file

> NOTE ch04-holes.c does direct binary I/O. This nicely illustrates the beauty of random access I/O: You can treat a disk file as if it were a very large array of binary data structures.
>
> In practice, storing live data by using binary I/O is a design decision that you should consider carefully. For example, suppose you need to move the data to a system using different byte orders for integers? Or different floating-point formats? Or to a system with different alignment requirements? Ignoring such issues can become significantly costly.

4.6 Creating Files

As described earlier, open() apparently opens existing files only. This section describes how brand-new files are created. There are two choices: creat() and open() with additional flags. Initially, creat() was the only way to create a file, but open() was later enhanced with this functionality as well. Both mechanisms require specification of the initial file permissions.

4.6.1 Specifying Initial File Permissions

As a GNU/Linux user, you are familiar with file permissions as printed by 'ls -l': read, write, and execute for each of user (the file's owner), group, and other. The various

---

[3] At least three of these blocks contain the data that we wrote out; the others are for use by the operating system in keeping track of where the data reside.

combinations are often expressed in octal, particularly for the chmod and umask commands. For example, file permissions -rw-r--r-- is equivalent to octal 0644 and -rwxr-xr-x is equivalent to octal 0755. (The leading 0 is C's notation for octal values.)

When you create a file, you must know the protections to be given to the new file. You can do this as a raw octal number if you choose, and indeed it's not uncommon to see such numbers in older code. However, it is better to use a bitwise OR of one or more of the symbolic constants from <sys/stat.h>, described in Table 4.5.

TABLE 4.5
POSIX symbolic constants for file modes

Symbolic constant	Value	Meaning
S_IRWXU	00700	User read, write, and execute permission.
S_IRUSR	00400	User read permission.
S_IREAD		Same as S_IRUSR.
S_IWUSR	00200	User write permission.
S_IWRITE		Same as S_IWUSR.
S_IXUSR	00100	User execute permission.
S_IEXEC		Same as S_IXUSR.
S_IRWXG	00070	Group read, write, and execute permission.
S_IRGRP	00040	Group read permission.
S_IWGRP	00020	Group write permission.
S_IXGRP	00010	Group execute permission.
S_IRWXO	00007	Other read, write, and execute permission.
S_IROTH	00004	Other read permission.
S_IWOTH	00002	Other write permission.
S_IXOTH	00001	Other execute permission.

The following fragment shows how to create variables representing permissions -rw-r--r-- and -rwxr-xr-x (0644 and 0755 respectively):

```
mode_t rw_mode, rwx_mode;

rw_mode  = S_IRUSR | S_IWUSR | S_IRGRP | S_IROTH;            /* 0644 */
rwx_mode = S_IRWXU | S_IRGRP | S_IXGRP | S_IROTH | S_IXOTH;  /* 0755 */
```

Older code used S_IREAD, S_IWRITE, and S_IEXEC together with bit shifting to produce the same results:

```
mode_t rw_mode, rwx_mode;

rw_mode  = (S_IREAD|S_IWRITE) | (S_IREAD >> 3) | (S_IREAD >> 6); /* 0644 */
rwx_mode = (S_IREAD|S_IWRITE|S_IEXEC) |
           ((S_IREAD|S_IEXEC) >> 3) | ((S_IREAD|S_IEXEC) >> 6);  /* 0755 */
```

Unfortunately, neither notation is incredibly clear. The modern version is preferred since each permission bit has its own name and there is less opportunity to do the bitwise operations incorrectly.

The additional permission bits shown in Table 4.6 are available for use when you are changing a file's permission, but they should not be used when you initially create a file. Whether these bits may be included varies wildly by operating system. It's best not to try; rather, you should explicitly change the permissions after the file is created. (Changing permission is described in Section 5.5.2, "Changing Permissions: chmod() and fchmod()," page 156. The meanings of these bits is discussed in Chapter 11, "Permissions and User and Group ID Numbers," page 403.)

TABLE 4.6
Additional POSIX symbolic constants for file modes

Symbolic constant	Value	Meaning
S_ISUID	04000	Set user ID.
S_ISGID	02000	Set group ID.
S_ISVTX	01000	Save text.

When standard utilities create files, the default permissions they use are -rw-rw-rw- (or 0666). Because most users prefer to avoid having files that are world-writable, each process carries with it a *umask*. The umask is a set of permission bits indicating those bits that should never be allowed *when new files are created*. (The umask is not used when changing permissions.) Conceptually, the operation that occurs is

```
actual_permissions = (requested_permissions & (~umask));
```

The umask is usually set by the umask command in $HOME/.profile when you log in. From a C program, it's set with the umask() system call:

```
#include <sys/types.h>                                        POSIX
#include <sys/stat.h>

mode_t umask(mode_t mask);
```

The return value is the old umask. Thus, to determine the current mask, you must set it to a value and then reset it (or change it, as desired):

```
mode_t mask = umask(0);      /* retrieve current mask */
(void) umask(mask);          /* restore it */
```

Here is an example of the umask in action, at the shell level:

```
$ umask                                Show the current mask
0022
$ touch newfile                        Create a file
$ ls -l newfile                        Show permissions of new file
-rw-r--r--    1 arnold    devel        0 Mar 24 15:43 newfile
$ umask 0                              Set mask to empty
$ touch newfile2                       Create a second file
$ ls -l newfile2                       Show permissions of new file
-rw-rw-rw-    1 arnold    devel        0 Mar 24 15:44 newfile2
```

4.6.2 Creating Files with `creat()`

The `creat()`[4] system call creates new files. It is declared as follows:

```
#include <sys/types.h>                                        POSIX
#include <sys/stat.h>
#include <fcntl.h>

int creat(const char *pathname, mode_t mode);
```

The `mode` argument represents the permissions for the new file (as discussed in the previous section). The file named by `pathname` is created, with the given permission as modified by the umask. It is opened for writing (only), and the return value is the file descriptor for the new file or -1 if there was a problem. In this case, `errno` indicates the error. If the file already exists, it will be truncated when opened.

In all other respects, file descriptors returned by `creat()` are the same as those returned by `open()`; they're used for writing and seeking and must be closed with `close()`:

---

[4] Yes, that's how it's spelled. Ken Thompson, one of the two "fathers" of Unix, was once asked what he would have done differently if he had it to do over again. He replied that he would have spelled `creat()` with an "e." Indeed, that is exactly what he did for the *Plan 9 From Bell Labs* operating system.

```
int fd, count;

/* Error checking omitted for brevity */
fd = creat("/some/new/file", 0666);
count = write(fd, "some data\n", 10);
(void) close(fd);
```

4.6.3 Revisiting open()

You may recall the declaration for open():

```
int open(const char *pathname, int flags, mode_t mode);
```

Earlier, we said that when opening a file for plain I/O, we could ignore the mode argument. Having seen creat(), though, you can probably guess that open() can also be used for creating files and that the mode argument is used in this case. This is indeed true.

Besides the O_RDONLY, O_WRONLY, and O_RDWR flags, additional flags may be bitwise OR'd when open() is called. The POSIX standard mandates a number of these additional flags. Table 4.7 presents the flags that are used for most mundane applications.

TABLE 4.7
Additional POSIX flags for open()

Flag	Meaning
O_APPEND	Force all writes to occur at the end of the file.
O_CREAT	Create the file if it doesn't exist.
O_EXCL	When used with O_CREAT, cause open() to fail if the file already exists.
O_TRUNC	Truncate the file (set it to zero length) if it exists.

Given O_APPEND and O_TRUNC, you can imagine how the shell might open or create files corresponding to the > and >> operators. For example:

```
int fd;
extern char *filename;
mode_t mode = S_IRUSR|S_IWUSR|S_IRGRP|S_IWGRP|S_IROTH|S_IWOTH;   /* 0666 */

fd = open(filename, O_CREAT|O_WRONLY|O_TRUNC, mode);              /* for > */

fd = open(filename, O_CREAT|O_WRONLY|O_APPEND, mode);             /* for >> */
```

Note that the O_EXCL flag would *not* be used here, since for both > and >>, it's not an error for the file to exist. Remember also that the system applies the umask to the requested permissions.

Also, it's easy to see that, at least conceptually, creat() could be written this easily:

```
int creat(const char *path, mode_t mode)
{
    return open(path, O_CREAT|O_WRONLY|O_TRUNC, mode);
}
```

> NOTE If a file is opened with O_APPEND, all data will be written at the end of the file, even if the current position has been reset with lseek().

Modern systems provide additional flags whose uses are more specialized. Table 4.8 describes them briefly.

TABLE 4.8
Additional advanced POSIX flags for open()

Flag	Meaning
O_NOCTTY	If the device being opened is a terminal, it does not become the process's controlling terminal. (This is a more advanced topic, discussed briefly in Section 9.2.1, page 312.)
O_NONBLOCK	Disables blocking of I/O operations in certain cases (see Section 9.4.3.4, page 333).
O_DSYNC	Ensure that data written to a file make it all the way to physical storage before write() returns.
O_RSYNC	Ensure that any data that read() would read, which may have been written to the file being read, have made it all the way to physical storage before read() returns.
O_SYNC	Like O_DSYNC, but also ensure that all file metadata, such as access times, have also been written to physical storage.

The O_DSYNC, O_RSYNC, and O_SYNC flags need some explanation. Unix systems (including Linux) maintain an internal cache of disk blocks, called the *buffer cache*. When the write() system call returns, the data passed to the operating system have been copied to a buffer in the buffer cache. They are not necessarily written out to the disk.

The buffer cache provides considerable performance improvement: Since disk I/O is often an order of magnitude or more slower than CPU and memory operations, programs would slow down considerably if they had to wait for every write to go all the way through to the disk. In addition, if data have recently been written to a file, a subsequent read of that same data will find the information already in the buffer cache, where it can be returned immediately instead of having to wait for an I/O operation to read it from the disk.

Unix systems also do *read-ahead*; since most reads are sequential, upon reading one block, the operating system will read several more consecutive disk blocks so that their information will already be in the buffer cache when a program asks for it. If multiple programs are reading the same file, they all benefit since they will all get their data from the same copy of the file's disk blocks in the buffer cache.

All of this caching is wonderful, but of course there's no free lunch. While data are in the buffer cache and before they have been written to disk, there's a small—but very real—window in which disaster can strike; for example, if the power goes out. Modern disk drives exacerbate this problem: Many have their own internal buffers, so while data may have made it to the drive, it may not have made it onto the media when the power goes out! This can be a significant issue for small systems that aren't in a data center with controlled power or that don't have an uninterruptible power supply (UPS).[5]

For most applications, the chance that data in the buffer cache might be inadvertently lost is acceptably small. However, for some applications, *any* such chance is not acceptable. Thus, the notion of *synchronous I/O* was added to Unix systems, whereby a program can be guaranteed that if a system call has returned, the data are safely written on a physical storage device.

The `O_DSYNC` flag guarantees data integrity; the data and any other information that the operating system needs to find the data are written to disk before `write()` returns. However, metadata, such as access and modification times, may not be written to disk. The `O_SYNC` flag requires that metadata also be written to disk before `write()` returns. (Here too there is no free lunch; synchronous writes can seriously affect the performance of a program, slowing it down noticeably.)

---

[5] If you don't have a UPS and you use your system for critical work, we highly recommend investing in one. You should also be doing regular backups.

The O_RSYNC flag is for data reads: If read() finds data in the buffer cache that were scheduled for writing to disk, then read() won't return that data until they have been written to disk. The other two flags can affect this: In particular, O_SYNC will cause read() to wait until the file metadata have been written out as well.

> NOTE As of kernel version 2.4, Linux treats all three flags the same, with essentially the meaning of O_SYNC. Furthermore, Linux defines additional flags that are Linux specific and intended for specialized uses. Check the GNU/Linux *open*(2) manpage for more information.

4.7 Forcing Data to Disk

Earlier, we described the O_DSYNC, O_RSYNC, and O_SYNC flags for open(). We noted that using these flags could slow a program down since each write() does not return until all data have been written to physical media.

For a slightly higher risk level, we can have our cake and eat it too. We do this by opening a file without one of the O_xSYNC flags and then using one of the following two system calls at whatever point it's necessary to have the data safely moved to physical storage:

```
#include <unistd.h>

int fsync(int fd);                                       POSIX FSC
int fdatasync(int fd);                                   POSIX SIO
```

The fdatasync() system call is like O_DSYNC: It forces all file data to be written to the final physical device. The fsync() system call is like O_SYNC, forcing not just file data, but also file metadata, to physical storage. The fsync() call is more portable; it has been around in the Unix world for longer and is more likely to exist across a broad range of systems.

You can use these calls with <stdio.h> file pointers by first calling fflush() and then using fileno() to obtain the underlying file descriptor. Here is an fpsync() function that can be used to wrap both operations in one call. It returns 0 on success:

```
/* fpsync --- sync a stdio FILE * variable */

int fpsync(FILE *fp)
{
    if (fp == NULL || fflush(fp) == EOF || fsync(fileno(fp)) < 0)
        return -1;

    return 0;
}
```

Technically, both of these calls are extensions to the base POSIX standard: `fsync()` in the "File Synchronization" extension (FSC), and `fdatasync()` in the "Synchronized Input and Output" extension. Nevertheless, you can use them on a GNU/Linux system without any problem.

4.8 Setting File Length

Two system calls make it possible to adjust the size of a file:

```
#include <unistd.h>
#include <sys/types.h>

int truncate(const char *path, off_t length);                    XSI
int ftruncate(int fd, off_t length);                             POSIX
```

As should be obvious from the parameters, `truncate()` takes a filename argument, whereas `ftruncate()` works on an open file descriptor. (The *xxx*() and f*xxxx*() naming convention for system call pairs that work on a filename or file descriptor is common. We see several examples in this and subsequent chapters.) For both, the `length` argument is the new size of the file.

This system call originated in 4.2 BSD Unix, and in early systems could only be used to shorten a file's length, hence the name. (It was created to simplify implementation of the truncate operation in Fortran.) On modern systems, including Linux, the name is a misnomer, since it's possible to extend the length of a file with these calls, not just shorten a file. (However, POSIX indicates that the ability to extend a file is an XSI extension.)

For these calls, the file being truncated must have write permission (for `truncate()`), or have been opened for writing (for `ftruncate()`). If the file is being shortened, any data past the new end of the file are lost. (Thus, you can't shorten the file, lengthen it again, and expect to find the original data.) If the file is extended, as with data written after an `lseek()`, the data between the old end of the file and the new end of file read as zeros.

These calls are very different from 'open(file, ...|O_TRUNC, mode)'. The latter truncates a file completely, throwing away all its data. These calls simply set the file's absolute length to the given value.

These functions are fairly specialized; they're used only four times in all of the GNU Coreutils code. We present an example use of ftruncate() in Section 5.5.3, "Changing Timestamps: utime()," page 157.

4.9 Summary

- When a system call fails, it usually returns -1, and the global variable errno is set to a predefined value indicating the problem. The functions perror() and strerror() can be used for reporting errors.

- Files are manipulated by small integers called file descriptors. File descriptors for standard input, standard output, and standard error are inherited from a program's parent process. Others are obtained with open() or creat(). They are closed with close(), and getdtablesize() returns the maximum number of allowed open files. The value of the umask (set with umask()) affects the permissions given to new files created with creat() or the O_CREAT flag for open().

- The read() and write() system calls read and write data, respectively. Their interface is simple. In particular, they do no interpretation of the data; files are linear streams of bytes. The lseek() system call provides random access I/O: the ability to move around within a file.

- Additional flags for open() provide for synchronous I/O, whereby data make it all the way to the physical storage media before write() or read() return. Data can also be forced to disk on a controlled basis with fsync() or fdatasync().

- The truncate() and ftruncate() system calls set the absolute length of a file. (On older systems, they can only be used to shorten a file; on modern systems they can also extend a file.)

Exercises

1. Using just open(), read(), write(), and close(), write a simple copy program that copies the file named by its first argument to the file named by its second.

2. Enhance the `copy` program to accept `"-"` to mean "standard input" if used as the first argument and "standard output" as the second. Does 'copy - -' work correctly?

3. Look at the *proc*(5) manpage on a GNU/Linux system. In particular the *fd* subsection. Do an 'ls -l /dev/fd' and examine the files in the /proc/self/fd directly. If /dev/stdin and friends had been around in the early versions of Unix, how would that have simplified the code for the V7 cat program? (Many other modern Unix systems have a /dev/fd directory or filesystem. If you're not using GNU/Linux, see what you can discover about your Unix version.)

4. Even though you don't understand it yet, try to copy the code segment from the V7 cat.c that uses the `struct stat` and the `fstat()` function into ch04-cat.c so that it too reports an error for 'cat file >> file'.

5. (Easy.) Assuming the existence of `strerror()`, write your own version of `perror()`.

6. What is the result of 'ulimit -n' on your system?

7. Write a simple version of the `umask` program, named `myumask`, that takes an octal mask on the command line. Use `strtol()` with a base of 8 to convert the character string command-line argument into an integer value. Change the umask to the new mask with the `umask()` system call.

   Compile and run `myumask`, and then examine the value of the umask with the regular `umask` command. Explain the results. (Hint: in Bash, enter 'type umask'.)

8. Change the simple `copy` program you wrote earlier to use `open()` with the O_SYNC flag. Using the `time` command, compare the performance of the original version and the new version on a large file.

9. For `ftruncate()`, we said that the file must have been opened for writing. How can a file be open for writing when the file itself doesn't have write permission?

10. Write a `truncate` program whose usage is 'truncate *filelength*'.

Chapter 5

Directories and File Metadata

In this chapter

T his chapter continues the climb up the learning curve toward the next plateau: understanding directories and information about files.

In this chapter we explore how file information is stored in a directory, how directories themselves are read, created, and removed, what information about files is available, and how to retrieve it. Finally, we explore other ways to update file metadata, such as the owner, group, permissions, and access and modification times.

5.1 Considering Directory Contents

All Unix systems, including Linux, use the same conceptual design for storing file information on disk. Although there is considerable variation in the implementation of the design, the interface at the C level remains consistent, making it possible to write portable programs that compile and run on many different systems.

5.1.1 Definitions

Copyright 1997–2004 © J.D. "Illiad" Frazer
Used with permission. http://www.userfriendly.org

We start the discussion by defining some terms.

Partition

> A unit of physical storage. *Physical partitions* are typically either part of a disk or an entire disk. Modern systems make it possible to create *logical partitions* from multiple physical ones.

Filesystem

A partition (physical or logical) that contains file data and *metadata*, information about files (as opposed to the file contents, which is information *in* the files). Such metadata include file ownership, permissions, size, and so on, as well as information for use by the operating system in locating file contents.

You place filesystems "in" partitions (a one-to-one correspondence) by writing standard information in them. This is done with a user-level program, such as `mke2fs` on GNU/Linux, or `newfs` on Unix. (The Unix `mkfs` command makes partitions but is difficult to use directly. `newfs` calls it with the correct parameters. If your system is a Unix system, see the *newfs*(8) and *mkfs*(8) manpages for the details.)

For the most part, GNU/Linux and Unix hide the existence of filesystems and partitions. (Further details are given in Section 8.1, "Mounting and Unmounting Filesystems," page 228). Everything is accessed by pathnames, without reference to which disk a file lives on. (Contrast this with almost every other commercial operating system, such as OpenVMS, or the default behavior of any Microsoft system.)

Inode

Short for "index node," initially abbreviated "i-node" and now written "inode." A small block of information describing everything about a file *except* the file's name(s). The number of inodes, and thus the number of unique files per filesystem, is set and made permanent when the filesystem is created. '`df -i`' can tell you how many inodes you have and how many are used.

Device

In the context of files, filesystems, and file metadata, a unique number representing an in-use ("mounted") filesystem. The (device, inode) pair *uniquely* identifies the file: Two different files are guaranteed to have different (device, inode) pairs. This is discussed in more detail later in this chapter.

Directory

A special file, containing a list of (inode number, name) pairs. Directories can be opened for reading but not for writing; the operating system makes all the changes to a directory's contents.

Conceptually, each disk block contains either some number of inodes, or file data. The inode, in turn, contains pointers to the blocks that contain the file's data. See Figure 5.1.

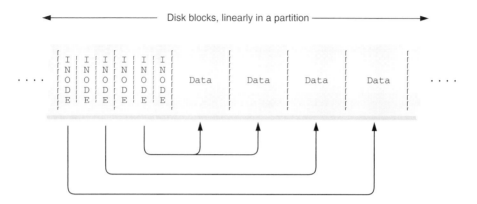

FIGURE 5.1
Conceptual view of inode and data blocks

The figure shows all the inode blocks at the front of the partition and the data blocks after them. Early Unix filesystems were indeed organized this way. However, while all modern systems still have inodes and data blocks, the organization has changed for improved efficiency and robustness. The details vary from system to system, and even within GNU/Linux systems there are multiple kinds of filesystems, but the concepts are the same.

5.1.2 Directory Contents

Directories make the connection between a filename and an inode. Directory entries contain an inode number and a filename. They also contain additional bookkeeping information that is not of interest to us here. See Figure 5.2.

Early Unix systems had two-byte inode numbers and up to 14-byte filenames. Here is the entire content of the V7 /usr/include/sys/dir.h:

Once a link is removed, creating a new file by the same name as the original file creates a new file:

```
$ rm message                                    Remove old name
$ echo "What's happenin?" > message             Reuse the name
$ ls -il msg message                            Show information
 228794 -rw-r--r--    1 arnold    devel        17 May  4 15:58 message
 228786 -rw-r--r--    1 arnold    devel        19 May  4 15:51 msg
```

Notice that the link counts for both files are now equal to 1.

At the C level, links are created with the `link()` system call:

```
#include <unistd.h>                                           POSIX

int link(const char *oldpath, const char *newpath);
```

The return value is 0 if the link was created successfully, or -1 otherwise, in which case `errno` reflects the error. An important failure case is one in which `newpath` already exists. The system won't remove it for you, since attempting to do so can cause inconsistencies in the filesystem.

5.1.3.1 The GNU `link` Program

The `ln` program is complicated and large. However, the GNU Coreutils contains a simple `link` program that just calls `link()` on its first two arguments. The following example shows the code from `link.c`, with some irrelevant parts deleted. Line numbers relate to the actual file.

```
20  /* Implementation overview:
21
22     Simply call the system 'link' function */
23
       ... #include statements omitted for brevity ...
34
35  /* The official name of this program (e.g., no `g' prefix).  */
36  #define PROGRAM_NAME "link"
37
38  #define AUTHORS "Michael Stone"
39
40  /* Name this program was run with.  */
41  char *program_name;
42
43  void
44  usage (int status)
45  {
       ... omitted for brevity ...
62  }
63
```

```
64  int
65  main (int argc, char **argv)
66  {
67    program_name = argv[0];
68    setlocale (LC_ALL, "");
69    bindtextdomain (PACKAGE, LOCALEDIR);
70    textdomain (PACKAGE);
71
72    atexit (close_stdout);
73
74    parse_long_options (argc, argv, PROGRAM_NAME, GNU_PACKAGE, VERSION,
75                        AUTHORS, usage);
76
77    /* The above handles --help and --version.
78       Since there is no other invocation of getopt, handle `--' here.  */
79    if (1 < argc && STREQ (argv[1], "--"))
80      {
81        --argc;
82        ++argv;
83      }
84
85    if (argc < 3)
86      {
87        error (0, 0, _("too few arguments"));
88        usage (EXIT_FAILURE);
89      }
90
91    if (3 < argc)
92      {
93        error (0, 0, _("too many arguments"));
94        usage (EXIT_FAILURE);
95      }
96
97    if (link (argv[1], argv[2]) != 0)
98      error (EXIT_FAILURE, errno, _("cannot create link %s to %s"),
99             quote_n (0, argv[2]), quote_n (1, argv[1]));
100
101   exit (EXIT_SUCCESS);
102 }
```

Lines 67–75 are typical Coreutils boilerplate, setting up internationalization, the final action upon exit, and parsing the arguments. Lines 79–95 make sure that link is called with only two arguments. The link() system call itself occurs on line 97. (The quote_n() function provides quoting of the arguments in a style suitable for the current locale; the details aren't important here.)

5.1.3.2 Dot and Dot-Dot

Rounding off the discussion of links, let's look at how the '.' and '..' special names are managed. They are really just hard links. In the first case, '.' is a hard link to the directory containing it, and '..' is a hard link to the parent directory. The operating system creates these links for you; as mentioned earlier, user-level code cannot create a hard link to a directory. This example illustrates the links:

```
$ pwd                                    Show current directory
/tmp
$ ls -ldi /tmp                           Show its inode number
 225345 drwxrwxrwt   14 root     root    4096 May   4 16:15 /tmp
$ mkdir x                                Create a new directory
$ ls -ldi x                              And show its inode number
  52794 drwxr-xr-x    2 arnold   devel   4096 May   4 16:27 x
$ ls -ldi x/. x/..                       Show . and .. inode numbers
  52794 drwxr-xr-x    2 arnold   devel   4096 May   4 16:27 x/.
 225345 drwxrwxrwt   15 root     root    4096 May   4 16:27 x/..
```

The root's parent directory (/..) is a special case; we defer discussion of it until Chapter 8, "Filesystems and Directory Walks," page 227.

5.1.4 File Renaming

Given the way in which directory entries map names to inode numbers, renaming a file is conceptually quite easy:

1. If the new name for the file names an existing file, remove the existing file first.

2. Create a new link to the file by the new name.

3. Remove the old name (link) for the file. (Removing names is discussed in the next section.)

Early versions of the mv command did work this way. However, when done this way, file renaming is not *atomic*; that is, it doesn't happen in one uninterruptible operation. And, on a heavily loaded system, a malicious user could take advantage of race conditions,[1] subverting the rename operation and substituting a different file for the original one.

---

[1] A *race condition* is a situation in which details of timing can produce unintended side effects or bugs. In this case, the directory, for a short period of time, is in an inconsistent state, and it is this inconsistency that introduces the vulnerability.

For this reason, 4.2 BSD introduced the `rename()` system call:

```
#include <stdio.h>                                           ISO C

int rename(const char *oldpath, const char *newpath);
```

On Linux systems, the renaming operation is atomic; the manpage states:

> If `newpath` already exists it will be atomically replaced ..., so that there is no point at which another process attempting to access `newpath` will find it missing.

> If `newpath` exists but the operation fails for some reason, `rename` guarantees to leave an instance of `newpath` in place.

> However, when overwriting there will probably be a window in which both `oldpath` and `newpath` refer to the file being renamed.

As with other system calls, a `0` return indicates success, and a return value of `-1` indicates an error.

5.1.5 File Removal

Removing a file means removing the file's entry in the directory and decrementing the file's link count (maintained in the inode). The contents of the file, and the disk blocks holding them, are not freed until the link count reaches zero.

The system call is named `unlink()`:

```
#include <unistd.h>                                          POSIX

int unlink(const char *pathname);
```

Given our discussion of file links, the name makes sense; this call removes the given link (directory entry) for the file. It returns `0` on success and `-1` on error.

The ability to remove a file requires write permission only for the directory and not for the file itself. This fact can be confusing, particularly for new Linux/Unix users. However, since the operation is one on the directory, this makes sense; it is the directory contents that are being modified, not the file's contents.[2]

---

[2] Indeed, the file's *metadata* are changed (the number of links), but that does not affect any other file attribute, nor does it affect the file's contents. Updating the link count is the only operation on a file that doesn't involve checking the file's permissions.

5.1.5.1 Removing Open Files

Since the earliest days of Unix, it has been possible to remove open files. Simply call `unlink()` with the filename after a successful call to `open()` or `creat()`.

At first glance, this seems to be a strange thing to do. Since the system frees the data blocks when a file's link count goes to zero, is it even possible to use the open file?

The answer is yes, you can continue to use the open file normally. The system knows that the file is open, and therefore it delays the release of the file's storage until the last file descriptor on the file is closed. Once the file is completely unused, the storage is freed.

This operation also happens to be a useful one: It is an easy way for a program to get temporary file storage that is guaranteed to be both private and automatically released when no longer needed:

```
/* Obtaining private temporary storage, error checking omitted for brevity */
int fd;
mode_t mode = O_CREAT|O_EXCL|O_TRUNC|O_RDWR;

fd = open("/tmp/myfile", mode, 0000);          Open the file
unlink("/tmp/myfile");                         Remove it

... continue to use file ...
close(fd);                                     Close file, free storage
```

The downside to this approach is that it's also possible for a runaway application to fill up a filesystem with an open but anonymous file, in which case the system administrator has to try to find and kill the process. In olden days, a reboot and filesystem consistency check might have been required; thankfully, this is exceedingly rare on modern systems.

5.1.5.2 Using ISO C: `remove()`

ISO C provides the `remove()` function for removing files; this is intended to be a general function, usable on any system that supports ISO C, not just Unix and GNU/Linux:

```
#include <stdio.h>                                        ISO C

int remove(const char *pathname);
```

While not technically a system call, the return value is in the same vein: 0 on success and -1 on error, with `errno` reflecting the value.

On GNU/Linux, `remove()` uses the `unlink()` system call to remove files, and the `rmdir()` system call (discussed later in the chapter) to remove directories. (On older GNU/Linux systems not using GLIBC, `remove()` is an alias for `unlink()`; this fails on directories. If you have such a system, you should probably upgrade it.)

5.1.6 Symbolic Links

We started the chapter with a discussion of partitions, filesystems, and inodes. We also saw that directory entries associate names with inode numbers. Because directory entries contain no other information, hard links are restricted to files *within the same filesystem*. This has to be; there is no way to distinguish inode 2341 on one filesystem from inode 2341 on another filesystem. Here is what happens when we try:

```
$ mount                                    Show filesystems in use
/dev/hda2 on / type ext3 (rw)
/dev/hda5 on /d type ext3 (rw)
...
$ ls -li /tmp/message                      Earlier example was on filesystem for /
 228786 -rw-r--r--    2 arnold   devel    19 May  4 15:51 /tmp/message
$ cat /tmp/message
Hi, how ya doin' ?
$ /bin/pwd                                 Current directory is on a different filesystem
/d/home/arnold
$ ln /tmp/message .                        Attempt the link
ln: creating hard link `./message' to `/tmp/message': Invalid cross-device link
```

Large systems often have many partitions, both on physically attached local disks and on remotely mounted network filesystems. The hard-link restriction to the same filesystem is inconvenient, for example, if some files or directories must be moved to a new location, but old software uses a hard-coded filename for the old location.

To get around this restriction, 4.2 BSD introduced *symbolic links*. A symbolic link (also referred to as a *soft link*) is a special kind of file (just as a directory is a special kind of file). The contents of the file are the *pathname* of the file being "pointed to." All modern Unix systems, including Linux, provide symbolic links; indeed they are now part of POSIX.

Symbolic links may refer to any file anywhere on the system. They may also refer to directories. This makes it easy to move directories from place to place, with a symbolic link left behind in the original location pointing to the new location.

When processing a filename, the system notices symbolic links and instead performs the action on the pointed-to file or directory. Symbolic links are created with the `-s` option to `ln`:

```
$ /bin/pwd                          Where are we
/d/home/arnold                      On a different filesystem
$ ln -s /tmp/message ./hello        Create a symbolic link
$ cat hello                         Use it
Hi, how ya doin' ?
$ ls -l hello                       Show information about it
lrwxrwxrwx   1 arnold   devel      12 May  4 16:41 hello -> /tmp/message
```

The file pointed to by the link need not exist. The system detects this at runtime and acts appropriately:

```
$ rm /tmp/message                   Remove pointed-to file
$ cat ./hello                       Attempt to use it by the soft link
cat: ./hello: No such file or directory
$ echo hi again > hello             Create new file contents
$ ls -l /tmp/message                Show pointed-to file info ...
-rw-r--r--   1 arnold   devel       9 May  4 16:45 /tmp/message
$ cat /tmp/message                  ... and contents
hi again
```

Symbolic links are created with the `symlink()` system call:

```
#include <unistd.h>                                              POSIX

int symlink(const char *oldpath, const char *newpath);
```

The `oldpath` argument names the pointed-to file or directory, and `newpath` is the name of the symbolic link to be created. The return value is `0` on success and `-1` on error; see your *symlink*(2) manpage for the possible `errno` values.

Symbolic links have their disadvantages:

- They take up extra disk space, requiring a separate inode and data block. Hard links take up only a directory slot.

- They add overhead. The kernel has to work harder to resolve a pathname containing symbolic links.

- They can introduce "loops." Consider the following:

```
$ rm -f a b                         Make sure 'a' and 'b' don't exist
$ ln -s a b                         Symlink old file 'a' to new file 'b'
$ ln -s b a                         Symlink old file 'b' to new file 'a'
$ cat a                             What happens?
cat: a: Too many levels of symbolic links
```

The kernel has to be able to detect this case and produce an error message.

- They are easy to break. If you move the pointed-to file to a different location or rename it, the symbolic link is no longer valid. This can't happen with a hard link.

5.2 Creating and Removing Directories

Creating and removing directories is straightforward. The two system calls, not surprisingly, are mkdir() and rmdir(), respectively:

```
#include <sys/types.h>                                   POSIX
#include <sys/stat.h>

int mkdir(const char *pathname, mode_t mode);

#include <unistd.h>                                       POSIX

int rmdir(const char *pathname);
```

Both return 0 on success and -1 on error, with errno set appropriately. For mkdir(), the mode argument represents the permissions to be applied to the directory. It is completely analogous to the mode arguments for creat() and open() discussed in Section 4.6, "Creating Files," page 106.

Both functions handle the '.' and '..' in the directory being created or removed. A directory must be empty before it can be removed; errno is set to ENOTEMPTY if the directory isn't empty. (In this case, "empty" means the directory contains only '.' and '..'.)

New directories, like all files, are assigned a group ID number. Unfortunately, how this works is complicated. We delay discussion until Section 11.5.1, "Default Group for New Files and Directories," page 412.

Both functions work *one directory level at a time.* If /somedir exists and /somedir/sub1 does not, 'mkdir("/somedir/sub1/sub2")' fails. Each component in a long pathname has to be created individually (thus the -p option to mkdir, see *mkdir*(1)).

Also, if pathname ends with a / character, mkdir() and rmdir() will fail on some systems and succeed on others. The following program, ch05-trymkdir.c, demonstrates both aspects.

```
1   /* ch05-trymkdir.c --- Demonstrate mkdir() behavior.
2                           Courtesy of Nelson H.F. Beebe. */
3
4   #include <stdio.h>
5   #include <stdlib.h>
6   #include <errno.h>
7
8   #if !defined(EXIT_SUCCESS)
9   #define EXIT_SUCCESS 0
10  #endif
11
12  void do_test(const char *path)
13  {
14      int retcode;
15
16      errno = 0;
17      retcode = mkdir(path, 0755);
18      printf("mkdir(\"%s\") returns %d: errno = %d [%s]\n",
19             path, retcode, errno, strerror(errno));
20  }
21
22  int main(void)
23  {
24      do_test("/tmp/t1/t2/t3/t4");                     Attempt creation in subdirs
25      do_test("/tmp/t1/t2/t3");
26      do_test("/tmp/t1/t2");
27      do_test("/tmp/t1");
28
29      do_test("/tmp/u1");                              Make subdirs
30      do_test("/tmp/u1/u2");
31      do_test("/tmp/u1/u2/u3");
32      do_test("/tmp/u1/u2/u3/u4");
33
34      do_test("/tmp/v1/");                             How is trailing '/' handled?
35      do_test("/tmp/v1/v2/");
36      do_test("/tmp/v1/v2/v3/");
37      do_test("/tmp/v1/v2/v3/v4/");
38
39      return (EXIT_SUCCESS);
40  }
```

Here are the results under GNU/Linux:

```
$ ch05-trymkdir
mkdir("/tmp/t1/t2/t3/t4") returns -1: errno = 2 [No such file or directory]
mkdir("/tmp/t1/t2/t3") returns -1: errno = 2 [No such file or directory]
mkdir("/tmp/t1/t2") returns -1: errno = 2 [No such file or directory]
mkdir("/tmp/t1") returns 0: errno = 0 [Success]
mkdir("/tmp/u1") returns 0: errno = 0 [Success]
mkdir("/tmp/u1/u2") returns 0: errno = 0 [Success]
```

```
mkdir("/tmp/u1/u2/u3") returns 0: errno = 0 [Success]
mkdir("/tmp/u1/u2/u3/u4") returns 0: errno = 0 [Success]
mkdir("/tmp/v1/") returns 0: errno = 0 [Success]
mkdir("/tmp/v1/v2/") returns 0: errno = 0 [Success]
mkdir("/tmp/v1/v2/v3/") returns 0: errno = 0 [Success]
mkdir("/tmp/v1/v2/v3/v4/") returns 0: errno = 0 [Success]
```

Note how GNU/Linux accepts a trailing slash. Not all systems do.

5.3 Reading Directories

On the original Unix systems, reading directory contents was easy. A program opened the directory with `open()` and read binary `struct direct` structures directly, 16 bytes at a time. The following fragment of code is from the V7 `rmdir` program,[3] lines 60–74. It shows the check for the directory being empty.

```
60  if((fd = open(name,0)) < 0) {
61      fprintf(stderr, "rmdir: %s unreadable\n", name);
62      ++Errors;
63      return;
64  }
65  while(read(fd, (char *)&dir, sizeof dir) == sizeof dir) {
66      if(dir.d_ino == 0) continue;
67      if(!strcmp(dir.d_name, ".") || !strcmp(dir.d_name, ".."))
68          continue;
69      fprintf(stderr, "rmdir: %s not empty\n", name);
70      ++Errors;
71      close(fd);
72      return;
73  }
74  close(fd);
```

Line 60 opens the directory for reading (a second argument of 0, equal to `O_RDONLY`). Line 65 reads the `struct direct`. Line 66 is the check for an empty directory slot; that is, one with an inode number of 0. Lines 67 and 68 check for '.' and '..'. Upon reaching line 69, we know that some other filename has been seen and, therefore, that the directory isn't empty.

(The test '`!strcmp(s1, s2)`' is a shorter way of saying '`strcmp(s1, s2) == 0`'; that is, testing that the strings are equal. For what it's worth, we consider the '`!strcmp(s1, s2)`' form to be poor style. As Henry Spencer once said, "`strcmp()` is not a boolean!")

---

[3] See `/usr/src/cmd/rmdir.c` in the V7 distribution.

When 4.2 BSD introduced a new filesystem format that allowed longer filenames and provided better performance, it also introduced several new functions to provide a directory-reading abstraction. This suite of functions is usable no matter what the underlying filesystem and directory organization are. The basic parts of it are what is standardized by POSIX, and programs using it are portable across GNU/Linux and Unix systems.

5.3.1 Basic Directory Reading

Directory entries are represented by a `struct dirent` (*not* the same as the V7 `struct direct`!):

```
struct dirent {
    ...
    ino_t d_ino;              /* XSI extension --- see text */
    char  d_name[...];        /* See text on the size of this array */
    ...
};
```

For portability, POSIX specifies only the d_name field, which is a zero-terminated array of bytes representing the filename part of the directory entry. The size of d_name is not specified by the standard, other than to say that there may be at most NAME_MAX bytes before the terminating zero. (NAME_MAX is defined in <limits.h>.) The XSI extension to POSIX provides for the d_ino inode number field.

In practice, since filenames can be of variable length and NAME_MAX is usually fairly large (like 255), the `struct dirent` contains additional members that aid in the bookkeeping of variable-length directory entries on disk. These additional members are not relevant for everyday code.

The following functions provide the directory-reading interface:

```
#include <sys/types.h>                                          POSIX
#include <dirent.h>

DIR *opendir(const char *name);          Open a directory for reading
struct dirent *readdir(DIR *dir);        Return one struct dirent at a time
int closedir(DIR *dir);                  Close an open directory
void rewinddir(DIR *dirp);               Return to the front of a directory
```

The DIR type is analogous to the FILE type in <stdio.h>. It is an *opaque type*, meaning that application code is not supposed to know what's inside it; its contents are for use by the other directory routines. If opendir() returns NULL, the named directory could not be opened for reading and errno is set to indicate the error.

Once you have an open DIR * variable, it can be used to retrieve a pointer to a struct dirent representing the next directory entry. readdir() returns NULL upon end-of-file or error.

Finally, closedir() is analogous to the fclose() function in <stdio.h>; it closes the open DIR * variable. The rewinddir() function can be used to start over at the beginning of a directory.

With these routines in hand (or at least in the C library), we can write a simple catdir program that "cats" the contents of a directory. Such a program is presented in ch05-catdir.c:

```
1   /* ch05-catdir.c --- Demonstrate opendir(), readdir(), closedir(). */
2
3   #include <stdio.h>        /* for printf() etc. */
4   #include <errno.h>        /* for errno */
5   #include <sys/types.h>    /* for system types */
6   #include <dirent.h>       /* for directory functions */
7
8   char *myname;
9   int process(char *dir);
10
11  /* main --- loop over directory arguments */
12
13  int main(int argc, char **argv)
14  {
15      int i;
16      int errs = 0;
17
18      myname = argv[0];
19
20      if (argc == 1)
21          errs = process(".");    /* default to current directory */
22      else
23          for (i = 1; i < argc; i++)
24              errs += process(argv[i]);
25
26      return (errs != 0);
27  }
```

This program is quite similar to ch04-cat.c (see Section 4.2, "Presenting a Basic Program Structure," page 84); the main() function is almost identical. The primary difference is that it defaults to using the current directory if there are no arguments (lines 20–21).

```
29   /*
30    * process --- do something with the directory, in this case,
31    *               print inode/name pairs on standard output.
32    *               Returns 0 if all ok, 1 otherwise.
33    */
34
35   int
36   process(char *dir)
37   {
38       DIR *dp;
39       struct dirent *ent;
40
41       if ((dp = opendir(dir)) == NULL) {
42           fprintf(stderr, "%s: %s: cannot open for reading: %s\n",
43                   myname, dir, strerror(errno));
44           return 1;
45       }
46
47       errno = 0;
48       while ((ent = readdir(dp)) != NULL)
49           printf("%8ld %s\n", ent->d_ino, ent->d_name);
50
51       if (errno != 0) {
52           fprintf(stderr, "%s: %s: reading directory entries: %s\n",
53                   myname, dir, strerror(errno));
54           return 1;
55       }
56
57       if (closedir(dp) != 0) {
58           fprintf(stderr, "%s: %s: closedir: %s\n",
59                   myname, dir, strerror(errno));
60           return 1;
61       }
62
63       return 0;
64   }
```

The `process()` function does all the work, and the majority of it is error-checking code. The heart of the function is lines 48 and 49:

```
while ((ent = readdir(dp)) != NULL)
    printf("%8ld %s\n", ent->d_ino, ent->d_name);
```

This loop reads directory entries, one at a time, until `readdir()` returns NULL. The loop body prints the inode number and filename of each entry. Here's what happens when the program is run:

```
$ ch05-catdir                      Default to current directory
  639063 .
  639062 ..
  639064 proposal.txt
  639012 lightsabers.url
  688470 code
  638976 progex.texi
  639305 texinfo.tex
  639007 15-processes.texi
  639011 00-preface.texi
  639020 18-tty.texi
  638980 Makefile
  639239 19-i18n.texi
  ...
```

The output is not sorted in any way; it represents the linear contents of the directory. (We describe how to sort the directory contents in Section 6.2, "Sorting and Searching Functions," page 181.)

5.3.1.1 Portability Considerations

There are several portability considerations. First, you should not assume that the first two entries returned by `readdir()` will always be '.' and '..'. Many filesystems use directory organizations that are different from that of the original Unix design, and '.' and '..' could be in the middle of the directory or possibly not even present.[4]

Second, the POSIX standard is silent about possible values for `d_ino`. It does say that the returned structures represent directory entries for files; this implies that empty slots are not returned by `readdir()`, and thus the GNU/Linux `readdir()` implementation doesn't bother returning entries when 'd_ino == 0'; it continues to the next valid directory entry.

So, on GNU/Linux and Unix systems at least, it is unlikely that `d_ino` will ever be zero. However, it is best to avoid using this field entirely if you can.

Finally, some systems use `d_fileno` instead of `d_ino` inside the `struct dirent`. Be aware of this if you have to port directory-reading code to such systems.

---

[4] GNU/Linux systems are capable of mounting filesystems from many non-Unix operating systems. Many commercial Unix systems can also mount MS-DOS filesystems. Assumptions about Unix filesystems don't apply in such cases.

Indirect System Calls

"Don't try this at home, kids!"
—**Mr. Wizard**—

Many system calls, such as open(), read(), and write(), are meant to be called directly from user-level application code: in other words, from code that you, as a GNU/Linux developer, would write.

However, other system calls exist only to make it possible to implement higher-level, standard library functions and should *not* be called directly. The GNU/Linux getdents() system call is one such; it reads multiple directory entries into a buffer provided by the caller—in this case, the code that implements readdir(). The readdir() code then returns valid directory entries from the buffer, one at a time, refilling the buffer as needed.

These for-library-use-only system calls can be distinguished from for-user-use system calls by their appearance in the manpage. For example, from *getdents*(2):

```
NAME
    getdents - get directory entries
SYNOPSIS
    #include <unistd.h>
    #include <linux/types.h>
    #include <linux/dirent.h>
    #include <linux/unistd.h>

    _syscall3(int, getdents, uint, fd, struct dirent *, dirp, uint, count);

    int getdents(unsigned int fd, struct dirent *dirp, unsigned int count);
```

Any system call that uses a _syscall*X*() macro should *not* be called by application code. (More information on these calls can be found in the *intro*(2) manpage; you should read that manpage if you haven't already.)

In the case of getdents(), many other Unix systems have a similar system call; sometimes with the same name, sometimes with a different name. Thus, trying to use these calls would only lead to a massive portability mess anyway; you're much better off in all cases using readdir(), whose interface is well defined, standard, and portable.

5.3.1.2 Linux and BSD Directory Entries

Although we just said that you should only use the d_ino and d_name members of the struct dirent, it's worth knowing about the d_type member in the BSD and Linux struct dirent. This is an unsigned char value that stores the type of the file named by the directory entry:

```
struct dirent {
    ...
    ino_t d_ino;               /* As before */
    char  d_name[...];         /* As before */
    unsigned char d_type;      /* Linux and modern BSD */
    ...
};
```

`d_type` can have any of the values described in Table 5.1.

TABLE 5.1
Values for `d_type`

Name	Meaning
`DT_BLK`	Block device file.
`DT_CHR`	Character device file.
`DT_DIR`	Directory.
`DT_FIFO`	FIFO or named pipe.
`DT_LNK`	Symbolic link.
`DT_REG`	Regular file.
`DT_SOCK`	Socket.
`DT_UNKNOWN`	Unknown file type.
`DT_WHT`	Whiteout entry (BSD systems only).

Knowing the file's type just by reading the directory entry is very handy; it can save a possibly expensive `stat()` system call. (The `stat()` call is described shortly, in Section 5.4.2, "Retrieving File Information," page 141.)

5.3.2 BSD Directory Positioning Functions

Occasionally, it's useful to mark the current position in a directory in order to be able to return to it later. For example, you might be writing code that traverses a directory tree and wish to recursively enter each subdirectory as you come across it. (How to distinguish files from directories is discussed in the next section.) For this reason, the original BSD interface included two additional routines:

```
#include <dirent.h>                                              XSI

/* Caveat Emptor: POSIX XSI uses long, not off_t, for both functions */
off_t telldir(DIR *dir);                     Return current position
void seekdir(DIR *dir, off_t offset);        Move to given position
```

These routines are similar to the `ftell()` and `fseek()` functions in `<stdio.h>`. They return the current position in a directory and set the current position to a previously retrieved value, respectively.

These routines are included in the XSI part of the POSIX standard, since they make sense only for directories that are implemented with linear storage of directory entries.

Besides the assumptions made about the underlying directory structure, these routines are riskier to use than the simple directory-reading routines. This is because the contents of a directory might be changing dynamically: As files are added to or removed from a directory, the operating system adjusts the contents of the directory. Since directory entries are of variable length, it may be that the absolute offset saved at an earlier time no longer represents the start of a directory entry! Thus, we don't recommend that you use these functions unless you have to.

5.4 Obtaining Information about Files

Reading a directory to retrieve filenames is only half the battle. Once you have a filename, you need to know how to retrieve the other information associated with a file, such as the file's type, its permissions, owner, and so on.

5.4.1 Linux File Types

Linux (and Unix) supports the following different kinds of file types:

Regular files

As the name implies; used for data, executable programs, and anything else you might like. In an 'ls -l' listing, they show up with a '-' in the first character of the permissions (mode) field.

Directories

Special files for associating file names with inodes. In an 'ls -l' listing, they show up with a d in the first character of the permissions field.

Symbolic links

As described earlier in the chapter. In an 'ls -l' listing, they show up with an l (letter "ell," not digit 1) in the first character of the permissions field.

Devices

Files representing both physical hardware devices and software pseudo-devices. There are two kinds:

Block devices

Devices on which I/O happens in chunks of some fixed physical record size, such as disk drives and tape drives. Access to such devices goes through the kernel's buffer cache. In an 'ls -l' listing, they show up with a b in the first character of the permissions field.

Character devices

Also known as *raw* devices. Originally, character devices were those on which I/O happened a few bytes at a time, such as terminals. However, the character device is also used for direct I/O to block devices such as tapes and disks, bypassing the buffer cache.[5] In an 'ls -l' listing, they show up with a c in the first character of the permissions field.

Named pipes

Also known as *FIFOs* ("first-in first-out") files. These special files act like pipes; data written into them by one program can be read by another; no data go to or from the disk. FIFOs are created with the mkfifo command; they are discussed in Section 9.3.2, "FIFOs," page 319. In an 'ls -l' listing, they show up with a p in the first character of the permissions field.

Sockets

Similar in purpose to named pipes,[6] they are managed with the socket interprocess communication (IPC) system calls and are not otherwise dealt with in this book. In an 'ls -l' listing, they show up with an s in the first character of the permissions field.

---

[5] Linux uses the block device for disks exclusively. Other systems use both.

[6] Named pipes and sockets were developed independently by the System V and BSD Unix groups, respectively. As Unix systems reconverged, both kinds of files became universally available.

5.4.2 Retrieving File Information

Three system calls return information about files:

```
#include <sys/types.h>                                    POSIX
#include <sys/stat.h>
#include <unistd.h>

int stat(const char *file_name, struct stat *buf);
int fstat(int filedes, struct stat *buf);
int lstat(const char *file_name, struct stat *buf);
```

The `stat()` function accepts a pathname and returns information about the given file. It *follows* symbolic links; that is, when applied to a symbolic link, `stat()` returns information about the pointed-to file, not about the link itself. For those times when you want to know if a file is a symbolic link, use the `lstat()` function instead; it does not follow symbolic links.

The `fstat()` function retrieves information about an already open file. It is particularly useful for file descriptors 0, 1, and 2, (standard input, output, and error) which are already open when a process starts up. However, it can be applied to any open file. (An open file descriptor will never relate to a symbolic link; make sure you understand why.)

The value passed in as the second parameter should be the address of a `struct stat`, declared in `<sys/stat.h>`. As with the `struct dirent`, the `struct stat` contains at least the following members:

```
struct stat {
    ...
    dev_t       st_dev;       /* device */
    ino_t       st_ino;       /* inode */
    mode_t      st_mode;      /* type and protection */
    nlink_t     st_nlink;     /* number of hard links */
    uid_t       st_uid;       /* user ID of owner */
    gid_t       st_gid;       /* group ID of owner */
    dev_t       st_rdev;      /* device type (block or character device) */
    off_t       st_size;      /* total size, in bytes */
    blksize_t   st_blksize;   /* blocksize for filesystem I/O */
    blkcnt_t    st_blocks;    /* number of blocks allocated */
    time_t      st_atime;     /* time of last access */
    time_t      st_mtime;     /* time of last modification */
    time_t      st_ctime;     /* time of last inode change */
    ...
};
```

(The layout may be different on different architectures.) This structure uses a number of `typedef`'d types. Although they are all (typically) integer types, the use of specially defined types allows them to have different sizes on different systems. This keeps user-level code that uses them portable. Here is a fuller description of each field.

st_dev

> The device for a mounted filesystem. Each mounted filesystem has a unique value for st_dev.

st_ino

> The file's inode number within the filesystem. The (st_dev, st_ino) pair *uniquely* identifies the file.

st_mode

> The file's type and its permissions encoded together in one field. We will shortly see how to extract this information.

st_nlink

> The number of hard links to the file (the link count). This can be zero if the file was unlinked after being opened.

st_uid

> The file's UID (owner number).

st_gid

> The file's GID (group number).

st_rdev

> The device type if the file is a block or character device. st_rdev encodes information about the device. We will shortly see how to extract this information. This field has no meaning if the file is not a block or character device.

st_size

> The logical size of the file. As mentioned in Section 4.5, "Random Access: Moving Around within a File," page 102, a file may have holes in it, in which case the size may not reflect the true amount of storage space that it occupies.

st_blksize

> The "block size" of the file. This represents the preferred size of a data block for I/O to or from the file. This is almost always larger than a physical disk sector. Older Unix systems don't have this field (or st_blocks) in the struct stat. For the Linux ext2 and ext3 filesystems, this value is 4096.

`st_blocks`

The number of "blocks" used by the file. On Linux, this is in units of 512-byte blocks. On other systems, the size of a block may be different; check your local *stat*(2) manpage. (This number comes from the `DEV_BSIZE` constant in `<sys/param.h>`. This constant isn't standardized, but it is fairly widely used on Unix systems.)

The number of blocks may be more than '`st_size / 512`'; besides the data blocks, a filesystem may use additional blocks to store the locations of the data blocks. This is particularly necessary for large files.

`st_atime`

The file's access time; that is, the last time the file's data were read.

`st_mtime`

The file's modification time; that is, the last time the file's data were written or truncated.

`st_ctime`

The file's inode change time. This indicates the last time when the file's metadata changed, such as the permissions or the owner.

> NOTE The `st_ctime` field is *not* the file's "creation time"! There is no such thing in a Linux or Unix system. Some early documentation referred to the `st_ctime` field as the creation time. This was a misguided effort to simplify the presentation of the file metadata.

The `time_t` type used for the `st_atime`, `st_mtime`, and `st_ctime` fields represents dates and times. These time-related values are sometimes termed *timestamps*. Discussion of how to use a `time_t` value is delayed until Section 6.1, "Times and Dates," page 166. Similarly, the `uid_t` and `gid_t` types represent user and group ID numbers, which are discussed in Section 6.3, "User and Group Names," page 195. Most of the other types are not of general interest.

5.4.3 Linux Only: Specifying Higher-Precision File Times

The 2.6 and later Linux kernel supplies three additional fields in the `struct stat`. These provide nanosecond resolution on the file times:

st_atime_nsec   The nanoseconds component of the file's access time.

st_mtime_nsec   The nanoseconds component of the file's modification time.

st_ctime_nsec   The nanoseconds component of the file's inode change time.

Some other systems also provide such high-resolution time fields, but the member names for the struct stat are *not* standardized, making it difficult to write portable code that uses these times. (See Section 14.3.2, "Microsecond File Times: utimes()," page 545, for a related advanced system call.)

5.4.4 Determining File Type

Recall that the st_mode field encodes both the file's type and its permissions. <sys/stat.h> defines a number of macros that determine the file's type. In particular, these macros return true or false when applied to the st_mode field. The macros correspond to each of the file types described earlier. Assume that the following code has been executed:

```
struct stat stbuf;
char filename[PATH_MAX];    /* PATH_MAX is from <limits.h> */

... fill in filename with a file name ...
if (stat(filename, & stbuf) < 0) {
    /* handle error */
}
```

Once stbuf has been filled in by the system, the following macros can be called, being passed stbuf.st_mode as the argument:

S_ISREG(stbuf.st_mode)
>   Returns true if filename is a regular file.

S_ISDIR(stbuf.st_mode)
>   Returns true if filename is a directory.

S_ISCHR(stbuf.st_mode)
>   Returns true if filename is a character device. Devices are shortly discussed in more detail.

S_ISBLK(stbuf.st_mode)
>   Returns true if filename is a block device.

S_ISFIFO(stbuf.st_mode)
>   Returns true if filename is a FIFO.

`S_ISLNK(stbuf.st_mode)`

   Returns true if `filename` is a symbolic link. (This can never return true if `stat()` or `fstat()` were used instead of `lstat()`.)

`S_ISSOCK(stbuf.st_mode)`

   Returns true if `filename` is a socket.

> **NOTE** It happens that on GNU/Linux, these macros return `1` for true and `0` for false. However, on other systems, it's possible that they return an arbitrary nonzero value for true, instead of `1`. (POSIX specifies only nonzero vs. zero.) Thus, you should always use these macros as standalone tests instead of testing the return value:
>
> ```
>     if (S_ISREG(stbuf.st_mode)) ...              Correct
>
>     if (S_ISREG(stbuf.st_mode) == 1) ...         Incorrect
> ```

Along with the macros, `<sys/stat.h>` provides two sets of bitmasks. One set is for testing permission, and the other set is for testing the type of a file. We saw the permission masks in Section 4.6, "Creating Files," page 106, when we discussed the `mode_t` type and values for `open()` and `creat()`. The bitmasks, their values for GNU/Linux, and their meanings are described in Table 5.2.

Several of these masks serve to isolate the different sets of bits encoded in the `st_mode` field:

- `S_IFMT` represents bits 12–15, which are where the different types of files are encoded.

- `S_IRWXU` represents bits 6–8, which are the user's permission (read, write, execute for User).

- `S_IRWXG` represents bits 3–5, which are the group's permission (read, write, execute for Group).

- `S_IRWXO` represents bits 0–2, which are the "other" permission (read, write, execute for Other).

The permission and file type bits are depicted graphically in Figure 5.3.

TABLE 5.2
POSIX file-type and permission bitmasks in `<sys/stat.h>`

Mask	Value	Meaning
S_IFMT	0170000	Bitmask for the file type bitfields.
S_IFSOCK	0140000	Socket.
S_IFLNK	0120000	Symbolic link.
S_IFREG	0100000	Regular file.
S_IFBLK	0060000	Block device.
S_IFDIR	0040000	Directory.
S_IFCHR	0020000	Character device.
S_IFIFO	0010000	FIFO.
S_ISUID	0004000	Setuid bit.
S_ISGID	0002000	Setgid bit.
S_ISVTX	0001000	Sticky bit.
S_IRWXU	0000700	Mask for owner permissions.
S_IRUSR	0000400	Owner read permission.
S_IWUSR	0000200	Owner write permission.
S_IXUSR	0000100	Owner execute permission.
S_IRWXG	0000070	Mask for group permissions.
S_IRGRP	0000040	Group read permission.
S_IWGRP	0000020	Group write permission.
S_IXGRP	0000010	Group execute permission.
S_IRWXO	0000007	Mask for permissions for others.
S_IROTH	0000004	Other read permission.
S_IWOTH	0000002	Other write permission.
S_IXOTH	0000001	Other execute permission.

The file-type masks are standardized primarily for compatibility with older code; they should not be used directly, because such code is less readable than the corresponding macros. It happens that the macros are implemented, logically enough, with the masks, but that's irrelevant for user-level code.

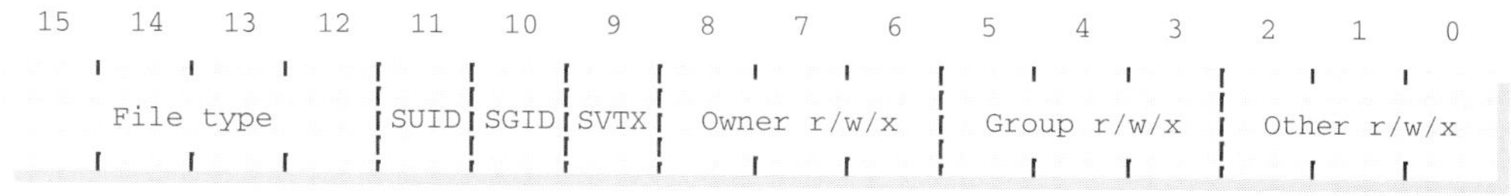

```
 15   14   13   12   11   10    9    8    7    6    5    4    3    2    1    0

     File type      |SUID|SGID|SVTX| Owner r/w/x  |  Group r/w/x  |  Other r/w/x
```

FIGURE 5.3
Permission and file-type bits

The POSIX standard explicitly states that no new bitmasks will be standardized in the future and that tests for any additional kinds of file types that may be added will be available only as S_ISxxx() macros.

5.4.4.1 Device Information

Because it is meant to apply to non-Unix systems as well as Unix systems, the POSIX standard doesn't define the meaning for the dev_t type. However, it's worthwhile to know what's in a dev_t.

When S_ISBLK(sbuf.st_mode) or S_ISCHR(sbuf.st_mode) is true, then the device information is found in the sbuf.st_rdev field. Otherwise, this field does not contain any useful information.

Traditionally, Unix device files encode a *major* device number and a *minor* device number within the dev_t value. The major number distinguishes the device type, such as "disk drive" or "tape drive." Major numbers also distinguish among different types of devices, such as SCSI disk vs. IDE disk. The minor number distinguishes the unit of that type, for example, the first disk or the second one. You can see these values with 'ls -l':

```
$ ls -1 /dev/hda /dev/hda?                    Show numbers for first hard disk
brw-rw----    1 root      disk      3,    0 Aug 31  2002 /dev/hda
brw-rw----    1 root      disk      3,    1 Aug 31  2002 /dev/hda1
brw-rw----    1 root      disk      3,    2 Aug 31  2002 /dev/hda2
brw-rw----    1 root      disk      3,    3 Aug 31  2002 /dev/hda3
brw-rw----    1 root      disk      3,    4 Aug 31  2002 /dev/hda4
brw-rw----    1 root      disk      3,    5 Aug 31  2002 /dev/hda5
brw-rw----    1 root      disk      3,    6 Aug 31  2002 /dev/hda6
brw-rw----    1 root      disk      3,    7 Aug 31  2002 /dev/hda7
brw-rw----    1 root      disk      3,    8 Aug 31  2002 /dev/hda8
brw-rw----    1 root      disk      3,    9 Aug 31  2002 /dev/hda9

$ ls -1 /dev/null                             Show info for /dev/null, too
crw-rw-rw-    1 root      root      1,    3 Aug 31  2002 /dev/null
```

Instead of the file size, `ls` displays the major and minor numbers. In the case of the hard disk, `/dev/hda` represents the whole drive. `/dev/hda1`, `/dev/hda2`, and so on, represent partitions within the drive. They all share the same major device number (3), but have different minor device numbers.

Note that the disk devices are block devices, whereas `/dev/null` is a character device. Block devices and character devices are separate entities; even if a character device and a block device share the same major device number, they are not necessarily related.

The major and minor device numbers can be extracted from a `dev_t` value with the `major()` and `minor()` functions defined in `<sys/sysmacros.h>`:

```
#include <sys/types.h>                              Common
#include <sys/sysmacros.h>

int major(dev_t dev);                          Major device number
int minor(dev_t dev);                          Minor device number
dev_t makedev(int major, int minor);           Create a dev_t value
```

(Some systems implement them as macros.)

The `makedev()` function goes the other way; it takes separate major and minor values and encodes them into a `dev_t` value. Its use is otherwise beyond the scope of this book; the morbidly curious should see *mknod*(2).

The following program, ch05-devnum.c, shows how to use the `stat()` system call, the file-type test macros, and finally, the `major()` and `minor()` macros.

```
/* ch05-devnum.c --- Demonstrate stat(), major(), minor(). */

#include <stdio.h>
#include <errno.h>
#include <sys/types.h>
#include <sys/stat.h>
#include <sys/sysmacros.h>
```

```c
int main(int argc, char **argv)
{
    struct stat sbuf;
    char *devtype;

    if (argc != 2) {
        fprintf(stderr, "usage: %s path\n", argv[0]);
        exit(1);
    }

    if (stat(argv[1], & sbuf) < 0) {
        fprintf(stderr, "%s: stat: %s\n", argv[1], strerror(errno));
        exit(1);
    }

    if (S_ISCHR(sbuf.st_mode))
        devtype = "char";
    else if (S_ISBLK(sbuf.st_mode))
        devtype = "block";
    else {
        fprintf(stderr, "%s is not a block or character device\n", argv[1]);
        exit(1);
    }

    printf("%s: major: %d, minor: %d\n", devtype,
            major(sbuf.st_rdev), minor(sbuf.st_rdev));

    exit(0);
}
```

Here is what happens when the program is run:

```
$ ch05-devnum /tmp                          Try a nondevice
/tmp is not a block or character device
$ ch05-devnum /dev/null                     Character device
char: major: 1, minor: 3
$ ch05-devnum /dev/hda2                     Block device
block: major: 3, minor: 2
```

Fortunately, the output agrees with that of ls, giving us confidence[7] that we have indeed written correct code.

Reproducing the output of ls is all fine and good, but is it really useful? The answer is yes. Any application that works with file hierarchies must be able to distinguish among all the different types of files. Consider an archiver such as tar or cpio. It would be disastrous if such a program treated a disk device file as a regular file, attempting to read it and store its contents in an archive! Or consider find, which can perform

---

[7] The technical term is *a warm fuzzy*.

arbitrary actions based on the type and other attributes of files it encounters. (find is a complicated program; see *find*(1) if you're not familiar with it.) Or even something as simple as a disk space accounting package has to distinguish regular files from everything else.

5.4.4.2 The V7 cat Revisited

In Section 4.4.4, "Example: Unix cat," page 99, we promised to return to the V7 cat program to review its use of the stat() system call. The first group of lines that used it were these:

```
31      fstat(fileno(stdout), &statb);
32      statb.st_mode &= S_IFMT;
33      if (statb.st_mode!=S_IFCHR && statb.st_mode!=S_IFBLK) {
34          dev = statb.st_dev;
35          ino = statb.st_ino;
36      }
```

This code should now make sense. Line 31 calls fstat() on the standard output to fill in the statb structure. Line 32 throws away all the information in statb.st_mode except the file type, by ANDing the mode with the S_IFMT mask. Line 33 checks that the file being used for standard output is *not* a device file. In that case, the program saves the device and inode numbers in dev and ino. These values are then checked for each input file in lines 50–56:

```
50          fstat(fileno(fi), &statb);
51          if (statb.st_dev==dev && statb.st_ino==ino) {
52              fprintf(stderr, "cat: input %s is output\n",
53                  fflg?"-": *argv);
54              fclose(fi);
55              continue;
56          }
```

If an input file's st_dev and st_ino values match those of the output file, then cat complains and continues to the next file named on the command line.

The check is done unconditionally, even though dev and ino are set only if the output is not a device file. This works out OK, because of how those variables are declared:

```
17      int dev, ino = -1;
```

Since `ino` is initialized to -1, no valid inode number will ever be equal to it.[8] That `dev` is not so initialized is sloppy, but not a problem, since the test on line 51 requires that both the device and inode be equal. (A good compiler will complain that `dev` is used without being initialized: '`gcc -Wall`' does.)

Note also that neither call to `fstat()` is checked for errors. This too is sloppy, although less so; it is unlikely that `fstat()` will fail on a valid file descriptor.

The test for input file equals output file is done only for nondevice files. This makes it possible to use `cat` to copy input from device files to themselves, such as with terminals:

```
$ tty                              Print current terminal device name
/dev/pts/3
$ cat /dev/pts/3 > /dev/pts/3      Copy keyboard input to screen
this is a line of text             Type in a line
this is a line of text             cat repeats it
```

5.4.5 Working with Symbolic Links

In general, symbolic links act like hard links; file operations such as `open()` and `stat()` apply to the pointed-to file instead of to the symbolic link itself. However, there are times when it really is necessary to work with the symbolic link instead of with the file the link points to.

For this reason, the `lstat()` system call exists. It behaves exactly like `stat()`, but if the file being checked happens to be a symbolic link, then the information returned applies to the symbolic link, and not to the pointed-to file. Specifically:

- `S_ISLNK(sbuf.st_mode)` will be true.
- `sbuf.st_size` is the number of bytes used by the name of the pointed-to file.

We already saw that the `symlink()` system call creates a symbolic link. But given an existing symbolic link, how can we retrieve the name of the file it points to? (`ls` obviously can, so we ought to be able to also.)

Opening the link with `open()` in order to read it with `read()` won't work; `open()` follows the link to the pointed-to file. Symbolic links thus necessitate an additional system call, named `readlink()`:

---

[8] This statement was true for V7; there are no such guarantees on modern systems.

```
#include <unistd.h>                                          POSIX

int readlink(const char *path, char *buf, size_t bufsiz);
```

`readlink()` places the contents of the symbolic link named by `path` into the buffer pointed to by `buf`. No more than `bufsiz` characters are copied. The return value is the number of characters placed in `buf` or `-1` if an error occurred. `readlink()` does *not* supply the trailing zero byte.

Note that if the buffer passed in to `readlink()` is too small, you will lose information; the full name of the pointed-to file won't be available. To properly use `readlink()`, your code should do the following:

1. Use `lstat()` to verify that you have a symbolic link.

2. Make sure that your buffer to hold the link contents is at least '`sbuf.st_size` + 1' bytes big; the '+ 1' is for the trailing zero byte to turn the buffer into a usable C string.

3. Call `readlink()`. It doesn't hurt to verify that the returned value is the same as `sbuf.st_size`.

4. Assign '`\0`' to the byte after the contents of the link, to make it into a C string.

Code to do all that would look something like this:

```
/* Error checking omitted for brevity */
int count;
char linkfile[PATH_MAX], realfile[PATH_MAX];  /* PATH_MAX is in <limits.h> */
strut stat sbuf;

... fill in linkfile with path to symbolic link of interest ...
lstat(linkfile, & sbuf);                        Get stat information
if (! S_ISLNK(sbuf.st_mode))                     Check that it's a symlink
    /* not a symbolic link, handle it */
if (sbuf.st_size + 1 > PATH_MAX)                 Check buffer size
    /* handle buffer size problems */

count = readlink(linkfile, realfile, PATH_MAX);  Read the link
if (count != sbuf.st_size)
    /* something weird going on, handle it */

realfile[count] = '\0';                          Make it into a C string
```

This example uses fixed-size buffers for simplicity of presentation. Real code would use `malloc()` to allocate a buffer of the correct size since the fixed-size arrays might be too small. The file `lib/xreadlink.c` in the GNU Coreutils does just this. It reads the contents of a symbolic link into storage allocated by `malloc()`. We show here just the function; most of the file is boilerplate definitions. Line numbers are relative to the start of the file:

```
55  /* Call readlink to get the symbolic link value of FILENAME.
56     Return a pointer to that NUL-terminated string in malloc'd storage.
57     If readlink fails, return NULL (caller may use errno to diagnose).
58     If realloc fails, or if the link value is longer than SIZE_MAX :-),
59     give a diagnostic and exit.  */
60
61  char *
62  xreadlink (char const *filename)
63  {
64    /* The initial buffer size for the link value.  A power of 2
65       detects arithmetic overflow earlier, but is not required.  */
66    size_t buf_size = 128;
67
68    while (1)
69      {
70        char *buffer = xmalloc (buf_size);
71        ssize_t link_length = readlink (filename, buffer, buf_size);
72
73        if (link_length < 0)
74          {
75            int saved_errno = errno;
76            free (buffer);
77            errno = saved_errno;
78            return NULL;
79          }
80
81        if ((size_t) link_length < buf_size)
82          {
83            buffer[link_length] = 0;
84            return buffer;
85          }
86
87        free (buffer);
88        buf_size *= 2;
89        if (SSIZE_MAX < buf_size || (SIZE_MAX / 2 < SSIZE_MAX && buf_size == 0))
90          xalloc_die ();
91      }
92  }
```

The function body consists of an infinite loop (lines 68–91), broken at line 84 which returns the allocated buffer. The loop starts by allocating an initial buffer (line 70) and reading the link (line 71). Lines 73–79 handle the error case, saving and restoring `errno` so that it can be used correctly by the calling code.

Lines 81–85 handle the "success" case, in which the link's contents' length is smaller than the buffer size. In this case, the terminating zero is supplied (line 83) and then the buffer returned (line 84), breaking the infinite loop. This ensures that the entire link contents have been placed into the buffer, since `readlink()` has no way to indicate "insufficient space in buffer."

Lines 87–88 free the buffer and double the buffer size for the next try at the top of the loop. Lines 89–90 handle the case in which the link's size is too big: `buf_size` is greater than `SSIZE_MAX`, or `SSIZE_MAX` is larger than the value that can be represented in a signed integer of the same size as used to hold `SIZE_MAX` and `buf_size` has wrapped around to zero. (These are unlikely conditions, but strange things do happen.) If either condition is true, the program dies with an error message. Otherwise, the function continues around to the top of the loop to make another try at allocating a buffer and reading the link.

Some further explanation: The '`SIZE_MAX / 2 < SSIZE_MAX`' condition is true only on systems on which '`SIZE_MAX < 2 * SSIZE_MAX`'; we don't know of any, but only on such a system can `buf_size` wrap around to zero. Since in practice this condition can't be true, the compiler can optimize away the whole expression, including the following '`buf_size == 0`' test. After reading this code, you might ask, "Why not use `lstat()` to retrieve the size of the symbolic link, allocate a buffer of the right size with `malloc()`, and be done?" Well, there are a number of reasons.[9]

- `lstat()` is a system call—it's best to avoid the overhead of making it since the contents of most symbolic links will fit in the initial buffer size of 128.

- Calling `lstat()` introduces a race condition: The link could change between the execution of `lstat()` and `readlink()`, forcing the need to iterate anyway.

- Some systems don't properly fill in the `st_size` member for symbolic links. (Sad, but true.) In a similar fashion, as we see in Section 8.4.2, "Getting the Current Directory: `getcwd()`," page 258, Linux provides special symbolic links under `/proc` whose `st_size` is zero, but for which `readlink()` does return valid content.

Finally, when the buffer isn't big enough, `xreadlink()` uses `free()` and `malloc()` with a bigger size, instead of `realloc()`, to avoid the useless copying that `realloc()`

---

[9] Thanks to Jim Meyering for explaining the issues.

does. (The comment on line 58 is thus out of date since `realloc()` isn't being used; this is fixed in the post-5.0 version of the Coreutils.)

5.5 Changing Ownership, Permission, and Modification Times

Several additional system calls let you change other file-related information: in particular, the owner and group of a file, the file's permissions, and the file's access and modification times.

5.5.1 Changing File Ownership: `chown()`, `fchown()`, and `lchown()`

File ownership and group are changed with three similar system calls:

```
#include <sys/types.h>                                    POSIX
#include <unistd.h>

int chown(const char *path, uid_t owner, gid_t group);
int fchown(int fd, uid_t owner, gid_t group);
int lchown(const char *path, uid_t owner, gid_t group);
```

`chown()` works on a pathname argument, `fchown()` works on an open file, and `lchown()` works on symbolic links instead of on the files pointed to by symbolic links. In all other respects, the three calls work identically, returning 0 on success and -1 on error.

It is noteworthy that one system call changes both the owner and group of a file. To change only the owner or only the group, pass in a value of -1 for the ID number that is to be left unchanged.

While you might think that you could pass in the corresponding value from a previously retrieved `struct stat` for the file or file descriptor, that method is more error prone. There's a race condition: The owner or group could have changed between the call to `stat()` and the call to `chown()`.

You might wonder, "Why be able to change ownership of a symbolic link? The permissions and ownership on them don't matter." But what happens if a user leaves, but all his files are still needed? It's necessary to be able to change the ownership on *all* the person's files to someone else, including symbolic links.

GNU/Linux systems normally do not permit ordinary (non-`root`) users to change the ownership of ("give away") their files. Changing the group to one of the user's groups is allowed, of course. The restriction on changing owners follows BSD systems, which also have this prohibition. The primary reason is that allowing users to give away files can defeat disk accounting. Consider a scenario like this:

```
$ mkdir mywork                          Make a directory
$ chmod go-rwx mywork                   Set permissions to drwx------
$ cd mywork                             Go there
$ myprogram > large_data_file           Create a large file
$ chmod ugo+rw large_data_file          Set permissions to -rw-rw-rw-
$ chown otherguy large_data_file        Give file away to otherguy
```

In this example, `large_data_file` now belongs to user `otherguy`. The original user can continue to read and write the file, because of the permissions. But `otherguy` will be charged for the disk space it occupies. However, since it's in a directory that belongs to the original user, which cannot be accessed by `otherguy`, there is no way for `otherguy` to remove the file.

Some System V systems do allow users to give away files. (Setuid and setgid files have the corresponding bit removed when the owner is changed.) This can be a particular problem when files are extracted from a `.tar` or `.cpio` archive; the extracted files end up belonging to the UID or GID encoded in the archive. On such systems, the `tar` and `cpio` programs have options that prevent this, but it's important to know that `chown()`'s behavior does vary across systems.

We will see in Section 6.3, "User and Group Names," page 195, how to relate user and group names to their corresponding numeric values.

5.5.2 Changing Permissions: `chmod()` and `fchmod()`

After all the discussion in Chapter 4, "Files and File I/O," page 83, and in this chapter, changing permissions is almost anticlimatic. It's done with one of two system calls, `chmod()` and `fchmod()`:

```
#include <sys/types.h>                                            POSIX
#include <sys/stat.h>

int chmod(const char *path, mode_t mode);
int fchmod(int fildes, mode_t mode);
```

`chmod()` works on a pathname argument, and `fchmod()` works on an open file. (There is no `lchmod()` call in POSIX, since the system ignores the permission settings on symbolic links. Some systems do have such a call, though.) As with most other system calls, these return `0` on success and `-1` on failure. Only the file's owner or `root` can change a file's permissions.

The `mode` value is created in the same way as for `open()` and `creat()`, as discussed in Section 4.6, "Creating Files," page 106. See also Table 5.2, which lists the permission constants.

The system will not allow setting the setgid bit (`S_ISGID`) if the group of the file does not match the effective group ID of the process or one of its supplementary groups. (We have not yet discussed these issues in detail; see Section 11.1.1, "Real and Effective IDs," page 405.) Of course, this check does not apply to `root` or to code running as `root`.

5.5.3 Changing Timestamps: `utime()`

The `struct stat` structure contains three fields of type `time_t`:

`st_atime`   The time the file was last accessed (read).

`st_mtime`   The time the file was last modified (written).

`st_ctime`   The time the file's inode was last changed (for example, renamed).

A `time_t` value represents time in "seconds since the Epoch." The *Epoch* is the Beginning of Time for computer systems. GNU/Linux and Unix use Midnight, January 1, 1970 UTC[10] as the Epoch. Microsoft Windows systems use Midnight January 1, 1980 (local time, apparently) as the Epoch.

`time_t` values are sometimes referred to as *timestamps*. In Section 6.1, "Times and Dates," page 166, we look at how these values are obtained and at how they're used. For now, it's enough to know what a `time_t` value is and that it represents seconds since the Epoch.

The `utime()` system call allows you to change a file's access and modification timestamps:

```
#include <sys/types.h>                                    POSIX
#include <utime.h>

int utime(const char *filename, struct utimbuf *buf);
```

A `struct utimbuf` looks like this:

---

[10] UTC is a language-independent acronym for Coordinated Universal Time. Older code (and sometimes older people) refer to this as "Greenwich Mean Time" (GMT), which is the time in Greenwich, England. When time zones came into widespread use, Greenwich was chosen as the location to which all other time zones are relative, either behind it or ahead of it.

```
struct utimbuf {
    time_t actime;  /* access time */
    time_t modtime; /* modification time */
};
```

If the call is successful, it returns 0; otherwise, it returns -1. If buf is NULL, then the system sets both the access time and the modification time to the current time.

To change one time but not the other, use the original value from the struct stat. For example:

```
/* Error checking omitted for brevity */
struct stat sbuf;
struct utimbuf ut;
time_t now;

time(& now);                              Get current time of day, see next chapter
stat("/some/file", & sbuf);               Fill in sbuf
ut.actime = sbuf.st_atime;                Access time unchanged

ut.modtime = now - (24 * 60 * 60);        Set modtime to 24 hours ago

utime("/some/file", & ut);                Set the values
```

About now, you may be asking yourself, "Why would anyone want to change a file's access and modification times?" Good question.

To answer it, consider the case of a program that creates backup archives, such as tar or cpio. These programs have to read the contents of a file in order to archive them. Reading the file, of course, changes the file's access time.

However, that file might not have been read *by a human* in 10 years. Someone doing an 'ls -lu', which displays the access time (instead of the default modification time), should see that the last time the file was read was 10 years ago. Thus, the backup program should save the original access and modification times, read the file in order to archive it, and then restore the original times with utime().

Similarly, consider the case of an archiving program *restoring* a file from an archive. The archive stores the file's original access and modification times. However, when a file is extracted from an archive to a newly created copy on disk, the new file has the current date and time of day for its access and modification times.

However, it's more useful if the newly created file *looks* as if it's the same age as the original file in the archive. Thus, the archiver needs to be able to set the access and modification times to those stored in the archive.

> **NOTE** In new code, you may wish to use the `utimes()` call (note the s in the name), which is described later in the book, in Section 14.3.2, "Microsecond File Times: `utimes()`," page 545.

5.5.3.1 Faking `utime(file, NULL)`

Some older systems don't set the access and modification times to the current time when the second argument to `utime()` is NULL. Yet, higher-level code (such as GNU `touch`) is simpler and more straightforward if it can rely on a single standardized interface.

The GNU Coreutils library thus contains a replacement function for `utime()` that handles this case, which can then be called by higher-level code. This reflects the "pick the best interface for the job" design principle we described in Section 1.5, "Portability Revisited," page 19.

The replacement function is in the file `lib/utime.c` in the Coreutils distribution. The following code is the version from Coreutils 5.0. Line numbers are relative to the start of the file:

```
24  #include <sys/types.h>
25
26  #ifdef HAVE_UTIME_H
27  # include <utime.h>
28  #endif
29
30  #include "full-write.h"
31  #include "safe-read.h"
32
33  /* Some systems (even some that do have <utime.h>) don't declare this
34     structure anywhere.  */
35  #ifndef HAVE_STRUCT_UTIMBUF
36  struct utimbuf
37  {
38    long actime;
39    long modtime;
40  };
41  #endif
42
43  /* Emulate utime (file, NULL) for systems (like 4.3BSD) that do not
44     interpret it to set the access and modification times of FILE to
45     the current time.  Return 0 if successful, -1 if not. */
46
```

```
47  static int
48  utime_null (const char *file)
49  {
50  #if HAVE_UTIMES_NULL
51    return utimes (file, 0);
52  #else
53    int fd;
54    char c;
55    int status = 0;
56    struct stat sb;
57
58    fd = open (file, O_RDWR);
59    if (fd < 0
60        || fstat (fd, &sb) < 0
61        || safe_read (fd, &c, sizeof c) == SAFE_READ_ERROR
62        || lseek (fd, (off_t) 0, SEEK_SET) < 0
63        || full_write (fd, &c, sizeof c) != sizeof c
64        /* Maybe do this -- it's necessary on SunOS4.1.3 with some combination
65           of patches, but that system doesn't use this code: it has utimes.
66           || fsync (fd) < 0
67        */
68        || (st.st_size == 0 && ftruncate (fd, st.st_size) < 0)
69        || close (fd) < 0)
70      status = -1;
71    return status;
72  #endif
73  }
74
75  int
76  rpl_utime (const char *file, const struct utimbuf *times)
77  {
78    if (times)
79      return utime (file, times);
80
81    return utime_null (file);
82  }
```

Lines 33–41 define the `struct utimbuf`; as the comment says, some systems don't declare the structure. The `utime_null()` function does the work. If the `utimes()` system call is available, it is used. (`utimes()` is a similar, but more advanced, system call, which is covered in Section 14.3.2, "Microsecond File Times: `utimes()`," page 545. It also allows NULL for the second argument, meaning use the current time.)

In the case that the times must be updated manually, the code does the update by first reading a byte from the file, and then writing it back. (The original Unix `touch` worked this way.) The operations are as follows:

1. Open the file, line 58.

2. Call `stat()` on the file, line 60.

3. Read one byte, line 61. For our purposes, `safe_read()` acts like `read()`; it's explained in Section 10.4.4, "Restartable System Calls," page 357.

4. Seek back to the front of the file with `lseek()`, line 62. This is done to write the just-read byte back on top of itself.

5. Write the byte back, line 63. `full_write()` acts like `write()`; it is also covered in Section 10.4.4, "Restartable System Calls," page 357.

6. If the file is of zero size, use `ftruncate()` to set it to zero size (line 68). This doesn't change the file, but it has the side effect of updating the access and modification times. (`ftruncate()` was described in Section 4.8, "Setting File Length," page 114.)

7. Close the file, line 69.

These steps are all done in one long successive chain of tests, inside an `if`. The tests are set up so that if any operation fails, `utime_null()` returns -1, like a regular system call. `errno` is automatically set by the system, for use by higher-level code.

The `rpl_utime()` function (lines 75–82) is the "replacement `utime()`." If the second argument is not `NULL`, then it calls the real `utime()`. Otherwise, it calls `utime_null()`.

5.5.4 Using `fchown()` and `fchmod()` for Security

The original Unix systems had only `chown()` and `chmod()` system calls. However, on heavily loaded systems, these system calls are subject to race conditions, by which an attacker could arrange to replace with a different file the file whose ownership or permissions were being changed.

However, once a file is opened, race conditions aren't an issue anymore. A program can use `stat()` on a pathname to obtain information about the file. If the information is what's expected, then after the file is opened, `fstat()` can verify that the file is the same (by comparing the `st_dev` and `st_ino` fields of the "before" and "after" `struct stat` structures).

Once the program knows that the files are the same, the ownership or permissions can then be changed with `fchown()` or `fchmod()`.

These system calls, as well as `lchown()`, are of relatively recent vintage;[11] older Unix systems won't have them, although modern, POSIX-compliant systems do.

There are no corresponding `futime()` or `lutime()` functions. In the case of `futime()`, this is (apparently) because the file timestamps are not critical to system security in the same way that ownership and permissions are. There is no `lutime()`, since the timestamps are irrelevant for symbolic links.

5.6 Summary

- The file and directory hierarchy as seen by the user is one logical tree, rooted at `/`. It is made up of one or more storage partitions, each of which contains a filesystem. Within a filesystem, inodes store information about files (metadata), including the location of file data blocks.

- Directories make the association between filenames and inodes. Conceptually, directory contents are just sequences of (inode, name) pairs. Each directory entry for a file is called a (hard) link, and files can have many links. Hard links, because they work only by inode number, must all be on the same filesystem. Symbolic (soft) links are pointers to files or directories that work based on filename, not inode number, and thus are not restricted to being on the same filesystem.

- Hard links are created with `link()`, symbolic links are created with `symlink()`, links are removed with `unlink()`, and files are renamed (possibly being moved to another directory) with `rename()`. A file's data blocks are not reclaimed until the link count goes to zero and the last open file descriptor for the file is closed.

- Directories are created with `mkdir()` and removed with `rmdir()`; a directory must be empty (nothing left but '.' and '..') before it can be removed. The GNU/Linux version of the ISO C `remove()` function calls `unlink()` or `rmdir()` as appropriate.

- Directories are processed with the `opendir()`, `readdir()`, `rewinddir()`, and `closedir()` functions. A `struct dirent` contains the inode number and the file's name. Maximally portable code uses only the filename in the d_name member. The BSD `telldir()` and `seekdir()` functions for saving and restoring the

---

[11] `fchown()` and `fchmod()` were introduced in 4.2 BSD but not picked up for System V until System V Release 4.

current position in a directory are widely available but are not as fully portable as the other directory processing functions.

- File metadata are retrieved with the `stat()` family of system calls; the `struct stat` structure contains all the information about a file *except* the filename. (Indeed, since a file may have many names or may even be completely unlinked, it's not possible to make the name available.)

- The `S_ISxxx()` macros in `<sys/stat.h>` make it possible to determine a file's type. The `major()` and `minor()` functions from `<sys/sysmacros.h>` make it possible to decode the `dev_t` values that represent block and character devices.

- Symbolic links can be checked for using `lstat()`, and the `st_size` field of the `struct stat` for a symbolic link returns the number of bytes needed to hold the name of the pointed-to file. The contents of a symbolic link are read with `readlink()`. Care must be taken to get the buffer size correct and to terminate the retrieved filename with a trailing zero byte so that it can be used as a C string.

- Several miscellaneous system calls update other information: the `chown()` family for the owner and group, the `chmod()` routines for the file permissions, and `utime()` to change file access and modification times.

Exercises

1. Write a routine 'const char *fmt_mode(mode_t mode)'. The input is a `mode_t` value as provided by the `st_mode` field in the `struct stat`; that is, it contains both the permission bits and the file type.

   The output should be a 10-character string identical to the first field of output from 'ls -l'. In other words, the first character identifies the file type, and the other nine the permissions.

   When the `S_ISUID` and `S_IXUSR` bits are set, use an s instead of an x; if only the `I_ISUID` bit is set, use an S. Similarly for the `S_ISGID` and `S_IXGRP` bits.

   If both the `S_ISVTX` and `S_IXOTH` bits are set, use t; for `S_ISVTX` alone, use T.

   For simplicity, you may use a `static` buffer whose contents are overwritten each time the routine is called.

2. Extend `ch05-catdir.c` to call `stat()` on each file name found. Then print the inode number, the result of `fmt_mode()`, the link count, and the file's name.

3. Extend `ch05-catdir.c` further such that if a file is a symbolic link, it will also print the name of the pointed-to file.

4. Add an option such that if a filename is that of a subdirectory, the program recursively enters the subdirectory and prints information about the subdirectory's files (and directories). Only one level of recursion is needed.

5. If you're not using a GNU/Linux system, run `ch05-trymkdir` (see Section 5.2, "Creating and Removing Directories," page 130) on your system and compare the results to those we showed.

6. Write the `mkdir` program. See your local *mkdir*(1) manpage and implement all its options.

7. In the root directory, `/`, both the device and inode numbers for '.' and '..' are the same. Using this bit of information, write the `pwd` program.

    The program has to start by finding the name of the current directory by reading the contents of the parent directory. It must then continue, working its way up the filesystem hierarchy, until it reaches the root directory.

    Printing the directory name backwards, from the current directory up to the root, is easy. How will your version of `pwd` manage to print the directory name in the correct way, from the root on down?

8. If you wrote `pwd` using recursion, write it again, using iteration. If you used iteration, write it using recursion. Which is better? (Hint: consider very deeply nested directory trees.)

9. Examine the `rpl_utime()` function (see Section 5.5.3.1, "Faking `utime(file, NULL)`," page 159) closely. What resource is not recovered if one of the tests in the middle of the `if` fails? (Thanks to Geoff Collyer.)

10. (Hard.) Read the *chmod*(1) manpage. Write code to parse the symbolic options argument, which allows adding, removing, and setting permissions based on user, group, other, and "all."

    Once you believe it works, write your own version of `chmod` that applies the permission specification to each file or directory named on the command line. Which function did you use, `chmod()`—or `open()` and `fchmod()`—and why?

## Chapter 6

General
Library Interfaces —
Part 1

In this chapter

W̲e saw in Chapter 5, "Directories and File Metadata," page 117, that directly reading a directory returns filenames in the order in which they're kept in the directory. We also saw that the `struct stat` contains all the information about a file, except its name. However, some components of that structure are not directly usable; they're just numeric values.

This chapter presents the rest of the APIs needed to make full use of the `struct stat` component values. In order, we cover the following topics: `time_t` values for representing times and the time formatting function; sorting and searching functions (for sorting filenames, or any other data); the `uid_t` and `gid_t` types for representing users and groups and the functions that map them to and from the corresponding user and group names; and finally, a function to test whether a file descriptor represents a terminal.

6.1 Times and Dates

Time values are kept in the type known as `time_t`. The ISO C standard guarantees that this is a numeric type but does not otherwise specify what it is (integer or floating-point), or the range or the precision of the values stored therein.

On GNU/Linux and Unix systems, `time_t` values represent "seconds since the Epoch." The *Epoch* is the beginning of recorded time, which is Midnight, January 1, 1970, UTC. On most systems, a `time_t` is a C `long int`. For 32-bit systems, this means that the `time_t` "overflows" sometime on January 19, 2038. By then, we hope, the `time_t` type will be redefined to be at least 64 bits big.

Various functions exist to retrieve the current time, compute the difference between two `time_t` values, convert `time_t` values into a more usable representation, and format both representations as character strings. Additionally, a date and time representation can be converted back into a `time_t`, and limited time-zone information is available.

A separate set of functions provides access to the current time with a higher resolution than one second. The functions work by providing two discrete values: the time as seconds since the Epoch, and the number of microseconds within the current second. These functions are described later in the book, in Section 14.3.1, "Microsecond Times: `gettimeofday()`," page 544.

6.1.1 Retrieving the Current Time: `time()` and `difftime()`

The `time()` system call retrieves the current date and time; `difftime()` computes the difference between two `time_t` values:

```
#include <time.h>                                          ISO C

time_t time(time_t *t);
double difftime(time_t time1, time_t time0);
```

`time()` returns the current time. If the `t` parameter is not `NULL`, then the value pointed to by `t` is also filled in with the current time. It returns `(time_t) -1` if there was an error, and `errno` is set.

Although ISO C doesn't specify what's in a `time_t` value, POSIX does indicate that it represents time in seconds. Thus, it's both common and portable to make this assumption. For example, to see if a time value represents something that is six months or more in the past, one might use code like this:

```
/* Error checking omitted for brevity */
time_t now, then, some_time;

time(& now);                               Get current time
then = now - (6L * 31 * 24 * 60 * 60);     Approximately six months ago

... set some_time, for example, via stat() ...
if (some_time < then)
    /* more than 6 months in the past */
else
    /* less than 6 months in the past */
```

However, since strictly portable code may need to run on non-POSIX systems, the `difftime()` function exists to produce the difference between two times. The same test, using `difftime()`, would be written this way:

```
time_t now, some_value;
const double six_months = 6.0 * 31 * 24 * 60 * 60;

time(& now);                               Get current time
... set some_time, for example, via stat() ...

if (difftime(now, some_time) >= six_months)
    /* more than 6 months in the past */
else
    /* less than 6 months in the past */
```

The return type of `difftime()` is a `double` because a `time_t` could possibly represent fractions of a second as well. On POSIX systems, it always represents whole seconds.

In both of the preceding examples, note the use of typed constants to force the computation to be done with the right type of math: `6L` in the first instance for `long` integers, `6.0` in the second, for floating point.

6.1.2 Breaking Down Times: `gmtime()` and `localtime()`

In practice, the "seconds since the Epoch" form of a date and time isn't very useful except for simple comparisons. Computing the components of a time yourself, such as the month, day, year, and so on, is error prone, since the local time zone (possibly with daylight-saving time) must be taken into account, leap years must be computed correctly, and so forth. Fortunately, two standard routines do this job for you:

```
#include <time.h>                                              ISO C

struct tm *gmtime(const time_t *timep);
struct tm *localtime(const time_t *timep);
```

`gmtime()` returns a pointer to a `struct tm` that represents UTC time. `localtime()` returns a pointer to a `struct tm` representing the local time; that is, it takes the current time zone and daylight-saving time into account. In effect, this is "wall-clock time," the date and time as it would be displayed on a wall clock or on a wristwatch. (How this works is discussed later, see Section 6.1.5, "Getting Time-Zone Information," page 178.)

Both functions return a pointer to a `struct tm`, which looks like this:

```
struct tm {
    int     tm_sec;        /* seconds */
    int     tm_min;        /* minutes */
    int     tm_hour;       /* hours */
    int     tm_mday;       /* day of the month */
    int     tm_mon;        /* month */
    int     tm_year;       /* year */
    int     tm_wday;       /* day of the week */
    int     tm_yday;       /* day in the year */
    int     tm_isdst;      /* daylight saving time */
};
```

The `struct tm` is referred to as a *broken-down time*, since the `time_t` value is "broken down" into its component parts. The component parts, their ranges, and their meanings are shown in Table 6.1.

TABLE 6.1
Fields in the `struct tm`

Member	Range	Meaning
tm_sec	0–60	Second within a minute. Second 60 allows for leap seconds. (C89 had the range as 0–61.)
tm_min	0–59	Minute within an hour.
tm_hour	0–23	Hour within the day.
tm_mday	1–31	Day of the month.
tm_mon	0–11	Month of the year.
tm_year	0–N	Year, in years since 1900.
tm_wday	0–6	Day of week, Sunday = 0.
tm_yday	0–365	Day of year, January 1 = 0.
tm_isdst	< 0, 0, > 0	Daylight Savings Time flag.

The ISO C standard presents most of these values as "x since y." For example, tm_sec is "seconds since the minute," tm_mon is "months since January," tm_wday is "days since Sunday," and so on. This helps to understand why all the values start at 0. (The single exception, logically enough, is tm_mday, the day of the month, which ranges from 1–31.) Of course, having them start at zero is also practical; since C arrays are zero-based, it makes using these values as indices trivial:

```
static const char *const days[] = {                    Array of day names
    "Sunday", "Monday", "Tuesday", "Wednesday",
    "Thursday", "Friday", "Saturday",
};
time_t now;
struct tm *curtime;

time(& now);                                           Get current time
curtime = gmtime(& now);                               Break it down
printf("Day of the week: %s\n", days[curtime->tm_wday]);    Index and print
```

Both gmtime() and localtime() return a pointer to a struct tm. The pointer points to a static struct tm maintained by each routine, and it is likely that these struct tm structures are overwritten each time the routines are called. Thus, it's a good idea to make a *copy* of the returned struct. Reusing the previous example:

```
static const char *const days[] = { /* As before */ };
time_t now;
struct tm curtime;                                    Structure, not pointer

time(& now);                                          Get current time
curtime = *gmtime(& now);                             Break it down and copy data
printf("Day of the week: %s\n", days[curtime.tm_wday]); Index and print, use . not ->
```

The tm_isdst field indicates whether or not daylight-saving time (DST) is currently in effect. A value of 0 means DST is not in effect, a positive value means it is, and a negative value means that no DST information is available. (The C standard is purposely vague, indicating only zero, positive, or negative; this gives implementors the most freedom.)

6.1.3   Formatting Dates and Times

The examples in the previous section showed how the fields in a struct tm could be used to index arrays of character strings for printing informative date and time values. While you could write your own code to use such arrays for formatting dates and times, standard routines alleviate the work.

6.1.3.1   Simple Time Formatting: asctime() and ctime()

The first two standard routines, listed below, produce output in a fixed format:

```
#include <time.h>                                     ISO C

char *asctime(const struct tm *tm);
char *ctime(const time_t *timep);
```

As with gmtime() and localtime(), asctime() and ctime() return pointers to static buffers that are likely to be overwritten upon each call. Furthermore, these two routines return strings in the same format. They differ only in the kind of argument they accept. asctime() and ctime() should be used when all you need is simple date and time information:

```
#include <stdio.h>
#include <time.h>

int main(void)
{
    time_t now;

    time(& now);
    printf("%s", ctime(& now));
}
```

When run, this program produces output of the form: 'Thu May 22 15:44:21 2003'. The terminating newline *is* included in the result. To be more precise, the return value points to an array of 26 characters, as shown in Figure 6.1.

```
0   1  2  3   4   5  6  7   8   9  10 11 12 13 14 15 16 17 18 19 20 21 22 23 24 25

T   h  u      M   a  y      2   2      1  5  :  4  4  :  2  1      2  0  0  3  \n \0
```

FIGURE 6.1
Return string from `ctime()` and `asctime()`

Much older Unix code relies on the fact that the values have a fixed position in the returned string. When using these routines, remember that they include a trailing newline. Thus, the small example program uses a simple `"%s"` format string for `printf()`, and not `"%s\n"`, as might be expected.

`ctime()` saves you the step of calling `localtime()`; it's essentially equivalent to

```
time_t now;
char *curtime;

time(& now);
curtime = asctime(localtime(& now));
```

6.1.3.2 Complex Time Formatting: `strftime()`

While `asctime()` and `ctime()` are often adequate, they are also limited:

- The output format is fixed. There's no way to rearrange the order of the elements.
- The output does not include time-zone information.
- The output uses abbreviated month and day names.
- The output assumes English names for the months and days.

For these reasons, C89 introduced the `strftime()` standard library routine:

```
#include <time.h>                                            ISO C

size_t strftime(char *s, size_t max, const char *format,
                const struct tm *tm);
```

`strftime()` is similar to `sprintf()`. The arguments are as follows:

`char *s`

   A buffer to hold the formatted string.

```
size_t max
```
    The size of the buffer.

```
const char *format
```
    The format string.

```
const struct tm *tm
```
    A `struct tm` pointer representing the broken-down time to be formatted.

The format string contains literal characters, intermixed with conversion specifiers that indicate what is to be placed into the string, such as the full weekday name, the hour according to a 24-hour or 12-hour clock, a.m. or p.m. designations, and so on. (Examples coming shortly.)

If the entire string can be formatted within `max` characters, the return value is the number of characters placed in `s`, *not* including the terminating zero byte. Otherwise, the return value is 0. In the latter case, the contents of `s` are "indeterminate." The following simple example gives the flavor of how `strftime()` is used:

```
#include <stdio.h>
#include <time.h>

int main(void)
{
    char buf[100];
    time_t now;
    struct tm *curtime;

    time(& now);
    curtime = localtime(& now);
    (void) strftime(buf, sizeof buf,
            "It is now %A, %B %d, %Y, %I:%M %p", curtime);

    printf("%s\n", buf);
    exit(0);
}
```

When run, this program prints something like:

```
It is now Thursday, May 22, 2003, 04:15 PM
```

Table 6.2 provides the full list of conversion specifiers, their possible alternative representations, and their meanings. In addition, the C99 standard added more specifiers to the list; those that are new in C99 are marked with a ✓ symbol.

TABLE 6.2
`strftime()` conversion format specifiers

Specifier(s)	C99	Meaning
`%a`		The locale's abbreviated weekday name.
`%A`		The locale's full weekday name.
`%b`		The locale's abbreviated month name.
`%B`		The locale's full month name.
`%c, %Ec`		The locale's "appropriate" date and time representation.
`%C, %EC`	✓	The century (00–99).
`%d, %Od`		The day of the month (01–31).
`%D`	✓	Same as `%m/%d/%y`.
`%e, %Oe`	✓	The day of the month. A single digit is preceded with a space (1–31).
`%F`	✓	Same as `%Y-%m-%d` (ISO 8601 date format).
`%g`	✓	The last two digits of week-based year (00–99).
`%G`	✓	The ISO 8601 week-based year.
`%h`	✓	Same as `%b`.
`%H, %OH`		The hour in a 24-hour clock (00–23).
`%I, %OI`		The hour in a 12-hour clock (01–12).
`%j`		The day of the year (001–366).
`%m, %Om`		The month as a number (01–12).
`%M, %OM`		The minute as a number (00–59).
`%n`	✓	A newline character (`'\n'`).
`%p`		The locale's a.m./p.m. designation.
`%r`	✓	The locale's 12-hour clock time.
`%R`	✓	Same as `%H:%M`.
`%S, %OS`		The second as a number (00–60).
`%t`	✓	A TAB character (`'\t'`).
`%T`	✓	Same as `%H:%M:%S` (ISO 8601 time format).
`%u, %Ou`	✓	ISO 8601 weekday number, Monday = 1 (1–7).
`%U, %OU`		Week number, first Sunday is first day of week 1 (00–53).

TABLE 6.2 *(Continued)*

Specifier(s)	C99	Meaning
`%V, %OV`	✓	ISO 8601 week number (`01–53`).
`%w, %Ow`		The weekday as a number, Sunday = 0 (`0–6`).
`%W, %OW`		Week number, first Monday is first day of week 1 (`00–53`).
`%x, %Ex`		The locale's "appropriate" date representation.
`%X, %EX`		The locale's "appropriate" time representation.
`%y, %Ey, %Oy`		The last two digits of the year (`00–99`).
`%Y, %EY`		The year as a number.
`%Z`		The locale's time zone, or no characters if no time-zone information is available.
`%%`		A single `%`.

A *locale* is a way of describing the current location, taking into account such things as language, character set, and defaults for formatting dates, times, and monetary amounts, and so on. We deal with them in Chapter 13, "Internationalization and Localization," page 485. For now, it's enough to understand that the results from `strftime()` for the same format string can vary, according to the current locale.

The versions starting with `%E` and `%O` are for "alternative representations." Some locales have multiple ways of representing the same thing; these specifiers provide access to the additional representations. If a particular locale does not support alternative representations, then `strftime()` uses the regular version.

Many Unix versions of `date` allow you to provide, on the command line, a format string that begins with a + character. `date` then formats the current date and time and prints it according to the format string:

```
$ date +'It is now %A, %B %d, %Y, %I:%M %p'
It is now Sunday, May 25, 2003, 06:44 PM
```

Most of the new C99 specifiers come from such existing Unix `date` implementations. The `%n` and `%t` formats are not strictly necessary in C, since the TAB and newline characters can be directly embedded in the string. However, in the context of a `date` format string on the command line, they make more sense. Thus, they're included in the specification for `strftime()` as well.

The ISO 8601 standard defines (among other things) how weeks are numbered within a year. According to this standard, weeks run Monday through Sunday, and Monday is day 1 of the week, not day 0. If the week in which January 1 comes out contains at least four days in the new year, then it is considered to be week 1. Otherwise, that week is the last week of the previous year, numbered 52 or 53. These rules are used for the computation of the %g, %G, and %V format specifiers. (While parochial Americans such as the author may find these rules strange, they are commonly used throughout Europe.)

Many of the format specifiers produce results that are specific to the current locale. In addition, several indicate that they produce the "appropriate" representation for the locale (for example, %x). The C99 standard defines the values for the "C" locale. These values are listed in Table 6.3.

TABLE 6.3
"C" locale values for certain strftime() formats

Specifier	Meaning
%a	The first three characters of %A.
%A	One of Sunday, Monday, ..., Saturday.
%b	The first three characters of %B.
%B	One of January, February, ..., December.
%c	Same as %a %b %e %T %Y.
%p	One of AM or PM.
%r	Same as %I:%M:%S %p.
%x	Same as %m/%d/%y.
%X	Same as %T.
%Z	Implementation-defined.

It should be obvious that strftime() provides considerable flexibility and control over date- and time-related output, in much the same way as printf() and sprintf() do. Furthermore, strftime() cannot overflow its buffer, since it checks against the passed-in size parameter, making it a safer routine than is sprintf().

As a simple example, consider the creation of program log files, when a new file is created every hour. The filename should embed the date and time of its creation in its name:

```
/* Error checking omitted for brevity */
char fname[PATH_MAX];        /* PATH_MAX is in <limits.h> */
time_t now;
struct tm *tm;
int fd;

time(& now);
tm = localtime(& now);
strftime(fname, sizeof fname, "/var/log/myapp.%Y-%m-%d-%H:%M", tm);
fd = creat(name, 0600);
...
```

The year-month-day-hour-minute format causes the filenames to sort in the order they were created.

> NOTE Some time formats are more useful than others. For example, 12-hour times are ambiguous, as are any purely numeric date formats. (What does '9/11' mean? It depends on where you live.) Similarly, two-digit years are also a bad idea. Use `strftime()` judiciously.

6.1.4 Converting a Broken-Down Time to a `time_t`

Obtaining seconds-since-the-Epoch values from the system is easy; that's how date and times are stored in inodes and returned from `time()` and `stat()`. These values are also easy to compare for equality or by < and > for simple earlier-than/later-than tests.

However, dates entered by humans are not so easy to work with. For example, many versions of the `touch` command allow you to provide a date and time to which `touch` should set a file's modification or access time (with `utime()`, as described in Section 5.5.3, "Changing Timestamps: `utime()`," page 157).

Converting a date as entered by a person into a `time_t` value is difficult: Leap years must be taken into account, time zones must be compensated for, and so on. Therefore, the C89 standard introduced the `mktime()` function:

```
#include <time.h>                                          ISO C

time_t mktime(struct tm *tm);
```

To use `mktime()`, fill in a `struct tm` with appropriate values: year, month, day, and so on. If you know whether daylight-saving time was in effect for the given date, set the tm_isdst field appropriately: 0 for "no," and positive for "yes." Otherwise, use a negative value for "don't know." The tm_wday and tm_yday fields are ignored.

mktime() assumes that the struct tm represents a local time, not UTC. It returns a time_t value representing the passed-in date and time, or it returns (time_t) -1 if the given date/time cannot be represented correctly. Upon a successful return, all the values in the struct tm are adjusted to be within the correct ranges, and tm_wday and tm_yday are set correctly as well. Here is a simple example:

```
1   /* ch06-echodate.c --- demonstrate mktime(). */
2
3   #include <stdio.h>
4   #include <time.h>
5
6   int main(void)
7   {
8       struct tm tm;
9       time_t then;
10
11      printf("Enter a Date/time as YYYY/MM/DD HH:MM:SS : ");
12      scanf("%d/%d/%d %d:%d:%d",
13          & tm.tm_year, & tm.tm_mon, & tm.tm_mday,
14          & tm.tm_hour, & tm.tm_min, & tm.tm_sec);
15
16      /* Error checking on values omitted for brevity. */
17      tm.tm_year -= 1900;
18      tm.tm_mon--;
19
20      tm.tm_isdst = -1;   /* Don't know about DST */
21
22      then = mktime(& tm);
23
24      printf("Got: %s", ctime(& then));
25      exit(0);
26  }
```

Line 11 prompts for a date and time, and lines 12–14 read it in. (Production code should check the return value from scanf().) Lines 17 and 18 compensate for the different basing of years and months, respectively. Line 22 indicates that we don't know whether or not the given date and time represent daylight-saving time. Line 22 calls mktime(), and line 24 prints the result of the conversion. When compiled and run, we see that it works:

```
$ ch06-echodate
Enter a Date/time as YYYY/MM/DD HH:MM:SS : 2003/5/25 19:07:23
Got: Sun May 25 19:07:23 2003
```

6.1.5 Getting Time-Zone Information

Early Unix systems embedded time-zone information into the kernel when it was compiled. The rules for daylight-saving time conversions were generally hard-coded, which was painful for users outside the United States or in places within the United States that didn't observe DST.

Modern systems have abstracted that information into binary files read by the C library when time-related functions are invoked. This technique avoids the need to recompile libraries and system executables when the rules change and makes it much easier to update the rules.

The C language interface to time-zone information evolved across different Unix versions, both System V and Berkeley, until finally it was standardized by POSIX as follows:

```
#include <time.h>                                        POSIX

extern char *tzname[2];
extern long timezone;
extern int daylight;

void tzset(void);
```

The `tzset()` function examines the `TZ` environment variable to find time-zone and daylight-saving time information.[1] If that variable isn't set, then `tzset()` uses an "implementation-defined default time zone," which is most likely the time zone of the machine you're running on.

After `tzset()` has been called, the local time-zone information is available in several variables:

`extern char *tzname[2]`

> The standard and daylight-saving time names for the time zone. For example, for U.S. locations in the Eastern time zone, the time-zone names are 'EST' (Eastern Standard Time) and 'EDT' (Eastern Daylight Time).

---

[1] Although POSIX standardizes `TZ`'s format, it isn't all that interesting, so we haven't bothered to document it here. After all, it is `tzset()` that has to understand the format, not user-level code. Implementations can, and do, use formats that extend POSIX.

`extern long timezone`

> The difference, in seconds, between the current time zone and UTC. The standard does not explain how this difference works. In practice, negative values represent time zones *east* of (ahead of, or later than) UTC; positive values represent time zones *west* of (behind, or earlier than) UTC. If you look at this value as "how much to change the local time to make it be the same as UTC," then the sign of the value makes sense.

`extern int daylight`

> This variable is zero if daylight-saving time conversions should never be applied in the current time zone, and nonzero otherwise.

> NOTE The `daylight` variable does *not* indicate whether daylight-saving time is currently in effect! Instead, it merely states whether the current time zone can even have daylight-saving time.

The POSIX standard indicates that `ctime()`, `localtime()`, `mktime()`, and `strftime()` all act "as if" they call `tzset()`. This means that they need not actually call `tzset()`, but they must behave as if it had been called. (The wording is intended to provide a certain amount of flexibility for implementors while guaranteeing correct behavior for user-level code.)

In practice, this means that you will almost never have to call `tzset()` yourself. However, it's there if you need it.

6.1.5.1 BSD Systems Gotcha: `timezone()`, Not `timezone`

Instead of the POSIX `timezone` variable, a number of systems derived from 4.4 BSD provide a `timezone()` function:

```
#include <time.h>                                              BSD

char *timezone(int zone, int dst);
```

The `zone` argument is the number of *minutes* west of GMT, and `dst` is true if daylight-saving time is in effect. The return value is a string giving the name of the indicated zone, or a value expressed relative to GMT. This function provides compatibility with the V7 function of the same name and behavior.

Local Time: How Does It Know?

GNU/Linux systems store time zone information in files and directories underneath
`/usr/share/zoneinfo`:

```
$ cd /usr/share/zoneinfo
$ ls -FC
Africa/       Canada/    Factory    Iceland     MST7MDT   Portugal    W-SU
America/      Chile/     GB         Indian/     Mexico/   ROC         WET
Antarctica/   Cuba       GB-Eire    Iran        Mideast/  ROK         Zulu
Arctic/       EET        GMT        Israel      NZ        Singapore   iso3166.tab
Asia/         EST        GMT+0      Jamaica     NZ-CHAT   SystemV/    posix/
Atlantic/     EST5EDT    GMT-0      Japan       Navajo    Turkey      posixrules
Australia/    Egypt      GMT0       Kwajalein   PRC       UCT         right/
Brazil/       Eire       Greenwich  Libya       PST8PDT   US/         zone.tab
CET           Etc/       HST        MET         Pacific/  UTC
CST6CDT       Europe/    Hongkong   MST         Poland    Universal
```

When possible, this directory uses hard links to provide the same data by multiple names.
For example, the files `EST5EDT` and `US/Eastern` are really the same:

```
$ ls -il EST5EDT US/Eastern
 724350 -rw-r--r--    5 root      root          1267 Sep  6  2002 EST5EDT
 724350 -rw-r--r--    5 root      root          1267 Sep  6  2002 US/Eastern
```

Part of the process of installing a system is to choose the time zone. The correct time-
zone data file is then placed in `/etc/localtime`:

```
$ file /etc/localtime
/etc/localtime: timezone data
```

On our system, this is a standalone copy of the time-zone file for our time zone. On
other systems, it may be a symbolic link to the file in `/usr/share/zoneinfo`. The
advantage of using a separate copy is that everything still works if `/usr` isn't mounted.

The `TZ` environment variable, if set, overrides the default time zone:

```
$ date                                   Date and time in default time zone
Wed Nov 19 06:44:50 EST 2003
$ export TZ=PST8PDT                       Change time zone to US West Coast
$ date                                    Print date and time
Wed Nov 19 03:45:09 PST 2003
```

This function's widespread existence makes portable use of the POSIX `timezone`
variable difficult. Fortunately, we don't see a huge need for it: `strftime()` should be
sufficient for all but the most unusual needs.

6.2 Sorting and Searching Functions

Sorting and searching are two fundamental operations, the need for which arises continually in many applications. The C library provides a number of standard interfaces for performing these tasks.

All the routines share a common theme; data are managed through void * pointers, and user-provided functions supply ordering. Note also that these APIs apply to *in-memory* data. Sorting and searching structures in files is considerably more involved and beyond the scope of an introductory text such as this one. (However, the sort command works well for text files; see the *sort*(1) manpage. Sorting binary files requires that a special-purpose program be written.)

Because no one algorithm works well for all applications, there are several different sets of library routines for maintaining searchable collections of data. This chapter covers only one simple interface for searching. Another, more advanced, interface is described in Section 14.4, "Advanced Searching with Binary Trees," page 551. Furthermore, we purposely don't explain the underlying algorithms, since this is a book on APIs, not algorithms and data structures. What's important to understand is that you can treat the APIs as "black boxes" that do a particular job, without needing to understand the details of how they do the job.

6.2.1 Sorting: qsort()

Sorting is accomplished with qsort():

```
#include <stdlib.h>                                          ISO C

void qsort(void *base, size_t nmemb, size_t size,
           int (*compare)(const void *, const void *));
```

The name qsort() comes from C.A.R. Hoare's Quicksort algorithm, which was used in the initial Unix implementation. (Nothing in the POSIX standard dictates the use of this algorithm for qsort(). The GLIBC implementation uses a highly optimized combination of Quicksort and Insertion Sort.)

qsort() sorts arrays of arbitrary objects. It works by shuffling opaque chunks of memory from one spot within the array to another and relies on you, the programmer, to provide a comparison function that allows it to determine the ordering of one array element relative to another. The arguments are as follows:

```
void *base
```
The address of the beginning of the array.

```
size_t nmemb
```
The total number of elements in the array.

```
size_t size
```
The size of each element in the array. The best way to obtain this value is with the C `sizeof` operator.

```
int (*compare)(const void *, const void *)
```
A possibly scary declaration for a *function pointer*. It says that "`compare` points to a function that takes two '`const void *`' parameters, and returns an `int`."

Most of the work is in writing a proper comparison function. The return value should mimic that of `strcmp()`: less than zero if the first value is "less than" the second, zero if they are equal, and greater than zero if the first value is "greater than" the second. It is the comparison function that defines the meaning of "less than" and "greater than" for whatever it is you're sorting. For example, to compare two `double` values, we could use this function:

```
int dcomp(const void *d1p, const void *d2p)
{
    const double *d1, *d2;

    d1 = (const double *) d1p;          Cast pointers to right type
    d2 = (const double *) d2p;

    if (*d1 < *d2)                      Compare and return right value
        return -1;
    else if (*d1 > *d2)
        return 1;
    else if (*d1 == *d2)
        return 0
    else
        return -1;       /* NaN sorts before real numbers */
}
```

This shows the general boilerplate for a comparison function: convert the arguments from `void *` to pointers to the type being compared and then return a comparison value.

For floating-point values, a simple subtraction such as '`return *d1 - *d2`' doesn't work, particularly if one value is very small or if one or both values are special "not a number" or "infinity" values. Thus, we have to do the comparison manually, including taking into account the not-a-number value (which doesn't even compare equal to itself!).

6.2.1.1 Example: Sorting Employees

For more complicated structures, a more involved function is necessary. For example, consider the following (rather trivial) `struct employee`:

```
struct employee {
    char lastname[30];
    char firstname[30];
    long emp_id;
    time_t start_date;
};
```

We might write a function to sort employees by last name, first name, and ID number:

```
int emp_name_id_compare(const void *e1p, const void *e2p)
{
    const struct employee *e1, *e2;
    int last, first;

    e1 = (const struct employee *) e1p;                  Convert pointers
    e2 = (const struct employee *) e2p;

    if ((last = strcmp(e1->lastname, e2->lastname)) != 0)  Compare last names
        return last;                                        Last names differ

    /* same last name, check first name */
    if ((first = strcmp(e1->firstname, e2->firstname)) != 0)  Compare first names
        return first;                                          First names differ

    /* same first name, check ID numbers */
    if (e1->emp_id < e2->emp_id)                          Compare employee ID
        return -1;
    else if (e1->emp_id == e2->emp_id)
        return 0;
    else
        return 1;
}
```

The logic here is straightforward, initially comparing on last names, then first names, and then using the employee ID number if the two names are the same. By using `strcmp()` on strings, we automatically get the right kind of negative/zero/positive value to return.

The employee ID comparison can't just use subtraction: suppose `long` is 64 bits and `int` is 32 bits, and the two values differ only in the upper 32 bits (say the lower 32 bits are zero). In such a case, the subtraction result would automatically be cast to `int`, throwing away the upper 32 bits and returning an incorrect value.

> NOTE We could have stopped with the comparison on first names, in which case all employees with the same last and first names would be grouped, but *without any other ordering*.
>
>   This point is important: `qsort()` does not guarantee a stable sort. A *stable* sort is one in which, if two elements compare equal based on some key value(s), they will maintain their original ordering, relative to each other, in the final sorted array. For example, consider three employees with the same first and last names, with employee numbers 17, 42, and 81. Their order in the original array might have been 42, 81, and 17. (Meaning, employee 42 is at a lower index than employee 81, who, in turn, is at a lower index than employee 17.) After sorting, the order might be 81, 42, and 17. If this is an issue, then the comparison routine must take *all* important key values into consideration. (Ours does.)

Simply by using a different function, we can sort employees by seniority:

```
int emp_seniority_compare(const void *e1p, const void *e2p)
{
    const struct employee *e1, *e2;
    double diff;

    e1 = (const struct employee *) e1p;          Cast pointers to correct type
    e2 = (const struct employee *) e2p;

    diff = difftime(e1->start_date, e2->start_date);   Compare times
    if (diff < 0)
        return -1;
    else if (diff > 0)
        return 1;
    else
        return 0;
}
```

For maximum portability we have used `difftime()`, which returns the difference in seconds between two `time_t` values. For this specific case, a cast such as—

```
    return (int) difftime(e1->start_date, e2->start_date);
```

—should do the trick, since `time_t` values are within reasonable ranges. Nevertheless, we instead use a full three-way `if` statement, just to be safe.

Here is a sample data file, listing five U.S. presidents:

```
$ cat presdata.txt
Bush George 43 980013600
Clinton William 42 727552800        Last name, first name, president number, inauguration
Bush George 41 601322400
Reagan Ronald 40 348861600
Carter James 39 222631200
```

`ch06-sortemp.c` shows a simple program that reads this file into a `struct employee` array and then sorts it, using the two different comparison functions just presented.

```
1   /* ch06-sortemp.c --- Demonstrate qsort() with two comparison functions. */
2
3   #include <stdio.h>
4   #include <stdlib.h>
5   #include <time.h>
6
7   struct employee {
8       char lastname[30];
9       char firstname[30];
10      long emp_id;
11      time_t start_date;
12  };
13
14  /* emp_name_id_compare --- compare by name, then by ID */
15
16  int emp_name_id_compare(const void *e1p, const void *e2p)
17  {
    ... as shown previously, omitted to save space ...
39  }
40
41  /* emp_seniority_compare --- compare by seniority */
42
43  int emp_seniority_compare(const void *e1p, const void *e2p)
44  {
    ... as shown previously, omitted to save space ...
58  }
59
60  /* main --- demonstrate sorting */
61
```

```
62   int main(void)
63   {
64   #define NPRES 10
65       struct employee presidents[NPRES];
66       int i, npres;
67       char buf[BUFSIZ];
68
69       /* Very simple code to read data: */
70       for (npres = 0; npres < NPRES && fgets(buf, BUFSIZ, stdin) != NULL;
71               npres++) {
72           sscanf(buf, "%s %s %ld %ld\n",
73               presidents[npres].lastname,
74               presidents[npres].firstname,
75               & presidents[npres].emp_id,
76               & presidents[npres].start_date);
77       }
78
79       /* npres is now number of actual lines read. */
80
81       /* First, sort by name */
82       qsort(presidents, npres, sizeof(struct employee), emp_name_id_compare);
83
84       /* Print output */
85       printf("Sorted by name:\n");
86       for (i = 0; i < npres; i++)
87           printf("\t%s %s\t%d\t%s",
88               presidents[i].lastname,
89               presidents[i].firstname,
90               presidents[i].emp_id,
91               ctime(& presidents[i].start_date));
92
93       /* Now, sort by seniority */
94       qsort(presidents, npres, sizeof(struct employee), emp_seniority_compare);
95
96       /* And print again */
97       printf("Sorted by seniority:\n");
98       for (i = 0; i < npres; i++)
99           printf("\t%s %s\t%d\t%s",
100              presidents[i].lastname,
101              presidents[i].firstname,
102              presidents[i].emp_id,
103              ctime(& presidents[i].start_date));
104  }
```

Lines 70–77 read in the data. Note that *any* use of scanf() requires "well behaved" input data. If, for example, any name is more than 29 characters, there's a problem. In this case, we're safe, but production code must be considerably more careful.

Line 82 sorts the data by name and employee ID, and then lines 84–91 print the sorted data. Similarly, line 94 re-sorts the data, this time by seniority, with lines 97–103 printing the results. When compiled and run, the program produces the following results:

```
$ ch06-sortemp < presdata.txt
Sorted by name:
     Bush George     41    Fri Jan 20 13:00:00 1989
     Bush George     43    Sat Jan 20 13:00:00 2001
     Carter James    39    Thu Jan 20 13:00:00 1977
     Clinton William 42    Wed Jan 20 13:00:00 1993
     Reagan Ronald   40    Tue Jan 20 13:00:00 1981
Sorted by seniority:
     Carter James    39    Thu Jan 20 13:00:00 1977
     Reagan Ronald   40    Tue Jan 20 13:00:00 1981
     Bush George     41    Fri Jan 20 13:00:00 1989
     Clinton William 42    Wed Jan 20 13:00:00 1993
     Bush George     43    Sat Jan 20 13:00:00 2001
```

(We've used 1:00 p.m. as an approximation for the time when all of the presidents started working.[2])

One point is worth mentioning: qsort() rearranges the data in the array. If each array element is a large structure, *a lot* of data will be copied back and forth as the array is sorted. It may pay, instead, to set up *a separate array of pointers*, each of which points at one element of the array. Then use qsort() to sort the pointer array, accessing the *unsorted* data through the *sorted* pointers.

The price paid is the extra memory to hold the pointers and modification of the comparison function to use an extra pointer indirection when comparing the structures. The benefit returned can be a considerable speedup, since only a four- or eight-byte pointer is moved around at each step, instead of a large structure. (Our struct employee is at least 68 bytes in size. Swapping four-byte pointers moves 17 times less data than does swapping structures.) For thousands of in-memory structures, the difference can be significant.

> NOTE If you're a C++ programmer, beware! qsort() may be dangerous to use with arrays of objects! qsort() does raw memory moves, copying bytes. It's completely unaware of C++ constructs such as copy constructors or operator=() functions. Instead, use one of the STL sorting functions, or use the separate-array-of-pointers technique.

---

[2] The output shown here is for U.S. Eastern Standard Time. You will get different results for the same program and data if you use a different time zone.

6.2.1.2 Example: Sorting Directory Contents

In Section 5.3, "Reading Directories," page 132, we demonstrated that directory entries are returned in physical directory order. Most of the time, it's much more useful to have directory contents sorted in some fashion, such as by name or by modification time. While not standardized by POSIX, several routines make it easy to do this, using `qsort()` as the underlying sorting agent:

```
#include <dirent.h>                                    Common

int scandir(const char *dir, struct dirent ***namelist,
        int (*select)(const struct dirent *),
        int (*compare)(const struct dirent **, const struct dirent **));
int alphasort(const void *a, const void *b);

int versionsort(const void *a, const void *b);        GLIBC
```

The `scandir()` and `alphasort()` functions were made available in 4.2 BSD and are widely supported.[3] `versionsort()` is a GNU extension.

`scandir()` reads the directory named by `dir`, creates an array of `struct dirent` pointers by using `malloc()`, and sets `*namelist` to point to the beginning of that array. Both the array of pointers and the pointed-to `struct dirent` structures are allocated with `malloc()`; it is up to the calling code to use `free()` to avoid memory leaks.

Use the `select` function pointer to choose entries of interest. When this value is NULL, all valid directory entries are included in the final array. Otherwise, `(*select)()` is called for each entry, and those entries for which it returns nonzero (true) are included in the array.

The `compare` function pointer compares two directory entries. It is passed to `qsort()` for use in sorting.

`alphasort()` compares filenames lexicographically. It uses the `strcoll()` function for comparison. `strcoll()` is similar to `strcmp()` but takes locale-related sorting rules into consideration (see Section 13.4, "Can You Spell That for Me, Please?", page 521).

`versionsort()` is a GNU extension, that uses the GNU `strverscmp()` function to compare filenames (see *strverscmp*(3)). To make a long story short, this function understands common filename versioning conventions and compares appropriately.

---

3 One notable exception is Sun's Solaris, where these two functions exist only in the hard-to-use BSD compatibility library.

ch06-sortdir.c shows a program similar to ch04-catdir.c. However, it uses scandir() and alphasort() to do the work.

```
1   /* ch06-sortdir.c --- Demonstrate scandir(), alphasort(). */
2
3   #include <stdio.h>            /* for printf() etc. */
4   #include <errno.h>            /* for errno */
5   #include <sys/types.h>        /* for system types */
6   #include <dirent.h>           /* for directory functions */
7
8   char *myname;
9   int process(const char *dir);
10
11  /* main --- loop over directory arguments */
12
13  int main(int argc, char **argv)
14  {
15      int i;
16      int errs = 0;
17
18      myname = argv[0];
19
20      if (argc == 1)
21          errs = process(".");    /* default to current directory */
22      else
23          for (i = 1; i < argc; i++)
24              errs += process(argv[i]);
25
26      return (errs != 0);
27  }
28
29  /* nodots --- ignore dot files, for use by scandir() */
30
31  int
32  nodots(const struct dirent *dp)
33  {
34      return (dp->d_name[0] != '.');
35  }
36
37  /*
38   * process --- do something with the directory, in this case,
39   *             print inode/name pairs on standard output.
40   *             Return 0 if all OK, 1 otherwise.
41   */
42
```

```
43  int
44  process(const char *dir)
45  {
46      DIR *dp;
47      struct dirent **entries;
48      int nents, i;
49
50      nents = scandir(dir, & entries, nodots, alphasort);
51      if (nents < 0) {
52          fprintf(stderr, "%s: scandir failed: %s\n", myname,
53                  strerror(errno));
54          return 1;
55      }
56
57      for (i = 0; i < nents; i++) {
58          printf("%8ld %s\n", entries[i]->d_ino, entries[i]->d_name);
59          free(entries[i]);
60      }
61
62      free(entries);
63
64      return 0;
65  }
```

The main() program (lines 1–27) follows the standard boilerplate we've used before. The nodots() function (lines 31–35) acts as the select parameter, choosing only filenames that don't begin with a period.

The process() function (lines 43–65) is quite simple, with scandir() doing most of the work. Note how each element is released separately with free() (line 59) and how the entire array is also released (line 62).

When run, the directory contents do indeed come out in sorted order, without '.' and '..':

```
$ ch06-sortdir                    Default actions displays current directory
 2097176 00-preface.texi
 2097187 01-intro.texi
 2097330 02-cmdline.texi
 2097339 03-memory.texi
 2097183 03-memory.texi.save
 2097335 04-fileio.texi
 2097334 05-fileinfo.texi
 2097332 06-general1.texi
 ...
```

6.2.2 Binary Searching: `bsearch()`

A *linear search* is pretty much what it sounds like: You start at the beginning, and walk through an array being searched until you find what you need. For something simple like finding integers, this usually takes the form of a `for` loop. Consider this function:

```
/* ifind --- linear search, return index if found or -1 if not */

int ifind(int x, const int array[], size_t nelems)
{
    size_t i;

    for (i = 0; i < nelems; i++)
        if (array[i] == x)   /* found it */
            return i;

    return -1;
}
```

The advantage to linear searching is that it's simple; it's easy to write the code correctly the first time. Furthermore, it always works. Even if elements are added to the end of the array or removed from the array, there's no need to sort the array.

The disadvantage to linear searching is that it's slow. On average, for an array containing `nelems` elements, a linear search for a random element does 'nelems / 2' comparisons before finding the desired element. This becomes prohibitively expensive, even on modern high-performance systems, as `nelems` becomes large. Thus, you should only use linear searching on small arrays.

Unlike a linear search, binary searching requires that the input array already be sorted. The disadvantage here is that if elements are added, the array must be re-sorted before it can be searched. (When elements are removed, the rest of the array contents must still be shuffled down. This is not as expensive as re-sorting, but it can still involve a lot of data motion.)

The advantage to binary searching, and it's a significant one, is that binary searching is blindingly fast, requiring at most $\log_2(N)$ comparisons, where N is the number of elements in the array. The `bsearch()` function is declared as follows:

```
#include <stdlib.h>                                        ISO C

void *bsearch(const void *key, const void *base, size_t nmemb,
              size_t size, int (*compare)(const void *, const void *));
```

The parameters and their purposes are similar to those of qsort():

const void *key
>   The object being searched for in the array.

const void *base
>   The start of the array.

size_t nmemb
>   The number of elements in the array.

size_t size
>   The size of each element, obtained with sizeof.

int (*compare)(const void *, const void *)
>   The comparison function. It must work the same way as the qsort() comparison
>   function, returning negative/zero/positive according to whether the first parameter
>   is less than/equal to/greater than the second one.

bsearch() returns NULL if the object is not found. Otherwise, it returns a pointer
to the found object. If more than one array element matches key, it is unspecified which
one is returned. Thus, as with qsort(), make sure that the comparison function ac-
counts for all relevant parts of the searched data structure.

ch06-searchemp.c shows bsearch() in practice, extending the struct employee
example used previously.

```
1   /* ch06-searchemp.c --- Demonstrate bsearch(). */
2
3   #include <stdio.h>
4   #include <errno.h>
5   #include <stdlib.h>
6
7   struct employee {
8       char lastname[30];
9       char firstname[30];
10      long emp_id;
11      time_t start_date;
12  };
13
14  /* emp_id_compare --- compare by ID */
15
```

```
16  int emp_id_compare(const void *e1p, const void *e2p)
17  {
18      const struct employee *e1, *e2;
19
20      e1 = (const struct employee *) e1p;
21      e2 = (const struct employee *) e2p;
22
23      if (e1->emp_id < e2->emp_id)
24          return -1;
25      else if (e1->emp_id == e2->emp_id)
26          return 0;
27      else
28          return 1;
29  }
30
31  /* print_employee --- print an employee structure */
32
33  void print_employee(const struct employee *emp)
34  {
35      printf("%s %s\t%d\t%s", emp->lastname, emp->firstname,
36          emp->emp_id, ctime(& emp->start_date));
37  }
```

Lines 7–12 define the `struct employee`; it's the same as before. Lines 16–29 serve as the comparison function, for both `qsort()` and `bsearch()`. It compares on employee ID number only. Lines 33–37 define `print_employee()`, which is a convenience function for printing the structure since this is done from multiple places.

```
39  /* main --- demonstrate sorting */
40
41  int main(int argc, char **argv)
42  {
43  #define NPRES 10
44      struct employee presidents[NPRES];
45      int i, npres;
46      char buf[BUFSIZ];
47      struct employee *the_pres;
48      struct employee key;
49      int id;
50      FILE *fp;
51
52      if (argc != 2) {
53          fprintf(stderr, "usage: %s datafile\n", argv[0]);
54          exit(1);
55      }
56
57      if ((fp = fopen(argv[1], "r")) == NULL) {
58          fprintf(stderr, "%s: %s: could not open: %s\n", argv[0],
59              argv[1], strerror(errno));
60          exit(1);
61      }
62
```

```
63     /* Very simple code to read data: */
64     for (npres = 0; npres < NPRES && fgets(buf, BUFSIZ, fp) != NULL;
65             npres++) {
66       sscanf(buf, "%s %s %ld %ld",
67             presidents[npres].lastname,
68             presidents[npres].firstname,
69             & presidents[npres].emp_id,
70             & presidents[npres].start_date);
71     }
72     fclose(fp);
73
74     /* npres is now number of actual lines read. */
75
76     /* First, sort by id */
77     qsort(presidents, npres, sizeof(struct employee), emp_id_compare);
78
79     /* Print output */
80     printf("Sorted by ID:\n");
81     for (i = 0; i < npres; i++) {
82         putchar('\t');
83         print_employee(& presidents[i]);
84     }
85
86     for (;;) {
87         printf("Enter ID number: ");
88         if (fgets(buf, BUFSIZ, stdin) == NULL)
89             break;
90
91         sscanf(buf, "%d\n", & id);
92         key.emp_id = id;
93         the_pres = (struct employee *) bsearch(& key, presidents, npres,
94                 sizeof(struct employee), emp_id_compare);
95
96         if (the_pres != NULL) {
97             printf("Found: ");
98             print_employee(the_pres);
99         } else
100            printf("Employee with ID %d not found!\n", id);
101     }
102
103     putchar('\n');  /* Print a newline on EOF. */
104
105     exit(0);
106 }
```

The `main()` function starts with argument checking (lines 52–55). It then reads the data from the named file (lines 57–72). Standard input cannot be used for the employee data, since that is reserved for prompting the user for the employee ID to search for.

Lines 77–84 sort the data and then print them. The program then goes into a loop, starting on line 86. It prompts for an employee ID number, exiting the loop upon end-of-file. To search the array, we use the `struct employee` named `key`. It's enough to set just its `emp_id` field to the entered ID number; none of the other fields are used in the comparison (line 92).

If an entry is found with the matching key, `bsearch()` returns a pointer to it. Otherwise it returns NULL. The return is tested on line 96, and appropriate action is then taken. Finally, line 102 prints a newline character so that the system prompt will come out on a fresh line. Here's a transcript of what happens when the program is compiled and run:

```
$ ch06-searchemp presdata.txt                          Run the program
Sorted by ID:
    Carter James      39    Thu Jan 20 13:00:00 1977
    Reagan Ronald     40    Tue Jan 20 13:00:00 1981
    Bush George       41    Fri Jan 20 13:00:00 1989
    Clinton William 42      Wed Jan 20 13:00:00 1993
    Bush George       43    Sat Jan 20 13:00:00 2001
Enter ID number: 42                                    Enter a valid number
Found: Clinton William  42   Wed Jan 20 13:00:00 1993  It's found
Enter ID number: 29                                    Enter an invalid number
Employee with ID 29 not found!                         It's not found
Enter ID number: 40                                    Try another good one
Found: Reagan Ronald     40   Tue Jan 20 13:00:00 1981 This one is found too
Enter ID number: ^D                                    CTRL-D entered for EOF
$                                                      Ready for next command
```

Additional, more advanced, APIs for searching data collections are described in Section 14.4, "Advanced Searching with Binary Trees," page 551.

6.3 User and Group Names

While the operating system works with user and group ID numbers for storage of file ownership and for permission checking, humans prefer to work with user and group *names*.

Early Unix systems kept the information that mapped names to ID numbers in simple text files, /etc/passwd and /etc/group. These files still exist on modern systems, and their format is unchanged from that of V7 Unix. However, they no longer tell the complete story. Large installations with many networked hosts keep the information in *network databases*: ways of storing the information on a small number of servers that are then accessed over the network.[4] However, this usage is *transparent* to most applications since access to the information is done through the same API as was used for retrieving the information from the text files. It is for this reason that POSIX standardizes only the APIs; the /etc/passwd and /etc/group files need not exist, as such, for a system to be POSIX compliant.

The APIs to the two databases are similar; most of our discussion focuses on the user database.

6.3.1 User Database

The traditional /etc/passwd format maintains one line per user. Each line has seven fields, each of which is separated from the next by a colon character:

```
$ grep arnold /etc/passwd
arnold:x:2076:10:Arnold D. Robbins:/home/arnold:/bin/bash
```

In order, the fields are as follows:

The user name
> This is what the user types to log in, what shows up for '1s -1' and in any other context that displays users.

The password field
> On older systems, this is the user's encrypted password. On newer systems, this field is likely to be an x (as shown), meaning that the password information is held in a different file. This separation is a security measure; if the encrypted password isn't available to nonprivileged users, it is much harder to "crack."

The user ID number
> This should be unique; one number per user.

The group ID number
> This is the user's initial group ID number. As is discussed later, on modern systems processes have multiple groups associated with them.

---

4 Common network databases include Sun Microsystems' Network Information Service (NIS) and NIS+, Kerberos (Hesiod), MacOS X NetInfo (versions up to and including 10.2), and LDAP, the Lightweight Directory Access Protocol. BSD systems keep user information in on-disk databases and generate the /etc/passwd and /etc/group files automatically.

The user's real name

This is at least a first and last name. Some systems allow for comma-separated fields, for office location, phone number, and so on, but this is not standardized.

The login directory

This directory becomes the home directory for users when they log in ($HOME—the default for the cd command).

The login program

The program to run when the user logs in. This is usually a shell, but it need not be. If this field is left empty, the default is /bin/sh.

Access to the user database is through the routines declared in <pwd.h>:

```
#include <sys/types.h>                                       XSI
#include <pwd.h>

struct passwd *getpwent(void);
void setpwent(void);
void endpwent(void);

struct passwd *getpwnam(const char *name);
struct passwd *getpwuid(uid_t uid);
```

The fields in the struct passwd used by the various API routines correspond directly to the fields in the password file:

```
struct passwd {
    char    *pw_name;       /* user name */
    char    *pw_passwd;     /* user password */
    uid_t   pw_uid;         /* user id */
    gid_t   pw_gid;         /* group id */
    char    *pw_gecos;      /* real name */
    char    *pw_dir;        /* home directory */
    char    *pw_shell;      /* shell program */
};
```

(The name pw_gecos is historical; when the early Unix systems were being developed, this field held the corresponding information for the user's account on the Bell Labs Honeywell systems running the GECOS operating system.)

The purpose of each routine is described in the following list.

struct passwd *getpwent(void)

Returns a pointer to an internal static struct passwd structure containing the "current" user's information. This routine reads through the entire password database, one record at a time, returning a pointer to a structure for each user.

The same pointer is returned each time; that is, the internal `struct passwd` is overwritten for each user's entry. When `getpwent()` reaches the end of the password database, it returns `NULL`. Thus, it lets you step through the entire database, one user at a time. The order in which records are returned is undefined.

`void setpwent(void)`

Resets the internal state such that the next call to `getpwent()` returns the first record in the password database.

`void endpwent(void)`

"Closes the database," so to speak, be it a simple file, network connection, or something else.

`struct passwd *getpwnam(const char *name)`

Looks up the user with a `pw_name` member equal to `name`, returning a pointer to a `static struct passwd` describing the user or `NULL` if the user is not found.

`struct passwd *getpwuid(uid_t uid)`

Similarly, looks up the user with the user ID number given by `uid`, returning a pointer to a `static struct passwd` describing the user or `NULL` if the user is not found.

`getpwuid()` is what's needed when you have a user ID number (such as from a `struct stat`) and you wish to print the corresponding user name. `getpwnam()` converts a name to a user ID number, for example, if you wish to use `chown()` or `fchown()` on a file. In theory, both of these routines do a linear search through the password database to find the desired information. This is true in practice when a password file is used; however, behind-the-scenes databases (network or otherwise, as on BSD systems) tend to use more efficient methods of storage, so these calls are possibly not as expensive in such a case.[5]

`getpwent()` is useful when you need to go through the entire password database. For instance, you might wish to read it all into memory, sort it, and then search it quickly with `bsearch()`. This is very useful for avoiding the multiple linear searches inherent in looking things up one at a time with `getpwuid()` or `getpwnam()`.

---

[5] Unfortunately, if performance is an issue, there's no standard way to know how your library does things, and indeed, the way it works can vary at runtime! (See the *nsswitch.conf* (5) manpage on a GNU/Linux system.) On the other hand, the point of the API is, after all, to hide the details.

> NOTE   The pointers returned by `getpwent()`, `getpwnam()`, and `getpwuid()`
> all point to internal `static` data. Thus, you should make a copy of their
> contents if you need to save the information.
>
>   Take a good look at the `struct passwd` definition. The members that
> represent character strings are pointers; they too point at internal `static` data,
> and if you're going to copy the structure, make sure to copy the data each
> member points to as well.

6.3.2 Group Database

The format of the `/etc/group` group database is similar to that of `/etc/passwd`,
but with fewer fields:

```
$ grep arnold /etc/group
mail:x:12:mail,postfix,arnold
uucp:x:14:uucp,arnold
floppy:x:19:arnold
devel:x:42:miriam,arnold
arnold:x:2076:arnold
```

Again, there is one line per group, with fields separated by colons. The fields are
as follows:

The group name
> This is the name of the group, as shown in '`ls -l`' or in any other context in
> which a group name is needed.

The group password
> This field is historical. It is no longer used.

The group ID number
> As with the user ID, this should be unique to each group.

The user list
> This is a comma-separated list of users who are members of the group.

In the previous example, we see that user `arnold` is a member of multiple groups.
This membership is reflected in practice in what is termed the *group set*. Besides the
main user ID and group ID number that processes have, the group set is a set of additional group ID numbers that each process carries around with it. The system checks
all of these group ID numbers against a file's group ID number when performing

permission checking. This subject is discussed in more detail in Chapter 11, "Permissions and User and Group ID Numbers," page 403.

The group database APIs are similar to those for the user database. The following functions are declared in `<grp.h>`:

```
#include <sys/types.h>                                            XSI
#include <grp.h>

struct group *getgrent(void);
void setgrent(void);
void endgrent(void);

struct group *getgrnam(const char *name);
struct group *getgrgid(gid_t gid);
```

The `struct group` corresponds to the records in `/etc/group`:

```
struct group {
    char    *gr_name;        /* group name */
    char    *gr_passwd;      /* group password */
    gid_t   gr_gid;          /* group id */
    char    **gr_mem;        /* group members */
};
```

The `gr_mem` field bears some explanation. While declared as a pointer to a pointer (`char **`), it is best thought of as an array of strings (like `argv`). The last element in the array is set to `NULL`. When no members are listed, the first element in the array is `NULL`.

`ch06-groupinfo.c` demonstrates how to use the `struct group` and the `gr_mem` field. The program accepts a single user name on the command line and prints all group records in which that user name appears:

```
 1   /* ch06-groupinfo.c --- Demonstrate getgrent() and struct group */
 2
 3   #include <stdio.h>
 4   #include <sys/types.h>
 5   #include <grp.h>
 6
 7   extern void print_group(const struct group *gr);
 8
 9   /* main --- print group lines for user named in argv[1] */
10
```

```
11  int
12  main(int argc, char **argv)
13  {
14      struct group *gr;
15      int i;
16
17      if (argc != 2) {                                        Check arguments
18          fprintf(stderr, "usage: %s user\n", argv[0]);
19          exit(1);
20      }
21
22      while ((gr = getgrent()) != NULL)                       Get each group record
23          for (i = 0; gr->gr_mem[i] != NULL; i++)             Look at each member
24              if (strcmp(gr->gr_mem[i], argv[1]) == 0)        If found the user ...
25                  print_group(gr);                           Print the record
26
27      endgrent();
28
29      exit(0);
30  }
```

The `main()` routine first does error checking (lines 17–20). The heart of the program is a nested loop. The outer loop (line 22) loops over all the group database records. The inner loop (line 23) loops over the members of the `gr_mem` array. If one of the members matches the name from the command line (line 24), then `print_group()` is called to print the record (line 25).

```
32  /* print_group --- print a group record */
33
34  void
35  print_group(const struct group *gr)
36  {
37      int i;
38
39      printf("%s:%s:%ld:", gr->gr_name, gr->gr_passwd, (long) gr->gr_gid);
40
41      for (i = 0; gr->gr_mem[i] != NULL; i++) {
42          printf("%s", gr->gr_mem[i]);
43          if (gr->gr_mem[i+1] != NULL)
44              putchar(',');
45      }
46
47      putchar('\n');
48  }
```

The `print_group()` function (lines 34–48) is straightforward, with logic similar to that of `main()` for printing the member list. Group list members are comma separated; thus, the loop body has to check that the *next* element in the array is not NULL before printing a comma. This code works correctly, even if there are no members in the group. However, for this program, we know there are members, or `print_group()` wouldn't have been called! Here's what happens when the program is run:

```
$ ch06-groupinfo arnold
mail:x:12:mail,postfix,arnold
uucp:x:14:uucp,arnold
floppy:x:19:arnold
devel:x:42:miriam,arnold
arnold:x:2076:arnold
```

6.4 Terminals: `isatty()`

The Linux/Unix standard input, standard output, standard error model discourages the special treatment of input and output devices. Programs generally should not need to know, or care, whether their output is a terminal, a file, a pipe, a physical device, or whatever.

However, there are times when a program really does need to know what kind of a file a file descriptor is associated with. The `stat()` family of calls often provides enough information: regular file, directory, device, and so on. Sometimes though, even that is not enough, and for interactive programs in particular, you may need to know if a file descriptor represents a tty

A *tty* (short for Teletype, one of the early manufacturers of computer terminals) is any device that represents a terminal, that is, something that a human would use to interact with the computer. This may be either a hardware device, such as the keyboard and monitor of a personal computer, an old-fashioned video display terminal connected to a computer by a serial line or modem, or a software *pseudoterminal*, such as is used for windowing systems and network logins.

The discrimination can be made with `isatty()`:

```
#include <unistd.h>                                          POSIX

int isatty(int desc);
```

This function returns 1 if the file descriptor `desc` represents a terminal, 0 otherwise. According to POSIX, `isatty()` may set `errno` to indicate an error; thus you should set `errno` to 0 before calling `isatty()` and then check its value if the return is 0. (The GNU/Linux *isatty*(3) manpage doesn't mention the use of `errno`.) The POSIX standard also points out that just because `isatty()` returns 1 doesn't mean there's a human at the other end of the file descriptor!

One place where `isatty()` comes into use is in modern versions of `ls`, in which the default is to print filenames in columns if the standard output is a terminal and to print them one per line if not.

6.5 Suggested Reading

1. *Mastering Algorithms With C*, by Kyle Loudon. O'Reilly & Associates, Sebastopol, California, USA, 1999. ISBN: 1-56592-453-3.

   This book provides a practical, down-to-earth introduction to algorithms and data structures using C, covering hash tables, trees, sorting, and searching, among other things.

2. *The Art of Computer Programming Volume 3: Sorting and Searching*, 2nd edition, by Donald E. Knuth. Addison-Wesley, Reading Massachusetts, USA, 1998. ISBN: 0-201-89685-0.

   This book is usually cited as the final word on sorting and searching. Bear in mind that it is considerably denser and harder to read than the Loudon book.

3. The GTK+ project[6] consists of several libraries that work together. GTK+ is the underlying toolkit used by the GNU GNOME Project.[7] At the base of the library hierarchy is Glib, a library of fundamental types and data structures and functions for working with them. Glib includes facilities for all the basic operations we've covered so far in this book, and many more, including linked lists and hash tables. To see the online documentation, start at the GTK+ Documentation Project's web site,[8] click on the "Download" link, and proceed to the online version.

6.6 Summary

- Times are stored internally as `time_t` values, representing "seconds since the Epoch." The Epoch is Midnight, January 1, 1970 UTC for GNU/Linux and Unix

---

[6] http://www.gtk.org

[7] http://www.gnome.org

[8] http://www.gtk.org/rdp

systems. The current time is retrieved from the system by the `time()` system call, and `difftime()` returns the difference, in seconds, between two `time_t` values.

- The `struct tm` structure represents a "broken-down time," which is a much more usable representation of a date and time. `gmtime()` and `localtime()` convert `time_t` values into `struct tm` values, and `mktime()` goes in the opposite direction.

- `asctime()` and `ctime()` do simplistic formatting of time values, returning a pointer to a fixed-size, fixed-format `static` character string. `strftime()` provides much more flexible formatting, including locale-based values.

- Time-zone information is made available by a call to `tzset()`. Since the standard routines act as if they call `tzset()` automatically, it is rare to need to call this function directly.

- The standard routine for sorting arrays is `qsort()`. By using a user-provided comparison function and being told the number of array elements and their size, `qsort()` can sort any kind of data. This provides considerable flexibility.

- `scandir()` reads an entire directory into an array of `struct dirent`. User-provided functions can be used to select which entries to include and can provide ordering of elements within the array. `alphasort()` is a standard function for sorting directory entries by name; `scandir()` passes the sorting function straight through to `qsort()`.

- The `bsearch()` function works similarly to `qsort()`. It does fast binary searching. Use it if the cost of linear searching outweighs the cost of sorting your data. (An additional API for searching data collections is described in Section 14.4, "Advanced Searching with Binary Trees," page 551.)

- The user and group databases may be kept in local disk files or may be made available over a network. The standard API purposely hides this distinction. Each database provides both linear scanning of the entire database and direct queries for a user/group name or user/group ID.

- Finally, for those times when `stat()` just isn't enough, `isatty()` can tell you whether or not an open file represents a terminal device.

Exercises

1. Write a simple version of the `date` command that accepts a format string on the command line and uses it to format and print the current time.

2. When a file is more than six months old, '`ls -l`' uses a simpler format for printing the modification time. The file GNU version of `ls.c` uses this computation:

```
3043  /* Consider a time to be recent if it is within the past six
3044     months.  A Gregorian year has 365.2425 * 24 * 60 * 60 ==
3045     31556952 seconds on the average.  Write this value as an
3046     integer constant to avoid floating point hassles.  */
3047  six_months_ago = current_time - 31556952 / 2;
```

Compare this to our example computation for computing the time six months in the past. What are the advantages and disadvantages of each method?

3. Write a simple version of the `touch` command that changes the modification time of the files named on the command line to the current time.

4. Add an option to your `touch` command that accepts a date and time specification on the command line and uses that value as the new modification time of the files named on the command line.

5. Add another option to your version of `touch` that takes a filename and uses the modification time of the given file as the new modification time for the files named on the command line.

6. Enhance `ch06-sortemp.c` to sort a separate array of pointers that point into the array of employees.

7. Add options to `ch06-sortdir.c` to sort by inode number, modification time, access time, and size. Add a "reverse option" such that time-based sorts make the most *recent* file first and other criteria (size, inode) sort by largest value first.

8. Write a simple version of the `chown` command. Its usage should be

```
chown user[:group] files ...
```

Here, *user* and *group* are user and group names representing the new user and group for the named files. The *group* is optional; if present it is separated from the *user* by a colon.

To test your version on a GNU/Linux system, you will have to work as `root`. Do so carefully!

9. Enhance your `chown` to allow numeric user or group numbers, as well as names.

10. Write functions to copy user and group structures, including pointed-to data. Use `malloc()` to allocate storage as needed.

11. Write a specialized user-lookup library that reads the entire user database into a dynamically allocated array. Provide *fast* lookup of users, by both user ID number and name. Be sure to handle the case in which a requested user isn't found.

12. Do the same thing for the group database.

13. Write a `stat` program that prints the contents of the `struct stat` for each file named on the command line. It should print all the values in human-readable format: `time_t` values as dates and times, `uid_t` and `gid_t` values as the corresponding names (if available), and the contents of symbolic links. Print the `st_mode` field the same way that `ls` would.

    Compare your program to the GNU Coreutils `stat` program, both by comparing outputs and by looking at the source code.

Chapter 7

Putting It
All Together:
`ls`

In this chapter

T he V7 `ls` command nicely ties together everything we've seen so far. It uses almost all of the APIs we've covered, touching on many aspects of Unix programming: memory allocation, file metadata, dates and times, user names, directory reading, and sorting.

7.1 V7 `ls` Options

In comparison to modern versions of `ls`, the V7 `ls` accepted only a handful of options and the meaning of some of them is different for V7 than for current `ls`. The options are as follows:

-a Print all directory entries. Without this, don't print '.' and '..'. Interestingly enough, V7 `ls` ignores only '.' and '..', while V1 through V6 ignore any file whose name begins with a period. This latter behavior is the default in modern versions of `ls`, as well.

-c Use the inode change time, instead of the modification time, with -t or -l.

-d For directory arguments, print information about the directory itself, not its contents.

-f "Force" each argument to be read as a directory, and print the name found in each slot. This options disables -l, -r, -s and -t, and enables -a. (This option apparently existed for filesystem debugging and repair.)

-g For '`ls -l`', use the group name instead of the user name.

-i Print the inode number in the first column along with the filename or the long listing.

-l Provide the familiar long format output. Note, however, that V7 '`ls -l`' printed only the user name, not the user and group names together.

-r Reverse the sort order, be it alphabetic for filenames or by time.

-s Print the size of the file in 512-byte blocks. The V7 *ls*(1) manpage states that *indirect blocks*—blocks used by the filesystem for locating the data blocks of large files—are also included in the computation, but, as we shall see, this statement was incorrect.

-t Sort the output by modification time, most recent first, instead of by name.

-u Use the access time instead of the modification time with -t and/or -l.

The biggest differences between V7 ls and modern ls concern the -a option and the -l option. Modern systems omit all dot files unless -a is given, and they include both user and group names in the -l long listing. On modern systems, -g is taken to mean print only the group name, and -o means print only the user name. For what it's worth, GNU ls has over 50 options!

7.2 V7 ls Code

The file /usr/src/cmd/ls.c in the V7 distribution contains the code. It is all of 425 lines long.

```
 1   /*
 2    * list file or directory
 3    */
 4
 5   #include <sys/param.h>
 6   #include <sys/stat.h>
 7   #include <sys/dir.h>
 8   #include <stdio.h>
 9
10   #define NFILES  1024
11   FILE      *pwdf, *dirf;
12   char      stdbuf[BUFSIZ];
13
14   struct lbuf {                                Collects needed info
15       union {
16           char      lname[15];
17           char      *namep;
18       } ln;
19       char      ltype;
20       short     lnum;
21       short     lflags;
22       short     lnl;
23       short     luid;
24       short     lgid;
25       long      lsize;
26       long      lmtime;
27   };
28
29   int aflg, dflg, lflg, sflg, tflg, uflg, iflg, fflg, gflg, cflg;
30   int rflg   = 1;
31   long    year;                                Global variables: auto init to 0
32   int flags;
33   int lastuid = -1;
34   char    tbuf[16];
35   long    tblocks;
36   int statreq;
37   struct  lbuf    *flist[NFILES];
38   struct  lbuf    **lastp = flist;
```

```
39   struct   lbuf     **firstp = flist;
40   char     *dotp    = ".";
41
42   char     *makename();
43   struct   lbuf *gstat();
44   char     *ctime();
45   long     nblock();
46
47   #define ISARG   0100000
```

char *makename(char *dir, char *file);
struct lbuf *gstat(char *file, int argfl);
char *ctime(time_t *t);
long nblock(long size);

The program starts with file inclusions (lines 5–8) and variable declarations. The struct lbuf (lines 14–27) encapsulates the parts of the struct stat that are of interest to ls. We see later how this structure is filled.

The variables aflg, dflg, and so on (lines 29 and 30) all indicate the presence of the corresponding option. This variable naming style is typical of V7 code. The flist, lastp, and firstp variables (lines 37–39) represent the files that ls reports information about. Note that flist is a fixed-size array, allowing no more than 1024 files to be processed. We see shortly how all these variables are used.

After the variable declarations come function declarations (lines 42–45), and then the definition of ISARG, which distinguishes a file named on the command line from a file found when a directory is read.

```
49   main(argc, argv)
50   char *argv[];
51   {
52       int i;
53       register struct lbuf *ep, **ep1;
54       register struct lbuf **slastp;
55       struct lbuf **epp;
56       struct lbuf lb;
57       char *t;
58       int compar();
59
60       setbuf(stdout, stdbuf);
61       time(&lb.lmtime);
62       year = lb.lmtime - 6L*30L*24L*60L*60L; /* 6 months ago */
```

int main(int argc, char **argv)

Variable and function declarations

Get current time

The main() function starts by declaring variables and functions (lines 52–58), setting the buffer for standard output, retrieving the time of day (lines 60–61), and computing the seconds-since-the-Epoch value for approximately six months ago (line 62). Note that all the constants have the L suffix, indicating the use of long arithmetic.

```
63       if (--argc > 0 && *argv[1] == '-') {
64           argv++;
65           while (*++*argv) switch (**argv) {
66
```

Parse options

```
 67            case 'a':                            All directory entries
 68                 aflg++;
 69                 continue;
 70
 71            case 's':                            Size in blocks
 72                 sflg++;
 73                 statreq++;
 74                 continue;
 75
 76            case 'd':                            Directory info, not contents
 77                 dflg++;
 78                 continue;
 79
 80            case 'g':                            Group name instead of user name
 81                 gflg++;
 82                 continue;
 83
 84            case 'l':                            Long listing
 85                 lflg++;
 86                 statreq++;
 87                 continue;
 88
 89            case 'r':                            Reverse sort order
 90                 rflg = -1;
 91                 continue;
 92
 93            case 't':                            Sort by time, not name
 94                 tflg++;
 95                 statreq++;
 96                 continue;
 97
 98            case 'u':                            Access time, not modification time
 99                 uflg++;
100                 continue;
101
102            case 'c':                            Inode change time, not modification time
103                 cflg++;
104                 continue;
105
106            case 'i':                            Include inode number
107                 iflg++;
108                 continue;
109
110            case 'f':                            Force reading each arg as directory
111                 fflg++;
112                 continue;
113
114            default:                             Ignore unknown option letters
115                 continue;
116            }
117            argc--;
118      }
```

Lines 63–118 parse the command-line options. Note the manual parsing code: getopt() hadn't been invented yet. The statreq variable is set to true when an option requires the use of the stat() system call.

Avoiding an unnecessary stat() call on each file is a big performance win. The stat() call was particularly expensive, because it could involve a disk seek to the inode location, a disk read to read the inode, and then a disk seek back to the location of the directory contents (in order to continue reading directory entries).

Modern systems have the inodes in groups, spread out throughout a filesystem instead of clustered together at the front. This makes a noticeable performance improvement. Nevertheless, stat() calls are still not free; you should use them as needed, but not any more than that.

```
119        if (fflg) {                              -f overrides -l, -s, -t, adds -a
120             aflg++;
121             lflg = 0;
122             sflg = 0;
123             tflg = 0;
124             statreq = 0;
125        }
126        if(lflg) {                               Open password or group file
127             t = "/etc/passwd";
128             if(gflg)
129                 t = "/etc/group";
130             pwdf = fopen(t, "r");
131        }
132        if (argc==0) {                            Use current dir if no args
133             argc++;
134             argv = &dotp - 1;
135        }
```

Lines 119–125 handle the -f option, turning off -l, -s, -t, and statreq. Lines 126–131 handle -l, setting the file to be read for user or group information. Remember that the V7 ls shows only one or the other, not both.

If no arguments are left, lines 132–135 set up argv such that it points at a string representing the current directory. The assignment 'argv = &dotp - 1' is valid, although unusual. The '- 1' compensates for the '++argv' on line 137. This avoids special case code for 'argc == 1' in the main part of the program.

```
136      for (i=0; i < argc; i++) {                    Get info about each file
137          if ((ep = gstat(*++argv, 1))==NULL)
138              continue;
139          ep->ln.namep = *argv;
140          ep->lflags |= ISARG;
141      }
142      qsort(firstp, lastp - firstp, sizeof *lastp, compar);
143      slastp = lastp;
144      for (epp=firstp; epp<slastp; epp++) {          Main code, see text
145          ep = *epp;
146          if (ep->ltype=='d' && dflg==0 || fflg) {
147              if (argc>1)
148                  printf("\n%s:\n", ep->ln.namep);
149              lastp = slastp;
150              readdir(ep->ln.namep);
151              if (fflg==0)
152                  qsort(slastp,lastp - slastp,sizeof *lastp,compar);
153              if (lflg || sflg)
154                  printf("total %D\n", tblocks);
155              for (ep1=slastp; ep1<lastp; ep1++)
156                  pentry(*ep1);
157          } else
158              pentry(ep);
159      }
160      exit(0);
161  }                                                  End of main()
```

Lines 136–141 loop over the arguments, gathering information about each one. The second argument to `gstat()` is a boolean: true if the name is a command-line argument, false otherwise. Line 140 adds the `ISARG` flag to the `lflags` field for each command-line argument.

The `gstat()` function adds each new `struct lbuf` into the global `flist` array (line 137). It also updates the `lastp` global pointer to point into this array at the current last element.

Lines 142–143 sort the array, using `qsort()`, and save the current value of `lastp` in `slastp`. Lines 144–159 loop over each element in the array, printing file or directory info, as appropriate.

The code for directories deserves further explication:

```
if (ep->ltype=='d' && dflg==0 || fflg) ...
```

Line 146. If the file type is directory and if `-d` was not provided *or* if `-f` was, then `ls` has to read the directory instead of printing information about the directory itself.

```
if (argc>1) printf("\n%s:\n", ep->ln.namep)
```
Lines 147–148. Print the directory name and a colon if multiple files were named on the command line.

```
lastp = slastp; readdir(ep->ln.namep)
```
Lines 149–150. Reset `lastp` from `slastp`. The `flist` array acts as a two-level stack of filenames. The command-line arguments are kept in `firstp` through `slastp - 1`. When `readdir()` reads a directory, it puts the `struct lbuf` structures for the directory contents onto the stack, starting at `slastp` and going through `lastp`. This is illustrated in Figure 7.1.

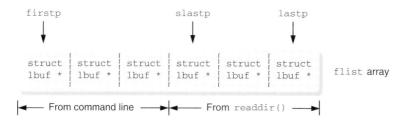

FIGURE 7.1
The `flist` array as a two-level stack

```
if (fflg==0) qsort(slastp,lastp - slastp,sizeof *lastp,compar)
```
Lines 151–152. Sort the subdirectory entries if -f is not in effect.

```
if (lflg || sflg) printf("total %D\n", tblocks)
```
Lines 153–154. Print the total number of blocks used by files in the directory, for -l or -s. This total is kept in the variable `tblocks`, which is reset for each directory. The %D format string for `printf()` is equivalent to %ld on modern systems; it means "print a long integer." (V7 also had %ld, see line 192.)

```
for (ep1=slastp; ep1<lastp; ep1++) pentry(*ep1)
```
Lines 155–156. Print the information about each file in the subdirectory. Note that the V7 ls descends only one level in a directory tree. It lacks the modern -R "recursive" option.

```
163  pentry(ap)                                          void pentry(struct lbuf *ap)
164  struct lbuf *ap;
165  {
166      struct { char dminor, dmajor;};              Unused historical artifact from V6 ls
167      register t;
168      register struct lbuf *p;
169      register char *cp;
170
171      p = ap;
172      if (p->lnum == -1)
173          return;
174      if (iflg)
175          printf("%5u ", p->lnum);                 Inode number
176      if (sflg)
177      printf("%4D ", nblock(p->lsize));            Size in blocks
```

The pentry() routine prints information about a file. Lines 172–173 check whether the lnum field is -1, and return if so. When 'p->lnum == -1' is true, the struct lbuf is not valid. Otherwise, this field is the file's inode number.

Lines 174–175 print the inode number if -i is in effect. Lines 176–177 print the total number of blocks if -s is in effect. (As we see below, this number may not be accurate.)

```
178      if (lflg) {                                 Long listing:
179          putchar(p->ltype);                      – File type
180          pmode(p->lflags);                       – Permissions
181          printf("%2d ", p->lnl);                 – Link count
182          t = p->luid;
183          if(gflg)
184              t = p->lgid;
185          if (getname(t, tbuf)==0)
186              printf("%-6.6s", tbuf);             – User or group
187          else
188              printf("%-6d", t);
189          if (p->ltype=='b' || p->ltype=='c')     – Device: major and minor numbers
190              printf("%3d,%3d", major((int)p->lsize), minor((int)p->lsize));
191          else
192              printf("%7ld", p->lsize);           – Size in bytes
193          cp = ctime(&p->lmtime);
194          if(p->lmtime < year)                    – Modification time
195              printf(" %-7.7s %-4.4s ", cp+4, cp+20); else
196              printf(" %-12.12s ", cp+4);
197      }
198      if (p->lflags&ISARG)                        – Filename
199          printf("%s\n", p->ln.namep);
200      else
201          printf("%.14s\n", p->ln.lname);
202  }
```

Lines 178–197 handle the -l option. Lines 179–181 print the file's type, permissions, and number of links. Lines 182–184 set t to the user ID or the group ID, based on the -g option. Lines 185–188 retrieve the corresponding name and print it if available. Otherwise, the program prints the numeric value.

Lines 189–192 check whether the file is a block or character device. If it is, they print the major and minor device numbers, extracted with the major() and minor() macros. Otherwise, they print the file's size.

Lines 193–196 print the time of interest. If it's older than six months, the code prints the month, day, and year. Otherwise, it prints the month, day, and time (see Section 6.1.3.1, "Simple Time Formatting: asctime() and ctime()," page 170, for the format of ctime()'s result).

Finally, lines 198–201 print the filename. For a command-line argument, we know it's a zero-terminated string, and %s can be used. For a file read from a directory, it may not be zero-terminated, and thus an explicit precision, %.14s, must be used.

```
204   getname(uid, buf)                                      int getname(int uid, char buf[])
205   int uid;
206   char buf[];
207   {
208       int j, c, n, i;
209
210       if (uid==lastuid)                                  Simple caching, see text
211           return(0);
212       if(pwdf == NULL)                                   Safety check
213           return(-1);
214       rewind(pwdf);                                      Start at front of file
215       lastuid = -1;
216       do {
217           i = 0;                                         Index in buf array
218           j = 0;                                         Counts fields in line
219           n = 0;                                         Converts numeric value
220           while((c=fgetc(pwdf)) != '\n') {               Read lines
221               if (c==EOF)
222                   return(-1);
223               if (c==':') {                              Count fields
224                   j++;
225                   c = '0';
226               }
227               if (j==0)                                  First field is name
228                   buf[i++] = c;
229               if (j==2)                                  Third field is numeric ID
230                   n = n*10 + c - '0';
231           }
232       } while (n != uid);                                Keep searching until ID found
```

```
233        buf[i++] = '\0';
234        lastuid = uid;
235        return(0);
236    }
```

The `getname()` function converts a user or group ID number into the corresponding name. It implements a simple caching scheme; if the passed-in `uid` is the same as the global variable `lastuid`, then the function returns 0, for OK; the buffer will already contain the name (lines 210–211). `lastuid` is initialized to -1 (line 33), so this test fails the first time `getname()` is called.

`pwdf` is already open on either `/etc/passwd` or `/etc/group` (see lines 126–130). The code here checks that the open succeeded and returns -1 if it didn't (lines 212–213).

Surprisingly, `ls` does *not* use `getpwuid()` or `getgrgid()`. Instead, it takes advantage of the facts that the format of `/etc/passwd` and `/etc/group` is identical for the first three fields (name, password, numeric ID) and that both use a colon as separator.

Lines 216–232 implement a linear search through the file. `j` counts the number of colons seen so far: 0 for the name and 2 for the ID number. Thus, while scanning the line, it fills in both the name and the ID number.

Lines 233–235 terminate the `name` buffer, set the global `lastuid` to the found ID number, and return 0 for OK.

```
238  long                                      long nblock(long size)
239  nblock(size)
240  long size;
241  {
242      return((size+511)>>9);
243  }
```

The `nblock()` function reports how many disk blocks the file uses. This calculation is based on the file's size as returned by `stat()`. The V7 block size was 512 bytes—the size of a physical disk sector.

The calculation on line 242 looks a bit scary. The '`>>9`' is a right-shift by nine bits. This divides by 512, to give the number of blocks. (On early hardware, a right-shift was much faster than division.) So far, so good. Now, a file of even one byte still takes up a whole disk block. However, '`1 / 512`' comes out as zero (integer division truncates), which is incorrect. This explains the '`size+511`'. By adding 511, the code ensures that the sum produces the correct number of blocks when it is divided by 512.

This calculation is only approximate, however. Very large files also have indirect blocks. Despite the claim in the V7 *ls*(1) manpage, this calculation does not account for indirect blocks.

Furthermore, consider the case of a file with large holes (created by seeking way past the end of the file with `lseek()`). Holes don't occupy disk blocks; however, this is not reflected in the size value. Thus, the calculation produced by `nblock()`, while usually correct, could produce results that are either smaller or larger than the real case.

For these reasons, the `st_blocks` member was added into the `struct stat` at 4.2 BSD, and then picked up for System V and POSIX.

```
245  int m1[] = { 1, S_IREAD>>0, 'r', '-' };
246  int m2[] = { 1, S_IWRITE>>0, 'w', '-' };
247  int m3[] = { 2, S_ISUID, 's', S_IEXEC>>0, 'x', '-' };
248  int m4[] = { 1, S_IREAD>>3, 'r', '-' };
249  int m5[] = { 1, S_IWRITE>>3, 'w', '-' };
250  int m6[] = { 2, S_ISGID, 's', S_IEXEC>>3, 'x', '-' };
251  int m7[] = { 1, S_IREAD>>6, 'r', '-' };
252  int m8[] = { 1, S_IWRITE>>6, 'w', '-' };
253  int m9[] = { 2, S_ISVTX, 't', S_IEXEC>>6, 'x', '-' };
254
255  int *m[] = { m1, m2, m3, m4, m5, m6, m7, m8, m9};
256
257  pmode(aflag)                                       void pmode(int aflag)
258  {
259      register int **mp;
260
261      flags = aflag;
262      for (mp = &m[0]; mp < &m[sizeof(m)/sizeof(m[0])];)
263          select(*mp++);
264  }
265
266  select(pairp)                                  void select(register int *pairp)
267  register int *pairp;
268  {
269      register int n;
270
271      n = *pairp++;
272      while (--n>=0 && (flags&*pairp++)==0)
273          pairp++;
274      putchar(*pairp);
275  }
```

Lines 245–275 print the file's permissions. The code is compact and rather elegant; it requires careful study.

- Lines 245–253: The arrays `m1` through `m9` encode the permission bits to check for along with the corresponding characters to print. There is one array per character to print in the file mode. The first element of each array is the number of (permission, character) pairs encoded in that particular array. The final element is the character to print in the event that none of the given permission bits are found.

  Note also how the permissions are specified as '`I_READ>>0`', '`I_READ>>3`', '`I_READ>>6`', and so on. The individual constants for each bit (`S_IRUSR`, `S_IRGRP`, etc.) had not been invented yet. (See Table 4.5 in Section 4.6.1, "Specifying Initial File Permissions," page 106.)

- Line 255: The `m` array points to each of the `m1` through `m9` arrays.

- Lines 257–264: The `pmode()` function first sets the global variable `flags` to the passed-in parameter `aflag`. It then loops through the `m` array, passing each element to the `select()` function. The passed-in element represents one of the `m1` to `m9` arrays.

- Lines 266–275: The `select()` function understands the layout of each `m1` through `m9` array. `n` is the number of pairs in the array (the first element); line 271 sets it. Lines 272–273 look for permission bits, checking the global variable `flags` set previously on line 261.

Note the use of the ++ operator, both in the loop test and in the loop body. The effect is to skip over pairs in the array as long as the permission bit in the first element of the pair is not found in `flags`.

When the loop ends, *either* the permission bit has been found, in which case `pairp` points at the second element of the pair, which is the correct character to print, *or* it has not been found, in which case `pairp` points at the default character. In either case, line 274 prints the character that `pairp` points to.

A final point worth noting is that in C, character constants (such as `'x'`) have type
`int`, not `char`.[1] So there's no problem putting such constants into an integer array;
everything works correctly.

```
277   char *                                          char *makename(char *dir, char *file)
278   makename(dir, file)
279   char *dir, *file;
280   {
281       static char dfile[100];
282       register char *dp, *fp;
283       register int i;
284
285       dp = dfile;
286       fp = dir;
287       while (*fp)
288           *dp++ = *fp++;
289       *dp++ = '/';
290       fp = file;
291       for (i=0; i<DIRSIZ; i++)
292           *dp++ = *fp++;
293       *dp = 0;
294       return(dfile);
295   }
```

Lines 277–295 define the `makename()` function. Its job is to concatenate a directory
name and a filename, separated by a slash character, and produce a string. It does this
in the `static` buffer `dfile`. Note that `dfile` is only 100 characters long and that no
error checking is done.

The code itself is straightforward, copying characters one at a time. `makename()` is
used by the `readdir()` function.

```
297   readdir(dir)                                     void readdir(char *dir)
298   char *dir;
299   {
300       static struct direct dentry;
301       register int j;
302       register struct lbuf *ep;
303
304       if ((dirf = fopen(dir, "r")) == NULL) {
305           printf("%s unreadable\n", dir);
306           return;
307       }
308       tblocks = 0;
```

---

[1] This is different in C++: There, character constants do have type `char`. This difference does not affect this particular code.

```
309        for(;;) {
310            if (fread((char *)&dentry, sizeof(dentry), 1, dirf) != 1)
311                break;
312            if (dentry.d_ino==0
313            || aflg==0 && dentry.d_name[0]=='.' && (dentry.d_name[1]=='\0'
314            || dentry.d_name[1]=='.' && dentry.d_name[2]=='\0'))
315                continue;
316            ep = gstat(makename(dir, dentry.d_name), 0);
317            if (ep==NULL)
318                continue;
319            if (ep->lnum != -1)
320                ep->lnum = dentry.d_ino;
321            for (j=0; j<DIRSIZ; j++)
322                ep->ln.lname[j] = dentry.d_name[j];
323        }
324        fclose(dirf);
325    }
```

Lines 297–325 define the `readdir()` function, whose job is to read the contents of directories named on the command line.

Lines 304–307 open the directory for reading, returning if `fopen()` fails. Line 308 initializes the global variable `tblocks` to 0. This was used earlier (lines 153–154) to print the total number of blocks used by files in a directory.

Lines 309–323 are a loop that reads directory entries and adds them to the `flist` array. Lines 310–311 read one entry, exiting the loop upon end-of-file.

Lines 312–315 skip uninteresting entries. If the inode number is zero, this slot isn't used. Otherwise, if -a was not given and the filename is either '.' or '..', skip it.

Lines 316–318 call `gstat()` with the full name of the file, and a second argument of false, indicating that it's not from the command line. `gstat()` updates the global `lastp` pointer and the `flist` array. A NULL return value indicates some sort of failure.

Lines 319–322 save the inode number and name in the `struct lbuf`. If `ep->lnum` comes back from `gstat()` set to -1, it means that the `stat()` operation on the file failed. Finally, line 324 closes the directory.

The following function, `gstat()` (lines 327–398), is the core function for the operation of retrieving and storing file information.

```
327   struct lbuf *                                    struct lbuf *gstat(char *file, int argfl)
328   gstat(file, argfl)
329   char *file;
330   {
331       extern char *malloc();
332       struct stat statb;
333       register struct lbuf *rep;
334       static int nomocore;
335
336       if (nomocore)                                Ran out of memory earlier
337           return(NULL);
338       rep = (struct lbuf *)malloc(sizeof(struct lbuf));
339       if (rep==NULL) {
340           fprintf(stderr, "ls: out of memory\n");
341           nomocore = 1;
342           return(NULL);
343       }
344       if (lastp >= &flist[NFILES]) {               Check whether too many files given
345           static int msg;
346           lastp--;
347           if (msg==0) {
348               fprintf(stderr, "ls: too many files\n");
349               msg++;
350           }
351       }
352       *lastp++ = rep;                              Fill in information
353       rep->lflags = 0;
354       rep->lnum = 0;
355       rep->ltype = '-';                            Default file type
```

The static variable nomocore [sic] indicates that malloc() failed upon an earlier call. Since it's static, it's automatically initialized to 0 (that is, false). If it's true upon entry, gstat() just returns NULL. Otherwise, if malloc() fails, ls prints an error message, sets nomocore to true, and returns NULL (lines 334–343).

Lines 344–351 make sure that there is still room left in the flist array. If not, ls prints a message (but only once; note the use of the static variable msg), and then reuses the last slot in flist.

Line 352 makes the slot lastp points to point to the new struct lbuf (rep). This also updates lastp, which is used for sorting in main() (lines 142 and 152). Lines 353–355 set default values for the flags, inode number, and type fields in the struct lbuf.

```
356      if (argfl || statreq) {
357          if (stat(file, &statb)<0) {                 stat() failed
358              printf("%s not found\n", file);
359              statb.st_ino = -1;
360              statb.st_size = 0;
361              statb.st_mode = 0;
362              if (argfl) {
363                  lastp--;
364                  return(0);
365              }
366          }
367          rep->lnum = statb.st_ino;                    stat() OK, copy info
368          rep->lsize = statb.st_size;
369          switch(statb.st_mode&S_IFMT) {
370
371          case S_IFDIR:
372              rep->ltype = 'd';
373              break;
374
375          case S_IFBLK:
376              rep->ltype = 'b';
377              rep->lsize = statb.st_rdev;
378              break;
379
380          case S_IFCHR:
381              rep->ltype = 'c';
382              rep->lsize = statb.st_rdev;
383              break;
384          }
385          rep->lflags = statb.st_mode & ~S_IFMT;
386          rep->luid = statb.st_uid;
387          rep->lgid = statb.st_gid;
388          rep->lnl = statb.st_nlink;
389          if(uflg)
390              rep->lmtime = statb.st_atime;
391          else if (cflg)
392              rep->lmtime = statb.st_ctime;
393          else
394              rep->lmtime = statb.st_mtime;
395          tblocks += nblock(statb.st_size);
396      }
397      return(rep);
398  }
```

Lines 356–396 handle the call to stat(). If this is a command-line argument or if statreq is true because of an option, the code fills in the struct lbuf as follows:

- Lines 357–366: Call stat() and if it fails, print an error message and set values as appropriate, then return NULL (expressed as 0).

- Lines 367–368: Set the inode number and size fields from the struct stat if the stat() succeeded.

- Lines 369–384: Handle the special cases of directory, block device, and character device. In all cases the code updates the ltype field. For devices, the lsize value is replaced with the st_rdev value.

- Lines 385–388: Fill in the lflags, luid, lgid, and lnl fields from the corresponding fields in the struct stat. Line 385 removes the file-type bits, leaving the 12 permissions bits (read/write/execute for user/group/other, and setuid, setgid, and save-text).

- Lines 389–394: Based on command-line options, use one of the three time fields from the struct stat for the lmtime field in the struct lbuf.

- Line 395: Update the global variable tblocks with the number of blocks in the file.

```
400   compar(pp1, pp2)                           int compar(struct lbuf **pp1,
401   struct lbuf **pp1, **pp2;                               struct lbuf **pp2)
402   {
403       register struct lbuf *p1, *p2;
404
405       p1 = *pp1;
406       p2 = *pp2;
407       if (dflg==0) {
408           if (p1->lflags&ISARG && p1->ltype=='d') {
409               if (!(p2->lflags&ISARG && p2->ltype=='d'))
410                   return(1);
411           } else {
412               if (p2->lflags&ISARG && p2->ltype=='d')
413                   return(-1);
414           }
415       }
416       if (tflg) {
417           if(p2->lmtime == p1->lmtime)
418               return(0);
419           if(p2->lmtime > p1->lmtime)
420               return(rflg);
421           return(-rflg);
422       }
423       return(rflg * strcmp(p1->lflags&ISARG? p1->ln.namep: p1->ln.lname,
424                   p2->lflags&ISARG? p2->ln.namep: p2->ln.lname));
425   }
```

The compar() function is dense: There's a lot happening in little space. The first thing to remember is the meaning of the return value: A negative value means that the first file should sort to an earlier spot in the array than the second, zero means the files are equal, and a positive value means that the second file should sort to an earlier spot than the first.

The next thing to understand is that `ls` prints the contents of directories *after* it prints information about files. Thus the result of sorting should be that all directories *named on the command line* follow all files named on the command line.

Finally, the `rflg` variable helps implement the `-r` option, which reverses the sorting order. It is initialized to `1` (line 30). If `-r` is used, `rflg` is set to `-1` (lines 89–91).

The following pseudocode describes the logic of `compar()`; the line numbers in the left margin correspond to those of `ls.c`:

```
407  if ls has to read directories  # dflg == 0
408      if p1 is a command-line arg and p1 is a directory
409          if p2 is not a command-line arg and is not a directory
410              return 1    # first comes after second
             else
                 fall through to time test
411      else
             # p1 is not a command-line directory
412          if p2 is a command-line arg and is a directory
413              return -1   # first comes before second
             else
                 fall through to time test

416  if sorting is based on time  # tflg is true
         # compare times:
417      if p2's time is equal to p1's time
418          return 0
419      if p2's time > p1's time
420          return the value of rflg (positive or negative)
         # p2's time < p1's time
421      return opposite of rflg (negative or positive)

423  Multiply rflg by the result of strcmp()
424  on the two names and return the result
```

The arguments to `strcmp()` on lines 423–424 look messy. What's going on is that different members of the `ln` union in the `struct lbuf` must be used, depending on whether the filename is a command-line argument or was read from a directory.

7.3 Summary

- The V7 `ls` is a relatively small program, yet it touches on many of the fundamental aspects of Unix programming: file I/O, file metadata, directory contents, users and groups, time and date values, sorting, and dynamic memory management.

- The most notable external difference between V7 ls and modern ls is the treatment of the -a and -l options. The V7 version has many fewer options than do modern versions; a noticeable lack is the -R recursive option.

- The management of flist is a clean way to use the limited memory of the PDP-11 architecture yet still provide as much information as possible. The struct lbuf nicely abstracts the information of interest from the struct stat; this simplifies the code considerably. The code for printing the nine permission bits is compact and elegant.

- Some parts of ls use surprisingly small limits, such as the upper bound of 1024 on the number of files or the buffer size of 100 in makename().

Exercises

1. Consider the getname() function. What happens if the requested ID number is 216 and the following two lines exist in /etc/passwd, in this order:

    ```
    joe:xyzzy:2160:10:Joe User:/usr/joe:/bin/sh
    jane:zzyxx:216:12:Jane User:/usr/jane:/bin/sh
    ```

2. Consider the makename() function. Could it use sprintf() to make the concatenated name? Why or why not?

3. Are lines 319–320 in readdir() really necessary?

4. Take the stat program you wrote for the exercises in "Exercises" for Chapter 6, page 205. Add the nblock() function from the V7 ls, and print the results along with the st_blocks field from the struct stat. Add a visible marker when they're different.

5. How would you grade the V7 ls on its use of malloc()? (Hint: how often is free() called? Where should it be called?)

6. How would you grade the V7 ls for code clarity? (Hint: how many comments are there?)

7. Outline the steps you would take to adapt the V7 ls for modern systems.

## Chapter 8

Filesystems
and
Directory Walks

In this chapter

This chapter completes the discussion of Linux (and Unix) filesystems and directories. We first describe how a disk partition containing a filesystem is added to (and removed from) the logical filesystem namespace, such that in general a user need neither know nor care where a file is physically located, along with the APIs for working with filesystems.

We then describe how to move around within the hierarchical file namespace, how to retrieve the full pathname of the current working directory, and how to easily process arbitrary directory hierarchies (trees), using the `nftw()` function. Finally, we describe the specialized but important `chroot()` system call.

8.1 Mounting and Unmounting Filesystems

The unified hierarchical file namespace is a great strength of the Linux/Unix design. This section looks at how administrative files, commands, and the operating system cooperate to build the namespace from separate physical devices that contain file data and metadata.

8.1.1 Reviewing the Background

Chapter 5, "Directories and File Metadata," page 117, introduced inodes for file metadata and described how directory entries link filenames to inodes. It also described partitions and filesystems, and you saw that hard links are restricted to working within a single filesystem because directories contain only inode numbers and inode numbers are not unique across the entire set of in-use filesystems.

Besides inodes and data blocks, filesystems also contain one or more copies of the *superblock*. This is a special disk block that describes the filesystem; its information is updated as the filesystem itself changes. For example, it contains counts of free and used inodes, free and used blocks, and other information. It also includes a *magic number*: a unique special value in a special location that identifies the type of the filesystem. (We'll see how this is relevant, shortly.)

Making a partition that contains a filesystem available for use is called *mounting* the filesystem. Removing a filesystem from use is called, not surprisingly, *unmounting* the filesystem.

These two jobs are accomplished with the mount and umount [sic] programs, named for the corresponding system calls. Every Unix system's mount() system call has a different interface. Because mounting and unmounting are considered implementation issues, POSIX purposely does not standardize these system calls.

You mount a filesystem onto a directory; such a directory is referred to as the filesystem's *mount point*. By convention the directory should be empty, but nothing enforces this. However, if the mount point is not empty, all of its contents become *completely inaccessible* while a filesystem is mounted on it.[1]

The kernel maintains a unique number, known as the *device number*, that identifies each mounted partition. For this reason, it is the (device, inode) pair that together uniquely identifies a file; when the struct stat structures for two filenames indicate that both numbers are the same, you can be sure that they do refer to the same file.

As mentioned earlier, user-level software places the inode structures and other metadata onto a disk partition, thereby creating the filesystem. This same software creates an initial root directory for the filesystem. Thus, we have to make a distinction between "the root directory named /," which is the topmost directory in the hierarchical filename namespace, and "the root directory of a filesystem," which is each filesystem's individual topmost directory. The / directory is also the "root directory" of the "root filesystem."

For reasons described in the sidebar, a filesystem's root directory *always* has inode number 2 (although this is not formally standardized). Since there can be multiple filesystems, each one's root directory has the same inode number, 2. When resolving a pathname, the kernel knows where each filesystem is mounted and arranges for the mount point's name to refer to the root directory of the mounted filesystem. Furthermore, '..' in the root of a mounted filesystem is made to refer to the parent directory of the mount point.

Figure 8.1 shows two filesystems: one for the root directory, and one for /usr, before /usr is mounted. Figure 8.2 shows the situation after /usr is mounted.

---

[1] GNU/Linux and Solaris allow you to mount one file on top of another; this has advanced uses, which we don't otherwise discuss.

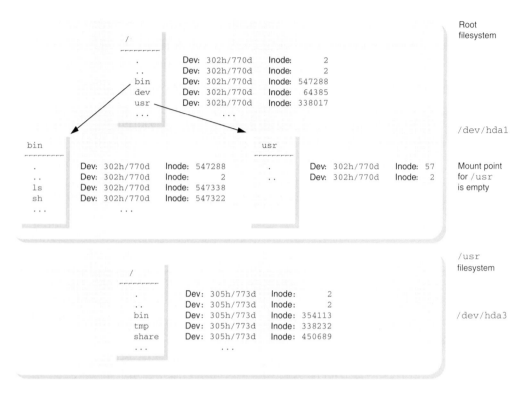

FIGURE 8.1
Separate filesystems, before mounting

The `/` directory, the root of the entire logical hierarchy, is special in an additional way: `/.` and `/..` refer to the same directory; this is not true of any other directory on the system. (Thus, after something like 'cd `/../../../..`', you're still in `/`.) This behavior is implemented in a simple fashion: Both `/.` and `/..` are hard links to the filesystem's root directory. (You can see this in both Figure 8.1 and Figure 8.2.) Every filesystem works this way, but the kernel treats `/` specially and does not treat as a special case the '`..`' directory for the filesystem mounted on `/`.

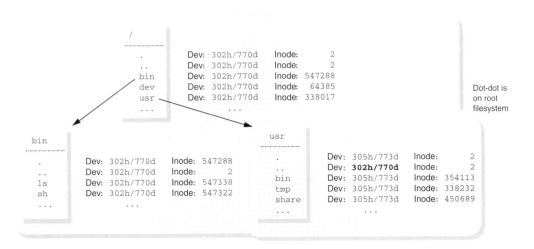

FIGURE 8.2
Separate filesystems, after mounting

Root Inode Numbers

The inode number for the root directory of a filesystem is always 2. Why is that? The answer has to do with both technology and history.

As mentioned in Section 5.3, "Reading Directories," page 132, a directory entry with an inode number of zero indicates an unused, or empty, slot. So inode 0 cannot be used for a real file or directory.

OK, so what about inode 1? Well, particularly in the 1970s and 1980s, disks were not as well made as they are now. When you bought a disk, it came with a (paper) list of *bad blocks*—known locations on the disk that were not usable. Each operating system had to have a way to keep track of those bad blocks and avoid using them.

Under Unix, you did this by creating a special-purpose file, whose data blocks were the ones known to be bad. This file was attached on inode 1, leaving inode 2 as the first inode usable for regular files or directories.

Modern disk drives have considerable built-in electronics and handle bad blocks on their own. Thus, technically, it would be feasible to use inode 1 for a file. However, since so much Unix software assumes that inode 2 is the inode for filesystem root directories, Linux follows this convention as well. (However, Linux sometimes uses inode 1 for nonnative filesystems, such as `vfat` or `/proc`.)

8.1.2 Looking at Different Filesystem Types

> NOTE The discussion in this section is specific to Linux. However, most modern Unix systems have similar features. We encourage you to explore your system's documentation.

Historically, V7 Unix supported only a single filesystem type; every partition's metadata and directory organization were structured the same way. 4.1 BSD used a filesystem with the same structure as that of V7, but with a 1024-byte block size instead of a 512-byte one. 4.2 BSD introduced the "BSD Fast Filesystem," which dramatically changed the layout of inodes and data on disk and enabled the use of much larger block sizes. (In general, using larger contiguous blocks of data provides better throughput, especially for file reads.)

Through 4.3 BSD and System V Release 2 in the early and mid-1980s, Unix systems continued to support just one filesystem type. To switch a computer from one filesystem to another,[2] you had to first back up each filesystem to archival media (9-track tape), upgrade the system, and then restore the data.

In the mid-1980s, Sun Microsystems developed a kernel architecture that made it possible to use multiple filesystem architectures at the same time. This design was implemented for their SunOS operating system, primarily to support Sun's Network File System (NFS). However, as a consequence it was also possible to support multiple on-disk architectures. System V Release 3 used a similar architecture to support the Remote File System (RFS), but it continued to support only one on-disk architecture.[3] (RFS was never widely used and is now only a historical footnote.)

Sun's general design became popular and widely implemented in commercial Unix systems, including System V Release 4. Linux and BSD systems use a variant of this design to support multiple on-disk filesystem formats. In particular, it's common for all Unix variants on Intel x86 hardware to be able to mount MS-DOS/Windows FAT filesystems, including those supplying long filenames, as well as ISO 9660-formatted CD-ROMs.

---

[2] For example, consider upgrading a VAX 11/780 from 4.1 BSD to 4.2 BSD.

[3] System V Release 3 supported two different block sizes: 512 bytes and 1024 bytes, but otherwise the disk organization was the same.

Linux has several native (that is, on-disk) filesystems. The most popular are the `ext2` and `ext3` filesystems. *Many* more filesystem types are available, however. You can find information about most of them in the `/usr/src/linux/Documentation/filesystems/` directory (if you have kernel source installed). Table 8.1 lists the various filesystem names, with brief descriptions of each. The abbreviation "RW" means "read/write" and "RO" means "read only."

TABLE 8.1
Supported in-kernel Linux filesystems (kernel 2.4.x)

Name	Support	Description
afs	RW	The Andrew File System.
adfs	RW	Acorn Advanced Disc Filing System.
affs	RO, RW	Amiga Fast File System. Read only vs. read/write depends upon the version of the filesystem.
autofs	RW	Filesystem for interacting with the automounter daemon.
befs	RO	BeOS Filesystem. Marked as *alpha* software.
bfs	RW	SCO UnixWare Boot Filesystem.
binfmt_misc	RW	Special filesystem for running interpreters on compiled files (for example, Java files).
efs	RW	A filesystem developed for SGI's Unix variant named Irix.
coda	RW	An experimental distributed filesystem developed at CMU.
cramfs	RO	A small filesystem for storing files in ROM.
devfs	RW	A way to dynamically provide device files for `/dev` (obsolete).
devpts	RW	Special filesystem for pseudo-ttys.
ext2	RW	The Second Extended Filesystem. This is the default GNU/Linux filesystem, although some distributions now use `ext3`.
ext3	RW	The `ext2` filesystem with journaling.
hfs	RW	Apple Mac OS Hierarchical File System.
hpfs	RW	The OS/2 High Performance File System.
intermezzo	RW	An experimental distributed filesystem for working while disconnected. See the InterMezzo web site (`http://www.inter-mezzo.org`).

TABLE 8.1 *(Continued)*

Name	Support	Description
`jffs`	RW	Journaled Flash Filesystem (for embedded systems).
`jffs2`	RW	Journaled Flash Filesystem 2 (also for embedded systems).
`iso9660`	RO	The ISO 9660 CD-ROM filesystem. The Rock Ridge extensions are also supported, making a CD-ROM that uses them look like a normal (but read-only) filesystem.
`jfs`	RW	IBM's Journaled File System for Linux.
`ncp`	RW	Novell's NCP protocol for NetWare; a remote filesystem client.
`ntfs`	RO	Support for Windows NTFS filesystem.
`openpromfs`	RO	A `/proc` filesystem for the PROM on SPARC systems.
`proc`	RW	Access to per-process and kernel information.
`qnx4`	RW	The QNX4 (a small, real-time operating system) filesystem.
`ramfs`	RW	A filesystem for creating RAM disks.
`reiserfs`	RW	An advanced journaling filesystem.
`romfs`	RO	A filesystem for creating simple read-only RAM disks.
`smbfs`	RW	Client support for SMB filesystems (Windows file shares).
`sysv`	RW	The System V Release 2, Xenix, Minix, and Coherent filesystems. `coherent`, `minix`, and `xenix` are aliases.
`tmpfs`	RW	A ramdisk filesystem, supporting dynamic growth.
`udf`	RO	The UDF filesystem format used by DVD-ROMs.
`ufs`	RO, RW	The BSD Fast Filesystem; read/write for modern systems.
`umsdos`	RW	An extension to `vfat` making it look more like a Unix filesystem.
`usbfs`	RW	A special filesystem for working with USB devices. The original name was `usbdevfs` and this name still appears, for example, in the output of `mount`.
`vfat`	RW	All variants of MS-DOS/Windows FAT filesystems. `msdos` and `fat` are components.
`vxfs`	RW	The Veritas VxFS journaling filesystem.
`xfs`	RW	A high-performance journaling filesystem developed by SGI for Linux. See the XFS web site (`http://oss.sgi.com/projects/xfs/`).

Not all of these filesystems are supported by the `mount` command; see *mount*(8) for the list of those that are supported.

Journaling is a technique, pioneered in database systems, for improving the performance of file updates, in such a way that filesystem recovery in the event of a crash can be done both correctly and quickly. As of this writing, several different journaling filesystems are available and competing for prominence in the GNU/Linux world. `ext3` is one such; it has the advantage of being upwardly compatible with existing `ext2` filesystems, and it's easy to convert a filesystem back and forth between the two types. (See *tune2fs*(8).) ReiserFS and XFS also have strong followings.

The `fat`, `msdos`, `umsdos`, and `vfat` filesystems all share common code. In general, you should use `vfat` to mount Windows FAT-32 (or other FAT-xx) partitions, and `umsdos` if you wish to use a FAT partition as the root filesystem for your GNU/Linux system.

The Coherent, MINIX, original System V, and Xenix filesystems all have similar on-disk structures. The `sysv` filesystem type supports all of them; the four names `coherent`, `minix`, `sysv`, and `xenix` are aliases one for the other. The `coherent` and `xenix` names will eventually be removed.

The BSD Fast Filesystem has evolved somewhat over the years. The `ufs` filesystem supports read/write operation for the version from 4.4 BSD, which is the basis for the three widely used BSD operating systems: FreeBSD, NetBSD, and OpenBSD. It also supports read/write operation for Sun's Solaris filesystem, for both SPARC and Intel x86 systems. The original BSD format and that from the NeXTStep operating system are supported read-only.

The "RO" designations for `befs` and `ntfs` mean that filesystems of those types can be mounted and read but files cannot be written on them or removed from them. (This may change with time; check your system's documentation.) The `cramfs`, `iso9660`, `romfs`, and `udf` filesystems are marked "RO" because the underlying media are inherently read-only.

Two filesystem types no longer exist: `ext`, which was the original Extended Filesystem, and `xiafs`, which extended the original MINIX filesystem for longer names and larger file sizes. `xiafs` and `ext2` came out approximately simultaneously, but `ext2` eventually became the dominant filesystem.[4]

8.1.3 Mounting Filesystems: `mount`

The `mount` command mounts filesystems, splicing their contents into the system file hierarchy at their mount points. Under GNU/Linux, it is somewhat complicated since it has to deal with all the known filesystem types and their options. Normally, only `root` can run `mount`, although it's possible to make exceptions for certain cases, as is discussed later in the chapter.

You specify the filesystem type with the `-t` option:

```
mount [ options ] device mount-point
```

For example (# is the `root` prompt):

```
# mount -t iso9660 /dev/cdrom /mnt/cdrom          Mount CD-ROM
# mount -t vfat /dev/fd0 /mnt/floppy              Mount MS-DOS floppy
# mount -t nfs files.example.com:/ /mnt/files     Mount NFS filesystem
```

You can use '`-t auto`' to force `mount` to guess the filesystem type. This usually works, although if you know for sure what kind of filesystem you have, it helps to supply the type and avoid the chance that `mount` will guess incorrectly. `mount` does this guessing by default, so '`-t auto`' isn't strictly necessary.

GNU/Linux systems provide a special kind of mounting by means of the *loopback* device. In this way, a filesystem image contained in a regular file can be mounted as if it were an actual disk device. This capability is very useful, for example, with CD-ROM images. It allows you to create one and try it out, without having to burn it to a writable CD and mount the CD. The following example uses the first CD image from the Red Hat 9 distribution of GNU/Linux:

```
# ls -l shrike-i386-disc1.iso                              Examine CD image file
-rw-r--r--    1 arnold    devel    668991488 Apr 11 05:13 shrike-i386-disc1.iso
# mount -t iso9660 -o ro,loop shrike-i386-disc1.iso /mnt/cdrom   Mount it on /mnt/cdrom
# cd /mnt/cdrom                                             Go there
# ls                                                       Look at files
autorun              README.it             RELEASE-NOTES-fr.html
dosutils             README.ja             RELEASE-NOTES.html
EULA                 README.ko             RELEASE-NOTES-it.html
```

---

[4] Source: `http://www.ife.ee.ethz.ch/music/software/sag/subsection2_5_4_3.html`.

```
GPL                       README.pt              RELEASE-NOTES-ja.html
images                    README.pt_BR           RELEASE-NOTES-ko.html
isolinux                  README.zh_CN           RELEASE-NOTES-pt_BR.html
README                    README.zh_TW           RELEASE-NOTES-pt.html
README-Accessibility      RedHat                 RELEASE-NOTES-zh_CN.html
README.de                 RELEASE-NOTES          RELEASE-NOTES-zh_TW.html
README.es                 RELEASE-NOTES-de.html  RPM-GPG-KEY
README.fr                 RELEASE-NOTES-es.html  TRANS.TBL
# cd                                                        Change out
# umount /mnt/cdrom                                         Unmount
```

Being able to mount an ISO 9660 image this way is particularly helpful when you are testing scripts that make CD images. You can create an image in a regular file, mount it, and verify that it's arranged correctly. Then, once you're sure it's correct, you can copy the image to a writable CD ("burn" the CD). The loopback facility is useful for mounting floppy disk images, too.

8.1.4 Unmounting Filesystems: umount

The umount command unmounts a filesystem, removing its contents from the system file hierarchy. The usage is as follows:

```
umount file-or-device
```

The filesystem being unmounted must not be *busy*. This means that there aren't any processes with open files on the filesystem and that no process has a directory on the filesystem as its current working directory:

```
$ mount                                              Show what's mounted
/dev/hda2 on / type ext3 (rw)                        / is on a real device
none on /proc type proc (rw)
usbdevfs on /proc/bus/usb type usbdevfs (rw)
/dev/hda5 on /d type ext3 (rw)                       So is /d
none on /dev/pts type devpts (rw,gid=5,mode=620)
none on /dev/shm type tmpfs (rw)
none on /proc/sys/fs/binfmt_misc type binfmt_misc (rw)
$ su                                                 Switch to superuser
Password:                                            Password does not echo
# cd /d                                              Make /d the current directory
# umount /d                                          Try to unmount /d
umount: /d: device is busy                           Doesn't work; it's still in use
# cd /                                               Change out of /d
# umount /d                                          Try to unmount /d again
#                                                    Silence is golden: unmount worked
```

8.2 Files for Filesystem Administration

The `/etc/fstab` file[5] lists filesystems that can be mounted. Most are automatically mounted when the system boots. The format is as follows:

```
device  mount-point  fs-type  options  dump-freq  fsck-pass
```

(The `dump-freq` and `fsck-pass` are administrative features that aren't relevant to the current discussion.) For example, on our system, the file looks like this:

```
$ cat /etc/fstab
# device        mount-point    type      options                         freq passno
/dev/hda3       /              ext3      defaults                        1 1      Root filesystem
/dev/hda5       /d             ext3      defaults                        1 2
none            /dev/pts       devpts    gid=5,mode=620                  0 0
none            /proc          proc      defaults                        0 0
none            /dev/shm       tmpfs     defaults                        0 0
# Windows partition:
/dev/hda1       /win           vfat      noauto,defaults,user,uid=2076,gid=10  0 0
/dev/hda3       swap           swap      defaults                        0 0
/dev/cdrom      /mnt/cdrom     iso9660   noauto,owner,ro                 0 0      World mountable
/dev/fd0        /mnt/floppy    auto      noauto,owner                    0 0      Floppy, same
```

Comments beginning with # are allowed. Discussion of the various options is provided shortly, in Section 8.2.1, "Using Mount Options," page 239.

This same file format is used for `/etc/mtab`, which is where mount writes information about filesystems as they are mounted; umount removes information from that file when a filesystem is unmounted:

```
$ cat /etc/mtab
/dev/hda2 / ext3 rw 0 0
none /proc proc rw 0 0
usbdevfs /proc/bus/usb usbdevfs rw 0 0
/dev/hda5 /d ext3 rw 0 0
none /dev/pts devpts rw,gid=5,mode=620 0 0
none /dev/shm tmpfs rw 0 0
none /proc/sys/fs/binfmt_misc binfmt_misc rw 0 0
/dev/hda1 /win vfat rw,noexec,nosuid,nodev,uid=2076,gid=10,user=arnold 0 0
```

The kernel makes (almost) the same information available in `/proc/mounts`, in the same format:

```
$ cat /proc/mounts
rootfs / rootfs rw 0 0
/dev/root / ext3 rw 0 0
/proc /proc proc rw 0 0
```

---

[5] On GNU/Linux and most systems. Solaris and some systems based on System V Release 4 use `/etc/vfstab`, possibly with a different format.

```
usbdevfs /proc/bus/usb usbdevfs rw 0 0
/dev/hda5 /d ext3 rw 0 0
none /dev/pts devpts rw 0 0
none /dev/shm tmpfs rw 0 0
none /proc/sys/fs/binfmt_misc binfmt_misc rw 0 0
/dev/hda1 /win vfat rw,nosuid,nodev,noexec 0 0
```

Note that `/etc/mtab` has some information that `/proc/mounts` doesn't. (For example, see the line for the `/win` mount point.) On the flip side, it's possible (using 'mount `-f`') to put entries into `/etc/mtab` that aren't real (this practice has its uses, see *mount*(8)). To sum up, `/proc/mounts` always describes what is really mounted; however, `/etc/mtab` contains information about mount options that `/proc/mounts` doesn't. Thus, to get the full picture, you may have to read *both* files.

8.2.1 Using Mount Options

The `mount` command supports options that control what operations the kernel will or will not allow for the filesystem. There are a fair number of these. Only two are really useful on the command line:

ro

> Mount the filesystem read-only. This is necessary for read-only media such as CD-ROMs and DVDs.

loop

> Use the loopback device for treating a regular file as a filesystem. We showed an example of this earlier (see Section 8.1.3, "Mounting Filesystems: `mount`," page 236).

Options are passed with the `-o` command-line option and can be grouped, separated by commas. For example, here is the command line used earlier:

```
mount -t iso9660 -o ro,loop shrike-i386-disc1.iso /mnt/cdrom
```

The rest of the options are intended for use in `/etc/fstab` (although they can also be used on the command line). The following list provides the ones we think are most important for day-to-day use.

auto, noauto

> Filesystems marked `auto` are to be mounted when the system boots through 'mount `-a`' (mount all filesystems). `noauto` filesystems must be mounted manually.

Such filesystems still appear in /etc/fstab along with the other filesystems. (See, for example, the entry for /win in our /etc/fstab file, shown previously.)

defaults
    Use the default options rw, suid, dev, exec, auto, nouser, and async. (async is an advanced option that increases I/O throughput.)

dev, nodev
    Allow (don't allow) the use of character or block device files on the filesystem.

exec, noexec
    Allow (don't allow) execution of binary executables on the filesystem.

user, nouser
    Allow (don't allow) any user to mount this filesystem. This is useful for CD-ROMs; even if you're on a single-user workstation, it's convenient to not have to switch to root just to mount a CD. Only the user who mounted the filesystem can un-mount it. user implies the noexec, nosuid, and nodev options.

suid, nosuid
    Support (don't support) the setuid and setgid bits on executables on the filesystem.

rw
    Mount the filesystem read-write.

The nodev, noexec, and nosuid options are particularly valuable for security on floppy-disk and CD-ROM filesystems. Consider a student environment in which students are allowed to mount their own floppies or CDs. It's trivial to craft a filesystem with a setuid-root shell or a world-writable device file for the hard disk that could let an enterprising user change permissions on system files.

Each filesystem has additional options specific to it. One important option for ext2 and ext3 is the grpid option. We defer discussion of this option until Section 11.5.1, "Default Group for New Files and Directories," page 412. The details for all supported filesystems can be found in the *mount*(8) manpage.

As a concrete example, reconsider the line for the Windows partition on our system:

```
# device    mount-point  type   options                            freq passno
/dev/hda1   /win         vfat   noauto,defaults,user,uid=2076,gid=10  0 0
```

The noauto option prevents the Windows partition from being mounted at boot time. The defaults option is the same as rw, suid, dev, exec, async. The user option allows us to mount the filesystem without being `root`. The `uid=` and `gid=` options force the files in `/win` to belong to us as a regular user so that we don't need to be `root` when working on that partition.

8.2.2 Working with Mounted Filesystems: `getmntent()`

Any of `/etc/fstab`, `/etc/mtab`, and `/proc/mounts` can be read programmatically with the `getmntent()` suite of routines:

```
#include <stdio.h>                                              GLIBC
#include <mntent.h>

FILE *setmntent(const char *filename, const char *type);
struct mntent *getmntent(FILE *filep);
int addmntent(FILE *filep, const struct mntent *mnt);
int endmntent(FILE *filep);
char *hasmntopt(const struct mntent *mnt, const char *opt);
```

`setmntent()` opens the file containing mount point entries. The `filename` argument is the file to open. The `type` argument is like the second argument to `fopen()`, indicating read, write, or read/write access. (Consider the `mount` command, which has to add an entry to `/etc/mtab` for each filesystem it mounts, and `umount`, which has to remove one.) The returned value of type `FILE *` is then used with the rest of the routines.

`getmntent()` reads through the file, returning a pointer to a `static struct mntent`, which is filled in with the appropriate values. This `static` storage is overwritten on each call. It returns `NULL` when there are no more entries. (This is similar to the routines for reading the password and group files; see Section 6.3, "User and Group Names," page 195.)

`addmntent()` is called to add more information to the end of the open file; it's intended for use by `mount`.

`endmntent()` closes the open file; call it when you're done processing. *Don't* just call `fclose()`; other internal data structures associated with the `FILE *` variable may need to be cleaned up.

`hasmntopt()` is a more specialized function. It scans the `struct mntent` passed as the first parameter for a mount option matching the second argument. If the option is found, it returns the address of the matching substring. Otherwise, it returns `NULL`.

The fields in the `struct mntent` correspond directly to the fields in the `/etc/fstab` file. It looks like this:

```
struct mntent {
    char *mnt_fsname;     /* Device or server for filesystem. */
    char *mnt_dir;        /* Directory mounted on. */
    char *mnt_type;       /* Type of filesystem: ufs, nfs, etc. */
    char *mnt_opts;       /* Comma-separated options for fs. */
    int mnt_freq;         /* Dump frequency (in days). */
    int mnt_passno;       /* Pass number for `fsck'. */
};
```

The normal paradigm for working with mounted filesystems is to write an outer loop that reads `/etc/mtab`, processing one `struct mntent` at a time. Our first example, `ch08-mounted.c`, does exactly that:

```
1   /* ch08-mounted.c --- print a list of mounted filesystems */
2
3   /* NOTE: GNU/Linux specific! */
4
5   #include <stdio.h>
6   #include <errno.h>
7   #include <mntent.h> /* for getmntent(), et al. */
8   #include <unistd.h> /* for getopt() */
9
10  void process(const char *filename);
11  void print_mount(const struct mntent *fs);
12
13  char *myname;
14
15  /* main --- process options */
16
17  int main(int argc, char **argv)
18  {
19      int c;
20      char *file = "/etc/mtab";    /* default file to read */
21
22      myname = argv[0];
23      while ((c = getopt(argc, argv, "f:")) != -1) {
24          switch (c) {
25          case 'f':
26              file = optarg;
27              break;
28          default:
29              fprintf(stderr, "usage: %s [-f fstab-file]\n", argv[0]);
30              exit(1);
31          }
32      }
33
34      process(file);
35      return 0;
36  }
```

```
37
38  /* process --- read struct mntent structures from file */
39
40  void process(const char *filename)
41  {
42      FILE *fp;
43      struct mntent *fs;
44
45      fp = setmntent(filename, "r");   /* read only */
46      if (fp == NULL) {
47          fprintf(stderr, "%s: %s: could not open: %s\n",
48              myname, filename, strerror(errno));
49          exit(1);
50      }
51
52      while ((fs = getmntent(fp)) != NULL)
53          print_mount(fs);
54
55      endmntent(fp);
56  }
57
58  /* print_mount --- print a single mount entry */
59
60  void print_mount(const struct mntent *fs)
61  {
62      printf("%s %s %s %s %d %d\n",
63          fs->mnt_fsname,
64          fs->mnt_dir,
65          fs->mnt_type,
66          fs->mnt_opts,
67          fs->mnt_freq,
68          fs->mnt_passno);
69  }
```

Unlike most of the programs that we've seen up to now, this one is Linux specific. Many Unix systems have similar routines, but they're not guaranteed to be identical.

By default, ch08-mounted reads /etc/mtab, printing the information about each mounted filesystem. The -f option allows you to specify a different file to read, such as /proc/mounts or even /etc/fstab.

The main() function processes the command line (lines 23–32) and calls process() on the named file. (This program follows our standard boilerplate.)

process(), in turn, opens the file (line 45), and loops over each returned filesystem (lines 52–53). When done, it closes the file (line 55).

The `print_mount()` function prints the information in the `struct mntent`. The output ends up being much the same as that of 'cat /etc/mtab':

```
$ ch08-mounted                              Run the program
/dev/hda2 / ext3 rw 0 0
none /proc proc rw 0 0
usbdevfs /proc/bus/usb usbdevfs rw 0 0
/dev/hda5 /d ext3 rw 0 0
none /dev/pts devpts rw,gid=5,mode=620 0 0
none /dev/shm tmpfs rw 0 0
none /proc/sys/fs/binfmt_misc binfmt_misc rw 0 0
/dev/hda1 /win vfat rw,noexec,nosuid,nodev,uid=2076,gid=10,user=arnold 0 0
```

8.3 Retrieving Per-Filesystem Information

Printing per-filesystem information is all fine and good, but it's not exciting. Once we know that a particular mount point represents a filesystem, we want information *about* the filesystem. This allows us to do things like print the information retrieved by `df` and 'df -i':

```
$ df                                                  Show free/used space
Filesystem          1K-blocks      Used Available Use% Mounted on
/dev/hda2            6198436    4940316    943248  84% /
/dev/hda5           61431520   27618536  30692360  48% /d
none                  256616          0    256616   0% /dev/shm
/dev/hda1            8369532    2784700   5584832  34% /win

$ df -i                                               Show free/used inodes
Filesystem           Inodes    IUsed    IFree IUse% Mounted on
/dev/hda2            788704   233216   555488   30% /
/dev/hda5           7815168   503243  7311925    7% /d
none                  64154        1    64153    1% /dev/shm
/dev/hda1                 0        0        0    -  /win
```

8.3.1 POSIX Style: `statvfs()` and `fstatvfs()`

Early Unix systems had only one kind of filesystem. For them, it was sufficient if `df` read the superblock of each mounted filesystem, extracted the relevant statistics, and formatted them nicely for printing. (The superblock was typically the second block in the filesystem; the first was the *boot block*, to hold bootstrapping code.)

However, in the modern world, such an approach would be untenable. POSIX provides an XSI extension to access this information. The main function is called statvfs(). (The "vfs" part comes from the underlying SunOS technology, later used in System V Release 4, called a *virtual filesystem*.) There are two functions:

```
#include <sys/types.h>                                    XSI
#include <sys/statvfs.h>

int statvfs(const char *path, struct statvfs *buf);
int fstatvfs(int fd, struct statvfs *buf);
```

statvfs() uses a pathname for any file; it returns information about the filesystem containing the file. fstatvfs() accepts an open file descriptor as its first argument; here too, the information returned is about the filesystem containing the open file. The struct statvfs contains the following members:

```
struct statvfs {
    unsigned long int f_bsize;          Block size
    unsigned long int f_frsize;         Fragment size ("fundamental block size")
    fsblkcnt_t f_blocks;                Total number of blocks
    fsblkcnt_t f_bfree;                 Total number of free blocks
    fsblkcnt_t f_bavail;                Number of available blocks (≤ f_bfree)
    fsfilcnt_t f_files;                 Total number of inodes
    fsfilcnt_t f_ffree;                 Total number of free inodes
    fsfilcnt_t f_favail;                Number of available inodes (≤ f_files)
    unsigned long int f_fsid;           Filesystem ID
    unsigned long int f_flag;           Flags: ST_RDONLY and/or ST_NOSUID
    unsigned long int f_namemax;        Maximum filename length
};
```

The information it contains is enough to write df:

unsigned long int f_bsize

> The block size is the preferred size for doing I/O. The filesystem attempts to keep at least f_bsize bytes worth of data in contiguous sectors on disk. (A *sector* is the smallest amount of addressable data on the disk. Typically, a disk sector is 512 bytes.)

unsigned long int f_frsize

> Some filesystems (such as the BSD Fast Filesystem) distinguish between blocks and *fragments* of blocks. Small files whose total size is smaller than a block reside in some number of fragments. This avoids wasting disk space (at the admitted cost of more complexity in the kernel code). The fragment size is chosen at the time the filesystem is created.

fsblkcnt_t f_blocks

> The total number of blocks (in units of f_bsize) in the filesystem.

`fsblkcnt_t f_bfree`
>   The total number of free blocks in the filesystem.

`fsblkcnt_t f_bavail`
>   The number of blocks that may actually be used. Some filesystems reserve a percentage of the filesystem's blocks for use by the superuser, in case the filesystem fills up. Modern systems reserve around 5 percent, although this number can be changed by an administrator. (See *tune2fs*(8) on a GNU/Linux system, and *tunefs*(8) on Unix systems.)

`fsfilcnt_t f_files`
>   The total number of inodes ("file serial numbers," in POSIX parlance) on the filesystem. This number is usually initialized and made permanent when the filesystem is created.

`fsfilcnt_t f_ffree`
>   The total number of free inodes.

`fsfilcnt_t f_favail`
>   The number of inodes that may actually be used. Some percentage of the inodes are reserved for the superuser, just as for blocks.

`unsigned long int f_fsid`
>   The filesystem ID. POSIX doesn't specify what this represents, and it's not used under Linux.

`unsigned long int f_flag`
>   Flags giving information about the filesystem. POSIX specifies two: `ST_RDONLY`, for a read-only filesystem (such as a CD-ROM), and `ST_NOSUID`, which disallows the use of the setuid and setgid permission bits on executables. GNU/Linux systems provide additional flags: They are listed in Table 8.2.

`unsigned long int f_namemax`
>   The maximum length of a filename. This refers to each individual component in a pathname; in other words, the maximum length for a directory entry.

TABLE 8.2
GLIBC values for `f_flag`

Flag	POSIX	Meaning
ST_MANDLOCK		Enforce mandatory locking (see Section 14.2, page 531).
ST_NOATIME		Don't update the access time field on each access.
ST_NODEV		Disallow access through device files.
ST_NODIRATIME		Don't update the access time field of directories.
ST_NOEXEC		Disallow execution of binaries.
ST_NOSUID	✓	Filesystem disallows the use of setuid and setgid bits.
ST_RDONLY	✓	Filesystem is read-only.
ST_SYNCHRONOUS		All writes are synchronous (see Section 4.6.3, page 110).

The `fsblkcnt_t` and `fsfilcnt_t` types are defined in `<sys/types.h>`. They are typically `unsigned long`, but on modern systems, they may be even be a 64-bit type, since disks have gotten very large. The following program, `ch08-statvfs.c`, shows how to use `statvfs()`:

```
1    /* ch08-statvfs.c --- demonstrate statvfs */
2
3    /* NOTE: GNU/Linux specific! */
4
5    #include <stdio.h>
6    #include <errno.h>
7    #include <mntent.h> /* for getmntent(), et al. */
8    #include <unistd.h> /* for getopt() */
9    #include <sys/types.h>
10   #include <sys/statvfs.h>
11
12   void process(const char *filename);
13   void do_statvfs(const struct mntent *fs);
14
15   int errors = 0;
16   char *myname;
17
18   /* main --- process options */
19
```

```
20  int main(int argc, char **argv)
21  {
22      int c;
23      char *file = "/etc/mtab";    /* default file to read */
24
25      myname = argv[0];
26      while ((c = getopt(argc, argv, "f:")) != -1) {
27          switch (c) {
28          case 'f':
29              file = optarg;
30              break;
31          default:
32              fprintf(stderr, "usage: %s [-f fstab-file]\n", argv[0]);
33              exit(1);
34          }
35      }
36
37      process(file);
38      return (errors != 0);
39  }
40
41  /* process --- read struct mntent structures from file */
42
43  void process(const char *filename)
44  {
45      FILE *fp;
46      struct mntent *fs;
47
48      fp = setmntent(filename, "r");   /* read only */
49      if (fp == NULL) {
50          fprintf(stderr, "%s: %s: could not open: %s\n",
51              myname, filename, strerror(errno));
52          exit(1);
53      }
54
55      while ((fs = getmntent(fp)) != NULL)
56          do_statvfs(fs);
57
58      endmntent(fp);
59  }
```

Lines 1–59 are essentially the same as ch08-mounted.c. main() handles the command line, and process() loops over each mounted filesystem. do_statvfs() does the real work, printing the struct statvfs for each interesting filesystem.

```
61  /* do_statvfs --- Use statvfs and print info */
62
63  void do_statvfs(const struct mntent *fs)
64  {
65      struct statvfs vfs;
66
67      if (fs->mnt_fsname[0] != '/')    /* skip nonreal filesystems */
68          return;
69
70      if (statvfs(fs->mnt_dir, & vfs) != 0) {
71          fprintf(stderr, "%s: %s: statvfs failed: %s\n",
72              myname, fs->mnt_dir, strerror(errno));
73          errors++;
74          return;
75      }
76
77      printf("%s, mounted on %s:\n", fs->mnt_dir, fs->mnt_fsname);
78      printf("\tf_bsize: %ld\n",   (long) vfs.f_bsize);
79      printf("\tf_frsize: %ld\n",  (long) vfs.f_frsize);
80      printf("\tf_blocks: %lu\n",  (unsigned long) vfs.f_blocks);
81      printf("\tf_bfree: %lu\n",   (unsigned long) vfs.f_bfree);
82      printf("\tf_bavail: %lu\n",  (unsigned long) vfs.f_bavail);
83      printf("\tf_files: %lu\n",   (unsigned long) vfs.f_files);
84      printf("\tf_ffree: %lu\n",   (unsigned long) vfs.f_ffree);
85      printf("\tf_favail: %lu\n",  (unsigned long) vfs.f_favail);
86      printf("\tf_fsid: %#lx\n",   (unsigned long) vfs.f_fsid);
87
88      printf("\tf_flag: ");
89      if (vfs.f_flag == 0)
90          printf("(none)\n");
91      else {
92          if ((vfs.f_flag & ST_RDONLY) != 0)
93              printf("ST_RDONLY ");
94          if ((vfs.f_flag & ST_NOSUID) != 0)
95              printf("ST_NOSUID");
96          printf("\n");
97      }
98
99      printf("\tf_namemax: %#ld\n", (long) vfs.f_namemax);
100 }
```

Lines 67–68 skip filesystems that are not based on a real disk device. This means that filesystems like /proc or /dev/pts are ignored. (Admittedly, this check is a heuristic, but it works: In /etc/mtab mounted devices are listed by the full device pathname: for example, /dev/hda1.) Line 70 calls statvfs() with appropriate error checking, and lines 77–99 print the information.

Lines 89–96 deal with *flags*: single bits of information that are or are not present. See the sidebar for a discussion of how flag bits are used in C code. Here is the output of ch08-statvfs:

```
$ ch08-statvfs                              Run the program
/, mounted on /dev/hda2:                    Results for ext2 filesystem
    f_bsize: 4096
    f_frsize: 4096
    f_blocks: 1549609
    f_bfree: 316663
    f_bavail: 237945
    f_files: 788704
    f_ffree: 555482
    f_favail: 555482
    f_fsid: 0
    f_flag: (none)
    f_namemax: 255
...
/win, mounted on /dev/hda1:                 Results for vfat filesystem
    f_bsize: 4096
    f_frsize: 4096
    f_blocks: 2092383
    f_bfree: 1391952
    f_bavail: 1391952
    f_files: 0
    f_ffree: 0
    f_favail: 0
    f_fsid: 0
    f_flag: ST_NOSUID
    f_namemax: 260
```

As of this writing, for GLIBC 2.3.2 and earlier, GNU df doesn't use statvfs(). This is because the code reads /etc/mtab, and calls stat() for each mounted filesystem, to find the one on which the device number matches that of the file (or file descriptor) argument. It needs to find the filesystem in order to read the mount options so that it can set the f_flag bits. The problem is that stat() on a remotely mounted filesystem whose server is not available can hang indefinitely, thus causing df to hang as well. This problem has since been fixed in GLIBC, but df won't change for a while so that it can continue to work on older systems.

> NOTE Although POSIX specifies statvfs() and fstatvfs(), not all systems support them or support them correctly. Many systems (including Linux, as described shortly), have their own system calls that provide similar information. GNU df uses a library routine to acquire filesystem information; the source file for that routine is full of #ifdefs for a plethora of different systems. With time, the portability situation should improve.

Bit Flags

A common technique, applicable in many cases, is to have a set of *flag* values; when a flag is *set* (that is, true), a certain fact is true or a certain condition applies. Flag values are defined with either `#defined` symbolic constants or `enums`. In this chapter, the `nftw()` API (described later) also uses flags. There are only two flags for the `struct statvfs` field `f_flag`:

```
#define ST_RDONLY    1    /* read-only filesystem */         Sample definitions
#define ST_NOSUID    2    /* setuid/setgid not allowed */
```

Physically, each symbolic constant represents a different bit position within the `f_flag` value. Logically, each value represents a separate bit of state information; that is, some fact or condition that is or isn't true for this particular instance of a `struct statvfs`.

Flags are set, tested, and cleared with the C bitwise operators. For example, `statvfs()` would set these flags, using the bitwise OR operator:

```
int statvfs(const char *path, struct statvfs *vfs)
{
    ... fill in most of *vfs ...
    vfs->f_flag = 0;                          Make sure it starts out as zero
    if (filesystem is read-only)
        vfs->f_flag |= ST_RDONLY;             Add the ST_RDONLY flag
    if (filesystem disallows setuid)
        vfs->f_flag |= ST_NOSUID;             Add the ST_NOSUID flag
    ... rest of routine ...
}
```

The bitwise AND operator tests whether a flag is set, and a combination of the bitwise AND and COMPLEMENT operators clears a flag:

```
if ((vfs.f_flag & ST_RDONLY) != 0)           True if ST_RDONLY flag is set
```

```
vfs.f_flag &= ~(ST_RDONLY|ST_NOSUID);        Clear both flags
```

The bitwise operators are daunting if you've not used them before. However, the example code just shown represents common C idioms. Study each operation carefully; perhaps draw yourself a few pictures showing how these operators work. Once you understand them, you can train yourself to recognize these operators as *high-level operations for managing flag values* instead of treating them as *low-level bit manipulations*.

The reason to use flag values is that they provide considerable savings in data space. The single `unsigned long` field lets you store at least 32 separate bits of information. GLIBC (as of this writing) defines 11 different flags for the `f_flag` field.[*] If you used a separate `char` field for each flag, that would use 11 bytes instead of just the four used by the `unsigned long`. If you had 32 flags, that would be 32 bytes instead of just four!

---

[*] See `/usr/include/bits/statvfs.h` on a GNU/Linux system.

8.3.2 Linux Style: `statfs()` and `fstatfs()`

The `statfs()` and `fstatfs()` system calls are Linux specific. Their declarations are as follows:

```
#include <sys/types.h>                                    GLIBC
#include <sys/vfs.h>

int statfs(const char *path, struct statfs *buf);
int fstatfs(int fd, struct statfs *buf);
```

As with `statvfs()` and `fstatvfs()`, the two versions work on a filename or an open file descriptor, respectively. The `struct statfs` looks like this:

```
struct statfs {
    long    f_type;      /* type of filesystem */
    long    f_bsize;     /* optimal transfer block size */
    long    f_blocks;    /* total data blocks in filesystem */
    long    f_bfree;     /* free blocks in fs */
    long    f_bavail;    /* free blocks avail to nonsuperuser */
    long    f_files;     /* total file nodes in file system */
    long    f_ffree;     /* free file nodes in fs */
    fsid_t  f_fsid;      /* filesystem id */
    long    f_namelen;   /* maximum length of filenames */
    long    f_spare[6];  /* spare for later */
};
```

The fields are analogous to those in the `struct statvfs`. At least through GLIBC 2.3.2, the POSIX `statvfs()` and `fstatvfs()` functions are wrappers around `statfs()` and `fstatfs()`, respectively, copying the values from one kind of `struct` to the other.

The advantage to using `statfs()` or `fstatfs()` is that they are system calls. The kernel returns the information directly. Since there is no `f_flag` field with mount options, it's not necessary to look at every mounted filesystem to find the right one. (In other words, in order to fill in the mount options, `statvfs()` must examine each mounted filesystem to find the one containing the file named by `path` or `fd`. `statfs()` doesn't need to do that, since it doesn't provide information about the mount options.)

There are two disadvantages to using these calls. First, they are Linux specific. Second, some of the information in the `struct statvfs` isn't in the `struct statfs`; most noticeably, the mount flags (`f_flag`) and the number of available inodes (`f_favail`). (Thus, the Linux `statvfs()` has to find mount options from other sources, such as `/etc/mtab`, and it "fakes" the information for the `struct statvfs` fields for which real information isn't available.)

One field in the `struct statfs` deserves special note. This is the `f_type` field, which indicates the type of the filesystem. The value is the filesystem's magic number, extracted from the superblock. The *statfs*(2) manpage provides a list of commonly used filesystems and their magic numbers, which we use in `ch08-statfs.c`. (Alas, there is no separate `#include` file.)

```
1   /* ch08-statfs.c --- demonstrate Linux statfs */
2
3   /* NOTE: GNU/Linux specific! */
4
5   #include <stdio.h>
6   #include <errno.h>
7   #include <mntent.h> /* for getmntent(), et al. */
8   #include <unistd.h> /* for getopt() */
9   #include <sys/types.h>
10  #include <sys/vfs.h>
11
12  /* Defines taken from statfs(2) man page: */
13  #define AFFS_SUPER_MAGIC     0xADFF
14  #define EFS_SUPER_MAGIC      0x00414A53
15  #define EXT_SUPER_MAGIC      0x137D
16  #define EXT2_OLD_SUPER_MAGIC 0xEF51
17  #define EXT2_SUPER_MAGIC     0xEF53
18  #define HPFS_SUPER_MAGIC     0xF995E849
19  #define ISOFS_SUPER_MAGIC    0x9660
20  #define MINIX_SUPER_MAGIC    0x137F /* orig. minix */
21  #define MINIX_SUPER_MAGIC2   0x138F /* 30-char minix */
22  #define MINIX2_SUPER_MAGIC   0x2468 /* minix V2 */
23  #define MINIX2_SUPER_MAGIC2  0x2478 /* minix V2, 30 char names */
24  #define MSDOS_SUPER_MAGIC    0x4d44
25  #define NCP_SUPER_MAGIC      0x564c
26  #define NFS_SUPER_MAGIC      0x6969
27  #define PROC_SUPER_MAGIC     0x9fa0
28  #define SMB_SUPER_MAGIC      0x517B
29  #define XENIX_SUPER_MAGIC    0x012FF7B4
30  #define SYSV4_SUPER_MAGIC    0x012FF7B5
31  #define SYSV2_SUPER_MAGIC    0x012FF7B6
32  #define COH_SUPER_MAGIC      0x012FF7B7
33  #define UFS_MAGIC            0x00011954
34  #define XFS_SUPER_MAGIC      0x58465342
35  #define _XIAFS_SUPER_MAGIC   0x012FD16D
36
37  void process(const char *filename);
38  void do_statfs(const struct mntent *fs);
39
```

```
40   int errors = 0;
41   char *myname;
42
```
... main() is unchanged, process() is almost identical ...
```
85
86   /* type2str --- convert fs type to printable string, from statfs(2) */
87
88   const char *type2str(long type)
89   {
90       static struct fsname {
91           long type;
92           const char *name;
93       } table[] = {
94           { AFFS_SUPER_MAGIC, "AFFS" },
95           { COH_SUPER_MAGIC, "COH" },
96           { EXT2_OLD_SUPER_MAGIC, "OLD EXT2" },
97           { EXT2_SUPER_MAGIC, "EXT2" },
98           { HPFS_SUPER_MAGIC, "HPFS" },
99           { ISOFS_SUPER_MAGIC, "ISOFS" },
100          { MINIX2_SUPER_MAGIC, "MINIX V2" },
101          { MINIX2_SUPER_MAGIC2, "MINIX V2 30 char" },
102          { MINIX_SUPER_MAGIC, "MINIX" },
103          { MINIX_SUPER_MAGIC2, "MINIX 30 char" },
104          { MSDOS_SUPER_MAGIC, "MSDOS" },
105          { NCP_SUPER_MAGIC, "NCP" },
106          { NFS_SUPER_MAGIC, "NFS" },
107          { PROC_SUPER_MAGIC, "PROC" },
108          { SMB_SUPER_MAGIC, "SMB" },
109          { SYSV2_SUPER_MAGIC, "SYSV2" },
110          { SYSV4_SUPER_MAGIC, "SYSV4" },
111          { UFS_MAGIC, "UFS" },
112          { XENIX_SUPER_MAGIC, "XENIX" },
113          { _XIAFS_SUPER_MAGIC, "XIAFS" },
114          { 0, NULL },
115      };
116      static char unknown[100];
117      int i;
118
119      for (i = 0; table[i].type != 0; i++)
120          if (table[i].type == type)
121              return table[i].name;
122
123      sprintf(unknown, "unknown type: %#x", type);
124      return unknown;
125  }
126
127  /* do_statfs --- Use statfs and print info */
128
```

```
129  void do_statfs(const struct mntent *fs)
130  {
131      struct statfs vfs;
132
133      if (fs->mnt_fsname[0] != '/')   /* skip nonreal filesystems */
134          return;
135
136      if (statfs(fs->mnt_dir, & vfs) != 0) {
137          fprintf(stderr, "%s: %s: statfs failed: %s\n",
138              myname, fs->mnt_dir, strerror(errno));
139          errors++;
140          return;
141      }
142
143      printf("%s, mounted on %s:\n", fs->mnt_dir, fs->mnt_fsname);
144
145      printf("\tf_type: %s\n", type2str(vfs.f_type));
146      printf("\tf_bsize: %ld\n", vfs.f_bsize);
147      printf("\tf_blocks: %ld\n", vfs.f_blocks);
148      printf("\tf_bfree: %ld\n", vfs.f_bfree);
149      printf("\tf_bavail: %ld\n", vfs.f_bavail);
150      printf("\tf_files: %ld\n", vfs.f_files);
151      printf("\tf_ffree: %ld\n", vfs.f_ffree);
152      printf("\tf_namelen: %ld\n", vfs.f_namelen);
153  }
```

To save space, we've omitted `main()`, which is unchanged from the other programs presented earlier, and we've also omitted `process()`, which now calls `do_statfs()` instead of `do_statvfs()`.

Lines 13–35 contain the list of filesystem magic numbers from the *statfs*(2) manpage. Although the numbers could be retrieved from kernel source code header files, such retrieval is painful (we tried), and the presentation here is easier to follow. Lines 86–125 define `type2str()`, which converts the magic number to a printable string. It does a simple linear search on a table of (value, string) pairs. In the (unlikely) event that the magic number isn't in the table, `types2str()` creates an "unknown type" message and returns that (lines 123–124).

`do_statfs()` (lines 129–153) prints the information from the `struct statfs`. The `f_fsid` member is omitted since `fsid_t` is an opaque type. The code is straightforward; line 145 uses `type2str()` to print the filesystem type. As for the similar program using `statvfs()`, this function ignores filesystems that aren't on local devices (lines 133–134). Here is the output on our system:

```
$ ch08-statfs                          Run the program
/, mounted on /dev/hda2:                Results for ext2 filesystem
    f_type: EXT2
    f_bsize: 4096
    f_blocks: 1549609
    f_bfree: 316664
    f_bavail: 237946
    f_files: 788704
    f_ffree: 555483
    f_namelen: 255
...
/win, mounted on /dev/hda1:             Results for vfat filesystem
    f_type: MSDOS
    f_bsize: 4096
    f_blocks: 2092383
    f_bfree: 1391952
    f_bavail: 1391952
    f_files: 0
    f_ffree: 0
    f_namelen: 260
```

In conclusion, whether to use `statvfs()` or `statfs()` in your own code depends on your requirements. As described in the previous section, GNU `df` doesn't use `statvfs()` under GNU/Linux and in general tends to use each Unix system's unique "get filesystem info" system call. Although this works, it isn't pretty. On the other hand, sometimes you have no choice: for example, the GLIBC problems we mentioned above. In this case, there is no perfect solution.

8.4 Moving Around in the File Hierarchy

Several system calls and standard library functions let you change your current directory and determine the full pathname of the current directory. More complicated functions let you perform arbitrary actions for every filesystem object in a directory hierarchy.

8.4.1 Changing Directory: `chdir()` and `fchdir()`

In Section 1.2, "The Linux/Unix Process Model," page 10, we said:

> The current working directory is the one to which relative pathnames (those that don't start with a /) are relative. This is the directory you are "in" whenever you issue a '`cd` *someplace*' command to the shell.

Each process has a current working directory. Each new process inherits its current directory from the process that started it (its parent). Two functions let you change to another directory:

```
#include <unistd.h>

int chdir(const char *path);                                    POSIX
int fchdir(int fd);                                             XSI
```

The chdir() function takes a string naming a directory, whereas fchdir() expects a file descriptor that was opened on a directory with open().[6] Both return 0 on success and -1 on error (with errno set appropriately). Typically, if open() on a directory succeeded, then fchdir() will also succeed, unless someone changed the permissions on the directory between the calls. (fchdir() is a relatively new function; older Unix systems won't have it.)

These functions are almost trivial to use. The following program, ch08-chdir.c, demonstrates both functions. It also demonstrates that fchdir() can fail if the permissions on the open directory don't include search (execute) permission:

```
 1  /* ch08-chdir.c --- demonstrate chdir() and fchdir().
 2                        Error checking omitted for brevity */
 3
 4  #include <stdio.h>
 5  #include <fcntl.h>
 6  #include <unistd.h>
 7  #include <sys/types.h>
 8  #include <sys/stat.h>
 9
10  int main(void)
11  {
12      int fd;
13      struct stat sbuf;
14
15      fd = open(".", O_RDONLY);    /* open directory for reading */
16      fstat(fd, & sbuf);           /* obtain info, need original permissions */
17      chdir("..");                 /* `cd ..' */
18      fchmod(fd, 0);               /* zap permissions on original directory */
19
20      if (fchdir(fd) < 0)          /* try to `cd' back, should fail */
21          perror("fchdir back");
22
```

---

[6] On GNU/Linux and BSD systems, you can apply the dirfd() function to a DIR * pointer to obtain the underlying file descriptor; see the GNU/Linux *dirfd*(3) manpage.

```
23      fchmod(fd, sbuf.st_mode & 07777);   /* restore original permissions */
24      close(fd);                       /* all done */
25
26      return 0;
27  }
```

Line 15 opens the current directory. Line 16 calls `fstat()` on the open directory so that we have a copy of its permissions. Line 17 uses `chdir()` to move up a level in the file hierarchy. Line 18 does the dirty work, turning off *all* permissions on the original directory.

Lines 20–21 attempt to change back to the original directory. It is expected to fail, since the current permissions don't allow it. Line 23 restores the original permissions. The '`sbuf.st_mode & 07777`' retrieves the low-order 12 permission bits; these are the regular 9 `rwxrwxrwx` bits, and the setuid, setgid, and "sticky" bits, which we discuss in Chapter 11, "Permissions and User and Group ID Numbers," page 403. Finally, line 24 cleans up by closing the open file descriptor. Here's what happens when the program runs:

```
$ ls -ld .                                              Show current permissions
drwxr-xr-x    2 arnold    devel        4096 Sep  9 16:42 .
$ ch08-chdir                                            Run the program
fchdir back: Permission denied                          Fails as expected
$ ls -ld .                                              Look at permissions again
drwxr-xr-x    2 arnold    devel        4096 Sep  9 16:42 .    Everything is back as it was
```

8.4.2 Getting the Current Directory: `getcwd()`

The aptly named `getcwd()` function retrieves the absolute pathname of the current working directory:

```
#include <unistd.h>                                          POSIX

char *getcwd(char *buf, size_t size);
```

The function fills in `buf` with the pathname; it expects `buf` to have `size` bytes. Upon success, it returns its first argument. Otherwise, if it needs more than `size` bytes, it returns `NULL` and sets `errno` to `ERANGE`. The intent is that if `ERANGE` happens, you should try to allocate a larger buffer (with `malloc()` or `realloc()`) and try again.

If any of the directory components leading to the current directory are not readable or searchable, then `getcwd()` can fail and `errno` will be `EACCES`. The following simple program demonstrates its use:

```
/* ch08-getcwd.c --- demonstrate getcwd().
                     Error checking omitted for brevity */

#include <stdio.h>
#include <fcntl.h>
#include <unistd.h>
#include <sys/types.h>
#include <sys/stat.h>

int main(void)
{
    char buf[PATH_MAX];
    char *cp;

    cp = getcwd(buf, sizeof(buf));
    printf("Current dir: %s\n", buf);

    printf("Changing to ..\n");
    chdir("..");              /* `cd ..' */

    cp = getcwd(buf, sizeof(buf));
    printf("Current dir is now: %s\n", buf);

    return 0;
}
```

This simple program prints the current directory, changes to the parent directory, and then prints the new current directory. (cp isn't really needed here, but in a real program it would be used for error checking.) When run, it produces the following output:

```
$ ch08-getcwd
Current dir: /home/arnold/work/prenhall/progex/code/ch08
Changing to ..
Current dir is now: /home/arnold/work/prenhall/progex/code
```

Formally, if the buf argument is NULL, the behavior of getcwd() is undefined. In this case, the GLIBC version of getcwd() will call malloc() for you, allocating a buffer of size size. Going even further out of its way to be helpful, if size is 0, then the buffer it allocates will be "big enough" to hold the returned pathname. In either case, you should call free() on the returned pointer when you're done with the buffer.

The GLIBC behavior is helpful, but it's not portable. For code that has to work across platforms, you can write a replacement function that provides the same functionality while having your replacement function call getcwd() directly if on a GLIBC system.

GNU/Linux systems provide the file `/proc/self/cwd`. This file is a symbolic link to the current directory:

```
$ cd /tmp                              Change directory someplace
$ ls -l /proc/self/cwd                 Look at the file
lrwxrwxrwx    1 arnold   devel     0 Sep  9 17:29 /proc/self/cwd -> /tmp
$ cd                                   Change to home directory
$ ls -l /proc/self/cwd                 Look at it again
lrwxrwxrwx    1 arnold   devel     0 Sep  9 17:30 /proc/self/cwd -> /home/arnold
```

This is convenient at the shell level but presents a problem at the programmatic level. In particular, the size of the file is zero! (This is because it's a file in `/proc`, which the kernel fakes; it's not a real file living on disk.)

Why is the zero size a problem? If you remember from Section 5.4.5, "Working with Symbolic Links," page 151, `lstat()` on a symbolic link returns the number of characters in the name of the linked-to file in the `st_size` field of the `struct stat`. This number can then be used to allocate a buffer of the appropriate size for use with `readlink()`. That won't work here, since the size is zero. You have to use (or allocate) a buffer that you guess is big enough. However, since `readlink()` does not fill in any more characters than you provide, *you can't tell* whether or not the buffer is big enough; `readlink()` does not fail when there isn't enough room. (See the Coreutils `xreadlink()` function in Section 5.4.5, "Working with Symbolic Links," page 151, which solves the problem.)

In addition to `getcwd()`, GLIBC has several other nonportable routines. These save you the trouble of managing buffers and provide compatibility with older BSD systems. For the details, see *getcwd*(3).

8.4.3 Walking a Hierarchy: `nftw()`

A common programming task is to process entire directory hierarchies: doing something for every file and every directory and subdirectory in an entire tree. Consider, for example, `du`, which prints disk usage information, '`chown -R`', which recursively changes ownership, or the `find` program, which finds files matching certain criteria.

At this point, you know enough to write your own code to manually open and read directories, call `stat()` (or `lstat()`) for each entry, and recursively process subdirectories. However, such code is challenging to get right; it's possible to run out of file descriptors if you leave parent directories open while processing subdirectories; you have to decide whether to process symbolic links as themselves or as the files they point to; you have to be able to deal with directories that aren't readable or searchable, and so on. It's also painful to have to write the same code over and over again if you need it for multiple applications.

8.4.3.1 The `nftw()` Interface

To obviate the problems, System V introduced the `ftw()` ("file tree walk") function. `ftw()` did all the work to "walk" a file tree (hierarchy). You supplied it with a pointer to a function, and it called the function for every file object it encountered. Your function could then process each filesystem object as it saw fit.

Over time, it became clear that the `ftw()` interface didn't quite do the full job;[7] for example, originally it didn't support symbolic links. For this reason, `nftw()` ("new `ftw()`" [sic]) was added to the X/Open Portability Guide; it's now part of POSIX. Here's the prototype:

```
#include <ftw.h>                              XSI

int nftw(const char *dir,                     Starting point
        int (*fn)(const char *file,           Function pointer to
                const struct stat *sb,        function of four arguments
                int flag, struct FTW *s),
        int depth, int flags);                Max open fds, flags
```

And here are the arguments:

`const char *dir`

A string naming the starting point of the hierarchy to process.

`int (*fn)(const char *file, const struct stat *sb, int flag, struct FTW *s)`

A pointer to a function with the given arguments. This function is called for every object in the hierarchy. Details below.

`int depth`

This argument is misnamed. To avoid running out of file descriptors, `nftw()` keeps no more than `depth` simultaneously open directories. This does *not* prevent

---

[7] POSIX standardizes the `ftw()` interface to support existing code, and GNU/Linux and commercial Unix systems continue to supply it. However, since it's underpowered, we don't otherwise discuss it. See *ftw*(3) if you're interested.

`nftw()` from processing hierarchies that are more than `depth` levels deep; but smaller values for `depth` mean that `nftw()` has to do more work.

`flags`

A set of flags, bitwise OR'd, that direct how `nftw()` should process the hierarchy.

The `nftw()` interface has two *disjoint* sets of flags. One set controls `nftw()` itself (the `flags` argument to `nftw()`). The other set is passed to the user-supplied function that `nftw()` calls (the `flag` argument to `(*fn)()`). However, the interface is confusing, because both sets of flags use names starting with the prefix 'FTW_'. We'll do our best to keep this clear as we go. Table 8.3 presents the flags that control `nftw()`.

TABLE 8.3
Control flags for `nftw()`

Flag	Meaning
FTW_CHDIR	When set, change to each directory before opening it. This action is more efficient, but the calling application has to be prepared to be in a different directory when `nftw()` is done.
FTW_DEPTH	When set, do a "depth-first search." This means that all of the files and subdirectories in a directory are processed before the directory itself is processed.
FTW_MOUNT	When set, stay within the same mounted filesystem. This is a more specialized option.
FTW_PHYS	When set, do not follow symbolic links.

FTW_CHDIR provides greater efficiency; when processing deep file hierarchies, the kernel doesn't have to process full pathnames over and over again when doing a `stat()` or opening a directory. The time savings on large hierarchies can be quite noticeable.[8]

FTW_DEPTH may or may not be what you need; for some applications it's just right. Consider 'chmod -R u-rx .'. This removes read and execute permission for the owner of all files and subdirectories in the current directory. If this permission change is applied to a directory before it's applied to the directory's contents, any subsequent attempt to process the contents will fail! Thus, it should be applied after the contents

---

[8] Some older GLIBC versions have problems with FTW_CHDIR. This is not true for GLIBC 2.3.2 and later, and it's unlikely that you'll encounter problems.

have been processed.[9] The GNU/Linux *nftw*(3) manpage notes for `FTW_PHYS` that "this is what you want." This lets you process symbolic links as themselves, which is usually what's necessary. (Consider `du`; it should count the link's space separately from that of the linked-to file.)

8.4.3.2 The `nftw()` Callback Function

As `nftw()` runs, it calls a function to which you supply a pointer. (Such functions are termed *callback functions* since they are "called back" from library code.) The callback function receives four arguments:

`const char *file`
> The name of the current file (directory, symbolic link, etc.) being processed.

`const struct stat *sb`
> A pointer to a `struct stat` for the file.

`int flag`
> One of several flag values (described below) indicating what kind of file this is or whether an error was encountered for the object.

`struct FTW *s`
> This structure provides two separate pieces of information:

```
struct FTW {
    int base;       /* Index in file of base part of filename */
    int level;      /* Depth of this item relative to starting point */
};
```

The `flag` parameter has one of the values listed in Table 8.4.

The `struct FTW *s` provides additional information that can be useful. `s->base` acts as an index into `file`; `file` is the full pathname of the object being processed (relative to the starting point). '`file + s->base`' points to the first character of the filename component of the file.

---

[9] Why anyone would want to make such a change, we don't know, but the "you asked for it, you got it" philosophy applies here too!

TABLE 8.4
Flag values for `nftw()` callback function

Flag	Meaning
FTW_F	Object is a regular file.
FTW_D	Object is a directory.
FTW_DNR	Object is a directory that wasn't readable.
FTW_SL	Object is a symbolic link.
FTW_NS	Object is not a symbolic link, and `stat()` failed.
FTW_DP	Object is a directory whose children have already been processed. This can only happen if `FTW_DEPTH` was used in the call to `nftw()`.
FTW_SLN	Object is a symbolic link pointing to a nonexistent file. This can only happen if `FTW_PHYS` was *not* used in the call to `nftw()`.

`s->level` indicates the current depth in the hierarchy; the original starting point is considered to be at level `0`.

The callback function should return `0` if all is well. Any nonzero return causes `nftw()` to stop its processing and to return the same nonzero value. The manpage notes that the callback function should stop processing only by using its return value so that `nftw()` has a chance to clean up: that is, free any dynamic storage, close open file descriptors, and so on. The callback function should not use `longjmp()` unless the program will immediately exit. (`longjmp()` is an advanced function, which we describe in Section 12.5, "Nonlocal Gotos," page 446.) The recommended technique for handling errors is to set a global variable indicating that there were problems, return `0` from the callback, and deal with the failures once `nftw()` has completed traversing the file hierarchy. (GNU `du` does this, as we see shortly.)

Let's tie all this together with an example program. `ch08-nftw.c` processes each file or directory named on the command line, running `nftw()` on it. The function that processes each file prints the filename and type with indentation, showing the hierarchical position of each file. For a change, we show the results first, and then we show and discuss the program:

```
$ pwd                                      Where we are
/home/arnold/work/prenhall/progex
$ code/ch08/ch08-nftw code                 Walk the 'code' directory
code (directory)                           Top-level directory
    ch02 (directory)                       Subdirectories one level indented
        ch02-printenv.c (file)             Files in subdirs two levels indented
    ch03 (directory)
        ch03-memaddr.c (file)
    ch04 (directory)
        ch04-holes.c (file)
        ch04-cat.c (file)
        ch04-maxfds.c (file)
        v7cat.c (file)
...
```

Here's the program itself:

```
1   /* ch08-nftw.c --- demonstrate nftw() */
2
3   #define _XOPEN_SOURCE 1                /* Required under GLIBC for nftw() */
4   #define _XOPEN_SOURCE_EXTENDED 1       /* Same */
5
6   #include <stdio.h>
7   #include <errno.h>
8   #include <getopt.h>
9   #include <ftw.h>            /* gets <sys/types.h> and <sys/stat.h> for us */
10  #include <limits.h>        /* for PATH_MAX */
11  #include <unistd.h>        /* for getdtablesize(), getcwd() declarations */
12
13  #define SPARE_FDS 5         /* fds for use by other functions, see text */
14
15  extern int process(const char *file, const struct stat *sb,
16             int flag, struct FTW *s);
17
18  /* usage --- print message and die */
19
20  void usage(const char *name)
21  {
22      fprintf(stderr, "usage: %s [-c] directory ...\n", name);
23      exit(1);
24  }
25
26  /* main --- call nftw() on each command-line argument */
27
28  int main(int argc, char **argv)
29  {
30      int i, c, nfds;
31      int errors = 0;
32      int flags = FTW_PHYS;
33      char start[PATH_MAX], finish[PATH_MAX];
34
```

```
35      while ((c = getopt(argc, argv, "c")) != -1) {
36          switch (c) {
37          case 'c':
38              flags |= FTW_CHDIR;
39              break;
40          default:
41              usage(argv[0]);
42              break;
43          }
44      }
45
46      if (optind == argc)
47          usage(argv[0]);
48
49      getcwd(start, sizeof start);
50
51      nfds = getdtablesize() - SPARE_FDS; /* leave some spare descriptors */
52      for (i = optind; i < argc; i++) {
53          if (nftw(argv[i], process, nfds, flags) != 0) {
54              fprintf(stderr, "%s: %s: stopped early\n",
55                  argv[0], argv[i]);
56              errors++;
57          }
58      }
59
60      if ((flags & FTW_CHDIR) != 0) {
61          getcwd(finish, sizeof finish);
62          printf("Starting dir: %s\n", start);
63          printf("Finishing dir: %s\n", finish);
64      }
65
66      return (errors != 0);
67  }
```

Lines 3–11 include header files. Through at least GLIBC 2.3.2, the `#defines` for
`_XOPEN_SOURCE` and `_XOPEN_SOURCE_EXTENDED` are necessary before *any* header file
inclusion. They make it possible to get the declarations and flag values that `nftw()`
provides over and above those of `ftw()`. This is specific to GLIBC. The need for it will
eventually disappear as GLIBC becomes fully compliant with the 2001 POSIX standard.

Lines 35–44 process options. The `-c` option adds the `FTW_CHDIR` flag to the `nftw()`
flags. This is an experiment to see if you can end up somewhere different from where
you started. It seems that if `nftw()` fails, you can; otherwise, you end up back where
you were. (POSIX doesn't document this explicitly, but the intent seems to be that you
do end up back where you started. The standard does say that the callback function
should not change the current directory.)

Line 49 saves the starting directory for later use, using `getcwd()`.

Line 51 computes the number of file descriptors `nftw()` can use. We don't want it to use all available file descriptors in case the callback function wants to open files too. The computation uses `getdtablesize()` (see Section 4.4.1, "Understanding File Descriptors," page 92) to retrieve the maximum available number and subtracts `SPARE_FDS`, which was defined earlier, on line 13.

This procedure warrants more explanation. In the normal case, at least three descriptors are already used for standard input, standard output, and standard error. `nftw()` needs some number of file descriptors for opening and reading directories; under the hood, `opendir()` uses `open()` to open a directory for reading. If the callback function also needs to open files, we have to prevent `nftw()` from using up all available file descriptors with open directories. We do this by subtracting some number from the maximum available. For this example, we chose five, but if the callback function needs to open files, a larger number should be used. (`nftw()` knows how to recover when it runs out of file descriptors; we don't have to worry about that case.)

Lines 52–58 are the main loop over the arguments; lines 53–57 check for errors; when they occur, the code prints a diagnostic and increments the `errors` variable.

Lines 60–64 are part of the experiment for `FTW_CHDIR`, printing the starting and finishing directories if `-c` was used.

The function of real interest is `process()`; this is the callback function that processes each file. It uses the basic template for an `nftw()` callback function, which is a `switch` statement on the `flag` value:

```
69  /* process --- print out each file at the right level */
70
71  int process(const char *file, const struct stat *sb,
72          int flag, struct FTW *s)
73  {
74      int retval = 0;
75      const char *name = file + s->base;
76
77      printf("%*s", s->level * 4, "");     /* indent over */
78
79      switch (flag) {
80      case FTW_F:
81          printf("%s (file)\n", name);
82          break;
83      case FTW_D:
84          printf("%s (directory)\n", name);
85          break;
```

```
86      case FTW_DNR:
87          printf("%s (unreadable directory)\n", name);
88          break;
89      case FTW_SL:
90          printf("%s (symbolic link)\n", name);
91          break;
92      case FTW_NS:
93          printf("%s (stat failed): %s\n", name, strerror(errno));
94          break;
95      case FTW_DP:
96      case FTW_SLN:
97          printf("%s: FTW_DP or FTW_SLN: can't happen!\n", name);
98          retval = 1;
99          break;
100     default:
101         printf("%s: unknown flag %d: can't happen!\n", name, flag);
102         retval = 1;
103         break;
104     }
105
106     return retval;
107 }
```

Line 75 uses 'file + s->base' to get at the name part of the full pathname. This pointer value is saved in the name variable for reuse throughout the function.

Line 77 produces the right amount of indentation, using a nice trick. Using %*s, printf() takes the field width from the first argument. This is computed dynamically as 'level * 4'. The string to be printed is "", the null string. The end result is that printf() produces the right amount of space for us, without our having to run a loop.

Lines 79–104 are the switch statement. In this case, it doesn't do anything terribly interesting except print the file's name and its type (file, directory, etc.).

Although this program doesn't use the struct stat, it should be clear that you could do anything you need to in the callback function.

> NOTE   Jim Meyering, the maintainer of the GNU Coreutils, notes that the nftw() design isn't perfect, because of its recursive nature. (It calls itself recursively when processing subdirectories.) If a directory hierarchy gets really deep, in the 20,000–40,000 level range (!), nftw() can run out of stack space, killing the program. There are other problems related to nftw()'s design as well. The post-5.0 version of the GNU Coreutils fixes this by using the BSD fts() suite of routines (see *fts*(3)).

8.5 Walking a File Tree: GNU du

The GNU version of du in the GNU Coreutils uses nftw() to traverse one or more file hierarchies, gathering and producing statistics concerning the amount of disk space used. It has a large number of options that control its behavior with respect to symbolic links, output format of numbers, and so on. This makes the code harder to decipher than a simpler version would be. (However, we're not going to let that stop us.) Here is a summary of du's options, which will be helpful shortly when we look at the code:

```
$ du --help
Usage: du [OPTION]... [FILE]...
Summarize disk usage of each FILE, recursively for directories.

Mandatory arguments to long options are mandatory for short options too.
  -a, --all             write counts for all files, not just directories
      --apparent-size   print apparent sizes, rather than disk usage; although
                          the apparent size is usually smaller, it may be
                          larger due to holes in (`sparse') files, internal
                          fragmentation, indirect blocks, and the like
  -B, --block-size=SIZE use SIZE-byte blocks
  -b, --bytes           equivalent to `--apparent-size --block-size=1'
  -c, --total           produce a grand total
  -D, --dereference-args  dereference FILEs that are symbolic links
  -h, --human-readable  print sizes in human readable format (e.g., 1K 234M 2G)
  -H, --si              likewise, but use powers of 1000 not 1024
  -k                    like --block-size=1K
  -l, --count-links     count sizes many times if hard linked
  -L, --dereference     dereference all symbolic links
  -S, --separate-dirs   do not include size of subdirectories
  -s, --summarize       display only a total for each argument
  -x, --one-file-system  skip directories on different filesystems
  -X FILE, --exclude-from=FILE  Exclude files that match any pattern in FILE.
      --exclude=PATTERN Exclude files that match PATTERN.
      --max-depth=N     print the total for a directory (or file, with --all)
                          only if it is N or fewer levels below the command
                          line argument;  --max-depth=0 is the same as
                          --summarize
      --help     display this help and exit
      --version  output version information and exit

SIZE may be (or may be an integer optionally followed by) one of following:
kB 1000, K 1024, MB 1,000,000, M 1,048,576, and so on for G, T, P, E, Z, Y.

Report bugs to <bug-coreutils@gnu.org>.
```

To complicate matters further, du uses a *private* version of nftw() that has some extensions. First, there are additional flag values for the callback function:

FTW_DCHP

This value signifies that nftw() could not execute 'chdir("..")'.

FTW_DCH

This value signifies that nftw() could not use chdir() to change into a directory itself.

FTW_DPRE

The private nftw() calls the callback function for directories, *twice*. This value is used the first time a directory is encountered. The standard FTW_DP value is used after all the directory's children have been processed.

The private nftw() also adds a new member, int skip, to the struct FTW. If the current object is a directory and the callback function sets the skip field to nonzero, nftw() will not process that directory any further. (The callback function should set skip this way when the flag is FTW_DPRE; doing it for FTW_DP is too late.)

With that explanation under our belt, here is the process_file() function from du.c. Line numbers are relative to the start of the function:

```
1   /* This function is called once for every file system object that nftw
2      encounters.  nftw does a depth-first traversal.  This function knows
3      that and accumulates per-directory totals based on changes in
4      the depth of the current entry.  */
5
6   static int
7   process_file (const char *file, const struct stat *sb, int file_type,
8                 struct FTW *info)
9   {
10    uintmax_t size;
11    uintmax_t size_to_print;
12    static int first_call = 1;
13    static size_t prev_level;
14    static size_t n_alloc;
15    static uintmax_t *sum_ent;
16    static uintmax_t *sum_subdir;
17    int print = 1;
18
19    /* Always define info->skip before returning.  */
20    info->skip = excluded_filename (exclude, file + info->base);   For --exclude
```

This function does a lot since it has to implement all of du's options. Line 17 sets print to true (1); the default is to print information about each file. Later code sets it to false (0) if necessary.

Line 20 sets info->skip based on the --exclude option. Note that this excludes subdirectories if a directory matches the pattern for --exclude.

```
22    switch (file_type)
23      {
24      case FTW_NS:
25        error (0, errno, _("cannot access %s"), quote (file));
26        G_fail = 1;                                    Set global var for later
27        return 0;                                      Return 0 to keep going
28
29      case FTW_DCHP:
30        error (0, errno, _("cannot change to parent of directory %s"),
31              quote (file));
32        G_fail = 1;
33        return 0;
34
35      case FTW_DCH:
36        /* Don't return just yet, since although nftw couldn't chdir into the
37           directory, it was able to stat it, so we do have a size.  */
38        error (0, errno, _("cannot change to directory %s"), quote (file));
39        G_fail = 1;
40        break;
41
42      case FTW_DNR:
43        /* Don't return just yet, since although nftw couldn't read the
44           directory, it was able to stat it, so we do have a size.  */
45        error (0, errno, _("cannot read directory %s"), quote (file));
46        G_fail = 1;
47        break;
48
49      default:
50        break;
51      }
52
53    /* If this is the first (pre-order) encounter with a directory,
54       return right away.  */
55    if (file_type == FTW_DPRE)
56      return 0;
```

Lines 22–51 are the standard `switch` statement. Errors for which there's no size information set the global variable `G_fail` to `1` and return `0` to keep going (see lines 24–27 and 29–33). Errors for which there is a size also set `G_fail` but then break out of the `switch` in order to handle the statistics (see lines 35–40 and 42–47).

Lines 55–56 return early if this is the first time a directory is encountered.

```
58      /* If the file is being excluded or if it has already been counted
59         via a hard link, then don't let it contribute to the sums.  */
60      if (info->skip
61          || (!opt_count_all
62              && 1 < sb->st_nlink
63              && hash_ins (sb->st_ino, sb->st_dev)))
64        {
65          /* Note that we must not simply return here.
66             We still have to update prev_level and maybe propagate
67             some sums up the hierarchy.  */
68          size = 0;
69          print = 0;
70        }
71      else
72        {
73          size = (apparent_size
74                    ? sb->st_size
75                    : ST_NBLOCKS (*sb) * ST_NBLOCKSIZE);
76        }
```

Now it starts to get interesting. By default, `du` counts the space used by hard-linked files just once. The `--count-links` option causes it to count each link's space; the variable `opt_count_all` is true when `--count-links` is supplied. To keep track of links, `du` maintains a hash table[10] of already seen (device, inode) pairs.

Lines 60–63 test whether a file should not be counted, either because it was excluded (`info->skip` is true, line 60) or because `--count-links` was not supplied (line 61) *and* the file has multiple links (line 62) *and* the file is already in the hash table (line 63). In this case, the size is set to `0`, so that it doesn't add to the running totals, and `print` is also set to false (lines 68–69).

If none of those conditions hold, the size is computed either according to the size in the `struct stat` or the number of disk blocks (lines 73–75). This decision is based on the `apparent_size` variable, which is set if the `--apparent-size` option is used.

---

[10] A hash table is a data structure that allows quick retrieval of stored information; the details are beyond the scope of this book.

```
78    if (first_call)
79      {
80        n_alloc = info->level + 10;                      Allocate arrays
81        sum_ent = XCALLOC (uintmax_t, n_alloc);          to hold sums
82        sum_subdir = XCALLOC (uintmax_t, n_alloc);
83      }
84    else
85      {
86        /* FIXME: it's a shame that we need these `size_t' casts to avoid
87           warnings from gcc about `comparison between signed and unsigned'.
88           Probably unavoidable, assuming that the members of struct FTW
89           are of type `int' (historical), since I want variables like
90           n_alloc and prev_level to have types that make sense.  */
91        if (n_alloc <= (size_t) info->level)
92          {
93            n_alloc = info->level * 2;                    Double amount
94            sum_ent = XREALLOC (sum_ent, uintmax_t, n_alloc);    And reallocate
95            sum_subdir = XREALLOC (sum_subdir, uintmax_t, n_alloc);
96          }
97      }
98
99    size_to_print = size;
```

Lines 78–97 manage the dynamic memory used to hold file size statistics. `first_call`
is a `static` variable (line 12) that is true the first time `process_file()` is called. In
this case, `calloc()` is called (through a wrapper macro on lines 81–82; this was discussed in Section 3.2.1.8, "Example: Reading Arbitrarily Long Lines," page 67). The
rest of the time, `first_call` is false, and `realloc()` is used (again, through a wrapper
macro, lines 91–96).

Line 99 sets `size_to_print` to `size`; this variable may be updated depending on
whether it has to include the sizes of any children. Although `size` could have been
reused, the separate variable makes the code easier to read.

```
101    if (! first_call)
102      {
103        if ((size_t) info->level == prev_level)
104          {
105            /* This is usually the most common case.  Do nothing.  */
106          }
107        else if ((size_t) info->level > prev_level)
108          {
109            /* Descending the hierarchy.
110               Clear the accumulators for *all* levels between prev_level
111               and the current one.  The depth may change dramatically,
112               e.g., from 1 to 10.  */
113            int i;
114            for (i = prev_level + 1; i <= info->level; i++)
115              sum_ent[i] = sum_subdir[i] = 0;
116          }
```

```
117          else /* info->level < prev_level */
118            {
119              /* Ascending the hierarchy.
120                 nftw processes a directory only after all entries in that
121                 directory have been processed.  When the depth decreases,
122                 propagate sums from the children (prev_level) to the parent.
123                 Here, the current level is always one smaller than the
124                 previous one.  */
125              assert ((size_t) info->level == prev_level - 1);
126              size_to_print += sum_ent[prev_level];
127              if (!opt_separate_dirs)
128                size_to_print += sum_subdir[prev_level];
129              sum_subdir[info->level] += (sum_ent[prev_level]
130                                         + sum_subdir[prev_level]);
131            }
132        }
```

Lines 101–132 compare the current level to the previous one. There are three possible cases.

The levels are the same.

In this case, there's no need to worry about child statistics. (Lines 103–106.)

The current level is higher than the previous level.

In this case, we've gone down the hierarchy, and the statistics must be reset (lines 107–116). The term "accumulator" in the comment is apt: each element accumulates the total disk space used at that level. (In the early days of computing, CPU registers were often termed "accumulators.")

The current level is lower than the previous level.

In this case, we've finished processing all the children in a directory and have just moved back up to the parent directory (lines 117–131). The code updates the totals, including `size_to_print`.

```
134    prev_level = info->level;                             Set static variables
135    first_call = 0;
136
137    /* Let the size of a directory entry contribute to the total for the
138       containing directory, unless --separate-dirs (-S) is specified.  */
139    if ( ! (opt_separate_dirs && IS_FTW_DIR_TYPE (file_type)))
140      sum_ent[info->level] += size;
141
142    /* Even if this directory is unreadable or we can't chdir into it,
143       do let its size contribute to the total, ... */
144    tot_size += size;
145
146    /* ... but don't print out a total for it, since without the size(s)
147       of any potential entries, it could be very misleading.  */
```

```
148     if (file_type == FTW_DNR || file_type == FTW_DCH)
149       return 0;
150
151     /* If we're not counting an entry, e.g., because it's a hard link
152        to a file we've already counted (and --count-links), then don't
153        print a line for it.  */
154     if (!print)
155       return 0;
```

Lines 134–135 set the `static` variables `prev_level` and `first_call` so that they'll have the correct values for a subsequent call to `process_file()`, ensuring that all the previous code works correctly.

Lines 137–144 adjust statistics on the basis of options and the file type. The comments and code are fairly straightforward. Lines 146–155 quit early if the information should not be printed.

```
157     /* FIXME: This looks suspiciously like it could be simplified.  */
158     if ((IS_FTW_DIR_TYPE (file_type) &&
159                       (info->level <= max_depth || info->level == 0))
160        || ((opt_all && info->level <= max_depth) || info->level == 0))
161       {
162         print_only_size (size_to_print);
163         fputc ('\t', stdout);
164         if (arg_length)
165           {
166             /* Print the file name, but without the `.' or `/.'
167                directory suffix that we may have added in main.  */
168             /* Print everything before the part we appended.  */
169             fwrite (file, arg_length, 1, stdout);
170             /* Print everything after what we appended.  */
171             fputs (file + arg_length + suffix_length
172                    + (file[arg_length + suffix_length] == '/'), stdout);
173           }
174         else
175           {
176             fputs (file, stdout);
177           }
178         fputc ('\n', stdout);
179         fflush (stdout);
180       }
181
182     return 0;
183   }
```

The condition on lines 158–160 is confusing, and the comment on line 157 notes this. The condition states: "If (1a) the file is a directory and (1b) the level is less than the maximum to print (the `--max-depth` and `max_depth` variable) or the level is zero, *or* (2a) all files should be printed and the level is less than the maximum to print, or

(2b) the level is zero," then print the file. (Yow! The post-5.0 version of du uses a slightly less complicated condition for this case.)

Lines 162–179 do the printing. Lines 162–163 print the size and a TAB character. Lines 164–173 handle a special case. This is explained later on in du.c, on lines 524–529 of the file:

```
524    /* When dereferencing only command line arguments, we're using
525       nftw's FTW_PHYS flag, so a symlink-to-directory specified on
526       the command line wouldn't normally be dereferenced.  To work
527       around that, we incur the overhead of appending `/.' (or `.')
528       now, and later removing it each time we output the name of
529       a derived file or directory name.  */
```

In this case, arg_length is true, so lines 164–173 have to print out the original name, not the modified one. Otherwise, lines 174–117 can print the name as it is.

Whew! That's a lot of code. We find this to be on the upper end of the complexity spectrum, at least as far as what can be easily presented in a book of this nature. However, it demonstrates that real-world code is often complex. The best way to manage such complexity is with clearly named variables and detailed comments. du.c is good in that respect; we were able to extract the code and examine it fairly easily, without having to show all 735 lines of the program!

8.6　Changing the Root Directory: chroot()

The current working directory, set with chdir() (see Section 8.4.1, "Changing Directory: chdir() and fchdir()," page 256), is an attribute of the process, just like the set of open files. It is also inherited by new processes.

Less well known is that every process also has a *current root directory*. It is this directory to which the pathname / refers. Most of the time, a process's root and the system root directories are identical. However, the superuser can change the root directory, with the (you guessed it) chroot() system call:

```
#include <unistd.h>                                    Common

int chroot(const char *path);
```

The return value is 0 upon success and –1 upon error.

As the GNU/Linux *chroot*(2) manpage points out, changing the root directory does not change the current directory: Programs that must make sure that they stay underneath the new root directory must also execute chdir() afterwards:

```
if (chroot("/new/root") < 0)          Set new root directory
    /* handle error */

if (chdir("/some/dir") < 0)           Pathnames now relative to new root
    /* handle error */
```

The `chroot()` system call is used most often for *daemons*—background programs that must run in a special, contained environment. For example, consider an Internet FTP daemon that allows anonymous FTP (connection by anyone, from anywhere, without a regular username and password). Obviously, such a connection should not be able to see all the files on the whole system. Instead, the FTP daemon does a `chroot()` to a special directory with just enough structure to allow it to function. (For example, its own `/bin/ls` for listing files, its own copy of the C runtime library if it's shared, and possibly its own copy of `/etc/passwd` and `/etc/group` to show a limited set of user and group names.)

POSIX doesn't standardize this system call, although GNU/Linux and all Unix systems support it. (It's been around since V7.) It is specialized, but when you need it, it's very handy.

8.7 Summary

- Filesystems are collections of free, inode, metadata, and data blocks, organized in a specific fashion. Filesystems correspond one-to-one with the (physical or logical) partitions in which they are made. Each filesystem has its own root directory; by convention the root directory always has inode number 2.

- The `mount` command mounts a filesystem, grafting it onto the logical hierarchical file namespace. The `umount` command detaches a filesystem. The kernel arranges for `/.` and `/..` to be the same; the root directory of the entire namespace is its own parent. In all other cases, the kernel arranges for '`..`' in the root of a mounted filesystem to point to the parent directory of the mount point.

- Modern Unix systems support multiple types of filesystems. In particular, Sun's Network File System (NFS) is universally supported, as is the ISO 9660 standard format for CD-ROMs, and MS-DOS FAT partitions are supported on all Unix systems that run on Intel x86 hardware. To our knowledge, Linux supports the largest number of different filesystems—well over 30! Many are specialized, but many others are for general use, including at least four different journaling filesystems.

- The `/etc/fstab` file lists each system's partitions, their mount points, and any relevant mount options. `/etc/mtab` lists those filesystems that are currently mounted, as does `/proc/mounts` on GNU/Linux systems. The `loop` option to `mount` is particularly useful under GNU/Linux for mounting filesystem images contained in regular files, such as CD-ROM images. Other options are useful for security and for mounting foreign filesystems, such as Windows `vfat` filesystems.

- The `/etc/fstab`-format files can be read with the `getmntent()` suite of routines. The GNU/Linux format is shared with several other commercial Unix variants, most notably Sun's Solaris.

- The `statvfs()` and `fstatvfs()` functions are standardized by POSIX for retrieving filesystem information, such as the number of free and used disk blocks, the number of free and used inodes, and so on. Linux has its own system calls for retrieving similar information: `statfs()` and `fstatfs()`.

- `chdir()` and `fchdir()` let a process change its current directory. `getcwd()` retrieves the absolute pathname of the current directory. These three functions are straightforward to use.

- The `nftw()` function centralizes the task of "walking a file tree," that is, visiting every filesystem object (file, device, symbolic link, directory) in an entire directory hierarchy. Different flags control its behavior. The programmer then has to provide a callback function that receives each file's name, a `struct stat` for the file, the file's type, and information about the file's name and level in the hierarchy. This function can then do whatever is necessary for each file. The Coreutils 5.0 version of GNU `du` uses an extended version of `nftw()` to do its job.

- Finally, the `chroot()` system call changes a process's current root directory. This is a specialized but important facility, which is particularly useful for certain daemon-style programs.

Exercises

1. Examine the *mount*(2) manpage under GNU/Linux and on as many other different Unix systems as you have access to. How do the system calls differ?

2. Enhance `ch08-statvfs.c` to take an option giving an open integer file descriptor; it should use `fstatvfs()` to retrieve filesystem information.

3. Enhance `ch08-statvfs.c` to not ignore NFS-mounted filesystems. Such filesystems have a device of the form `server.example.com:/big/disk`.

4. Modify `ch08-statfs.c` (the one that uses the Linux-specific `statfs()` call) to produce output that looks like that from `df`.

5. Add a `-i` option to the program you wrote for the previous exercise to produce output like that of '`df -i`'.

6. Using `opendir()`, `readdir()`, `stat()` or `fstat()`, `dirfd()`, and `fchdir()`, write your own version of `getcwd()`. How will you compute the total size the buffer needs to be? How will you move through the directory hierarchy?

7. Enhance your version of `getcwd()` to allocate a buffer for the caller if the first argument is NULL.

8. Can you use `nftw()` to write `getcwd()`? If not, why not?

9. Using `nftw()`, write your own version of `chown` that accepts a `-R` option to recursively process entire directory trees. Make sure that without `-R`, '`chown user directory`' does *not* recurse. How will you test it?

10. The BSD `fts()` ("file tree stream") suite of routines provides a different way to process directory hierarchies. It has a somewhat heftier API, in terms of both the number of functions and the `struct` it makes available to the user-level function that calls it. These functions are available as a standard part of GLIBC.

    Read the *fts*(3) manpage. (It may help you to print it and have it handy.) Rewrite your private version of `chown` to use `fts()`.

11. Look at the *find*(1) manpage. If you were to try to write `find` from scratch, which file tree suite would you prefer, `nftw()` or `fts()`? Why?

Part II

Processes, IPC, and Internationalization

Process Management and Pipes

In this chapter

As we said in Chapter 1, "Introduction," page 3, if you were to summarize Unix (and thus Linux) in three words, they would have to be "files and processes." Now that we've seen how to work with files and directories, it's time to look at the rest of the story: processes. In particular, we examine how processes are created and managed, how they interact with open files, and how they can communicate with each other. Subsequent chapters examine signals—a coarse way for one process (or the kernel) to let another know that some event has occurred—and permission checking.

In this chapter the picture begins to get more complicated. In particular, to be fairly complete, we must mention things that aren't covered until later in the chapter or later in the book. In such cases, we provide forward references, but you should be able to get the gist of each section without looking ahead.

9.1 Process Creation and Management

Unlike many predecessor and successor operating systems, process creation in Unix was intended to be (and is) cheap. Furthermore, Unix separated the idea of "create a new process" from that of "run a given program in a process." This was an elegant design decision, one that simplifies many operations.

9.1.1 Creating a Process: `fork()`

The first step in starting a new program is calling `fork()`:

POSIX

```
#include <sys/types.h>
#include <unistd.h>

pid_t fork(void);
```

Using `fork()` is simple. Before the call, one process, which we term the *parent*, is running. When `fork()` returns, there are two processes: the parent and the *child*.

Here is the key: *The two processes both run the same program*. The two processes can distinguish themselves based on the return value from `fork()`:

Negative
> If there is an error, `fork()` returns -1, and no new process is created. The original process continues running.

Zero
> In the child, `fork()` returns 0.

Positive

In the parent, `fork()` returns the positive process identification number (PID) of the child.

Boilerplate code for creating a child process looks like this:

```
pid_t child;

if ((child = fork()) < 0)
    /* handle error */
else if (child == 0)
    /* this is the new process */
else
    /* this is the original parent process */
```

The `pid_t` is a signed integer type for holding PID values. It is most likely a plain `int`, but it makes code more self-documenting and should be used instead of `int`.

In Unix parlance, besides being the name of a system call, the word "fork" is both a verb and a noun. We might say that "one process forks another," and that "after the fork, two processes are running." (Think "fork in a road" and not "fork, knife and spoon.")

9.1.1.1   After the `fork()`: Shared and Distinct Attributes

The child "inherits" identical copies of a large number of attributes from the parent. Many of these attributes are specialized and irrelevant here. Thus, the following list in purposely incomplete. The following attributes are the relevant ones:

- The environment; see Section 2.4, "The Environment," page 40.

- All open files and open directories; see Section 4.4.1, "Understanding File Descriptors," page 92, and see Section 5.3.1, "Basic Directory Reading," page 133.

- The umask setting; see Section 4.6, "Creating Files," page 106.

- The current working directory; see Section 8.4.1, "Changing Directory: `chdir()` and `fchdir()`," page 256.

- The root directory; see Section 8.6, "Changing the Root Directory: `chroot()`," page 276.

- The current priority (a.k.a. "nice value"; we discuss this shortly; see Section 9.1.3, "Setting Process Priority: `nice()`," page 291).

- The controlling terminal. This is the terminal device (physical console or terminal-emulator window) that is allowed to send signals to a process (such as CTRL-Z to stop running jobs). This is discussed later, in Section 9.2.1, "Job Control Overview," page 312.

- The process signal mask and all current signal dispositions (not discussed yet; see Chapter 10, "Signals," page 347).

- The real, effective, and saved set-user and set-group IDs and the supplemental group set (not discussed yet; see Chapter 11, "Permissions and User and Group ID Numbers," page 403).

Besides the `fork()` return value, the two processes differ in the following ways:

- Each one has a unique process ID and parent process ID (PID and PPID). These are described in Section 9.1.2, "Identifying a Process: `getpid()` and `getppid()`," page 289.

- The child's PID will not equal that of any existing process group ID (see Section 9.2, "Process Groups," page 312).

- The accumulated CPU times for the child process and its future children are initialized to zero. (This makes sense; after all, it is a brand-new process.)

- Any signals that were pending in the parent are cleared in the child, as are any pending alarms or timers. (We haven't covered these topics yet; see Chapter 10, "Signals," page 347, and see Section 14.3.3, "Interval Timers: `setitimer()` and `getitimer()`," page 546.)

- File locks held by the parent are not duplicated in the child (also not discussed yet; see Section 14.2, "Locking Files," page 531).

9.1.1.2 File Descriptor Sharing

The attributes that the child inherits from the parent are all set to the same values they had in the parent at the time of the `fork()`. From then on, though, the two processes proceed on their merry ways, (mostly) independent of each other. For example, if the child changes directory, the parent's directory is not affected. Similarly, if the child changes its environment, the parent's environment is *not* changed.

Open files are a significant exception to this rule. Open file descriptors are *shared*, and an action by one process on a shared file descriptor affects the state of the file for the other process as well. This is best understood after study of Figure 9.1.

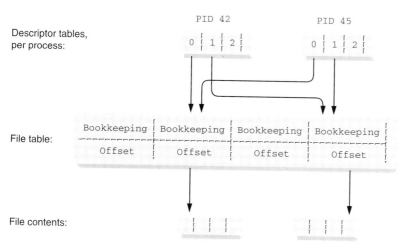

FIGURE 9.1
File descriptor sharing

The figure displays the kernel's internal data structures. The key data structure is the *file table*. Each element refers to an open file. Besides other bookkeeping data, the file table maintains the current position (read/write offset) in the file. This is adjusted either automatically each time a file is read or written or directly with `lseek()` (see Section 4.5, "Random Access: Moving Around within a File," page 102).

The file descriptor returned by `open()` or `creat()` acts as an index into a per-process array of pointers into the file table. This per-process array won't be any larger than the value returned by `getdtablesize()` (see Section 4.4.1, "Understanding File Descriptors," page 92).

Figure 9.1 shows two processes sharing standard input and standard output; for each, both point to the same entries in the file table. Thus, when process 45 (the child) does a `read()`, the shared offset is updated; the next time process 42 (the parent) does a `read()`, it starts at the position where process 45's `read()` finished.

This can be seen easily at the shell level:

```
$ cat data                                          Show demo data file contents
line 1
line 2
line 3
line 4
$ ls -l test1 ; cat test1                           Mode and contents of test program
-rwxr-xr-x   1 arnold   devel   93 Oct 20 22:11 test1
#! /bin/sh
read line ; echo p: $line                           Read a line in parent shell, print it
( read line ; echo c: $line )                       Read a line in child shell, print it
read line ; echo p: $line                           Read a line in parent shell, print it
$ test1 < data                                      Run the program
p: line 1                                           Parent starts at beginning
c: line 2                                           Child picks up where parent left off
p: line 3                                           Parent picks up where child left off
```

The first executable line of test1 reads a line from standard input, changing the offset in the file. The second line of test1 runs the commands enclosed between the parentheses in a *subshell*. This is a separate shell process created—you guessed it—with fork(). The child subshell inherits standard input from the parent, including the current file offset. This process reads a line and updates the *shared* offset into the file. When the third line, back in the parent shell, reads the file, it starts where the child left off.

Although the read command is built into the shell, things work the same way with external commands. Some early Unix systems had a line command that read one line of input (one character at a time!) for use within shell scripts; if the file offset weren't shared, it would be impossible to use such a command in a loop.

File descriptor sharing and inheritance play a pivotal role in shell I/O redirection; the system calls and their semantics make the shell-level primitives straightforward to implement in C, as we see later in the chapter.

9.1.1.3 File Descriptor Sharing and close()

The fact that multiple file descriptors can point at the same open file has an important consequence: *A file is not closed until all its file descriptors are closed.*

We see later in the chapter that multiple descriptors for the same file can exist not only across processes but even within the same process; this rule is particularly important for working with pipes.

If you need to know if two descriptors are open on the same file, you can use fstat() (see Section 5.4.2, "Retrieving File Information," page 141) on the two descriptors with two different `struct stat` structures. If the corresponding `st_dev` and `st_ino` fields are equal, they're the same file.

We complete the discussion of file descriptor manipulation and the file descriptor table later in the chapter.

9.1.2 Identifying a Process: `getpid()` and `getppid()`

Each process has a unique process ID number (the PID). Two system calls provide the current PID and the PID of the parent process:

```
#include <sys/types.h>                                     POSIX
#include <unistd.h>

pid_t getpid(void);
pid_t getppid(void);
```

The functions are about as simple as they come:

`pid_t getpid(void)`   Returns the PID of the current process.

`pid_t getppid(void)`   Returns the parent's PID.

PID values are unique; by definition there cannot be two running processes with the same PID. PIDs usually increase in value, in that a child process generally has a higher PID than its parent. On many systems, however, PID values *wrap around*; when the system maximum value for PIDs is exceeded, the next process created will have the lowest unused PID number. (Nothing in POSIX requires this behavior, and some systems assign unused PID numbers randomly.)

If the parent dies or exits, the child is given a new parent, `init`. In this case, the new parent PID will be 1, which is `init`'s PID. Such a child is termed an *orphan*. The following program, `ch09-reparent.c`, demonstrates this. This is also the first example we've seen of `fork()` in action:

```
1   /* ch09-reparent.c --- show that getppid() can change values */
2
3   #include <stdio.h>
4   #include <errno.h>
5   #include <sys/types.h>
6   #include <unistd.h>
7
8   /* main --- do the work */
9
```

```
10  int main(int argc, char **argv)
11  {
12      pid_t pid, old_ppid, new_ppid;
13      pid_t child, parent;
14
15      parent = getpid();       /* before fork() */
16
17      if ((child = fork()) < 0) {
18          fprintf(stderr, "%s: fork of child failed: %s\n",
19              argv[0], strerror(errno));
20          exit(1);
21      } else if (child == 0) {
22          old_ppid = getppid();
23          sleep(2);            /* see Chapter 10 */
24          new_ppid = getppid();
25      } else {
26          sleep(1);
27          exit(0);             /* parent exits after fork() */
28      }
29
30      /* only the child executes this */
31      printf("Original parent: %d\n", parent);
32      printf("Child: %d\n", getpid());
33      printf("Child's old ppid: %d\n", old_ppid);
34      printf("Child's new ppid: %d\n", new_ppid);
35
36      exit(0);
37  }
```

Line 15 retrieves the PID of the initial process, using getpid(). Lines 17–20 fork the child, checking for an error return.

Lines 21–24 are executed by the child: Line 22 retrieves the PPID. Line 23 suspends the process for two seconds (see Section 10.8.1, "Alarm Clocks: sleep(), alarm(), and SIGALRM," page 382, for information about sleep()), and then line 24 retrieves the PPID again.

Lines 25–27 run in the parent. Line 26 delays the parent for one second, giving the child enough time to make the first getppid() call. Line 27 then exits the parent.

Lines 31–34 print the values. Note that the parent variable, which was set before the fork, still maintains its value in the child. After forking, the two processes have identical but independent copies of their address spaces. Here's what happens when the program runs:

```
$ ch09-reparent                              Run the program
$ Original parent: 6582                      Program finishes: shell prompts and child prints
Child: 6583
Child's old ppid: 6582
Child's new ppid: 1
```

Remember that the two programs execute *in parallel*. This is depicted graphically in Figure 9.2.

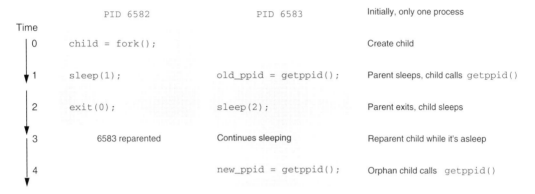

FIGURE 9.2
Two processes running in parallel after forking

> NOTE   The use of `sleep()` to have one process outlive another works most of the time. However, occasionally it fails, leading to hard-to-reproduce and hard-to-find bugs. The only way to guarantee correct behavior is explicit synchronization with `wait()` or `waitpid()`, which are described further on in the chapter (see Section 9.1.6.1, "Using POSIX Functions: `wait()` and `waitpid()`," page 306).

9.1.3 Setting Process Priority: `nice()`

As processes run, the kernel dynamically changes each process's *priority*. As in life, higher-priority items get attention before lower-priority ones. In brief, each process is allotted a small amount of time in which to run, called its *time slice*. When the time slice finishes, if the current process is still the one with the highest priority, it is allowed to continue running.

Linux, like Unix, provides *preemptive multitasking*. This means that the kernel can preempt a process (pause it) if it's time to let another process run. Processes that have been running a lot (for example, compute-intensive processes) have their priority lowered at the end of their time slice, to let other processes have a chance at the processor. Similarly, processes that have been idle while waiting for I/O (such as an interactive text editor) are given a higher priority so that they can respond to the I/O when it happens. In short, the kernel makes sure that all processes, averaged over time, get their "fair share" of the CPU. Raising and lowering priorities are part of this process.

Designing a good process scheduler for the kernel is an art; the nitty-gritty details are beyond the scope of this book. However, a process can influence the kernel's priority assignment algorithm by way of its *nice value*.

The nice value is an indication of "how nice" the process is willing to be toward other processes. Thus, higher nice values indicate increasingly more patient processes; that is, ones that are increasingly nice toward others, lowering their priority with respect to that of other processes.

A negative nice value, on the other hand, indicates that a process wishes to be "less nice" towards others. Such a process is more selfish, wanting more CPU time for itself.[1] Fortunately, while users can increase their nice value (be more nice), only `root` can decrease the nice value (be less nice).

The nice value is only one factor in the equation used by the kernel to compute the priority; the nice value is not the priority itself, which varies over time, based on the process's behavior and the state of other processes in the system. To change the nice value, use the `nice()` system call:

```
#include <unistd.h>                                          XSI

int nice(int inc);
```

The default nice value is 0. The allowed range for nice values is -20 to 19. This takes some getting used to. The more negative the value, the higher the process's priority: -20 is the highest priority (least nice), and 19 is the lowest priority (most nice).

The `inc` argument is the increment by which to change the nice value. Use '`nice(0)`' to retrieve the current value without changing it. If the result of '`current_nice_value + inc`' would be outside the range -20 to 19, the system forces the result to be inside the range.

---

[1] Such processes often display childlike behavior.

The return value is the new nice value or -1 if there was an error. Since -1 is also a valid nice value, when calling `nice()` you must explicitly set `errno` to zero first, and then check it afterwards to see if there was a problem:

```
int niceval;
int inc = /* whatever */;

errno = 0;
if ((niceval = nice(inc)) < 0 && errno != 0) {
    fprintf(stderr, "nice(%d) failed: %s\n", inc, strerror(errno));
    /* other recovery */
}
```

This example can fail if `inc` has a negative value and the process is not running as `root`.

9.1.3.1 POSIX vs. Reality

The nice value range of -20 to 19 that Linux uses is historical; it dates back at least as far as V7. POSIX expresses the situation in more indirect language, which allows for implementation flexibility while maintaining historical compatibility. It also makes the standard harder to read and understand, but then, that's why you're reading this book. So, here's how POSIX describes it.

First, the *process's nice value* as maintained by the system ranges from 0 to '(2 * NZERO) - 1'. The constant `NZERO` is defined in `<limits.h>` and must be at least 20. This gives us the range 0–39.

Second, as we described, the sum of the current nice value and the `incr` increment is forced into this range.

Finally, the return value from `nice()` is the process nice value *minus* `NZERO`. With an `NZERO` value of 20, this gives us the original -20 to 19 range that we initially described.

The upshot is that `nice()`'s return value actually ranges from '-NZERO' to 'NZERO-1', and it's best to write your code in terms of that symbolic constant. However, practically speaking, you're unlikely to find a system where `NZERO` is not 20.

9.1.4 Starting New Programs: The `exec()` Family

Once a new process is running (through `fork()`), the next step is to start a different program running in the process. There are multiple functions that serve different purposes:

```
#include <unistd.h>                                        POSIX

int execve(const char *filename, char *const argv[],        System call
           char *const envp[]);

int execl(const char *path, const char *arg, ...);          Wrappers
int execlp(const char *file, const char *arg, ...);
int execle(const char *path, const char *arg, ..., char *const envp[]);
int execv(const char *path, char *const argv[]);
int execvp(const char *file, char *const argv[]);
```

We refer to these functions as the "exec() family." There is no function named exec(); instead we use this function name to mean any of the above listed functions. As with fork(), "exec" is used in Unix parlance as a verb, meaning to execute (run) a program, and as a noun.

9.1.4.1 The execve() System Call

The simplest function to explain is execve(). It is also the underlying system call. The others are wrapper functions, as is explained shortly.

```
int execve(const char *filename, char *const argv[],
    char *const envp[])
```

   filename is the name of the program to execute. It may be a full or relative pathname. The file must be in an executable format that the kernel understands. Modern systems uses the ELF (Extensible Linking Format) executable format. GNU/Linux understands ELF and several others. Interpreted scripts can be executed with execve() if they use the '#!' special first line that names the interpreter to use. (Scripts that don't start with '#!' will fail.) Section 1.1.3, "Executable Files," page 7, provides an example use of '#!'.

   argv is a standard C argument list—an array of character pointers to argument strings, *including the value to use for* argv[0], terminated with a NULL pointer.

   envp is the environment to use for the new process, with the same layout as the environ global variable (see Section 2.4, "The Environment," page 40). In the new program, this environment becomes the initial value of environ.

A call to exec() should not return. If it does, there was a problem. Most commonly, either the requested program doesn't exist, or it exists but it isn't executable (ENOENT and EACCES for errno, respectively). Many more things can go wrong; see the *execve*(2) manpage.

Assuming that the call succeeds, the current contents of the process's address space are thrown away. (The kernel does arrange to save the `argv` and `envp` data in a safe place first.) The kernel loads the executable code for the new program, along with any global and `static` variables. Next, the kernel initializes the environment with that passed to `execve()`, and then it calls the new program's `main()` routine with the `argv` array passed to `execve()`. It counts the number of arguments and passes that value to `main()` in `argc`.

At that point, the new program is running. It doesn't know (and can't find out) what program was running in the process before it. Note that the process ID *does not change*. Many other attributes remain in place across the exec; we cover this in more detail shortly.

In a loose analogy, `exec()` is to a process what life roles are to a person. At different times during the day, a single person might function as parent, spouse, friend, student or worker, store customer, and so on. Yet it is the same underlying person performing the different roles. So too, the process—its PID, open files, current directory, etc.—doesn't change, while the particular job it's doing—the program run with `exec()`—can.

9.1.4.2 Wrapper Functions: `execl()` et al.

Five additional functions, acting as wrappers, provide more convenient interfaces to `execve()`. The first group all take a list of arguments, each one passed as an explicit function parameter:

```
int execl(const char *path, const char *arg, ...)
```
The first argument, `path`, is the pathname of the file to execute. Subsequent arguments, starting with `arg`, are the individual elements to be placed in `argv`. As before, `argv[0]` must be explicitly included. You must pass a terminating `NULL` pointer as the final argument so that `execl()` can tell where the argument list ends. The new program inherits whatever environment is in the current program's `environ` variable.

```
int execlp(const char *file, const char *arg, ...)
```
This function is like `execl()`, but it simulates the shell's command searching mechanism, looking for `file` in each directory named in the `PATH` environment variable. If `file` contains a / character, this search is not done. If `PATH` isn't present

in the environment, `execlp()` uses a default path. On GNU/Linux, the default is `":/bin:/usr/bin"` but it may be different on other systems. (Note that the leading colon in PATH means that the current directory is searched *first*.)

Furthermore, if the file is found and has execute permission but cannot be exec'd because it isn't in a known executable format, `execlp()` assumes that the program is a shell script, and execs the shell with the filename as an argument.

```
int execle(const char *path, const char *arg, ...,
    char *const envp[])
```
This function is also like `execl()`, but it accepts an additional argument, `envp`, which becomes the new program's environment. As with `execl()`, you must supply the terminating NULL pointer to end the argument list, before `envp`.

The second group of wrapper functions accepts an `argv` style array:

```
int execv(const char *path, char *const argv[])
```
This function is like `execve()`, but the new program inherits whatever environment is in the current program's `environ` variable.

```
int execvp(const char *file, char *const argv[])
```
This function is like `execv()`, but it does the same PATH search that `execlp()` does. It also does the same falling back to exec'ing the shell if the found file cannot be executed directly.

Table 9.1 summarizes the six `exec()` functions.

TABLE 9.1
Alphabetical `exec()` family summary

Function	Path search	Uses environ	Purpose
`execl()`		✓	Execute arg list.
`execle()`			Execute arg list with environment.
`execlp()`	✓	✓	Execute arg list by path search.
`execv()`		✓	Execute with `argv`.
`execve()`			Execute with `argv` and environment (system call).
`execvp()`	✓	✓	Execute with `argv` by path search.

The execlp() and execvp() functions are best avoided unless you know that the PATH environment variable contains a reasonable list of directories.

9.1.4.3 Program Names and argv[0]

Until now, we have always treated argv[0] as the program name. We know that it may or may not contain a / character, depending on how the program is invoked; if it does, then that's usually a good clue as to the pathname used to invoke the program.

However, as should be clear by now, argv[0] being the filename is *only a convention*. There's nothing stopping you from passing an arbitrary string to the exec'd program for argv[0]. The following program, ch09-run.c, demonstrates passing an arbitrary string:

```
1   /* ch09-run.c --- run a program with a different name and any arguments */
2
3   #include <stdio.h>
4   #include <errno.h>
5   #include <unistd.h>
6
7   /* main --- adjust argv and run named program */
8
9   int main(int argc, char **argv)
10  {
11      char *path;
12
13      if (argc < 3) {
14          fprintf(stderr, "usage: %s path arg0 [ arg ... ]\n", argv[0]);
15          exit(1);
16      }
17
18      path = argv[1];
19
20      execv(path, argv + 2);  /* skip argv[0] and argv[1] */
21
22      fprintf(stderr, "%s: execv() failed: %s\n", argv[0],
23          strerror(errno));
24      exit(1);
25  }
```

The first argument is the pathname of the program to run and the second is the new name for the program (which most utilities ignore, other than for error messages); any other arguments are passed on to the program being exec'd.

Lines 13–16 do error checking. Line 18 saves the path in path. Line 20 does the exec; if lines 22–23 run, it's because there was a problem. Here's what happens when we run the program:

```
$ ch09-run /bin/grep whoami foo          Run grep
a line                                   Input line doesn't match
a line with foo in it                    Input line that does match
a line with foo in it                    It's printed
^D                                       EOF

$ ch09-run nonexistent-program foo bar   Demonstrate failure
ch09-run: execv() failed: No such file or directory
```

This next example is a bit bizarre: we have ch09-run run *itself*, passing 'foo' as the program name. Since there aren't enough arguments for the second run, it prints the usage message and exits:

```
$ ch09-run ./ch09-run foo
usage: foo path arg0 [ arg ... ]
```

While not very useful, ch09-run clearly shows that argv[0] need not have any relationship to the file that is actually run.

In System III (circa 1980), the cp, ln, and mv commands were one executable file, with three links by those names in /bin. The program would examine argv[0] and decide what it should do. This saved a modest amount of disk space, at the expense of complicating the source code and forcing the program to choose a default action if invoked by an unrecognized name. (Some current commercial Unix systems continue this practice!) Without stating an explicit reason, the *GNU Coding Standards* recommends that a program *not* base its behavior upon its name. One reason we see is that administrators often install the GNU version of a utility alongside the standard ones on commercial Unix systems, using a g prefix: gmake, gawk, and so on. If such programs expect only the standard names, they'll fail when run with a different name.

Also, today, disk space is cheap; if two almost identical programs can be built from the same source code, it's better to do it that way, using #ifdef or what-have-you. For example, grep and egrep share considerable code, but the GNU version builds two separate executables.

9.1.4.4 Attributes Inherited across exec()

As with fork(), a number of attributes remain in place after a program does an exec:

- All open files and open directories; see Section 4.4.1, "Understanding File Descriptors," page 92, and see Section 5.3.1, "Basic Directory Reading," page 133. (This doesn't include files marked close-on-exec, as described later in the chapter; see Section 9.4.3.1, "The Close-on-exec Flag," page 329.)

- The umask setting; see Section 4.6, "Creating Files," page 106.

- The current working directory; see Section 8.4.1, "Changing Directory: `chdir()` and `fchdir()`," page 256.

- The root directory; see Section 8.6, "Changing the Root Directory: `chroot()`," page 276.

- The current nice value.

- The process ID and parent process ID.

- The process group ID; see Section 9.2, "Process Groups," page 312.

- The session ID and the controlling terminal; for both, see Section 9.2.1, "Job Control Overview," page 312.

- The process signal mask and any pending signals, as well as any unexpired alarms or timers (not discussed yet; see Chapter 10, "Signals," page 347).

- The real user ID and group IDs and the supplemental group set. The effective user and group IDs (and thus the saved set-user and set-group IDs) can be set by the setuid and setgid bits on the file being exec'd. (None of this has been discussed yet; see Chapter 11, "Permissions and User and Group ID Numbers," page 403).

- File locks remain in place (also not discussed yet; see Section 14.2, "Locking Files," page 531).

- Accumulated CPU times for the process and its children don't change.

After an exec, signal disposition changes; see Section 10.9, "Signals Across `fork()` and `exec()`," page 398, for more information.

All open files and directories remain open and available after the exec. This is how programs inherit standard input, output, and error: They're in place when the program starts up.

Most of the time, when you fork and exec a separate program, you don't want it to inherit anything but file descriptors 0, 1, and 2. In this case, you can manually close all other open files in the child, after the fork but before the exec. Alternatively, you can mark a file descriptor to be automatically closed by the system upon an exec; this latter option is discussed later in the chapter (see Section 9.4.3.1, "The Close-on-exec Flag," page 329).

9.1.5 Terminating a Process

Process termination involves two steps: The process exits, passing an exit status to the system, and the parent process recovers the information.

9.1.5.1 Defining Process Exit Status

The *exit status* (also known variously as the *exit value*, *return code*, and *return value*) is an 8-bit value that the parent can recover when the child exits (in Unix parlance, "when the child dies"). By convention, an exit status of 0 means that the program ran with no problems. Any nonzero exit status indicates some sort of failure; the program determines the values to use and their meanings, if any. (For example, grep uses 0 to mean that it matched the pattern at least once, 1 to mean that it did not match the pattern at all, and 2 to mean that an error occurred.) This exit status is available at the shell level (for Bourne-style shells) in the special variable $?.

The C standard defines two constants, which are all you should use for strict portability to non-POSIX systems:

EXIT_SUCCESS
>   The program exited with no problems. Zero can also be used to mean success.

EXIT_FAILURE
>   The program had some kind of problem.

In practice, using only these values is rather constraining. Instead, you should pick a small set of return codes, document their meanings, and use them. (For example, 1 for command-line option and argument errors, 2 for I/O errors, 3 for bad data errors, and so on.) For readability, it pays to use #defined constants or an enum for them. Having too large a list of errors makes using them cumbersome; most of the time the invoking program (or user) only cares about zero vs. nonzero.

When the binary success/failure distinction is adequate, the pedantic programmer uses EXIT_SUCCESS and EXIT_FAILURE. Our own style is more idiomatic, using the explicit constants 0 or 1 with return and exit(). This is so common that it is learned early on and quickly becomes second nature. However, you should make your own decision for your own projects.

> NOTE   Only the least-significant eight bits of the value are available to the parent process. Thus, you should use values in the range 0–255. As we'll see shortly, `126` and `127` have a conventional meaning (above and beyond plain "unsuccessful"), to which your programs should adhere.
>
> Since only the least-significant eight bits matter, you should *never* use a negative exit status. When the last eight bits are retrieved from small negative numbers, they become large positive values! (For example, –1 becomes 255, and –5 becomes 251.) We have seen C programming books that get this wrong—don't be misled.

9.1.5.2 Returning from `main()`

A program can terminate voluntarily in one of two ways: by using one of the functions described next or by returning from `main()`. (A third, more drastic, way, is described later, in Section 12.4, "Committing Suicide: `abort()`," page 445.) In the latter case, you should use an explicit return value instead of falling off the end of the function:

```
/* Good: */                          /* Bad: */
int main(int argc, char **argv)      int main(int argc, char **argv)
{                                     {
    /* code here */                       /* code here */
    return 0;                             /* ?? What does main() return ?? */
}                                     }
```

The 1999 C standard indicates that when `main()` returns by falling off the end, the behavior is as if it had returned 0. (This is also true for C++; however, the 1989 C standard leaves this case purposely undefined.) In all cases, it's poor practice to rely on this behavior; one day you may be programming for a system with meager C runtime support or an embedded system, or somewhere else where it will make a difference. (In general, falling off the end of any non-`void` function is a bad idea; it can only lead to buggy code.)

The value returned from `main()` is automatically passed back to the system, from which the parent can recover it later. We describe how in Section 9.1.6.1, "Using POSIX Functions: `wait()` and `waitpid()`," page 306.

> NOTE   On GNU/Linux systems, the `c99` compiler-driver command runs the compiler with the appropriate options such that the return value when falling off the end is 0. Plain `gcc` doesn't do this.

9.1.5.3 Exiting Functions

The other way to voluntarily terminate a program is by calling an exiting function. The C standard defines the following functions:

```
#include <stdlib.h>                                      ISO C

void exit(int status);
void _Exit(int status);
int atexit(void (*function)(void));
```

The functions work as follows:

`void exit(int status)`

>   This function terminates the program. `status` is passed to the system for recovery by the parent. Before the program exits, `exit()` calls all functions registered with `atexit()`, flushes and closes all open `<stdio.h>` `FILE *` streams, and removes any temporary files created with `tmpfile()` (see Section 12.3.2, "Creating and Opening Temporary Files (Good)," page 441). When the process exits, the kernel closes any remaining open files (those opened by `open()`, `creat()`, or file descriptor inheritance), frees up its address space, and releases any other resources it may have been using. `exit()` never returns.

`void _Exit(int status)`

>   This function is essentially identical to the POSIX `_exit()` function; we delay discussion of it for a short while.

`int atexit(void (*function)(void))`

>   `function` is a pointer to a callback function to be called at program exit. `exit()` invokes the callback function before it closes files and terminates. The idea is that an application can provide one or more cleanup functions to be run before finally shutting down. Providing a function is called *registering* it. (Callback functions for `nftw()` were described in Section 8.4.3.2, "The `nftw()` Callback Function," page 263; it's the same idea here, although `atexit()` invokes each registered function only once.)
>
>   `atexit()` returns 0 on success or -1 on error, and sets `errno` appropriately.

The following program does no useful work, but it does demonstrate how `atexit()` works:

```
/* ch09-atexit.c --- demonstrate atexit().
                     Error checking omitted for brevity. */

/*
 * The callback functions here just answer roll call.
 * In a real application, they would do more.
 */

void callback1(void) { printf("callback1 called\n"); }
void callback2(void) { printf("callback2 called\n"); }
void callback3(void) { printf("callback3 called\n"); }

/* main --- register functions and then exit */

int main(int argc, char **argv)
{
    printf("registering callback1\n");  atexit(callback1);
    printf("registering callback2\n");  atexit(callback2);
    printf("registering callback3\n");  atexit(callback3);

    printf("exiting now\n");
    exit(0);
}
```

Here's what happens when it's run:

```
$ ch09-atexit
registering callback1                   Main program runs
registering callback2
registering callback3
exiting now
callback3 called                        Callback functions run in reverse order
callback2 called
callback1 called
```

As the example demonstrates, functions registered with atexit() run in the reverse order in which they were registered: most recent one first. (This is also termed *last-in first-out*, abbreviated LIFO.)

POSIX defines the _exit() function. Unlike exit(), which invokes callback functions and does <stdio.h> cleanup, _exit() is the "die immediately" function:

```
#include <unistd.h>                                        POSIX

void _exit(int status);
```

The status is given to the system, just as for exit(), but the process terminates immediately. The kernel still does the usual cleanup: All open files are closed, the memory used by the address space is released, and any other resources the process was using are also released.

In practice, the ISO C `_Exit()` function is identical to `_exit()`. The C standard says it's implementation defined as to whether `_Exit()` calls functions registered with `atexit()` and closes open files. For GLIBC systems, it does not, behaving like `_exit()`.

The time to use `_exit()` is when an exec fails in a forked child. In this case, you *don't* want to use regular `exit()`, since that flushes any buffered data held by `FILE *` streams. When the parent later flushes its copies of the buffers, the buffered data ends up being written *twice*; obviously this is not good.

For example, suppose you wish to run a shell command and do the fork and exec yourself. Such code would look like this:

```
char *shellcommand = "...";
pid_t child;

if ((child = fork()) == 0) {   /* child */
    execl("/bin/sh", "sh", "-c", shellcommand, NULL);
    _exit(errno == ENOENT ? 127 : 126);
}
/* parent continues */
```

The `errno` test and exit values follow conventions used by the POSIX shell. If a requested program doesn't exist (`ENOENT`—no entry for it in a directory), then the exit value is `127`. Otherwise, the file exists but couldn't be exec'd for some other reason, so the exit status is `126`. It's a good idea to follow this convention in your own programs too.

Briefly, to make good use of `exit()` and `atexit()`, you should do the following:

- Define a small set of exit status values that your program will use to communicate information to its caller. Use `#defined` constants or an `enum` for them in your code.

- Decide if having callback functions for use with `atexit()` makes sense. If it does, register them in `main()` at the appropriate point; for example, after parsing options, and after initializing whatever data structures the callback functions are supposed to clean up. Remember that the functions are called in LIFO (last-in first-out) order.

- Use `exit()` everywhere to exit from the program when something goes wrong, and exiting is the correct action to take. Use the error codes that you defined.

- An exception is `main()`, for which you can use `return` if you wish. Our own style is generally to use `exit()` when there are problems and 'return 0' at the end of `main()` if everything has gone well.

- Use `_exit()` or `_Exit()` in a child process if `exec()` fails.

9.1.6 Recovering a Child's Exit Status

When a process dies, the normal course of action is for the kernel to release all its resources. The kernel does retain the dead process's exit status, as well as information about the resources it used during its lifetime, and the PID continues to be counted as being in use. Such a dead process is termed a *zombie*.

The parent process, be it the original parent or `init`, can recover the child's exit status. Or, by use of BSD functions that aren't standardized by POSIX, the exit status together with the resource usage information can be recovered. Status recovery is done by waiting for the process to die: This is also known as *reaping* the process.[2]

There is considerable interaction between the mechanisms that wait for children to die and the signal mechanisms we haven't described yet. Which one to describe first is a bit of a chicken-and-egg problem; we've chosen to talk about the child-waiting mechanisms first, and Chapter 10, "Signals," page 347, provides the full story on signals.

For now, it's enough to understand that a signal is a way to notify a process that some event has occurred. Processes can generate signals that get sent to themselves, or signals can be sent externally by other processes or by a user at a terminal. For example, CTRL-C sends an "interrupt" signal, and CTRL-Z sends a job control "stop" signal.

By default, many signals, such as the interrupt signal, cause the receiving process to die. Others, such as the job control signals, cause it to change state. The child waiting mechanisms can determine whether a process suffered death-by-signal, and, if so, which signal it was. The same is true for processes stopping and, on some systems, when a process continues.

---

[2] We are not making this up. The terminology is indeed rather morbid, but such was the original Unix designers' sense of humor.

9.1.6.1 Using POSIX Functions: `wait()` and `waitpid()`

The original V7 system call was `wait()`. The newer POSIX call, based on BSD functionality, is `waitpid()`. The function declarations are:

```
#include <sys/types.h>                               POSIX
#include <sys/wait.h>

pid_t wait(int *status);
pid_t waitpid(pid_t pid, int *status, int options);
```

`wait()` waits for *any* child process to die; the information as to how it died is returned in `*status`. (We discuss how to interpret `*status` shortly.) The return value is the PID of the process that died or -1 if an error occurred.

If there is no child process, `wait()` returns -1 with `errno` set to `ECHILD` (no child process). Otherwise, it waits for the first child to die or for a signal to come in.

The `waitpid()` function lets you wait for a specific child process to exit. It provides considerable flexibility and is the preferred function to use. It too returns the PID of the process that died or -1 if an error occurred. The arguments are as follows:

`pid_t pid`

    The value specifies which child to wait for, both by real `pid` and by process group. The `pid` value has the following meanings:

    `pid < −1`   Wait for any child process with a process group ID equal to the absolute value of `pid`.

    `pid = −1`   Wait for any child process. This is the way `wait()` works.

    `pid = 0`   Wait for any child process with a process group ID equal to that of the parent process's process group.

    `pid > 0`   Wait for the specific process with the PID equal to `pid`.

`int *status`

    This is the same as for `wait()`. `<sys/wait.h>` defines various macros that interpret the value in `*status`, which we describe soon.

`int options`

    This should be either `0` or the bitwise OR of one or more of the following flags:

WNOHANG

> If no child has exited, return immediately. That way you can check periodically to see if any children have died. (Such periodic checking is known as *polling* for an event.)

WUNTRACED

> Return information about a child process that has stopped but that hasn't exited yet. (For example, with job control.)

WCONTINUED

> (XSI.) Return information about a child process that has continued if the status of the child has not been reported since it changed. This too is for job control. This flag is an XSI extension and is not available under GNU/Linux.

Multiple macros work on the filled-in *status value to determine what happened. They tend to come in pairs: one macro to determine if something occurred, and if that macro is true, one or more macros that retrieve the details. The macros are as follows:

WIFEXITED(status)

> This macro is nonzero (true) if the process exited (as opposed to changing state).

WEXITSTATUS(status)

> This macro gives the exit status; it equals the least-significant eight bits of the value passed to exit() or returned from main(). You should use this macro only if WIFEXITED(status) is true.

WIFSIGNALED(status)

> This macro is nonzero if the process suffered death-by-signal.

WTERMSIG(status)

> This macro provides the signal number that terminated the process. You should use this macro only if WIFSIGNALED(status) is true.

WIFSTOPPED(status)

> This macro is nonzero if the process was stopped.

WSTOPSIG(status)

> This macro provides the signal number that stopped the process. (Several signals can stop a process.) You should use this macro only if WIFSTOPPED(status) is

true. Job control signals are discussed in Section 10.8.2, "Job Control Signals," page 383.

`WIFCONTINUED(status)`

(XSI.) This macro is nonzero if the process was continued. There is no corresponding `WCONTSIG()` macro, since only one signal can cause a process to continue.

Note that this macro is an XSI extension. In particular, it is *not* available on GNU/Linux. Therefore, if you wish to use it, bracket your code inside '`#ifdef WIFCONTINUED ... #endif`'.

`WCOREDUMP(status)`

(Common.) This macro is nonzero if the process dumped core. A *core dump* is the memory image of a running process created when the process terminates. It is intended for use later for debugging. Unix systems name the file `core`, whereas GNU/Linux systems use `core.`*pid*, where *pid* is the process ID of the process that died. Certain signals terminate a process and produce a core dump automatically.

Note that this macro is nonstandard. GNU/Linux, Solaris, and BSD systems support it, but some other Unix systems do not. Thus, here too, if you wish to use it, bracket your code inside '`#ifdef WCOREDUMP ... #endif`'.

Most programs don't care *why* a child process died; they merely care *that* it died, perhaps noting if it exited successfully or not. The GNU Coreutils `install` program demonstrates such straightforward use of `fork()`, `execlp()`, and `wait()`. The `-s` option causes `install` to run the `strip` program on the binary executable being installed. (`strip` removes debugging and other information from an executable file. This can save considerable space, relatively speaking. On modern systems with multi-gigabyte disk drives, it's rarely necessary to strip executables upon installation.) Here is the `strip()` function from `install.c`:

```
513    /* Strip the symbol table from the file PATH.
514       We could dig the magic number out of the file first to
515       determine whether to strip it, but the header files and
516       magic numbers vary so much from system to system that making
517       it portable would be very difficult.  Not worth the effort. */
518
```

```
519   static void
520   strip (const char *path)
521   {
522     int status;
523     pid_t pid = fork ();
524
525     switch (pid)
526       {
527       case -1:
528         error (EXIT_FAILURE, errno, _("fork system call failed"));
529         break;
530       case 0:                        /* Child. */
531         execlp ("strip", "strip", path, NULL);
532         error (EXIT_FAILURE, errno, _("cannot run strip"));
533         break;
534       default:                       /* Parent. */
535         /* Parent process. */
536         while (pid != wait (&status)) /* Wait for kid to finish. */
537           /* Do nothing. */ ;
538         if (status)
539           error (EXIT_FAILURE, 0, _("strip failed"));
540         break;
541       }
542   }
```

Line 523 calls `fork()`. The `switch` statement then takes the correct action for error return (lines 527–529), child process (lines 530–533), and parent process (lines 534–539).

The idiom on lines 536–537 is common; it waits until the specific child of interest exits. `wait()`'s return value is the PID of the reaped child. This is compared with that of the forked child. `status` is unused other than to see if it's nonzero (line 538), in which case the child exited unsuccessfully. (The test, while correct, is coarse but simple. A test like '`if (WIFEXITED(status) && WEXITSTATUS(status) != 0)`' would be more pedantically correct.)

From the description and code presented so far, it may appear that parent programs must choose a specific point to wait for any child processes to die, possibly polling in a loop (as `install.c` does), waiting for all children. In Section 10.8.3, "Parental Supervision: Three Different Strategies," page 385, we'll see that this is not necessarily the case. Rather, signals provide a range of mechanisms to use for managing parent notification when a child process dies.

9.1.6.2 Using BSD Functions: `wait3()` and `wait4()`

The BSD `wait3()` and `wait4()` system calls are useful if you're interested in the resources used by a child process. They are nonstandard (meaning not part of POSIX) but widely available, including on GNU/Linux. The declarations are as follows:

```
#include <sys/types.h>                                              Common
#include <sys/time.h>          Not needed under GNU/Linux, but improves portability
#include <sys/resource.h>
#include <sys/wait.h>

pid_t wait3(int *status, int options, struct rusage *rusage);
pid_t wait4(pid_t pid, int *status, int options, struct rusage *rusage);
```

The `status` variable is the same as for `wait()` and `waitpid()`. All the macros described earlier (`WIFEXITED()`, etc.) can also be used with it.

The `options` value is also the same as for `waitpid()`: either `0` or the bitwise OR of one or both of `WNOHANG` and `WUNTRACED`.

`wait3()` behaves like `wait()`, retrieving information about the first available zombie child, and `wait4()` is like `waitpid()`, retrieving information about a particular process. Both return the PID of the reaped child, `-1` on error, or `0` if no process is available and `WNOHANG` was used. The `pid` argument can take on the same values as the `pid` argument for `waitpid()`.

The key difference is the `struct rusage` pointer. If not `NULL`, the system fills it in with information about the process. This structure is described in POSIX and in the *getrusage*(2) manpage:

```
struct rusage {
    struct timeval ru_utime; /* user time used */
    struct timeval ru_stime; /* system time used */
    long   ru_maxrss;        /* maximum resident set size */
    long   ru_ixrss;         /* integral shared memory size */
    long   ru_idrss;         /* integral unshared data size */
    long   ru_isrss;         /* integral unshared stack size */
    long   ru_minflt;        /* page reclaims */
    long   ru_majflt;        /* page faults */
    long   ru_nswap;         /* swaps */
    long   ru_inblock;       /* block input operations */
    long   ru_oublock;       /* block output operations */
    long   ru_msgsnd;        /* messages sent */
    long   ru_msgrcv;        /* messages received */
    long   ru_nsignals;      /* signals received */
    long   ru_nvcsw;         /* voluntary context switches */
    long   ru_nivcsw;        /* involuntary context switches */
};
```

Pure BSD systems (4.3 Reno and later) support all of the fields. Table 9.2 describes the availability of the various fields in the `struct rusage` for POSIX and Linux.

TABLE 9.2
Availability of `struct rusage` fields

Field	POSIX	Linux		Field	POSIX	Linux
ru_utime	✓	≥ 2.4		ru_nswap		≥ 2.4
ru_stime	✓	≥ 2.4		ru_nvcsw		≥ 2.6
ru_minflt		≥ 2.4		ru_nivcsw		≥ 2.6
ru_majflt		≥ 2.4				

Only the fields marked "POSIX" are defined by the standard. While Linux defines the full structure, the 2.4 kernel maintains only the user-time and system-time fields. The 2.6 kernel also maintains the fields related to context switching.[3]

The fields of most interest are `ru_utime` and `ru_stime`, the user and system CPU times, respectively. (User CPU time is time spent executing user-level code. System CPU time is time spent in the kernel on behalf of the process.)

These two fields use a `struct timeval`, which maintains time values down to microsecond intervals. See Section 14.3.1, "Microsecond Times: `gettimeofday()`," page 544, for more information on this structure.

In 4.2 and 4.3 BSD, the `status` argument to `wait()` and `wait3()` was a `union wait`. It fit into an `int` and provided access to the same information as the modern `WIFEXITED()` etc. macros do, but through the union's members. Not all members were valid in all situations. The members and their uses are described in Table 9.3.

POSIX doesn't standardize the `union wait`, and 4.4 BSD doesn't document it, instead using the POSIX macros. GLIBC jumps through several hoops to make old code using it continue to work. We describe it here primarily so that you'll recognize it if you see it; new code should use the macros described in Section 9.1.6.1, "Using POSIX Functions: `wait()` and `waitpid()`," page 306.

---

[3] Double-check the *getrusage*(2) manpage if your kernel is newer, because this behavior may have changed.

TABLE 9.3
The 4.2 and 4.3 BSD `union wait`

POSIX macro	Union member	Usage	Meaning
`WIFEXITED()`	`w_termsig`	`w.w_termsig == 0`	True if normal exit.
`WEXITSTATUS()`	`w_retcode`	`code = w.w_retcode`	Exit status if not by signal.
`WIFSIGNALED()`	`w_termsig`	`w.w_termsig != 0`	True if death by signal.
`WTERMSIG()`	`w_termsig`	`sig = w.w_termsig`	Signal that caused termination.
`WIFSTOPPED()`	`w_stopval`	`w.w_stopval == WSTOPPED`	True if stopped.
`WSTOPSIG()`	`w_stopsig`	`sig = w.w_stopsig`	Signal that caused stopping.
`WCOREDUMP()`	`w_coredump`	`w.w_coredump != 0`	True if child dumped core.

9.2 Process Groups

A *process group* is a group of related processes that should be treated together for job control purposes. Processes with the same process group ID are members of the process group, and the process whose PID is the same as the process group ID is the *process group leader*. New processes inherit the process group ID of their parent process.

We have already seen that `waitpid()` allows you to wait for any process in a given process group. In Section 10.6.7, "Sending Signals: `kill()` and `killpg()`," page 376, we'll also see that you can send a signal to all the processes in a particular process group as well. (Permission checking always applies; you can't send a signal to a process you don't own.)

9.2.1 Job Control Overview

Job control is an involved topic, one that we've chosen not to delve into for this volume. However, here's a quick conceptual overview.

The terminal device (physical or otherwise) with a user working at it is called the *controlling terminal*.

A *session* is a collection of process groups associated with the controlling terminal. There is only one session per terminal, with multiple process groups in the session. One process is designated the *session leader*; this is normally a shell that can do job control, such as Bash, `pdksh`, `zsh`, or `ksh93`.[4] We refer to such a shell as a *job control shell*.

Each job started by a job control shell, be it a single program or a pipeline, receives a separate process group identifier. That way, the shell can manipulate the job as a single entity, although it may have multiple processes.

The controlling terminal also has a process group identifier associated with it. When a user types a special character such as CTRL-C for "interrupt" or CTRL-Z for "stop," the kernel sends the given signal to the processes in the terminal's process group.

The process group whose process group ID is the same as that of the controlling terminal is allowed to read from and write to the terminal. This is called the *foreground process group*. (It also receives the keyboard-generated signals.) Any other process groups in the session are *background process groups* and cannot read from or write to the terminal; they receive special signals that stop them if they try.

Jobs move in and out of the foreground, *not* by a change to an attribute of the job, but rather by a change to the controlling terminal's process group. It is the job control shell that makes this change, and if the new process group was stopped, the shell continues it by sending a "continue" signal to all members of the process group.

In days of yore, users often used serial terminals connected to modems to dial in to centralized minicomputer Unix systems. When the user closed the connection (hung up the phone), the serial line detected the disconnection and the kernel sent a "hangup" signal to all processes connected to the terminal.

This concept remains: If a hangup occurs (serial hardware does still exist and is still in use), the kernel sends the hangup signal to the foreground process group. If the session leader exits, the same thing happens.

An *orphaned process group* is one where, for every process in the group, that process's parent is also in the group or the parent is in a different session. (This can happen if a job control shell exits with background jobs running.) Running processes in an orphaned process group are allowed to run to completion. If there are any already stopped processes in an orphaned process group when it becomes orphaned, the kernel sends those

---

[4] Well, `csh` and `tcsh` can be included in this category too, but we prefer Bourne-style shells.

processes a hangup signal and then a continue signal. This causes them to wake up so that they can exit instead of remaining stopped forever.

9.2.2 Process Group Identification: `getpgrp()` and `getpgid()`

For compatibility with older systems, POSIX provides multiple ways to retrieve process group information:

```
#include <unistd.h>

pid_t getpgrp(void);                                              POSIX
pid_t getpgid(pid_t pid);                                         XSI
```

The `getpgrp()` function returns the current process's process group ID. `getpgid()` is an XSI extension. It returns the process group ID of the given process `pid`. A `pid` of `0` means "the current process's process group." Thus `getpgid(0)` is the same as `getpgrp()`. For general programming, `getpgrp()` should be used.

4.2 and 4.3 BSD also have a `getpgrp()` function, but it acts like the POSIX `getpgid()` function, requiring a `pid` argument. Since modern systems support POSIX, you should use the POSIX version in new code. (If you think this is confusing, you're right. Multiple ways to do the same thing are a normal result of design-by-committee, since the committee feels that it must please everyone.)

9.2.3 Process Group Setting: `setpgid()` and `setpgrp()`

Two functions set the process group:

```
#include <unistd.h>

int setpgid(pid_t pid, pid_t pgid);                               POSIX
int setpgrp(void);                                                XSI
```

The `setpgrp()` function is simple: It sets the process group ID to be the same as the process ID. Doing so creates a new process group in the same session, and the calling process becomes the process group leader.

The `setpgid()` function is intended for job control use. It allows one process to set the process group of another. A process may change only its own process group ID or the process group ID of a child process, and then only if that child process has not yet done an exec. Job control shells make this call after the fork, in *both* the parent and the child. For one of them the call succeeds, and the process group ID is changed. (Otherwise, there's no way to guarantee the ordering, such that the parent could change the child's process group ID before the child execs. If the parent's call succeeds first, it can move on to the next task, such as manipulating other jobs or the terminal.)

With `setpgid()`, `pgid` must be an existing process group that is part of the current session, effectively joining `pid` to that process group. Otherwise, `pgid` must be equal to `pid`, creating a new process group.

There are some special case values for both `pid` and `pgid`:

pid = 0   In this case, `setpgid()` changes the process group of the calling process to `pgid`. It's equivalent to '`setpgid(getpid(), pgid)`'.

pgid = 0   This sets the process group ID for the given process to be the same as its PID. Thus, '`setpgid(pid, 0)`' is the same as '`setpgid(pid, pid)`'. This causes the process with PID `pid` to become a process group leader.

In all cases, session leaders are special; their PID, process group ID, and session ID values are all identical, and the process group ID of a session leader cannot be changed. (Session IDs are set with `setsid()` and retrieved with `getsid()`. These are specialized calls: see the *setsid*(2) and *getsid*(2) manpages.)

9.3 Basic Interprocess Communication: Pipes and FIFOs

Interprocess communication (IPC) is what it sounds like: a way for two separate processes to communicate. The oldest IPC mechanism on Unix systems is the *pipe*: a one-way communication channel. Data written into one end of the channel come out the other end.

9.3.1 Pipes

Pipes manifest themselves as regular file descriptors. Without going to special lengths, you can't tell if a file descriptor is a file or a pipe. This is a feature; programs that read standard input and write standard output don't have to know or care that they may be communicating with another process. Should you need to know, the canonical way to check is to attempt '`lseek(fd, 0L, SEEK_CUR)`' on the file descriptor; this call attempts to seek zero bytes from the current position, that is, a do-nothing operation.[5] This operation fails for pipes and does no damage for other files.

---

[5] Such an operation is often referred to as a *no-op*, short for "no operation."

9.3.1.1 Creating Pipes

The `pipe()` system call creates a pipe:

```
#include <unistd.h>                                          POSIX

int pipe(int filedes[2]);
```

The argument value is the address of a two-element integer array. `pipe()` returns 0 upon success and -1 if there was an error.

If the call was successful, the process now has two additional open file descriptors. The value in `filedes[0]` is the *read end* of the pipe, and `filedes[1]` is the *write end*. (A handy mnemonic device is that the read end uses index 0, analogous to standard input being file descriptor 0, and the write end uses index 1, analogous to standard output being file descriptor 1.)

As mentioned, data written into the write end are read from the read end. When you're done with a pipe, you close both ends with a call to `close()`. The following simple program, `ch09-pipedemo.c`, demonstrates pipes by creating one, writing data to it, and then reading the data back from it:

```
1   /* ch09-pipedemo.c --- demonstrate I/O with a pipe. */
2
3   #include <stdio.h>
4   #include <errno.h>
5   #include <unistd.h>
6
7   /* main --- create a pipe, write to it, and read from it. */
8
9   int main(int argc, char **argv)
10  {
11      static const char mesg[] = "Don't Panic!";  /* a famous message */
12      char buf[BUFSIZ];
13      ssize_t rcount, wcount;
14      int pipefd[2];
15      size_t l;
16
17      if (pipe(pipefd) < 0) {
18          fprintf(stderr, "%s: pipe failed: %s\n", argv[0],
19              strerror(errno));
20          exit(1);
21      }
22
23      printf("Read end = fd %d, write end = fd %d\n",
24          pipefd[0], pipefd[1]);
25
```

```
26        l = strlen(mesg);
27        if ((wcount = write(pipefd[1], mesg, l)) != l) {
28            fprintf(stderr, "%s: write failed: %s\n", argv[0],
29                strerror(errno));
30            exit(1);
31        }
32
33        if ((rcount = read(pipefd[0], buf, BUFSIZ)) != wcount) {
34            fprintf(stderr, "%s: read failed: %s\n", argv[0],
35                strerror(errno));
36            exit(1);
37        }
38
39        buf[rcount] = '\0';
40
41        printf("Read <%s> from pipe\n", buf);
42        (void) close(pipefd[0]);
43        (void) close(pipefd[1]);
44
45        return 0;
46   }
```

Lines 11–15 declare local variables; of most interest is mesg, which is the text that will traverse the pipe.

Lines 17–21 create the pipe, with error checking; lines 23–24 print the values of the new file descriptors (just to prove that they won't be 0, 1, or 2).

Line 26 gets the length of the message, to use with write(). Lines 27–31 write the message down the pipe, again with error checking.

Lines 33–37 read the contents of the pipe, again with error checking.

Line 39 supplies a terminating zero byte, so that the read data can be used as a regular string. Line 41 prints the data, and lines 42–43 close both ends of the pipe. Here's what happens when the program runs:

```
$ ch09-pipedemo
Read end = fd 3, write end = fd 4
Read <Don't Panic!> from pipe
```

This program doesn't do anything useful, but it does demonstrate the basics. Note that there are no calls to open() or creat() and that the program isn't using its three inherited file descriptors. Yet the write() and read() succeed, proving that the file descriptors are valid and that data that go into the pipe do come out of it.[6] Of course,

---

[6] We're sure you weren't worried. After all, you probably use pipelines from the shell dozens of times a day.

had the message been too big, our program wouldn't have worked. This is because pipes have only so much room in them, a fact we discuss in the next section.

Like other file descriptors, those for a pipe are inherited by a child after a fork and if not closed, are still available after an exec. We see shortly how to make use of this fact and do something interesting with pipes.

9.3.1.2 Pipe Buffering

Pipes *buffer* their data, meaning that data written to the pipe are held by the kernel until they are read. However, a pipe can hold only so much written but not yet read data. We can call the writing process the *producer*, and the reading process the *consumer*. How does the system manage full and empty pipes?

When the pipe is full, the system automatically *blocks* the producer the next time it attempts to `write()` data into the pipe. Once the pipe empties out, the system copies the data into the pipe and then allows the `write()` system call to return to the producer.

Similarly, if the pipe is empty, the consumer blocks in the `read()` until there is more data in the pipe to be read. (The blocking behavior can be turned off; this is discussed in Section 9.4.3.4, "Nonblocking I/O for Pipes and FIFOs," page 333.)

When the producer does a `close()` on the pipe's write end, the consumer can successfully read any data still buffered in the pipe. After that, further calls to `read()` return `0`, indicating end of file.

Conversely, if the consumer closes the read end, a `write()` to the write end fails—drastically. In particular, the kernel sends the producer a "broken pipe" signal, whose default action is to terminate the process.

Our favorite analogy for pipes is that of a husband and wife washing and drying dishes together. One spouse washes the dishes, placing the clean but wet plates into a dish drainer by the sink. The other spouse takes the dishes from the drainer and dries them. The dish washer is the producer, the dish drainer is the pipe, and the dish dryer is the consumer.[7]

If the drying spouse is faster than the washing one, the drainer becomes empty, and the dryer has to wait until more dishes are available. Conversely, if the washing spouse

---

[7] What they ate for dinner is left unspecified.

is faster, then the drainer becomes full, and the washer has to wait until it empties out before putting more clean dishes into it. This is depicted in Figure 9.3.

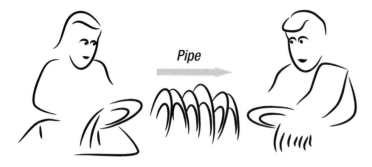

Pipe

FIGURE 9.3
Synchronization of pipe processes

9.3.2 FIFOs

With traditional pipes, the only way for two separate programs to have access to the same pipe is through file descriptor inheritance. This means that the processes must be the children of a common parent or one must be an ancestor of the other.

This can be a severe limitation. Many system services run as *daemons*, disconnected long-running processes. There needs to be an easy way to send data to such processes (and possibly receive data from them). Files are inappropriate for this; synchronization is difficult or impossible, and pipes can't be created to do the job, since there are no common ancestors.

To solve this problem, System III invented the notion of a FIFO. A *FIFO*,[8] or *named pipe*, is a file in the filesystem that acts like a pipe. In other words, one process opens the FIFO for writing, while another opens it for reading. Data then written to the FIFO are read by the reader. The data are buffered by the kernel, not stored on disk.

Consider a line printer spooler. The spooler daemon controls the physical printers, creating print jobs that print one by one. To add a job to the queue, user-level line-printer software has to communicate with the spooler daemon. One way to do this is for the spooler to create a FIFO with a well-known filename. The user software can

---

[8] FIFO is an acronym for "first in first out." This is the way pipes work.

then open the FIFO, write a request to it, and close it. The spooler sits in a loop, reading requests from the FIFO and processing them.

The `mkfifo()` function creates FIFO files:

```
#include <sys/types.h>                                           POSIX
#include <sys/stat.h>

int mkfifo(const char *pathname, mode_t mode);
```

The `pathname` argument is the name of the FIFO file to create, and `mode` is the permissions to give it, analogous to the second argument to `creat()` or the third argument to `open()` (see Section 4.6, "Creating Files," page 106). FIFO files are removed like any other, with `remove()` or `unlink()` (see Section 5.1.5.1, "Removing Open Files," page 127).

The GNU/Linux *mkfifo*(3) manpage points out that the FIFO must be open both for reading and writing at the same time, before I/O can be done: "Opening a FIFO for reading normally blocks until some other process opens the same FIFO for writing, and vice versa." Once a FIFO file is opened, it acts like a regular pipe; that is, it's just another file descriptor.

The `mkfifo` command brings this system call to the command level. This makes it easy to show a FIFO file in action:

```
$ mkfifo afifo                    Create a FIFO file
$ ls -l afifo                     Show type and permissions, note leading 'p'
prw-r--r--    1 arnold    devel    0 Oct 23 15:49 afifo
$ cat < afifo &                   Start a reader in the background
[1] 22100
$ echo It was a Blustery Day > afifo    Send data to FIFO
$ It was a Blustery Day           Shell prompts, cat prints data
                                  Press ENTER to see job exit status
[1]+  Done                cat <afifo      cat exited
```

9.4 File Descriptor Management

At this point, the pieces of the puzzle are almost complete. `fork()` and `exec()` create processes and run programs in them. `pipe()` creates a pipe that can be used for IPC. What's still missing is a way to move the pipe's file descriptors into place as standard output and standard input for a pipeline's producer and consumer.

The `dup()` and `dup2()` system calls, together with `close()`, let you move (well, copy) an open file descriptor to another number. The `fcntl()` system call lets you do the same thing and manipulate several important attributes of open files.

9.4.1 Duplicating Open Files: dup() and dup2()

Two system calls create a copy of an open file descriptor:

```
#include <unistd.h>
```
POSIX

```
int dup(int oldfd);
int dup2(int oldfd, int newfd);
```

The functions are as follows:

int dup(int oldfd)

Returns the lowest unused file descriptor value; it is a copy of oldfd. dup() returns a nonnegative integer on success or -1 on failure.

int dup2(int oldfd, int newfd)

Makes newfd be a copy of oldfd; if newfd is open, it's closed first, as if by close(). dup2() returns the new descriptor or -1 if there was a problem.

Remember Figure 9.1, in which two processes shared pointers to the same file entry in the kernel's file table? Well, dup() and dup2() create the same situation, within a single process. See Figure 9.4.

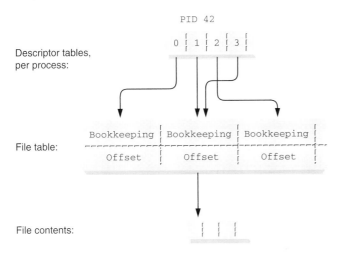

FIGURE 9.4
File descriptor sharing after 'dup2(1, 3)'

In this figure, the process executed 'dup2(1, 3)' to make file descriptor 3 a copy of standard output, file descriptor 1. Exactly as described before, the two descriptors share the file offset for the open file.

In Section 4.4.2, "Opening and Closing Files," page 93, we mentioned that `open()`
(and `creat()`) *always* returns the lowest unused integer file descriptor value for the file
being opened. Almost all system calls that return new file descriptors follow this rule,
not just `open()` and `creat()`. (`dup2()` is an exception since it provides a way to get
a particular new file descriptor, even if it's not the lowest unused one.)

Given the "return lowest unused number" rule combined with `dup()`, it's now easy
to move a pipe's file descriptors into place as standard input and output. Assuming that
the current process is a shell and that it needs to fork two children to set up a simple
two-stage pipeline, here are the steps:

1. Create the pipe with `pipe()`. This must be done first so that the two children
    can inherit the open file descriptors.

2. Fork what we'll call the "left-hand child." This is the one whose standard output
    goes down the pipe. In this child, do the following:

    a. Use '`close(pipefd[0])`' since the read end of the pipe isn't needed in
        the left-hand child.

    b. Use '`close(1)`' to close the original standard output.

    c. Use '`dup(pipefd[1])`' to copy the write end of the pipe to file descriptor 1.

    d. Use '`close(pipefd[1])`' since we don't need two copies of the open
        descriptor.

    e. Exec the program to be run.

3. Fork what we'll call the "right-hand child." This is the one whose standard input
    comes from the pipe. The steps in this child are the mirror image of those in
    the left-hand child:

    a. Use '`close(pipefd[1])`' since the write end of the pipe isn't needed in
        the right-hand child.

    b. Use '`close(0)`' to close the original standard input.

    c. Use '`dup(pipefd[0])`' to copy the read end of the pipe to file descriptor 0.

    d. Use '`close(pipefd[0])`' since we don't need two copies of the open
        descriptor.

    e. Exec the program to be run.

4. In the parent, close both ends of the pipe: `close(pipefd[0]); close(pipefd[1])`.

5. Finally, use `wait()` in the parent to wait for both children to finish.

Note how important it is to close the unused copies of the pipe's file descriptors. As we pointed out earlier, a file isn't closed until the last open file descriptor for it is closed. This is true even though multiple processes share the file descriptors. Closing unused file descriptors matters because the process reading from the pipe won't get an end-of-file indication until *all* the copies of the write end have been closed.

In our case, after the two children are forked, there are three processes, each of which has copies of the two pipe file descriptors: the parent and the two children. The parent closes both ends since it doesn't need the pipe. The left-hand child is writing down the pipe, so it has to close the read end. The right-hand child is reading from the pipe, so it has to close the write end. This leaves exactly one copy of each file descriptor open.

When the left-hand child finishes, it exits. The system then closes all of its file descriptors. When that happens, the right-hand child finally receives the end-of-file notification, and it too can then finish up and exit.

The following program, `ch09-pipeline.c`, creates the equivalent of the following shell pipeline:

```
$ echo hi there | sed s/hi/hello/g
hello there
```

Here's the program:

```
1   /* ch09-pipeline.c --- fork two processes into their own pipeline.
2                          Minimal error checking for brevity. */
3
4   #include <stdio.h>
5   #include <errno.h>
6   #include <sys/types.h>
7   #include <sys/wait.h>
8   #include <unistd.h>
9
10  int pipefd[2];
11
12  extern void left_child(void), right_child(void);
13
14  /* main --- fork children, wait for them to finish */
15
```

```
16  int main(int argc, char **argv)
17  {
18      pid_t left_pid, right_pid;
19      pid_t ret;
20      int status;
21
22      if (pipe(pipefd) < 0) {          /* create pipe, very first thing */
23          perror("pipe");
24          exit(1);
25      }
26
27      if ((left_pid = fork()) < 0) {   /* fork left-hand child */
28          perror("fork");
29          exit(1);
30      } else if (left_pid == 0)
31          left_child();
32
33      if ((right_pid = fork()) < 0) {  /* fork right-hand child */
34          perror("fork");
35          exit(1);
36      } else if (right_pid == 0)
37          right_child();
38
39      close(pipefd[0]);                /* close parent's copy of pipe */
40      close(pipefd[1]);
41
42      while ((ret = wait(& status)) > 0) {    /* wait for children */
43          if (ret == left_pid)
44              printf("left child terminated, status: %x\n", status);
45          else if (ret == right_pid)
46              printf("right child terminated, status: %x\n", status);
47          else
48              printf("yow! unknown child %d terminated, status %x\n",
49                  ret, status);
50      }
51
52      return 0;
53  }
```

Lines 22–25 create the pipe. This has to be done first.

Lines 27–31 create the left-hand child, and lines 33–37 create the right-hand child. In both instances, the parent continues a linear execution path through `main()` while the child calls the appropriate function to manipulate file descriptors and do the exec.

Lines 39–40 close the parent's copy of the pipe.

Lines 42–50 loop, reaping children, until `wait()` returns an error.

```
55  /* left_child --- do the work for the left child */
56
57  void left_child(void)
58  {
59      static char *left_argv[]  = { "echo", "hi", "there", NULL };
60
61      close(pipefd[0]);
62      close(1);
63      dup(pipefd[1]);
64      close(pipefd[1]);
65
66      execvp("echo", left_argv);
67      _exit(errno == ENOENT ? 127 : 126);
68  }
69
70  /* right_child --- do the work for the right child */
71
72  void right_child(void)
73  {
74      static char *right_argv[] = { "sed", "s/hi/hello/g", NULL };
75
76      close(pipefd[1]);
77      close(0);
78      dup(pipefd[0]);
79      close(pipefd[0]);
80
81      execvp("sed", right_argv);
82      _exit(errno == ENOENT ? 127 : 126);
83  }
```

Lines 57–68 are the code for the left-hand child. The procedure follows the steps given above to close the unneeded end of the pipe, close the original standard output, dup() the pipe's write end to 1, and then close the original write end. At that point, line 66 calls execvp(), and if it fails, line 67 calls _exit(). (Remember that line 67 is never executed if execvp() succeeds.)

Lines 72–83 do the similar steps for the right-hand child. Here's what happens when it runs:

```
$ ch09-pipeline                        Run the program
left child terminated, status: 0       Left child finishes before output (!)
hello there                            Output from right child
right child terminated, status: 0
$ ch09-pipeline                        Run the program again
hello there                            Output from right child and ...
right child terminated, status: 0      Right child finishes before left one
left child terminated, status: 0
```

Note that the order in which the children finish isn't deterministic. It depends on the system load and many other factors that can influence process scheduling. You should be careful to avoid making ordering assumptions when you write code that creates multiple processes, particularly the code that calls one of the `wait()` family of functions.

The whole process is illustrated in Figure 9.5.

Figure 9.5 (a) depicts the situation after the parent has created the pipe (lines 22–25) and the two children (lines 27–37).

Figure 9.5 (b) shows the situation after the parent has closed the pipe (lines 39–40) and started to wait for the children (lines 42–50). Each child has moved the pipe into place as standard output (left child, lines 61–63) and standard input (lines 76–78).

Finally, Figure 9.5 (c) depicts the situation after the children have closed off the original pipe (lines 64 and 79) and called `execvp()` (lines 66 and 81).

9.4.2 Creating Nonlinear Pipelines: /dev/fd/XX

Many modern Unix systems, including GNU/Linux, support special files in the `/dev/fd` directory.[9] These files represent open file descriptors, with names such as `/dev/fd/0`, `/dev/fd/1`, and so on. Passing such a name to `open()` returns a new file descriptor that is effectively the same as calling `dup()` on the given file descriptor number.

These special files find their use at the shell level: The Bash, `ksh88` (some versions) and `ksh93` shells supply a feature called *process substitution* that makes it possible to create *nonlinear* pipelines. The notation at the shell level is '`<(...)`' for input pipelines, and '`>(...)`' for output pipelines. For example, suppose you wish to apply the `diff` command to the output of two commands. You would normally have to use temporary files:

```
command1 > /tmp/out.$$.1
command2 > /tmp/out.$$.2
diff /tmp/out.$$.1 /tmp/out.$$.2
rm /tmp/out.$$.1 /tmp/out.$$.2
```

With process substitution, it looks like this:

---

[9] On GNU/Linux systems, `/dev/fd` is a symbolic link to `/proc/self/fd`, but since `/dev/fd` is the common place, that's what you should use in your code.

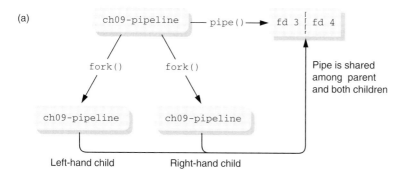

(a)

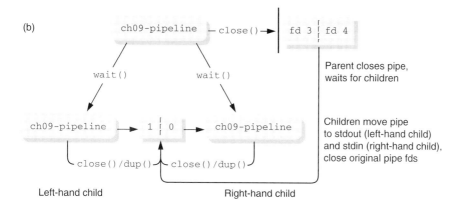

(b)

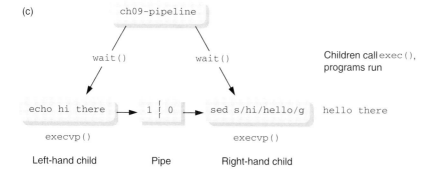

(c)

FIGURE 9.5
Parent creating a pipeline

```
diff <(command1) <(command2)
```

No messy temporary files to remember to clean up. For example, the following command shows that our home directory is a symbolic link to a different directory:

```
$ diff <(pwd) <(/bin/pwd)
1c1
< /home/arnold/work/prenhall/progex
---
> /d/home/arnold/work/prenhall/progex
```

The plain `pwd` is the one built in to the shell: It prints the current logical pathname as managed by the shell with `cd`. The `/bin/pwd` program does a physical filesystem walk to print the pathname.

How does process substitution work? The shell creates the subsidiary commands[10] ('pwd' and '/bin/pwd'). Each one's output is connected to a pipe, with the read end open on a new file descriptor for the main process ('`diff`'). The shell then passes *the names of files in* `/dev/fd` to the main process as the command-line argument. We can see this by turning on execution tracing in the shell:

```
$ set -x                                    Turn on execution tracing
$ diff <(pwd) <(/bin/pwd)                   Run command
+ diff /dev/fd/63 /dev/fd/62                Shell trace: main program, note arguments
++ pwd                                       Shell trace: subsidiary programs
++ /bin/pwd
1c1                                          Output from diff
< /home/arnold/work/prenhall/progex
---
> /d/home/arnold/work/prenhall/progex
```

This is illustrated in Figure 9.6.

If your system has `/dev/fd`, you may be able to take advantage of this facility as well. Do be careful, though, to document what you're doing. The file descriptor manipulation at the C level is considerably less transparent than the corresponding shell notations!

9.4.3 Managing File Attributes: `fcntl()`

The `fcntl()` ("file control") system call provides control over miscellaneous attributes of either the file descriptor itself or the underlying open file. The GNU/Linux *fcntl*(2) manpage describes it this way:

---

[10] Although we've shown simple commands, arbitrary pipelines are allowed.

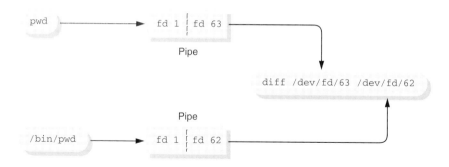

FIGURE 9.6
Process substitution

```
#include <unistd.h>                                          POSIX
#include <fcntl.h>

int fcntl(int fd, int cmd);
int fcntl(int fd, int cmd, long arg);
int fcntl(int fd, int cmd, struct flock *lock);
```

In other words, it takes at least two arguments; based on the second argument, it may take a third one.

The last form, in which the third argument is a pointer to a `struct flock`, is for doing file locking. File locking is a large topic in it own right; we delay discussion until Section 14.2, "Locking Files," page 531.

9.4.3.1 The Close-on-exec Flag

After a `fork()` and before an `exec()`, you should make sure that the new program inherits only the open files it needs. You don't want a child process messing with the parent's open files unless it's supposed to. On the flip side, if a parent has lots of files open, that will artificially limit the number of new files the child can open. (See the accompanying sidebar.)

Organizationally, this behavior may present a problem. The part of your program that starts a new child shouldn't particularly need access to the other part(s) of your program that manipulate open files. And a loop like the following is painful, since there may not be any open files:

```
int j;

for (j = getdtablesize(); j >= 3; j--)    /* close all but 0, 1, 2 */
    (void) close(j);
```

The solution is the *close-on-exec flag*. This is an attribute of the *file descriptor itself*, not the underlying open file. When this flag is set, the system automatically closes the file when the process does an exec. By setting this flag as soon as you open a file, you don't have to worry about any child processes accidentally inheriting it. (The shell automatically sets this flag for all file descriptors it opens numbered 3 and above.)

The cmd argument has two values related to the close-on-exec flag:

F_GETFD

> Retrieves the file descriptor flags. The return value is the setting of all the file descriptor flags or -1 on error.

F_SETFD

> Sets the file descriptor flags to the value in arg (the third argument). The return value is 0 on success or -1 on error.

At the moment, only one "file descriptor flag" is defined: FD_CLOEXEC. This symbolic constant is a POSIX invention,[11] and most code uses a straight 1 or 0:

```
if (fcntl(fd, F_SETFD, 1) < 0) ...  /* set close-on-exec, handle any errors */

if (fcntl(fd, F_GETFD) == 1) ...    /* close-on-exec bit is already set */
```

However, the POSIX definition allows for future extension, and thus the correct way to write such code is more along these lines:

```
int fd;
long fd_flags;

if ((fd_flags = fcntl(fd, F_GETFD)) < 0)          Retrieve flags
    /* handle error */

fd_flags |= FD_CLOEXEC;                           Add close-on-exec flag
if (fcntl(fd, F_SETFD, fd_flags) < 0)             Set flags
    /* handle error */
```

---

[11] The POSIX standard purposely does not give it a value. However, for old code to continue to work, the only value any implementation could sensibly use is 1.

> NOTE The close-on-exec flag is a property of the *descriptor*, not the underlying *file*. Thus, the new descriptor returned by dup() or dup2() (or by fcntl() with F_DUPD, as we're about to see) does *not* inherit the close-on-exec flag setting of the original descriptor. If you want it set for the new file descriptor also, you must remember to do it yourself. This behavior makes sense: If you've just called dup(), copying one end of a pipe to 0 or 1, you don't want the system to close it for you as soon as the process does an exec!

A Close-on-exec War Story from gawk

6 Within the awk language, I/O statements use a redirection notation similar to that of the shell. This includes one-way pipes to and from subprocesses:

```
print "something brilliant" > "/some/file"        Output to file
getline my_record < "/some/other/file"            Input from file

print "more words of wisdom" | "a_reader process" Output to subprocess
"a_writer process" | getline some_input           Input from subprocess
```

The awk interpreter has an open file descriptor for all file redirections, and for the pipe notations that create a subprocess, the awk interpreter creates a pipe and then does a fork and exec of a shell to run the command as given by the string.

Now, on modern systems, part of the C runtime startup code (that runs before main() is called) needs to temporarily open files in order to manage the use of shared libraries. This means that there *must* be at least one or two unused file descriptors available to a brand-new program after an exec, or the program just won't run.

One day, a user reported that when the awk program had the maximum number of files open, any child process that it tried to fork and exec for a pipeline would fail to start!

You can probably guess what was happening. The child shell inherited all the open file descriptors that gawk itself was using for its redirections. We modified gawk to set the close-on-exec flag for all file and pipe redirections, and that fixed the problem.

9.4.3.2 File Descriptor Duplication

When fcntl()'s cmd argument is F_DUPFD, the behavior is similar, but not quite identical, to dup2(). In this case, arg is a file descriptor representing the *lowest acceptable value* for the new file descriptor:

```
int new_fd = fcntl(old_fd, F_DUPFD, 7);    Return value is between 7 and maximum, or failure

int new_fd = dup2(old_fd, 7);              Return value is 7, or failure
```

You can simulate the behavior of `dup()`, which returns the lowest free file descriptor, by using '`fcntl(old_fd, F_DUPFD, 0)`'.

If you remember that file descriptors are just indexes into an internal table, understanding how this function works should be clear. The third argument merely provides the index at which the kernel should start its search for an unused file descriptor.

Whether to use `fcntl()` with `F_DUPFD` or `dup()` or `dup2()` in your own code is largely a matter of taste. All three APIs are part of POSIX and widely supported. We have a mild preference for `dup()` and `dup2()` since those are more specific in their action, and thus are more self-documenting. But because all of them are pretty simple, this reasoning may not convince you.

9.4.3.3 Manipulation of File Status Flags and Access Modes

In Section 4.6.3, "Revisiting `open()`," page 110, we provided the full list of O_*xx* flags that `open()` accepts. POSIX breaks these down by function, classifying them as described in Table 9.4.

TABLE 9.4
O_*xx* flags for `open()`, `creat()` and `fcntl()`

Category	Functions	Flags
File access	`open()`, `fcntl()`	O_RDONLY, O_RDWR, O_WRONLY
File creation	`open()`	O_CREAT, O_EXCL, O_NOCTTY, O_TRUNC
File status	`open()`, `fcntl()`	O_APPEND, O_DSYNC, O_NONBLOCK, O_RSYNC, O_SYNC

Besides setting the various flags initially with `open()`, you can use `fcntl()` to retrieve the current settings, as well as to change them. This is done with the `F_GETFL` and `F_SETFL` values for `cmd`, respectively. For example, you might use these commands to change the setting of the nonblocking flag, O_NONBLOCK, like so:

```
int fd_flags;

if ((fd_flags = fcntl(fd, F_GETFL)) < 0)
    /* handle error */

if ((fd_flags & O_NONBLOCK) != 0) {          /* Nonblocking flag is set */
    fd_flags &= ~O_NONBLOCK;                  /* Clear it */
    if (fcntl(fd, F_SETFL, fd_flags) != 0)    /* Give kernel new value */
        /* handle error */
}
```

Besides the modes themselves, the `O_ACCMODE` symbolic constant is a *mask* you can use to retrieve the file access modes from the return value:

```
fd_flags = fcntl(fd, F_GETFL);

switch (fd_flags & O_ACCESS) {
case O_RDONLY:
    ... action for read-only ...
    break;
case O_WRONLY:
    ... action for write-only ...
    break;
case O_RDWR:
    ... action for read-write ...
    break;
}
```

POSIX requires that `O_RDONLY`, `O_RDWR`, and `O_WRONLY` be bitwise distinct; thus, code such as just shown is guaranteed to work and is an easy way to determine how an arbitrary file descriptor was opened.

By using `F_SETFL`, you can change these modes as well, although permission checking still applies. According to the GNU/Linux *fcntl*(2) manpage, the `O_APPEND` flag cannot be cleared if it was used when the file was opened.

9.4.3.4 Nonblocking I/O for Pipes and FIFOs

Earlier, we used the metaphor of two people washing and drying dishes, and using a dish drainer to describe the way a pipe works; when the drainer fills up, the dishwasher stops, and when it empties out, the dishdryer stops. This is *blocking* behavior: The producer or consumer blocks in the call to `write()` or `read()`, waiting either for more room in the pipe or for more data to come into it.

In the real world, a human being waiting for the dish drainer to empty out or fill up would not just stand by, immobile.[12] Rather, the idle one would go and find some other kitchen task to do (such as sweeping up all the kids' crumbs on the floor) until the dish drainer was ready again.

In Unix/POSIX parlance, this concept is termed *nonblocking I/O*. That is, the requested I/O either completes or returns an error value indicating no data (for the reader) or no room (for the writer). Nonblocking I/O applies to pipes and FIFOs, not to regular

---

[12] Well, we're ignoring the idea that two spouses might want to talk and enjoy each other's company.

disk files. It can also apply to certain devices, such as terminals, and to network connections, both of which are beyond the scope of this volume.

The `O_NONBLOCK` flag can be used with `open()` to specify nonblocking I/O, and it can be set or cleared with `fcntl()`. For `open()` and `read()`, nonblocking I/O is straightforward.

Opening a FIFO with `O_NONBLOCK` set or clear displays the following behavior:

`open("/fifo/file", O_RDONLY, mode)`
    Blocks until the FIFO is opened for writing.

`open("/fifo/file", O_RDONLY|O_NONBLOCK, mode)`
    Opens the file, returning immediately.

`open("/fifo/file", O_WRONLY, mode)`
    Blocks until the FIFO is opened for reading.

`open("/fifo/file", O_WRONLY|O_NONBLOCK, mode)`
    If the FIFO has been opened for reading, opens the FIFO and returns immediately. Otherwise, returns an error (return value of –1 and `errno` set to `ENXIO`).

As described for regular pipes, a `read()` of a FIFO that is no longer open for writing returns end-of-file (a return value of 0). The `O_NONBLOCK` flag is irrelevant in this case. Things get more interesting for an *empty* pipe or FIFO: one that is still open for writing but that has no data in it:

`read(fd, buf, count)`, and `O_NONBLOCK` clear
    The `read()` blocks until more data come into the pipe or FIFO.

`read(fd, buf, count)`, and `O_NONBLOCK` set
    The `read()` returns –1 immediately, with `errno` set to `EAGAIN`.

Finally, `write()` behavior is more complicated. To discuss it we have to first introduce the concept of an *atomic write*. An atomic write is one in which all the requested data are written together, without being interleaved with data from other writes. POSIX defines the constant `PIPE_BUF` in `<unistd.h>`. Writes of amounts less than or equal to `PIPE_BUF` bytes to a pipe or FIFO either succeed or block, according to the details we get into shortly. The minimum value for `PIPE_BUF` is `_POSIX_PIPE_BUF`, which is `512`. `PIPE_BUF` itself can be larger; current GLIBC systems define it to be `4096`, but in any case you should use the symbolic constant and not expect `PIPE_BUF` to be the same value across different systems.

In all cases, for pipes and FIFOs, a `write()` appends data to the end of the pipe. This derives from the fact that pipes don't have file offsets: They aren't seekable.

Also in all cases, as mentioned, writes of up to `PIPE_BUF` are atomic: The data are not interleaved with the data from other writes. Data from a write of more than `PIPE_BUF` bytes can be interleaved with the data from other writes *on arbitrary boundaries*. This last means that you *cannot* expect every `PIPE_BUF` subchunk of a large amount of data to be written atomically. The `O_NONBLOCK` setting does not affect this rule.

As with `read()`, when `O_NONBLOCK` is not set, `write()` blocks until all the data are written.

Things are most complicated with `O_NONBLOCK` set. For a pipe or FIFO, the behavior is as follows:

	space ≥ nbytes	space < nbytes
`nbytes` ≤ `PIPE_BUF`	`write()` succeeds	`write()` returns –1/EAGAIN
	space > 0	space = 0
`nbytes` > `PIPE_BUF`	`write()` writes what it can	`write()` returns –1/EAGAIN

For nonpipe and non-FIFO files to which `O_NONBLOCK` can be applied, the behavior is as follows:

space > 0   `write()` writes what it can.

space = 0   `write()` returns –1/EAGAIN.

Although there is a bewildering array of behavior changes based on pipe/nonpipe, `O_NONBLOCK` set or clear, the space available in the pipe, and the size of the attempted write, the rules are intended to make programming straightforward:

- End-of-file is always distinguishable: `read()` returns zero bytes.
- If no data are available to be read, `read()` either succeeds or returns a "nothing to read" indication: EAGAIN, which means "try again later."
- If there's no room to write data, `write()` either blocks until it can succeed (`O_NONBLOCK` clear) or it fails with a "no room right now" error: EAGAIN.

- When there's room, as much data will be written as can be, so that eventually all the data can be written out.

In summary, if you intend to use nonblocking I/O, any code that uses `write()` has to be able to handle a short write, where less than the requested amount is successfully written. Robust code should be written this way anyway: Even for a regular file it's possible that a disk could become full and that a `write()` will only partially succeed.

Furthermore, you should be prepared to handle EAGAIN, understanding that in this case `write()` failing isn't necessarily a fatal error. The same is true of code that uses nonblocking I/O for reading: recognize that EAGAIN isn't fatal here either. (It may pay, though, to count such occurrences, giving up after too many.)

Nonblocking I/O does complicate your life, no doubt about it. But for many applications, it's a necessity that lets you get your job done. Consider the print spooler again. The spooler daemon can't afford to sit in a blocking `read()` on the FIFO file to which incoming jobs are submitted. It has to be able to monitor running jobs as well and possibly periodically check the status of the printer devices (for example, to make sure they have paper or aren't jammed).

9.4.3.5 `fcntl()` Summary

The `fcntl()` system call is summarized in Table 9.5.

TABLE 9.5
`fcntl()` **summary**

cmd value	arg value	Returns
F_DUPFD	Lowest new descriptor	Duplicate of the `fd` argument.
F_GETFD		Retrieve file descriptor flags (close-on-exec).
F_SETFD	New flag value	Set file descriptor flags (close-on-exec).
F_GETFL		Retrieve flags on underlying file.
F_SETFL	New flag value	Set flags on underlying file.

The file creation, status, and access flags are copied when a file descriptor is duplicated. The close-on-exec flag is not.

9.5 Example: Two-Way Pipes in gawk

A *two-way pipe* connects two processes bidirectionally. Typically, for at least one of the processes, both standard input and standard output are set up on pipes to the other process. The Korn shell (ksh) introduced two-way pipes at the language level, with what it terms a *coprocess*:

```
database engine command and arguments |&        Start coprocess in background
print -p "database command"                     Write to coprocess
read -p db_response                              Read from coprocess
```

Here, `database engine` represents any back-end program that can be driven by a front end, in this case the ksh script. `database engine` has standard input and standard output connected to the shell by way of two separate one-way pipes.[13] This is illustrated in Figure 9.7.

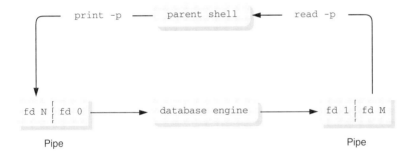

FIGURE 9.7
Korn shell coprocess

In regular awk, pipes to or from subprocesses are one-way: There's no way to send data to a program and read a response back from it—you have to use a temporary file. GNU awk (gawk) borrows the '|&' notation from ksh to extend the awk language:

```
print "a command" |& "database engine"          Start coprocess, write to it
"database engine" |& getline db_response         Read from coprocess
```

gawk also uses the '|&' notation for TCP/IP sockets and BSD portals, which aren't covered in this volume. The following code from io.c in the gawk 3.1.3 distribution

---

[13] There is only one default coprocess (accessible with 'read -p' and 'print -p') at a time. Shell scripts can use the exec command with a special redirection notation to move the coprocess's file descriptors to specific numbers. Once this is done, another coprocess can be started.

is the part of the `two_way_open()` function that sets up a simple coprocess: It creates two pipes, forks the child process, and does all the file descriptor manipulation. We have omitted a number of irrelevant pieces of code (this function is bigger than it should be):

```
1561  static int
1562  two_way_open(const char *str, struct redirect *rp)
1563  {
          ...
1827      /* case 3: two way pipe to a child process */
1828      {
1829      int ptoc[2], ctop[2];
1830      int pid;
1831      int save_errno;
1835
1836      if (pipe(ptoc) < 0)
1837          return FALSE;    /* errno set, diagnostic from caller */
1838
1839      if (pipe(ctop) < 0) {
1840          save_errno = errno;
1841          close(ptoc[0]);
1842          close(ptoc[1]);
1843          errno = save_errno;
1844          return FALSE;
1845      }
```

The first step is to create the two pipes. `ptoc` is "parent to child," and `ctop` is "child to parent." Bear in mind as you read the code that index 0 is the read end and that index 1 is the write end.

Lines 1836–1837 create the first pipe, `ptoc`. Lines 1839–1845 create the second one, closing the first one if this fails. This is important. Failure to close an open but unused pipe leads to *file descriptor leaks*. Like memory, file descriptors are a finite resource, and once you run out of them, they're gone.[14] The same is true of open files: Make sure that all your error-handling code always closes any open files or pipes that you won't need when a failure happens.

`save_errno` saves the `errno` values as set by `pipe()`, on the off chance that `close()` might fail (line 1840). `errno` is then restored on line 1843.

---

[14] Well, you can close them, obviously. But if you don't know they're open, then they're lost just as effectively as memory through a memory leak.

```
1906        if ((pid = fork()) < 0) {
1907            save_errno = errno;
1908            close(ptoc[0]); close(ptoc[1]);
1909            close(ctop[0]); close(ctop[1]);
1910            errno = save_errno;
1911            return FALSE;
1912        }
```

Lines 1906–1912 fork the child, this time closing both pipes if `fork()` failed. Here too, the original `errno` value is saved and restored for later use in producing a diagnostic.

```
1914        if (pid == 0) { /* child */
1915            if (close(1) == -1)
1916                fatal(_("close of stdout in child failed (%s)"),
1917                    strerror(errno));
1918            if (dup(ctop[1]) != 1)
1919                fatal(_("moving pipe to stdout in child failed (dup: %s)"),
1920                        strerror(errno));
1920            if (close(0) == -1)
1921                fatal(_("close of stdin in child failed (%s)"),
1922                    strerror(errno));
1923            if (dup(ptoc[0]) != 0)
1924                fatal(_("moving pipe to stdin in child failed (dup: %s)"),
                            strerror(errno));
1925            if (   close(ptoc[0]) == -1 || close(ptoc[1]) == -1
1926                || close(ctop[0]) == -1 || close(ctop[1]) == -1)
1927                fatal(_("close of pipe failed (%s)"), strerror(errno));
1928            /* stderr does NOT get dup'ed onto child's stdout */
1929            execl("/bin/sh", "sh", "-c", str, NULL);
1930            _exit(errno == ENOENT ? 127 : 126);
1931        }
```

Lines 1914–1931 handle the child's code, with appropriate error checking and messages at each step. Line 1915 closes standard output. Line 1918 copies the child-to-parent pipe write end to `1`. Line 1920 closes standard input, and line 1923 copies the parent-to-child read end to `0`. If this all works, the child's standard input and output are now in place, connected to the parent.

Lines 1925–1926 close all four original pipe file descriptors since they're no longer needed. Line 1928 reminds us that standard error remains in place. This is the best decision, since the user will see errors from the coprocess. An `awk` program that must capture standard error can use the '`2>&1`' shell notation in the command to redirect the coprocess's standard error or send it to a separate file.

Finally, lines 1929–1930 attempt to run `execl()` on the shell and exit appropriately if that fails.

```
1934      /* parent */
1935      rp->pid = pid;
1936      rp->iop = iop_alloc(ctop[0], str, NULL);
1937      if (rp->iop == NULL) {
1938          (void) close(ctop[0]);
1939          (void) close(ctop[1]);
1940          (void) close(ptoc[0]);
1941          (void) close(ptoc[1]);
1942          (void) kill(pid, SIGKILL);  /* overkill? (pardon pun) */
1943
1944          return FALSE;
1945      }
```

The first step in the parent is to manage the input end, from the coprocess. The `rp` pointer points to a `struct redirect`, which maintains a field to hold the child's PID, a `FILE *` for output, and an `IOBUF *` pointer named `iop`. The `IOBUF` is a `gawk` internal data structure for doing input. It, in turn, keeps a copy of the underlying file descriptor.

Line 1935 saves the process ID value. Line 1936 allocates a new `IOBUF` for the given file descriptor and command string. The third argument here is `NULL`: It allows the use of a preallocated `IOBUF` if necessary.

If the allocation fails, lines 1937–1942 clean up by closing the pipes and sending a "kill" signal to the child process to cause it to terminate. (The `kill()` function is described in Section 10.6.7, "Sending Signals: `kill()` and `killpg()`," page 376.)

```
1946      rp->fp = fdopen(ptoc[1], "w");
1947      if (rp->fp == NULL) {
1948          iop_close(rp->iop);
1949          rp->iop = NULL;
1950          (void) close(ctop[0]);
1951          (void) close(ctop[1]);
1952          (void) close(ptoc[0]);
1953          (void) close(ptoc[1]);
1954          (void) kill(pid, SIGKILL);  /* overkill? (pardon pun) */
1955
1956          return FALSE;
1957      }
```

Lines 1946–1957 are analogous. They set up the parent's output to the child, saving the file descriptor for the parent-to-child pipe write end in a `FILE *` by means of `fdopen()`. If this fails, lines 1947–1957 take the same action as before: closing all the pipe descriptors and sending a signal to the child.

From this point on, the write end of the parent-to-child pipe, and the read end of the child-to-parent pipe are held down in the larger structures: the `FILE *` and `IOBUF`, respectively. They are closed automatically by the regular routines that close these structures. However, two tasks remain:

```
1960        os_close_on_exec(ctop[0], str, "pipe", "from");
1961        os_close_on_exec(ptoc[1], str, "pipe", "from");
1962
1963        (void) close(ptoc[0]);
1964        (void) close(ctop[1]);
1966
1967        return TRUE;
1968        }
            ...
1977  }
```

Lines 1960–1961 set the close-on-exec flag for the two descriptors that will remain open. `os_close_on_exec()` is a simple wrapper routine that does the job on Unix and POSIX-compatible systems, but does nothing on systems that don't have a close-on-exec flag. This buries the portability issue in a single place and avoids lots of messy `#ifdefs` throughout the code here and elsewhere in `io.c`.

Finally, lines 1963–1964 close the ends of the pipes that the parent doesn't need, and line 1967 returns `TRUE`, for success.

9.6 Suggested Reading

Job control is complicated, involving process groups, sessions, the wait mechanisms, signals, and manipulation of the terminal's process group. As such, we've chosen not to get into the details. However, you may wish to look at these books:

1. *Advanced Programming in the UNIX Environment*, 2nd edition, by W. Richard Stevens and Stephen Rago. Addison-Wesley, Reading Massachusetts, USA, 2004. ISBN: 0-201-43307-9.

    This book is both complete and thorough, covering elementary and advanced Unix programming. It does an excellent job of covering process groups, sessions, job control, and signals.

2. *The Design and Implementation of the 4.4 BSD Operating System*, by Marshall Kirk McKusick, Keith Bostic, Michael J. Karels, and John S. Quarterman. Addison-Wesley, Reading, Massachusetts, USA, 1996. ISBN: 0-201-54979-4.

    This book gives a good overview of the same material, including a discussion of kernel data structures, which can be found in section 4.8 of that book.

9.7 Summary

- New processes are created with `fork()`. After a fork, both processes run the same code, the only difference being the return value: `0` in the child and a positive PID number in the parent. The child process inherits copies of almost all the parent's attributes, of which the open files are perhaps the most important.

- Inherited shared file descriptors make possible much of the higher-level Unix semantics and elegant shell control structures. This is one of the most fundamental parts of the original Unix design. Because of descriptor sharing, a file isn't really closed until the last open file descriptor is closed. This particularly affects pipes, but it also affects the release of disk blocks for unlinked but still open files.

- The `getpid()` and `getppid()` calls return the current and parent process ID numbers, respectively. A process whose parent dies is reparented to the special `init` process, PID 1. Thus, it's possible for the PPID to change, and applications should be prepared for this.

- The `nice()` system call lets you adjust your process's priority. The nicer you are to other processes, the lower your priority, and vice versa. Only the superuser can be less nice to other processes. On modern systems, especially single-user ones, there's no real reason to change the nice value.

- The `exec()` system calls starts a new program running in an existing process. Six different versions of the call provide flexibility in the setup of argument and environment lists, at the cost of initial confusion as to which one is best to use. Two variants simulate the shell's path searching mechanism and fall back to the use of the shell to interpret the file in case it isn't a binary executable; these variants should be used with care.

- The new program's value for `argv[0]` normally comes from the filename being executed, but this is only convention. As with `fork()`, a significant but not identical set of attributes is inherited across an exec. Other attributes are reset to reasonable default values.

- The `atexit()` function registers callback functions to run in LIFO order when a program terminates. The `exit()`, `_exit()`, and `_Exit()` functions all terminate the program, passing an exit status back to the parent. `exit()` cleans up open `FILE *` streams and runs functions registered with `atexit()`. The other two functions exit immediately and should be used only when an exec has failed in a forked child. Returning from `main()` is like calling `exit()` with the given return value. In C99 and C++, falling off the end of `main()` is the same as 'exit(0)' but is bad practice.

- `wait()` and `waitpid()` are the POSIX functions for recovering a child's exit status. Various macros let you determine whether the child exited normally, and if so, to determine its exit status, or whether the child suffered death-by-signal and if so, which signal committed the crime. With specific options, `waitpid()` also provides information about children that haven't died but that have changed state.

- GNU/Linux and most Unix systems support the BSD `wait3()` and `wait4()` functions. GNU/Linux also supports the obsolescent `union wait`. The BSD functions provide a `struct rusage`, allowing access to CPU time information, which can be handy. If `waitpid()` will suffice though, it's the most portable way to go.

- Process groups are part of the larger job control mechanism, which includes signals, sessions, and manipulation of the terminal's state. `getpgrp()` returns the current process's process group ID, and `getpgid()` returns the PGID of a specific process. Similarly, `setpgrp()` sets the current process's PGID to its PID, making it a process group leader; `setpgid()` lets a parent process set the PGID of a child that hasn't yet exec'd.

- Pipes and FIFOs provide a one-way communications channel between two processes. Pipes must be set up by a common ancestor, whereas a FIFO can be used by any two processes. Pipes are created with `pipe()`, and FIFO files are created with `mkfifo()`. Pipes and FIFOs buffer their data, stopping the producer or consumer as the pipe fills up or empties out.

- `dup()` and `dup2()` create copies of open file descriptors. In combination with `close()`, they enable pipe file descriptors to be put in place as standard input and output for pipelines. For pipes to work correctly, all copies of unused ends of the pipes must be closed before exec'ing the target program(s). `/dev/fd` can be used to create nonlinear pipelines, as demonstrated by the Bash and Korn shells' process substitution capability.

- `fcntl()` is a catchall function for doing miscellaneous jobs. It manages attributes of both the file descriptor itself and the file underlying the descriptor. In this chapter, we saw that `fcntl()` is used for the following:

  - Duplicating a file descriptor, simulating `dup()` and almost simulating `dup2()`.

  - Retrieving and setting the close-on-exec flag. The close-on-exec flag is the only current file descriptor attribute, but it's an important one. It is not copied by a `dup()` action but should be explicitly set on any file descriptors that should not remain open after an exec. In practice, this should be done for most file descriptors.

  - Retrieving and setting flags controlling the underlying file. Of these, `O_NONBLOCK` is perhaps the most useful, at least for FIFOs and pipes. It is definitely the most complicated flag.

Exercises

1. Write a program that prints as much information as possible about the current process: PID, PPID, open files, current directory, nice value, and so on. How can you tell which files are open? If multiple file descriptors reference the same file, so indicate. (Again, how can you tell?)

2. How do you think `atexit()` stores the pointers to the callback functions? Implement `atexit()`, keeping the GNU "no arbitrary limits" principle in mind. Sketch an outline (pseudocode) for `exit()`. What information (`<stdio.h>` library internals) are you missing, the absence of which prevents you from writing `exit()`?

3. The `xargs` program is designed to run a command and arguments multiple times, when there would be too many arguments to pass directly on the command line. It does this by reading lines from standard input, treating each line as a separate argument for the named command, and bundling arguments until there are just enough to still be below the system maximum. For example:

```
$ grep ARG_MAX /usr/include/*.h /usr/include/*/*.h     Command line
bash: /bin/grep: Argument list too long                Shell's error message

$ find /usr/include -name '*.h' | xargs grep ARG_MAX   find and xargs works
/usr/include/sys/param.h:#define        NCARGS         ARG_MAX
...
```

The constant ARG_MAX in <limits.h> represents the combined total memory used by the environment and the command-line arguments. The POSIX standard doesn't say whether this includes the pointer arrays or just the strings themselves.

Write a simple version of xargs that works as described. Don't forget the environment when calculating how much space you have. Be sure to manage your memory carefully.

4. The layout of the status value filled in by wait() and waitpid() isn't defined by POSIX. Historically though, it's a 16-bit value that looks as shown in Figure 9.8.

FIGURE 9.8
Layout of status value from wait()

- A nonzero value in bits 0–7 indicates death-by-signal.
- All 1-bits in the signal field indicates that the child process stopped. In this case, bits 9–15 contain the signal number.
- A 1-bit in bit 8 indicates death with core dump.
- If bits 0–7 are zero, the process exited normally. In this case, bits 9–15 are the exit status.

Given this information, write the POSIX WIFEXITED() et al. macros.

5. Remembering that dup2() closes the requested file descriptor first, implement dup2() using close() and fcntl(). How will you handle the case that fcntl() returns a value lower than the one requested?

6. Does your system have a /dev/fd directory? If so, how is it implemented?

7. Write a new version of ch09-pipeline.c that forks only one process. After forking, the parent should rearrange its file descriptors and exec one of the new programs itself.

8. (Hard.) How can you tell if your process ever called `chroot()`? Write a program that checks and prints a message indicating yes or no. Can your program be fooled? If so, how?

9. Does your system have a `/proc` directory? If so, what kind of per-process information does it make available?

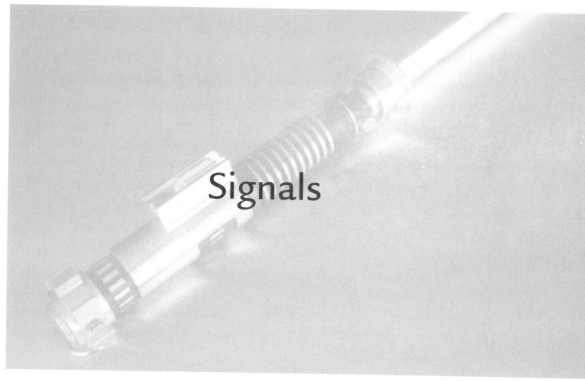
Signals

In this chapter

$\mathbf{T}$his chapter covers the ins and outs of signals, an important but complicated part of the GNU/Linux API.

10.1 Introduction

A *signal* is an indication that some event has happened, for example, an attempt to reference a memory address that isn't part of your program's address space, or when a user presses CTRL-C to stop your program (called *generating an interrupt*).

Your program can tell only that a particular signal has happened at least once. Generally, you can't tell if the same signal has happened multiple times. You can distinguish one signal from another, and control the way in which your program reacts to different signals.

Signal handling mechanisms have evolved over time. As is the case with almost all such mechanisms, both the original and the newer APIs are standardized and available. However, of the fundamental APIs, signal handling displays possibly the broadest change; there's a lot to get a handle on to be able to use the most capable APIs. As a result, this is perhaps the most difficult chapter in the book. We'll do our best to make a coherent presentation, but it'll help if you work your way through this chapter more carefully than usual.

Unlike most of the chapters in this book, our presentation here is historical, covering the APIs as they evolved, *including some APIs that you should never use in new code*. We do this because it simplifies the presentation, making it straightforward to understand why the POSIX `sigaction()` API supports all the facilities that it does.

10.2 Signal Actions

Every signal (we provide a full list shortly) has a default *action* associated with it. POSIX terms this the signal's *disposition*. This action is what the kernel does for the process when a particular signal arrives. The default actions vary:

Termination
> The process is terminated.

Ignored
> The signal is ignored. The program is never aware that anything happened.

Core dump

> The process is terminated, and the kernel creates a `core` file (in the process's current directory) containing the image of the running program at the time the signal arrived. The core dump can be used later with a debugger for examination of the state of the program (see Chapter 15, "Debugging," page 567).

> By default, GNU/Linux systems create files named `core.pid`, where *pid* is the process ID of the killed process. (This can be changed; see *sysctl*(8).) This naming lets you store multiple `core` files in the same directory, at the expense of the disk space involved.[1] Traditional Unix systems name the file `core`, and it's up to you to save any `core` files for later reexamination if there's a chance that more will be created in the same directory.

Stopped

> The process is stopped. It may be continued later. (If you've used shell job control with CTRL-Z, `fg`, and `bg`, you understand stopping a process.)

10.3 Standard C Signals: `signal()` and `raise()`

The ISO C standard defines the original V7 signal management API and a new API for sending signals. You should use them for programs that have to work on non-POSIX systems, or for cases in which the functionality provided by the ISO C APIs is adequate.

10.3.1 The `signal()` Function

You change a signal's action with the `signal()` function. You can change the action to one of "ignore this signal," "restore the system's default action for this signal," or "call my function with the signal number as a parameter when the signal occurs."

A function you provide to deal with the signal is called a *signal handler* (or just a *handler*), and putting a handler in place is arranging to *catch the signal*.

With that introduction, let's proceed to the APIs. The `<signal.h>` header file provides macro definitions for supported signals and declares the signal management function provided by Standard C:

---

[1] At least one vendor of GNU/Linux distributions disables the creation of `core` files "out of the box." To reenable them, put the line 'ulimit -S -c unlimited' into your ~/.profile file.

```
#include <signal.h>                                          ISO C

void (*signal(int signum, void (*func)(int)))(int);
```

This declaration for `signal()` is almost impossible to read. Thus, the GNU/Linux *signal*(2) manpage defines it this way:

```
typedef void (*sighandler_t)(int);

sighandler_t signal(int signum, sighandler_t handler);
```

Now it's more intelligible. The type `sighandler_t` is a pointer to a function returning `void`, which accepts a single integer argument. This integer is the number of the arriving signal.

The `signal()` function accepts a signal number as its first parameter and a pointer to a function (the new handler) as its second argument. If not a function pointer, the second argument may be either `SIG_DFL`, which means "restore the default action," or `SIG_IGN`, which means "ignore the signal."

`signal()` changes the action for `signum` and returns the previous action. (This allows you to later restore the previous action if you so desire.) The return value may also be `SIG_ERR`, which indicates that something went wrong. (Some signals can't be caught or ignored; supplying a signal handler for them, or an invalid `signum`, generates this error return.) Table 10.1 lists the signals available under GNU/Linux, their numeric values, each one's default action, the formal standard or modern operating system that defines them, and each one's meaning.

Older versions of the Bourne shell (`/bin/sh`) associated *traps*, which are shell-level signal handlers, directly with signal numbers. Thus, the well-rounded Unix programmer needed to know not only the signal names for use from C code but also the corresponding signal numbers! POSIX requires the `trap` command to understand symbolic signal names (without the 'SIG' prefix), so this is no longer necessary. However (mostly against our better judgment), we have provided the numbers in the interest of completeness and because you may one day have to deal with a pre-POSIX shell script or ancient C code that uses signal numbers directly.

> NOTE For some of the newer signals, from 16 on up, the association between signal number and signal name isn't necessarily the same across platforms! Check your system header files and manpages. Table 10.1 is correct for GNU/Linux.

TABLE 10.1
GNU/Linux signals

Name	Value	Default	Source	Meaning
SIGHUP	1	Term	POSIX	Hangup.
SIGINT	2	Term	ISO C	Interrupt.
SIGQUIT	3	Core	POSIX	Quit.
SIGILL	4	Core	ISO C	Illegal instruction.
SIGTRAP	5	Core	POSIX	Trace trap.
SIGABRT	6	Core	ISO C	Abort.
SIGIOT	6	Core	BSD	IOT trap.
SIGBUS	7	Core	BSD	Bus error.
SIGFPE	8	Core	ISO C	Floating-point exception.
SIGKILL	9	Term	POSIX	Kill, unblockable.
SIGUSR1	10	Term	POSIX	User-defined signal 1.
SIGSEGV	11	Core	ISO C	Segmentation violation.
SIGUSR2	12	Term	POSIX	User-defined signal 2.
SIGPIPE	13	Term	POSIX	Broken pipe.
SIGALRM	14	Term	POSIX	Alarm clock.
SIGTERM	15	Term	ISO C	Termination.
SIGSTKFLT	16	Term	Linux	Stack fault on a processor (unused).
SIGCHLD	17	Ignr	POSIX	Child process status changed.
SIGCLD	17	Ignr	System V	Same as SIGCHLD (for compatibility only).
SIGCONT	18		POSIX	Continue if stopped.
SIGSTOP	19	Stop	POSIX	Stop, unblockable.
SIGTSTP	20	Stop	POSIX	Keyboard stop.
SIGTTIN	21	Stop	POSIX	Background read from tty.
SIGTTOU	22	Stop	POSIX	Background write to tty.
SIGURG	23	Ignr	BSD	Urgent condition on socket.
SIGXCPU	24	Core	BSD	CPU limit exceeded.
SIGXFSZ	25	Core	BSD	File size limit exceeded.

TABLE 10.1 *(Continued)*

Name	Value	Default	Source	Meaning
SIGVTALRM	26	Term	BSD	Virtual alarm clock.
SIGPROF	27	Term	BSD	Profiling alarm clock.
SIGWINCH	28	Ignr	BSD	Window size change.
SIGIO	29	Term	BSD	I/O now possible.
SIGPOLL	29	Term	System V	Pollable event occurred: same as SIGIO (for compatibility only).
SIGPWR	30	Term	System V	Power failure restart.
SIGSYS	31	Core	POSIX	Bad system call.

Key: **Core**:   Terminate the process and produce a core file.
          Ignr: Ignore the signal.
          Stop: Stop the process.
          Term: Terminate the process.

Some systems also define other signals, such as SIGEMT, SIGLOST, and SIGINFO. The GNU/Linux *signal*(7) manpage provides a complete listing; if your program needs to handle signals not supported by GNU/Linux, the way to do it is with an #ifdef:

```
#ifdef SIGLOST
... handle SIGLOST here ...
#endif
```

With the exception of SIGSTKFLT, the signals listed in Table 10.1 are widely available and don't need to be bracketed with #ifdef.

SIGKILL and SIGSTOP cannot be caught or ignored (or blocked, as described later in the chapter). They always perform the default action listed in Table 10.1.

You can use 'kill -l' to see a list of supported signals. From one of our GNU/Linux systems:

```
$ kill -l
 1) SIGHUP       2) SIGINT       3) SIGQUIT      4) SIGILL
 5) SIGTRAP      6) SIGABRT      7) SIGBUS       8) SIGFPE
 9) SIGKILL     10) SIGUSR1     11) SIGSEGV     12) SIGUSR2
13) SIGPIPE     14) SIGALRM     15) SIGTERM     17) SIGCHLD
18) SIGCONT     19) SIGSTOP     20) SIGTSTP     21) SIGTTIN
22) SIGTTOU     23) SIGURG      24) SIGXCPU     25) SIGXFSZ
26) SIGVTALRM   27) SIGPROF     28) SIGWINCH    29) SIGIO
```

```
30) SIGPWR       31) SIGSYS       32) SIGRTMIN     33) SIGRTMIN+1
34) SIGRTMIN+2   35) SIGRTMIN+3   36) SIGRTMIN+4   37) SIGRTMIN+5
38) SIGRTMIN+6   39) SIGRTMIN+7   40) SIGRTMIN+8   41) SIGRTMIN+9
42) SIGRTMIN+10  43) SIGRTMIN+11  44) SIGRTMIN+12  45) SIGRTMIN+13
46) SIGRTMIN+14  47) SIGRTMIN+15  48) SIGRTMAX-15  49) SIGRTMAX-14
50) SIGRTMAX-13  51) SIGRTMAX-12  52) SIGRTMAX-11  53) SIGRTMAX-10
54) SIGRTMAX-9   55) SIGRTMAX-8   56) SIGRTMAX-7   57) SIGRTMAX-6
58) SIGRTMAX-5   59) SIGRTMAX-4   60) SIGRTMAX-3   61) SIGRTMAX-2
62) SIGRTMAX-1   63) SIGRTMAX
```

The SIGRT*XXX* signals are real-time signals, an advanced topic that we don't cover.

10.3.2 Sending Signals Programmatically: raise()

Besides being generated externally, a program can send itself a signal directly, using the Standard C function raise():

```
#include <signal.h>                                          ISO C

int raise(int sig);
```

This function sends the signal sig to the calling process. (This action has its uses; we show an example shortly.)

Because raise() is defined by Standard C, it is the most portable way for a process to send itself a signal. There are other ways, which we discuss further on in the chapter.

10.4 Signal Handlers in Action

Much of the complication and variation shows up once a signal handler is in place, as it is invoked, and after it returns.

10.4.1 Traditional Systems

After putting a signal handler in place, your program proceeds on its merry way. Things don't get interesting until a signal comes in (for example, the user pressed CTRL-C to interrupt your program or a call to raise() was made).

Upon receipt of the signal, the kernel stops the process wherever it may be. It then simulates a procedure call to the signal handler, passing it the signal number as its sole argument. The kernel arranges things such that a normal return from the signal handler function (either through return or by falling off the end of the function) returns to the point in the program at which the signal happened.

Once a signal has been handled, what happens the next time the same signal comes in? Does the handler remain in place? Or is the signal's action reset to its default? The answer, for historical reasons, is "it depends." In particular, the C standard leaves it as implementation defined.

In practice, V7 and traditional System V systems, such as Solaris, reset the signal's action to the default.

Let's see a simple signal handler in action under Solaris. The following program, `ch10-catchint.c`, catches `SIGINT`. You normally generate this signal by typing CTRL-C at the keyboard.

```
1   /* ch10-catchint.c --- catch a SIGINT, at least once. */
2
3   #include <signal.h>
4   #include <string.h>
5   #include <unistd.h>
6
7   /* handler --- simple signal handler. */
8
9   void handler(int signum)
10  {
11      char buf[200], *cp;
12      int offset;
13
14      /* Jump through hoops to avoid fprintf(). */
15      strcpy(buf, "handler: caught signal ");
16      cp = buf + strlen(buf); /* cp points at terminating '\0' */
17      if (signum > 100)        /* unlikely */
18          offset = 3;
19      else if (signum > 10)
20          offset = 2;
21      else
22          offset = 1;
23      cp += offset;
24
25      *cp-- = '\0';            /* terminate string */
26      while (signum > 0) {     /* work backwards, filling in digits */
27          *cp-- = (signum % 10) + '0';
28          signum /= 10;
29      }
30      strcat(buf, "\n");
31      (void) write(2, buf, strlen(buf));
32  }
33
```

```
34  /* main --- set up signal handling and go into infinite loop */
35
36  int main(void)
37  {
38      (void) signal(SIGINT, handler);
39
40      for (;;)
41          pause();     /* wait for a signal, see later in the chapter */
42
43      return 0;
44  }
```

Lines 9–32 define the signal handling function (cleverly named `handler()`). All this function does is print the caught signal's number and return. It does a lot of manual labor to generate the message, since `fprintf()` is not "safe" for calling from within a signal handler. (This is described shortly, in Section 10.4.6, "Additional Caveats," page 363.)

The `main()` function sets up the signal handler (line 38) and then goes into an infinite loop (lines 40–41). Here's what happens when it's run:

```
$ ssh solaris.example.com              Log in to a handy Solaris system
Last login: Fri Sep 19 04:33:25 2003 from 4.3.2.1.
Sun Microsystems Inc.   SunOS 5.9      Generic May 2002
$ gcc ch10-catchint.c                  Compile the program
$ a.out                                Run it
^Chandler: caught signal 2             Type ^C, handler is called
^C                                     Try again, but this time ...
$                                      The program dies
```

Because V7 and other traditional systems reset the signal's action to the default, when you wish to receive the signal again in the future, the handler function should immediately reinstall itself:

```
void handler(int signum)
{
    char buf[200], *cp;
    int offset;

    (void) signal(signum, handler);        /* reinstall handler */

    ... rest of function as before ...
}
```

10.4.2 BSD and GNU/Linux

4.2 BSD changed the way `signal()` worked.[2] On BSD systems, the signal handler remains in place after the handler returns. GNU/Linux systems follow the BSD behavior. Here's what happens under GNU/Linux:

```
$ ch10-catchint                         Run the program
handler: caught signal 2                Type ^C, handler is called
handler: caught signal 2                And again ...
handler: caught signal 2                And again!
handler: caught signal 2                Help!
handler: caught signal 2                How do we stop this?!
Quit (core dumped)                      ^\, generate SIGQUIT. Whew
```

On a BSD or GNU/Linux system, a signal handler doesn't need the extra '`signal(signum, handler)`' call to reinstall the handler. However, the extra call also doesn't hurt anything, since it maintains the status quo.

In fact, POSIX provides a `bsd_signal()` function, which is identical to `signal()`, except that it guarantees that the signal handler stays installed:

```
#include <signal.h>                                        XSI, Obsolescent

void (*bsd_signal(int sig, void (*func)(int)))(int);
```

This eliminates the portability issues. If you know your program will run only on POSIX systems, you may wish to use `bsd_signal()` instead of `signal()`.

One caveat is that this function is also marked "obsolescent," meaning that it can be withdrawn from a future standard. In practice, even if it's withdrawn, vendors will likely continue to support it for a long time. (As we'll see, the POSIX `sigaction()` API provides enough facilities to let you write a workalike version, should you need to.)

10.4.3 Ignoring Signals

More practically, when a signal handler is invoked, it usually means that the program should finish up and exit. It would be annoying if most programs, upon receipt of a `SIGINT`, printed a message and continued; the point of the signal is that they should stop!

---

[2] Changing the behavior was a bad idea, thoroughly criticized at the time, but it was too late. Changing the semantics of a defined interface always leads to trouble, as it did here. While especially true for operating system designers, *anyone* designing a general-purpose library should keep this lesson in mind as well.

For example, consider the `sort` program. `sort` may have created any number of temporary files for use in intermediate stages of the sorting process. Upon receipt of a `SIGINT`, `sort` should remove the temporary files and then exit. Here is a simplified version of the signal handler from the GNU Coreutils `sort.c`:

```
/* Handle interrupts and hangups. */     Simplified for presentation

static void
sighandler (int sig)
{
  signal (sig, SIG_IGN);                  Ignore this signal from now on
  cleanup ();                             Clean up after ourselves
  signal (sig, SIG_DFL);                  Restore default action
  raise (sig);                            Now resend the signal
}
```

Setting the action to `SIG_IGN` ensures that any further `SIGINT` signals that come in won't affect the clean-up action in progress. Once `cleanup()` is done, resetting the action to `SIG_DFL` allows the system to dump core if the signal that came in would do so. Calling `raise()` regenerates the signal. The regenerated signal then invokes the default action, which most likely terminates the program. (We show the full `sort.c` signal handler later in this chapter.)

10.4.4 Restartable System Calls

The `EINTR` value for `errno` (see Section 4.3, "Determining What Went Wrong," page 86) indicates that a system call was interrupted. While a large number of system calls can fail with this error value, the two most important ones are `read()` and `write()`. Consider the following code:

```
void handler(int signal) { /* handle signals */ }

int main(int argc, char **argv)
{
    signal(SIGINT, handler);
    ...
    while ((count = read(fd, buf, sizeof buf)) > 0) {
        /* process the buffer */
    }
    if (count == 0)
        /* end of file, clean up etc. */
    else if (count == -1)
        /* failure */
    ...
}
```

Suppose that the system has successfully read (and filled in) part of the buffer when a SIGINT occurs. The read() system call has not yet returned from the kernel to the program, but the kernel decides that it can deliver the signal. handler() is called, runs, and returns into the middle of the read(). What does read() return?

In days of yore (V7, earlier System V systems), read() would return -1 and set errno to EINTR. There was *no way to tell* that data had been transferred. In this case, V7 and System V act as if nothing happened: No data are transferred to or from the user's buffer, and the file offset isn't changed.

4.2 BSD changed this. There were two cases:

Slow devices

> A "slow device" is essentially a terminal or almost anything but a regular file. In this case, read() could fail with EINTR *only* if no data were transferred when the signal arrived. Otherwise, the system call would be *restarted*, and read() would return normally.

Regular files

> The system call would be restarted. In this case, read() would return normally; the return value would be either as many bytes as were requested or the number of bytes actually readable (such as when reading close to the end of the file).

The BSD behavior is clearly valuable; you can always tell how much data you've read.

The POSIX behavior is similar, but not identical, to the original BSD behavior. POSIX indicates that read()[3] fails with EINTR only if a signal occurred before any data were transferred. Although POSIX doesn't say anything about "slow devices," in practice, this condition only occurs on such devices.

Otherwise, if a signal interrupts a partially successful read(), the return is the number of bytes read so far. For this reason (as well as being able handle short files), you should always check the return value from read() and never assume that it read the full number of bytes requested. (The POSIX sigaction() API, described later, allows you to get the behavior of BSD restartable system calls if you want it.)

---

[3] Although we are describing read(), the rules apply to all system calls that can fail with EINTR, such as those of the wait() family.

10.4.4.1 Example: GNU Coreutils `safe_read()` and `safe_write()`

The GNU Coreutils use two routines, `safe_read()` and `safe_write()`, to handle the `EINTR` case on traditional systems. The code is a bit complicated by the fact that the same file, by means of `#include` and macros, implements both functions. From `lib/safe-read.c` in the Coreutils distribution:

```
 1   /* An interface to read and write that retries after interrupts.
 2      Copyright (C) 1993, 1994, 1998, 2002 Free Software Foundation, Inc.
     ... lots of boilerplate stuff omitted ...
56
57   #ifdef SAFE_WRITE
58   # include "safe-write.h"
59   # define safe_rw safe_write          Create safe_write()
60   # define rw write                    Use write() system call
61   #else
62   # include "safe-read.h"
63   # define safe_rw safe_read           Create safe_read()
64   # define rw read                     Use read() system call
65   # undef const
66   # define const /* empty */
67   #endif
68
69   /* Read(write) up to COUNT bytes at BUF from(to) descriptor FD, retrying if
70      interrupted.  Return the actual number of bytes read(written), zero for EOF,
71      or SAFE_READ_ERROR(SAFE_WRITE_ERROR) upon error.  */
72   size_t
73   safe_rw (int fd, void const *buf, size_t count)
74   {
75     ssize_t result;
76
77     /* POSIX limits COUNT to SSIZE_MAX, but we limit it further, requiring
78        that COUNT <= INT_MAX, to avoid triggering a bug in Tru64 5.1.
79        When decreasing COUNT, keep the file pointer block-aligned.
80        Note that in any case, read(write) may succeed, yet read(write)
81        fewer than COUNT bytes, so the caller must be prepared to handle
82        partial results.  */
83     if (count > INT_MAX)
84       count = INT_MAX & ~8191;
85
86     do
87       {
88         result = rw (fd, buf, count);
89       }
90     while (result < 0 && IS_EINTR (errno));
91
92     return (size_t) result;
93   }
```

Lines 57–67 handle the definitions, creating `safe_read()` and `safe_write()`, as appropriate (see `safe_write.c`, below).

Lines 77–84 are indicative of the kinds of complications found in the real world. Here, one particular Unix variant can't handle count values greater than INT_MAX, so lines 83–84 perform two operations at once: reducing the count to below INT_MAX and keeping the amount a multiple of 8192. The latter operation maintains the efficiency of the I/O operations: Doing I/O in multiples of the fundamental disk block size is always more efficient than doing it in odd amounts. As the comment notes, the code maintains the semantics of read() and write(), where the returned count may be less than the requested count.

Note that the count parameter can indeed be greater than INT_MAX, since count is a size_t, which is unsigned. INT_MAX is a plain int, which on all modern systems is signed.

Lines 86–90 are the actual loop, performing the operation repeatedly, as long as it fails with EINTR. The IS_EINTR() macro isn't shown, but it handles the case for systems on which EINTR isn't defined. (There must be at least one out there or the code wouldn't bother setting up the macro; it was probably done for a Unix or POSIX emulation on top of a non-Unix system.)

Here is safe_write.c:

```
1    /* An interface to write that retries after interrupts.
2       Copyright (C) 2002 Free Software Foundation, Inc.
     ... lots of boilerplate stuff omitted ...
17
18   #define SAFE_WRITE
19   #include "safe-read.c"
```

The #define on line 18 defines SAFE_WRITE; this ties in to lines 57–60 in safe-read.c.

10.4.4.2 GLIBC Only: TEMP_FAILURE_RETRY()

The GLIBC <unistd.h> file defines a macro, TEMP_FAILURE_RETRY(), that you can use to encapsulate any system call that can fail and set errno to EINTR. Its "declaration" is as follows:

```
#include <unistd.h>                                                     GLIBC

long int TEMP_FAILURE_RETRY(expression);
```

Here is the macro's definition:

```
/* Evaluate EXPRESSION, and repeat as long as it returns -1 with `errno'
   set to EINTR.   */

# define TEMP_FAILURE_RETRY(expression) \
  (__extension__                                            \
    ({ long int __result;                                   \
       do __result = (long int) (expression);         \
       while (__result == -1L && errno == EINTR);     \
       __result; }))
```

The macro uses a GCC extension to the C language (as marked by the
__extension__ keyword) which allows brace-enclosed statements inside parentheses
to return a value, thus acting like a simple expression.

Using this macro, we might rewrite safe_read() as follows:

```
size_t safe_read(int fd, void const *buf, size_t count)
{
    ssize_t result;

    /* Limit count as per comment earlier. */
    if (count > INT_MAX)
        count = INT_MAX & ~8191;

    result = TEMP_FAILURE_RETRY(read(fd, buf, count));

    return (size_t) result;
}
```

10.4.5 Race Conditions and sig_atomic_t (ISO C)

So far, handling one signal at a time looks straightforward: install a signal handler
in main() and (optionally) have the signal handler reinstall itself (or set the action to
SIG_IGN) as the first thing it does.

What happens though if *two* identical signals come in, right after the other? In particular, what if your system resets the signal's action to the default, and the second one
comes in *after* the signal handler is called but *before* it can reinstall itself?

Or, suppose you're using bsd_signal(), so the handler stays installed, but the
second signal is different from the first one? Usually, the first signal handler needs to
complete its job before the second one runs, and every signal handler shouldn't have
to temporarily ignore all other possible signals!

Both of these are race conditions. One workaround for these problems is to make
signal handlers as simple as possible. You can do this by creating flag variables that

indicate that a signal occurred. The signal handler sets the variable to true and returns. Then the main logic checks the flag variable at strategic points:

```
int sig_int_flag = 0;            /* signal handler sets to true */

void int_handler(int signum)
{
    sig_int_flag = 1;
}

int main(int argc, char **argv)
{
    bsd_signal(SIGINT, int_handler);
    ... program proceeds on ...
    if (sig_int_flag) {
        /* SIGINT occurred, handle it */
    }
    ... rest of logic ...
}
```

(Note that this strategy *reduces* the window of vulnerability but does not eliminate it.)

Standard C introduces a special type—`sig_atomic_t`—for use with such flag variables. The idea behind the name is that assignments to variables of this type are *atomic*: That is, they happen in one indivisible action. For example, on most machines, assignment to an `int` value happens atomically, whereas a structure assignment is likely to be done either by copying all the bytes with a (compiler-generated) loop, or by issuing a "block move" instruction that can be interrupted. Since assignment to a `sig_atomic_t` value is atomic, once started, it completes before another signal can come in and interrupt it.

Having a special type is only part of the story. `sig_atomic_t` variables should also be declared `volatile`:

```
volatile sig_atomic_t sig_int_flag = 0;  /* signal handler sets to true */
... rest of code as before ...
```

The `volatile` keyword tells the compiler that the variable can be changed externally, behind the compiler's back, so to speak. This keeps the compiler from doing optimizations that might otherwise affect the code's correctness.

Structuring an application exclusively around `sig_atomic_t` variables is not reliable. The correct way to deal with signals is shown later, in Section 10.7, "Signals for Interprocess Communication," page 379.

10.4.6 Additional Caveats

The POSIX standard provides several caveats for signal handlers:

- It is undefined what happens when handlers for SIGFPE, SIGILL, SIGSEGV, or any other signals that represent "computation exceptions" return.

- If a handler was invoked as a result of calls to abort(), raise(), or kill(), the handler cannot call raise(). abort() is described in Section 12.4, "Committing Suicide: abort()," page 445, and kill() is described later in this chapter. (The sigaction() API, with the three-argument signal handler described later, makes it possible to tell if this is the case.)

- Signal handlers can only call the functions in Table 10.2. In particular, they should avoid <stdio.h> functions. The problem is that an interrupt may come in while a <stdio.h> function is running, when the internal state of the library is in the middle of being updated. Further calls to <stdio.h> functions could corrupt the internal state.

The list in Table 10.2 comes from Section 2.4 of the *System Interfaces* volume of the 2001 POSIX standard. Many of these functions are advanced APIs not otherwise covered in this volume.

10.4.7 Our Story So Far, Episode I

Signals are a complicated topic, and it's about to get more confusing. So, let's pause for a moment, take a step back, and summarize what we've discussed so far:

- Signals are an indication that some external event has occurred.

- raise() is the ISO C function for sending signals *to the current process*. We have yet to describe how to send signals to other processes.

- signal() controls the disposition of a signal: that is, the process's reaction to the signal when it comes in. The signal may be left set to the system default, ignored, or caught.

- A handler function runs when a signal is caught. Here is where complexity starts to rear its ugly head:

  - ISO C leaves as unspecified whether signal disposition is restored to its default before the handler runs or whether the disposition remains in place. The former

TABLE 10.2
Functions that can be called from a signal handler

_Exit()	fpathconf()	raise()	sigqueue()
_exit()	fstat()	read()	sigset()
accept()	fsync()	readlink()	sigsuspend()
access()	ftruncate()	recv()	sleep()
aio_error()	getegid()	recvfrom()	socket()
aio_return()	geteuid()	recvmsg()	socketpair()
aio_suspend()	getgid()	rename()	stat()
alarm()	getgroups()	rmdir()	symlink()
bind()	getpeername()	select()	sysconf()
cfgetispeed()	getpgrp()	sem_post()	tcdrain()
cfgetospeed()	getpid()	send()	tcflow()
cfsetispeed()	getppid()	sendmsg()	tcflush()
cfsetospeed()	getsockname()	sendto()	tcgetattr()
chdir()	getsockopt()	setgid()	tcgetpgrp()
chmod()	getuid()	setpgid()	tcsendbreak()
chown()	kill()	setsid()	tcsetattr()
clock_gettime()	link()	setsockopt()	tcsetpgrp()
close()	listen()	setuid()	time()
connect()	lseek()	shutdown()	timer_getoverrun()
creat()	lstat()	sigaction()	timer_gettime()
dup()	mkdir()	sigaddset()	timer_settime()
dup2()	mkfifo()	sigdelset()	times()
execle()	open()	sigemptyset()	umask()
execve()	pathconf()	sigfillset()	uname()
fchmod()	pause()	sigismember()	unlink()
fchown()	pipe()	signal()	utime()
fcntl()	poll()	sigpause()	wait()
fdatasync()	posix_trace_event()	sigpending()	waitpid()
fork()	pselect()	sigprocmask()	write()

is the behavior of V7 and modern System V systems such as Solaris. The latter is the BSD behavior also found on GNU/Linux. (The POSIX `bsd_signal()` function may be used to force BSD behavior.)

- What happens when a system call is interrupted by a signal also varies along the traditional vs. BSD line. Traditional systems return -1 with `errno` set to `EINTR`. BSD systems restart the system call after the handler returns. The GLIBC `TEMP_FAILURE_RETRY()` macro can help you write code to handle system calls that return -1 with `errno` set to `EINTR`.

  POSIX requires that a system call that has partially completed return a success value indicating how much succeeded. A system call that hasn't started yet is restarted.

- The `signal()` mechanism provides fertile ground for growing race conditions. The ISO C `sig_atomic_t` data type helps with this situation but doesn't solve it, and the mechanism as defined can't be made safe from race conditions.

- A number of additional caveats apply, and in particular, only a subset of the standard library functions can be *safely* called from within a signal handler.

Despite the problems, for simple programs, the `signal()` interface is adequate, and it is still widely used.

10.5 The System V Release 3 Signal APIs: `sigset()` et al.

4.0 BSD (circa 1980) introduced additional APIs to provide "reliable" signals.[4] In particular, it became possible to *block* signals. In other words, a program could tell the kernel, "hang on to these particular signals for the next little while, and then deliver them to me when I'm ready to take them." A big advantage is that this feature simplifies signal handlers, which automatically run with their own signal blocked (to avoid the two-signals-in-a-row problem) and possibly with others blocked as well.

System V Release 3 (circa 1984) picked up these APIs and popularized them; in most Unix-related documentation and books, you'll probably see these APIs referred to as being from System V Release 3. The functions are as follows:

---

[4] The APIs required linking with a separate library, `-ljobs`, in order to be used.

```
#include <signal.h>                                                          XSI

int sighold(int sig);                                          Add sig to process signal mask
int sigrelse(int sig);                                         Remove sig from process signal mask

int sigignore(int sig);                                        Short for sigset(sig, SIG_IGN)
int sigpause(int sig);                                         Suspend process, allow sig to come in
void (*sigset(int sig, void (*disp)(int)))(int);   sighandler_t sigset(int sig, sighandler_t disp);
```

The POSIX standard for these functions describes their behavior in terms of each process's *process signal mask*. The process signal mask tracks which signals (if any) a process currently has blocked. This is described in more detail in Section 10.6.2, "Signal Sets: `sigset_t` and Related Functions," page 368. In the System V Release 3 API there is no way to retrieve or modify the process signal mask as a whole. The functions work as follows:

int sighold(int sig)
:   Adds `sig` to the list of blocked processes (the process signal mask).

int sigrelse(int sig)
:   Removes (releases) `sig` from the process signal mask.

int sigignore(int sig)
:   Ignores `sig`. This is a convenience function.

int sigpause(int sig)
:   Removes `sig` from the process signal mask, and then suspends the process until a signal comes in (see Section 10.7, "Signals for Interprocess Communication," page 379).

sighandler_t sigset(int sig, sighandler_t disp)
:   Is a replacement for `signal()`. (We've used the GNU/Linux manpage notation here to make the declaration easier to read.)

For `sigset()`, the `handler` argument can be `SIG_DFL`, `SIG_IGN`, or a function pointer, just as for `signal()`. However, it may also be `SIG_HOLD`. In this case, `sig` is added to the process's process signal mask, but its associated action is otherwise unchanged. (In other words, if it had a handler, the handler is still in place; if it was the default action, that has not changed.)

When `sigset()` is used to install a signal handler and the signal comes in, the kernel first adds the signal to the process signal mask, blocking any additional receipt of that signal. The handler runs, and when it returns, the kernel restores the process signal mask to what it was before the handler ran. (In the POSIX model, if a signal handler changes the signal mask, that change is overridden by the restoration of the previous mask when the handler returns.)

`sighold()` and `sigrelse()` may be used together to bracket so-called *critical sections* of code: chunks of code that should not be interrupted by particular signals so that no data structures are corrupted by code from a signal handler.

> NOTE POSIX standardizes these APIs, since a major goal of POSIX is to formalize existing practice, wherever possible. However, the `sigaction()` APIs described shortly let you do everything that these APIs do, and more. You should not use these APIs in new programs. Instead, use `sigaction()`. (We note that there isn't even a *sigset*(2) GNU/Linux manpage!)

10.6 POSIX Signals

The POSIX API is based on the `sigvec()` API from 4.2 and 4.3 BSD. With minor changes, this API was able to subsume the functionality of both the V7 and System V Release 3 APIs. POSIX made these changes and renamed the API `sigaction()`. Because the `sigvec()` interface was not widely used, we don't describe it. Instead, this section describes only `sigaction()`, which is what you should use anyway. (Indeed, the 4.4 BSD manuals from 1994 mark `sigvec()` as obsolete, pointing the reader to `sigaction()`.)

10.6.1 Uncovering the Problem

What's wrong with the System V Release 3 APIs? After all, they provide signal blocking, so signals aren't lost and any given signal can be handled reliably.

The answer is that the API works with only *one signal at a time*. Programs generally handle more than one signal. And when you're in the middle of handling one signal, you don't want to have to worry about handling another one. (Suppose you've just answered your office phone when your cell phone starts ringing: You'd prefer to have the phone system tell your caller you're on another line and you'll be there shortly, instead of having to do it yourself.)

With the `sigset()` API, each signal handler would have to temporarily block *all* the other signals, do its job, and then unblock them. The problem is that in the interval between any two calls to sighold(), a not-yet-blocked signal could come up. The scenario is rife, once again, with race conditions.

The solution is to make it possible to work with groups of signals atomically, that is, with one system call. You effect this by working with signal sets and the process signal mask.

10.6.2 Signal Sets: sigset_t and Related Functions

The *process signal mask* is a list of signals that a process currently has blocked. The strength of the POSIX API is that the process signal mask can be manipulated atomically, as a whole.

The process signal mask is represented programmatically with a *signal set*. This is the sigset_t type. Conceptually, it's just a bitmask, with 0 and 1 values in the mask representing a particular signal's absence or presence in the mask:

```
/* Signal mask manipulated directly.  DO NOT DO THIS! */
int mask = (1 << SIGHUP) | (1 << SIGINT);   /* bitmask for SIGHUP and SIGINT */
```

However, because a system can have more signals than can be held in a single int or long and because heavy use of the bitwise operators is hard to read, several APIs exist to manipulate signal sets:

```
#include <signal.h>                                          POSIX

int sigemptyset(sigset_t *set);
int sigfillset(sigset_t *set);
int sigaddset(sigset_t *set, int signum);
int sigdelset(sigset_t *set, int signum);
int sigismember(const sigset_t *set, int signum);
```

The functions are as follows:

int sigemptyset(sigset_t *set)
    Empties out a signal set. Upon return, *set has no signals in it. Returns 0 on success or -1 on error.

int sigfillset(sigset_t *set)
    Completely fills in a signal set. Upon return, *set contains all the signals defined by the system. Returns 0 on success or -1 on error.

int sigaddset(sigset_t *set, int signum)
    Adds signum to the process signal mask in *set. Returns 0 on success or -1 on error.

```
int sigdelset(sigset_t *set, int signum)
```
    Removes `signum` from the process signal mask in `*set`. Returns 0 on success or
    -1 on error.

```
int sigismember(const sigset_t *set, int signum)
```
    Returns true/false if `signum` is or isn't present in `*set`.

You must always call one of `sigemptyset()` or `sigfillset()` before doing anything
else with a `sigset_t` variable. Both interfaces exist because sometimes you want to
start out with an empty set and then just work with one or two signals, and other times
you want to work with all signals, possibly taking away one or two.

10.6.3 Managing the Signal Mask: `sigprocmask()` et al.

The process signal mask starts out empty—initially, no signals are blocked. (This is
a simplification; see Section 10.9, "Signals Across `fork()` and `exec()`," page 398.)
Three functions let you work directly with the process signal mask:

```
#include <signal.h>                                              POSIX

int sigprocmask(int how, const sigset_t *set, sigset_t *oldset);
int sigpending(sigset_t *set);
int sigsuspend(const sigset_t *set);
```

The functions are as follows:

```
int sigprocmask(int how, const sigset_t *set, sigset_t *oldset)
```
    If `oldset` is not NULL, the current process signal mask is retrieved and placed in
    `*oldset`. The process signal mask is then updated, according to the contents of
    `set` and the value of `how`, which must be one of the following:

    SIG_BLOCK   Merge the signals in `*set` with the current process signal mask.
                 The new mask is the union of the current mask and `*set`.

    SIG_UNBLOCK   Remove the signals in `*set` from the process signal mask. It
                 is not a problem if `*set` contains a signal that is not currently
                 in the process signal mask.

    SIG_SETMASK   Replace the process signal mask with the contents of `*set`.

    If `set` is NULL and `oldset` isn't, the value of `how` isn't important. This combination
    retrieves the current process signal mask without changing it. (This is explicit in
    the POSIX standard but isn't clear from the GNU/Linux manpage.)

```
int sigpending(sigset_t *set)
```
This function lets you see which signals are *pending*: That is, `*set` is filled in with those signals that have been sent but that haven't yet been delivered since they're blocked.

```
int sigsuspend(const sigset_t *set)
```
This function *temporarily* replaces the process's process signal mask with `*set`, and then suspends the process until a signal is received. By definition, only a signal not in `*set` can cause the function to return (see Section 10.7, "Signals for Inter-process Communication," page 379).

10.6.4 Catching Signals: `sigaction()`

Finally, we're ready to look at the `sigaction()` function. This function is complicated, and we intentionally omit many details that are only for advanced uses. The POSIX standard and the *sigaction*(2) manpage provide full details, although you must carefully read both to fully absorb everything.

```
#include <signal.h>                                            POSIX

int sigaction(int signum, const struct sigaction *act, struct sigaction *oldact);
```
The arguments are as follows:

```
int signum
```
The signal of interest, as with the other signal handling functions.

```
const struct sigaction *act
```
The new handler specification for signal `signum`.

```
struct sigaction *oldact
```
The current handler specification. If not NULL, the system fills in `*oldact` before installing `*act`. `*act` can be NULL, in which case `*oldact` is filled in, but nothing else changes.

Thus, `sigaction()` both sets the new handler and retrieves the old one, in one shot. The `struct sigaction` looks like this:

```
/* NOTE: Order in struct may vary. There may be other fields too! */
struct sigaction {
    sigset_t sa_mask;                                    Additional signals to block
    int sa_flags;                                        Control behavior
    void (*sa_handler)(int);                             May be union with sa_sigaction
    void (*sa_sigaction)(int, siginfo_t *, void *);      May be union with sa_handler
}
```

The fields are as follows:

`sigset_t sa_mask`

A set of *additional* signals to block when the signal handler function runs. Thus, when the handler is invoked, the total set of blocked signals is the union of those in the process signal mask, those in `act->sa_mask`, and, if `SA_NODEFER` is clear, `signum`.

`int sa_flags`

Flags that control the kernel's handling of the signal. See the discussion further on.

`void (*sa_handler)(int)`

A pointer to a "traditional" handler function. It has the same *signature* (return type and parameter list) as the handler functions for `signal()`, `bsd_signal()`, and `sigset()`.

`void (*sa_sigaction)(int, siginfo_t *, void *)`

A pointer to a "new style" handler function. The function takes three arguments, as described shortly.

Which of `act->sa_handler` and `act->sa_sigaction` is used depends on the `SA_SIGINFO` flag in `act->sa_flags`. When present, `act->sa_sigaction` is used; otherwise, `act->sa_handler` is used. Both POSIX and the GNU/Linux manpage point out that these two fields may overlap in storage (that is, be part of a `union`). Thus, you should *never* use both fields in the same `struct sigaction`.

The `sa_flags` field is the bitwise OR of one or more of the flag values listed in Table 10.3.

When the `SA_SIGINFO` flag is set in `act->sa_flags`, then the `act->sa_sigaction` field is a pointer to a function declared as follows:

TABLE 10.3
Flag values for `sa_flags`

Flag	Meaning
SA_NOCLDSTOP	This flag is only meaningful for SIGCHLD. When set, the parent does not receive the signal when a child process is stopped by SIGSTOP, SIGTSTP, SIGTTIN, or SIGTTOU. These signals are discussed later, in Section 10.8.2, page 383.
SA_NOCLDWAIT	This flag is only meaningful for SIGCHLD. Its behavior is complicated. We delay explanation until later in the chapter; see Section 10.8.3, page 385.
SA_NODEFER	Normally, the given signal is blocked while the signal handler runs. When one of these flags is set, the given signal is not blocked while the signal handler runs. SA_NODEFER is the official POSIX name of the flag (which you should use).
SA_NOMASK	An alternative name for SA_NODEFER.[*]
SA_SIGINFO	The signal handler takes three arguments. As mentioned, with this flag set, the sa_sigaction field should be used instead of sa_handler.
SA_ONSTACK	This is an advanced feature. Signal handlers can be called, using user-provided memory as an "alternative signal stack." Such memory is given to the kernel for this use with sigaltstack() (see *sigaltstack*(2)). This feature is not otherwise described in this volume.
SA_RESETHAND	This flag provides the V7 behavior: The signal's action is reset to its default when the handler is called. SA_RESETHAND is the official POSIX name of the flag (which you should use).
SA_ONESHOT	An alternative name for SA_RESETHAND.
SA_RESTART	This flag provides BSD semantics: System calls that can fail with EINTR, and that receive this signal, are restarted.

---

[*] As far as we could determine, the names SA_NOMASK and SA_ONESHOT are specific to GNU/Linux. If anyone knows differently, please inform us!

```
void action_handler(int sig, siginfo_t *info, void *context)
{
    /* handler body here */
}
```

The `siginfo_t` structure provides a wealth of information about the signal:

```
/* POSIX 2001 definition.  Actual contents likely to vary across systems. */
typedef struct {
    int si_signo;              /* signal number */
    int si_errno;              /* <errno.h> value if an error */
    int si_code;               /* signal code; see text */
    pid_t si_pid;              /* process ID of process that sent signal */
    uid_t si_uid;              /* real UID of sending process */
    void *si_addr;             /* address of instruction that faulted */
    int si_status;             /* exit value, may include death-by-signal */
    long si_band;              /* band event for SIGPOLL/SIGIO */
    union sigval si_value;     /* signal value (advanced) */
} siginfo_t;
```

The `si_signo`, `si_code`, and `si_value` fields are available for all signals. The other fields can be members of a `union` and thus should be used only for the signals for which they're defined. There may also be other fields in the `siginfo_t` structure.

Almost all the fields are for advanced uses. The full details are in the POSIX standard and in the *sigaction*(2) manpage. However, we can describe a straightforward use of the `si_code` field.

For `SIGBUS`, `SIGCHLD`, `SIGFPE`, `SIGILL`, `SIGPOLL`, `SIGSEGV`, and `SIGTRAP`, the `si_code` field can take on any of a set of predefined values specific to each signal, indicating the cause of the signal. Frankly, the details are a bit overwhelming; everyday code doesn't really need to deal with them (although we'll look at the values for `SIGCHLD` later on). For all other signals, the `si_code` member has one of the values in Table 10.4.

TABLE 10.4
Signal origin values for `si_code`

Value	GLIBC only	Meaning
SI_ASYNCIO		Asynchronous I/O completed (advanced).
SI_KERNEL	✓	Kernel sent the signal.
SI_MESGQ		Message queue state changed (advanced).
SI_QUEUE		Signal sent from `sigqueue()` (advanced).
SI_SIGIO	✓	A `SIGIO` was queued (advanced).
SI_TIMER		A timer expired.
SI_USER		Signal sent by `kill()`. `raise()` and `abort()` are allowed to produce this too, but are not required to.

In particular, the `SI_USER` value is useful; it allows a signal handler to tell if the signal was sent by `raise()` or `kill()` (described later). You can use this information to avoid calling `raise()` or `kill()` a second time.

The third argument to a three-argument signal handler, `void *context`, is an advanced feature, not otherwise discussed in this volume.

Finally, to see `sigaction()` in use, examine the full text of the signal handler for `sort.c`:

```
2074  static void
2075  sighandler (int sig)
2076  {
2077  #ifndef SA_NOCLDSTOP                    On old style system ...
2078    signal (sig, SIG_IGN);               — Use signal() to ignore sig
2079  #endif                                  — Otherwise, sig automatically blocked
2080
2081    cleanup ();                           Run cleanup code
2082
2083  #ifdef SA_NOCLDSTOP                      On POSIX style system ...
2084    {
2085      struct sigaction sigact;
2086
2087      sigact.sa_handler = SIG_DFL;        — Set action to default
2088      sigemptyset (&sigact.sa_mask);      — No additional signals to block
2089      sigact.sa_flags = 0;                — No special action to take
2090      sigaction (sig, &sigact, NULL);     — Put it in place
2091    }
2092  #else                                   On old style system ...
2093    signal (sig, SIG_DFL);               — Set action to default
2094  #endif
2095
2096    raise (sig);                          Resend the signal
2097  }
```

Here is the code in `main()` that puts the handler in place:

```
2214  #ifdef SA_NOCLDSTOP                      On a POSIX system ...
2215    {
2216      unsigned i;
2217      sigemptyset (&caught_signals);
2218      for (i = 0; i < nsigs; i++)          — Block all signals
2219        sigaddset (&caught_signals, sigs[i]);
2220      newact.sa_handler = sighandler;      — Signal handling function
2221      newact.sa_mask = caught_signals;     — Set process signal mask for handler
2222      newact.sa_flags = 0;                 — No special flags
2223    }
2224  #endif
2225
```

```
2226     {
2227        unsigned i;
2228        for (i = 0; i < nsigs; i++)              For all signals ...
2229          {
2230            int sig = sigs[i];
2231  #ifdef SA_NOCLDSTOP
2232            sigaction (sig, NULL, &oldact);       – Retrieve old handler
2233            if (oldact.sa_handler != SIG_IGN)     – If not ignoring this signal
2234              sigaction (sig, &newact, NULL);     – Install our handler
2235  #else
2236            if (signal (sig, SIG_IGN) != SIG_IGN)
2237              signal (sig, sighandler);           – Same logic with old API
2238  #endif
2239          }
2240     }
```

We note that lines 2216–2219 and 2221 could be replaced with the single call:

```
sigfillset(& newact.sa_mask);
```

We don't know why the code is written the way it is.

Also of interest are lines 2233–2234 and 2236–2237, which show the correct way to check whether a signal is being ignored and to install a handler only if it's not.

> NOTE   The `sigaction()` API and the `signal()` API should not be used together for the same signal. Although POSIX goes to great lengths to make it possible to use `signal()` initially, retrieve a `struct sigaction` representing the disposition from `signal()`, and restore it, it's still a bad idea. Code will be easier to read, write, and understand if you use one API or the other, exclusively.

10.6.5 Retrieving Pending Signals: `sigpending()`

The `sigpending()` system call, described earlier, lets you retrieve the set of signals that are pending, that is, those that have come in, but are not yet delivered because they were blocked:

```
#include <signal.h>                                               POSIX

int sigpending(sigset_t *set);
```

Besides unblocking the pending signals so that they get delivered, you may choose to ignore them. Setting the action for a pending signal to `SIG_IGN` causes the pending signal to be discarded (even if it was blocked). Similarly, for those signals for which the default action is to ignore the signal, setting the action to `SIG_DFL` causes such a pending signal to also be discarded.

10.6.6 Making Functions Interruptible: `siginterrupt()`

As a convenience, the `siginterrupt()` function can be used to make functions interruptible for a particular signal or to make them restartable, depending on the value of the second argument. The declaration is:

```
#include <signal.h>                                           XSI

int siginterrupt(int sig, int flag);
```

According to the POSIX standard, the behavior of `siginterrupt()` is equivalent to the following code:

```
int siginterrupt(int sig, int flag)
{
    int ret;
    struct sigaction act;

    (void) sigaction(sig, NULL, &act);        Retrieve old setting

    if (flag)                                 If flag is true ...
        act.sa_flags &= ~SA_RESTART;          Disable restarting
    else                                      Otherwise ...
        act.sa_flags |= SA_RESTART;           Enable restarting

    ret = sigaction(sig, &act, NULL);         Put new setting in place
    return ret;                               Return result
}
```

The return value is 0 on success or –1 on error.

10.6.7 Sending Signals: `kill()` and `killpg()`

The traditional Unix function for sending a signal is named `kill()`. The name is something of a misnomer; all it does is send a signal. (Often, the result is that the signal's recipient dies, but that need not be true. However, it's way too late now to change the name.) The `killpg()` function sends a signal to a specific process group. The declarations are:

```
#include <sys/types.h>                                        POSIX
#include <signal.h>

int kill(pid_t pid, int sig);
int killpg(int pgrp, int sig);                                XSI
```

The `sig` argument is either a signal name or 0. In the latter case, no signal is sent, but the kernel still performs error checking. In particular, this is the correct way to verify that a given process or process group exists, as well as to verify that you have permission to send signals to the process or process group. `kill()` returns 0 on success and -1 on error; `errno` then indicates the problem.

The rules for the `pid` value are a bit complicated:

pid > 0   `pid` is a process number, and the signal is sent to that process.

pid = 0   The signal is sent to every process in the sending process's process group.

pid = −1   The signal is sent to every process on the system except for any special system processes. Permission checking still applies. On GNU/Linux systems, only the `init` process (PID 1) is excluded, but other systems may have other special processes.

pid < −1   The signal is sent to the process group represented by the absolute value of `pid`. Thus, you can send a signal to an entire process group, duplicating `killpg()`'s functionality. This nonorthogonality provides historical compatibility.

The meanings of `pid` for `kill()` are similar to those of `waitpid()` (see Section 9.1.6.1, "Using POSIX Functions: `wait()` and `waitpid()`," page 306).

The Standard C function `raise()` is essentially equivalent to

```
int raise(int sig)
{
    return kill(getpid(), sig);
}
```

The C standards committee chose the name `raise()` because C also has to work in non-Unix environments, and `kill()` was considered specific to Unix. It was also a good opportunity to use a more descriptive name for the function.

`killpg()` sends a signal to a process group. As long as the `pgrp` value is greater than 1, it's equivalent to '`kill(-pgrp, sig)`'. The GNU/Linux *killpg*(2) manpage states that if `pgrp` is 0, the signal is sent to the sending processes's process group. (This is the same as `kill()`.)

As you might imagine, you cannot send signals to arbitrary processes (unless you are the superuser, `root`). For ordinary users, the real or effective UID of the sending process must match the real or saved set-user-ID of the receiving process. (The different UIDs are described in Section 11.1.1, "Real and Effective IDs," page 405.)

However, `SIGCONT` is a special case: As long as the receiving process is a member of the same session as the sender, the signal will go through. (Sessions were described briefly in Section 9.2.1, "Job Control Overview," page 312.) This special rule allows a job control shell to continue a stopped descendant process, even if that stopped process is running with a different user ID.

10.6.8 Our Story So Far, Episode II

The System V Release 3 API was intended to remedy the various problems presented by the original V7 signal APIs. The notion of signal blocking, in particular, is an important additional concept.

However, those APIs didn't go far enough, since they worked on only one signal at a time, leaving wide open plenty of windows through which undesired signals could arrive. The POSIX APIs, by working *atomically* on multiple signals (the process signal mask, represented programmatically by the `sigset_t` type), solves this problem, closing the windows.

The first set of functions we examined manipulate `sigset_t` values: `sigfillset()`, `sigemptyset()`, `sigaddset()`, `sigdelset()`, and `sigismember()`.

The next set works with the process signal mask: `sigprocmask()` sets and retrieves the process signal mask. `sigpending()` retrieves the set of pending signals, and `sigsuspend()` puts a process to sleep, temporarily replacing the process signal mask with the one in its parameter.

The POSIX `sigaction()` API is (severely) complicated by the need to supply

- Backward-compatible behavior: `SA_RESETHAND` and `SA_RESTART` in the `sa_flags` field.

- A choice as to whether or not the received signal is also blocked: `SA_NODEFER` for `sa_flags`.

- The ability to have two different kinds of signal handlers: one-argument or three-argument.

- A choice of behaviors for managing `SIGCHLD`: `SA_NOCLDSTOP` and `SA_NOCLDWAIT` for `sa_flags`.

The `siginterrupt()` function is a convenience API for enabling or disabling restartable system calls for a given signal.

Finally, `kill()` and `killpg()` can be used to send signals, not just to the current process but to other processes as well (permissions permitting, of course).

10.7 Signals for Interprocess Communication

> "THIS IS A TERRIBLE IDEA! SIGNALS ARE NOT MEANT
> FOR THIS! Just say NO."
> **—Geoff Collyer—**

One of the primary mechanisms for interprocess communication (IPC) is the pipe, which is described in Section 9.3, "Basic Interprocess Communication: Pipes and FIFOs," page 315. It is possible to use signals for very simple IPC as well.[5] Doing so is rather clumsy; the recipient can only tell that a particular signal came in. While the `sigaction()` API does allow the recipient to learn the PID and owner of the process that sent the signal, such information usually isn't terribly helpful.

> NOTE As the opening quote indicates, using signals for IPC is almost always a bad idea. We recommend avoiding it if possible. But our goal is to teach you how to use the Linux/Unix facilities, including their negative points, leaving it to you to make an informed decision about what to use.

Signals as IPC may sometimes be the only choice for many programs. In particular, pipes are not an option if two communicating programs were not started by a common parent, and FIFO files may not be an option if one of the communicating programs only works with standard input and output. (One instance in which signals are commonly used is with certain system daemon programs, such as `xinetd`, which accepts several signals advising that it should reread its control file, do a consistency check, and so on. See *xinetd*(8) on a GNU/Linux system, and *inetd*(8) on a Unix system.)

The typical high-level structure of a signal-based application looks like this:

```
for (;;) {
    Wait for signal

    Process signal
}
```

The original V7 interface to wait for a signal is `pause()`:

---

[5] Our thanks to Ulrich Drepper for helping us understand the issues involved.

```
#include <unistd.h>                                              POSIX

int pause(void);
```

pause() suspends a process; it only returns after both a signal has been delivered and the signal handler has returned. pause(), by definition, is only useful with caught signals—ignored signals are ignored when they come in, and signals with a default action that terminates the process (with or without a core file) still do so.

The problem with the high-level application structure just described is the *Process signal* part. When that code is running, you don't want to have to handle another signal; you want to finish processing the current signal before going on to the next one. One solution is to structure the signal handler to set a flag and check for that flag within the main loop:

```
volatile sig_atomic_t signal_waiting = 0;   /* true if undealt-with signals */

void handler(int sig)
{
    signal_waiting = 1;
    Set up any other data indicating which signal
}
```

In the mainline code, check the flag:

```
for (;;) {
    if (! signal_waiting) {                 If another signal came in
        pause();                            This code is skipped
        signal_waiting = 1;
    }

    Determine which signal came in
    signal_waiting = 0;
    Process the signal
}
```

Unfortunately, this code is rife with race conditions:

```
for (;;) {
    if (! signal_waiting) {
        <-----------------------  Signal could arrive here, after condition checked!
        pause();                  pause() would be called anyway
        signal_waiting = 1;
    }

    Determine which signal came in  <----  A signal here could overwrite global data
    signal_waiting = 0;
    Process the signal              <----  Same here, especially if multiple signals
}
```

The solution is to keep the signal of interest blocked at all times, *except* when waiting for it to arrive. For example, suppose SIGINT is the signal of interest:

```
void handler(int sig)
{
    /* sig is automatically blocked with sigaction() */
    Set any global data about this signal
}

int main(int argc, char **argv)
{
    sigset_t set;
    struct sigaction act;

    ... usual setup, process options, etc. ...

    sigemptyset(& set);                           Initialize set to empty
    sigaddset(& set, SIGINT);                     Add SIGINT to set
    sigprocmask(SIG_BLOCK, & set, NULL);          Block it

    act.sa_mask = set;                            Set up handler
    act.sa_handler = handler;
    act.sa_flags = 0;
    sigaction(sig, & act, NULL);                  Install it

    ...                                           Possibly install separate handlers
    ...                                           For other signals

    sigemptyset(& set);                           Reset to empty, allows SIGINT to arrive

    for (;;) {
        sigsuspend(& set);                        Wait for SIGINT to arrive

        Process signal                            SIGINT is again blocked here
    }

    ... any other code ...
    return 0;
}
```

The key to this working is that sigsuspend() *temporarily* replaces the process signal mask with the one passed in as its argument. This allows SIGINT to arrive. Once it does, it's handled; the signal handler returns and then sigsuspend() returns as well. By the time sigsuspend() returns, the original process signal mask is back in place.

You can easily extend this paradigm to multiple signals by blocking all signals of interest during main() and during the signal handlers, and unblocking them only in the call to sigsuspend().

Given all this, you should not use `pause()` in new code. `pause()` is standardized by POSIX primarily to support old code. The same is true of the System V Release 3 `sigpause()`. Rather, if you need to structure your application to use signals for IPC, use the `sigsuspend()` and `sigaction()` APIs exclusively.

> NOTE   The example code above presumes that the process signal mask starts out empty. Production code should instead work with whatever signal mask is in place when the program starts.

10.8 Important Special-Purpose Signals

Several signals serve special purposes. We describe the most important ones here.

10.8.1 Alarm Clocks: `sleep()`, `alarm()`, and `SIGALRM`

It is often necessary to write programs of the form

```
while (some condition isn't true) {
    wait for a while
}
```

This need comes up frequently in shell scripting, for example, to wait until a particular user has logged in:

```
until who | grep '^arnold' > /dev/null
do
    sleep 10
done
```

Two mechanisms, one lower level and one higher level, let a running process know when a given number of seconds have passed.

10.8.1.1 Harder but with More Control: `alarm()` and `SIGALRM`

The most basic building block is the `alarm()` system call:

```
#include <unistd.h>                                              POSIX

unsigned int alarm(unsigned int seconds);
```

After `alarm()` returns, the program keeps running. However, when `seconds` seconds have elapsed, the kernel sends a `SIGALRM` to the process. The default action is to terminate the process, but most likely, you will instead have installed a signal handler for SIGALRM.

The return value is either 0, or if a previous alarm had been set, the number of seconds remaining before it would have gone off. However, there is only one such alarm for a process; the previous alarm is canceled and the new one is put in place.

The advantage here is that with your own handler in place, you can do anything you wish when the signal comes in. The disadvantage is that you have to be prepared to work in multiple contexts: that of the mainline program and that of the signal handler.

10.8.1.2 Simple and Easy: sleep()

An easier way to wait a fixed amount of time is with sleep():

```
#include <unistd.h>                                              POSIX

unsigned int sleep(unsigned int seconds);
```

The return value is 0 if the process slept for the full amount of time. Otherwise, the return value is the remaining time left to sleep. This latter return value can occur if a signal came in while the process was napping.

> NOTE   The sleep() function is often implemented with a combination of signal(), alarm(), and pause(). This approach makes it dangerous to mix sleep() with your own calls to alarm() (or the setitimer() advanced function, described in Section 14.3.3, "Interval Timers: setitimer() and getitimer()," page 546). To learn about the nanosleep() function now, see Section 14.3.4, "More Exact Pauses: nanosleep()," page 550).

10.8.2 Job Control Signals

Several signals are used to implement *job control*—the ability to start and stop jobs, and move them to and from the background and foreground. At the user level, you have undoubtedly done this: using CTRL-Z to stop a job, bg to put it in the background, and occasionally using fg to move a background or stopped job into the foreground.

Section 9.2.1, "Job Control Overview," page 312, describes generally how job control works. This section completes the overview by describing the job control signals, since you may occasionally wish to catch them directly:

SIGTSTP

> This signal effects a "terminal stop." It is the signal the kernel sends to the process when the user at the terminal (or window emulating a terminal) types a particular key. Normally, this is CTRL-Z, just as CTRL-C normally sends a SIGINT.
>
> The default action for SIGTSTP is to stop (suspend) the process. However, you can catch this signal, just like any other. It is a good idea to do so if your program changes the state of the terminal. For example, consider the vi or Emacs screen editors, which put the terminal into character-at-a-time mode. Upon receipt of SIGTSTP, they should restore the terminal to its normal line-at-a-time mode, and then suspend themselves.

SIGSTOP

> This signal also stops a process, but it cannot be caught, blocked, or ignored. It can be used manually (with the kill command) as a last resort, or programmatically. For example, the SIGTSTP handler just discussed, after restoring the terminal's state, could then use 'raise(SIGSTOP)' to stop the process.

SIGTTIN, SIGTTOU

> These signals were defined earlier as "background read from tty" and "background write to tty." A *tty* is a terminal device. On job control systems, processes running in the background are blocked from reading from or writing to the terminal. When a process attempts either operation, the kernel sends it the appropriate signal. For both of them, the default action is to stop the process. You may catch these signals if you wish, but there is rarely a reason to do so.

SIGCONT

> This signal continues a stopped process. It is ignored if the process is not stopped. You can catch it if you wish, but again, for most programs, there's little reason to do so. Continuing our example, the SIGCONT handler for a screen editor should put the terminal back into character-at-a-time mode before returning.

When a process is stopped, any other signals sent to it become pending. The exception to this is SIGKILL, which is always delivered to the process and which cannot be caught, blocked, or ignored. Assuming that signals besides SIGKILL have been sent, upon receipt of a SIGCONT, the pending signals are delivered and the process then continues execution after they've been handled.

10.8.3 Parental Supervision: Three Different Strategies

As described in Section 9.1.1, "Creating a Process: `fork()`," page 284, one side effect of calling `fork()` is the creation of parent-child relationships among processes. A parent process can wait for one or more of its children to die and recover the child's exit status by one of the `wait()` family of system calls.

Dead child processes that haven't been waited for are termed *zombies*. Normally, every time a child process dies, the kernel sends a `SIGCHLD` signal to the parent process.[6] The default action is to ignore this signal. In this case, zombie processes accrue until the parent does a `wait()` or until the parent itself dies. In the latter case, the zombie children are reparented to the `init` system process (PID 1), which reaps them as part of its normal work. Similarly, active children are also reparented to `init` and will be reaped when they exit.

`SIGCHLD` is used for more than death-of-children notification. Any time a child is stopped (by one of the job control signals discussed earlier), `SIGCHLD` is also sent to the parent. The POSIX standard indicates that `SIGCHLD` "may be sent" when a child is continued as well; apparently there are differences among historical Unix systems.

A combination of flags for the `sa_flags` field in the `struct sigaction`, and the use of `SIG_IGN` as the action for `SIGCHLD` allows you to change the way the kernel deals with children stopping, continuing, or dying.

As with signals in general, the interfaces and mechanisms described here are complicated because they have evolved over time.

10.8.3.1 Poor Parenting: Ignoring Children Completely

The simplest thing you can do is to change the action for `SIGCHLD` to `SIG_IGN`. In this case, children that terminate do not become zombies. Instead, their exit status is thrown away, and they are removed from the system entirely. Another option that produces the same effect is use of the `SA_NOCLDWAIT` flag. In code:

---

[6] Historically, BSD systems used the name `SIGCHLD`, and this is what POSIX uses. System V had a similar signal named `SIGCLD`. GNU/Linux `#defines` the latter to be the former—see Table 10.1.

```
/* Old style: */                          /* New style: */
                                          struct sigaction sa;
                                          sa.sa_handler = SIG_IGN;
signal(SIGCHLD, SIG_IGN);                 sa.sa_flags = SA_NOCLDWAIT;
                                          sigemptyset(& sa.sa_mask);
                                          sigaction(SIGCHLD, & sa, NULL);
```

10.8.3.2 Permissive Parenting: Supervising Minimally

Alternatively, you may only care about child termination and not be interested in simple state changes (stopped, and continued). In this case, use the SA_NOCLDSTOP flag, and set up a signal handler that calls wait() (or one of its siblings) to reap the process.

In general, you *cannot* expect to get one SIGCHLD per child that dies. You should treat SIGCHLD as meaning "at least one child has died" and be prepared to reap as many children as possible whenever you process SIGCHLD.

The following program, ch10-reap1.c, blocks SIGCHLD until it's ready to recover the children.

```
 1   /* ch10-reap1.c --- demonstrate SIGCHLD management, using a loop */
 2
 3   #include <stdio.h>
 4   #include <errno.h>
 5   #include <signal.h>
 6   #include <string.h>
 7   #include <sys/types.h>
 8   #include <sys/wait.h>
 9
10   #define MAX_KIDS    42
11   #define NOT_USED    -1
12
13   pid_t kids[MAX_KIDS];
14   size_t nkids = 0;
```

The kids array tracks the process IDs of children processes. If an element is NOT_USED, then it doesn't represent an unreaped child. (Lines 89–90, below, initialize it.) nkids indicates how many values in kids should be checked.

```
16    /* format_num --- helper function since can't use [sf]printf() */
17
18    const char *format_num(int num)
19    {
20    #define NUMSIZ   30
21        static char buf[NUMSIZ];
22        int i;
23
24        if (num <= 0) {
25            strcpy(buf, "0");
26            return buf;
27        }
28
29        i = NUMSIZ - 1;
30        buf[i--] = '\0';
31
32        /* Generate digits backwards into string. */
33        do {
34            buf[i--] = (num % 10) + '0';
35            num /= 10;
36        } while (num > 0);
37
38        return & buf[i+1];
39    }
```

Because signal handlers should not call any member of the `printf()` family, we provide a simple "helper" function, `format_num()`, to turn a decimal signal or PID number into a string. This is primitive, but it works.

```
41    /* childhandler --- catch SIGCHLD, reap all available children */
42
43    void childhandler(int sig)
44    {
45        int status, ret;
46        int i;
47        char buf[100];
48        static const char entered[] = "Entered childhandler\n";
49        static const char exited[] = "Exited childhandler\n";
50
51        write(1, entered, strlen(entered));
52        for (i = 0; i < nkids; i++) {
53            if (kids[i] == NOT_USED)
54                continue;
55
```

```
56      retry:
57          if ((ret = waitpid(kids[i], & status, WNOHANG)) == kids[i]) {
58              strcpy(buf, "\treaped process ");
59              strcat(buf, format_num(ret));
60              strcat(buf, "\n");
61              write(1, buf, strlen(buf));
62              kids[i] = NOT_USED;
63          } else if (ret == 0) {
64              strcpy(buf, "\tpid ");
65              strcat(buf, format_num(kids[i]));
66              strcat(buf, " not available yet\n");
67              write(1, buf, strlen(buf));
68          } else if (ret == -1 && errno == EINTR) {
69              write(1, "\tretrying\n", 10);
70              goto retry;
71          } else {
72              strcpy(buf, "\twaitpid() failed: ");
73              strcat(buf, strerror(errno));
74              strcat(buf, "\n");
75              write(1, buf, strlen(buf));
76          }
77      }
78      write(1, exited, strlen(exited));
79  }
```

Lines 51 and 58 print "entered" and "exited" messages, so that we can clearly see when the signal handler is invoked. Other messages start with a leading TAB character.

The main part of the signal handler is a large loop, lines 52–77. Lines 53–54 check for NOT_USED and continue the loop if the current slot isn't in use.

Line 57 calls waitpid() on the PID in the current element of kids. We supply the WNOHANG option, which causes waitpid() to return immediately if the requested child isn't available. This call is necessary since it's possible that not all of the children have exited.

Based on the return value, the code takes the appropriate action. Lines 57–62 handle the case in which the child is found, by printing a message and marking the appropriate slot in kids as NOT_USED.

Lines 63–67 handle the case in which the requested child is not available. The return value is 0 in this case, so we print a message and keep going.

Lines 68–70 handle the case in which the system call was interrupted. In this case, a `goto` back to the `waitpid()` call is the cleanest way to handle things. (Since `main()` causes all signals to be blocked when the signal handler runs [line 96], this interruption shouldn't happen. But this example shows you how to deal with all the cases.)

Lines 71–76 handle any other error, printing an appropriate error message.

```
 81    /* main --- set up child-related information and signals, create children */
 82
 83    int main(int argc, char **argv)
 84    {
 85        struct sigaction sa;
 86        sigset_t childset, emptyset;
 87        int i;
 88
 89        for (i = 0; i < nkids; i++)
 90            kids[i] = NOT_USED;
 91
 92        sigemptyset(& emptyset);
 93
 94        sa.sa_flags = SA_NOCLDSTOP;
 95        sa.sa_handler = childhandler;
 96        sigfillset(& sa.sa_mask);    /* block everything when handler runs */
 97        sigaction(SIGCHLD, & sa, NULL);
 98
 99        sigemptyset(& childset);
100        sigaddset(& childset, SIGCHLD);
101
102        sigprocmask(SIG_SETMASK, & childset, NULL); /* block it in main code */
103
104        for (nkids = 0; nkids < 5; nkids++) {
105            if ((kids[nkids] = fork()) == 0) {
106                sleep(3);
107                _exit(0);
108            }
109        }
110
111        sleep(5);    /* give the kids a chance to terminate */
112
113        printf("waiting for signal\n");
114        sigsuspend(& emptyset);
115
116        return 0;
117    }
```

Lines 89–90 initialize `kids`. Line 92 initializes `emptyset`. Lines 94–97 set up and install the signal handler for `SIGCHLD`. Note the use of `SA_NOCLDSTOP` on line 94, while line 96 blocks all signals when the handler is running.

Lines 99–100 create a signal set representing just `SIGCHLD`, and line 102 installs it as the process signal mask for the program.

Lines 104–109 create five child processes, each of which sleeps for three seconds. Along the way, it updates the `kids` array and `nkids` variable.

Line 111 then gives the children a chance to terminate by sleeping longer than they did. (This doesn't *guarantee* that the children will terminate, but the chances are pretty good.)

Finally, lines 113–114 print a message and then pause, replacing the process signal mask that blocks `SIGCHLD` with an empty one. This allows the `SIGCHLD` signal to come through, in turn causing the signal handler to run. Here's what happens:

```
$ ch10-reap1                                    Run the program
waiting for signal
Entered childhandler
        reaped process 23937
        reaped process 23938
        reaped process 23939
        reaped process 23940
        reaped process 23941
Exited childhandler
```

The signal handler reaps all of the children in one go.

The following program, `ch10-reap2.c` is similar to `ch10-reap1.c`. The difference is that it allows `SIGCHLD` to arrive at any time. This behavior increases the chance of receiving more than one `SIGCHLD` but does *not* guarantee it. As a result, the signal handler still has to be prepared to reap multiple children in a loop.

```
 1  /* ch10-reap2.c --- demonstrate SIGCHLD management, one signal per child */
 2
    ... unchanged code omitted ...
12
13  pid_t kids[MAX_KIDS];
14  size_t nkids = 0;
15  size_t kidsleft = 0;                    /* <<< Added */
16
    ... unchanged code for format_num() omitted ...
41
42  /* childhandler --- catch SIGCHLD, reap all available children */
43
```

```
44  void childhandler(int sig)
45  {
46      int status, ret;
47      int i;
48      char buf[100];
49      static const char entered[] = "Entered childhandler\n";
50      static const char exited[] = "Exited childhandler\n";
51
52      write(1, entered, strlen(entered));
53      for (i = 0; i < nkids; i++) {
54          if (kids[i] == NOT_USED)
55              continue;
56
57      retry:
58          if ((ret = waitpid(kids[i], & status, WNOHANG)) == kids[i]) {
59              strcpy(buf, "\treaped process ");
60              strcat(buf, format_num(ret));
61              strcat(buf, "\n");
62              write(1, buf, strlen(buf));
63              kids[i] = NOT_USED;
64              kidsleft--;             /* <<< Added */
65          } else if (ret == 0) {
    ... unchanged code omitted ...
80      write(1, exited, strlen(exited));
81  }
```

This is identical to the previous version, except we have a new variable, `kidsleft`, indicating how many unreaped children there are. Lines 15 and 64 flag the new code.

```
83  /* main --- set up child-related information and signals, create children */
84
85  int main(int argc, char **argv)
86  {
    ... unchanged code omitted ...
100
101     sigemptyset(& childset);
102     sigaddset(& childset, SIGCHLD);
103
104 /*  sigprocmask(SIG_SETMASK, & childset, NULL); /* block it in main code */
105
106     for (nkids = 0; nkids < 5; nkids++) {
107         if ((kids[nkids] = fork()) == 0) {
108             sleep(3);
109             _exit(0);
110         }
111         kidsleft++;                     /* <<< Added */
112     }
113
114 /*  sleep(5);   /* give the kids a chance to terminate */
115
```

```
116        while (kidsleft > 0) {         /* <<< Added */
117            printf("waiting for signals\n");
118            sigsuspend(& emptyset);
119        }                              /* <<< Added */
120
121        return 0;
122  }
```

Here too, the code is almost identical. Lines 104 and 114 are commented out from the earlier version, and lines 111, 116, and 119 were added. Surprisingly, when run, the behavior varies by kernel version!

```
$ uname -a                            Display system version
Linux example1 2.4.20-8 #1 Thu Mar 13 17:54:28 EST 2003 i686 i686 i386 GNU/Linux
$ ch10-reap2                          Run the program
waiting for signals
Entered childhandler                  Reap one child
        reaped process 2702
        pid 2703 not available yet
        pid 2704 not available yet
        pid 2705 not available yet
        pid 2706 not available yet
Exited childhandler
waiting for signals
Entered childhandler                  And the next
        reaped process 2703
        pid 2704 not available yet
        pid 2705 not available yet
        pid 2706 not available yet
Exited childhandler
waiting for signals
Entered childhandler                  And so on
        reaped process 2704
        pid 2705 not available yet
        pid 2706 not available yet
Exited childhandler
waiting for signals
Entered childhandler
        reaped process 2705
        pid 2706 not available yet
Exited childhandler
waiting for signals
Entered childhandler
        reaped process 2706
Exited childhandler
```

In this example, exactly one SIGCHLD is delivered per child process! While this is lovely, and completely reproducible on this system, it's also unusual. On both an earlier and a later kernel and on Solaris, the program receives one signal for more than one child:

```
$ uname -a                                    Display system version
Linux example2 2.4.22-1.2115.nptl #1 Wed Oct 29 15:42:51 EST
        2003 i686 i686 i386 GNU/Linux
$ ch10-reap2                                  Run the program
waiting for signals
Entered childhandler                          Signal handler only called once
        reaped process 9564
        reaped process 9565
        reaped process 9566
        reaped process 9567
        reaped process 9568
Exited childhandler
```

> NOTE The code for `ch10-reap2.c` has one important flaw—a race condition.
> Take another look at lines 106–112 in `ch10-reap2.c`. What happens if a
> SIGCHLD comes in while this code is running? It's possible for the `kids` array
> and `nkids` and `kidsleft` variables to become corrupted: The main code adds
> in a new process, but the signal handler takes one away.
>
>   This piece of code is an excellent example of a critical section; it must run
> uninterrupted. The correct way to manage this code is to bracket it with calls
> that first block, and then unblock, SIGCHLD.

10.8.3.3 Strict Parental Control

The `siginfo_t` structure and three argument signal catcher make it possible to learn
what happened to a child. For SIGCHLD, the `si_code` field of the `siginfo_t` indicates
the reason the signal was sent (child stopped, continued, exited, etc.). Table 10.5 presents
the full list of values. All of these are defined as an XSI extension in the POSIX standard.

The following program, `ch10-status.c`, demonstrates the use of the `siginfo_t`
structure.

```
1   /* ch10-status.c --- demonstrate SIGCHLD management, use 3 argument handler */
2
3   #include <stdio.h>
4   #include <errno.h>
5   #include <signal.h>
6   #include <string.h>
7   #include <sys/types.h>
8   #include <sys/wait.h>
9
10  void manage(siginfo_t *si);
11

        ... unchanged code for format_num() omitted ...
```

TABLE 10.5
XSI si_code values for SIGCHLD

Value	Meaning
CLD_CONTINUED	A stopped child has been continued.
CLD_DUMPED	Child terminated abnormally and dumped core.
CLD_EXITED	Child exited normally.
CLD_KILLED	Child was killed by a signal.
CLD_STOPPED	The child process was stopped.
CLD_TRAPPED	A child being traced has stopped. (This condition occurs if a program is being traced—either from a debugger or for real-time monitoring. In any case, you're not likely to see it in run-of-the-mill situations.)

Lines 3–8 include standard header files, line 10 declares manage(), which deals with the child's status changes, and the format_num() function is unchanged from before.

```
37  /* childhandler --- catch SIGCHLD, reap just one child */
38
39  void childhandler(int sig, siginfo_t *si, void *context)
40  {
41      int status, ret;
42      int i;
43      char buf[100];
44      static const char entered[] = "Entered childhandler\n";
45      static const char exited[] = "Exited childhandler\n";
46
47      write(1, entered, strlen(entered));
48  retry:
49      if ((ret = waitpid(si->si_pid, & status, WNOHANG)) == si->si_pid) {
50          strcpy(buf, "\treaped process ");
51          strcat(buf, format_num(si->si_pid));
52          strcat(buf, "\n");
53          write(1, buf, strlen(buf));
54          manage(si);            /* deal with what happened to it */
55      } else if (ret > 0) {
56          strcpy(buf, "\treaped unexpected pid ");
57          strcat(buf, format_num(ret));
58          strcat(buf, "\n");
59          write(1, buf, strlen(buf));
60          goto retry;      /* why not? */
61      } else if (ret == 0) {
62          strcpy(buf, "\tpid ");
63          strcat(buf, format_num(si->si_pid));
64          strcat(buf, " changed status\n");
65          write(1, buf, strlen(buf));
66          manage(si);            /* deal with what happened to it */
```

```
67        } else if (ret == -1 && errno == EINTR) {
68            write(1, "\tretrying\n", 10);
69            goto retry;
70        } else {
71            strcpy(buf, "\twaitpid() failed: ");
72            strcat(buf, strerror(errno));
73            strcat(buf, "\n");
74            write(1, buf, strlen(buf));
75        }
76
77        write(1, exited, strlen(exited));
78 }
```

The signal handler is similar to those shown earlier. Note the argument list (line 39), and that there is no loop.

Lines 49–54 handle process termination, including calling `manage()` to print the status.

Lines 55–60 handle the case of an unexpected child dying. This case shouldn't happen, since this signal handler is passed information specific to a particular child process.

Lines 61–66 are what interest us: The return value is 0 for status changes. `manage()` deals with the details (line 66).

Lines 67–69 handle interrupts, and lines 70–75 deal with errors.

```
80  /* child --- what to do in the child */
81
82  void child(void)
83  {
84      raise(SIGCONT);      /* should be ignored */
85      raise(SIGSTOP);       /* go to sleep, parent wakes us back up */
86      printf("\t---> child restarted <---\n");
87      exit(42);             /* normal exit, let parent get value */
88  }
```

The `child()` function handles the child's behavior, taking actions of the sort to cause the parent to be notified.[7] Line 84 sends `SIGCONT`, which might cause the parent to get a `CLD_CONTINUED` event. Line 85 sends a `SIGSTOP`, which stops the process (the signal is uncatchable) and causes a `CLD_STOPPED` event for the parent. Once the parent restarts the child, the child prints a message to show it's active again and then exits with a distinguished exit status.

---

[7] Perhaps `child_at_school()` would be a better function name.

```
90   /* main --- set up child-related information and signals, create child */
91
92   int main(int argc, char **argv)
93   {
94       pid_t kid;
95       struct sigaction sa;
96       sigset_t childset, emptyset;
97
98       sigemptyset(& emptyset);
99
100      sa.sa_flags = SA_SIGINFO;
101      sa.sa_sigaction = childhandler;
102      sigfillset(& sa.sa_mask);    /* block everything when handler runs */
103      sigaction(SIGCHLD, & sa, NULL);
104
105      sigemptyset(& childset);
106      sigaddset(& childset, SIGCHLD);
107
108      sigprocmask(SIG_SETMASK, & childset, NULL); /* block it in main code */
109
110      if ((kid = fork()) == 0)
111          child();
112
113      /* parent executes here */
114      for (;;) {
115          printf("waiting for signals\n");
116          sigsuspend(& emptyset);
117      }
118
119      return 0;
120  }
```

The `main()` program sets everything up. Lines 100–103 put the handler in place.
Line 100 sets the `SA_SIGINFO` flag so that the three-argument handler is used. Lines
105–108 block `SIGCHLD`.

Line 110 creates the child process. Lines 113–117 continue in the parent, using
`sigsuspend()` to wait for signals to come in.

```
123  /* manage --- deal with different things that could happen to child */
124
125  void manage(siginfo_t *si)
126  {
127      char buf[100];
128
129      switch (si->si_code) {
130      case CLD_STOPPED:
131          write(1, "\tchild stopped, restarting\n", 27);
132          kill(si->si_pid, SIGCONT);
133          break;
134
```

```
135        case CLD_CONTINUED: /* not sent on Linux */
136            write(1, "\tchild continued\n", 17);
137            break;
138
139        case CLD_EXITED:
140            strcpy(buf, "\tchild exited with status ");
141            strcat(buf, format_num(si->si_status));
142            strcat(buf, "\n");
143            write(1, buf, strlen(buf));
144            exit(0);    /* we're done */
145            break;
146
147        case CLD_DUMPED:
148            write(1, "\tchild dumped\n", 14);
149            break;
150
151        case CLD_KILLED:
152            write(1, "\tchild killed\n", 14);
153            break;
154
155        case CLD_TRAPPED:
156            write(1, "\tchild trapped\n", 15);
157            break;
158        }
159  }
```

Through the `manage()` function, the parent deals with the status change in the child. `manage()` is called when the status changes and when the child has exited.

Lines 130–133 handle the case in which the child stopped; the parent restarts the child by sending SIGCONT.

Lines 135–137 print a notification that the child continued. This event doesn't happen on GNU/Linux systems, and the POSIX standard uses wishy-washy language about it, merely saying that this event *can* occur, not that it *will.*

Lines 139–145 handle the case in which the child exits, printing the exit status. For this program, the parent is done too, so the code exits, although in a larger program, that's not the right action to take.

The other cases are more specialized. In the event of CLD_KILLED, the status value filled in by `waitpid()` would be useful in determining more details.

Here is what happens when it runs:

```
$ ch10-status                                Run the program
waiting for signals
Entered childhandler                         Signal handler entered
        pid 24279 changed status
        child stopped, restarting            Handler takes action
Exited childhandler
waiting for signals
        ---> child restarted <---            From the child
Entered childhandler
        reaped process 24279                 Parent's handler reaps child
        child exited with status 42
```

Unfortunately, because there is no way to guarantee the delivery of one SIGCHLD per process, your program has to be prepared to recover multiple children at one shot.

10.9 Signals Across `fork()` and `exec()`

When a program calls `fork()`, the signal situation in the child is almost identical to that of the parent. Installed handlers remain in place, blocked signals remain blocked, and so on. However, any signals pending for the parent are cleared for the child, including time left as set by `alarm()`. This is straightforward, and it makes sense.

When a process calls one of the `exec()` functions, the disposition in the new program is as follows:

- Signals set to their default action stay set to their default.

- Any caught signals are reset to their default action.

- Signals that are ignored stay ignored. SIGCHLD is a special case. If SIGCHLD is ignored before the `exec()`, it may stay ignored after it. Alternatively, it may be reset to the default action. What actually happens is purposely unspecified by POSIX. (The GNU/Linux manpages don't state what Linux does, and because POSIX leaves it as unspecified, any code you write that uses SIGCHLD should be prepared to handle either case.)

- Signals that are blocked before the `exec()` remain blocked after it. In other words, the new program inherits the process's existing process signal mask.

- Any pending signals (those that have arrived but that were blocked) are cleared. The new program won't get them.

- The time remaining for an `alarm()` remains in place. (In other words, if a process sets an alarm and then calls `exec()` directly, the new image will eventually get the SIGALRM. If it does a fork() first, the parent keeps the alarm setting, while the child, which does the exec(), does not.)

> NOTE Many, if not most, programs assume that signal actions are initialized to their defaults and that no signals are blocked. Thus, particularly if you didn't write the program being run with exec(), it's a good idea to unblock all signals before doing the exec().

10.10 Summary

> "Our story so far, Episode III."
> —Arnold Robbins—

- Signal handling interfaces have evolved from simple but prone-to-race conditions to complicated but reliable. Unfortunately, the multiplicity of interfaces makes them harder to learn than many other Linux/Unix APIs.

- Each signal has an action associated with it. The action is one of the following: ignore the signal; perform the system default action; or call a user-provided handler. The system default action, in turn, is one of the following: ignore the signal; kill the process; kill the process and dump core; stop the process; or continue the process if stopped.

- signal() and raise() are standardized by ISO C. signal() manages actions for particular signals; raise() sends a signal to the current process. Whether signal handlers stay installed upon invocation, or are reset to their default values is up to the implementation. signal() and raise() are the simplest interfaces, and they suffice for many applications.

- POSIX defines the bsd_signal() function, which is like signal() but guarantees that the handler stays installed.

- What happens after a signal handler returns varies according to the type of system. Traditional systems (V7, Solaris, and likely others) reset signal dispositions to their default. On those systems, interrupted system calls return -1, setting errno to EINTR. BSD systems leave the handler installed and only return -1 with errno set to EINTR when no data were transferred; otherwise, they restart the system call.

- GNU/Linux follows POSIX, which is similar but not identical to BSD. If no data were transferred, the system call returns `-1`/`EINTR`. Otherwise, it returns a count of the amount of data transferred. The BSD "always restart" behavior is available in the `sigaction()` interface but is not the default.

- Signal handlers used with `signal()` are prone to race conditions. Variables of type `volatile sig_atomic_t` should be used exclusively inside signal handlers. (For expositional purposes, we did not follow this rule in some of our examples.) Similarly, only the functions in Table 10.2 are safe to call from within a signal handler.

- The System V Release 3 signal API (lifted from 4.0 BSD) was an initial attempt at reliable signals. Don't use it in new code.

- The POSIX API has multiple components:

  - the process signal mask, which lists the currently blocked signals,

  - the `sigset_t` type to represent signal masks, and the `sigfillset()`, `sigemptyset()`, `sigaddset()`, `sigdelset()`, and `sigismember()` functions for working with it,

  - the `sigprocmask()` function to set and retrieve the process signal mask,

  - the `sigpending()` function to retrieve the set of pending signals,

  - the `sigaction()` API and `struct sigaction` in all their glory.

  These facilities together use signal blocking and the process signal mask to provide reliable signals. Furthermore, through various flags, it's possible to get restartable system calls and a more capable signal handler that receives more information about the reason for a particular signal (the `siginfo_t` structure).

- `kill()` and `killpg()` are the POSIX mechanisms for sending signals. These differ from `raise()` in two ways: (1) one process may send a signal to another process or an entire process group (permissions permitting, of course), and (2) sending signal `0` does not send anything but does do the checking. Thus, these functions provide a way to verify the existence of a particular process or process group, and the ability to send it (them) a signal.

- Signals can be used as an IPC mechanism, although such use is a poor way to structure your application and is prone to race conditions. If someone holds a gun

to your head to make you work that way, use careful signal blocking and the
`sigaction()` interface to do it correctly.

- `SIGALRM` and the `alarm()` system call provide a low-level mechanism for notification after a certain number of seconds have passed. `pause()` suspends a process until any signal comes in. `sleep()` uses these to put a process to sleep for a given amount of time: `sleep()` and `alarm()` should not be used together. `pause()` itself opens up race conditions; signal blocking and `sigsuspend()` should be used instead.

- Job control signals implement job control for shells. Most of the time you should leave them set to their default, but it's helpful to understand that occasionally it makes sense to catch them.

- Catching `SIGCHLD` lets a parent know what its children processes are doing. Using '`signal(SIGCHLD, SIG_IGN)`' (or `sigaction()` with `SA_NOCLDWAIT`) ignores children altogether. Using `sigaction()` with `SA_NOCLDSTOP` provides notification only about termination. In the latter case, whether or not `SIGCHLD` is blocked, signal handlers for `SIGCHLD` should be prepared to reap multiple children at once. Finally, using `sigaction()` without `SA_NOCLDSTOP` with a three-argument signal handler gives you the reason for receipt for the signal. (Whew!)

- After a `fork()`, signal disposition in the child remains the same, except that pending signals and alarms are cleared. After an `exec()`, it's a little more complicated—essentially everything that can be left alone is; anything else is reset to its defaults.

Exercises

1. Implement `bsd_signal()` by using `sigaction()`.

2. If you're not running GNU/Linux, run `ch10-catchint` on your system. Is your system traditional or BSD?

3. Implement the System V Release 3 functions `sighold()`, `sigrelse()`, `sigignore()`, `sigpause()`, and `sigset()` by using `sigaction()` and the other related functions in the POSIX API.

4. Practice your bit-bashing skills. Assuming that there is no signal 0 and that there are no more than 31 signals, provide a `typedef` for `sigset_t` and

write `sigemptyset()`, `sigfillset()`, `sigaddset()`, `sigdelset()`, and `sigismember()`.

5. Practice your bit-bashing skills some more. Repeat the previous exercise, this time assuming that the highest signal is `42`.

6. Now that you've done the previous two exercises, find `sigemptyset()` et al. in your `<signal.h>` header file. (You may have to search for them; they could be in files `#included` by `<signal.h>`.) Are they macros or functions?

7. In Section 10.7, "Signals for Interprocess Communication," page 379, we mentioned that production code should work with the initial process signal mask, adding signals to be blocked and removing them except in the call to `sigsuspend()`. Rewrite the example, using the appropriate calls to do this.

8. Write your own version of the `kill` command. The interface should be

   `kill [ -s` *signal-name* `]` *pid* `...`

   Without a specific signal, the program should send `SIGTERM`.

9. Why do you think modern shells such as Bash and `ksh93` have `kill` as a built-in command?

10. (Hard). Implement `sleep()`, using `alarm()`, `signal()`, and `pause()`. What if a signal handler for `SIGALRM` is already in place?

11. Experiment with `ch10-reap.c`, changing the amount of time each child sleeps and arranging to call `sigsuspend()` enough times to reap all the children.

12. See if you can get `ch10-reap2.c` to corrupt the information in `kids`, `nkids`, and `kidsleft`. Now add blocking/unblocking around the critical section and see if it makes a difference.

Chapter

11

Permissions and User and Group ID Numbers

In this chapter

L inux, following Unix, is a *multiuser system*. Unlike most operating systems for personal computers,[1] in which there is only one user and whoever is physically in front of the computer has complete control, Linux and Unix separate files and processes by the owners and groups to which they belong. In this chapter, we examine permission checking and look at the APIs for retrieving and setting the owner and group identifiers.

11.1 Checking Permissions

As we saw in Section 5.4.2, "Retrieving File Information," page 141, the filesystem stores a file's user identifier and group identifier as numeric values; these are the types `uid_t` and `gid_t`, respectively. For brevity, we use the abbreviations UID and GID for "user identifier" and "group identifier."

Every process has several user and group identifiers associated with it. As a simplification, one particular UID and GID are used for permission checking; when the UID of a process matches the UID of a file, the file's user permission bits dictate what the process can do with the file. If they don't match, the system checks the GID of the process against the GID of the file; if they match, the group permissions apply; otherwise the "other" permissions apply.

Besides files, the UID controls how one process can affect another by sending it a signal. Signals are described in Chapter 10, "Signals," page 347.

Finally, the superuser, `root`, is a special case. `root` is identified by a UID of 0. When a process has UID 0, the kernel lets it do whatever it wants to: read, write, or remove files, send signals to arbitrary processes, and so on. (POSIX is more obtuse about this, referring to processes with "appropriate privilege." This language in turn has filtered down into the GNU/Linux manpages and the GLIBC online Info manual. Some operating systems do separate privilege by user, and Linux is moving in this direction as well. Nevertheless, in current practice, "appropriate privilege" just means processes with UID 0.)

---

[1] MacOS X and Windows XP are both multiuser systems, but this is a rather recent development.

11.1.1 Real and Effective IDs

UID and GID numbers are like personal identification. Sometimes you need to carry more than one bit of identification around with you. For instance, you may have a driver's license or government identity card.[2] In addition, your university or company may have issued you an identification card. Such is the case with processes too; they carry multiple UID and GID numbers around with them, as follows:

Real user ID

> The UID of the user that forked the process.

Effective user ID

> The UID used for most permission checking. Most of the time, the effective and real UIDs are the same. The effective UID can be different from the real one at startup if the *setuid* bit of the executable program's file is set and the file is owned by someone other than the user running the program. (More details soon.)

Saved set-user ID

> The original effective UID at program startup (after the exec). This plays a role in permission checking when a process needs to swap its real and effective UIDs back and forth. This concept came from System V.

Real group ID

> The GID of the user that created the process, analogous to the real UID.

Effective group ID

> The GID used for permission checking, analogous to the effective UID.

Saved set-group ID

> The original effective GID at program startup, analogous to the saved set-user ID.

Supplemental group set

> 4.2 BSD introduced the idea of a *group set*. Besides the real and effective GIDs, each process has some set of additional groups to which it *simultaneously* belongs. Thus, when permission checking is done for a file's group permissions, not only does the kernel check the effective GID, but it also checks all of the GIDs in the group set.

---

[2] Although the United States doesn't have official identity cards, many countries do.

Any process can retrieve all of these values. A regular (non-superuser) process can switch its real and effective user and group IDs back and forth. A `root` process (one with an effective UID of 0) can also set the values however it needs to (although this can be a one-way operation).

11.1.2 Setuid and Setgid Bits

The *setuid* and *setgid* bits[3] in the file permissions cause a process to acquire an effective UID or GID that is different from the real one. These bits are applied manually to a file with the `chmod` command:

```
$ chmod u+s myprogram                    Add setuid bit
$ chmod g+s myprogram                    Add setgid bit
$ ls -l myprogram
-rwsr-sr-x    1 arnold    devel          4573 Oct  9 18:17 myprogram
```

The `s` character where an `x` character usually appears indicates the presence of the setuid/setgid bits.

As mentioned in Section 8.2.1, "Using Mount Options," page 239, the `nosuid` option to `mount` for a filesystem prevents the kernel from honoring both the setuid and setgid bits. This is a security feature; for example, a user with a home GNU/Linux system might handcraft a floppy with a copy of the shell executable made setuid to `root`. But if the GNU/Linux system in the office or the lab will only mount floppy filesystems with the `nosuid` option, then running this shell won't provide `root` access.[4]

The canonical (and probably overused) motivating example of a setuid program is a game program. Suppose you've written a really cool game, and you wish to allow users on the system to play it. The game keeps a score file, listing the highest scores.

If you're not the system administrator, you can't create a separate group of just those users who are allowed to play the game and thus write to the score file. But if you make the file world-writable so that anyone can play the game, then anyone can also cheat and put any name at the top.

---

3 Dennis Ritchie, the inventor of C and a cocreator of Unix, received a patent for the setuid bit: *Protection of Data File Contents*, US Patent number 4,135,240. See `http://www.delphion.com/details?pn=US04135240__` and also `http://www.uspto.gov`. AT&T assigned the patent to the public, allowing anyone to use its technology.

4 Security for GNU/Linux and Unix systems is a deep topic in and of itself. This is just an example; see Section 11.9, "Suggested Reading," page 423.

However, by making the game program setuid to yourself, users running the game have your UID as their effective UID. The game program can then open and update the file as needed, but arbitrary users can't come along and edit it. (You also open yourself up to most of the dangers of setuid programming; for example, if the game program has a hole that can be exploited to produce a shell running as you, *all* your files are available for deletion or change. This is a justifiably scary thought.)

The same logic applies to setgid programs, although in practice setgid programs are much less used than setuid ones. (This is too bad; many things that are done with setuid root programs could easily be done with setgid programs or programs that are setuid to a regular user, instead.[5])

11.2 Retrieving User and Group IDs

Getting the UID and GID information from the system is straightforward. The functions are as follows:

```
#include <unistd.h>                                    POSIX

uid_t getuid(void);                    Real and effective UID
uid_t geteuid(void);

gid_t getgid(void);                    Real and effective GID
gid_t getegid(void);

int getgroups(int size, gid_t list[]);   Supplemental group list
```

The functions are:

uid_t getuid(void)
    Returns the real UID.

uid_t geteuid(void)
    Returns the effective UID.

gid_t getgid(void)
    Returns the real GID.

gid_t getegid(void)
    Returns the effective GID.

---

[5] One program designed for this purpose is GNU userv (ftp://ftp.gnu.org/gnu/userv/).

```
int getgroups(int size, gid_t list[])
```
Fills in up to `size` elements of `list` from the process's supplemental group set. The return value is the number of elements filled in or -1 if there's an error. It is implementation defined whether the effective GID is also included in the set.

On POSIX-compliant systems, you can pass in a `size` value of zero; in this case, `getgroups()` returns the number of groups in the process's group set. You can then use that value to dynamically allocate an array that's big enough.

On non-POSIX systems, the constant `NGROUPS_MAX` defines the maximum necessary size for the `list` array. This constant can be found in `<limits.h>` on modern systems or in `<sys/param.h>` on older ones. We present an example shortly.

You may have noticed that there are no calls to get the saved set-user ID or saved set-group ID values. These are just the original values of the effective UID and effective GID. Thus, you can use code like this at program startup to obtain the six values:

```
uid_t ruid, euid, saved_uid;
gid_t rgid, egid, saved_gid;

int main(int argc, char **argv)
{
    ruid = getuid();
    euid = saved_uid = geteuid();

    rgid = getgid();
    egid = saved_gid = getegid();

    ... rest of program ...
}
```

Here is an example of retrieving the group set. As an extension, `gawk` provides `awk`-level access to the real and effective UID and GID values and the supplemental group set. To do this, it has to retrieve the group set. The following function is from `main.c` in the `gawk` 3.1.3 distribution:

```
1080  /* init_groupset --- initialize groupset */
1081
1082  static void
1083  init_groupset()
1084  {
1085  #if defined(HAVE_GETGROUPS) && defined(NGROUPS_MAX) && NGROUPS_MAX > 0
1086  #ifdef GETGROUPS_NOT_STANDARD
1087      /* For systems that aren't standards conformant, use old way. */
1088      ngroups = NGROUPS_MAX;
```

```
1089    #else
1090        /*
1091         * If called with 0 for both args, return value is
1092         * total number of groups.
1093         */
1094        ngroups = getgroups(0, NULL);
1095    #endif
1096        if (ngroups == -1)
1097            fatal(_("could not find groups: %s"), strerror(errno));
1098        else if (ngroups == 0)
1099            return;
1100
1101        /* fill in groups */
1102        emalloc(groupset, GETGROUPS_T *, ngroups * sizeof(GETGROUPS_T),
1103                "init_groupset");
1104        ngroups = getgroups(ngroups, groupset);
1105        if (ngroups == -1)
1106            fatal(_("could not find groups: %s"), strerror(errno));
1107    #endif
1108    }
```

The `ngroups` and `groupset` variables are global; their declaration isn't shown. The `GETGROUPS_T` macro (line 1102) is the type to use for the second argument; it's `gid_t` on a POSIX system, `int` otherwise.

Lines 1085 and 1107 bracket the entire function body; on ancient systems that don't have group sets at all, the function has an empty body.

Lines 1086–1088 handle non-POSIX systems; `GETGROUPS_NOT_STANDARD` is defined by the configuration mechanism before the program is compiled. In this case, the code uses `NGROUPS_MAX`, as described earlier. (As late as 2004, such systems still exist and are in use; thankfully though, they are diminishing in number.)

Lines 1089–1094 are for POSIX systems, using a `size` parameter of zero to retrieve the number of groups.

Lines 1096–1099 do error checking. If the return value was 0, there aren't any supplemental groups, so `init_groupset()` merely returns early.

Finally, line 1102 uses `malloc()` (through an error-checking wrapper macro, see Section 3.2.1.8, "Example: Reading Arbitrarily Long Lines," page 67) to allocate an array that's large enough. Line 1104 then fills in the array.

11.3 Checking As the Real User: `access()`

Most of the time, the effective and real UID and GID values are the same. Thus, it doesn't matter that file-permission checking is performed against the effective ID and not the real one.

However, when writing a setuid or setgid application, you sometimes want to check whether a file operation that's OK for the effective UID and GID is also OK for the *real* UID and GID. This is the job of the `access()` function:

```
#include <unistd.h>                                              POSIX

int access(const char *path, int amode);
```

The `path` argument is the pathname of the file to check the real UID and GID against. `amode` is the bitwise OR of one or more of the following values:

`R_OK`   The real UID/GID can read the file.

`W_OK`   The real UID/GID can write the file.

`X_OK`   The real UID/GID can execute the file, or if a directory, search through the directory.

`F_OK`   Check whether the file exists.

Each component in the pathname is checked, and on some implementations, when checking for `root`, `access()` might act as if `X_OK` is true, even if no execute bits are set in the file's permissions. (Strange but true: In this case, forewarned is forearmed.) Linux doesn't have this problem.

If `path` is a symbolic link, `access()` checks the file that the symbolic link points to.

The return value is `0` if the operation is permitted to the real UID and GID or `-1` otherwise. Thus, if `access()` returns `-1`, a setuid program can deny access to a file that the effective UID/GID would otherwise be able to work with:

```
if (access("/some/special/file", R_OK|W_OK) < 0) {
    fprintf(stderr, "Sorry: /some/special/file: %s\n", strerror(errno));
    exit(1);
}
```

At least with the 2.4 series of Linux kernels, when the `X_OK` test is applied to a filesystem mounted with the `noexec` option (see Section 8.2.1, "Using Mount Options," page 239), the test succeeds if the file's permissions indicate execute permission. This is true even though an attempt to execute the file will fail. Caveat emptor.

> NOTE   While using access() before opening a file is proper practice, a race
> condition exists: The file being opened could be swapped out in between the
> check with access() and the call to open(). Careful programming is required,
> such as checking owner and permission with stat() and fstat() before and
> after the calls to access() and open().

For example, the pathchk program checks pathnames for validity. The GNU version
uses access() to check that the directory components of given pathnames are valid.
From the Coreutils pathchk.c:

```
244   /* Return 1 if PATH is a usable leading directory, 0 if not,
245      2 if it doesn't exist.  */
246
247   static int
248   dir_ok (const char *path)
249   {
250     struct stat stats;
251
252     if (stat (path, &stats))                          Nonzero return = failure
253       return 2;
254
255     if (!S_ISDIR (stats.st_mode))
256       {
257         error (0, 0, _("`%s' is not a directory"), path);
258         return 0;
259       }
260
261     /* Use access to test for search permission because
262        testing permission bits of st_mode can lose with new
263        access control mechanisms.  Of course, access loses if you're
264        running setuid. */
265     if (access (path, X_OK) != 0)
266       {
267         if (errno == EACCES)
268           error (0, 0, _("directory `%s' is not searchable"), path);
269         else
270           error (0, errno, "%s", path);
271         return 0;
272       }
273
274     return 1;
275   }
```

The code is straightforward. Lines 252–253 check whether the file exists. If stat()
fails, then the file doesn't exist. Lines 255–259 verify that the file is indeed a directory.

The comment on lines 261–264 explains the use of access(). Checking the st_mode
bits isn't enough: The file could be on a filesystem that was mounted read-only, on a

remote filesystem, or on a non-Linux or non-Unix filesystem, or the file could have file attributes that prevent access. Thus, only the kernel can really tell if the access would work. Lines 265–272 do the check, with the error message being determined by the value of `errno` (lines 267–270).

11.4 Checking as the Effective User: `euidaccess()` (GLIBC)

GLIBC provides an additional function that works like `access()` but that checks according to the effective UID, GID and group set:

```
#include <unistd.h>                                          GLIBC

int euidaccess(const char *path, int amode);
```

The arguments and return value have the same meaning as for `access()`. When the effective and real UIDs are equal and the effective and real GIDs are equal, `euidaccess()` calls `access()` to do the test. This has the advantage that the kernel can test for read-only filesystems or other conditions that are not reflected in the file's ownership and permissions.

Otherwise, `euidaccess()` checks the file's owner and group values against those of the effective UID and GID and group set, using the appropriate permission bits. This test is based on the file's `stat()` information.

If you're writing a portable program but prefer to use this interface, it's easy enough to extract the source file from the GLIBC archive and adapt it for general use.

11.5 Setting Extra Permission Bits for Directories

On modern systems, the setgid and "sticky" bits each have special meaning when applied to directories.

11.5.1 Default Group for New Files and Directories

In the original Unix system, when `open()` or `creat()` created a new file, the file received the effective UID and GID of the process creating it.

V7, BSD through 4.1 BSD, and System V through Release 3 all treated directories like files. However, with the addition of the supplemental group set in 4.2 BSD, the way new directories were created changed: new directories inherited the group of the parent directory. Furthermore, new files also inherited the group ID of the parent directory and *not* the effective GID of the creating process.

The idea behind having multiple groups and directories that work this way is to facilitate group cooperation. Each organizational project using a system would have a separate group assigned to it. The top-level directory for each project would be in that project's group, and files for the project would all have group read and write (and if necessary, execute) permission. In addition, new files automatically get the group of the parent directory. By being simultaneously in multiple groups (the group set), a user could move among projects at will with a simple cd command, and all files and directories would maintain their correct group.

What happens on modern systems? Well, this is another of the few cases where it's possible to have our cake and eat it too. SunOS 4.0 invented a mechanism that was included in System V Release 4; it is used today by at least Solaris and GNU/Linux. These systems give meaning to the setgid bit on the parent directory of the new file or directory, as follows:

Setgid bit on parent directory clear
    New files and directories receive the creating process's effective GID.

Setgid bit on parent directory set
    New files and directories receive the parent directory's GID. New directories also inherit the setgid bit being on.

(Until SunOS 4.0, the setgid bit on a directory had no defined meaning.) The following session shows the setgid bit in action:

```
$ cd /tmp                                               Move to /tmp
$ ls -ld .                                              Check its permissions
drwxrwxrwt    8 root     root      4096 Oct 16 17:40 .
$ id                                                    Check out current groups
uid=2076(arnold) gid=42(devel) groups=19(floppy),42(devel),2076(arnold)
$ mkdir d1 ; ls -ld d1                                  Make a new directory
drwxr-xr-x    2 arnold   devel     4096 Oct 16 17:40 d1 Effective group ID inherited
$ chgrp arnold d1                                       Change the group
$ chmod g+s d1                                          Add setgid bit
$ ls -ld d1                                             Verify change
drwxr-sr-x    2 arnold   arnold    4096 Oct 16 17:40 d1
$ cd d1                                                 Change into it
$ echo this should have group arnold on it > f1         Create a new file
$ ls -l f1                                              Check permissions
-rw-r--r--    1 arnold   arnold      36 Oct 16 17:41 f1 Inherited from parent
```

```
$ mkdir d2                                                    Make a directory
$ ls -ld d2                                                   Check permissions
drwxr-sr-x    2 arnold  arnold    4096 Oct 16 17:51 d2        Group and setgid inherited
```

The `ext2` and `ext3` filesystems for GNU/Linux work as just shown. In addition they support special mount options, `grpid` and `bsdgroups`, which make the "use parent directory group" semantics the default. (The two names mean the same thing.) In other words, when these mount options are used, then parent directories do not have to have their setgid bits set.

The opposite mount options are `nogrpid` and `sysvgroups`. This is the default behavior; however, the setgid bit is still honored if it's present. (Here, too, the two names mean the same thing.)

POSIX specifies that new files and directories inherit either the effective GID of the creating process or the group of the parent directory. However, implementations have to provide a way to make new directories inherit the group of the parent directory. Furthermore, the standard recommends that applications not rely on one behavior or the other, but in cases where it matters, applications should use `chown()` to force the ownership of the new file or directory's group to the desired GID.

11.5.2 Directories and the Sticky Bit

> "Sherman, set the wayback machine for 1976."
> —Mr. Peabody—

The *sticky bit* originated in the PDP-11 versions of Unix and was applied to regular executable files.[6] This bit was applied to programs that were expected to be heavily used, such as the shell and the editor. When a program had this bit set, the kernel would keep a copy of the program's executable code on the swap device, from which it could be quickly loaded into memory for reuse. (Loading from the filesystem took longer: The image on the swap device was stored in contiguous disk blocks, whereas the image in the filesystem might be spread all over the disk.) The executable images "stuck" to the swap device, hence the name.

Thus, even if the program was not currently in use, it was expected that it would be in use again shortly when another user went to run it, so it would be loaded quickly.

---

6 Images come to mind of happy youthful programs, their faces and hands covered in chocolate.

Modern systems have considerably faster disk and memory hardware than the PDP-11s of yore. They also use a technique called *demand paging* to load into memory only those parts of an executable program that are being executed. Thus, today, the sticky bit on a regular executable file serves no purpose, and indeed it has no effect.

However, in Section 1.1.2, "Directories and Filenames," page 6, we mentioned that the sticky bit on an otherwise writable directory prevents file removal from that directory, or file renaming within it, by anyone except the file's owner, or `root`. Here is an example:

```
$ ls -ld /tmp                                              Show /tmp's permissions
drwxrwxrwt   19 root     root          4096 Oct 20 14:04 /tmp
$ cd /tmp                                                  Change there
$ echo this is my file > arnolds-file                      Create a file
$ ls -l arnolds-file                                       Show its permissions
-rw-r--r--    1 arnold   devel           16 Oct 20 14:14 arnolds-file
$ su - miriam                                              Change to another user
Password:
$ cd /tmp                                                  Change to /tmp
$ rm arnolds-file                                          Attempt to remove file
rm: remove write-protected regular file `arnolds-file'? y  rm is cautious
rm: cannot remove `arnolds-file': Operation not permitted  Kernel disallows removal
```

The primary purpose of this feature is exactly for directories such as `/tmp`, where multiple users wish to place their files. On the one hand, the directory needs to be world-writable so that anyone can create files in it. On the other hand, once it's world-writable, any user can remove any other user's files! The directory sticky bit solves this problem nicely. Use 'chmod +t' to add the sticky bit to a file or directory:

```
$ mkdir mytmp                                              Create directory
$ chmod a+wxt mytmp                                        Add all-write, sticky bits
$ ls -ld mytmp                                             Verify result
drwxrwxrwt    2 arnold   devel         4096 Oct 20 14:23 mytmp
```

Finally, note that the directory's owner can also remove files, even if they don't belong to him.

11.6 Setting Real and Effective IDs

Things get interesting once a process has to change its UID and GID values. Setting the group set is straightforward. Changing real and effective UID and GID values around is more involved.

11.6.1 Changing the Group Set

The `setgroups()` function installs a new group set:

```
#include <sys/types.h>                                    Common
#include <unistd.h>
#include <grp.h>

int setgroups(size_t size, const gid_t *list);
```

The `size` parameter indicates how many items there are in the `list` array. The return value is `0` if all went well, `-1` with `errno` set otherwise.

Unlike the functions for manipulating the real and effective UID and GID values, this function may only be called by a process running as `root`. This is one example of what POSIX terms a *privileged operation*; as such it's not formally standardized by POSIX.

`setgroups()` is used by any program that does a login to a system, such as `/bin/login` for console logins or `/bin/sshd` for remote logins with `ssh`.

11.6.2 Changing the Real and Effective IDs

Running with two different user IDs presents a challenge to the application programmer. There are things that a program may need to do when working with the effective UID, and other things that it may need to do when working using the real UID.

For example, before Unix systems had job control, many programs provided *shell escapes*, that is, a way to run a command or interactive shell from within the current program. The `ed` editor is a good example of this: Typing a command line beginning with `!` ran the rest of the line as a shell command. Typing '`!sh`' gave you an interactive shell. (This still works—try it!) Suppose the hypothetical game program described earlier also provides a shell escape: the shell should be run as the real user, *not* the effective one. Otherwise, it again becomes trivial for the game player to directly edit the score file or do lots more worse things!

Thus, there is a clear need to be able to change the effective UID to be the real UID. Furthermore, it's helpful to be able to switch the effective UID *back* to what it was originally. (This is the reason for having a saved set-user ID in the first place; it becomes possible to regain the original privileges that the process had when it started out.)

As with many Unix APIs, different systems solved the problem in different ways, sometimes by using the same API but with different semantics and sometimes by introducing different APIs. Delving into the historic details is only good for producing headaches, so we don't bother. Instead, we look at what POSIX provides and how each API works. Furthermore, our discussion focuses on the real and effective UID values; the GID values work analogously, so we don't bother to repeat the details for those system calls. The functions are as follows:

```
#include <sys/types.h>                              POSIX
#include <unistd.h>

int seteuid(uid_t euid);                     Set effective ID
int setegid(gid_t egid);

int setuid(uid_t uid);                       Set effective ID, if root, set all
int setgid(gid_t gid);

int setreuid(uid_t ruid, uid_t euid);        BSD compatibility, set both
int setregid(gid_t rgid, gid_t egid);
```

There are three sets of functions. The first two were created by POSIX:

`int seteuid(uid_t euid)`

This function sets only the effective UID. A regular (non-root) user can only set the ID to one of the real, effective, or saved set-user ID values. Applications that will switch the effective UID around should use this function exclusively.

A process with an effective UID of zero can set the effective UID to any value. Since it is also possible to set the effective UID to the saved set-user ID, the process can regain its root privileges with another call to seteuid().

`int setegid(gid_t egid)`

This function does for the effective group ID what seteuid() does for the effective user ID.

The next set of functions offers the original Unix API for changing the real and effective UID and GID. Under the POSIX model, these functions are what a setuid-root program should use to make a *permanent* change of real and effective UID:

`int setuid(uid_t uid)`

For a regular user, this function also sets only the effective UID. As with seteuid(), the effective UID may be set to any of the current real, effective, or saved set-user ID values. The change is not permanent; the effective UID can be changed to another value (from the same source set) with a subsequent call.

However, for `root`, this function sets *all three* of the real, effective, and saved set-user IDs to the given value. Furthermore, the change is permanent; the IDs cannot be changed back. (This makes sense: Once the saved set-user ID is changed, there isn't a different ID to change back to.)

`int setgid(gid_t gid)`

This function does for the effective group ID what `setuid()` does for the effective user ID. The same distinction between regular users and `root` applies.

> NOTE The ability to change the group ID hinges on the *effective user ID*. An effective GID of 0 has no special privileges.

Finally, POSIX provides two functions from 4.2 BSD for historical compatibility. It is best not to use these in new code. However, since you are likely to see older code which does use these functions, we describe them here.

`int setreuid(uid_t ruid, uid_t euid)`

Sets the real and effective UIDs to the given values. A value of –1 for `ruid` or `euid` leaves the respective ID unchanged. (This is similar to `chown()`; see Section 5.5.1, "Changing File Ownership: `chown()`, `fchown()`, and `lchown()`," page 155.)

`root` is allowed to set both the real and the effective IDs to any value. According to POSIX, non-`root` users may only change the effective ID; it is "unspecified" what happens if a regular user attempts to change the real UID. However, the GNU/Linux *setreuid*(2) manpage spells out the Linux behavior: The real UID may be set to either the real or effective UID, and the effective UID may be set to any of the real, effective, or saved set-user IDs. (For other systems, see the *setreuid*(2) manpage.)

`int setregid(gid_t rgid, gid_t egid)`

Does for the real and effective group IDs what `setreuid()` does for the real and effective user ID. The same distinction between regular users and `root` applies.

The saved set-user ID didn't exist in the BSD model, so the idea behind `setreuid()` and `setregid()` was to make it simple to swap the real and effective IDs:

```
setreuid(geteuid(), getuid());  /* swap real and effective */
```

However, given POSIX's adoption of the saved set-user ID model and the `seteuid()` and `setegid()` functions, the BSD functions should not be used in new code. Even the 4.4 BSD documentation marks these functions as obsolete, recommending `seteuid()`/`setuid()` and `setegid()`/`setgid()` instead.

11.6.3 Using the Setuid and Setgid Bits

There are important cases in which a program running as `root` must *irrevocably* change all three of the real, effective, and saved set-user IDs to that of a regular user. The most obvious is the `login` program, which you use every time you log in to a GNU/Linux or Unix system (either directly, or remotely). There is a hierarchy of programs, as outlined in Figure 11.1.

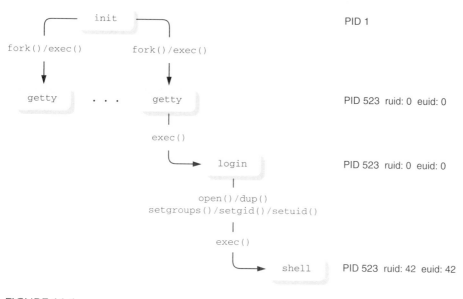

FIGURE 11.1
From `init` to `getty` to `login` to shell

The code for `login` is too complicated to be shown here, since it deals with a number of tasks that aren't relevant to the current discussion. But we can outline the steps that happen at login time, as follows:

1. `init` is the primordial process. It has PID 1. All other processes are descended from it. The kernel handcrafts process 1 at boot time and runs `init` in it. It runs with both the real and effective UID set to zero, that is, as `root`.

2. `init` reads `/etc/inittab`, which, among other things, tells `init` on which hardware devices it should start a `getty` process. For each such device (such as the console, serial terminals, or virtual consoles on a GNU/Linux system), `init` forks a new process. This new process then uses `exec()` to run `getty` ("get tty," that is, a terminal). On many GNU/Linux systems, this command is named `mingetty`. The program opens the device, resets its state, and prints the '`login:`' prompt.

3. Upon reading a login name, `getty` execs `login`. The `login` program looks up the username in the password file, prompts for a password, and verifies the password. If they match, the login process continues.

4. `login` changes to the user's home directory, sets up the initial environment, and then sets up the initial set of open files. It closes all file descriptors, opens the terminal, and uses `dup()` to copy the terminal's file descriptor to 0, 1, and 2. This is where the already opened standard input, output, and error file descriptors come from.

5. `login` then uses `setgroups()` to set the supplemental group set, `setgid()` to set the real, effective, and saved set-group IDs to those of the user, and finally `setuid()` to set all three of the real, effective, and saved set-user IDs to those of the logging-in user. Note that the call to `setuid()` must come *last* so that the other two calls succeed.

6. Finally, `login` execs the user's login shell. Bourne-style shells then read `/etc/profile` and `$HOME/.profile`, if those files exist. Finally, the shell prints a prompt.

Note how one process changes its nature from system process to user process. Each child of `init` starts out as a copy of `init`. By using `exec()`, the same process does different jobs. By calling `setuid()` to change from `root` to a regular user, the process finally goes directly to work for the user. When you exit the shell (by CTRL-D or `exit`), the process simply dies. `init` then restarts the cycle, spawning a fresh `getty`, which prints a fresh '`login:`' prompt.

> NOTE Open files remain open and usable, even after a process has changed any or all of its UIDs or GIDs. Thus, setuid programs should open any necessary files up front, change their IDs to those of the real user, and continue with the rest of their job without any extra privilege.

Table 11.1 summarizes the six standard functions for manipulating UID and GID values.

TABLE 11.1
API summary for setting real and effective IDs

Function	Sets	Permanent	Regular user	Root
`seteuid()`	E	No	From R, E, S	Any value
`setegid()`	E	No	From R, E, S	Any value
`setuid()`	Root: R, E, S	Root: yes	From R, E	Any value
	Other: E	Other: no		
`setgid()`	Root: R, E, S	Root: yes	From R, E	Any value
	Other: E	Other: no		
`setreuid()`	E, may set R	No	From R, E	Any value
`setregid()`	E, may set R	No	From R, E	Any value

11.7 Working with All Three IDs: `getresuid()` and `setresuid()` (Linux)

Linux provides additional system calls by which you can work directly with the real, effective, and saved user and group IDs:

```
#include <sys/types.h>                                        Linux
#include <unistd.h>

int getresuid(uid_t *ruid, uid_t *euid, uid_t *suid);
int getresgid(gid_t *rgid, gid_t *egid, gid_t *sgid);

int setresuid(uid_t ruid, uid_t euid, uid_t suid);
int setresgid(gid_t rgid, gid_t egid, gid_t sgid);
```

The functions are as follows:

```
int getresuid(uid_t *ruid, uid_t *euid, uid_t *suid)
```
    Retrieves the real, effective, and saved set-user ID values. The return value is `0` on success or `-1` if an error, with `errno` indicating the problem.

```
int getresgid(gid_t *rgid, gid_t *egid, gid_t *sgid)
```
    Retrieves the real, effective, and saved set-group ID values. The return value is `0` on success or `-1` if an error, with `errno` indicating the problem.

```
int setresuid(uid_t ruid, uid_t euid, uid_t suid)
```
    Sets the real, effective, and saved set-user ID values respectively. When a parameter value is `-1`, the corresponding UID is left unchanged.

    When the process is running as `root`, the parameters can be any arbitrary values. (However, using a nonzero value for `euid` causes a permanent, irrevocable loss of `root` privilege.) Otherwise, the parameters must be one of the current real, effective, or saved set-user ID values.

```
int setresgid(gid_t rgid, gid_t egid, gid_t sgid)
```
    Sets the real, effective, and saved set-group ID values respectively. When a parameter value is `-1`, the corresponding GID is left unchanged.

    This function is analogous to `setresuid()`.

The `setresuid()` and `setresgid()` functions are particularly valuable because the semantics are clearly defined. A programmer knows exactly what the effect of the call will be.

Furthermore, the calls are "all or nothing" operations: They either succeed completely, making the desired change, or fail completely, leaving the current situation as it was. This improves reliability since, again, it's possible to be sure of exactly what happened.

11.8 Crossing a Security Minefield: Setuid `root`

Real minefields are difficult, but not impossible, to cross. However, it's not something to attempt lightly, without training or experience.

So, too, writing programs that run setuid to `root` is a difficult task. There are many, many issues to be aware of, and almost anything can have unexpected security consequences. Such an endeavor should be undertaken carefully.

In particular, it pays to read up on Linux/Unix security issues and to invest time in learning how to write setuid `root` programs. If you dive straight into such a challenge having read this book and nothing else, rest assured that your system will be broken into, *easily and immediately*. It's unlikely that either you or your customers will be happy.

Here are a few guiding principles:

- Do as little as possible as `root`. Use your super powers sparingly, only where they're absolutely needed.

- Design your program properly. Compartmentalize your program so that all of the `root` operations can be done up front, with the rest of the program running as a regular user.

- When changing or dropping privileges, use `setresuid()` if you have it. Otherwise use `setreuid()`, since those two functions have the cleanest semantics. Use `setuid()` only when you want the change to be permanent.

- Change from `root` to regular user in the proper order: set the group set and GID values first, and then the UID values.

- Be especially careful with `fork()` and `exec()`; the real and effective UIDs are not changed across them unless you explicitly change them.

- Consider using setgid permissions and a special group for your application. If that will work, it'll save you much headache.

- Consider throwing out the inherited environment. If you must keep some environment variables around, keep as few as possible. Be sure to provide reasonable values for the `PATH` and `IFS` environment variables.

- Avoid `execlp()` and `execvp()`, which depend upon the value of the `PATH` environment variable (although this is less problematic if you've reset `PATH` yourself).

These are just a few of the many tactics for traversing a danger zone notable for pitfalls, booby-traps, and landmines. See the next section for pointers to other sources of information.

11.9 Suggested Reading

Unix (and thus GNU/Linux) security is a topic that requires knowledge and experience to handle properly. It has gotten only harder in the Internet Age, not easier.

1. *Practical UNIX & Internet Security*, 3rd edition, by Simson Garfinkel, Gene Spafford, and Alan Schwartz, O'Reilly & Associates, Sebastopol, CA, USA, 2003. ISBN: 0-596-00323-4.

   This is the standard book on Unix security.

2. *Building Secure Software: How to Avoid Security Problems the Right Way*, by John Viega and Gary McGraw. Addison-Wesley, Reading, Massachusetts, USA, 2001. ISBN: 0-201-72152-X.

   This is a good book on writing secure software and it includes how to deal with setuid issues. It assumes you are familiar with the basic Linux/Unix APIs; by the time you finish reading our book, you should be ready to read it.

3. "Setuid Demystified," by Hao Chen, David Wagner, and Drew Dean. *Proceedings of the 11th USENIX Security Symposium*, August 5–9, 2002. `http://www.cs.berkeley.edu/~daw/papers/setuid-usenix02.pdf`.

   Garfinkel, Spafford, and Schwartz recommend reading this paper "before you even think about writing code that tries to save and restore privileges." We most heartily agree with them.

11.10 Summary

- The use of user and group ID values (UIDs and GIDs) to identify files and processes is what makes Linux and Unix into multiuser systems. Processes carry both real and effective UID and GID values, as well as a supplemental group set. It is generally the effective UID that determines how one process might affect another, and the effective UID, GID, and group set that are checked against a file's permissions. Users with an effective UID of zero, known as `root` or the *superuser*, are allowed to do what they like; the system doesn't apply permission checks to such a user.

- The saved set-user ID and saved set-group ID concepts came from System V and have been adopted by POSIX with full support in GNU/Linux. Having these separate ID values makes it possible to easily and correctly swap real and effective UIDs (and GIDs) as necessary.

- Setuid and setgid programs create processes in which the effective and real IDs differ. The programs are marked as such with additional bits in the file permissions. The setuid and setgid bits must be added to a file after it is created.

- `getuid()` and `geteuid()` retrieve the real and effective UID values, respectively, and `getgid()` and `getegid()` retrieve the real and effective GID values, respectively. `getgroups()` retrieves the supplemental group set and in a POSIX environment, can query the system as to how many members the group set contains.

- The `access()` function does file permission checking as the *real* user, making it possible for setuid programs to check the real user's permissions. Note that, often, examining the information as retrieved by `stat()` may not provide the full picture, given that the file may reside on a nonnative or network filesystem.

- The GLIBC `euidaccess()` function is similar to `access()` but does the checking on the base of the effective UID and GID values.

- The setgid and sticky bits, when applied to directories, introduce extra semantics. When a directory has its setgid bit on, new files in that directory inherit the directory's group. New directories do also, and they automatically inherit the setting of the setgid bit. Without the setgid bit, new files and directories receive the effective GID of the creating process. The sticky bit on otherwise writable directories restricts file removal to the file's owner, the directory's owner, and to `root`.

- The group set is changed with `setgroups()`. This function isn't standardized by POSIX, but it exists on all modern Unix systems. Only `root` may use it.

- Changing UIDs and GIDs is considerably involved. The semantics of various system calls have changed over the years. New applications that will change only their effective UID/GID should use `seteuid()` and `setegid()`. Non-root applications can also set their effective IDs with `setuid()` and `setgid()`. The `setreuid()` and `setregid()` calls from BSD were intended for swapping the UID and GID values; their use in new programs is discouraged.

- Applications running as `root` can permanently change the real, effective, and saved ID values with `setuid()` and `setgid()`. One example of this is `login`, which has to change from a system program running as `root` to a nonprivileged login shell running as a regular user.

- The Linux `setresuid()` and `setresgid()` functions should be used when they're available, since they provide the cleanest and most reliable behavior.

- Writing setuid-`root` applications is not a task for a novice. If you need to do such a thing, read up on security issues first; the sources cited previously are excellent.

Exercises

1. Write a simple version of the `id` command. Its action is to print the user and group IDs, with the group names, to standard output. When the effective and real IDs are different, both are printed. For example:

    ```
    $ id
    uid=2076(arnold) gid=42(devel) groups=19(floppy),42(devel),2076(arnold)
    ```

    Its usage is:

    ```
    id [ user ]
    id -G [ -nr ] [ user ]
    id -g [ -nr ] [ user ]
    id -u [ -nr ] [ user ]
    ```

    With *user*, that user's information is displayed; otherwise, `id` prints the invoking user's information. The options are as follows:

    -G   Print all the group values as numeric values only, no names.

    -n   Print the name only, no numeric values. Applies to user and group values.

    -g   Print just the effective GID.

    -u   Print just the effective UID.

2. Write a simple program, named `sume`, that is setuid to yourself. It should prompt for a password (see *getpass*(3)), which for the purposes of this exercise, can be hardwired into the program's source code. If the person running the program correctly enters the password, `sume` should exec a shell. Get another user to help you test it.

3. How do you feel about making `sume` available to your friends? To your fellow students or coworkers? To every user on your system?

12

General Library Interfaces — Part 2

In this chapter

C hapter 6, "General Library Interfaces — Part 1," page 165, presented the first set of general-purpose library APIs. In a sense, those APIs support working with the fundamental objects that Linux and Unix systems manage: the time of day, users and groups for files, and sorting and searching.

This chapter is more eclectic; the APIs covered here are not particularly related to each other. However, all are useful for day-to-day Linux/Unix programming. Our presentation moves from simpler, more general APIs to more complicated and more specialized ones.

12.1 Assertion Statements: `assert()`

An *assertion* is a statement you make about the state of your program at certain points in time during its execution. The use of assertions for programming was originally developed by C.A.R. Hoare.[1] The general idea is part of "program verification": That as you design and develop a program, you can show that it's correct by making carefully reasoned statements about the effects of your program's code. Often, such statements are made about *invariants*—facts about the program's state that are supposed to remain true throughout the execution of a chunk of code.

Assertions are particularly useful for describing two kinds of invariants: *preconditions* and *postconditions*: conditions that must hold true before and after, respectively, the execution of a code segment. A simple example of preconditions and postconditions is linear search:

```
/* lsearch --- return index in array of value, or -1 if not found */

int lsearch(int *array, size_t size, int value)
{
    size_t i;

    /* precondition: array != NULL */
    /* precondition: size > 0 */
    for (i = 0; i < size; i++)
        if (array[i] == value)
            return i;

    /* postcondition: i == size */

    return -1;
}
```

---

[1] In his 1981 ACM Turing Award lecture, however, Dr. Hoare states that Alan Turing himself promoted this idea.

This example states the conditions using comments. But wouldn't it be better to be able to test the conditions by using code? This is the job of the `assert()` macro:

```
#include <assert.h>                                              ISO C

void assert(scalar expression);
```

When the *scalar expression* is false, the `assert()` macro prints a diagnostic message and exits the program (with the `abort()` function; see Section 12.4, "Committing Suicide: `abort()`," page 445). `ch12-assert.c` provides the `lsearch()` function again, this time with assertions and a `main()` function:

```
1   /* ch12-assert.c --- demonstrate assertions */
2
3   #include <stdio.h>
4   #include <assert.h>
5
6   /* lsearch --- return index in array of value, or -1 if not found */
7
8   int lsearch(int *array, size_t size, int value)
9   {
10      size_t i;
11
12      assert(array != NULL);
13      assert(size > 0);
14      for (i = 0; i < size; i++)
15          if (array[i] == value)
16              return i;
17
18      assert(i == size);
19
20      return -1;
21  }
22
23  /* main --- test out assertions */
24
25  int main(void)
26  {
27  #define NELEMS  4
28      static int array[NELEMS] = { 1, 17, 42, 91 };
29      int index;
30
31      index = lsearch(array, NELEMS, 21);
32      assert(index == -1);
33
34      index = lsearch(array, NELEMS, 17);
35      assert(index == 1);
36
```

```
37        index = lsearch(NULL, NELEMS, 10);   /* won't return */
38
39        printf("index = %d\n", index);
40
41        return 0;
42    }
```

When compiled and run, the assertion on line 12 "fires:"

```
$ ch12-assert                                   Run the program
ch12-assert: ch12-assert.c:12: lsearch: Assertion `array != ((void *)0)' failed.
Aborted (core dumped)
```

The message from assert() varies from system to system. For GLIBC on GNU/Linux, the message includes the program name, the source code filename and line number, the function name, and then the text of the failed assertion. (In this case, the symbolic constant NULL shows up as its macro expansion, '((void *)0)'.)

The 'Aborted (core dumped)' message means that ch12-assert created a core file; that is, a snapshot of the process's address space right before it died.[2] This file can be used later, with a debugger; see Section 15.3, "GDB Basics," page 570. Core file creation is a purposeful side effect of assert(); the assumption is that something went drastically wrong, and you'll want to examine the process with a debugger to determine what.

You can disable assertions by compiling your program with the command-line option '-DNDEBUG'. When this macro is defined before <assert.h> is included, the assert() macro expands into code that does nothing. For example:

```
$ gcc -DNDEBUG=1 ch12-assert.c -o ch12-assert      Compile with -DNDEBUG
$ ch12-assert                                       Run it
Segmentation fault (core dumped)                    What happened?
```

Here, we got a real core dump! We know that assertions were disabled; there's no "failed assertion" message. So what happened? Consider line 15 of lsearch(), when called from line 37 of main(). In this case, the array variable is NULL. Accessing memory through a NULL pointer is an error. (Technically, the various standards leave as "undefined" what happens when you dereference a NULL pointer. Most modern systems do what GNU/Linux does; they kill the process by sending it a SIGSEGV signal; this in turn produces a core dump. This process is described in Chapter 10, "Signals," page 347.)

---

2 As mentioned in Section 10.2, "Signal Actions," page 348, some GNU/Linux distributions disable creation of core files. To reenable them, put the line 'ulimit -S -c unlimited' into your ~/.profile file.

This case raises an important point about assertions. Frequently, programmers mistakenly use assertions *instead of* runtime error checking. In our case, the test for 'array != NULL' should be a runtime check:

```
if (array == NULL)
    return -1;
```

The test for 'size > 0' (line 13) is less problematic; if size is 0 or less than 0, the loop never executes and lsearch() (correctly) returns -1. (In truth, this assertion isn't needed because the code correctly handles the case in which 'size <= 0'.)

The logic behind turning off assertions is that the extra checking can slow program performance and that therefore they should be disabled for the production version of a program. C.A.R. Hoare[3] made this observation, however:

> Finally, it is absurd to make elaborate security checks on debugging runs, when no trust is put in the results, and then remove them in production runs, when an erroneous result could be expensive or disastrous. What would we think of a sailing enthusiast who wears his lifejacket when training on dry land, but takes it off as soon as he goes to sea?

Given these sentiments, our recommendation is to use assertions thoughtfully: First, for any given assertion, consider whether it should instead be a runtime check. Second, place your assertions carefully so that you won't mind leaving assertion checking enabled, even in the production version of your program.

Finally, we'll note the following, from the "BUGS" section of the GNU/Linux *assert*(3) manpage:

> assert() is implemented as a macro; if the expression tested has side effects, program behavior will be different depending on whether NDEBUG is defined. This may create Heisenbugs which go away when debugging is turned on.

Heisenberg's famous Uncertainty Principle from physics indicates that the more precisely you can determine a particle's velocity, the less precisely you can determine its position, and vice versa. In layman's terms, it states that the mere act of observing the particle affects it.

---

[3] *Hints On Programming Language Design*, C.A.R. Hoare. Stanford University Computer Science Technical Report CS-73-403 (ftp://reports.stanford.edu/pub/cstr/reports/cs/tr/73/403/CS-TR-73-403.pdf), December, 1973.

A similar phenomenon occurs in programming, not related to particle physics: The act of compiling a program for debugging, or running it with debugging enabled can change the program's behavior. In particular, the original bug can disappear. Such a bug is known colloquially as a *heisenbug*.

The manpage is warning us against putting expressions with side effects into `assert()` calls:

```
assert(*p++ == '\n');
```

The side-effect here is that the `p` pointer is incremented as part of the test. When NDEBUG is defined, the expression argument *disappears* from the source code; it's never executed. This can lead to an unexpected failure. However, as soon as assertions are reenabled in preparation for debugging, things start working again! Such problems are painful to track down.

12.2 Low-Level Memory: The memXXX() Functions

Several functions provide low-level services for working with arbitrary blocks of memory. Their names all start with the prefix 'mem':

```
#include <string.h>                                        ISO C

void *memset(void *buf, int val, size_t count);
void *memcpy(void *dest, const void *src, size_t count);
void *memmove(void *dest, const void *src, size_t count);
void *memccpy(void *dest, const void *src, int val, size_t count);
int memcmp(const void *buf1, const void *buf2, size_t count);
void *memchr(const void *buf, int val, size_t count);
```

12.2.1 Setting Memory: memset()

The `memset()` function copies the value `val` (treated as an `unsigned char`) into the first `count` bytes of `buf`. It is particularly useful for zeroing out blocks of dynamic memory:

```
void *p = malloc(count);
if (p != NULL)
    memset(p, 0, count);
```

However, `memset()` can be used on any kind of memory, not just dynamic memory. The return value is the first argument: `buf`.

12.2.2 Copying Memory: memcpy(), memmove(), and memccpy()

Three functions copy one block of memory to another. The first two differ in their handling of *overlapping* memory areas; the third copies memory but stops upon seeing a particular value.

`void *memcpy(void *dest, const void *src, size_t count)`
> This is the simplest function. It copies count bytes from src to dest. It does not handle overlapping memory areas. It returns dest.

`void *memmove(void *dest, const void *src, size_t count)`
> Similar to memcpy(), it also copies count bytes from src to dest. However, it does handle overlapping memory areas. It returns dest.

`void *memccpy(void *dest, const void *src, int val, size_t count)`
> This copies bytes from src to dest stopping *either* after copying val into dest *or* after copying count bytes. If it found val, it returns a pointer to the position in dest just beyond where val was placed. Otherwise, it returns NULL.

Now, what's the issue with overlapping memory? Consider Figure 12.1.

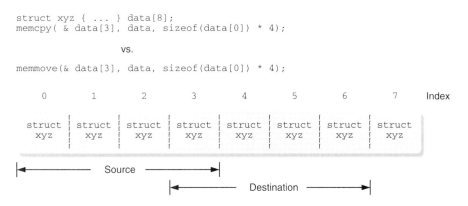

```
struct xyz { ... } data[8];
memcpy( & data[3], data, sizeof(data[0]) * 4);
```
vs.
```
memmove(& data[3], data, sizeof(data[0]) * 4);
```

FIGURE 12.1
Overlapping copies

The goal is to copy the four instances of struct xyz in data[0] through data[3] into data[3] through data[6]. data[3] is the problem here; a byte-by-byte copy moving forward in memory from data[0] will clobber data[3] before it can be safely copied into data[6]! (It's also possible to come up with a scenario where a backwards copy through memory destroys overlapping data.)

The `memcpy()` function was the original System V API for copying blocks of memory; its behavior for overlapping blocks of memory wasn't particularly defined one way or the other. For the 1989 C standard, the committee felt that this lack of defined behavior was a problem; thus they invented `memmove()`. For historical compatibility, `memcpy()` was left alone, with the behavior for overlapping memory specifically stated as undefined, and `memmove()` was invented to provide a routine that would correctly deal with problem cases.

Which one should you use in your own code? For a library function that has no knowledge of the memory areas being passed into it, you should use `memmove()`. That way, you're guaranteed that there won't be any problems with overlapping areas. For application-level code that "knows" that two areas don't overlap, it's safe to use `memcpy()`.

For both `memcpy()` and `memmove()` (as for `strcpy()`), the destination buffer is the first argument and the source is the second one. To remember this, note that the order is the same as for an assignment statement:

```
dest = src;
```

(Many systems have manpages that don't help, providing the prototype as 'void `*memcpy(void *buf1, void *buf2, size_t n)`' and relying on the prose to explain which is which. Fortunately, the GNU/Linux manpage uses better names.)

12.2.3 Comparing Memory Blocks: `memcmp()`

The `memcmp()` function compares `count` bytes from two arbitrary buffers of data. Its return value is like `strcmp()`: negative, zero, or positive if the first buffer is less than, equal to, or greater than the second one.

You may be wondering "Why not use `strcmp()` for such comparisons?" The difference between the two functions is that `memcmp()` doesn't care about zero bytes (the `'\0'` string terminator). Thus, `memcmp()` is the function to use when you need to compare arbitrary binary data.

Another advantage to memcmp() is that it's faster than the typical C implementation:

```
/* memcmp --- example C implementation, NOT for real use */

int memcmp(const void *buf1, const void *buf2, size_t count)
{
    const unsigned char *cp1 = (const unsigned char *) buf1;
    const unsigned char *cp2 = (const unsigned char *) buf2;
    int diff;

    while (count-- != 0) {
        diff = *cp1++ - *cp2++;
        if (diff != 0)
            return diff;
    }

    return 0;
}
```

The speed can be due to special "block memory compare" instructions that many architectures support or to comparisons in units larger than bytes. (This latter operation is tricky and is best left to the library's author.)

For these reasons, you should *always* use your library's version of memcmp() instead of rolling your own. Chances are excellent that the library author knows the machine better than you do.

12.2.4 Searching for a Byte Value: memchr()

The memchr() function is similar to the strchr() function: It returns the location of a particular value within an arbitrary buffer. As for memcmp() vs. strcmp(), the principal reason to use memchr() is that you have arbitrary binary data.

GNU wc uses memchr() when counting only lines and bytes,[4] and this allows wc to be quite fast. From wc.c in the GNU Coreutils:

---

[4] See *wc*(1). wc counts lines, words, and characters.

```
257    else if (!count_chars && !count_complicated)
258      {
259        /* Use a separate loop when counting only lines or lines and bytes --
260           but not chars or words.  */
261        while ((bytes_read = safe_read (fd, buf, BUFFER_SIZE)) > 0)
262          {
263            register char *p = buf;
264
265            if (bytes_read == SAFE_READ_ERROR)
266              {
267                error (0, errno, "%s", file);
268                exit_status = 1;
269                break;
270              }
271
272            while ((p = memchr (p, '\n', (buf + bytes_read) - p)))
273              {
274                ++p;
275                ++lines;
276              }
277            bytes += bytes_read;
278          }
279      }
```

The outer loop (lines 261–278) reads data blocks from the input file. The inner loop (lines 272–276) uses memchr() to find and count newline characters. The complicated expression '(buf + bytes_read) - p' resolves to the number of bytes left between the current value of p and the end of the buffer.

The comment on lines 259–260 needs some explanation. Briefly, modern systems can use characters that occupy more than one byte in memory and on disk. (This is discussed in a little more detail in Section 13.4, "Can You Spell That for Me, Please?", page 521.) Thus, wc has to use different code if it's distinguishing characters from bytes: This code deals with the counting-bytes case.

12.3 Temporary Files

A *temporary file* is exactly what it sounds like: A file that while a program runs, holds data that isn't needed once the program exits. An excellent example is the sort program. sort reads standard input if no files are named on the command line or if you use '-' as the filename. Yet sort has to read *all* of its input data before it can output the sorted results. (Think about this a bit and you'll see that it's true.) While standard input is being read, the data must be stored somewhere until sort can sort it; this is the perfect use for a temporary file. sort also uses temporary files for storing intermediate sorted results.

Amazingly, there are *five* different functions for creating temporary files. Three of them work by creating strings representing (supposedly) unique filenames. As we'll see, these should generally be avoided. The other two work by creating and opening the temporary file; these functions are preferred.

12.3.1 Generating Temporary Filenames (Bad)

There are three functions whose purpose is to create the *name* of a unique, nonexistent file. Once you have such a filename, you can use it to create a temporary file. Since the name is unique, you're "guaranteed" exclusive use of the file. Here are the function declarations:

```
#include <stdio.h>

char *tmpnam(char *s);                                                   ISO C
char *tempnam(const char *dir, const char *pfx);                         XSI
char *mktemp(char *template);                                            ISO C
```

The functions all provide different variations of the same theme: They fill in or create a buffer with the path of a unique temporary filename. The file is unique in that the created name doesn't exist as of the time the functions create the name and return it. The functions work as follows:

`char *tmpnam(char *s)`

Generates a unique filename. If s is not NULL, it should be at least L_tmpnam bytes in size and the unique name is copied into it. If s is NULL, the name is generated in an internal `static` buffer that can be overwritten on subsequent calls. The directory prefix of the path will be P_tmpdir. Both P_tmpdir and L_tmpnam are defined in <stdio.h>.

`char *tempnam(const char *dir, const char *pfx)`

Like tmpnam(), lets you specify the directory prefix. If dir is NULL, P_tmpdir is used. The pfx argument, if not NULL, specifies up to five characters to use as the leading characters of the filename.

tempnam() allocates storage for the filenames it generates. The returned pointer can be used later with free() (and should be if you wish to avoid memory leaks).

`char *mktemp(char *template)`

Generates unique filenames based on a template. The last six characters of template must be 'XXXXXX'; these characters are replaced with a unique suffix.

> NOTE The `template` argument to `mktemp()` is overwritten in place. Thus, it should *not* be a string constant. Many pre-Standard C compilers put string constants into the data segment, along with regular global variables. Although defined as constants in the source code, they were *writable*; thus, code like the following was not uncommon:
>
> ```
> /* Old-style code: don't do this. */
> char *tfile = mktemp("/tmp/myprogXXXXXX");
> ... use tfile ...
> ```
>
> On modern systems, such code will likely fail; string constants nowadays find themselves in read-only segments of memory.

Using these functions is quite straightforward. The file `ch12-mktemp.c` demonstrates `mktemp()`; changes to use the other functions are not difficult:

```
1   /* ch12-mktemp.c --- demonstrate naive use of mktemp().
2                        Error checking omitted for brevity */
3
4   #include <stdio.h>
5   #include <fcntl.h>      /* for open flags */
6   #include <limits.h>     /* for PATH_MAX */
7
8   int main(void)
9   {
10      static char template[] = "/tmp/myfileXXXXXX";
11      char fname[PATH_MAX];
12      static char mesg[] =
13          "Here's lookin' at you, kid!\n";      /* beats "hello, world" */
14      int fd;
15
16      strcpy(fname, template);
17      mktemp(fname);
18
19      /* RACE CONDITION WINDOW OPENS */
20
21      printf("Filename is %s\n", fname);
22
23      /* RACE CONDITION WINDOW LASTS TO HERE */
24
25      fd = open(fname, O_CREAT|O_RDWR|O_TRUNC, 0600);
26      write(fd, mesg, strlen(mesg));
27      close(fd);
28
29      /* unlink(fname); */
30
31      return 0;
32  }
```

The `template` variable (line 10) defines the filename template; the 'xxxxxx' will be replaced with a unique value. Line 16 copies the template into `fname`, which isn't `const`: It can be modified. Line 18 calls `mktemp()` to generate the filename, and line 21 prints it so we can see what it is. (We explain the comments on lines 19 and 23 shortly.)

Line 25 opens the file, creating it if necessary. Line 26 writes the message in `mesg`, and line 27 closes the file. In a program in which the file should be removed when we're done with it, line 29 would not be commented out. (Sometimes, a temporary file should not be unlinked; for example, if the file will be renamed once it's completely written.) We've commented it out so that we can run this program and look at the file afterwards. Here's what happens when the program runs:

```
$ ch12-mktemp                          Run the program
Filename is /tmp/myfileQES4WA          Filename printed
$ cat /tmp/myfileQES4WA
Here's lookin' at you, kid!            Contents are what we expect
$ ls -l /tmp/myfileQES4WA             So are owner and permissions
-rw-------    1 arnold   devel          28 Sep 18 09:27 /tmp/myfileQES4WA
$ rm /tmp/myfileQES4WA                Remove it
$ ch12-mktemp                          Is same filename reused?
Filename is /tmp/myfileic7xCy          No. That's good
$ cat /tmp/myfileic7xCy               Check contents again
Here's lookin' at you, kid!
$  ls -l /tmp/myfileic7xCy            Check owner and permissions again
-rw-------    1 arnold   devel          28 Sep 18 09:28 /tmp/myfileic7xCy
```

Everything seems to be working fine. `mktemp()` gives back a unique name, `ch12-mktemp` creates the file with the right permissions, and the contents are what's expected. So what's the problem with all of these functions?

Historically, `mktemp()` used a simple, *predictable* algorithm to generate the replacement characters for the 'xxxxxx' in the template. Furthermore, the interval between the time the filename is *generated* and the time the file itself is *created* creates a race condition.

How? Well, Linux and Unix systems use *time slicing*, a technique that shares the processor among all the executing processes. This means that, although a program *appears* to be running all the time, in actuality, there are times when processes are *sleeping*, that is, waiting to run on the processor.

Now, consider a professor's program for tracking student grades. Both the professor and a malicious student are using a heavily loaded, multiuser system at the same time.

The professor's program uses `mktemp()` to create temporary files, and the student, having in the past watched the grading program create and remove temporary files, has figured out the algorithm that `mktemp()` uses. (The GLIBC version doesn't have this problem, but not all systems use GLIBC!) Figure 12.2 illustrates the race condition and how the student takes advantage of it.

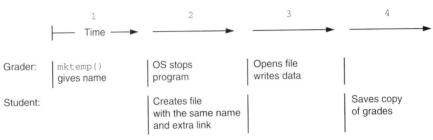

FIGURE 12.2
Race condition with `mktemp()`

Here's what happened.

1. The grading program uses `mktemp()` to generate a filename. Upon return from `mktemp()`, the race condition window is now open (line 19 in `ch12-mktemp.c`).

2. The kernel stops the grader so that other programs on the system can run. This happens before the call to `open()`.

   While the grader is stopped, the student creates the file with the same name `mktemp()` returned to the grader program. (Remember, the algorithm was easy to figure out.) The student creates the file with an extra link to it, so that when the grading program unlinks the file, it will still be available for perusal.

3. The grader program now opens the file and writes data to it. The student created the file with `-rw-rw-rw-` permissions, so this isn't a problem.

4. When the grader program is finished, it unlinks the temporary file. However, the student still has a copy. For example, there may be a profit opportunity to sell classmates their grades in advance.

Our example is simplistic; besides just stealing the grade data, a clever (if immoral) student might be able to *change* the data in place. If the professor doesn't double-check his program's results, no one would be the wiser.

> NOTE We do not recommend doing any of this! If you are a student, *don't try any of this*. First and foremost, it is unethical. Second, it's likely to get you kicked out of school. Third, your professors are probably not so naive as to have used `mktemp()` to code their programs. The example is for illustration only!

For the reasons given, and others, all three functions described in this section should never be used. They exist in POSIX and in GLIBC only to support old programs that were written before the dangers of these routines were understood. To this end, GNU/Linux systems generate a warning at link time:

```
$ cc ch12-mktemp.c -o ch12-mktemp          Compile the program
/tmp/cc1XCvD9.o(.text+0x35): In function `main':
: the use of `mktemp' is dangerous, better use `mkstemp'
```

(We cover `mkstemp()` in the next subsection.)

Should your system not have `mkstemp()`, think about how you might use these interfaces to simulate it. (See also "Exercises" for Chapter 12, page 482, at the end of the chapter.)

12.3.2 Creating and Opening Temporary Files (Good)

There are two functions that don't have race condition problems. One is intended for use with the `<stdio.h>` library:

```
#include <stdio.h>                                              ISO C

FILE *tmpfile(void);
```

The second function is for use with the file-descriptor-based system calls:

```
#include <stdlib.h>                                             XSI

int mkstemp(char *template);
```

`tmpfile()` returns a `FILE *` value representing a unique, open temporary file. The file is opened in `"w+b"` mode. The `w+` means "open for reading and writing, truncate the file first," and the `b` means binary mode, not text mode. (There's no difference on a GNU/Linux or Unix system, but there is on other systems.) The file is automatically deleted when the file pointer is closed; there is no way to get to the file's name to save its contents. The program in `ch12-tmpfile.c` demonstrates `tmpfile()`:

```
/* ch12-tmpfile.c --- demonstrate tmpfile().
                      Error checking omitted for brevity */

#include <stdio.h>

int main(void)
{
    static char mesg[] =
        "Here's lookin' at you, kid!";  /* beats "hello, world" */
    FILE *fp;
    char buf[BUFSIZ];

    fp = tmpfile();                     /* Get temp file */
    fprintf(fp, "%s", mesg);            /* Write to it */
    fflush(fp);                         /* Force it out */

    rewind(fp);                         /* Move to front */
    fgets(buf, sizeof buf, fp);         /* Read contents */

    printf("Got back <%s>\n", buf);     /* Print retrieved data */

    fclose(fp);                         /* Close file, goes away */
    return 0;                           /* All done */
}
```

The returned FILE * value is no different from any other FILE * returned by
fopen(). When run, the results are what's expected:

```
$ ch12-tmpfile
Got back <Here's lookin' at you, kid!>
```

We saw earlier that the GLIBC authors recommend the use of mkstemp() function:

```
$ cc ch12-mktemp.c -o ch12-mktemp        Compile the program
/tmp/cc1XCvD9.o(.text+0x35): In function `main':
: the use of `mktemp' is dangerous, better use `mkstemp'
```

This function is similar to mktemp() in that it takes a filename ending in 'XXXXXX'
and replaces those characters with a unique suffix to create a unique filename. However,
it goes one step further. It *creates and opens the file*. The file is created with mode 0600
(that is, -rw------). Thus, only the user running the program can access the file.

Furthermore, and this is what makes mkstemp() more secure, the file is created using
the O_EXCL flag, which guarantees that the file doesn't exist and keeps anyone else from
opening the file.

The return value is an open file descriptor that can be used for reading and writing.
The pathname now stored in the buffer passed to mkstemp() should be used to remove
the file when you're done. This is all demonstrated in ch12-mkstemp.c, which is a
straightforward modification of ch12-tmpfile.c:

```
/* ch12-mkstemp.c --- demonstrate mkstemp().
                       Error checking omitted for brevity */

#include <stdio.h>
#include <fcntl.h>   /* for open flags */
#include <limits.h>  /* for PATH_MAX */

int main(void)
{
    static char template[] = "/tmp/myfileXXXXXX";
    char fname[PATH_MAX];
    static char mesg[] =
        "Here's lookin' at you, kid!\n"; /* beats "hello, world" */
    int fd;
    char buf[BUFSIZ];
    int n;

    strcpy(fname, template);              /* Copy template */
    fd = mkstemp(fname);                  /* Create and open temp file */
    printf("Filename is %s\n", fname);    /* Print it for information */

    write(fd, mesg, strlen(mesg));        /* Write something to file */

    lseek(fd, 0L, SEEK_SET);              /* Rewind to front */
    n = read(fd, buf, sizeof(buf));       /* Read data back; NOT '\0' terminated! */
    printf("Got back: %.*s", n, buf);     /* Print it out for verification */

    close(fd);                            /* Close file */
    unlink(fname);                        /* Remove it */

    return 0;
}
```

When run, the results are as expected:

```
$ ch12-mkstemp
Filename is /tmp/myfileuXFW1N
Got back: Here's lookin' at you, kid!
```

12.3.3 Using the TMPDIR Environment Variable

Many standard utilities pay attention to the TMPDIR environment variable, using the directory it names as the place in which to put their temporary files. If TMPDIR isn't set, then the default directory for temporary files is usually /tmp, although most modern systems have a /var/tmp directory as well. /tmp is usually cleared of all files and directories by administrative shell scripts at system startup.

Many GNU/Linux systems provide a directory /dev/shm that uses the tmpfs filesystem type:

```
$ df
Filesystem          1K-blocks      Used Available Use% Mounted on
/dev/hda2            6198436    5136020    747544  88% /
/dev/hda5           61431520   27720248  30590648  48% /d
none                  256616          0    256616   0% /dev/shm
```

The `tmpfs` filesystem type provides a *RAM disk*: a portion of memory used as if it were a disk. Furthermore, the `tmpfs` filesystem uses the Linux kernel's virtual memory mechanisms to allow it to grow beyond a fixed size limit. If you have lots of RAM in your system, this approach can provide a noticeable speedup. To test performance we started with the `/usr/share/dict/linux.words` file, which is a sorted list of correctly spelled words, one per line. We then randomized this file so that it was no longer sorted and created a larger file containing 500 copies of the random version of the file:

```
$ ls -l /tmp/randwords.big                                       Show size
-rw-r--r--    1 arnold   devel    204652500 Sep 18 16:02 /tmp/randwords.big
$ wc -l  /tmp/randwords.big                                      How many words?
22713500 /tmp/randwords.big                                      Over 22 million!
```

We then sorted the file, first using the default `/tmp` directory, and then with TMPDIR set to `/dev/shm`:[5]

```
$ time sort /tmp/randwords.big > /dev/null                       Use real files

real    1m32.566s
user    1m23.137s
sys     0m1.740s
$ time TMPDIR=/dev/shm sort /tmp/randwords.big > /dev/null        Use RAM disk

real    1m28.257s
user    1m18.469s
sys     0m1.602s
```

Interestingly, using the RAM disk was only marginally faster than using regular files. (On some further tests, it was actually slower!) We conjecture that the kernel's buffer cache (see Section 4.6.2, "Creating Files with `creat()`," page 109) comes into the picture, quite effectively speeding up file I/O.[6]

---

5   This use of `/dev/shm` is really an *abuse* of it; it's intended for use in implementing shared memory, not for use as a RAM disk. Nevertheless, it's helpful for illustrating our point.

6   Our system has 512 megabytes of RAM, which to old fogies like the author seems like a lot. However, RAM prices have fallen, and systems with one or more gigabytes of RAM are not uncommon, at least for software developers.

The RAM disk has a significant disadvantage: It is limited by the amount of *swap space* configured on your system.[7] When we tried to sort a file containing 1,000 copies of the randomized words file, the RAM disk ran out of room, whereas the regular `sort` finished successfully.

Using `TMPDIR` for your own programs is straightforward. We offer the following outline:

```
const char template[] = "myprog.XXXXXX";
char *tmpdir, *tfile;
size_t count;
int fd;

if ((tmpdir = getenv("TMPDIR")) == NULL)          Use TMPDIR value if there
    tmpdir = "/tmp";                              Otherwise, default to /tmp

count = strlen(tmpdir) + strlen(template) + 2;    Compute size of filename
tfile = (char *) malloc(count);                   Allocate space for it
if (tfile == NULL)                                Check for error
    /* recover */

sprintf(tfile, "%s/%s", tmpdir, template);        Create final template
fd = mkstemp(tfile);                              Create and open file
... use tempfile via fd ...
close(fd);                                        Clean up
unlink(tfile);
free(tfile);
```

Depending on your application's needs, you may wish to unlink the file immediately after opening it instead of doing so as part of the cleanup.

12.4 Committing Suicide: `abort()`

There are times when a program just can't continue. Generally, the best thing to do is to generate an error message and call `exit()`. However, particularly for errors that are likely to be programming problems, it's helpful to not just exit but also to produce a core dump, which saves the state of the running program in a file for later examination with a debugger. This is the job of the `abort()` function:

```
#include <stdlib.h>                                          ISO C

void abort(void);
```

---

[7] Swap space consists of one or more dedicated chunks of disk, used to hold the parts of executing processes that are not currently in memory.

The `abort()` function sends a `SIGABRT` signal to the process itself. This happens even if `SIGABRT` is blocked or ignored. The normal action for `SIGABRT`, which is to produce a core dump, then takes place.

An example of `abort()` in action is the `assert()` macro described at the beginning of this chapter. When `assert()` finds that its expression is false, it prints an error message and then calls `abort()` to dump core.

According to the C standard, it is implementation defined whether or not `abort()` does any cleanup actions. Under GNU/Linux it does: All `<stdio.h>` `FILE *` streams are closed before the program exits. Note, however, that nothing is done for open files that use the file descriptor-based system calls. (Nothing needs to be done if all that are open are files or pipes. Although we don't discuss it, file descriptors are also used for network connections, and not closing them cleanly is poor practice.)

12.5 Nonlocal Gotos

> "Go directly to jail. Do not pass GO. Do not collect $200."
> —Monopoly—

You undoubtedly know what a `goto` is: a transfer of control flow to a label somewhere else within the current function. `goto` statements, when used sparingly, can contribute to the readability and correctness of a function. (For example, when all error checks use a `goto` to a label at the end of a function, such as `clean_up`, the code at that label then cleans things up [closing files, etc.] and returns.) When used poorly, `goto` statements can lead to so-called spaghetti code, the logic of which becomes impossible to follow.

The `goto` statement is constrained by the C language to jump to a label within the current function. Many languages in the Algol family, such as Pascal, allow a `goto` to "jump out" of a nested function into an earlier calling function. However in C, there is no way, within the syntax of the language itself, to jump to a location in a different function, even a calling one. Such a jump is termed a *nonlocal goto*.

Why is a nonlocal goto useful? Consider an interactive program that reads commands and processes them. Suppose the user starts a long-running task, gets frustrated or changes his mind about doing the task, and then presses CTRL-C to generate a `SIGINT` signal. When the signal handler runs, it can jump back to the start of the main read-commands-and-process-them loop. The `ed` line editor provides a straightforward example of this:

```
$ ed -p '> ' sayings                Start ed, use '>' as prompt
sayings: No such file or directory
> a                                 Append text
Hello, world
Don't panic
^C                                  Generate SIGINT
?                                   The "one size fits all" error message
> 1,$p                              ed returns to command loop
Hello, world                        '1,$p' prints all the lines
Don't panic
> w                                 Save file
25
> q                                 All done
```

Internally, `ed` sets up a return point before the command loop, and the signal handler then does a nonlocal goto back to the return point.

12.5.1 Using Standard Functions: `setjmp()` and `longjmp()`

Nonlocal gotos are accomplished with the `setjmp()` and `longjmp()` functions. These functions come in two flavors. The traditional routines are defined by the ISO C standard:

```
#include <setjmp.h>                                        ISO C

int setjmp(jmp_buf env);
void longjmp(jmp_buf env, int val);
```

The `jmp_buf` type is `typedef`'d in `<setjmp.h>`. `setjmp()` saves the current "environment" in `env`. `env` is typically a global or file-level `static` variable so that it can be used from a called function. This environment includes whatever information is necessary for jumping to the location at which `setjmp()` is called. The contents of a `jmp_buf` are by nature machine dependent; thus, `jmp_buf` is an opaque type: something you use without knowing what's inside it.

`setjmp()` returns 0 when it is called to save the current environment in a `jmp_buf`. It returns nonzero when a nonlocal jump is made using the environment:

```
jmp_buf command_loop;               At global level
... then in main() ...
if (setjmp(command_loop) == 0)      State saved OK, proceed on
    ;
else                                We get here via nonlocal goto
    printf("?\n");                  ed's famous message
... now start command loop ...
```

longjmp() makes the jump. The first parameter is a jmp_buf that must have been initialized by setjmp(). The second is an integer *nonzero* value that setjmp() returns in the original environment. This is so that code such as that just shown can distinguish between setting the environment and arriving by way of a nonlocal jump.

The C standard states that even if longjmp() is called with a second argument of 0, setjmp() still returns nonzero. In such a case, it instead returns 1.

The ability to pass an integer value and have that come back from the return of setjmp() is useful; it lets user-level code distinguish the reason for the jump. For instance, gawk uses this capability to handle the break and continue statements inside loops. (The awk language is deliberately similar to C in its syntax for loops, with while, do-while, and for loops, and break and continue.) The use of setjmp() looks like this (from eval.c in the gawk 3.1.3 distribution):

```
507   case Node_K_while:
508       PUSH_BINDING(loop_tag_stack, loop_tag, loop_tag_valid);
509
510       stable_tree = tree;
511       while (eval_condition(stable_tree->lnode)) {
512           INCREMENT(stable_tree->exec_count);
513           switch (setjmp(loop_tag)) {
514           case 0: /* normal non-jump */
515               (void) interpret(stable_tree->rnode);
516               break;
517           case TAG_CONTINUE:   /* continue statement */
518               break;
519           case TAG_BREAK:      /* break statement */
520               RESTORE_BINDING(loop_tag_stack, loop_tag, loop_tag_valid);
521               return 1;
522           default:
523               cant_happen();
524           }
525       }
526       RESTORE_BINDING(loop_tag_stack, loop_tag, loop_tag_valid);
527       break;
```

This code fragment represents a while loop. Line 508 manages nested loops by means of a stack of saved jmp_buf variables. Lines 511–524 run the while loop (using a C while loop!). Line 511 tests the loop's condition. If it's true, line 513 does a switch on the setjmp() return value. If it's 0 (lines 514–516), then line 515 runs the statement's body. However, when setjmp() returns either TAG_BREAK or TAG_CONTINUE, the `switch` statement handles them appropriately (lines 517–518 and 519–521, respectively).

An awk-level `break` statement passes `TAG_BREAK` to `longjmp()`, and the awk-level `continue` passes `TAG_CONTINUE`. Again, from `eval.c`, with some irrelevant details omitted:

```
657  case Node_K_break:
658      INCREMENT(tree->exec_count);
            ...
675          longjmp(loop_tag, TAG_BREAK);
676      break;
677
678  case Node_K_continue:
679      INCREMENT(tree->exec_count);
            ...
696          longjmp(loop_tag, TAG_CONTINUE);
697      break;
```

You can think of `setjmp()` as placing the label, and `longjmp()` as the `goto`, with the extra advantage of being able to tell where the code "came from" (by the return value).

12.5.2 Handling Signal Masks: `sigsetjmp()` and `siglongjmp()`

For historical reasons that would most likely bore you to tears, the 1999 C standard is silent about the effect of `setjmp()` and `longjmp()` on the state of a process's signals, and POSIX states explicitly that their effect on the process signal mask (see Section 10.6, "POSIX Signals," page 367) is undefined.

In other words, if a program changes its process signal mask between the first call to `setjmp()` and a call to `longjmp()`, what is the state of the process signal mask after the `longjmp()`? Is it the mask in effect when `setjmp()` was first called? Or is it the current mask? POSIX says explicitly "there's no way to know."

To make handling of the process signal mask explicit, POSIX introduced two additional functions and one `typedef`:

```
#include <setjmp.h>                                    POSIX

int sigsetjmp(sigjmp_buf env, int savesigs);    Note: sigjmp_buf, not jmp_buf!
void siglongjmp(sigjmp_buf env, int val);
```

The main difference is the `savesigs` argument to `sigsetjmp()`. If nonzero, then the current set of blocked signals is saved in `env`, along with the rest of the environment that would be saved by `setjmp()`. A `siglongjmp()` with an `env` where `savesigs` was true restores the saved process signal mask.

> NOTE POSIX is also clear that if `savesigs` is zero (false), it's *undefined* whether the process signal mask is saved and restored, just like `setjmp()`/`longjmp()`. This in turn implies that if you're going to use '`sigsetjmp(env, 0)`' you may as well not bother: The whole point is to have control over saving and restoring the process signal mask!

12.5.3 Observing Important Caveats

There are several technical caveats to be aware of:

First, because the environment saving and restoring can be messy, machine-dependent tasks, `setjmp()` and `longjmp()` are allowed to be macros.

Second, the C standard limits the use of `setjmp()` to the following situations:

- As the sole controlling expression of a loop or condition statement (`if`, `switch`).

- As one operand of a comparison expression (`==`, `<`, etc.), with the other operand as an integer constant. The comparison expression can be the sole controlling expression of a loop or condition statement.

- As the operand of the unary `!` operator, with the resulting expression being the sole controlling expression of a loop or condition statement.

- As the entire expression of an expression statement, possibly cast to `void`. For example:

```
(void) setjmp(buf);
```

Third, if you wish to change a local variable in the function that calls `setjmp()`, *after* the call, and you want that variable to maintain its most recently assigned value after a `longjmp()`, you must declare the variable to be `volatile`. Otherwise, any non-`volatile` local variables changed after `setjmp()` was initially called have indeterminate values. (Note that the `jmp_buf` variable itself need not be declared `volatile`.) For example:

```
1   /* ch12-setjmp.c --- demonstrate setjmp()/longjmp() and volatile. */
2
3   #include <stdio.h>
4   #include <setjmp.h>
5
6   jmp_buf env;
7
8   /* comeback --- do a longjmp */
9
10  void comeback(void)
11  {
12      longjmp(env, 1);
13      printf("This line is never printed\n");
14  }
15
16  /* main --- call setjmp, fiddle with vars, print values */
17
18  int main(void)
19  {
20      int i = 5;
21      volatile int j = 6;
22
23      if (setjmp(env) == 0) {      /* first time */
24          i++;
25          j++;
26          printf("first time: i = %d, j = %d\n", i, j);
27          comeback();
28      } else                 /* second time */
29          printf("second time: i = %d, j = %d\n", i, j);
30
31      return 0;
32  }
```

In this example, only j (line 21) is guaranteed to maintain its value for the second call to printf(). The value of i (line 20), according to the 1999 C standard, is indeterminate. It may be 6, it may be 5, or it may even be something else!

Fourth, as described in Section 12.5.2, "Handling Signal Masks: sigsetjmp() and siglongjmp()," page 449, the 1999 C standard makes no statement about the effect, if any, of setjmp() and longjmp() on the state of the program's signals. If that's important, you have to use sigsetjmp() and siglongjmp() instead.

Fifth, these routines provide amazing potential for memory leaks! Consider a program in which main() calls setjmp() and then calls several nested functions, each of which allocates dynamic memory with malloc(). If the most deeply nested function does a longjmp() back into main(), the pointers to the dynamic memory are lost. Consider ch12-memleak.c:

```
1    /* ch12-memleak.c --- demonstrate memory leaks with setjmp()/longjmp(). */
2
3    #include <stdio.h>
4    #include <malloc.h>       /* for definition of ptrdiff_t on GLIBC */
5    #include <setjmp.h>
6    #include <unistd.h>
7
8    jmp_buf env;
9
10   void f1(void), f2(void);
11
12   /* main --- leak memory with setjmp() and longjmp() */
13
14   int main(void)
15   {
16       char *start_break;
17       char *current_break;
18       ptrdiff_t diff;
19
20       start_break = sbrk((ptrdiff_t) 0);
21
22       if (setjmp(env) == 0)        /* first time */
23           printf("setjmp called\n");
24
25       current_break = sbrk((ptrdiff_t) 0);
26
27       diff = current_break - start_break;
28       printf("memsize = %ld\n", (long) diff);
29
30       f1();
31
32       return 0;
33   }
34
35   /* f1 --- allocate some memory, make a nested call */
36
37   void f1(void)
38   {
39       char *p = malloc(1024);
40
41       f2();
42   }
43
44   /* f2 --- allocate some memory, make longjmp */
45
46   void f2(void)
47   {
48       char *p = malloc(1024);
49
50       longjmp(env, 1);
51   }
```

This program sets up an infinite loop, using setjmp() and longjmp(). Line 20 uses sbrk() (see Section 3.2.3, "System Calls: brk() and sbrk()," page 75) to find the current start of the heap, and then line 22 calls setjmp(). Line 25 gets the current start of the heap; this location changes each time through since the code is entered repeatedly by longjmp(). Lines 27–28 compute how much memory has been allocated and print the amount. Here's what happens when it runs:

```
$ ch12-memleak              Run the program
setjmp called
memsize = 0
memsize = 6372
memsize = 6372
memsize = 6372
memsize = 10468
memsize = 10468
memsize = 14564
memsize = 14564
memsize = 18660
memsize = 18660
...
```

The program leaks memory like a sieve. It runs until interrupted from the keyboard or until it runs out of memory (at which point it produces a massive core dump).

Functions f1() and f2() each allocate memory, and f2() does the longjmp() back to main() (line 51). Once that happens, the *local* pointers (lines 41 and 49) to the allocated memory are gone! Such memory leaks can be difficult to track down because they are often for small amounts of memory, and as such, they can go unnoticed literally for years.[8]

This code is clearly pathological, but it's intended to illustrate our point: setjmp() and longjmp() can lead to hard-to-find memory leaks. Suppose that f1() called free() correctly. It would then be far from obvious that the memory would never be freed. In a larger, more realistic program, in which longjmp() might be called only by an if, such a leak becomes even harder to find.

In the presence of setjmp() and longjmp(), dynamic memory must thus be managed by global variables, and you must have code that detects entry with longjmp() (by checking the setjmp() return value). Such code should then clean up any dynamically allocated memory that's no longer needed.

---

[8] We had such a leak in gawk. Fortunately, it's fixed.

Sixth, `longjmp()` and `siglongjmp()` should not be used from any functions registered with `atexit()` (see Section 9.1.5.3, "Exiting Functions," page 302).

Seventh, `setjmp()` and `longjmp()` can be costly operations on machines with lots of registers.

Given all of these issues, you should take a hard look at your program's design. If you don't need to use `setjmp()` and `longjmp()`, then you're probably better off not doing so. However, if their use is the best way to structure your program, then go ahead and use them, but do so carefully.

12.6 Pseudorandom Numbers

Many applications need sequences of random numbers. For example, game programs that simulate rolling a die, dealing cards, or turning the wheels on a slot machine need to be able to pick one of a set of possible values at random. (Consider the `fortune` program, which has a large collection of pithy sayings; it prints a different one "at random" each time it's called.) Many cryptographic algorithms also require "high quality" random numbers. This section describes different ways to get sequences of random numbers.

> NOTE The nature of randomness, generation of random numbers, and the "quality" of random numbers are all broad topics, beyond the scope of this book. We provide an introduction to the available APIs, but that's about all we can do. See Section 12.9, "Suggested Reading," page 480, for other sources of more detailed information.

Computers, by design, are *deterministic*. The same calculation, with the same inputs, should produce the same outputs, every time. Thus, they are not good at generating truly random numbers, that is, sequences of numbers in which each number in the sequence is completely independent of the number (or numbers) that came before it. Instead, the kinds of numbers usually dealt with at the programmatic level are called *pseudorandom* numbers. That is, within any given sequence, the numbers appear to be independent of each other, but the sequence as a whole is repeatable. (This repeatability can be an asset; it provides determinism for the program as a whole.)

Many methods of producing pseudorandom number sequences work by performing the same calculation each time on a starting, or *seed*, value. The stored seed value is then updated for use next time. APIs provide a way to specify a new seed. Each initial seed produces the same sequence of pseudorandom numbers, although different seeds (should) produce different sequences.

12.6.1 Standard C: `rand()` and `srand()`

Standard C defines two related functions for pseudorandom numbers:

```
#include <stdlib.h>                                            ISO C

int rand(void);
void srand(unsigned int seed);
```

`rand()` returns a pseudorandom number between 0 and `RAND_MAX` (inclusive, as far as we can tell from the C99 standard) each time it's called. The constant `RAND_MAX` must be at least 32,767; it can be larger.

`srand()` seeds the random number generator with `seed`. If `srand()` is never called by the application, `rand()` behaves as if the initial seed were 1.

The following program, `ch12-rand.c`, uses `rand()` to print die faces.

```
1   /* ch12-rand.c --- generate die rolls, using rand(). */
2
3   #include <stdio.h>
4   #include <stdlib.h>
5
6   char *die_faces[] = {    /* ASCII graphics rule! */
7       "           ",
8       "     *     ",   /* 1 */
9       "           ",
10
11      "           ",
12      " *       * ",   /* 2 */
13      "           ",
14
15      "           ",
16      " * * * * ",   /* 3 */
17      "           ",
18
19      " *       * ",
20      "           ",   /* 4 */
21      " *       * ",
22
23      " *       * ",
24      "     *     ",   /* 5 */
25      " *       * ",
26
```

```
27        " *   *   * ",
28        "         ",   /* 6 */
29        " *   *   * ",
30   };
31
32   /* main --- print N different die faces */
33
34   int main(int argc, char **argv)
35   {
36        int nfaces;
37        int i, j, k;
38
39        if (argc != 2) {
40            fprintf(stderr, "usage: %s number-die-faces\n", argv[0]);
41            exit(1);
42        }
43
44        nfaces = atoi(argv[1]);
45
46        if (nfaces <= 0) {
47            fprintf(stderr, "usage: %s number-die-faces\n", argv[0]);
48            fprintf(stderr, "\tUse a positive number!\n");
49            exit(1);
50        }
51
52        for (i = 1; i <= nfaces; i++) {
53            j = rand() % 6;      /* force to range 0 <= j <= 5 */
54            printf("+-------+\n");
55            for (k = 0; k < 3; k++)
56                printf("|%s|\n", die_faces[(j * 3) + k]);
57            printf("+-------+\n\n");
58        }
59
60        return 0;
61   }
```

This program uses simple ASCII graphics to print out the semblance of a die face. You call it with the number of die faces to print. This is computed on line 44 with `atoi()`. (In general, `atoi()` should be avoided for production code since it does no error or overflow checking nor does it do any input validation.)

The key line is line 53, which converts the `rand()` return value into a number between zero and five, using the remainder operator, `%`. The value '`j * 3`' acts a starting index into the `die_faces` array for the three strings that make up each die's face. Lines 54 and 57 print out surrounding top and bottom lines, and the loop on lines 55 and 56 prints the face itself. When run, it produces output like the following:

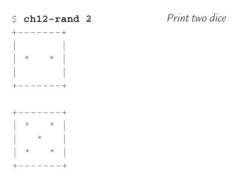

```
$ ch12-rand 2              Print two dice
+-------+
|       |
|  *  * |
|       |
+-------+

+-------+
| *   * |
|   *   |
| *   * |
+-------+
```

The `rand()` interface dates back to V7 and the PDP-11. In particular, on many systems the result is only a 16-bit number, which severely limits the range of numbers that can be returned. Furthermore, the algorithm it used is considered "weak" by modern standards. (The GLIBC version of `rand()` doesn't have these problems, but portable code needs to be written with the awareness that `rand()` isn't the best API to use.)

`ch12-rand.c` uses a simple technique to obtain a value within a certain range: the `%` operator. This technique uses the low bits of the returned value (just as in decimal division, where the remainder of dividing by 10 or 100 uses the lowest one or two decimal digits). It turns out that the historical `rand()` generator did a better job of producing random values in the middle and higher-order bits than in the lower bits. Thus, if you must use `rand()`, try to avoid the lower bits. The GNU/Linux *rand*(3) manpage cites *Numerical Recipes in C*,[9] which recommends this technique:

```
j = 1+(int) (10.0*rand()/(RAND_MAX+1.0));  /* for a number between 1 and 10 */
```

12.6.2 POSIX Functions: `random()` and `srandom()`

4.3 BSD introduced `random()` and its partner functions. These functions use a much better random number generator, which returns a 31-bit value. They are now an XSI extension standardized by POSIX:

```
#include <stdlib.h>                                        XSI

long random(void);
void srandom(unsigned int seed);
char *initstate(unsigned int seed, char *state, size_t n);
char *setstate(char *state);
```

---

[9] *Numerical Recipes in C: The Art of Scientific Computing*, 2nd edition, by William H. Press, Brian P. Flannery, Saul A. Teukolsky, and William T. Vetterling. Cambridge University Press, USA, 1993. ISBN: 0-521-43108-5.

The first two functions correspond closely to `rand()` and `srand()` and can be used similarly. However, instead of a single seed value that produces the sequence of pseudo-random numbers, these functions use a seed value along with a *state array*: an array of bytes that holds state information for calculating the pseudorandom numbers. The last two functions let you manage the state array.

`long random(void);`

> Returns a number between 0 and $2^{31} - 1$. (Although the GNU/Linux *random*(3) manpage says between 0 and `RAND_MAX`, this is only true for GLIBC systems where `RAND_MAX` equals $2^{31} - 1$. On other systems, `RAND_MAX` might be smaller. POSIX is explicit that the range is 0 to $2^{31} - 1$.)

`void srandom(unsigned int seed);`

> Sets the seed. If `srandom()` is never called, the default seed is `1`.

`char *initstate(unsigned int seed, char *state, size_t n);`

> Initializes the `state` array with information for use in generating random numbers. `seed` is the seed value to use, as for `srandom()`, and `n` is the number of bytes in the `state` array.
>
> n should be one of the values `8`, `32`, `64`, `128`, or `256`. Larger values produce better sequences of random numbers. Values less than `8` cause `random()` to use a simple random number generator similar to that of `rand()`. Values larger than `8` that are not equal to a value in the list are rounded down to the nearest appropriate value.

`char *setstate(char *state);`

> Sets the internal state to the `state` array, which must have been initialized by `initstate()`. This lets you switch back and forth between different states at will, providing multiple random number generators.

If `initstate()` and `setstate()` are never called, `random()` uses an internal state array of size 128.

The `state` array is opaque; you initialize it with `initstate()` and pass it to the `random()` function with `setstate()`, but you don't otherwise need to look inside it. If you use `initstate()` and `setstate()`, you don't have to also call `srandom()`, since the seed is included in the state information. `ch12-random.c` uses these routines instead of `rand()`. It also uses a common technique, which is to seed the random number generator with the time of day, added to the PID.

```
1    /* ch12-random.c --- generate die rolls, using random(). */
2
3    #include <stdio.h>
4    #include <stdlib.h>
5    #include <sys/types.h>
6    #include <unistd.h>
7
8    char *die_faces[] = {    /* ASCII graphics rule! */
         ... as before ...
32   };
33
34   /* main --- print N different die faces */
35
36   int main(int argc, char **argv)
37   {
38       int nfaces;
39       int i, j, k;
40       char state[256];
41       time_t now;
42
         ... check args, compute nfaces, as before ...
55
56       (void) time(& now); /* seed with time of day and PID */
57       (void) initstate((unsigned int) (now + getpid()), state, sizeof state);
58       (void) setstate(state);
59
60       for (i = 1; i <= nfaces; i++) {
61           j = random() % 6;        /* force to range 0 <= j <= 5 */
62           printf("+-------+\n");
63           for (k = 0; k < 3; k++)
64               printf("|%s|\n", die_faces[(j * 3) + k]);
65           printf("+-------+\n\n");
66       }
67
68       return 0;
69   }
```

Including the PID as part of the seed value guarantees that you'll get different results, even when two programs are started within the same second.

Because it produces a higher-quality sequence of random numbers, `random()` is preferred over `rand()`, and GNU/Linux and all modern Unix systems support it.

12.6.3 The /dev/random and /dev/urandom Special Files

Both rand() and srandom() are pseudorandom number generators. Their output, for the same seed, is a reproducible sequence of numbers. Some applications, like cryptography, require their random numbers to be (more) truly random. To this end, the Linux kernel, as well as various BSD and commercial Unix systems, provide special device files that provide access to an "entropy pool" of random bits that the kernel collects from physical devices and other sources. From the *random*(4) manpage:

/dev/random

> [Bytes read from this file are] within the estimated number of bits of noise in the entropy pool. /dev/random should be suitable for uses that need high quality randomness such as one-time pad or key generation. When the entropy pool is empty, reads to /dev/random will block until additional environmental noise is gathered.

/dev/urandom

> [This device will] return as many bytes as are requested. As a result, if there is not sufficient entropy in the entropy pool, the returned values are theoretically vulnerable to a cryptographic attack on the algorithms used by the driver. Knowledge of how to do this is not available in the current non-classified literature, but it is theoretically possible that such an attack may exist. If this is a concern in your application, use /dev/random instead.

For most applications, reading from /dev/urandom should be good enough. If you're going to be writing high-quality cryptographic algorithms, you should read up on cryptography and randomness first; don't rely on the cursory presentation here! Here's our die rolling program, once more, using /dev/urandom:

```
1   /* ch12-devrandom.c --- generate die rolls, using /dev/urandom. */
2
3   #include <stdio.h>
4   #include <fcntl.h>
5   #include <stdlib.h>
6
7   char *die_faces[] = {   /* ASCII graphics rule! */
        ... as before ...
31  };
32
33  /* myrandom --- return data from /dev/urandom as unsigned long */
34
```

```
35  unsigned long myrandom(void)
36  {
37      static int fd = -1;
38      unsigned long data;
39
40      if (fd == -1)
41          fd = open("/dev/urandom", O_RDONLY);
42
43      if (fd == -1 || read(fd, & data, sizeof data) <= 0)
44          return random();    /* fall back */
45
46      return data;
47  }
48
49  /* main --- print N different die faces */
50
51  int main(int argc, char **argv)
52  {
53      int nfaces;
54      int i, j, k;
55
        ... check args, compute nfaces, as before ...
68
69      for (i = 1; i <= nfaces; i++) {
70          j = myrandom() % 6;      /* force to range 0 <= j <= 5 */
71          printf("+-------+\n");
72          for (k = 0; k < 3; k++)
73              printf("|%s|\n", die_faces[(j * 3) + k]);
74          printf("+-------+\n");
75          putchar('\n');
76      }
77
78      return 0;
79  }
```

Lines 35–47 provide a function-call interface to /dev/urandom, reading an unsigned long's worth of data each time. The cost is one file descriptor that remains open throughout the program's life.

12.7 Metacharacter Expansions

Three sets of functions, of increasing complexity, provide the ability to match shell wildcard patterns. Many programs need such library functions. One example is find: 'find . -name '*.c' -print'. Another is the --exclude option in many programs that accepts a wildcard pattern of files to exclude from some action or other. This section looks at each set of functions in turn.

12.7.1 Simple Pattern Matching: `fnmatch()`

We start with the `fnmatch()` ("filename match") function:

```
#include <fnmatch.h>                                          POSIX

int fnmatch(const char *pattern, const char *string, int flags);
```

This function matches `string` against `pattern`, which is a regular shell wildcard pattern. The `flags` value (described shortly) modifies the function's behavior. The return value is `0` if `string` matches `pattern`, `FNM_NOMATCH` if it doesn't, and a nonzero value if an error occurred. Unfortunately, POSIX doesn't define any specific errors; thus, you can only tell that something went wrong, but not what.

The `flags` variable is the bitwise-OR of one or more of the flags listed in Table 12.1.

TABLE 12.1
Flag values for `fnmatch()`

Flag name	GLIBC only	Meaning
FNM_CASEFOLD	✓	Do case-insensitive matching.
FNM_FILE_NAME	✓	This is a GNU synonym for FNM_PATHNAME.
FNM_LEADING DIR	✓	This is a flag for internal use by GLIBC; don't use it in your programs. See *fnmatch*(3) for the details.
FNM_NOESCAPE		Backslash is an ordinary character, not an escape character.
FNM_PATHNAME		Slash in `string` must match slash in `pattern`; it cannot be matched by *, ?, or '[...]'.
FNM_PERIOD		A leading period in `string` is matched only if `pattern` also has a leading period. The period must be the first character in `string`. However, if FNM_PATHNAME is also set, a period following a slash is treated as a leading period.

`fnmatch()` works with strings from any source; strings to be matched need not be actual filenames. In practice though, you would use `fnmatch()` from code that reads a directory with `readdir()` (see Section 5.3.1, "Basic Directory Reading," page 133):

```
struct dirent dp;
DIR *dir;
char pattern[100];
... fill pattern, open directory, check for errors ...
while ((dp = readdir(dir)) != NULL) {
    if (fnmatch(pattern, dir->d_name, FNM_PERIOD) == 0)
        /* filename matches pattern */
    else
        continue;    /* doesn't match */
}
```

GNU ls uses fnmatch() to implement its --ignore option. You can provide multiple patterns to ignore (with multiple options). ls tests each filename against all the patterns. It does this with the file_interesting() function in ls.c:

```
2269  /* Return nonzero if the file in `next' should be listed. */
2270
2271  static int
2272  file_interesting (const struct dirent *next)
2273  {
2274    register struct ignore_pattern *ignore;
2275
2276    for (ignore = ignore_patterns; ignore; ignore = ignore->next)
2277      if (fnmatch (ignore->pattern, next->d_name, FNM_PERIOD) == 0)
2278        return 0;
2279
2280    if (really_all_files
2281        || next->d_name[0] != '.'
2282        || (all_files
2283            && next->d_name[1] != '\0'
2284            && (next->d_name[1] != '.' || next->d_name[2] != '\0')))
2285      return 1;
2286
2287    return 0;
2288  }
```

The loop on lines 2276–2278 tests the filename against the list of patterns for files to ignore. If any of the patterns matches, the file is *not* interesting and file_interesting() returns false (that is, 0).

The all_files variable corresponds to the -A option, which shows files whose names begin with a period but that aren't '.' and '..'. The really_all_files variable corresponds to the -a option, which implies -A, and also shows '.' and '..'. Given this information, the condition on lines 2280–2284 can be represented with the following pseudocode:

```
if (    show every file, no matter what its name (-a)
    OR the first character of the name isn't a period
    OR (    show dot files (-A)
         AND there are multiple characters in the filename
         AND (    the second character isn't a period
               OR the third character doesn't end the name)))
                 return TRUE;
```

> **NOTE** fnmatch() can be an expensive function if it's used in a locale that uses a multibyte character set. We discuss multibyte character sets in Section 13.4, "Can You Spell That for Me, Please?", page 521.

12.7.2 Filename Expansion: glob() and globfree()

The glob() and globfree() functions are more elaborate than fnmatch():

```
#include <glob.h>                                                    POSIX

int glob(const char *pattern, int flags,
         int (*errfunc)(const char *epath, int eerrno),
         glob_t *pglob);
void globfree(glob_t *pglob);
```

The glob() function does directory scanning and wildcard matching, returning a list of all pathnames that match the pattern. Wildcards can be included at multiple points in the pathame, not just for the last component (for example, '/usr/*/*.so'). The arguments are as follows:

const char *pattern
    The pattern to expand.

int flags
    Flags that control glob()'s behavior, described shortly.

int (*errfunc)(const char *epath, int eerrno)
    A pointer to a function to use for reporting errors. This value may be NULL. If it's not, and if (*errfunc)() returns nonzero or if GLOB_ERR is set in flags, then glob() stops processing.

    The arguments to (*errfunc)() are the pathname that caused a problem and the value of errno set by opendir(), readdir(), or stat().

glob_t *pglob
    A pointer to a glob_t structure used to hold the results.

The `glob_t` structure holds the list of pathnames that `glob()` produces:

```
typedef struct {                                              POSIX
    size_t gl_pathc;         Count of paths matched so far
    char **gl_pathv;         List of matched pathnames
    size_t gl_offs;          Slots to reserve in gl_pathv
} glob_t;
```

`size_t gl_pathc`

   The number of paths that were matched.

`char **gl_pathv`

   An array of matched pathnames. `gl_pathv[gl_pathc]` is always NULL.

`size_t gl_offs`

   "Reserved slots" in `gl_pathv`. The idea is to reserve slots *at the front* of `gl_pathv` for the application to fill in later, such as with a command name and options. The list can then be passed directly to `execv()` or `execvp()` (see Section 9.1.4, "Starting New Programs: The `exec()` Family," page 293). Reserved slots are set to NULL. For all this to work, `GLOB_DOOFFS` must be set in `flags`.

   Table 12.2 lists the standard flags for `glob()`.

TABLE 12.2
Flags for `glob()`

Flag name	Meaning
GLOB_APPEND	Append current call's results to those of a previous call.
GLOB_DOOFFS	Reserve `gl_offs` spots at the front of `gl_pathv`.
GLOB_MARK	Append a / character to the end of each pathname that is a directory.
GLOB_NOCHECK	If the pattern doesn't match any filename, return it unchanged.
GLOB_NOESCAPE	Treat backslash as a literal character. This makes it impossible to escape wildcard metacharacters.
GLOB_NOSORT	Don't sort the results; the default is to sort them.

The GLIBC version of the `glob_t` structure contains additional members:

```
typedef struct {                                              GLIBC
/* POSIX components: */
    size_t gl_pathc;         Count of paths matched so far
    char **gl_pathv;         List of matched pathnames
    size_t gl_offs;          Slots to reserve in gl_pathv
```

```
/* GLIBC components: */
  int gl_flags;                              Copy of flags, additional GLIBC flags
  void (*gl_closedir)(DIR *);                Private version of closedir()
  struct dirent *(*gl_readdir)(DIR *);       Private version of readdir()
  DIR *(*gl_opendir)(const char *);          Private version of opendir()
  int (*gl_lstat)(const char *, struct stat *);   Private version of lstat()
  int (*gl_stat) (const char *, struct stat *);   Private version of stat()
} glob_t;
```

The members are as follows:

int gl_flags

Copy of flags. Also includes GLOB_MAGCHAR if pattern included any metacharacters.

void (*gl_closedir)(DIR *)

Pointer to alternative version of closedir().

struct dirent *(*gl_readdir)(DIR *)

Pointer to alternative version of readdir().

DIR *(*gl_opendir)(const char *)

Pointer to alternative version of opendir().

int (*gl_lstat)(const char *, struct stat *)

Pointer to alternative version of lstat().

int (*gl_stat) (const char *, struct stat *)

Pointer to alternative version of stat().

The pointers to private versions of the standard functions are mainly for use in implementing GLIBC; it is highly unlikely that you will ever need to use them. Because GLIBC provides the gl_flags field and additional flag values, the manpage and Info manual document the rest of the GLIBC glob_t structure. Table 12.3 lists the additional flags.

The GLOB_ONLYDIR flag functions as a *hint* to the implementation that the caller is only interested in directories. Its primary use is by other functions within GLIBC, and a caller still has to be prepared to handle nondirectory files. You should not use it in your programs.

glob() can be called more than once: The first call should *not* have the GLOB_APPEND flag set, and all subsequent calls *must* have it set. You cannot change gl_offs between

TABLE 12.3
Additional GLIBC flags for `glob()`

Flag name	Meaning
GLOB_ALTDIRFUNC	Use alternative functions for directory access (see text).
GLOB_BRACE	Perform `csh`- and Bash-style brace expansions.
GLOB_MAGCHAR	Set in `gl_flags` if metacharacters were found.
GLOB_NOMAGIC	Return the pattern if it doesn't contain metacharacters.
GLOB_ONLYDIR	If possible, only match directories. See text.
GLOB_PERIOD	Allow metacharacters like `*` and `?` to match a leading period.
GLOB_TILDE	Do shell-style tilde expansions.
GLOB_TILDE_CHECK	Like GLOB_TILDE, but if there are problems with the named home directory, return GLOB_NOMATCH instead of placing `pattern` into the list.

calls, and if you modify any values in `gl_pathv` or `gl_pathc`, you must restore them before making a subsequent call to `glob()`.

The ability to call `glob()` multiple times allows you to build up the results in a single list. This is quite useful; it approaches the power of the shell's wildcard expansion facility, but at the C programming level.

`glob()` returns 0 if there were no problems or one of the values in Table 12.4 if there were.

TABLE 12.4
`glob()` return values

Constant	Meaning
GLOB_ABORTED	Scanning stopped early because GLOB_ERR was set or because `(*errfunc)()` returned nonzero.
GLOB_NOMATCH	No filenames matched `pattern`, and GLOB_NOCHECK was not set in the flags.
GLOB_NOSPACE	There was a problem allocating dynamic memory.

`globfree()` releases all the memory that `glob()` dynamically allocated. The following program, `ch12-glob.c`, demonstrates `glob()`:

```
1   /* ch12-glob.c --- demonstrate glob(). */
2
3   #include <stdio.h>
4   #include <errno.h>
5   #include <glob.h>
6
7   char *myname;
8
9   /* globerr --- print error message for glob() */
10
11  int globerr(const char *path, int eerrno)
12  {
13      fprintf(stderr, "%s: %s: %s\n", myname, path, strerror(eerrno));
14      return 0;    /* let glob() keep going */
15  }
16
17  /* main() --- expand command-line wildcards and print results */
18
19  int main(int argc, char **argv)
20  {
21      int i;
22      int flags = 0;
23      glob_t results;
24      int ret;
25
26      if (argc == 1) {
27          fprintf(stderr, "usage: %s wildcard ...\n", argv[0]);
28          exit(1);
29      }
30
31      myname = argv[0];    /* for globerr() */
32
33      for (i = 1; i < argc; i++) {
34          flags |= (i > 1 ? GLOB_APPEND : 0);
35          ret = glob(argv[i], flags, globerr, & results);
36          if (ret != 0) {
37              fprintf(stderr, "%s: problem with %s (%s), stopping early\n",
38                  myname, argv[i],
39      /* ugly: */ (ret == GLOB_ABORTED ? "filesystem problem" :
40                   ret == GLOB_NOMATCH ? "no match of pattern" :
41                   ret == GLOB_NOSPACE ? "no dynamic memory" :
42                   "unknown problem"));
43              break;
44          }
45      }
46
47      for (i = 0; i < results.gl_pathc; i++)
48          printf("%s\n", results.gl_pathv[i]);
49
50      globfree(& results);
51      return 0;
52  }
```

Line 7 defines `myname`, which points to the program's name; this variable is for error messages from `globerr()`, defined on lines 11–15.

Lines 33–45 are the heart of the program. They loop over the patterns given on the command line, calling `glob()` on each one to append its results to the list. Most of the loop is error handling (lines 36–44). Lines 47–48 print the resulting list, and lines 50–51 clean up and return.

Lines 39–41 aren't pretty; a separate function that converts the integer constant to a string should be used; we've done it this way primarily to save space. Code like this is tolerable in a small program, but a larger program should use a function.

If you think about all the work going on under the hood (opening and reading directories, matching patterns, dynamic allocation to grow the list, sorting the list), you can start to appreciate how much `glob()` does for you! Here are some results:

```
$ ch12-glob '/usr/lib/x*.so' '../../*.texi'
/usr/lib/xchat-autob5.so
/usr/lib/xchat-autogb.so
../../00-preface.texi
../../01-intro.texi
../../02-cmdline.texi
../../03-memory.texi
...
```

Note that we have to quote the arguments to keep the shell from doing the expansion!

Globbing? What's That?

In days of yore, circa V6 Unix, the shell used a separate program to perform wildcard expansion behind the scenes. This program was named `/etc/glob`, and according to the V6 source code,[*] the name "glob" is short for "global."

The verb "to glob" thus passed into the Unix lexicon, with the meaning "to perform wildcard expansion." This in turn gives us the function names `glob()` and `globfree()`. The usually understated sense of humor that occasionally peeked through from the Unix manual therefore lives on, formally enshrined in the POSIX standard. (Can you imagine anyone at IBM, in the 1970s or 1980s, naming a system routine `glob()`?)

---

[*] See `/usr/source/s1/glob.c` in the V6 distribution.

12.7.3 Shell Word Expansion: `wordexp()` and `wordfree()`

Many members of the POSIX committee felt that `glob()` didn't do enough: They wanted a library routine capable of doing everything the shell can do: tilde expansion ('echo ~arnold'), shell variable expansion ('echo $HOME'), and command substitution ('echo $(cd ; pwd)'). Many others felt that `glob()` wasn't the right function for this purpose. To "satisfy" everyone, POSIX supplies an additional two functions that do everything:

```
#include <wordexp.h>                                          POSIX

int wordexp(const char *words, wordexp_t *pwordexp, int flags);
void wordfree(wordexp_t *wordexp);
```

These functions work similarly to `glob()` and `globfree()`, but on a `wordexp_t` structure:

```
typedef struct {
    size_t we_wordc;          Count of words matched
    char **we_wordv;          List of expanded words
    size_t we_offs;           Slots to reserve in we_wordv
} wordexp_t;
```

The members are completely analogous to those of the `glob_t` described earlier; we won't repeat the whole description here.

As with `glob()`, several flags control `wordexp()`'s behavior. The flags are listed in Table 12.5.

TABLE 12.5
Flags for `wordexp()`

Constant	Meaning
WRDE_APPEND	Append current call's results to those of a previous call.
WRDE_DOOFFS	Reserve `we_offs` spots at the front of `we_wordv`.
WRDE_NOCMD	Don't allow command substitution.
WRDE_REUSE	Reuse the storage already pointed to by `we_wordv`.
WRDE_SHOWERR	Don't be silent about errors during expansion.
WRDE_UNDEF	Cause undefined shell variables to produce an error.

The return value is 0 if everything went well or one of the values in Table 12.6 if not.

TABLE 12.6
wordexp() **error return values**

Constant	Meaning
WRDE_BADCHAR	A metacharacter (one of newline, '|', &, ;, <, >, (,), {, or }) appeared in an invalid location.
WRDE_BADVAL	A variable was undefined and WRDE_UNDEF is set.
WRDE_CMDSUB	Command substitution was attempted and WRDE_NOCMD was set.
WRDE_NOSPACE	There was a problem allocating dynamic memory.
WRDE_SYNTAX	There was a shell syntax error.

We leave it to you as an exercise (see later) to modify ch12-glob.c to use wordexp() and wordfree(). Here's our version in action:

```
$ ch12-wordexp 'echo $HOME'                  Shell variable expansion
echo
/home/arnold
$ ch12-wordexp 'echo $HOME/*.gz'             Variables and wildcards
echo
/home/arnold/48000.wav.gz
/home/arnold/ipmasq-HOWTO.tar.gz
/home/arnold/rc.firewall-examples.tar.gz
$ ch12-wordexp 'echo ~arnold'                Tilde expansion
echo
/home/arnold
$ ch12-wordexp 'echo ~arnold/.p*'            Tilde and wildcards
echo
/home/arnold/.postitnotes
/home/arnold/.procmailrc
/home/arnold/.profile
$ ch12-wordexp "echo '~arnold/.p*'"          Quoting works
echo
~arnold/.p*
```

12.8 Regular Expressions

A *regular expression* is a way to describe patterns of text to be matched. If you've used GNU/Linux or Unix for any time at all, you're undoubtedly familiar with regular expressions: They are a fundamental part of the Unix programmer's toolbox. They are integral to such everyday programs as grep, egrep, sed, awk, Perl, and the ed, vi, vim, and Emacs editors. If you're not at all familiar with regular expressions, we suggest you take a detour to some of the books or URLs named in Section 12.9, "Suggested Reading," page 480.

POSIX defines two flavors of regular expressions: *basic* and *extended*. Programs such as grep, sed, and the ed line editor use basic regular expressions. Programs such as egrep and awk use extended regular expressions. The following functions give you the ability to use either flavor in your programs:

```
#include <sys/types.h>                                            POSIX
#include <regex.h>

int regcomp(regex_t *preg, const char *regex, int cflags);
int regexec(const regex_t *preg,  const char *string, size_t nmatch,
            regmatch_t pmatch[], int eflags);
size_t regerror(int errcode, const regex_t *preg,
                char *errbuf, size_t errbuf_size);
void regfree(regex_t *preg);
```

To do regular expression matching, you must first *compile* a string version of the regular expression. Compilation converts the regular expression into an internal form. The compiled form is then *executed* against a string to see whether it matches the original regular expression. The functions are as follows:

int regcomp(regex_t *preg, const char *regex, int cflags)

Compiles the regular expression regex into the internal form, storing it in the regex_t structure pointed to by preg. cflags controls how the compilation is done; its value is 0 or the bitwise OR of one or more of the flags in Table 12.7.

int regexec(const regex_t *preg, const char *string, size_t nmatch, regmatch_t pmatch[], int eflags)

Executes the compiled regular expression in *preg against the string string. eflags controls how the execution is done; its value is 0 or the bitwise OR of one or more of the flags in Table 12.8. We discuss the other arguments shortly.

size_t regerror(int errcode, const regex_t *preg, char *errbuf, size_t errbuf_size)

Converts an error returned by either regcomp() or regexec() into a string that can be printed for a human to read.

void regfree(regex_t *preg)

Frees dynamic memory used by the compiled regular expression in *preg.

The `<regex.h>` header file defines a number of flags. Some are for use with `regcomp()`; others are for use with `regexec()`. However, they all start with the prefix 'REG_'. Table 12.7 lists the flags for regular expression compilation with `regcomp()`.

TABLE 12.7
Flags for `regcomp()`

Constant	Meaning
REG_EXTENDED	Use extended regular expressions. The default is basic regular expressions.
REG_ICASE	Matches with `regexec()` ignore case.
REG_NEWLINE	Operators that can match any character *don't* match newline.
REG_NOSUB	Subpattern start and end information isn't needed (see text).

The flags for regular expression matching with `regexec()` are given in Table 12.8.

TABLE 12.8
Flags for `regexec()`

Constant	Meaning
REG_NOTBOL	Don't allow the ^ (beginning of line) operator to match.
REG_NOTEOL	Don't allow the $ (end of line) operator to match.

The `REG_NEWLINE`, `REG_NOTBOL`, and `REG_NOTEOL` flags interact with each other. It's a little complicated, so we take it one step at a time.

- When `REG_NEWLINE` is not included in `cflags`, the newline character acts like an ordinary character. The '.' (match any character) metacharacter can match it, as can complemented character lists ('[^...]'). Also, $ does not match immediately before an embedded newline, and ^ does not match immediately after one.

- When `REG_NOTBOL` is set in `eflags`, the ^ operator does not match the beginning of the string. This is useful when the `string` parameter is the address of a character in the middle of the text being matched.

- Similarly, when `REG_NOTEOL` is set in `eflags`, the $ operator does not match the end of the string.

- When `REG_NEWLINE` is included in `cflags`, then:

- Newline is not matched by '.' or by a complemented character list.
- The ^ operator always matches immediately following an embedded newline, no matter the setting of REG_BOL.
- The $ operator always matches immediately before an embedded newline, no matter the setting of REG_EOL.

When you're doing line-at-a-time I/O, such as by grep, you can leave REG_NEWLINE out of cflags. If you have multiple lines in a buffer and want to treat each one as a separate string, with ^ and $ matching within them, then you should include REG_NEWLINE.

The regex_t structure is mostly opaque. It has one member that user-level code can examine; the rest is for internal use by the regular expression routines:

```
typedef struct {
    ... internal stuff here ...
    size_t re_nsub;
    ... internal stuff here ...
} regex_t;
```

The regmatch_t structure has at least two members for use by user-level code:

```
typedef struct {
    ... possible internal stuff here ...
    regoff_t rm_so;        Byte offset to start of substring
    regoff_t rm_eo;        Byte offset to first character after substring end
    ... possible internal stuff here ...
} regmatch_t;
```

Both the re_nsub field and the regmatch_t structure are for *subexpression matching*. Consider an extended regular expression such as:

```
[[:space:]]+([[:digit:]]+)[[:space:]]+([[:alpha:]])+
```

The two parenthesized subexpressions can each match one or more characters. Furthermore, the text matching each subexpression can start and end at arbitrary positions within the string.

regcomp() sets the re_nsub field to the number of parenthesized subexpressions in the regular expression. regexec() fills in the pmatch array of regmatch_t structures with the start and ending byte offsets of the text that matched the corresponding subexpressions. Together, these data allow you to do text substitution—deletion of matched text or replacement of matched text with other text, just as in your favorite text editor.

pmatch[0] describes the portion of string that matched the entire regular expression. pmatch[1] through pmatch[preg->re_nsub] describe the portions that matched each parenthesized subexpression. (Thus, subexpressions are numbered from 1.) Unused elements in the pmatch array have their rm_so and rm_eo elements set to -1.

regexec() fills in no more than nmatch - 1 elements of pmatch; you should thus ensure that there are at least as many elements (plus 1) as in preg->re_nsub.

Finally, the REG_NOSUB flag for regcomp() indicates that starting and ending information isn't necessary. You should use this flag when you don't need the information; it can potentially improve the performance of regexec(), making a significant difference.

In other words, if all you need to know is "did it match?" then include REG_NOSUB. However, if you also need to know "where is the matching text?" then omit it.

Finally, both regcomp() and regexec() return 0 if they were successful or a specific error code if not. The error codes are listed in Table 12.9.

TABLE 12.9
Error codes for regcomp() and regexec()

Constant	Meaning
REG_BADBR	The contents of '\{...\}' are invalid.
REG_BADPAT	The regular expression is invalid.
REG_BADRPT	A ?, +, or * is not preceded by valid regular expression.
REG_EBRACE	Braces ('\{...\}') are not balanced correctly.
REG_EBRACK	Square brackets ('[...]') are not balanced correctly.
REG_ECOLLATE	The pattern used an invalid collating element.
REG_ECTYPE	The pattern used an invalid character class.
REG_EESCAPE	The pattern has a trailing \ character.
REG_EPAREN	Grouping parentheses ('(...)' or '\(...\)') are not balanced correctly.
REG_ERANGE	The endpoint in a range expression is invalid.
REG_ESPACE	The function ran out of memory.
REG_ESUBREG	The digit in '\digit' is invalid.
REG_NOMATCH	regexec() did not match the string to the pattern.

To demonstrate the regular expression routines, `ch12-grep.c` provides a basic reimplementation of the standard `grep` program, which searches files for a pattern. Our version uses basic regular expressions by default. It accepts a `-E` option to use extended regular expressions instead and a `-i` option to ignore case. Like the real `grep`, if no files are provided on the command line, our `grep` reads standard input, and as in the real `grep`, a filename of '`-`' can be used to mean standard input. (This technique is useful for searching standard input along with other files.) Here's the program:

```
 1   /* ch12-grep.c --- Simple version of grep using POSIX R.E. functions. */
 2
 3   #define _GNU_SOURCE 1          /* for getline() */
 4   #include <stdio.h>
 5   #include <errno.h>
 6   #include <regex.h>
 7   #include <unistd.h>
 8   #include <sys/types.h>
 9
10   char *myname;                  /* for error messages */
11   int ignore_case = 0;           /* -i option: ignore case */
12   int extended = 0;              /* -E option: use extended RE's */
13   int errors = 0;                /* number of errors */
14
15   regex_t pattern;               /* pattern to match */
16
17   void compile_pattern(const char *pat);
18   void process(const char *name, FILE *fp);
19   void usage(void);
```

Lines 10–15 declare the program's global variables. The first set (lines 10–13) are for options and error messages. Line 15 declares `pattern`, which holds the compiled pattern. Lines 17–19 declare the program's other functions.

```
21   /* main --- process options, open files */
22
23   int main(int argc, char **argv)
24   {
25       int c;
26       int i;
27       FILE *fp;
28
29       myname = argv[0];
```

```
30      while ((c = getopt(argc, argv, ":iE")) != -1) {
31          switch (c) {
32          case 'i':
33              ignore_case = 1;
34              break;
35          case 'E':
36              extended = 1;
37              break;
38          case '?':
39              usage();
40              break;
41          }
42      }
43
44      if (optind == argc)      /* sanity check */
45          usage();
46
47      compile_pattern(argv[optind]);  /* compile the pattern */
48      if (errors)             /* compile failed */
49          return 1;
50      else
51          optind++;
```

Line 29 sets `myname`, and lines 30–45 parse the options. Lines 47–51 compile the regular expression, placing the results into `pattern`. `compile_pattern()` increments `errors` if there was a problem. (Coupling the functions by means of a global variable like this is generally considered bad form. It's OK for a small program such as this one, but such coupling can become a problem in larger programs.) If there was no problem, line 51 increments `optind` so that the remaining arguments are the files to be processed.

```
53      if (optind == argc)      /* no files, default to stdin */
54          process("standard input", stdin);
55      else {
56          /* loop over files */
57          for (i = optind; i < argc; i++) {
58              if (strcmp(argv[i], "-") == 0)
59                  process("standard input", stdin);
60              else if ((fp = fopen(argv[i], "r")) != NULL) {
61                  process(argv[i], fp);
62                  fclose(fp);
63              } else {
64                  fprintf(stderr, "%s: %s: could not open: %s\n",
65                      argv[0], argv[i], strerror(errno));
66                  errors++;
67              }
68          }
69      }
70
71      regfree(& pattern);
72      return errors != 0;
73  }
```

Lines 53–69 process the files, searching for lines that match the pattern. Lines 53–54 handle the case in which no files are provided: The program reads standard input. Otherwise, lines 57–68 loop over the files. Line 58 handles the special casing of '–' to mean standard input, lines 60–62 handle regular files, and lines 63–67 handle problems.

```
75  /* compile_pattern --- compile the pattern */
76
77  void compile_pattern(const char *pat)
78  {
79      int flags = REG_NOSUB;  /* don't need where-matched info */
80      int ret;
81  #define MSGBUFSIZE  512      /* arbitrary */
82      char error[MSGBUFSIZE];
83
84      if (ignore_case)
85          flags |= REG_ICASE;
86      if (extended)
87          flags |= REG_EXTENDED;
88
89      ret = regcomp(& pattern, pat, flags);
90      if (ret != 0) {
91          (void) regerror(ret, & pattern, error, sizeof error);
92          fprintf(stderr, "%s: pattern `%s': %s\n", myname, pat, error);
93          errors++;
94      }
95  }
```

Lines 75–95 define the `compile_pattern()` function. It first sets `flags` to `REG_NOSUB` since all we need to know is "did a line match?" and not "where in the line is the matching text?".

Lines 84–85 add additional flags in accordance with the command-line options. Line 89 compiles the pattern, and lines 90–94 report any problems.

```
97  /* process --- read lines of text and match against the pattern */
98
99  void process(const char *name, FILE *fp)
100 {
101     char *buf = NULL;
102     size_t size = 0;
103     char error[MSGBUFSIZE];
104     int ret;
105
```

```
106        while (getline(& buf, &size, fp) != -1) {
107            ret = regexec(& pattern, buf, 0, NULL, 0);
108            if (ret != 0) {
109                if (ret != REG_NOMATCH) {
110                    (void) regerror(ret, & pattern, error, sizeof error);
111                    fprintf(stderr, "%s: file %s: %s\n", myname, name, error);
112                    free(buf);
113                    errors++;
114                    return;
115                }
116            } else
117                printf("%s: %s", name, buf);    /* print matching lines */
119        }
119        free(buf);
120    }
```

Lines 97–120 define `process()`, which reads the file and does the regular expression match. The outer loop (lines 106–119) reads input lines. We use `getline()` (see Section 3.2.1.9, "GLIBC Only: Reading Entire Lines: `getline()` and `getdelim()`," page 73) to avoid line-length problems. Line 107 calls `regexec()`. A nonzero return indicates either failure to match or some other error. Thus, lines 109–115 check for REG_NOMATCH and print an error only if some *other* problem occurred—failure to match isn't an error.

If the return value was 0, the line matched the pattern and thus line 117 prints the filename and matching line.

```
122  /* usage --- print usage message and exit */
123
124  void usage(void)
125  {
126      fprintf(stderr, "usage: %s [-i] [-E] pattern [ files ... ]\n", myname);
127      exit(1);
128  }
```

The `usage()` function prints a usage message and exits. It's called when invalid options are provided or if no pattern is provided (lines 38–40 and 44–45).

That's it! A modest, yet useful version of `grep`, in under 130 lines of code.

12.9 Suggested Reading

1. *Programming Pearls*, 2nd edition, by Jon Louis Bentley. Addison-Wesley, Reading, Massachusetts, USA, 2000. ISBN: 0-201-65788-0. See also this book's web site.[10]

   Program design with assertions is one of the fundamental themes in the book.

2. *Building Secure Software: How to Avoid Security Problems the Right Way*, by John Viega and Gary McGraw. Addison-Wesley, Reading, Massachusetts, USA, 2001. ISBN: 0-201-72152-X.

   Race conditions are only one of many issues to worry about when you are writing secure software. Random numbers are another. This book covers both, among other things. (We mentioned it in the previous chapter.)

3. *The Art of Computer Programming: Volume 2: Seminumerical Algorithms*, 3rd edition, by Donald E. Knuth. Addison-Wesley, Reading, Massachusetts, USA, 1998. ISBN: 0-201-89684-2. See also the book's web site.[11]

   This is the classic reference on random number generation.

4. *Random Number Generation and Monte Carlo Methods*, 2nd edition, by James E. Gentle. Springer-Verlag, Berlin, Germany, 2003. ISBN: 0-387-00178-6.

   This book has wide coverage of the methods for generating and testing pseudo-random numbers. While it still requires background in mathematics and statistics, the level is not as high as that in Knuth's book. (Thanks to Nelson H.F. Beebe for the pointer to this reference.)

5. *sed & awk*, 2nd edition, by Dale Dougherty and Arnold Robbins. O'Reilly and Associates, Sebastopol, California, USA, 1997. ISBN: 1-56592-225-5.

   This book gently introduces regular expressions and text processing, starting with `grep`, and moving on to the more powerful `sed` and `awk` tools.

6. *Mastering Regular Expressions*, 2nd edition, by Jeffrey E.F. Friedl. O'Reilly and Associates, Sebastopol, California, USA, 2002. ISBN: 0-59600-289-0.

---

[10] `http://www.cs.bell-labs.com/cm/cs/pearls/`

[11] `http://www-cs-faculty.stanford.edu/~knuth/taocp.html`

Regular expressions are an important part of Unix. For learning how to chop, slice, and dice text using regular expressions, we recommend this book.

7. The online manual for GNU `grep` also explains regular expressions. On a GNU/Linux system, you can use 'info grep' to look at the local copy. Or use a web browser to read the GNU Project's online documentation for `grep`.[12]

12.10 Summary

- Assertions provide a way to make statements about the expected state of a program. They are a useful design and debugging tool and should generally be left in production code. Be careful, however, not to confuse assertions with runtime checks for possible failure conditions.

- The `memXXX()` functions provide analogues to the better-known `strXXX()` functions. Their greatest value is that they can work on binary data; zero bytes are no different from other bytes. Of particular note is `memcpy()` vs. `memmove()` and the handling of overlapping copies.

- Temporary files are useful in many applications. The `tmpfile()` and `mkstemp()` APIs are the preferred way to create temporary files while avoiding race conditions and their security implications. Many programs use the `TMPDIR` environment variable to specify the location for their temporary files, with a meaningful default (usually `/tmp`) if that variable isn't defined. This is a good convention, one you should adopt for your own programs.

- The `abort()` function sends a `SIGABRT` to the calling process. The effect is to kill the process and create a core dump, presumably for debugging.

- `setjmp()` and `longjmp()` provide a nonlocal goto. This is a powerful facility that must be used with care. `sigsetjmp()` and `siglongjmp()` save and restore the process signal mask when a program does a nonlocal jump. The problems with nonlocal gotos sometimes outweigh their benefits; thus, use these routines only if there isn't a better way to structure your application.

- Random numbers are useful in a variety of applications. Most software uses pseudorandom numbers—sequences of numbers that appear random but that can

---

[12] http://www.gnu.org/software/grep/doc/grep.html

be reproduced by starting with the same seed each time. `rand()` and `srand()` are the original API, standardized by the C language. On many systems, `rand()` uses a subpar algorithm. `random()` and `srandom()` use a better algorithm, are included in the POSIX standard, and are preferred over `rand()` and `srand()`. Use the `/dev/random` and `/dev/urandom` special files (a) if they're available and (b) if you need high-quality random numbers.

- Three APIs provide increasingly powerful facilities for metacharacter expansion (wildcarding).

  - `fnmatch()` is the simplest, returning true/false as a given string does or doesn't match a shell wildcard pattern.

  - `glob()` works its way through the filesystem, returning a list of pathnames that match a given wildcard. When the standard `glob()` functionality is all that's needed, it should be used. While the GLIBC version of `glob()` has some extensions, portable programs needing the extra power should use `wordexp()` instead. (Programs that will only run on GNU/Linux systems should feel free to use the full power of the GLIBC `glob()`.)

  - `wordexp()` not only does what `glob()` does, but it also does full shell word expansion, including tilde expansion, shell variable expansion, and command substitution.

- The `regcomp()` and `regexec()` functions give you access to POSIX basic and extended regular expressions. By using one or the other, you can make your program behave identically to the standard utilities, making it much easier for programmers familiar with GNU/Linux and Unix to use your program.

Exercises

1. Use `read()` and `memcmp()` to write a simple version of the `cmp` program that compares two files. Your version need not support any options.

2. Use the `<stdio.h>` `getc()` macro and direct comparison of each read character to write another version of `cmp` that compares two files. Compare the performance of this version against the one you wrote for the previous exercise.

3. (Medium.) Consider the `<stdio.h>` `fgets()` and GLIBC `getline()` functions. Would `memccpy()` be useful for implementing them? Sketch a possible implementation of `fgets()` using it.

4. (Hard.) Find the source to the GLIBC version of `memcmp()`. This should be on one of the source code CD-ROMs in your GNU/Linux distribution, or you can find it by a Web search. Examine the code, and explain it.

5. Test your memory. How does `tmpfile()` arrange for the file to be deleted when the file pointer is closed?

6. Using `mkstemp()` and `fdopen()` and any other functions or system calls you think necessary, write your own version of `tmpfile()`. Test it too.

7. Describe the advantages and disadvantages of using `unlink()` on the filename created by `mkstemp()` immediately after `mkstemp()` returns.

8. Write your own version of `mkstemp()`, using `mktemp()` and `open()`. How can you make the same guarantees about uniqueness that `mkstemp()` does?

9. Programs using `mkstemp()` should arrange to clean up the file when they exit. (Assume that the file is not immediately unlinked after opening, for whatever reason.) This includes the case in which a terminating signal could arrive. So, as part of a signal catcher, the file should be removed. How do you do this?

10. (Hard.) Even with the first-cut signal-handling cleanup, there's still a race condition. There's a small window between the time `mkstemp()` creates the temporary file and the time its name is returned and recorded (for use by the signal handling function) in a variable. If an uncaught signal is delivered in that window, the program dies and leaves behind the temporary file. How do you close that window? (Thanks to Jim Meyering.)

11. Try compiling and running `ch12-setjmp.c` on as many different systems with as many different compilers as you have access to. Try compiling with and without different levels of optimizations. What variations in behavior, if any, did you see?

12. Look at the file `/usr/src/libc/gen/sleep.c` in the V7 Unix source distribution. It implements the `sleep()` function described in Section 10.8.1, "Alarm Clocks: `sleep()`, `alarm()`, and `SIGALRM`," page 382. Print it, and annotate it in the style of our examples to explain how it works.

13. On a GNU/Linux or System V Unix system, look at the *lrand48*(3) manpage. Does this interface look easier or harder to use than `random()`?

14. Take `ch08-nftw.c` from Section 8.4.3, "Walking a Hierarchy: `nftw()`," page 260, and add a `--exclude=`*pat* option. Files matching the pattern should not be printed.

15. (Hard.) Why would GLIBC need pointers to private versions of the standard directory and `stat()` calls? Can't it just call them directly?

16. Modify `ch12-glob.c` to use the `wordexp()` API. Experiment with it by doing some of the extra things it provides. Be sure to quote your command-line arguments so that `wordexp()` is really doing all the work!

17. The standard `grep` prints the filename only when more than one file is provided on the command line. Make `ch12-grep.c` perform the same way.

18. Look at the *grep*(1) manpage. Add the standard `-e`, `-s`, and `-v` options to `ch12-grep.c`.

19. Write a simple substitution program:

    ```
    subst [-g] pattern replacement [ files ... ]
    ```

    It should read lines of text from the named *files* or from standard input if no files are given. It should search each line for a match of *pattern*. If it finds one, it should replace it with *replacement*.

    With `-g`, it should replace not just the first match but *all* matches on the line.

## Chapter 13

Internationalization and Localization

E arly computing systems generally used English for their output (prompts, error messages) and input (responses to queries, such as "yes" and "no"). This was true of Unix systems, even into the mid-1980s. In the late 1980s, beginning with the first ISO standard for C and continuing with the POSIX standards of the 1990s and the current POSIX standard, facilities were developed to make it possible for programs to work in multiple languages, without a requirement to maintain multiple versions of the same program. This chapter describes how modern programs should deal with multiple-language issues.

13.1 Introduction

The central concept is the *locale*, the place in which a program is run. Locales encapsulate information about the following: the local character set; how to display date and time information; how to format and display monetary amounts; and how to format and display numeric values (with or without a thousands separator, what character to use as the decimal point, and so on).

Internationalization is the process of writing (or modifying) a program so that it can function in multiple locales. *Localization* is the process of tailoring an internationalized program for a specific locale. These terms are often abbreviated *i18n* and *l10n*, respectively. (The numeric values indicate how many characters appear in the middle of the word, and these abbreviations bear a minor visual resemblance to the full terms. They're also considerably easier to type.) Another term that appears frequently is *native language support*, abbreviated *NLS*; NLS refers to the programmatic support for doing i18n and l10n.

Additionally, some people use the term *globalization* (abbreviated *g10n*) to mean the process of preparing all possible localizations for an internationalized program. In other words, making it ready for global use.

NLS facilities exist at two levels. The first level is the C library. It provides information about the locale; routines to handle much of the low-level detail work for formatting date/time, numeric and monetary values; and routines for locale-correct regular expression matching and character classification and comparison. It is the library facilities that appear in the C and POSIX standards.

At the application level, GNU `gettext` provides commands and a library for localizing a program: that is, making all output messages available in one or more natural languages. GNU `gettext` is based on a design originally done by Sun Microsystems for Solaris;[1] however it was implemented from scratch and now provides extensions to the original Solaris `gettext`. GNU `gettext` is a de facto standard for program localization, particularly in the GNU world.

In addition to locales and `gettext`, Standard C provides facilities for working with multiple character sets and their *encodings*—ways to represent large character sets with fewer bytes. We touch on these issues, briefly, at the end of the chapter.

13.2 Locales and the C Library

You control locale-specific behavior by setting environment variables to describe which locale(s) to use for particular kinds of information. The number of available locales offered by any particular operating system ranges from fewer than ten on some commercial Unix systems to hundreds of locales on GNU/Linux systems. (`locale -a` prints the full list of available locales.)

Two locales, `"C"` and `"POSIX"`, are guaranteed to exist. They act as the default locale, providing a 7-bit ASCII environment whose behavior is the same as traditional, non-locale-aware Unix systems. Otherwise, locales specify a language, country, and, optionally, character set information. For example, `"it_IT"` is for Italian in Italy using the system's default character set, and `"it_IT.UTF-8"` uses the UTF-8 character encoding for the Unicode character set.

More details on locale names can be found in the GNU/Linux *setlocale*(3) manpage. Typically, GNU/Linux distributions set the default locale for a system when it's installed, based on the language chosen by the installer, and users don't need to worry about it anymore.

13.2.1 Locale Categories and Environment Variables

The `<locale.h>` header file defines the locale functions and structures. Locale *categories* define the kinds of information about which a program will be locale-aware. The categories are available as a set of symbolic constants. They are listed in Table 13.1.

---

[1] An earlier design, known as `catgets()`, exists. Although this design is standardized by POSIX, it is much harder to use, and we don't recommend it.

TABLE 13.1
ISO C locale category constants defined in `<locale.h>`

Category	Meaning
LC_ALL	This category includes all possible locale information. This consists of the rest of the items in this table.
LC_COLLATE	The category for string collation (discussed below) and regular expression ranges.
LC_CTYPE	The category for classifying characters (upper case, lower case, etc.). This affects regular expression matching and the is*XXX*() functions in `<ctype.h>`.
LC_MESSAGES	The category for locale-specific messages. This category comes into play with GNU `gettext`, discussed later in the chapter.
LC_MONETARY	The category for formatting monetary information, such as the local and international symbols for the local currency (for example, $ vs. USD for U.S. dollars), how to format negative values, and so on.
LC_NUMERIC	The category for formatting numeric values.
LC_TIME	The category for formatting dates and times.

These categories are the ones defined by the various standards. Some systems may support additional categories, such LC_TELEPHONE or LC_ADDRESS. However, these are not standardized; any program that needs to use them but that still needs to be portable should use `#ifdef` to enclose the relevant sections.

By default, C programs and the C library act as if they are in the `"C"` or `"POSIX"` locale, to provide compatibility with historical systems and behavior. However, by calling `setlocale()` (as described below), a program can enable locale awareness. Once a program does this, the user can, by setting environment variables, enable and disable the degree of locale functionality that the program will have.

The environment variables have the same names as the locale categories listed in Table 13.1. Thus, the command—

```
export LC_NUMERIC=en_DK LC_TIME=C
```

—specifies that numbers should be printed according to the `"en_DK"` (English in Denmark) locale, but that date and time values should be printed according to the regular `"C"` locale. (This example merely illustrates that you *can* specify different locales for different categories; it's not necessarily something that you *should* do.)

The environment variable LC_ALL overrides all other LC_*xxx* variables. If LC_ALL isn't set, then the library looks for the specific variables (LC_CTYPE, LC_MONETARY, and so on). Finally, if none of those is set, the library looks for the variable LANG. Here is a small demonstration, using gawk:

```
$ unset LC_ALL LANG                                      Remove default variables
$ export LC_NUMERIC=en_DK LC_TIME=C                      European numbers, default date, time
$ gawk 'BEGIN { print 1.234 ; print strftime() }'        Print a number, current date, time
1,234
Wed Jul 09 09:32:18 PDT 2003
$ export LC_NUMERIC=it_IT LC_TIME=it_IT                  Italian numbers, date, time
$ gawk 'BEGIN { print 1.234 ; print strftime() }'        Print a number, current date, time
1,234
mer lug 09 09:32:40 PDT 2003
$ export LC_ALL=C                                        Set overriding variable
$ gawk 'BEGIN { print 1.234 ; print strftime() }'        Print a number, current date, time
1.234
Wed Jul 09 09:33:00 PDT 2003
```

(For awk, the POSIX standard states that numeric constants in the source code always use '.' as the decimal point, whereas numeric output follows the rules of the locale.)

Almost all GNU versions of the standard Unix utilities are locale-aware. Thus, particularly on GNU/Linux systems, setting these variables gives you control over the system's behavior.[2]

13.2.2 Setting the Locale: setlocale()

As mentioned, if you do nothing, C programs and the C library act as if they're in the "C" locale. The setlocale() function enables locale awareness:

```
#include <locale.h>                                              ISO C

char *setlocale(int category, const char *locale);
```

The category argument is one of the locale categories described in Section 13.2.1, "Locale Categories and Environment Variables," page 487. The locale argument is a string naming the locale to use for that category. When locale is the empty string (""), setlocale() inspects the appropriate environment variables.

If locale is NULL, the locale information is not changed. Instead, the function returns a string representing the current locale for the given category.

---

[2] Long-time C and Unix programmers may prefer to use the "C" locale, even if they are native English speakers; the English locales produce different results from what grizzled, battle-scarred Unix veterans expect.

Because each category can be set individually, the application's author decides how locale-aware the program will be. For example, if `main()` *only* does this—

```
setlocale(LC_TIME, "");        /* Be locale-aware for time, but that's it. */
```

—then, no matter what other LC_*xxx* variables are set in the environment, only the time and date functions obey the locale. All others act as if the program is still in the `"C"` locale. Similarly, the call:

```
setlocale(LC_TIME, "it_IT");   /* For the time, we're always in Italy. */
```

overrides the `LC_TIME` environment variable (as well as `LC_ALL`), forcing the program to be Italian for time/date computations. (Although Italy may be a great place to be, programs are better off using `""` so that they work correctly everywhere; this example is here just to explain *how* `setlocale()` works.)

You can call `setlocale()` individually for each category, but the simplest thing to do is set everything in one fell swoop:

```
/* When in Rome, do as the Romans do, for *everything*. :-) */
setlocale(LC_ALL, "");
```

`setlocale()`'s return value is the current setting of the locale. This is either a string value passed in from an earlier call or an *opaque* value representing the locale in use at startup. This same value can then later be passed back to `setlocale()`. For later use, the return value should be copied into local storage since it is a pointer to internal data:

```
char *initial_locale;

initial_locale = strdup(setlocale(LC_ALL, ""));   /* save copy */
...
(void) setlocale(LC_ALL, initial_locale);          /* restore it */
```

Here, we've saved a copy by using the POSIX `strdup()` function (see Section 3.2.2, "String Copying: `strdup()`," page 74).

13.2.3 String Collation: `strcoll()` and `strxfrm()`

The familiar `strcmp()` function compares two strings, returning negative, zero, or positive values if the first string is less than, equal to, or greater than the second one.

This comparison is based on the numeric values of characters in the machine's character set. Because of this, strcmp()'s result *never varies*.

However, in a locale-aware world, simple numeric comparison isn't enough. Each locale defines the *collating sequence* for characters within it, in other words, the relative order of characters within the locale. For example, in simple 7-bit ASCII, the two characters A and a have the decimal numeric values 65 and 97, respectively. Thus, in the fragment

```
int i = strcmp("A", "a");
```

i has a negative value. However, in the "en_US.UTF-8" locale, A comes *after* a, not before it. Thus, using strcmp() for applications that need to be locale-aware is a bad idea; we might say it returns a locale-ignorant answer.

The strcoll() (string collate) function exists to compare strings in a locale-aware fashion:

```
#include <string.h>                                         ISO C

int strcoll(const char *s1, const char *s2);
```

Its return value is the same negative/zero/positive as strcmp(). The following program, ch13-compare.c, interactively demonstrates the difference:

```
 1  /* ch13-compare.c --- demonstrate strcmp() vs. strcoll() */
 2
 3  #include <stdio.h>
 4  #include <locale.h>
 5  #include <string.h>
 6
 7  int main(void)
 8  {
 9  #define STRBUFSIZE  1024
10      char locale[STRBUFSIZE], curloc[STRBUFSIZE];
11      char left[STRBUFSIZE], right[STRBUFSIZE];
12      char buf[BUFSIZ];
13      int count;
14
15      setlocale(LC_ALL, "");                  /* set to env locale */
16      strcpy(curloc, setlocale(LC_ALL, NULL));   /* save it */
17
18      printf("--> "); fflush(stdout);
```

```
19      while (fgets(buf, sizeof buf, stdin) != NULL) {
20          locale[0] = '\0';
21          count = sscanf(buf, "%s %s %s", left, right, locale);
22          if (count < 2)
23              break;
24
25          if (*locale) {
26              setlocale(LC_ALL, locale);
27              strcpy(curloc, locale);
28          }
29
30          printf("%s: strcmp(\"%s\", \"%s\") is %d\n", curloc, left,
31                  right, strcmp(left, right));
32          printf("%s: strcoll(\"%s\", \"%s\") is %d\n", curloc, left,
33                  right, strcoll(left, right));
34
35          printf("\n--> "); fflush(stdout);
36      }
37
38      exit(0);
39  }
```

The program reads input lines, which consist of two words to compare and, optionally, a locale to use for the comparison. If the locale is given, that becomes the locale
for subsequent entries. It starts out with whatever locale is set in the environment.

The curloc array saves the current locale for printing results; left and right are
the left- and right-hand words to compare (lines 10–11). The main part of the program
is a loop (lines 19–36) that reads lines and does the work. Lines 20–23 split up the input
line. locale is initialized to the empty string, in case a third value isn't provided.

Lines 25–28 set the new locale if there is one. Lines 30–33 print the comparison results, and line 35 prompts for more input. Here's a demonstration:

```
$ ch13-compare                              Run the program
--> ABC abc                                 Enter two words
C: strcmp("ABC", "abc") is -1               Program started in "C" locale
C: strcoll("ABC", "abc") is -1              Identical results in "C" locale

--> ABC abc en_US                           Same words, "en_US" locale
en_US: strcmp("ABC", "abc") is -1           strcmp() results don't change
en_US: strcoll("ABC", "abc") is 2           strcoll() results do!

--> ABC abc en_US.UTF-8                      Same words, "en_US.UTF-8" locale
en_US.UTF-8: strcmp("ABC", "abc") is -1
en_US.UTF-8: strcoll("ABC", "abc") is 6      Different value, still positive

--> junk JUNK                               New words
en_US.UTF-8: strcmp("junk", "JUNK") is 1     Previous locale used
en_US.UTF-8: strcoll("junk", "JUNK") is -6
```

This program clearly demonstrates the difference between strcmp() and strcoll(). Since strcmp() works in accordance with the numeric character values, it always returns the same result. strcoll() understands collation issues, and its result varies according to the locale. We see that in both en_US locales, the uppercase letters come after the lowercase ones.

> NOTE   Locale-specific string collation is also an issue in regular-expression matching. Regular expressions allow character ranges within bracket expressions, such as '[a-z]' or '["-/]'. The exact meaning of such a construct (the characters numerically between the start and end points, inclusive) is defined only for the "C" and "POSIX" locales.
>
> For non-ASCII locales, a range such as '[a-z]' can also match uppercase letters, not just lowercase ones! The range '["-/]' is valid in ASCII, but not in "en_US.UTF-8".
>
> The long-term most portable solution is to use POSIX character classes, such as '[[:lower:]]' and '[[:punct:]]'. If you find yourself needing to use range expressions on systems that are locale-aware and on older systems that are not, but without having to change your program, the solution is to use brute force and list each character individually within the brackets. It isn't pretty, but it works.

Locale-based collation is potentially expensive. If you expect to be doing lots of comparisons, where at least one of the strings will not change or where string values will be compared against each other multiple times (such as in sorting a list), then you should consider using the strxfrm() function to convert your strings to versions that can be used with strcmp(). The strxfrm() function is declared as follows:

```
#include <string.h>                                                          ISO C

size_t strxfrm(char *dest, const char *src, size_t n);
```

The idea is that strxfrm() transforms the first n characters of src, placing them into dest. The return value is the number of characters necessary to hold the transformed characters. If this is more than n, then the contents of dest are "indeterminate."

The POSIX standard explicitly allows n to be zero and dest to be NULL. In this case, strxfrm() returns the size of the array needed to hold the transformed version of src (not including the final '\0' character). Presumably, this value would then be used with malloc() for creating the dest array or for checking the size against a predefined array bound. (When doing this, obviously, `src` must have a terminating zero byte.) This fragment illustrates how to use `strxfrm()`:

```
#define STRBUFSIZE ...
char s1[STRBUFSIZE], s2[STRBUFSIZE];              Original strings
char s1x[STRBUFSIZE], s2x[STRBUFSIZE];            Transformed copies
size_t len1, len2;
int cmp;

... fill in s1 and s2 ...
len1 = strlen(s1);
len2 = strlen(s2);

if (strxfrm(s1x, s1, len1) >= STRBUFSIZE || strxfrm(s2x, s2, len2) >= STRBUFSIZE)
    /* too big, recover */

cmp = strcmp(s1x, s2x);
if (cmp == 0)
    /* equal */
else if (cmp < 0)
    /* s1 < s2 */
else
    /* s1 > s2 */
```

For one-time comparisons, it is probably faster to use `strcoll()` directly. But if strings will be compared multiple times, then using `strxfrm()` once and `strcmp()` on the transformed values will be faster.

There are no locale-aware collation functions that correspond to `strncmp()` or `strcasecmp()`.

13.2.4 Low-Level Numeric and Monetary Formatting: `localeconv()`

Correctly formatting numeric and monetary values requires a fair amount of low-level information. Said information is available in the `struct lconv`, which is retrieved with the `localeconv()` function:

```
#include <locale.h>                                         ISO C

struct lconv *localeconv(void);
```

Similarly to the `ctime()` function, this function returns a pointer to internal `static` data. You should make a copy of the returned data since subsequent calls could return different values if the locale has been changed. Here is the `struct lconv` (condensed slightly), direct from GLIBC's `<locale.h>`:

```
struct lconv {
  /* Numeric (non-monetary) information.  */
  char *decimal_point;           /* Decimal point character.  */
  char *thousands_sep;           /* Thousands separator.  */
  /* Each element is the number of digits in each group;
     elements with higher indices are farther left.
     An element with value CHAR_MAX means that no further grouping is done.
     An element with value 0 means that the previous element is used
     for all groups farther left.  */
  char *grouping;

  /* Monetary information.  */
  /* First three chars are a currency symbol from ISO 4217.
     Fourth char is the separator.  Fifth char is '\0'.  */
  char *int_curr_symbol;
  char *currency_symbol;         /* Local currency symbol.  */
  char *mon_decimal_point;       /* Decimal point character.  */
  char *mon_thousands_sep;       /* Thousands separator.  */
  char *mon_grouping;            /* Like `grouping' element (above).  */
  char *positive_sign;           /* Sign for positive values.  */
  char *negative_sign;           /* Sign for negative values.  */
  char int_frac_digits;          /* Int'l fractional digits.  */
  char frac_digits;              /* Local fractional digits.  */
  /* 1 if currency_symbol precedes a positive value, 0 if succeeds.  */
  char p_cs_precedes;
  /* 1 iff a space separates currency_symbol from a positive value.  */
  char p_sep_by_space;
  /* 1 if currency_symbol precedes a negative value, 0 if succeeds.  */
  char n_cs_precedes;
  /* 1 iff a space separates currency_symbol from a negative value.  */
  char n_sep_by_space;
  /* Positive and negative sign positions:
     0 Parentheses surround the quantity and currency_symbol.
     1 The sign string precedes the quantity and currency_symbol.
     2 The sign string follows the quantity and currency_symbol.
     3 The sign string immediately precedes the currency_symbol.
     4 The sign string immediately follows the currency_symbol.  */
  char p_sign_posn;
  char n_sign_posn;
  /* 1 if int_curr_symbol precedes a positive value, 0 if succeeds.  */
  char int_p_cs_precedes;
  /* 1 iff a space separates int_curr_symbol from a positive value.  */
  char int_p_sep_by_space;
  /* 1 if int_curr_symbol precedes a negative value, 0 if succeeds.  */
  char int_n_cs_precedes;
  /* 1 iff a space separates int_curr_symbol from a negative value.  */
  char int_n_sep_by_space;
```

```
    /* Positive and negative sign positions:
        0 Parentheses surround the quantity and int_curr_symbol.
        1 The sign string precedes the quantity and int_curr_symbol.
        2 The sign string follows the quantity and int_curr_symbol.
        3 The sign string immediately precedes the int_curr_symbol.
        4 The sign string immediately follows the int_curr_symbol.  */
    char int_p_sign_posn;
    char int_n_sign_posn;
};
```

The comments make it fairly clear what's going on. Let's look at the first several fields in the struct lconv:

decimal_point

> The decimal point character to use. In the United States and other English-speaking countries, it's a period, but many countries use a comma.

thousands_sep

> The character to separate each 3 digits in a value.

grouping

> An array of single-byte integer values. Each element indicates how many digits to group. As the comment says, CHAR_MAX means no further grouping should be done, and 0 means reuse the last element. (We show some sample code later in the chapter.)

int_curr_symbol

> This is the international symbol for the local currency. For example, 'USD' for U.S. dollars.

currency_symbol

> This is the local symbol for the local currency. For example, $ for U.S. dollars.

mon_decimal_point, mon_thousands_sep, mon_grouping

> These correspond to the earlier fields, providing the same information, but for monetary amounts.

Most of the rest of the values are not useful for day-to-day programming. The following program, ch13-lconv.c, prints some of these values, to give you a feel for what kind of information is available:

```
/* ch13-lconv.c --- show some of the components of the struct lconv */

#include <stdio.h>
#include <limits.h>
#include <locale.h>

int main(void)
{
    struct lconv l;
    int i;

    setlocale(LC_ALL, "");
    l = *localeconv();

    printf("decimal_point = [%s]\n", l.decimal_point);
    printf("thousands_sep = [%s]\n", l.thousands_sep);

    for (i = 0; l.grouping[i] != 0 && l.grouping[i] != CHAR_MAX; i++)
        printf("grouping[%d] = [%d]\n", i, l.grouping[i]);

    printf("int_curr_symbol = [%s]\n", l.int_curr_symbol);
    printf("currency_symbol = [%s]\n", l.currency_symbol);
    printf("mon_decimal_point = [%s]\n", l.mon_decimal_point);
    printf("mon_thousands_sep = [%s]\n", l.mon_thousands_sep);
    printf("positive_sign = [%s]\n", l.positive_sign);
    printf("negative_sign = [%s]\n", l.negative_sign);
}
```

When run with different locales, not surprisingly we get different results:

```
$ LC_ALL=en_US ch13-lconv          Results for the United States
decimal_point = [.]
thousands_sep = [,]
grouping[0] = [3]
grouping[1] = [3]
int_curr_symbol = [USD ]
currency_symbol = [$]
mon_decimal_point = [.]
mon_thousands_sep = [,]
positive_sign = []
negative_sign = [-]

$ LC_ALL=it_IT ch13-lconv          Results for Italy
decimal_point = [.]
thousands_sep = []
int_curr_symbol = []
currency_symbol = []
mon_decimal_point = []
mon_thousands_sep = []
positive_sign = []
negative_sign = []
```

Note how the value for int_curr_symbol in the "en_US" locale includes a trailing space character that acts to separate the symbol from the following monetary value.

13.2.5 High-Level Numeric and Monetary Formatting: strfmon() and printf()

After looking at all the fields in the struct lconv, you may be wondering, "Do I *really* have to figure out how to use all that information just to format a monetary value?" Fortunately, the answer is no.[3] The strfmon() function does all the work for you:

```
#include <monetary.h>                                        POSIX

ssize_t strfmon(char *s, size_t max, const char *format, ...);
```

This routine is much like strftime() (see Section 6.1.3.2, "Complex Time Formatting: strftime()," page 171), using format to copy literal characters and formatted numeric values into s, placing no more than max characters into it. The following simple program, ch13-strfmon.c, demonstrates how strfmon() works:

```
/* ch13-strfmon.c --- demonstrate strfmon() */

#include <stdio.h>
#include <locale.h>
#include <monetary.h>

int main(void)
{
    char buf[BUFSIZ];
    double val = 1234.567;

    setlocale(LC_ALL, "");
    strfmon(buf, sizeof buf, "You owe me %n (%i)\n", val, val);

    fputs(buf, stdout);
    return 0;
}
```

When run in two different locales, it produces this output:

```
$ LC_ALL=en_US ch13-strfmon              In the United States
You owe me $1,234.57 (USD 1,234.57)
$ LC_ALL=it_IT ch13-strfmon              In Italy
You owe me EUR 1.235 (EUR  1.235)
```

---

3 We're as happy as you are, since we don't have to provide example code that uses this, er, full-featured struct.

As you can see, `strfmon()` is like `strftime()`, copying regular characters unchanged into the destination buffer and formatting arguments according to its own formatting specifications. There are only three:

`%n`   Print the national (that is, local) form of the currency value.

`%i`   Print the international form of the currency value.

`%%`   Print a literal `%` character.

The values to be formatted must be of type `double`. We see the difference between `%n` and `%i` in the `"en_US"` locale: `%n` uses a `$` character, whereas `%i` uses USD, which stands for "U.S. Dollars."

Flexibility—and thus a certain amount of complexity—comes along with many of the APIs that were developed for POSIX, and `strfmon()` is no exception. As with `printf()`, several optional items that can appear between the `%` and the `i` or `n` provide increased control. The full forms are as follows:

```
%[flags][field width][#left-prec][.right-prec]i
%[flags][field width][#left-prec][.right-prec]n
%%                                                        No flag, field width, etc., allowed
```

The flags are listed in Table 13.2.

TABLE 13.2
Flags for `strfmon()`

Flag	Meaning
=c	Use the character c for the numeric fill character, for use with the left precision. The default fill character is a space. A common alternative fill character is 0.
^	Disable the use of the grouping character (for example, a comma in the United States).
(	Enclose negative amounts in parentheses. Mutually exclusive with the + flag.
+	Handle positive/negative values normally. Use the locale's positive and negative signs. Mutually exclusive with the (flag.
!	Do not include the currency symbol. This flag is useful if you wish to use `strfmon()` to get more flexible formatting of regular numbers than what `sprintf()` provides.
−	Left-justify the result. The default is right justification. This flag has no effect without a field width.

The field width is a decimal digit string, providing a minimum width. The default is to use as many characters as necessary based on the rest of the specification. Values smaller than the field width are padded with spaces on the left (or on the right, if the '–' flag was given).

The left precision consists of a # character and a decimal digit string. It indicates the minimum number of digits to appear to the left of the decimal point character;[4] if the converted value is smaller than this, the result is padded with the numeric fill character. The default is a space, but the = flag can be used to change it. Grouping characters are not included in the count.

Finally, the right precision consists of a '.' character and a decimal digit string. This indicates how many digits to round the value to before it is formatted. The default is provided by the `frac_digits` and `int_frac_digits` fields in the `struct lconv`. If this value is 0, no decimal point character is printed.

`strfmon()` returns the number of characters placed into the buffer, not including the terminating zero byte. If there's not enough room, it returns -1 and sets `errno` to `E2BIG`.

Besides `strfmon()`, POSIX (but *not* ISO C) provides a special flag—the single-quote character, '—for the `printf()` formats %i, %d, %u, %f, %F, %g, and %G. In locales that supply a thousands separator, this flag adds the locale's thousands separator. The following simple program, `ch13-quoteflag.c`, demonstrates the output:

```
/* ch13-quoteflag.c --- demonstrate printf's quote flag */

#include <stdio.h>
#include <locale.h>

int main(void)
{
    setlocale(LC_ALL, "");      /* Have to do this, or it won't work */
    printf("%'d\n", 1234567);
    return 0;
}
```

Here's what happens for two different locales: one that does not supply a thousands separator and one that does:

---

[4] The technical term used in the standards is *radix point*, since numbers in different bases may have fractional parts as well. However, for monetary values, it seems pretty safe to use the term "decimal point."

```
$ LC_ALL=C ch13-quoteflag              Traditional environment, no separator
1234567
$ LC_ALL=en_US ch13-quoteflag          English in United States locale, has separator
1,234,567
```

As of this writing, only GNU/Linux and Solaris support the ' flag. Double-check your system's *printf*(3) manpage.

13.2.6 Example: Formatting Numeric Values in gawk

gawk implements its own version of the `printf()` and `sprintf()` functions. For full locale awareness, gawk must support the ' flag, as in C. The following fragment, from the file `builtin.c` in gawk 3.1.4, shows how gawk uses the `struct lconv` for numeric formatting:

```
1   case 'd':
2   case 'i':
3       ...
4       tmpval = force_number(arg);
5
6       ...
7       uval = (uintmax_t) tmpval;
8       ...
9       ii = jj = 0;
10      do {
11          *--cp = (char) ('0' + uval % 10);
12  #ifdef HAVE_LOCALE_H
13          if (quote_flag && loc.grouping[ii] && ++jj == loc.grouping[ii]) {
14              *--cp = loc.thousands_sep[0]; /* XXX - assumption it's one char */
15              if (loc.grouping[ii+1] == 0)
16                  jj = 0;   /* keep using current val in loc.grouping[ii] */
17              else if (loc.grouping[ii+1] == CHAR_MAX)
18                  quote_flag = FALSE;
19              else {
20                  ii++;
21                  jj = 0;
22              }
23          }
24  #endif
25          uval /= 10;
26      } while (uval > 0);
```

(The line numbers are relative to the start of the fragment.) Some parts of the code that aren't relevant to the discussion have been omitted to make it easier to focus on the parts that are important.

The variable `loc`, used in lines 13–17, is a `struct lconv`. It's initialized in `main()`. Of interest to us here are `loc.thousands_sep`, which is the thousands-separator character, and `loc.grouping`, which is an array describing how many digits between separators. A zero element means "use the value in the previous element for all subsequent digits," and a value of `CHAR_MAX` means "stop inserting thousands separators."

With that introduction, let's look at the code. Line 7 sets `uval`, which is an `unsigned` version of the value to be formatted. `ii` and `jj` keep track of the position in `loc.grouping` and the number of digits in the current group that have been converted, respectively.[5] `quote_flag` is true when a `'` character has been seen in a conversion specification.

The `do-while` loop generates digit characters in reverse, filling in a buffer from the back end toward the front end. Each digit is generated on line 11. Line 25 then divides by 10, shifting the value right by one decimal digit.

Lines 12–24 are what interest us. The work is done only on a system that supports locales, as indicated by the presence of the `<locale.h>` header file. The symbolic constant `HAVE_LOCALE_H` will be true on such a system.[6]

When the condition on line 13 is true, it's time to add in a thousands-separator character. This condition can be read in English as "if grouping is requested, *and* the current position in `loc.grouping` indicates an amount for grouping, *and* the current count of digits equals the grouping amount." If this condition is true, line 14 adds the thousands separator character. The comment notes an assumption that is probably true but that might come back to haunt the maintainer at some later time. (The 'XXX' is a traditional way of marking dangerous or doubtful code. It's easy to search for and very noticeable to readers of the code.)

Once the current position in `loc.grouping` has been used, lines 15–22 look ahead at the value in the next position. If it's 0, then the current position's value should continue to be used. We specify this by resetting `jj` to 0 (line 16). On the other hand, if the next position is `CHAR_MAX`, no more grouping should be done, and line 18 turns it off entirely by setting `quote_flag` to false. Otherwise, the next value is a grouping value, so line 20 resets `jj` to 0, and line 21 increments `ii`.

---

[5] We probably should have chosen more descriptive names than just `ii` and `jj`. Since the code that uses them is short, our lack of imagination is not a significant problem.

[6] This is set by the Autoconf and Automake machinery. Autoconf and Automake are powerful software suites that make it possible to support a wide range of Unix systems in a systematic fashion.

This is low-level, detailed code. However, once you understand how the information in the `struct lconv` is presented, the code is straightforward to read (and it was straightforward to write).

13.2.7 Formatting Date and Time Values: `ctime()` and `strftime()`

Section 6.1, "Times and Dates," page 166, described the functions for retrieving and formatting time and date values. The `strftime()` function is also locale-aware if `setlocale()` has been called appropriately. The following simple program, `ch13-times.c` demonstrates this:

```
/* ch13-times.c --- demonstrate locale-based times */

#include <stdio.h>
#include <locale.h>
#include <time.h>

int main(void)
{
    char buf[100];
    time_t now;
    struct tm *curtime;

    setlocale(LC_ALL, "");
    time(& now);
    curtime = localtime(& now);
    (void) strftime(buf, sizeof buf,
            "It is now %A, %B %d, %Y, %I:%M %p", curtime);

    printf("%s\n", buf);

    printf("ctime() says: %s", ctime(& now));
    exit(0);
}
```

When the program is run, we see that indeed the `strftime()` results vary while the `ctime()` results do not:

```
$ LC_ALL=en_US ch13-times                          Time in the United States
It is now Friday, July 11, 2003, 10:35 AM
ctime() says: Fri Jul 11 10:35:55 2003

$ LC_ALL=it_IT ch13-times                          Time in Italy
It is now venerdì, luglio 11, 2003, 10:36
ctime() says: Fri Jul 11 10:36:00 2003

$ LC_ALL=fr_FR ch13-times                          Time in France
It is now vendredi, juillet 11, 2003, 10:36
ctime() says: Fri Jul 11 10:36:05 2003
```

The reason for the lack of variation is that `ctime()` (and `asctime()`, upon which `ctime()` is based) are legacy interfaces; they exist to support old code. `strftime()`, being a newer interface (developed initially for C89), is free to be locale-aware.

13.2.8 Other Locale Information: `nl_langinfo()`

Although we said earlier that the `catgets()` API is hard to use, one part of that API is generally useful: `nl_langinfo()`. It provides additional locale-related information, above and beyond that which is available from the `struct lconv`:

```
#include <nl_types.h>                                            XSI
#include <langinfo.h>

char *nl_langinfo(nl_item item);
```

The `<nl_types.h>` header file defines the `nl_item` type. (This is most likely an `int` or an `enum`.) The `item` parameter is one of the symbolic constants defined in `<langinfo.h>`. The return value is a string that can be used as needed, either directly or as a format string for `strftime()`.

The available information comes from several locale categories. Table 13.3 lists the item constants, the corresponding locale category, and the item's meaning.

An *era* is a particular time in history. As it relates to dates and times, it makes the most sense in countries ruled by emperors or dynasties.[7]

POSIX era specifications can describe eras before A.D. 1. In such a case, the start date has a higher absolute numeric value than the end date. For example, Alexander the Great ruled from 336 B.C. to 323 B.C.

The value returned by '`nl_langinfo(ERA)`', if not `NULL`, consists of one or more era specifications. Each specification is separated from the next by a `;` character. Components of each era specification are separated from each other by a `:` character. The components are described in Table 13.4.

---

[7] Although Americans often refer to the eras of particular presidents, these are not a formal part of the national calendar in the same sense as in pre-World War II Japan or pre-Communist China.

TABLE 13.3
Item values for `nl_langinfo()`

Item name	Category	Meaning
ABDAY_1, ..., ABDAY_7	LC_TIME	The abbreviated names of the days of the week. Sunday is Day 1.
ABMON_1, ..., ABMON_12	LC_TIME	The abbreviated names of the months.
ALT_DIGITS	LC_TIME	Alternative symbols for digits; see text.
AM_STR, PM_STR	LC_TIME	The a.m./p.m. notations for the locale.
CODESET	LC_TYPE	The name of the locale's *codeset*; that is, the character set and encoding in use.
CRNCYSTR	LC_MONETARY	The local currency symbol, described below.
DAY_1, ..., DAY_7	LC_TIME	The names of the days of the week. Sunday is Day 1.
D_FMT	LC_TIME	The date format.
D_T_FMT	LC_TIME	The date and time format.
ERA_D_FMT	LC_TIME	The era date format.
ERA_D_T_FMT	LC_TIME	The era date and time format.
ERA_T_FMT	LC_TIME	The era time format.
ERA	LC_TIME	Era description segments; see text.
MON_1, ..., MON_12	LC_TIME	The names of the months.
RADIXCHAR	LC_NUMERIC	The radix character. For base 10, this is the decimal point character.
THOUSEP	LC_NUMERIC	The thousands-separator character.
T_FMT_AMPM	LC_TIME	The time format with a.m./p.m. notation.
T_FMT	LC_TIME	The time format.
YESEXPR, NOEXPR	LC_MESSAGES	Strings representing positive and negative responses.

TABLE 13.4
Era specification components

Component	Meaning
Direction	A + or '–' character. A + indicates that the era runs from a numerically lower year to a numerically higher one, and a '–' indicates the opposite.
Offset	The year closest to the start date of the era.
Start date	The date when the era began, in the form '*yyyy*/*mm*/*dd*'. These are the year, month, and day, respectively. Years before A.D. 1 use a negative value for *yyyy*.
End date	The date when the era ended, in the same form. Two additional special forms are allowed: `-*` means the "beginning of time," and `+*` means the "end of time."
Era name	The name of the era, corresponding to `strftime()`'s `%EC` conversion specification.
Era format	The format of the year within the era, corresponding to `strftime()`'s `%EY` conversion specification.

The `ALT_DIGITS` value also needs some explanation. Some locales provide for "alternative digits." (Consider Arabic, which uses the decimal numbering system but different glyphs for the digits 0–9. Or consider a hypothetical "Ancient Rome" locale using roman numerals.) These come up, for example, in `strftime()`'s various `%Oc` conversion specifications. The return value for '`nl_langinfo(ALT_DIGITS)`' is a semicolon-separated list of character strings for the alternative digits. The first should be used for 0, the next for 1, and so on. POSIX states that up to 100 alternative symbols may be provided. The point is to avoid restricting locales to the use of the ASCII digit characters when a locale has its own numbering system.

Finally, '`nl_langinfo(CRNCYSTR)`' returns the local currency symbol. The first character of the return value, if it's a '–', +, or '.', indicates how the symbol should be used:

– The symbol should appear before the value.

+ The symbol should appear after the value.

. The symbol should replace the radix character (decimal point).

13.3 Dynamic Translation of Program Messages

The standard C library interfaces just covered solve the easy parts of the localization problem. Monetary, numeric, and time and date values, as well as string collation issues, all lend themselves to management through tables of locale-specific data (such as lists of month and day names).

However, most user interaction with a text-based program occurs in the form of the messages it outputs, such as prompts or error messages. The problem is to avoid having multiple versions of the same program that differ only in the contents of the message strings. The de facto solution in the GNU world is GNU gettext. (GUI programs face similar issues with the items in menus and menu bars; typically, each major user interface toolkit has its own way to solve that problem.)

GNU gettext enables translation of program messages into different languages at runtime. Within the code for a program, this translation involves several steps, each of which uses different library functions. Once the program itself has been properly prepared, several shell-level utilities facilitate the preparation of translations into different languages. Each such translation is referred to as a *message catalog*.

13.3.1 Setting the Text Domain: textdomain()

A complete application may contain multiple components: individual executables written in C or C++ or in scripting languages that can also access gettext facilities, such as gawk or the Bash shell. The components of the application all share the same *text domain*, which is a string that uniquely identifies the application. (Examples might be "gawk" or "coreutils"; the former is a single program, and the latter is a whole suite of programs.) The text domain is set with textdomain():

```
#include <libintl.h>                                          GLIBC

char *textdomain(const char *domainname);
```

Each component should call this function with a string naming the text domain as part of the initial startup activity in main(). The return value is the current text domain. If the domainname argument is NULL, then the current domain is returned; otherwise, it is set to the new value and that value is then returned. A return value of NULL indicates an error of some sort.

If the text domain is not set with textdomain(), the default domain is "messages".

13.3.2 Translating Messages: `gettext()`

The next step after setting the text domain is to use the `gettext()` function (or a variant) for *every* string that should be translated. Several functions provide translation services:

```
#include <libintl.h>                                         GLIBC

char *gettext(const char *msgid);
char *dgettext(const char *domainname, const char *msgid);
char *dcgettext(const char *domainname, const char *msgid, int category);
```

The arguments used in these functions are as follows:

`const char *msgid`
> The string to be translated. It acts as a key into a database of translations.

`const char *domainname`
> The text domain from which to retrieve the translation. Thus, even though `main()` has called `textdomain()` to set the application's own domain, messages can be retrieved from other text domains. (This is most applicable to messages that might be in the text domain for a third-party library, for example.)

`int category`
> One of the domain categories described earlier (`LC_TIME`, etc.).

The default text domain is whatever was set with `textdomain()` (`"messages"` if `textdomain()` was never called). The default category is `LC_MESSAGES`. Assume that `main()` makes the following call:

```
textdomain("killerapp");
```

Then, '`gettext("my message")`' is equivalent to '`dgettext("killerapp", "my message")`'. Both of these, in turn, are equivalent to '`dcgettext("killerapp", "my message", LC_MESSAGES)`'.

You will want to use `gettext()` 99.9 percent of the time. However, the other functions give you the flexibility to work with other text domains or locale categories. You are most likely to need this flexibility when doing library programming, since a standalone library will almost certainly be in its own text domain.

All the functions return a string. The string is either the translation of the given `msgid` or, if no translation exists, the original string. Thus, there is always some output, even if it's just the original (presumably English) message. For example:

```
/* The canonical first program, localized version. */

#include <stdio.h>
#include <locale.h>
#include <libintl.h>

int main(void)
{
    setlocale(LC_ALL, "");
    printf("%s\n", gettext("hello, world"));
    return 0;
}
```

Although the message is a simple string, we don't use it directly as the `printf()` control string, since in general, translations can contain `%` characters.

Shortly, in Section 13.3.4, "Making `gettext()` Easy to Use," page 510, we'll see how to make `gettext()` easier to use in large-scale, real-world programs.

13.3.3 Working with Plurals: `ngettext()`

Translating plurals provides special difficulties. Naive code might look like this:

```
printf("%d word%s misspelled\n", nwords, nwords > 1 ? "s" : "");
/* or */
printf("%d %s misspelled\n", nwords, nwords == 1 ? "word" : "words");
```

This is reasonable for English, but translation becomes difficult. First of all, many languages don't use as simple a plural form as English (adding an `s` suffix for most words). Second, many languages, particularly in Eastern Europe, have multiple plural forms, each indicating how many objects the form designates. Thus, even code like this isn't enough:

```
if (nwords == 1)
    printf("one word misspelled\n");
else
    printf("%d words misspelled\n", nwords);
```

The solution is a parallel set of routines specifically for formatting plural values:

```
#include <libintl.h>                                              GLIBC

char *ngettext(const char *msgid, const char *msgid_plural,
               unsigned long int n);
char *dngettext(const char *domainname, const char *msgid,
                const char *msgid_plural, unsigned long int n);
char *dcngettext(const char *domainname, const char *msgid,
                 const char *msgid_plural, unsigned long int n, int category);
```

Besides the original `msgid` argument, these functions accept additional arguments:

`const char *msgid_plural`
> The default string to use for plural values. Examples shortly.

`unsigned long int n`
> The number of items there are.

Each locale's message catalog specifies how to translate plurals.[8] The `ngettext()` function (and its variants) examines `n` and, based on the specification in the message catalog, returns the appropriate translation of `msgid`. If the catalog does not have a translation for `msgid`, or in the `"C"` locale, `ngettext()` returns `msgid` if 'n == 1'; otherwise, it returns `msgid_plural`. Thus, our misspelled words example looks like this:

```
printf("%s\n", ngettext("%d word misspelled", "%d words misspelled", nwords),
        nwords);
```

Note that `nwords` must be passed to `ngettext()` to select a format string, and then to `printf()` for formatting. In addition, be careful not to use a macro or expression whose value changes each time, like 'n++'! Such a thing could happen if you're doing global editing to add calls to `ngettext()` and you don't pay attention.

13.3.4 Making `gettext()` Easy to Use

The call to `gettext()` in program source code serves two purposes. First, it does the translation at runtime, which is the main point, after all. However, it also serves to *mark* the strings that need translating. The `xgettext` utility reads program source code and extracts all the original strings that need translation. (We briefly cover the mechanics of this later in the chapter.)

Consider the case, though, of `static` strings that aren't used directly:

```
static char *copyrights[] = {
    "Copyright 2004, Jane Programmer",
    "Permission is granted ...",
    ...                                   LOTS of legalese here
    NULL
};
```

---

[8] The details are given in the GNU `gettext` documentation. Here, we're focusing on the developer's needs, not the translator's.

```
void copyright(void)
{
    int i;

    for (i = 0; copyrights[i] != NULL, i++)
        printf("%s\n", gettext(copyrights[i]));
}
```

Here, we'd like to be able to print the translations of the copyright strings if they're available. However, how is the `xgettext` extractor supposed to find these strings? We can't enclose them in calls to `gettext()` because that won't work at compile time:

```
/* BAD CODE: won't compile */
static char *copyrights[] = {
    gettext("Copyright 2004, Jane Programmer"),
    gettext("Permission is granted ..."),
    ...                                  LOTS of legalese here
    NULL
};
```

13.3.4.1 Portable Programs: `"gettext.h"`

We assume here that you wish to write a program that can be used along with the GNU `gettext` library on any Unix system, not just GNU/Linux systems. The next section describes what to do for GNU/Linux-only programs.

The solution to marking strings involves two steps. The first is the use of the `gettext.h` convenience header that comes in the GNU `gettext` distribution. This file handles several portability and compilation issues, making it easier to use `gettext()` in your own programs:

```
#define ENABLE_NLS 1          ENABLE_NLS must be true for gettext() to work
#include "gettext.h"          Instead of <libintl.h>
```

If the `ENABLE_NLS` macro is not defined[9] or it's set to zero, then `gettext.h` expands calls to `gettext()` into the first argument. This makes it possible to port code using `gettext()` to systems that have neither GNU `gettext` installed nor their own version. Among other things, this header file defines the following macro:

---

[9] This macro is usually automatically defined by the `configure` program, either in a special header or on the compiler command line. `configure` is generated with Autoconf and Automake.

```
/* A pseudo function call that serves as a marker for the automated
   extraction of messages, but does not call gettext().  The run-time
   translation is done at a different place in the code.
   The argument, String, should be a literal string.  Concatenated strings
   and other string expressions won't work.
   The macro's expansion is not parenthesized, so that it is suitable as
   initializer for static 'char[]' or 'const char[]' variables.  */
#define gettext_noop(String) String
```

The comment is self-explanatory. With this macro, we can now proceed to the second step. We rewrite the code as follows:

```
#define ENABLE_NLS 1
#include "gettext.h"

static char copyrights[] =
    gettext_noop("Copyright 2004, Jane Programmer\n"
    "Permission is granted ...\n"
    ...                                 LOTS of legalese here
    "So there.");

void copyright(void)
{
    printf("%s\n", gettext(copyrights));
}
```

Note that we made two changes. First, `copyrights` is now one long string, built up by using the Standard C string constant concatenation feature. This single string is then enclosed in the call to `gettext_noop()`. We need a single string so that the legalese can be translated as a single entity.

The second change is to print the translation directly, as one string in `copyright()`.

By now, you may be thinking, "Gee, having to type '`gettext(...)`' each time is pretty painful." Well, you're right. Not only is it extra work to type, it makes program source code harder to read as well. Thus, once you are using the `gettext.h` header file, the GNU `gettext` manual recommends the introduction of two more macros, named `_()` and `N_()`, as follows:

```
#define ENABLE_NLS 1
#include "gettext.h"
#define _(msgid)  gettext(msgid)
#define N_(msgid) msgid
```

This approach reduces the burden of using `gettext()` to just three extra characters per translatable string constant and only four extra characters for `static` strings:

```
#include <stdio.h>
#define ENABLE_NLS 1
#include "gettext.h"
#define _(msgid)  gettext(msgid)
#define N_(msgid) msgid
...
static char copyrights[] =
    N_("Copyright 2004, Jane Programmer\n"
    "Permission is granted ...\n"
    ...                              LOTS of legalese here
    "So there.");

void copyright(void)
{
   printf("%s\n", gettext(copyrights));
}

int main(void)
{
    setlocale(LC_ALL, "");        /* gettext.h gets <locale.h> for us too */
    printf("%s\n", _("hello, world"));
    copyright();
    exit(0);
}
```

These macros are unobtrusive, and in practice, all GNU programs that use GNU
gettext use this convention. If you intend to use GNU gettext, you too should
follow this convention.

13.3.4.2 GLIBC Only: `<libintl.h>`

For a program that will only be used on systems with GLIBC, the header file usage
and macros are similar, but simpler:

```
#include <stdio.h>
#include <libintl.h>
#define _(msgid)  gettext(msgid)
#define N_(msgid) msgid
... everything else is the same ...
```

As we saw earlier, the `<libintl.h>` header file declares gettext() and the other
functions. You still have to define _() and N_(), but you don't have to worry about
ENABLE_NLS, or distributing gettext.h with your program's source code.

13.3.5 Rearranging Word Order with `printf()`

When translations are produced, sometimes the word order that is natural in English is incorrect for other languages. For instance, while in English an adjective appears before the noun it modifies, in many languages it appears *after* the noun. Thus, code like the following presents a problem:

```
char *animal_color, *animal;

if (...) {
    animal_color = _("brown");
    animal = _("cat");
} else if (...) {
    ...
} else {
    ...
}
printf(_("The %s %s looks at you enquiringly.\n"), animal_color, color);
```

Here, the format string, `animal_color` and `animal` are all properly enclosed in calls to `gettext()`. However, the statement will still be incorrect when translated, since *the order of the arguments cannot be changed at runtime.*

To get around this, the POSIX (but *not* ISO C) version of the `printf()` family allows you to provide a *positional specifier* within a format specifier. This takes the form of a decimal number followed by a `$` character *immediately* after the initial `%` character. For example:

```
printf("%2$s, %1$s\n", "world", "hello");
```

The positional specifier indicates which argument in the argument list to use; counts begin at 1 and don't include the format string itself. This example prints the famous '`hello, world`' message in the correct order.

GLIBC and Solaris implement this capability. As it's part of POSIX, if your Unix vendor's `printf()` doesn't have it, it should be appearing soon.

Any of the regular `printf()` flags, a field width, and a precision may follow the positional specifier. The rules for using positional specifiers are these:

- The positional specifier form may not be mixed with the nonpositional form. In other words, either every format specifier includes a positional specifier or none of them do. Of course, `%%` can always be used.

- If the *N*'th argument is used in the format string, all the arguments up to *N* must also be used by the string. Thus, the following is invalid:

  ```
  printf("%3$s %1$s\n", "hello", "cruel", "world");
  ```

- A particular argument may be referenced with a positional specifier multiple times. Nonpositional format specifications always move through the argument list sequentially.

This facility isn't intended for direct use by application programmers, but rather by translators. For example, a French translation for the previous format string, `"The %s %s looks at you enquiringly.\n"`, might be:

```
"Le %2$s %1$s te regarde d'un aire interrogateur.\n"
```

(Even this translation isn't perfect: the article "Le" is gender specific. Preparing a program for translation is a hard job!)

13.3.6 Testing Translations in a Private Directory

The collection of messages in a program is referred to as the *message catalog*. This term also applies to each translation of the messages into a different language. When a program is installed, each translation is also installed in a standard location, where `gettext()` can find the right one at runtime.

It can be useful to place translations in a directory other than the standard one, particularly for program testing. Especially on larger systems, a regular developer probably does not have the permissions necessary to install files in system directories. The `bindtextdomain()` function gives `gettext()` an alternative place to look for translations:

```
#include <libintl.h>                                             GLIBC

char *bindtextdomain(const char *domainname, const char *dirname);
```

Useful directories include '.' for the current directory and `/tmp`. It might also be handy to get the directory from an environment variable, like so:

```
char *td_dir;

setlocale(LC_ALL, "");
textdomain("killerapp");
if ((td_dir = getenv("KILLERAPP_TD_DIR")) != NULL)
    bindtextdomain("killerapp", td_dir);
```

`bindtextdomain()` should be called before any calls to the `gettext()` family of functions. We see an example of how to use it in Section 13.3.8, "Creating Translations," page 517.

13.3.7 Preparing Internationalized Programs

So far, we've looked at all the components that go into an internationalized program. This section summarizes the process.

1. Adopt the `gettext.h` header file into your application, and add definitions for the `_()` and `N_()` macros to a header file that is included by all your C source files. Don't forget to define the `ENABLE_NLS` symbolic constant.

2. Call `setlocale()` as appropriate. It is easiest to call '`setlocale(LC_ALL, "")`', but occasionally an application may need to be more picky about which locale categories it enables.

3. Pick a text domain for the application, and set it with `textdomain()`.

4. If testing, bind the text domain to a particular directory with `bindtextdomain()`.

5. Use `strfmon()`, `strftime()`, and the `'` flag for `printf()` as appropriate. If other locale information is needed, use `nl_langinfo()`, particularly in conjunction with `strftime()`.

6. Mark all strings that should be translated with calls to `_()` or `N_()`, as appropriate.

   A few should not be so marked though. For example, if you use `getopt_long()` (see Section 2.1.2, "GNU Long Options," page 27), you probably *don't* want the long option names to be marked for translation. Also, simple format strings like `"%d %d\n"` don't need to be translated, nor do debugging messages.

7. When appropriate, use `ngettext()` (or its variants) for dealing with values that can be either 1 or greater than 1.

8. Make life easier for your translators by using multiple strings representing complete sentences instead of doing word substitutions with `%s` and `?:`. For example:

```
if (an error occurred) {          /* RIGHT */
    /* Use multiple strings to make translation easier. */
    if (input_type == INPUT_FILE)
        fprintf(stderr, _("%s: cannot read file: %s\n"),
                        argv[0], strerror(errno));
    else
        fprintf(stderr, _("%s: cannot read pipe: %s\n"),
                        argv[0], strerror(errno));
}
```

This is better than

```
if (an error occurred) {          /* WRONG */
    fprintf(stderr, _("%s: cannot read %s: %s\n"), argv[0],
            input_type == INPUT_FILE ? _("file") : _("pipe"),
            strerror(errno));
}
```

As just shown, it's a good idea to include a comment stating that there are multiple messages on purpose—to make it easier to translate the messages.

13.3.8 Creating Translations

Once your program has been internationalized, it's necessary to prepare translations. This is done with several shell-level tools. We start with an internationalized version of `ch06-echodate.c`, from Section 6.1.4, "Converting a Broken-Down Time to a `time_t`," page 176:

```
/* ch13-echodate.c --- demonstrate translations */

#include <stdio.h>
#include <time.h>
#include <locale.h>
#define ENABLE_NLS 1
#include "gettext.h"
#define _(msgid) gettext(msgid)
#define N_(msgid) msgid
```

```
int main(void)
{
    struct tm tm;
    time_t then;

    setlocale(LC_ALL, "");
    bindtextdomain("echodate", ".");
    textdomain("echodate");

    printf("%s", _("Enter a Date/time as YYYY/MM/DD HH:MM:SS : "));
    scanf("%d/%d/%d %d:%d:%d",
        & tm.tm_year, & tm.tm_mon, & tm.tm_mday,
        & tm.tm_hour, & tm.tm_min, & tm.tm_sec);

    /* Error checking on values omitted for brevity. */
    tm.tm_year -= 1900;
    tm.tm_mon -= 1;

    tm.tm_isdst = -1;   /* Don't know about DST */

    then = mktime(& tm);

    printf(_("Got: %s"), ctime(& then));
    exit(0);
}
```

We have purposely used "gettext.h" and not <gettext.h>. If our application ships with a private copy of the gettext library, then "gettext.h" will find it, avoiding the system's copy. On the other hand, if there is only a system copy, it will be found if there is no local copy. The situation is admittedly complicated by the fact that Solaris systems also have a gettext library which is not as featureful as the GNU version.

Moving on to creating translations, the first step is to extract the translatable strings. This is done with the xgettext program:

```
$ xgettext --keyword=_ --keyword=N_ \
> --default-domain=echodate ch13-echodate.c
```

The --keyword options tell xgettext to look for the _() and N_() macros. It already knows to extract strings from gettext() and its variants, as well as from gettext_noop().

The output from xgettext is called a *portable object* file. The default filename is messages.po, corresponding to the default text domain of "messages". The --default-domain option indicates the text domain, for use in naming the output file. In this case, the file is named echodate.po. Here are its contents:

```
# SOME DESCRIPTIVE TITLE.                              Boilerplate, to be edited
# Copyright (C) YEAR THE PACKAGE'S COPYRIGHT HOLDER
# This file is distributed under the same license as the PACKAGE package.
# FIRST AUTHOR <EMAIL@ADDRESS>, YEAR.
#
#, fuzzy
msgid ""                                               Detailed information
msgstr ""                                              Each translator completes
"Project-Id-Version: PACKAGE VERSION\n"
"Report-Msgid-Bugs-To: \n"
"POT-Creation-Date: 2003-07-14 18:46-0700\n"
"PO-Revision-Date: YEAR-MO-DA HO:MI+ZONE\n"
"Last-Translator: FULL NAME <EMAIL@ADDRESS>\n"
"Language-Team: LANGUAGE <LL@li.org>\n"
"MIME-Version: 1.0\n"
"Content-Type: text/plain; charset=CHARSET\n"
"Content-Transfer-Encoding: 8bit\n"

#: ch13-echodate.c:19                                  Message location
msgid "Enter a Date/time as YYYY/MM/DD HH:MM:SS : "    Original message
msgstr ""                                              Translation goes here

#: ch13-echodate.c:32                                  Same for each message
#, c-format
msgid "Got: %s"
msgstr ""
```

This original file is reused for each translation. It is thus a *template* for translations, and by convention it should be renamed to reflect this fact, with a `.pot` (*portable object template*) suffix:

```
$ mv echodate.po echodate.pot
```

Given that we aren't fluent in many languages, we have chosen to translate the messages into pig Latin. Thus, the next step is to produce a translation. We do this by copying the template file and adding translations to the new copy:

```
$ cp echodate.pot piglat.po
$ vi piglat.po              Add translations, use your favorite editor
```

The filename convention is `language.po` where `language` is the two- or three-character international standard abbreviation for the language. Occasionally the form `language_country.po` is used: for example, `pt_BR.po` for Portugese in Brazil. As pig Latin isn't a real language, we've called the file `piglat.po`. Here are the contents, after the translations have been added:

```
# echodate translations into pig Latin
# Copyright (C) 2004 Prentice-Hall
# This file is distributed under the same license as the echodate package.
# Arnold Robbins <arnold@example.com> 2004
#
#, fuzzy
msgid ""
msgstr ""
"Project-Id-Version: echodate 1.0\n"
"Report-Msgid-Bugs-To: arnold@example.com\n"
"POT-Creation-Date: 2003-07-14 18:46-0700\n"
"PO-Revision-Date: 2003-07-14 19:00+8\n"
"Last-Translator: Arnold Robbins <arnold@example.com>\n"
"Language-Team: Pig Latin <piglat@li.example.org>\n"
"MIME-Version: 1.0\n"
"Content-Type: text/plain; charset=ASCII\n"
"Content-Transfer-Encoding: 8bit\n"

#: ch13-echodate.c:19
msgid "Enter a Date/time as YYYY/MM/DD HH:MM:SS : "
msgstr "Enteray A Ateday/imetay asay YYYY/MM/DD HH:MM:SS : "

#: ch13-echodate.c:32
#, c-format
msgid "Got: %s"
msgstr "Otgay: %s"
```

While it would be possible to do a linear search directly in the portable object file, such a search would be slow. For example, `gawk` has approximately 350 separate messages, and the GNU Coreutils have over 670. Linear searching a file with hundreds of messages would be noticeably slow. Therefore, GNU `gettext` uses a binary format for fast message lookup. `msgfmt` does the compilation, producing a *message object* file:

```
$ msgfmt piglat.po -o piglat.mo
```

As program maintenance is done, the strings used by a program change: new strings are added, others are deleted or changed. At the very least, a string's location in the source file may move around. Thus, translation `.po` files will likely get out of date. The `msgmerge` program merges an old translation file with a new `.pot` file. The result can then be updated. This example does a merge and then recompiles:

```
$ msgmerge piglat.po echodate.pot -o piglat.new.po     Merge files
$ mv piglat.new.po piglat.po                           Rename the result
$ vi piglat.po                                         Bring translations up to date
$ msgfmt piglat.po -o piglat.mo                        Recreate .mo file
```

Compiled `.mo` files are placed in the file *base*/*locale*/*category*/*textdomain*.mo. On GNU/Linux systems, *base* is `/usr/share/locale`. *locale* is the language, such as 'es', 'fr', and so on. *category* is a locale category; for messages, it is LC_MESSAGES.

textdomain is the text domain of the program: in our case, `echodate`. As a real example, the GNU Coreutils Spanish translation is in `/usr/share/locale/es/LC_MESSAGES/coreutils.mo`.

The `bindtextdomain()` function changes the *base* part of the location. In `ch13-echodate.c`, we change it to '.'. Thus, it's necessary to make the appropriate directories, and place the pig Latin translation there:

```
$ mkdir -p en_US/LC_MESSAGES                    Have to use a real locale
$ cp piglat.mo en_US/LC_MESSAGES/echodate.mo    Put the file in the right place
```

A real locale must be used;[10] thus, we "pretend" by using `"en_US"`. With the translation in place, we set `LC_ALL` appropriately, cross our fingers, and run the program:

```
$ LC_ALL=en_US ch13-echodate                    Run the program
Enteray A Ateday/imetay asay YYYY/MM/DD HH:MM:SS : 2003/07/14 21:19:26
Otgay: Mon Jul 14 21:19:26 2003
```

The latest version of GNU `gettext` can be found in the GNU `gettext` distribution directory.[11]

This section has necessarily only skimmed the surface of the localization process. GNU `gettext` provides many tools for working with translations, and in particular for making it easy to keep translations up to date as program source code evolves.

The manual process for updating translations is workable but tedious. This task is easily automated with `make`; in particular GNU `gettext` integrates well with Autoconf and Automake to provide this functionality, removing considerable development burden from the programmer.

We recommend reading the GNU `gettext` documentation to learn more about both of these issues in particular and about GNU `gettext` in general.

13.4 Can You Spell That for Me, Please?

In the very early days of computing, different systems assigned different correspondences between numeric values and *glyphs*—symbols such as letters, digits, and punctuation used for communication with humans. Eventually, two widely used standards emerged: the EBCDIC encoding used on IBM and workalike mainframes, and ASCII,

---

[10] We spent a frustrating 30 or 45 minutes attempting to use a `piglat/LC_MESSAGES` directory and setting 'LC_ALL=piglat', all to no effect, until we figured this out.

[11] `ftp://ftp.gnu.org/gnu/gettext`

used on everything else. Today, except on mainframes, ASCII is the basis for all other character sets currently in use.

The original seven-bit ASCII character set suffices for American English and most punctuation and special characters (such as $, but there is no character for the "cent" symbol). However, there are many languages and many countries with different character set needs. ASCII doesn't handle the accented versions of the roman characters used in Europe, and many Asian languages have *thousands* of characters. New technologies have evolved to solve these deficiencies.

The i18n literature abounds with references to three fundamental terms. Once we define them and their relationship to each other, we can present a general description of the corresponding C APIs.

Character set

A definition of the meaning assigned to different integer values; for example, that A is 65. Any character set that uses more than eight bits per character is termed a *multibyte character set*.

Character set encoding

ASCII uses a single byte to represent characters. Thus, the integer value is stored as itself, directly in disk files. More recent character sets, most notably different versions of Unicode,[12] use 16-bit or even 32-bit integer values for representing characters. For most of the defined characters, one, two, or even three of the higher bytes in the integer are zero, making direct storage of their values in disk files expensive. The encoding describes a mechanism for converting 16- or 32-bit values into one to six bytes for storage on disk, such that overall there is a significant space savings.

Language

The rules for a given language dictate character set usage. In particular, the rules affect the ordering of characters. For example, in French, e, é, and è should all come between d and f, no matter what numerical values are assigned to those characters. Different languages can (and do) assign different orderings to the same glyphs.

---

[12] http://www.unicode.org

Various technologies have evolved over time for supporting multibyte character sets. Computing practice is slowly converging on Unicode and its encoding, but Standard C and POSIX support both past and present techniques. This section provides a conceptual overview of the various facilities. We have not had to use them ourselves, so we prefer to merely introduce them and provide pointers to more information.

13.4.1 Wide Characters

We start with the concept of a *wide character*. A wide character is an integer type that can hold any value of the particular multibyte character set being used.

Wide characters are represented in C with the type wchar_t. C99 provides a corresponding wint_t type, which can hold any value that a wchar_t can hold, and the special value WEOF, which is analogous to regular EOF from <stdio.h>. The various types are defined in the <wchar.h> header file. A number of functions similar to those of <ctype.h> are defined by the <wctype.h> header file, such as iswalnum(), and many more.

Wide characters may be 16 to 32 bits in size, depending on the implementation. As mentioned, they're intended for manipulating data in memory and are not usually stored directly in files.

For wide characters, the C standard provides a large number of functions and macros that correspond to the traditional functions that work on char data. For example, wprintf(), iswlower(), and so on. These are documented in the GNU/Linux manpages and in books on Standard C.

13.4.2 Multibyte Character Encodings

Strings of wide characters are stored on disk by being converted to a multibyte character set encoding in memory, and the converted data is then written to a disk file. Similarly, such strings are read in from disk through low-level block I/O, and converted in memory from the encoded version to the wide-character version.

Many defined encodings represent multibyte characters by using *shift states*. In other words, given an input byte stream, byte values represent themselves until a special control value is encountered. At that point, the interpretation changes according to the current shift state. Thus, the same eight-bit value can have two meanings: one for the normal, unshifted state, and another for the shifted state. Correctly encoded strings are supposed to start and end in the same shift state.

A significant advantage to Unicode is that its encodings are self-correcting; the encondings don't use shift states, so a loss of data in the middle does not corrupt the subsequent encoded data.

The initial versions of the multibyte-to-wide-character and wide-character-to-multibyte functions maintained a private copy of the state of the translation (for example, the shift state, and anything else that might be necessary). This design limits the functions' use to one kind of translation throughout the life of the program. Examples are mblen() (multibyte-character length), mbtowc() (multibyte to wide character), and wctomb() (wide character to multibyte), mbstowcs() (multibyte string to wide-character string), and wcstombs() (wide-character string to multibyte string).

The newer versions of these routines are termed *restartable*. This means that the user-level code maintains the state of the translation in a separate object, of type mbstate_t. The corresponding examples are mbrlen(), mbrtowc(), and wcrtomb(), mbsrtowcs() and wcsrtombs(). (Note the r, for "restartable," in their names.)

13.4.3 Languages

Language issues are controlled by the locale. We've already seen setlocale() earlier in the chapter. POSIX provides an elaborate mechanism for defining the rules by which a locale works; see the GNU/Linux *locale*(5) manpage for some of the details and the POSIX standard itself for the full story.

The truth is, you really don't want to know the details. Nor should you, as an application developer, need to worry about them; it is up to the library implementors to make things work. All you need to do is understand the concepts and make your code use the appropriate functions, such as strcoll() (see Section 13.2.3, "String Collation: strcoll() and strxfrm()," page 490).

Current GLIBC systems provide excellent locale support, including a multibyte-aware suite of regular expression matching routines. For example, the POSIX extended regular expression [[:alpha:]][[:alnum:]]+ matches a letter followed by one or more letters or digits (an alphabetic character followed by one or more alphanumeric ones). The definition of which characters matches these classes depends on the locale. For example, this regular expression would match the two characters 'eè', whereas the traditional Unix, ASCII-oriented regular expression `[a-zA-Z][a-A-Zz0-9]+` most likely would not. The POSIX character classes are listed in Table 13.5.

TABLE 13.5
POSIX regular expression character classes

Class name	Matches
`[:alnum:]`	Alphanumeric characters.
`[:alpha:]`	Alphabetic characters.
`[:blank:]`	Space and TAB characters.
`[:cntrl:]`	Control characters.
`[:digit:]`	Numeric characters.
`[:graph:]`	Characters that are both printable and visible. (A newline is printable but not visible, whereas a $ is both.)
`[:lower:]`	Lowercase alphabetic characters.
`[:print:]`	Printable characters (not control characters).
`[:punct:]`	Punctuation characters (not letters, digits, control characters, or space characters).
`[:space:]`	Space characters (such as space, TAB, newline, and so on).
`[:upper:]`	Uppercase alphabetic characters.
`[:xdigit:]`	Characters from the set `abcdefABCDEF0123456789`.

13.4.4 Conclusion

You may never have to deal with different character sets and encodings. On the other hand, the world is rapidly becoming a "global village," and software authors and vendors can't afford to be parochial. It pays, therefore, to be aware of internationalization issues and character set issues and the way in which they affect your system's behavior. Already, at least one vendor of GNU/Linux distributions sets the default locale to be `en_US.UTF-8` for systems in the United States.

13.5 Suggested Reading

1. *C, A Reference Manual*, 5th edition, by Samuel P. Harbison III and Guy L. Steele, Jr., Prentice-Hall, Upper Saddle River, New Jersey, USA, 2002. ISBN: 0-13-089592-X.

   We have mentioned this book before. It provides a concise and comprehensible description of the evolution and use of the multibyte and wide-character facilities in the C standard library. This is particularly valuable on modern systems supporting C99 because the library was significantly enhanced for the 1999 C standard.

2. *GNU gettext tools*, by Ulrich Drepper, Jim Meyering, François Pinard, and Bruno Haible. This is the manual for GNU `gettext`. On a GNU/Linux system, you can see the local copy with `'info gettext'`. Or download and print the latest version (from `ftp://ftp.gnu.org/gnu/gettext/`).

13.6 Summary

- Program internationalization and localization fall under the general heading of *native language support*. *i18n*, *l10n*, and *NLS* are popular acronyms. The central concept is the *locale*, which customizes the character set, date, time, and monetary and numeric information for the current language and country.

- Locale awareness must be enabled with `setlocale()`. Different locale categories provide access to the different kinds of locale information. Locale-unaware programs act as if they were in the `"C"` locale, which produces results typical of Unix systems before NLS: 7-bit ASCII, English names for months and days, and so on. The `"POSIX"` locale is equivalent to the `"C"` one.

- Locale-aware string comparisons are done with `strcoll()` or with the combination of `strxfrm()` and `strcmp()`. Library facilities provide access to locale information (`localeconv()` and `nl_langinfo()`) as well as locale-specific information formatting (`strfmon()`, `strftime()`, and `printf()`).

- The flip side of retrieving locale-related information is producing messages in the local language. The System V `catgets()` design, while standardized by POSIX, is difficult to use and not recommended.[13] Instead, GNU `gettext` implements and extends the original Solaris design.

- With `gettext()`, the original English message string acts as a key into a binary translation file from which to retrieve the string's translation. Each application specifies a unique text domain so that `gettext()` can find the correct translation file (known as a "message catalog"). The text domain is set with `textdomain()`. For testing, or as otherwise needed, the location for message catalogs can be changed with `bindtextdomain()`.

- Along with `gettext()`, variants provide access to translations in different text domains or different locale categories. Additionally, the `ngettext()` function and its variants enable correct plural translations without overburdening the developer. The positional specifier within `printf()` format specifiers enables translation of format strings where arguments need to be printed in a different order from the one in which they're provided.

- In practice, GNU programs use the `gettext.h` header file and `_()` and `N_()` macros for marking translatable strings in their source files. This practice keeps program source code readable and maintainable while still providing the benefits of i18n and l10n.

- GNU `gettext` provides numerous tools for the creation and management of translation databases (portable object files) and their binary equivalents (message object files).

- Finally, it pays to be aware of character set and encoding issues. Software vendors can no longer afford to assume that their users are willing to work in only one language.

Exercises

1. Does your system support locales? If so, what is the default locale?

2. Look at the *locale*(1) manpage if you have it. How many locales are there if you count them with '`locale -a | wc -l`'?

---

[13] GNU/Linux supports it, but only for compatibility.

3. Experiment with `ch13-strings.c`, `ch13-lconv.c`, `ch13-strfmon.c`, `ch13-quoteflag.c`, and `ch13-times.c` in different locales. What is the most "unusual" locale you can find, and why?

4. Take one of your programs. Internationalize it to use GNU `gettext`. Try to find someone who speaks another language to translate the messages for you. Compile the translation, and test it by using `bindtextdomain()`. What was your translator's reaction upon seeing the translations in use?

Chapter 14

Extended Interfaces

In this chapter

This chapter describes several extended APIs. The APIs here are similar in nature to those described earlier in the book or provide additional facilities. Some of them could not be discussed easily until after the prerequisite topics were covered.

The presentation order here parallels the order of the chapters in the first half of the book. The topics are not otherwise related to each other. We cover the following topics: dynamically allocating aligned memory; file locking; a number of calls that work with subsecond time values; and a more advanced suite of functions for storing and retrieving arbitrary data values. Unless stated otherwise, all the APIs in this chapter are included in the POSIX standard.

14.1 Allocating Aligned Memory: `posix_memalign()` and `memalign()`

For most tasks, the standard allocation routines, `malloc()`, `realloc()`, and so on, are fine. Occasionally, though, you may need memory that is *aligned* a certain way. In other words, the address of the first allocated byte is a multiple of some number. (For example, on some systems, memory copies are significantly faster into and out of word-aligned buffers.) Two functions offer this service:

```
#include <stdlib.h>

int posix_memalign(void **memptr, size_t alignment, size_t size);     POSIX ADV
void *memalign(size_t boundary, size_t size);                         Common
```

`posix_memalign()` is a newer function; it's part of yet another optional extension, the "Advisory Information" (ADV) extension. The function works differently from most other allocation Linux APIs. It does not return -1 when there's a problem. Rather, the return value is 0 on success *or an* `errno` *value on failure*. The arguments are as follows:

`void **memptr`

A pointer to a `void *` variable. The pointed-to variable will have the address of the allocated storage placed into it. The allocated storage can be released with `free()`.

`size_t alignment`

The required alignment. It must be a multiple of `sizeof(void *)` and a power of 2.

```
size_t size
```
   The number of bytes to allocate.

   `memalign()` is a nonstandard but widely available function that works similarly. The return value is `NULL` on failure or the requested storage on success, with `boundary` (a power of 2) indicating the alignment and `size` indicating the requested amount of memory.

   Traditionally, storage allocated with `memalign()` could *not* be released with `free()`, since `memalign()` would allocate storage with `malloc()` and return a pointer to a suitably-aligned byte somewhere within that storage. The GLIBC version does not have this problem. Of the two, you should use `posix_memalign()` if you have it.

14.2 Locking Files

   Modern Unix systems, including GNU/Linux, allow you to lock part or all of a file for reading and writing. Like many parts of the Unix API that developed after V7, there are multiple, conflicting ways to do file locking. This section covers the possibilities.

14.2.1 File Locking Concepts

   Just as the lock in your front door prevents unwanted entry into your home, a *lock* on a file prevents access to data within the file. File locking was added to Unix after the development of V7 (from which all modern Unix systems are descended) and thus, for a while, multiple, conflicting file-locking mechanisms were available and in use on different Unix systems. Both BSD Unix and System V had their own incompatible locking calls. Eventually, POSIX formalized the System V way of doing file locks. Fortunately, the names of the calls were different between System V and BSD, so GNU/Linux, in an effort to please everyone, supports both kinds of locks.

   Table 14.1 summarizes the different kinds of locks.

   There are multiple aspects to locking, as follows:

Record locking
   A record lock is a lock on a portion of the file. Since Unix files are just byte streams, it would be more correct to use the term *range lock* since the lock is on a range of bytes. Nevertheless, the term "record lock" is in common use.

TABLE 14.1
File locking functions

Source	Function	Record	Whole file	R/W	Advisory	Mandatory
BSD	`flock()`		✓	✓	✓	
POSIX	`fcntl()`	✓	✓	✓	✓	✓
POSIX	`lockf()`	✓	✓	✓	✓	✓

Whole file locking

   A whole file lock, as the name implies, locks the entire file, even if its size changes
   while the lock is held. The BSD interface provides only whole-file locking. To
   lock the whole file using the POSIX interface, specify a length of zero. This is
   treated specially to mean "the entire file."

Read locking

   A read lock prevents writing on the area being read. There may be multiple read
   locks on a file, and even on the same region of a file, without them interfering
   with each other, since data are only being accessed and not changed.

Write locking

   A write lock provides exclusive access to the area being written. If that area is
   blocked with a read lock, the attempt to acquire a write lock either blocks or fails,
   depending on the type of lock request. Once a write lock has been acquired, an
   attempt to acquire a read lock fails.

Advisory locking

   An advisory lock closely matches your front-door lock. It's been said that "locks
   keep honest people honest," meaning that if someone *really* wishes to break into
   your house, he will probably find a way to do so, despite the lock in your front
   door. So too with an advisory lock; it only works when everyone attempting to
   access the locked file first attempts to acquire the lock. However, it's possible for
   a program to completely ignore any advisory locks and do what it pleases with the
   file (as long as the file permissions allow it, of course).

Mandatory locking

   A mandatory lock is a stronger form of lock: When a mandatory lock is in place,
   no other process can access the locked file. Any process that attempts to ignore

the lock either blocks until the lock becomes available or will have its operation fail. (Under GNU/Linux, at least, this includes `root`!)

Advisory locking is adequate for cooperating programs that share a private file, when no other application is expected to use the file. Mandatory locking is advisable in situations in which avoiding conflicting file use is critical, such as in commercial database systems.

POSIX standardizes only advisory locking. Mandatory locking is available on GNU/Linux, as well as on a number of commercial Unix systems, but the details vary. We cover the GNU/Linux details later in this section.

14.2.2 POSIX Locking: `fcntl()` and `lockf()`

The `fcntl()` (file control) system call is used for file locking. (Other uses for `fnctl()` were described in Section 9.4.3, "Managing File Attributes: `fcntl()`," page 328.) It is declared as follows:

```
#include <unistd.h>                               POSIX
#include <fcntl.h>

int fcntl(int fd, int cmd);                       Not relevant for file locking
int fcntl(int fd, int cmd, long arg);             Not relevant for file locking
int fcntl(int fd, int cmd, struct flock *lock);
```

The arguments are as follows:

fd   The file descriptor for the open file.

cmd   One of the symbolic constants defined in `<fcntl.h>`. These are described
        in more detail below.

lock   A pointer to a `struct flock` describing the desired lock.

14.2.2.1 Describing a Lock

Before looking at how to get a lock, let's examine how to describe a lock to the operating system. You do so with the `struct flock` structure, which describes the byte range to be locked and the kind of lock being requested. The POSIX standard states that a `struct flock` contains "at least" certain members. This allows implementations to provide additional structure members if so desired. From the *fcntl*(3) manpage, slightly edited:

```
struct flock {
    ...
    short  l_type;          Type of lock: F_RDLCK, F_WRLCK, F_UNLCK
    short  l_whence;        How to interpret l_start: SEEK_SET, SEEK_CUR, SEEK_END
    off_t  l_start;         Starting offset for lock
    off_t  l_len;           Number of bytes to lock; 0 means from start to end-of-file
    pid_t  l_pid;           PID of process blocking our lock (F_GETLK only)
    ...
};
```

The `l_start` field is the starting byte offset for the lock. `l_len` is the length of the byte range, that is, the total number of bytes to lock. `l_whence` specifies the point in the file that `l_start` is relative to; the values are the same as for the `whence` argument to `lseek()` (see Section 4.5, "Random Access: Moving Around within a File," page 102), hence the name for the field. The structure is thus self-contained: The `l_start` offset and `l_whence` value are *not* related to the current file offset for reading and writing. Some example code might look like this:

```
struct employee { /* whatever */ };     /* Describe an employee */
struct flock lock;                       /* Lock structure */
...
/* Lock sixth struct employee */
lock.l_whence = SEEK_SET;                /* Absolute position */
lock.l_start = 5 * sizeof(struct employee);     /* Start of 6th structure */
lock.l_len = sizeof(struct employee);    /* Lock one record */
```

Using `SEEK_CUR` or `SEEK_END`, you can lock ranges relative to the current position in the file, or relative to the end of the file, respectively. For these two cases, `l_start` may be negative, as long as the absolute starting position is not less than zero. Thus, to lock the last record in a file:

```
/* Lock last struct employee */
lock.l_whence = SEEK_END;                /* Relative to EOF */
lock.l_start = -1 * sizeof(struct employee);    /* Start of last structure */
lock.l_len = sizeof(struct employee);    /* Lock one record */
```

Setting `l_len` to 0 is a special case. It means lock the file from the starting position indicated by `l_start` and `l_whence` through the end of the file. This includes any positions past the end of the file, as well. (In other words, if the file grows while the lock is held, the lock is extended so that it continues to cover the entire file.) Thus, locking the entire file is a degenerate case of locking a single record:

```
lock.l_whence = SEEK_SET;                /* Absolute position */
lock.l_start = 0;                         /* Start of file */
lock.l_len = 0;                           /* Through end of file */
```

The *fnctl*(3) manpage has this note:

> POSIX 1003.1–2001 allows `l_len` to be negative. (And if it is, the interval described by the lock covers bytes `l_start + l_len` up to and including `l_start − 1`.) However, for current kernels the Linux system call returns `EINVAL` in this situation.

(We note that the manpage refers to the 2.4.x series of kernels; it may pay to check the current manpage if your system is newer.)

Now that we know how to describe *where* in the file to lock, we can describe the *type* of the lock with `l_type`. The possible values are as follows:

`F_RDLCK`   A read lock. The file must have been opened for reading to apply a read lock.

`F_WRLCK`   A write lock. The file must have been opened for writing to apply a write lock.

`F_UNLCK`   Release a previously held lock.

Thus, the complete specification of a lock involves setting a total of four fields in the `struct flock` structure: three to specify the byte range and the fourth to describe the desired lock type.

The `F_UNLCK` value for `l_type` releases locks. In general, it's easiest to release exactly the same locks that you acquired earlier, but it is possible to "split" a lock by releasing a range of bytes in the middle of a larger, previously locked range. For example:

```
struct employee { /* whatever */ };         /* Describe an employee */
struct flock lock;                          /* Lock structure */
...
/* Lock struct employees 6-8 */
lock.l_whence = SEEK_SET;                    /* Absolute position */
lock.l_start = 5 * sizeof(struct employee);  /* Start of 6th structure */
lock.l_len = sizeof(struct employee) * 3;    /* Lock three records */
... obtain lock (see next section) ...
/* Release record 7: this splits the previous lock into two: */
lock.l_whence = SEEK_SET;                    /* Absolute position */
lock.l_start = 6 * sizeof(struct employee);  /* Start of 7th structure */
lock.l_len = sizeof(struct employee) * 1;    /* Unlock one record */
... release lock (see next section) ...
```

14.2.2.2 Obtaining and Releasing Locks

Once the `struct flock` has been filled in, the next step is to request the lock. This step is done with an appropriate value for the `cmd` argument to `fcntl()`:

`F_GETLK`   Inquire if it's possible to obtain a lock.

`F_SETLK`   Obtain or release a lock.

`F_SETLKW`   Obtain a lock, waiting until it's available.

The `F_GETLK` command is the "Mother may I?" command. It inquires whether the lock described by the `struct flock` is available. If it is, the lock is *not* placed; instead, the operating system changes the `l_type` field to `F_UNLCK`. The other fields are left unchanged.

If the lock is not available, then the operating system fills in the various fields with information describing an already held lock that blocks the requested lock from being obtained. In this case, `l_pid` contains the PID of the process holding the described lock.[1] There's not a lot to be done if the lock is being held, other than to wait awhile and try again to obtain the lock, or print an error message and give up.

The `F_SETLK` command attempts to acquire the specified lock. If `fcntl()` returns 0, then the lock has been successfully acquired. If it returns -1, then another process holds a conflicting lock. In this case, `errno` is set to either `EAGAIN` (try again later) or `EACCES` (access denied). Two values are possible, to cater to historical systems.

The `F_SETLKW` command also attempts to acquire the specified lock. It differs from `F_SETLK` in that it will wait until the lock becomes available.

Once you've chosen the appropriate value for the `cmd` argument, pass it as the second argument to `fcntl()`, with a pointer to a filled-in `struct flock` as the third argument:

```
struct flock lock;
int fd;
... open file, fill in struct flock ...
if (fcntl(fd, F_SETLK, & lock) < 0) {
    /* Could not acquire lock, attempt to recover */
}
```

---

[1] The GNU/Linux *fcntl*(3) manpage points out that this may not be enough information; the process could be residing on another machine! There are other issues with locks held across a network; in general, using locks on filesystems mounted from remote computers is not a good idea.

The lockf() function[2] provides an alternative way to acquire a lock *at the current file position*:

```
#include <sys/file.h>                                    XSI

int lockf(int fd, int cmd, off_t len);
```

The file descriptor, fd, must have been opened for writing. len specifies the number of bytes to lock: from the current position (call it pos) to pos + len bytes if len is positive, or from pos - len to pos - 1 if len is negative. The commands are as follows:

F_LOCK   Sets an exclusive lock on the range. The call blocks until the lock becomes available.

F_TLOCK   Tries the lock. This is like F_LOCK, but if the lock isn't available, F_TLOCK returns an error.

F_ULOCK   Unlocks the indicated section. This can cause lock splitting, as described earlier.

F_TEST   Sees if the lock is available. If it is, returns 0 and acquires the lock. Otherwise, it returns -1 and sets errno to EACCES.

The return value is 0 on success and -1 on error, with errno set appropriately. Possible error returns include:

EAGAIN   The file is locked, for F_TLOCK or F_TEST.

EDEADLK   For F_TLOCK, this operation would cause a deadlock.[3]

ENOLCK   The operating system is unable to allocate a lock.

The combination of F_TLOCK and EDEADLK is useful: If you know that there can never be potential for deadlock, then use F_LOCK. Otherwise, it pays to be safe and use F_TLOCK. If the lock is available, you'll get it, but if it's not, you have a chance to recover instead of blocking, possibly forever, waiting for the lock.

When you're done with a lock, you should release it. With fcntl(), take the original struct lock used to acquire the lock, and change the l_type field to F_UNLCK. Then use F_SETLK as the cmd argument:

---

[2] On GNU/Linux, lockf() is implemented as a "wrapper" around fcntl().

[3] A *deadlock* is a situation in which two processes would both block, each waiting on the other to release a resource.

```
lock.l_whence = ... ;       /* As before */
lock.l_start = ... ;        /* As before */
lock.l_len = ... ;          /* As before */
lock.l_type = F_UNLCK;      /* Unlock */
if (fcntl(fd, F_SETLK, & lock) < 0) {
    /* handle error */
}
/* Lock has been released */
```

Code using `lockf()` is a bit simpler. For brevity, we've omitted the error checking:

```
off_t curpos, len;

curpos = lseek(fd, (off_t) 0, SEEK_CUR);        Retrieve current position
len = ... ;                                     Set correct number of bytes to lock

lockf(fd, F_LOCK, len);                         Acquire lock
... use locked area here ...
lseek(fd, curpos, SEEK_SET);                    Return to position of lock

lockf(fd, F_ULOCK, len);                        Unlock file
```

If you don't explicitly release a lock, the operating system will do it for you in two cases. The first is when the process exits (either by `main()` returning or by the `exit()` function, which was covered in Section 9.1.5.1, "Defining Process Exit Status," page 300). The other case is when you call `close()` on the file descriptor: more on this in the next section.

14.2.2.3 Observing Locking Caveats

There are several caveats to be aware of when doing file locking:

- As described previously, advisory locking is just that. An uncooperative process can do anything it wants behind the back (so to speak) of processes that are doing locking.

- These calls should *not* be used in conjunction with the `<stdio.h>` library. This library does its own buffering, and while you can retrieve the underlying file descriptor with `fileno()`, the actual position in the file may not be where you think it is. In general, the Standard I/O library doesn't understand file locks.

- Bear in mind that locks are *not* inherited by child processes after a fork but that they *do* remain in place after an exec.

- A `close()` of *any* file descriptor open on the file removes *all* of the process's locks on a file, even if other file descriptors remain open on it.

That `close()` works this way is unfortunate, but because this is how `fcntl()` locking was originally implemented, POSIX standardizes it. Making this behavior the standard avoids breaking existing Unix code.

14.2.3 BSD Locking: `flock()`

4.2 BSD Unix introduced its own file locking mechanism, `flock()`.[4] It is declared as follows:

```
#include <sys/file.h>                                    Common

int flock(int fd, int operation);
```

The file descriptor `fd` represents the open file. These are the operations:

LOCK_SH   Creates a shared lock. There can be multiple shared locks.

LOCK_EX   Creates an exclusive lock. There can be only one such lock.

LOCK_UN   Removes the previous lock.

LOCK_NB   When bitwise-OR'd with LOCK_SH or LOCK_EX avoids blocking if the lock isn't available.

By default, the lock requests will block (not return) if a competing lock exists. Once the competing lock is removed and the requested lock is obtained, the call returns. (This implies that, by default, there is potential for deadlock.) To attempt to obtain a lock without blocking, perform a bitwise OR of LOCK_NB with one of the other values for `operation`.

The salient points about `flock()` are as follows:

- `flock()` locking is also advisory locking; a program that does no locking can come in and blast, with no errors, a file locked with `flock()`.

- The whole file is locked. There is no mechanism for locking or unlocking just a part of the file.

---

[4] It is fortunate that `flock()` is a different name from `lockf()`, since the semantics are different. It is also terribly confusing. Keep your manual handy.

- How the file was opened has no effect on the type of lock that may be placed. (Compare this to `fcntl()`, whereby the file must have been opened for reading for a read lock, or opened for writing for a write lock.)

- Multiple file descriptors open on the same file share the lock. Any one of them can be used to remove the lock. Unlike `fcntl()`, when there is no explicit unlock, the lock is not removed until *all* open file descriptors for the file have been closed.

- Only one `flock()` lock can be held by a process on a file; calling `flock()` successively with two different lock types changes the lock to the new type.

- On GNU/Linux systems, `flock()` locks are *completely independent* of `fcntl()` locks. Many commercial Unix systems implement `flock()` as a "wrapper" on top of `fcntl()`, but the semantics are not the same.

We don't recommend using `flock()` in new programs, because the semantics are not as flexible and because the call is not standardized by POSIX. Support for it in GNU/Linux is primarily for compatibility with software written for older BSD Unix systems.

> NOTE The GNU/Linux *flock*(2) manpage warns that `flock()` locks do *not* work for remotely mounted files. `fcntl()` locks do, provided you have a recent enough version of Linux and an NFS server that supports locking.

14.2.4 Mandatory Locking

Most commercial Unix systems support mandatory file locking, in addition to advisory file locking. Mandatory locking works only with `fcntl()` locks. Mandatory locking for a file is controlled by the file's permission settings, in particular, by addition of the setgid bit to a file with the `chmod` command:

```
$ echo hello, world > myfile                                          Create file
$ ls -l myfile                                                        Show permissions
-rw-r--r--    1 arnold    devel           13 Apr  3 17:11 myfile
$ chmod g+s myfile                                                    Add setgid bit
$ ls -l myfile                                                        Show new permissions
-rw-r-Sr--    1 arnold    devel           13 Apr  3 17:11 myfile
```

The group execute bit should be left turned off. The `S` shows that the setgid bit is turned on but that execute permission isn't; an `s` would be used if both were on.

The combination of setgid on and group execute off is generally meaningless. For this reason, it was chosen by the System V developers to mean "enforce mandatory locking." And indeed, adding this bit is enough to cause a commercial Unix system, such as Solaris, to enforce file locks.

On GNU/Linux systems, the story is a little different. The setgid bit must be applied to a file for mandatory locking, but that alone is not enough. The filesystem containing the file must also be mounted with the `mand` option to the `mount` command.

We have already covered filesystems, disk partitions, mounting, and the `mount` command, mostly in Section 8.1, "Mounting and Unmounting Filesystems," page 228. We can demonstrate mandatory locking with a small program and a test filesystem on a floppy disk. First, here's the program:

```
 1   /* ch14-lockall.c --- Demonstrate mandatory locking. */
 2
 3   #include <stdio.h>           /* for fprintf(), stderr, BUFSIZ */
 4   #include <errno.h>           /* declare errno */
 5   #include <fcntl.h>           /* for flags for open() */
 6   #include <string.h>          /* declare strerror() */
 7   #include <unistd.h>          /* for ssize_t */
 8   #include <sys/types.h>
 9   #include <sys/stat.h>        /* for mode_t */
10
11   int
12   main(int argc, char **argv)
13   {
14       int fd;
15       int i, j;
16       mode_t rw_mode;
17       static char message[] = "hello, world\n";
18       struct flock lock;
19
20       if (argc != 2) {
21           fprintf(stderr, "usage: %s file\n", argv[0]);
22           exit(1);
23       }
24
25       rw_mode = S_IRUSR | S_IWUSR | S_IRGRP | S_IROTH;    /* 0644 */
26       fd = open(argv[1], O_RDWR|O_TRUNC|O_CREAT|O_EXCL, rw_mode);
27       if (fd < 0) {
28           fprintf(stderr, "%s: %s: cannot open for read/write: %s\n",
29                   argv[0], argv[1], strerror(errno));
30           (void) close(fd);
31           return 1;
32       }
33
```

```
34      if (write(fd, message, strlen(message)) != strlen(message)) {
35          fprintf(stderr, "%s: %s: cannot write: %s\n",
36                  argv[0], argv[1], strerror(errno));
37          (void) close(fd);
38          return 1;
39      }
40
41      rw_mode |= S_ISGID; /* add mandatory lock bit */
42
43      if (fchmod(fd, rw_mode) < 0) {
44          fprintf(stderr, "%s: %s: cannot change mode to %o: %s\n",
45                  argv[0], argv[1], rw_mode, strerror(errno));
46          (void) close(fd);
47          return 1;
48      }
49
50      /* lock the file */
51      memset(& lock, '\0', sizeof(lock));
52      lock.l_whence = SEEK_SET;
53      lock.l_start = 0;
54      lock.l_len = 0;          /* whole-file lock */
55      lock.l_type = F_WRLCK;     /* write lock */
56
57      if (fcntl(fd, F_SETLK, & lock) < 0) {
58          fprintf(stderr, "%s: %s: cannot lock the file: %s\n",
59                  argv[0], argv[1], strerror(errno));
60          (void) close(fd);
61          return 1;
62      }
63
64      pause();
65
66      (void) close(fd);
67
68      return 0;
69  }
```

The program sets the permissions and creates the file named on the command line (lines 25 and 26). It then writes some data into the file (line 34). Line 41 adds the setgid bit to the permissions, and line 43 changes them. (The `fchmod()` system call was discussed in Section 5.5.2, "Changing Permissions: `chmod()` and `fchmod()`," page 156.)

Lines 51–55 set up the `struct flock` to lock the whole file, and then the lock is actually requested on line 57. Once we have the lock, the program goes to sleep, using the `pause()` system call (see Section 10.7, "Signals for Interprocess Communication," page 379). When done, the program closes the file descriptor and returns. Here is an annotated transcript demonstrating the use of mandatory file locking:

```
$ fdformat /dev/fd0                                          Format floppy disk
Double-sided, 80 tracks, 18 sec/track. Total capacity 1440 kB.
Formatting ...   done
Verifying ...    done
$ /sbin/mke2fs /dev/fd0                                      Make a Linux filesystem
... lots of output, omitted ...
$ su                                                         Become root, to use mount
Password:                                                    Password does not echo
# mount -t ext2 -o mand /dev/fd0 /mnt/floppy                 Mount floppy, with locking
# suspend                                                    Suspend root shell

[1]+  Stopped                 su
$ ch14-lockall /mnt/floppy/x &                              Background program
[2] 23311                                                    holds lock
$ ls -l /mnt/floppy/x                                        Look at file
-rw-r-Sr--    1 arnold   devel          13 Apr  6 14:23 /mnt/floppy/x
$ echo something > /mnt/floppy/x                            Try to modify file
bash2: /mnt/floppy/x: Resource temporarily unavailable      Error returned
$ kill %2                                                    Kill program holding lock
$                                                            Press ENTER
[2]-  Terminated            ch14-lockall /mnt/floppy/x       Program died
$ echo something > /mnt/floppy/x                            Retry modification, works
$ fg                                                         Return to root shell
su
# umount /mnt/floppy                                         Unmount floppy
# exit                                                       Done with root shell
$
```

As long as ch14-lockall is running, it holds the lock. Since it's a mandatory lock, the shell's I/O redirection fails. Once ch14-lockall exits, the lock is released, and the I/O redirection succeeds. As mentioned earlier, under GNU/Linux, not even root can override a mandatory file lock.

As an aside, floppy disks make excellent test beds for learning how to use tools that manipulate filesystems. If you do something that destroys the data on a floppy, it's not likely to be catastrophic, whereas experimenting with live partitions on regular hard disks is much riskier.

14.3 More Precise Times

The time() system call and time_t type represent times in seconds since the Epoch format. A *resolution* of one second really isn't enough; today's machines are fast, and it's often useful to distinguish subsecond time intervals. Starting with 4.2 BSD, Berkeley Unix introduced a series of system calls that make it possible to retrieve and use subsecond times. These calls are available on all modern Unix systems, including GNU/Linux.

14.3.1 Microsecond Times: `gettimeofday()`

The first task is to retrieve the time of day:

```
#include <sys/time.h>                                              XSI

int gettimeofday(struct timeval *tv, void *tz);      POSIX definition, not GLIBC's
```

`gettimeofday()` gets the time of day.[5] The return value is 0 on success, -1 for an error. The arguments are as follows:

`struct timeval *tv`

> This argument is a pointer to a `struct timeval`, described shortly, into which the system places the current time.

`void *tz`

> This argument is no longer used; thus, it's of type `void *` and you should always pass `NULL` for it. (The manpage describes what it used to be and then proceeds to state that it's obsolete. Read it if you're interested in the details.)

The time is represented by a `struct timeval`:

```
struct timeval {
    long tv_sec;       /* seconds */
    long tv_usec;      /* microseconds */
};
```

The `tv_sec` value represents seconds since the Epoch; `tv_usec` is the number of microseconds within the second.

The GNU/Linux *gettimeofday*(2) manpage also documents the following macros:

```
#define  timerisset(tvp) ((tvp)->tv_sec || (tvp)->tv_usec)

#define  timercmp(tvp, uvp, cmp) \
        ((tvp)->tv_sec cmp (uvp)->tv_sec || \
        (tvp)->tv_sec == (uvp)->tv_sec && \
        (tvp)->tv_usec cmp (uvp)->tv_usec)

#define timerclear(tvp) ((tvp)->tv_sec = (tvp)->tv_usec = 0)
```

These macros work on `struct timeval *` values; that is, pointers to structures, and their use should be obvious both from their names and the code. The `timercmp()` macro is particularly interesting: The third argument is a comparison operator to indicate

---

[5] The *gettimeofday*(2) manpage documents a corresponding `settimeofday()` function, for use by the superuser (`root`) to set the time of day for the whole system.

the kind of comparison. For example, consider the determination of whether one struct timeval is less than another:

```
struct timeval t1, t2;
...
if (timercmp(& t1, & t2, <))
    /* t1 is less than t2 */
```

The macro expands to

```
((& t1)->tv_sec < (& t2)->tv_sec || \
 (& t1)->tv_sec == (& t2)->tv_sec && \
 (& t1)->tv_usec < (& t2)->tv_usec)
```

This says "if t1.tv_sec is less than t2.tv_sec, OR if they are equal and t1.tv_usec is less than t2.tv_usec, then ...."

14.3.2 Microsecond File Times: utimes()

Section 5.5.3, "Changing Timestamps: utime()," page 157, describes the utime() system call for setting the access and modification times of a given file. Some filesystems store these times with microsecond (or greater) resolution. Such systems provide the utimes() system call (note the trailing s in the name) to set the access and modification times with microsecond values:

```
#include <sys/time.h>                                        XSI

int utimes(char *filename, struct timeval tvp[2]);
```

The tvp argument should point to an array of two struct timeval structures; the values are used for the access and modification times, respectively. If tvp is NULL, then the system uses the current time of day.

POSIX marks this as a "legacy" function, meaning that it's standardized only to support old code and should not be used for new applications. The primary reason seems to be that there is no defined interface for *retrieving* file access and modification times that includes the microseconds value; the struct stat contains only time_t values, not struct timeval values.

However, as mentioned in Section 5.4.3, "Linux Only: Specifying Higher-Precision File Times," page 143, Linux 2.6 (and later) does provide access to nanosecond resolution timestamps with the stat() call. Some other systems (such as Solaris) do as well.[6] Thus, `utimes()` is more useful than it first appears, and despite its official "legacy" status, there's no reason not to use it in your programs.

14.3.3 Interval Timers: `setitimer()` and `getitimer()`

The `alarm()` function (see Section 10.8.1, "Alarm Clocks: `sleep()`, `alarm()`, and `SIGALRM`," page 382) arranges to send `SIGALRM` after the given number of seconds has passed. Its smallest resolution is one second. Here too, 4.2 BSD introduced a function and three different timers that accept subsecond times.

An *interval timer* is like a repeating alarm clock. You set the first time it should "go off" as well as how frequently after that the timer should repeat. Both of these values use `struct timeval` objects; that is, they (potentially) have microsecond resolution. The timer "goes off" by delivering a signal; thus, you have to install a signal handler for the timer, preferably before setting the timer itself.

Three different timers exist, as described in Table 14.2.

TABLE 14.2
Interval timers

Timer	Signal	Function
`ITIMER_REAL`	`SIGALRM`	Runs in real time.
`ITIMER_VIRTUAL`	`SIGVTALRM`	Runs when a process is executing in user mode.
`ITIMER_PROF`	`SIGPROF`	Runs when a process is in either user or system mode.

The use of the first timer, `ITIMER_REAL`, is straightforward. The timer runs down in real time, sending `SIGALRM` after the given amount of time has passed. (Because `SIGALRM` is sent, you cannot mix calls to `setitimer()` with calls to `alarm()`, and mixing them with calls to `sleep()` is also dangerous; see Section 10.8.1, "Alarm Clocks: `sleep()`, `alarm()`, and `SIGALRM`," page 382.)

The second timer, `ITIMER_VIRTUAL`, is also fairly straightforward. It runs down when the process is running, but only in user-level (application) code. If a process is

---

6 Unfortunately, there seems to be no current standard for the names of the members in the `struct stat`, making it an unportable operation.

blocked doing I/O, such as to a disk or, more importantly, to a terminal, the timer is suspended.

The third timer, `ITIMER_PROF`, is more specialized. It runs down whenever the process is running, even if the operating system is doing something on behalf of the process (such as I/O). According to the POSIX standard, it is "designed to be used by interpreters in statistically profiling the execution of interpreted programs." By setting both `ITIMER_VIRTUAL` and `ITIMER_PROF` to identical intervals and computing the difference between the times when the two timers go off, an interpreter can tell how much time it's spending in system calls on behalf of the executing interpreted program.[7] (As stated, this is quite specialized.) The two system calls are:

```
#include <sys/time.h>                                    XSI

int getitimer(int which, struct itimerval *value);
int setitimer(int which, const struct itimerval *value,
                         struct itimerval *ovalue);
```

The `which` argument is one of the symbolic constants listed earlier naming a timer. `getitimer()` fills in the `struct itimerval` pointed to by `value` with the given timer's current settings. `setitimer()` sets the given timer with the value in `value`. If `ovalue` is provided, the function fills it in with the timer's current value. Use an `ovalue` of `NULL` if you don't care about the current value. Both functions return 0 on success or −1 on error.

A `struct itimerval` consists of two `struct timeval` members:

```
struct itimerval {
   struct timeval it_interval; /* next value */
   struct timeval it_value;    /* current value */
};
```

Application programs should not expect timers to be exact to the microsecond. The *getitimer*(2) manpage provides this explanation:

> Timers will never expire before the requested time, instead expiring some short, constant time afterwards, dependent on the system timer resolution (currently 10ms). Upon expiration, a signal will be generated and the timer reset. If the timer expires while the process is active (always true for `ITIMER_VIRT`) the signal will be delivered immediately when generated.

---

[7] Doing profiling correctly is nontrivial; if you're thinking about writing an interpreter, it pays to do your research first.

Otherwise the delivery will be offset by a small time dependent on the system loading.

Of the three timers, ITIMER_REAL seems most useful. The following program, ch14-timers.c, shows how to read data from a terminal, but with a *timeout* so that the program won't hang forever waiting for input:

```
 1   /* ch14-timers.c ---- demonstrate interval timers */
 2
 3   #include <stdio.h>
 4   #include <assert.h>
 5   #include <signal.h>
 6   #include <sys/time.h>
 7
 8   /* handler --- handle SIGALRM */
 9
10   void handler(int signo)
11   {
12       static const char msg[] = "\n*** Timer expired, you lose ***\n";
13
14       assert(signo == SIGALRM);
15
16       write(2, msg, sizeof(msg) - 1);
17       exit(1);
18   }
19
20   /* main --- set up timer, read data with timeout */
21
22   int main(void)
23   {
24       struct itimerval tval;
25       char string[BUFSIZ];
26
27       timerclear(& tval.it_interval); /* zero interval means no reset of timer */
28       timerclear(& tval.it_value);
29
30       tval.it_value.tv_sec = 10;   /* 10 second timeout */
31
32       (void) signal(SIGALRM, handler);
33
34       printf("You have ten seconds to enter\nyour name,
                   rank, and serial number: ");
35
36       (void) setitimer(ITIMER_REAL, & tval, NULL);
```

```
37          if (fgets(string, sizeof string, stdin) != NULL) {
38              (void) setitimer(ITIMER_REAL, NULL, NULL);   /* turn off timer */
39              /* process rest of data, diagnostic print for illustration */
40              printf("I'm glad you are being cooperative.\n");
41          } else
42              printf("\nEOF, eh?  We won't give up so easily!\n");
43
44          exit(0);
45      }
```

Lines 10–18 are the signal handler for SIGALRM; the assert() call makes sure that the signal handler was set up properly. The body of the handler prints a message and exits, but it could do anything appropriate for a larger-scale program.

In the main() program, lines 27–28 clear out the two struct timeval members of the struct itimerval structure, tval. Then line 30 sets the timeout to 10 seconds. Having tval.it_interval set to 0 means there is no repeated alarm; it only goes off once. Line 32 sets the signal handler, and line 34 prints the prompt.

Line 36 sets the timer, and lines 37–42 print appropriate messages based on the user's action. A real program would do its work at this point. What's important to note is line 38, which cancels the timer because valid data was entered.

> NOTE   There is a deliberate race condition between lines 37 and 38. The whole point is that if the user doesn't enter a line within the timer's expiration period, the signal will be delivered and the signal handler will print the "you lose" message.

Here are three successive runs of the program:

```
$ ch14-timers                              First run, enter nothing
You have ten seconds to enter
your name, rank, and serial number:
*** Timer expired, you lose ***

$ ch14-timers                              Second run, enter data
You have ten seconds to enter
your name, rank, and serial number: James Kirk, Starfleet Captain, 1234
I'm glad you are being cooperative.

$ ch14-timers                              Third run, enter EOF (^D)
You have ten seconds to enter
your name, rank, and serial number: ^D
EOF, eh?  We won't give up so easily!
```

POSIX leaves it undefined as to how the interval timers interact with the `sleep()` function, if at all. GLIBC does not use `alarm()` to implement `sleep()`, so on GNU/Linux systems, `sleep()` does not interact with the interval timer. However, for portable programs, you cannot make this assumption.

14.3.4 More Exact Pauses: `nanosleep()`

The `sleep()` function (see Section 10.8.1, "Alarm Clocks: `sleep()`, `alarm()`, and `SIGALRM`," page 382) lets a program sleep for a given number of seconds. But as we saw, it only took an integral number of seconds, making it impossible to delay for a short period, and it also can potentially interact with `SIGALRM` handlers. The `nanosleep()` function makes up for these deficiencies:

```
#include <time.h>                                          POSIX TMR

int nanosleep(const struct timespec *req, struct timespec *rem);
```

This function is part of the optional "Timers" (TMR) extension to POSIX. The two arguments are the requested sleep time and the amount of time remaining should the sleep return early (if `rem` is not `NULL`). Both of these are `struct timespec` values:

```
struct timespec {
    time_t tv_sec;          /* seconds */
    long   tv_nsec;         /* nanoseconds */
};
```

The `tv_nsec` value must be in the range 0–999,999,999. As with `sleep()`, the amount of time slept can be more than the requested amount of time, depending on when and how the kernel schedules processes for execution.

Unlike `sleep()`, `nanosleep()` has no interactions with any signals, making it generally safer and easier to use.

The return value is 0 if the process slept for the full time. Otherwise, it is -1, with `errno` indicating the error. In particular, if `errno` is `EINTR`, then `nanosleep()` was interrupted by a signal. In this case, if `rem` is not `NULL`, the `struct timespec` it points to is filled in with the remaining sleep time. This facilitates calling `nanosleep()` again to continue napping.

Although it looks a little strange, it's perfectly OK to use the same structure for both parameters:

```
struct timespec sleeptime = /* whatever */ ;
int ret;

ret = nanosleep(& sleeptime, & sleeptime);
```

The `struct timeval` and `struct timespec` are similar to each other, differing only in the units of the second component. The GLIBC `<sys/time.h>` header file defines two useful macros for converting between them:

```
#include <sys/time.h>                                              GLIBC

void TIMEVAL_TO_TIMESPEC(struct timeval *tv, struct timespec *ts);
void TIMEPSEC_TO_TIMEVAL(struct timespec *ts, struct timeval *tv);
```

Here they are:

```
# define TIMEVAL_TO_TIMESPEC(tv, ts) {                    \
        (ts)->tv_sec = (tv)->tv_sec;                      \
        (ts)->tv_nsec = (tv)->tv_usec * 1000;       \
}
# define TIMESPEC_TO_TIMEVAL(tv, ts) {                    \
        (tv)->tv_sec = (ts)->tv_sec;                      \
        (tv)->tv_usec = (ts)->tv_nsec / 1000;       \
}
#endif
```

> NOTE It is indeed confusing that some system calls use microsecond resolution and others use nanosecond resolution. This reason is historical: The microsecond calls were developed on systems whose hardware clocks did not have any higher resolution, whereas the nanosecond calls were developed more recently, for systems with much higher resolution clocks. C'est la vie. About all you can do is to keep your manual handy.

14.4 Advanced Searching with Binary Trees

In Section 6.2, "Sorting and Searching Functions," page 181, we presented functions for searching and sorting arrays. In this section, we cover a more advanced facility.

14.4.1 Introduction to Binary Trees

Arrays are about the simplest kind of structured data. They are easy to understand and use. They have a disadvantage, though, which is that their size is fixed at compile time. Thus, if you have more data than will fit in the array, you're out of luck. If you have considerably less data than the size of your array, you're wasting memory. (Although modern systems have large memories, consider the constraints of programmers writing software for embedded systems, such as microwave ovens or cell phones. On the other end of the spectrum, consider the problems of programmers dealing with very large amounts of inputs, such as weather simulations.)

The computer science field has invented numerous *dynamic data structures*, structures that grow and shrink in size on demand, that are more flexible than simple arrays, even arrays created and resized dynamically with `malloc()` and `realloc()`. Arrays also require re-sorting should new elements be added or removed.

One such structure is the *binary search tree*, which we'll just call a "binary tree" for short. A binary tree maintains items in sorted order, inserting them in the proper place in the tree as they come in. Lookup in a binary tree is also fast, similar in time to binary search on an array. Unlike arrays, binary trees do not have to be re-sorted from scratch every time you add an item.

Binary trees have one disadvantage. In the case in which the input data is *already sorted*, the lookup time of binary trees reduces to that of linear searching. The technicalities of this have to do with how binary trees are managed internally, described shortly.

Some more formal data-structure terminology is now unavoidable. Figure 14.1 shows a binary tree. In computer science, trees are drawn starting at the top and growing downwards. The further down the tree you go, the higher *depth* you have. Each object within the tree is termed a *node*. At the top of the tree is the *root node*, with depth `0`. At the bottom are the *leaf nodes*, with varying depth. In between the root and the leaves are zero or more *internal nodes*. Leaf nodes are distinguished by the fact that they have no *subtrees* hanging off them, whereas internal nodes have at least one subtree. Nodes with subtrees are sometimes referred to as *parent* nodes, with the subnodes being called *children*.

Plain binary trees are distinguished by the fact that nodes have no more than two children. (Trees with more than two nodes are useful but aren't relevant here.) The children are referred to as the left and right children, respectively.

Binary search trees are further distinguished by the fact that the values stored in a left subchild are always less than the value stored in the node itself, and the values stored in the right subchild are always greater than the value in the node itself. This implies that there are no duplicate values within the tree. This fact also explains why trees don't

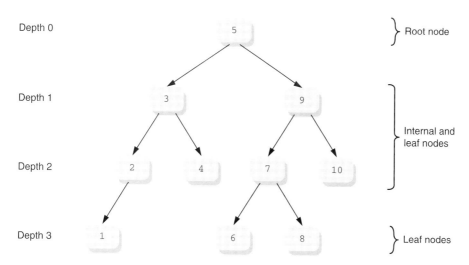

FIGURE 14.1
A binary tree

handle presorted data well: Depending on the sort order, each new data item ends up stored either to the left or to the right of the one before it, forming a simple linear list.

The operations on a binary tree are as follows:

Insertion

Adding a new item to the tree.

Lookup

Finding an item in the tree.

Removal

Removing an item from the tree.

Traversal

Doing something with every item that has been stored in the tree. Tree traversals are also referred to as *tree walks*. There are multiple ways to "visit" the items stored in a tree. The functions discussed here only implement one such way. We have more to say about this, later.

14.4.2 Tree Management Functions

The operations just described correspond to the following functions:

```
#include <search.h>                                                  XSI

void *tsearch(const void *key, void **rootp,
              int (*compare)(const void *, const void *));
void *tfind(const void *key, const void **rootp,
              int (*compare)(const void *, const void *));
void *tdelete(const void *key, void **rootp,
              int (*compare)(const void *, const void *));

typedef enum { preorder, postorder, endorder, leaf } VISIT;
void twalk(const void *root,
       void (*action)(const void *nodep, const VISIT which, const int depth));

void tdestroy(void *root, void (*free_node)(void *nodep));        GLIBC
```

These functions were first defined for System V and are now formally standardized by POSIX. They follow the pattern of the others we saw in Section 6.2, "Sorting and Searching Functions," page 181: using `void *` pointers for pointing at arbitrary data types, and user-provided comparison functions to determine ordering. As for `qsort()` and `bsearch()`, the comparison function must return a negative/zero/positive value when the `key` is compared with a value in a tree node.

14.4.3 Tree Insertion: `tsearch()`

These routines allocate storage for the tree nodes. To use them with multiple trees, you have to give them a pointer to a `void *` variable which they fill in with the address of the root node. When creating a new tree, initialize this pointer to NULL:

```
void *root = NULL;                              Root of new tree
void *val;                                      Pointer to returned data

extern int my_compare(const void *, const void *);   Comparison function
extern char key[], key2[];                      Values to insert in tree

val = tsearch(key, & root, my_compare);         Insert first item in tree
... fill key2 with a different value. DON'T modify root ...
val = tsearch(key2, & root, my_compare);        Insert subsequent item in tree
```

As shown, the `root` variable should be set to NULL only the first time and then left alone after that. On each subsequent call, `tsearch()` uses it to manage the tree.

When the `key` being sought is found, both `tsearch()` and `tfind()` return pointers to the node containing it. They differ when the `key` is not found: `tfind()` returns

NULL, and `tsearch()` inserts the new value into the tree and returns a pointer to it. The pointers returned by `tsearch()` and `tfind()` are to the internal tree nodes. They can be used as the value of `root` in subsequent calls in order to work on subtrees. As we will see shortly, the `key` value can be a pointer to an arbitrary structure; it's not restricted to a character string as the previous example might imply.

These routines store only *pointers* to the data used for keys. Thus, it is up to you to manage the storage holding the data values, usually with `malloc()`.

> NOTE   Since the tree functions keep pointers, be extra careful *not* to use `realloc()` for values that have been used as keys! `realloc()` could move the data around, returning a new pointer, but the tree routines would still be maintaining *dangling pointers* into the old data.

14.4.4 Tree Lookup and Use of A Returned Pointer: `tfind()` and `tsearch()`

The `tfind()` and `tsearch()` functions search a binary tree for a given key. They take the same list of arguments: a `key` to search for; a pointer to the root of the tree, `rootp`; and `compare`, a pointer to a comparison function. Both functions return a pointer to the node that matches `key`.

Just how do you use the pointer returned by `tfind()` or `tsearch()`? What exactly does it point to, anyway? The answer is that it points to a node in the tree. This is an *internal* type; you can't see how it's defined. However, POSIX guarantees that this pointer can be cast to *a pointer to a pointer* to whatever you're using for a key. Here is some fragmentary code to demonstrate, and then we show how this works:

```
struct employee {                              From Chapter 6
        char lastname[30];
        char firstname[30];
        long emp_id;
        time_t start_date;
};

/* emp_name_id_compare --- compare by name, then by ID */

int emp_name_id_compare(const void *e1p, const void *e2p)
{
... also from Chapter 6, reproduced in full later on ...
}

struct employee key = { ... };
```

```
void *vp, *root;
struct employee *e;
... fill tree with data ...

vp = tfind(& key, root, emp_name_id_compare);
if (vp != NULL) {   /* it's there, use it */
    e = *((struct employee **) vp);          Retrieve stored data from tree
    /* use info in *e ... */
}
```

How can a pointer to a node double as a pointer to a pointer to the data? Well, consider how a binary tree's node would be implemented. Each node maintains at least a pointer to the user's data item and pointers to potential left and right subchildren. So, it has to look approximately like this:

```
struct binary_tree {
    void *user_data;                  Pointer to user's data
    struct binary_tree *left;         Left subchild or NULL
    struct binary_tree *right;        Right subchild or NULL
    ... possibly other fields here ...
} node;
```

C and C++ guarantee that fields within a `struct` are laid out in increasing address order. Thus, it's true that '`& node.left < & node.right`'. Furthermore, the address of the `struct` is *also* the address of its first field (in other words, ignoring type issues, '`& node == & node.user_data`').

Conceptually, then, here's what '`e = *((struct employee **) vp);`' means:

1. `vp` is a `void *`, that is, a generic pointer. It is the address of the internal tree node, but it's *also* the address of the part of the node (most likely another `void *`) that points to the user's data.

2. '`(struct employee **) vp`' casts the address of the internal pointer to the correct type; it remains a pointer to a pointer, but now to a `struct employee`. Remember that casts from one pointer type to another don't change any values (bit patterns); they only change how the compiler treats the values for type considerations.

3. '`*((struct employee **) vp)`' indirects through the newly minted `struct employee **`, returning a usable `struct employee *` pointer.

4. '`e = *((struct employee **) vp)`' stores this value in `e` for direct use later.

The concept is illustrated in Figure 14.2.

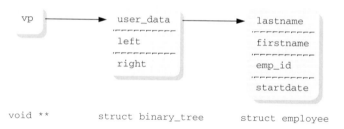

FIGURE 14.2
Tree nodes and their pointers

You might consider defining a macro to simplify the use of the returned pointer:

```
#define tree_data(ptr, type) (*(type **) (ptr))
...
struct employee *e;
void *vp;

vp = tfind(& key, root, emp_name_id_compare);
if (vp != NULL) {   /* it's there, use it */
    e = tree_data(vp, struct employee);
    /* use info in *e ... */
}
```

14.4.5 Tree Traversal: `twalk()`

The `twalk()` function is declared as follows in `<search.h>`:

```
typedef enum { preorder, postorder, endorder, leaf } VISIT;
void twalk(const void *root,
        void (*action)(const void *nodep, const VISIT which, const int depth));
```

The first parameter is the root of the tree (*not* a pointer to the root). The second is a pointer to a callback function, which is called with three arguments: a pointer to the tree node being visited, an enumerated type indicating how the given node is being visited, and an integer indicating the depth of the current node (the root is at depth 0, as explained earlier).

The use here of a callback function is the same as for `nftw()` (see Section 8.4.3.2, "The `nftw()` Callback Function," page 263). There, the callback function is called for each object in the filesystem. Here, the callback function is called for each object stored in the tree.

There are several ways to traverse, or "walk," a binary tree:

• Left child, node itself, right child.

- Node itself, left child, right child.

- Left child, right child, node itself.

The GLIBC `twalk()` function uses the second of these: the node first, then the left child, then the right child. Each time a node is encountered, the node is said to be *visited*.[8] In the course of visiting a node's child, the function must visit the node itself. Thus the values of type `VISIT` indicate at what stage this node is being encountered:

preorder   Before visiting any children.

postorder   After visiting the first child but before visiting the second child.

endorder   After visiting both children.

leaf   This node is a leaf node, without children.

> NOTE The terminology used here does not exactly match that used in formal data-structures texts. There, the terms used are *inorder*, *preorder*, and *postorder*, referring respectively to the three ways listed earlier for traversing a tree. Thus, `twalk()` uses a preorder traversal, but uses the preorder, etc., symbolic constants to indicate at what stage a node is being visited. This can be confusing.

The following program, `ch14-tsearch.c`, demonstrates building and traversing a tree. It reuses the `struct employee` structure and `emp_name_id_compare()` function from Section 6.2, "Sorting and Searching Functions," page 181.

```
 1  /* ch14-tsearch.c --- demonstrate tree management */
 2
 3  #include <stdio.h>
 4  #include <search.h>
 5  #include <time.h>
 6
 7  struct employee {
 8          char lastname[30];
 9          char firstname[30];
10          long emp_id;
11          time_t start_date;
12  };
13
```

---

8 Images come to mind of little binary data structures sitting down with each other over tea and cookies. Or at least that happens if you've been spending too much time in front of your computer…

```
14  /* emp_name_id_compare --- compare by name, then by ID */
15
16  int emp_name_id_compare(const void *e1p, const void *e2p)
17  {
18      const struct employee *e1, *e2;
19      int last, first;
20
21      e1 = (const struct employee *) e1p;
22      e2 = (const struct employee *) e2p;
23
24      if ((last = strcmp(e1->lastname, e2->lastname)) != 0)
25          return last;
26
27      /* same last name, check first name */
28      if ((first = strcmp(e1->firstname, e2->firstname)) != 0)
29          return first;
30
31      /* same first name, check ID numbers */
32      if (e1->emp_id < e2->emp_id)
33          return -1;
34      else if (e1->emp_id == e2->emp_id)
35          return 0;
36      else
37          return 1;
38  }
39
40  /* print_emp --- print an employee structure during a tree walk */
41
42  void print_emp(const void *nodep, const VISIT which, const int depth)
43  {
44      struct employee *e = *((struct employee **) nodep);
45
46      switch (which) {
47      case leaf:
48      case postorder:
49          printf("Depth: %d. Employee:\n", depth);
50          printf("\t%s, %s\t%d\t%s\n", e->lastname, e->firstname,
51              e->emp_id, ctime(& e->start_date));
52          break;
53      default:
54          break;
55      }
56  }
```

Lines 7–12 define the struct employee, and lines 14–38 define emp_name_id_compare().

Lines 40–56 define print_emp(), the callback function that prints a struct employee, along with the depth in the tree of the current node. Note the magic cast on line 44 to retrieve the pointer to the stored data.

```
58  /* main --- demonstrate maintaining data in binary tree */
59
60  int main(void)
61  {
62  #define NPRES 10
63      struct employee presidents[NPRES];
64      int i, npres;
65      char buf[BUFSIZ];
66      void *root = NULL;
67
68      /* Very simple code to read data: */
69      for (npres = 0; npres < NPRES && fgets(buf, BUFSIZ, stdin) != NULL;
70                      npres++) {
71          sscanf(buf, "%s %s %ld %ld\n",
72              presidents[npres].lastname,
73              presidents[npres].firstname,
74              & presidents[npres].emp_id,
75              & presidents[npres].start_date);
76      }
77
78      for (i = 0; i < npres; i++)
79          (void) tsearch(& presidents[i], & root, emp_name_id_compare);
80
81      twalk(root, print_emp);
82      return 0;
83  }
```

The goal of printing the tree is to print the contained elements in sorted order. Remember that `twalk()` visits intermediate nodes three times and that the left child is less than the node itself, while the right child is greater than the node. Thus, the `switch` statement prints the node's information only if `which` is `leaf`, for a leaf node, or `postorder`, indicating that the left child has been visited, but not yet the right child.

The data used is the list of presidents, also from Section 6.2, "Sorting and Searching Functions," page 181. To refresh your memory, the fields are last name, first name, employee number, and start time as a seconds-since-the-Epoch timestamp:

```
$ cat presdata.txt
Bush George 43 980013600
Clinton William 42 727552800
Bush George 41 601322400
Reagan Ronald 40 348861600
Carter James 39 222631200
```

The data are sorted based on last name, then first name, and then seniority. When run,[9] the program produces this output:

---

[9] This output is for the U.S. Eastern Time zone.

```
$ ch14-tsearch < presdata.txt
Depth: 1. Employee:
      Bush, George        41        Fri Jan 20 13:00:00 1989

Depth: 0. Employee:
      Bush, George        43        Sat Jan 20 13:00:00 2001

Depth: 2. Employee:
      Carter, James       39        Thu Jan 20 13:00:00 1977

Depth: 1. Employee:
      Clinton, William          42        Wed Jan 20 13:00:00 1993

Depth: 2. Employee:
      Reagan, Ronald  40        Tue Jan 20 13:00:00 1981
```

14.4.6 Tree Node Removal and Tree Deletion: `tdelete()` and `tdestroy()`

Finally, you can remove items from a tree and, on GLIBC systems, delete the entire tree itself:

```
void *tdelete(const void *key, void **rootp,
              int (*compare)(const void *, const void *));

/* GLIBC extension, not in POSIX: */
void tdestroy (void *root, void (*free_node)(void *nodep));
```

The arguments to `tdelete()` are the same as for `tsearch()`: the key, the address of the tree's root, and the comparison function. If the given item is found in the tree, it is removed and `tdelete()` returns a pointer to the *parent* of the given node. Otherwise, it returns NULL. This behavior has to be managed carefully in your code if you need the original item being deleted, for example, to free its storage:

```
struct employee *e, key;                          Variable declarations
void *vp, *root;
... fill in key for item to remove from tree ...
vp = tfind(& key, root, emp_name_id_compare);     Find item to remove
if (vp != NULL) {
    e = *((struct employee **) vp);               Convert pointer
    free(e);                                      Free storage
}
(void) tdelete(& key, & root, emp_name_id_compare);  Now remove it from tree
```

Although not specified in the manpages or in the POSIX standard, under GNU/Linux, if you delete the item stored in the root node, the returned value is that of the new root node. For portable code, you should not necessarily rely on this behavior.

The `tdestroy()` function is a GLIBC extension. It allows you to destroy a whole tree. The first argument is the root of the tree. The second is a pointer to a function that releases the *data* pointed to by each node in the tree. If nothing needs to be done with these data (for example, they're held in a regular array, as in our earlier example program), then this function should do nothing. Do *not* pass in a NULL pointer! Doing so results in a crash.

14.5 Summary

- Occasionally, it's necessary to allocate memory aligned at a certain boundary. `posix_memalign()` does this. Its return value is different from that of most of the functions covered in this book: Caveat emptor. `memalign()` also allocates aligned memory, but not all systems support releasing that memory with `free()`.

- File locking with `fcntl()` provides record locks, down to the level of the ability to lock single bytes within a file. Read locks prevent writing of the locked area, and a write lock prevents other processes from reading and writing the locked area. Locking is advisory by default, and POSIX standardizes only advisory locking. Most modern Unix systems support mandatory locking, using the setgid permission bit on the file and possibly additional filesystem mount options.

- On GNU/Linux, the `lockf()` function acts as a wrapper around POSIX locking with `fcntl()`; the BSD `flock()` function's locks are (on GNU/Linux) completely independent of `fcntl()` locks. BSD `flock()` locks are whole-file locks only and do not work on remote filesystems. For these reasons, `flock()` locks are not recommended.

- `gettimeofday()` retrieves the time of day as a (seconds, microseconds) pair in a `struct timeval`. These values are used by `utimes()` to update a file's accessed and modification times. The `getitimer()` and `setitimer()` system calls use pairs of `struct timevals` in a `struct itimerval` to create interval timers—alarm clocks that "go off" at a set time and continue to go off at a set interval thereafter. Three different timers provide control over the states in which the timer continues to run down.

- The `nanosleep()` function uses a `struct timespec`, which specifies time in seconds and nanoseconds, to pause a process for a given amount of time. It has the happy trait of not interacting at all with the signal mechanism.

- The tree API is an additional set of data storage and search functions that maintains data in binary trees, the effect of which is to keep data sorted. The tree API is very flexible, allowing use of multiple trees and arbitrary data.

Exercises

1. Write the `lockf()` function, using `fcntl()` to do the locking.

2. The directory `/usr/src/linux/Documentation` contains a number of files that describe different aspects of the operating system's behavior. Read the files `locks.txt` and `mandatory.txt` for more information about Linux's handling of file locks.

3. Run the `ch14-lockall` program on your system, without mandatory locking, and see if you can change the operand file.

4. If you have a non-Linux system that supports mandatory locking, try the `ch14-lockall` program on it.

5. Write a function named `strftimes()`, with the following API:

   ```
   size_t strftimes(char *buf, size_t size, const char *format,
                    const struct timeval *tp);
   ```

   It should behave like the standard `strftime()` function, except that it allows `%q` to mean "the current number of microseconds."

6. Using the `strftimes()` function you just wrote, write an enhanced version of `date` that accepts a format string beginning with a leading + and formats the current date and time. (See *date*(1).)

7. The handling of the timeout in `ch14-timers.c` is rather primitive. Rewrite the program to use `setjmp()` after printing the prompt and `longjmp()` from within the signal handler. Does this improve the structure or clarity of the program?

8. We noted that `ch14-timers.c` contains a deliberate race condition. Suppose the user enters a response within the right time period, but `ch14-timers` is suspended before the alarm can be canceled. What call can you make to cut down the size of the problem window?

9. Draw the tree as shown by the output of `ch14-tsearch` in Section 14.4.5, "Tree Traversal: `twalk()`," page 557.

10. Examine the file `/usr/share/dict/words` on a GNU/Linux system. (This is the spelling dictionary for `spell`; it might be in a different place on different systems.) The words exist in the file, one per line, in sorted order.

    First, use this `awk` program to create a new list, in random order:

    ```
    $ awk '{ list[$0]++ }
    > END { for (i in list) print i }' /usr/share/dict/words > /tmp/wlist
    ```

    Next, write two programs. Each should read the new list and store each word read into a tree and an array, respectively. The second program should use `qsort()` to sort the array and `bsearch()` to search it.

    Retrieve the word 'gravy' from the tree or array. Time the two programs to see which one runs faster. You may need to put the word retrieval inside a loop that runs multiple times (say 1,000), to get running times that are long enough to show a difference.

    Use the output of `ps` to see how much memory each program uses.

11. Rerun the two programs, using the original sorted dictionary file, and see how, if at all, the timing results change.

Part

III

Debugging and Final Project

15

Debugging

In this chapter

There are many practices, starting with program logic and data design, through code breakdown and organization, and finally implementation, that can help minimize errors and problems. We encourage you to study these; find good books on software design and software engineering, and put their advice into practice! Any program over a few hundred lines in size should be carefully thought out and designed, instead of just hacked on until it appears to work.

However, since programmers are human, programming errors are unavoidable. *Debugging* is the process of tracking down and removing errors in programs. Even well-designed, well-implemented programs occasionally don't work; when something's going wrong and you can't figure out why, it's a good idea to point a debugger at the code, and watch it fail.

This chapter covers a range of topics, starting off with basic debugging advice and techniques (compiling for debugging and elementary use of GDB, the GNU debugger), moving on to a range of techniques for use during program development and debugging that make debugging easier, and then looking at a number of tools that help the debugging process. It then closes with a brief introduction to software testing, and a wonderful set of "debugging rules," extracted from a book that we highly recommend.

Most of our advice is based on our long-term experience as a volunteer for the GNU project, maintaining gawk (GNU awk). Most, if not all, the specific examples we present come from that program.

Throughout the chapter, specific recommendations are marked **Recommendation**.

15.1 First Things First

When a program misbehaves, you may be at a loss as to what to do first. Often, strange behavior is due to misusing memory—using uninitialized values, reading or writing outside the bounds of dynamic memory, and so on. Therefore, you may get faster results by trying out a memory-debugging tool *before* you crank up a debugger.

The reason is that memory tools can point you directly at the failing line of code, whereas using a debugger is more like embarking on a search-and-destroy mission, in which you first have to isolate the problem and then fix it. Once you're sure that memory problems aren't the issue, you can proceed to using a debugger.

Because the debugger is a more general tool, we cover it first. We discuss a number of memory-debugging tools later in the chapter.

15.2 Compilation for Debugging

For a source code debugger to be used, the executable being debugged (the *debuggee*, if you will) must be compiled with the compiler's -g option. This option causes the compiler to emit extra *debugging symbols* into the object code; that is, extra information giving the names and types of variables, constants, functions, and so on. The debugger then uses this information to match source code locations with the code being executed and to retrieve or store variable values in the running program.

On many Unix systems, the -g compiler option is mutually exclusive with the -O option, which turns on optimizations. This is because optimizations can cause rearrangement of bits and pieces of the object code, such that there is no longer a direct relationship between what's being executed and a linear reading of the source code. By disabling optimizations, you make it much easier for the debugger to relate the object code to the source code, and in turn, single-stepping through a program's execution works in the obvious way. (Single-stepping is described shortly.)

GCC, the GNU Compiler Collection, does allow -g and -O together. However, this introduces exactly the problem we wish to avoid when debugging: that following the execution in a debugger becomes considerably more difficult. The advantage of allowing the two together is that you can leave the debugging symbols in an optimized, for-production-use executable. They occupy only disk space, not memory. Then, an installed executable can still be debugged in an emergency.

In our experience, if you need to use a debugger, it's better to recompile the application from scratch, with only the -g option. This makes tracing considerably easier; there's enough detail to keep track of just going through the program as it's written, without also having to worry about how the compiler rearranged the code.

There is one caveat: *Be sure the program still misbehaves.* Reproducibility is the key to debugging; if you can't reproduce the problem, it's *much* harder to track it down and fix it. Rarely, compiling a program without -O can cause it to stop failing.[1] Typically, the problem persists when compiled without -O, meaning there is indeed a logic bug of some kind, waiting to be discovered.

15.3 GDB Basics

A *debugger* is a program that allows you to control the execution of another program and examine and change the subordinate program's state (such as variable values). There are two kinds of debuggers: *machine-level debuggers*, which work on the level of machine instructions, and *source-level debuggers*, which work in terms of the program's source code. For example, in a machine-level debugger, to change a variable's value, you specify its address in memory. In a source-level debugger, you just use the variable's name.

Historically, V7 Unix had adb, which was a machine-level debugger. System III had sdb, which was a source-level debugger, and BSD Unix provided dbx, also a source-level debugger. (Both continued to provide adb.) dbx survives on some commercial Unix systems.

GDB, the GNU Debugger, is a source-level debugger. It has many more features, is more broadly portable, and is more usable than either sdb or dbx.[2]

Like its predecessors, GDB is a command-line debugger. It prints one line of source code at a time, prints a prompt, and reads one line of input containing a command to execute.

There are graphical debuggers; these provide a larger view of the source code and usually provide the ability to manipulate the program both through a command-line window and through GUI components such as buttons and menus. The ddd debugger[3] is one such; it is built on top of GDB, so if you learn GDB, you can make some use of ddd right away. (ddd has its own manual, which you should read if you'll be using it

---

[1] Compiler optimizations are a notorious scapegoat for logic bugs. In the past, finger-pointing at the compiler was more justified. In our experience, using modern systems and compilers, it is *very* unusual to find a case in which compiler optimization introduces bugs into working code.

[2] We're speaking of the original BSD dbx. We have used GDB exclusively for well over a decade.

[3] ddd comes with many GNU/Linux systems. The source code is available from the GNU Project's FTP site for ddd (ftp://ftp.gnu.org/gnu/ddd/).

heavily.) Another graphical debugger is Insight,[4] which uses Tcl/Tk to provide a graphical interface on top of GDB. (You should use a graphical debugger if one is available to you and you like it. Since our intent is to provide an introduction to debuggers and debugging, we've chosen to go with a simple interface that can be presented in print.)

GDB understands C and C++, including support for *name demangling*, which means that you can use the regular C++ source code names for class member functions and overloaded functions. In particular, GDB understands C expression syntax, which is useful when you wish to look at the value of complicated expressions, such as '`*ptr->x.a[1]->q`'. It also understands Fortran 77, although you may have to append an underscore character to the Fortran variable and function names. GDB has partial support for Modula-2, and limited support for Pascal.

If you're running GNU/Linux or a BSD system (and you installed the development tools), then you should have a recent version of GDB already installed and ready to use. If not, you can download the GDB source code from the GNU Project's FTP site for GDB[5] and build it yourself.

GDB comes with its own manual, which is over 300 pages long. You can generate the printable version of the manual in the GDB source code directory and print it yourself. You can also buy printed and bound copies from the Free Software Foundation; your purchase helps the FSF and contributes directly to the production of more free software. (See the FSF web site[6] for ordering information.) This section describes the basics of GDB; we recommend reading the manual to learn how to take full advantage of GDB's capabilities.

15.3.1 Running GDB

The basic usage is this:

```
gdb [ options ] [ executable [ core-file-name ]]
```

Here, `executable` is the executable program to be debugged. If provided, `core-file-name` is the name of a `core` file created when a program was killed by the

---

[4] `http://sources.redhat.com/insight/`

[5] `ftp://ftp.gnu.org/gnu/gdb/`

[6] `http://www.gnu.org`

operating system and dumped core. Under GNU/Linux, such files (by default) are named core.*pid*,[7] where *pid* is the process ID number of the running program that died. The *pid* extension means you can have multiple core dumps in the same directory, which is helpful, but also good for consuming disk space!

If you forget to name the files on the command line, you can use 'file *executable*' to tell GDB the name of the executable file, and 'core-file *core-file-name*' to tell GDB the name of the core file.

With a core dump, GDB indicates where the program died. The following program, ch15-abort.c, creates a few nested function calls and then purposely dies by abort() to create a core dump:

```
/* ch15-abort.c --- produce a core dump */

#include <stdio.h>
#include <stdlib.h>

/* recurse --- build up some function calls */

void recurse(void)
{
    static int i;

    if (++i == 3)
        abort();
    else
        recurse();
}

int main(int argc, char **argv)
{
    recurse();
}
```

Here's a short GDB session with this program:

```
$ gcc -g ch15-abort.c -o ch15-abort          Compile, no -O
$ ch15-abort                                 Run the program
Aborted (core dumped)                        It dies miserably
$ gdb ch15-abort core.4124                   Start GDB on it
GNU gdb 5.3
Copyright 2002 Free Software Foundation, Inc.
GDB is free software, covered by the GNU General Public License, and you are
welcome to change it and/or distribute copies of it under certain conditions.
Type "show copying" to see the conditions.
```

---

7 See *sysctl*(8) if you wish to change this behavior.

```
There is absolutely no warranty for GDB.  Type "show warranty" for details.
This GDB was configured as "i686-pc-linux-gnu"...
Core was generated by `ch15-abort'.
Program terminated with signal 6, Aborted.
Reading symbols from /lib/i686/libc.so.6...done.
Loaded symbols for /lib/i686/libc.so.6
Reading symbols from /lib/ld-linux.so.2...done.
Loaded symbols for /lib/ld-linux.so.2
#0  0x42028cc1 in kill () from /lib/i686/libc.so.6
(gdb) where                                              Print stack trace
#0  0x42028cc1 in kill () from /lib/i686/libc.so.6
#1  0x42028ac8 in raise () from /lib/i686/libc.so.6
#2  0x4202a019 in abort () from /lib/i686/libc.so.6
#3  0x08048342 in recurse () at ch15-abort.c:13          <--- We need to examine here
#4  0x08048347 in recurse () at ch15-abort.c:15
#5  0x08048347 in recurse () at ch15-abort.c:15
#6  0x0804835f in main (argc=1, argv=0xbffff8f4) at ch15-abort.c:20
#7  0x420158d4 in __libc_start_main () from /lib/i686/libc.so.6
```

The `where` command prints a *stack trace*, that is, a list of all the functions called, most recent first. Note that there are three invocations of the `recurse()` function. The command `bt`, for "back trace," is an alias for `where`; it's easier to type.

Each function invocation in the stack is referred to as a *frame*. This term comes from the compiler field, in which each function's parameters, local variables, and return address, grouped on the stack, are referred to as a *stack frame*. The GDB `frame` command lets you examine a particular frame. In this case, we want frame 3. This is the most recent invocation of `recurse()`, which called `abort()`:

```
(gdb) frame 3                                            Move to frame 3
#3  0x08048342 in recurse () at ch15-abort.c:13
13                  abort();                             GDB prints source location in frame
(gdb) list                                               Show several lines of source code
8       void recurse(void)
9       {
10          static int i;
11
12          if (++i == 3)
13              abort();
14          else
15              recurse();
16      }
17
(gdb)                                                    Pressing ENTER repeats the last command
18      int main(int argc, char **argv)
19      {
20          recurse();
21      }
(gdb) quit                                               Leave the debugger (for now)
```

As demonstrated, pressing ENTER repeats the last command, in this case, `list`, to show source code lines. This is an easy way to step through the source code.

GDB uses the `readline` library for command-line editing, so you can use Emacs or `vi` commands (as you prefer) for recalling and editing previous lines. The Bash shell uses the same library, so if you're familiar with command-line editing at the shell prompt, GDB's works the same way. This feature saves considerable typing.

15.3.2 Setting Breakpoints, Single-Stepping, and Setting Watchpoints

Often, program failures produce a core dump. The first step is to use GDB on the `core` file to determine the routine in which the program died. If the original binary was not compiled for debugging (that is, no `-g`), all GDB can tell you is the function's name, but no other details.

The next step is to then recompile the program with debugging and without optimization, and *verify that it still fails*. Assuming it does, you'll want to run the program under the control of the debugger and set a breakpoint in the failing routine.

A *breakpoint* is a point at which execution should break, or stop. You can set breakpoints by function name, source code line number, source code file and line number together, as well as in other ways.

After setting the breakpoint, you start the program running, using the `run` command, possibly followed by any command-line arguments to be passed on to the debuggee. (GDB conveniently remembers the arguments for you; if you wish to start the program over again from the beginning, all you need do is type the `run` command by itself, and GDB will start a fresh copy with the same arguments as before.) Here's a short session using `gawk`:

```
$ gdb gawk                                            Start GDB on gawk
GNU gdb 5.3
...
(gdb) break do_print                                  Set breakpoint in do_print
Breakpoint 1 at 0x805a36a: file builtin.c, line 1504.
(gdb) run 'BEGIN { print "hello, world" }'            Start the program running
Starting program: /home/arnold/Gnu/gawk/gawk-3.1.3/gawk 'BEGIN { print
    "hello, world" }'

Breakpoint 1, do_print (tree=0x8095290) at builtin.c:1504
1504              struct redirect *rp = NULL;         Execution reaches breakpoint
(gdb) list                                            Show source code
1499
```

```
1500    void
1501    do_print(register NODE *tree)
1502    {
1503        register NODE **t;
1504        struct redirect *rp = NULL;
1505        register FILE *fp;
1506        int numnodes, i;
1507        NODE *save;
1508        NODE *tval;
```

Once the breakpoint is reached, you proceed through the program by *single-stepping* it. This means that GDB allows the program to execute one source code statement at a time. GDB prints the line it's about to execute and then prints its prompt. To run the statement, use the next command:

```
(gdb) next                                              Run current statement (1504, above)
1510        fp = redirect_to_fp(tree->rnode, & rp);     GDB prints next statement
(gdb)                                                   Hit ENTER to run it, and go to next
1511        if (fp == NULL)
(gdb)                                                   ENTER again
1519        save = tree = tree->lnode;
(gdb)                                                   And again
1520        for (numnodes = 0; tree != NULL; tree = tree->rnode)
```

The step command is an alternative command for single-stepping. There is an important difference between next and step. next executes the next statement. If that statement contains a function call, the function is called and returns before GDB regains control of the running program.

On the other hand, when you use step on a statement with a function call, GDB descends into the called function, allowing you to continue single-stepping (or *tracing*) the program. If a statement doesn't contain a function call, then step is the same as next.

> NOTE It's easy to forget which command you're using and keep pressing ENTER to run each subsequent statement. If you're using step, you can accidentally enter a library function, such as strlen() or printf(), which you really don't want to bother with. In such a case, you can use the command finish, which causes the program to run until the current function returns.

You can print memory contents by using the print command. GDB understands C expression syntax, which makes it easy and natural to examine structures pointed to by pointers:

```
(gdb) print *save                                    Print the structure pointed to by save
$1 = {sub = {nodep = {l = {lptr = 0x8095250, param_name = 0x8095250 "pR\t\b",
        ll = 134828624}, r = {rptr = 0x0, pptr = 0, preg = 0x0, hd = 0x0,
        av = 0x0, r_ent = 0}, x = {extra = 0x0, xl = 0, param_list = 0x0},
      name = 0x0, number = 1, reflags = 0}, val = {
      fltnum = 6.6614191194446594e-316, sp = 0x0, slen = 0, sref = 1,
      idx = 0}, hash = {next = 0x8095250, name = 0x0, length = 0, value = 0x0,
      ref = 1}}, type = Node_expression_list, flags = 1}
```

Finally, the `cont` (continue) command lets you continue the program's execution. It will run until the next breakpoint or until it exits normally if it doesn't hit any breakpoints. This example picks up where the previous one left off:

```
1520          for (numnodes = 0; tree != NULL; tree = tree->rnode)
(gdb) cont                                           Continue
Continuing.
hello, world

Program exited normally.                             Informative message from GDB
(gdb) quit                                           Leave the debugger
```

A *watchpoint* is like a breakpoint, but for data instead of executable code. You set a watchpoint on a variable (or field in a `struct` or `union`, or array element), and when it changes, GDB notifies you. GDB checks the value of the watchpoint as it single-steps the program, and stops when the value changes. For example, the `do_lint_old` variable in `gawk` is true when the `--lint-old` option was issued. This variable is set to true by `getopt_long()`. (We covered `getopt_long()` in Section 2.1.2, "GNU Long Options," page 27.) In `gawk`'s `main.c` file:

```
int do_lint_old = FALSE;          /* warn about stuff not in V7 awk */
...
static const struct option optab[] = {
    ...
    { "lint-old", no_argument, & do_lint_old, 1 },
    ...
};
```

Here's a sample session, showing a watchpoint in action:

```
$ gdb gawk                                           Start GDB on gawk
GNU gdb 5.3
...
(gdb) watch do_lint_old                              Set watchpoint on variable
Hardware watchpoint 1: do_lint_old
(gdb) run --lint-old 'BEGIN { print "hello, world" }'    Run the program
Starting program: /home/arnold/Gnu/gawk/gawk-3.1.4/gawk --lint-old
    'BEGIN { print "hello, world" }'
Hardware watchpoint 1: do_lint_old
Hardware watchpoint 1: do_lint_old
Hardware watchpoint 1: do_lint_old                   Watchpoint checked as program runs
```

```
Hardware watchpoint 1: do_lint_old
Hardware watchpoint 1: do_lint_old

Old value = 0                                    Watchpoint stops the program
New value = 1
0x420c4219 in _getopt_internal () from /lib/i686/libc.so.6
(gdb) where                                      Stack trace
#0  0x420c4219 in _getopt_internal () from /lib/i686/libc.so.6
#1  0x420c4e83 in getopt_long () from /lib/i686/libc.so.6
#2  0x080683a1 in main (argc=3, argv=0xbffff8a4) at main.c:293
#3  0x420158d4 in __libc_start_main () from /lib/i686/libc.so.6
(gdb) quit                                       We're done for now
The program is running.  Exit anyway? (y or n) y Yes, really
```

GDB can do much more than we've shown here. Although the GDB manual is large, it is worthwhile to read it in its entirety at least once, to familiarize yourself with its commands and capabilities. After that, it's probably sufficient to look at the NEWS file in each new GDB distribution to see what's new or changed.

It's also worth printing the GDB reference card which comes in the file gdb/doc/refcard.tex within the GDB source distribution. You can create a printable PostScript version of the reference card, after extracting the source and running configure, by using these commands:

```
$ cd gdb/doc                                     Change to doc subdirectory
$ make refcard.ps                                Format the reference card
```

The reference card is meant to be printed dual-sided, on 8.5 x 11 inch ("letter") paper, in landscape format. It provides a six-column summary of the most useful GDB commands. We recommend printing it and having it by your keyboard as you work with GDB.

15.4 Programming for Debugging

There are many techniques for making source code easier to debug, ranging from simple to involved. We look at a number of them in this section.

15.4.1 Compile-Time Debugging Code

Several techniques relate to the source code itself.

15.4.1.1 Use Debugging Macros

Perhaps the simplest compile-time technique is the use of the preprocessor to provide conditionally compiled code. For example:

```
#ifdef DEBUG
    fprintf(stderr, "myvar = %d\n", myvar);
    fflush(stderr);
#endif /* DEBUG */
```

Adding -DDEBUG to the compiler command line causes the call to fprintf() to execute when the program runs.

Recommendation: Send debug messages to stderr so that they aren't lost down a pipeline and so that they can be captured with an I/O redirection. Be sure to use fflush() so that messages are forced to the output as soon as possible.

> NOTE   The symbol DEBUG, while obvious, is also highly overused. It's a better idea to use a symbol specific to your program, such as MYAPPDEBUG. You can even use different symbols for debugging code in different parts of your program, such as file I/O, data verification, memory management, and so on.

Scattering lots of #ifdef statements throughout your code quickly becomes painful. And too many #ifdefs obscure the main program logic. There's got to be a better way, and indeed, a technique that's often used is to conditionally define special macros for printing:

```
/* TECHNIQUE 1 --- commonly used but not recommended, see text */
/* In application header file: */
#ifdef MYAPPDEBUG
#define DPRINT0(msg)                 fprintf(stderr, msg)
#define DPRINT1(msg, v1)             fprintf(stderr, msg, v1)
#define DPRINT2(msg, v1, v2)         fprintf(stderr, msg, v1, v2)
#define DPRINT3(msg, v1, v2, v3)     fprintf(stderr, msg, v1, v2, v3)
#else /* ! MYAPPDEBUG */
#define DPRINT0(msg)
#define DPRINT1(msg, v1)
#define DPRINT2(msg, v1, v2)
#define DPRINT3(msg, v1, v2, v3)
#endif /* ! MYAPPDEBUG */

/* In application source file: */
DPRINT1("myvar = %d\n", myvar);
...
DPRINT2("v1 = %d, v2 = %f\n", v1, v2);
```

There are multiple macros, one for each different number of arguments, up to whatever limit you wish to provide. When MYAPPDEBUG is defined, the calls to the DPRINT*x*() macros expand into calls to fprintf(). When MYAPPDEBUG isn't defined, then those same calls expand to nothing. (This is essentially how `assert()` works; we described `assert()` in Section 12.1, "Assertion Statements: `assert()`," page 428.)

This technique works; we have used it ourselves and seen it recommended in textbooks. However, it can be refined a bit further, reducing the number of macros down to one:

```
/* TECHNIQUE 2 --- most portable; recommended */
/* In application header file: */
#ifdef MYAPPDEBUG
#define DPRINT(stuff)    fprintf stuff
#else
#define DPRINT(stuff)
#endif

/* In application source file: */
DPRINT((stderr, "myvar = %d\n", myvar));        Note the double parentheses
```

Note how the macro is invoked, with two sets of parentheses! By making the entire argument list for `fprintf()` into a single argument, you no longer need to have an arbitrary number of debugging macros.

If you are using a compiler that conforms to the 1999 C standard, you have an additional choice, which produces the cleanest-looking debugging code:

```
/* TECHNIQUE 3 --- cleanest, but C99 only */
/* In application header file: */
#ifdef MYAPPDEBUG
#define DPRINT(mesg, ...)   fprintf(stderr, mesg, __VA_ARGS__)
#else
#define DPRINT(mesg, ...)
#endif

/* In application source file: */
DPRINT("myvar = %d\n", myvar);
...
DPRINT("v1 = %d, v2 = %f\n", v1, v2);
```

The 1999 C standard provides *variadic macros*; that is, macros that can accept a variable number of arguments. (This is similar to variadic functions, like `printf()`.) In the macro definition, the three periods, '`...`', indicate that there will be zero or more arguments. In the macro body, the special identifier `__VA_ARGS__` is replaced with the provided arguments, however many there are.

The advantage to this mechanism is that only one set of parentheses is necessary when the debugging macro is invoked, making the code read much more naturally.

It also preserves the ability to have just one macro name, instead of multiple names that vary according to the number of arguments. The disadvantage is that C99 compilers are not yet widely available, reducing the portability of this construct. (However, this situation will improve with time.)

Recommendation: Current versions of GCC do support C99 variadic macros. Thus, if you know that you will never be using anything but GCC (or some other C99 compiler) to compile your program, you can use the C99 mechanism. However, as of this writing, C99 compilers are still not commonplace. So, if your code has to be compiled by different compilers, you should use the double-parentheses-style macro.

15.4.1.2 Avoid Expression Macros If Possible

In general, C preprocessor macros are a rather sharp, two-edged sword. They provide you with great power, but they also provide a great opportunity to injure yourself.[8]

For efficiency or code clarity, it's common to see macros such as this:

```
#define RS_is_null   (RS_node->var_value == Nnull_string)
...
if (RS_is_null || today == TUESDAY) ...
```

At first glance, this looks fine. The condition 'RS_is_null' is clear and easy to understand, and abstracts the details inherent in the test. The problem comes when you try to print the value in GDB:

```
(gdb) print RS_is_null
No symbol "RS_is_null" in current context.
```

In such a case, you have to track down the definition of the macro and print the expanded value.

Recommendation: Use variables to represent important conditions in your program, with explicit code to change the variable values when the conditions change.

Here is an abbreviated example, from `io.c` in the `gawk` distribution:

---

8 Bjarne Stroustrup, the creator of C++, worked hard to make the use of the C preprocessor completely unnecessary in C++. In our opinion, he didn't quite succeed: `#include` is still needed, but regular macros aren't. For C, the preprocessor remains a valuable tool, but it should be used judiciously.

```
void set_RS()
{
    ...
    RS_is_null = FALSE;
    ...
    if (RS->stlen == 0) {
        RS_is_null = TRUE;
        matchrec = rsnullscan;
    }
    ...
}
```

Once `RS_is_null` is set and maintained, it can be tested by code *and* printed from within a debugger.

> NOTE   Beginning with GCC 3.1 and version 5 of GDB, if you compile your program with the options `-gdwarf-2` and `-g3`, you *can* use macros from within GDB. The GDB manual states that the GDB developers hope to eventually find a more compact representation for macros, and that the `-g3` option will be subsumed into `-g`.
>
> However, only the combination of GCC, GDB, and the special options allows you to use macros this way: If you're not using GCC (or if you're using an older version), you still have the problem. We stand by our recommendation to avoid such macros if you can.

The problem with macros extends to code fragments as well. If a macro defines multiple statements, you can't set a breakpoint inside the middle of the macro. This is also true of C99 and C++ `inline` functions: If the compiler substitutes the body of an `inline` function into the generated code, it is again difficult or impossible to set a breakpoint inside it. This ties in with our advice to compile with `-g` alone; in this case, compilers usually don't do function inlining.

Along similar lines, it's common to have a variable that represents a particular state. It's easy, and encouraged by many C programming books, to `#define` symbolic constants for these states. For example:

```
/* The various states to be in when scanning for the end of a record. */
#define NOSTATE    1     /* scanning not started yet (all) */
#define INLEADER   2     /* skipping leading data (RS = "") */
#define INDATA     3     /* in body of record (all) */
#define INTERM     4     /* scanning terminator (RS = "", RS = regexp) */
int state;
...
state = NOSTATE;
...
state = INLEADER;
...
if (state != INTERM) ...
```

At the source code level, this looks great. But again, there is a problem when you look at the code from within GDB:

```
(gdb) print state
$1 = 2
```

Here too, you're forced to go back and look at the header file to figure out what the 2 means. So, what's the alternative?

Recommendation: Use enums instead of macros to define symbolic constants. The source code usage is the same, and the debugger can print the enums' values too.

An example, also from io.c in gawk:

```
typedef enum scanstate {
    NOSTATE,     /* scanning not started yet (all) */
    INLEADER,    /* skipping leading data (RS = "") */
    INDATA,      /* in body of record (all) */
    INTERM,      /* scanning terminator (RS = "", RS = regexp) */
} SCANSTATE;
SCANSTATE state;
... rest of code remains unchanged! ...
```

Now, when looking at state from within GDB, we see something useful:

```
(gdb) print state
$1 = NOSTATE
```

15.4.1.3 Reorder Code If Necessary

It's not uncommon to have a condition in an if or while consist of multiple component tests, separated by && or ||. If these tests are function calls (or even if they're not), it's impossible to single-step each separate part of the condition. GDB's step and next commands work on the basis of *statements*, not *expressions*. (Splitting such things across lines doesn't help, either.)

Recommendation: Rewrite the original code, using explicit temporary variables that store return values or conditional results so that you can examine them in a debugger. The original code should be maintained in a comment so that you (or some later programmer) can tell what's going on.

Here's a concrete example: the function do_input() from gawk's file io.c:

```
1   /* do_input --- the main input processing loop */
2
3   void
4   do_input()
5   {
6       IOBUF *iop;
7       extern int exiting;
8       int rval1, rval2, rval3;
9
10      (void) setjmp(filebuf); /* for `nextfile' */
11
12      while ((iop = nextfile(FALSE)) != NULL) {
13          /*
14           * This was:
15          if (inrec(iop) == 0)
16              while (interpret(expression_value) && inrec(iop) == 0)
17                  continue;
18           * Now expand it out for ease of debugging.
19           */
20          rval1 = inrec(iop);
21          if (rval1 == 0) {
22              for (;;) {
23                  rval2 = rval3 = -1; /* for debugging */
24                  rval2 = interpret(expression_value);
25                  if (rval2 != 0)
26                      rval3 = inrec(iop);
27                  if (rval2 == 0 || rval3 != 0)
28                      break;
29              }
30          }
31          if (exiting)
32              break;
33      }
34  }
```

(The line numbers are relative to the start of the routine, not the file.) This function is the heart of gawk's main processing loop. The outer loop (lines 12 and 33) steps through the command-line data files. The comment on lines 13–19 shows the original code, which reads each record from the current file and processes it.

A 0 return value from `inrec()` indicates an OK status, while a nonzero return value from `interpret()` indicates an OK status. When we tried to step through this loop, verifying the record reading process, it became necessary to perform each step individually.

Lines 20–30 are the rewritten code, which calls each function separately, storing the return values in local variables so that they can be printed from the debugger. Note how line 23 forces these variables to have known, invalid values each time around the loop: Otherwise, they would retain their values from previous loop iterations. Line 27 is the exit test; because the code has changed to an infinite loop (compare line 22 to line 16), the test for breaking out of the loop is the opposite of the original test.

As an aside, we admit to having had to study the rewrite carefully when we made it, to make sure it did exactly the same as the original code; it did. It occurs to us now that perhaps this version of the loop might be closer to the original:

```
/* Possible replacement for lines 22 - 29 */
do {
    rval2 = rval3 = -1; /* for debugging */
    rval2 = interpret(expression_value);
    if (rval2 != 0)
        rval3 = inrec(iop);
} while (rval2 != 0 && rval3 == 0);
```

The truth is, both versions are harder to read than the original and thus potentially in error. However, since the current code works, we decided to leave well enough alone.

Finally, we note that not all expert programmers would agree with our advice here. When each component of a condition is a function call, you can set a breakpoint on each one, use `step` to step into each function, and then use `finish` to complete the function. GDB will tell you the function's return value, and from that point you can use `cont` or `step` to continue. We like our approach because the results are kept in variables, which can be checked (and rechecked) after the function calls, and even a few statements later.

15.4.1.4 Use Debugging Helper Functions

A common technique, applicable in many cases, is to have a set of *flag* values; when a flag is *set* (that is, true), a certain fact is true or a certain condition applies. This is commonly done with `#defined` symbolic constants and the C bitwise operators.

(We discussed the use of bit flags and the bit manipulation operators in the sidebar in Section 8.3.1, "POSIX Style: `statvfs()` and `fstatvfs()`," page 244.)

For example, `gawk`'s central data structure is called a NODE. It has a large number of fields, the last of which is a set of flag values. From the file `awk.h`:

```
typedef struct exp_node {
    ...                                 Lots of stuff omitted
    unsigned short flags;
#       define  MALLOC  1           /* can be free'd */
#       define  TEMP    2           /* should be free'd */
#       define  PERM    4           /* can't be free'd */
#       define  STRING  8           /* assigned as string */
#       define  STRCUR  16          /* string value is current */
#       define  NUMCUR  32          /* numeric value is current */
#       define  NUMBER  64          /* assigned as number */
#       define  MAYBE_NUM 128       /* user input: if NUMERIC then
                                     * a NUMBER */
#       define  ARRAYMAXED 256      /* array is at max size */
#       define  FUNC    512         /* this parameter is really a
                                     * function name; see awkgram.y */
#       define  FIELD   1024        /* this is a field */
#       define  INTLSTR 2048        /* use localized version */
} NODE;
```

The reason to use flag values is that they provide considerable savings in data space. If the NODE structure used a separate `char` field for each flag, that would use 12 bytes instead of the 2 used by the `unsigned short`. The current size of a NODE (on an Intel x86) is 32 bytes. Adding 10 more bytes would bump that to 42 bytes. Since `gawk` can allocate potentially hundreds of thousands (or even millions) of NODEs,[9] keeping the size down is important.

What does this have to do with debugging? Didn't we just recommend using `enums` for symbolic constants? Well, in the case of OR'd values `enums` are no help, since they're no longer individually recognizable!

Recommendation: Provide a function to convert flags to a string. If you have multiple independent flags, set up a general-purpose routine.

---

[9] Seriously! People often run megabytes of data through `gawk`. Remember, *no arbitrary limits!*

> NOTE   What's unusual about these debugging functions is that *application code*
> *never calls them.* They exist *only* so that they can be called from a debugger. Such
> functions should always be compiled in, without even a surrounding #ifdef,
> so that you can use them without having to take special steps. The (usually
> minimal) extra code size is justified by the developer's time savings.

First we'll show you how we did this initially. Here is (an abbreviated version of)
flags2str() from an earlier version of gawk (3.0.6):

```
1   /* flags2str --- make a flags value readable */
2
3   char *
4   flags2str(flagval)
5   int flagval;
6   {
7       static char buffer[BUFSIZ];
8       char *sp;
9
10      sp = buffer;
11
12      if (flagval & MALLOC) {
13          strcpy(sp, "MALLOC");
14          sp += strlen(sp);
15      }
16      if (flagval & TEMP) {
17          if (sp != buffer)
18              *sp++ = '|';
19          strcpy(sp, "TEMP");
20          sp += strlen(sp);
21      }
22      if (flagval & PERM) {
23          if (sp != buffer)
24              *sp++ = '|';
25          strcpy(sp, "PERM");
26          sp += strlen(sp);
27      }
        ... much more of the same, omitted for brevity ...
82
83      return buffer;
84  }
```

(The line numbers are relative to the start of the function.) The result is a string,
something like "MALLOC|PERM|NUMBER". Each flag is tested separately, and if present,
each one's action is the same: test if not at the beginning of the buffer so we can add

the '|' character, copy the string into place, and update the pointer. Similar functions existed for formatting and displaying the other kinds of flags in the program.

The code is both repetitive and error prone, and for gawk 3.1 we were able to simplify and generalize it. Here's how gawk now does it. Starting with this definition in awk.h:

```
/* for debugging purposes */
struct flagtab {
    int val;                      Integer flag value
    const char *name;             String name
};
```

This structure can be used to represent any set of flags with their corresponding string values. Each different group of flags has a corresponding function that returns a printable representation of the flags that are currently set. From eval.c:

```
/* flags2str --- make a flags value readable */

const char *
flags2str(int flagval)
{
    static const struct flagtab values[] = {
        { MALLOC, "MALLOC" },
        { TEMP, "TEMP" },
        { PERM, "PERM" },
        { STRING, "STRING" },
        { STRCUR, "STRCUR" },
        { NUMCUR, "NUMCUR" },
        { NUMBER, "NUMBER" },
        { MAYBE_NUM, "MAYBE_NUM" },
        { ARRAYMAXED, "ARRAYMAXED" },
        { FUNC, "FUNC" },
        { FIELD, "FIELD" },
        { INTLSTR, "INTLSTR" },
        { 0,    NULL },
    };

    return genflags2str(flagval, values);
}
```

flags2str() defines an array that maps flag values to strings. By convention, a 0 flag value indicates the end of the array. The code calls genflags2str() ("general flags to string") to do the work. genflags2str() is a general-purpose routine that converts a flag value into a string. From eval.c:

```
 1   /* genflags2str --- general routine to convert a flag value to a string */
 2
 3   const char *
 4   genflags2str(int flagval, const struct flagtab *tab)
 5   {
 6       static char buffer[BUFSIZ];
 7       char *sp;
 8       int i, space_left, space_needed;
 9
10       sp = buffer;
11       space_left = BUFSIZ;
12       for (i = 0; tab[i].name != NULL; i++) {
13           if ((flagval & tab[i].val) != 0) {
14               /*
15                * note the trick, we want 1 or 0 for whether we need
16                * the '|' character.
17                */
18               space_needed = (strlen(tab[i].name) + (sp != buffer));
19               if (space_left < space_needed)
20                   fatal(_("buffer overflow in genflags2str"));
21
22               if (sp != buffer) {
23                   *sp++ = '|';
24                   space_left--;
25               }
26               strcpy(sp, tab[i].name);
27               /* note ordering! */
28               space_left -= strlen(sp);
29               sp += strlen(sp);
30           }
31       }
32
33       return buffer;
34   }
```

(Line numbers are relative to the start of the function, not the file.) As with the previous version, the idea here is to fill in a `static` buffer with a string value such as `"MALLOC|PERM|STRING|MAYBE_NUM"` and return the address of that buffer. We discuss the reasons for using a `static` buffer shortly; first let's examine the code.

The `sp` pointer tracks the position of the next empty spot in the buffer, while `space_left` tracks how much room is left; this keeps us from overflowing the buffer.

The bulk of the function is a loop (line 12) through the array of flag values. When a flag is found (line 13), the code computes how much space is needed for the string (line 18) and tests to see if that much room is left (lines 19–20).

The test 'sp != buffer' fails on the first flag value found, returning 0. On subsequent flags, the test has a value of 1. This tells us if we need the '|' separator character between values. By adding the result (1 or 0) to the length of the string, we get the correct value for space_needed. The same test, for the same reason, is used on line 22 to control lines 23 and 24, which insert the '|' character.

Finally, lines 26–29 copy in the string value, adjust the amount of space left, and update the sp pointer. Line 33 returns the address of the buffer, which contains the printable representation of the string.

Now, what about that static buffer? Normally, good programming practice discourages the use of functions that return the address of static buffers: It's easy to have multiple calls to such a function overwrite the buffer each time, forcing the caller to copy the returned data.

Furthermore, a static buffer is by definition a buffer of fixed size. What happened to the GNU "no arbitrary limits" principle?

The answer to both of these questions is to remember that this is a *debugging* function. Normal code *never* calls genflags2str(); it's only called by a human using a debugger. No caller holds a pointer to the buffer; as a developer doing debugging, we don't care that the buffer gets overwritten each time we call the function.

In practice, the fixed size isn't an issue either; we know that BUFSIZ is big enough to represent all the flags that we use. Nevertheless, being experienced and knowing that things can change, genflags2str() has code to protect itself from overrunning the buffer. (The space_left variable and the code on lines 18–20.)

As an aside, the use of BUFSIZ is arguable. That constant should be used exclusively for I/O buffers, but it is often used for general string buffers as well. Such code would be better off defining explicit constants, such as FLAGVALSIZE, and using 'sizeof(buffer)' on line 11.

Here is an abbreviated GDB session showing flags2str() in use:

```
$ gdb gawk                                              Start GDB on gawk
GNU gdb 5.3
...
(gdb) break do_print                                    Set a breakpoint
Breakpoint 1 at 0x805a584: file builtin.c, line 1547.
(gdb) run 'BEGIN { print "hello, world" }'              Start it running
Starting program: /home/arnold/Gnu/gawk/gawk-3.1.4/gawk 'BEGIN { print
    "hello, world" }'

Breakpoint 1, do_print (tree=0x80955b8) at builtin.c:1547   Breakpoint hit
1547            struct redirect *rp = NULL;
(gdb) print *tree                                       Print NODE
$1 = {sub = {nodep = {l = {lptr = 0x8095598, param_name = 0x8095598 "xU\t\b",
        ll = 134829464}, r = {rptr = 0x0, pptr = 0, preg = 0x0, hd = 0x0,
        av = 0x0, r_ent = 0}, x = {extra = 0x0, xl = 0, param_list = 0x0},
      name = 0x0, number = 1, reflags = 0}, val = {
      fltnum = 6.6614606209589101e-316, sp = 0x0, slen = 0, sref = 1,
      idx = 0}, hash = {next = 0x8095598, name = 0x0, length = 0, value = 0x0,
      ref = 1}}, type = Node_K_print, flags = 1}
(gdb) print flags2str(tree->flags)                      Print flag value
$2 = 0x80918a0 "MALLOC"
(gdb) next                                              Keep going
1553            fp = redirect_to_fp(tree->rnode, & rp);
...
1588                 efwrite(t[i]->stptr, sizeof(char), t[i]->stlen, fp,
                        "print", rp, FALSE);
(gdb) print *t[i]                                       Print NODE again
$4 = {sub = {nodep = {l = {lptr = 0x8095598, param_name = 0x8095598 "xU\t\b",
        ll = 134829464}, r = {rptr = 0x0, pptr = 0, preg = 0x0, hd = 0x0,
        av = 0x0, r_ent = 0}, x = {extra = 0x8095ad8, xl = 134830808,
        param_list = 0x8095ad8}, name = 0xc <Address 0xc out of bounds>,
      number = 1, reflags = 4294967295}, val = {
      fltnum = 6.6614606209589101e-316, sp = 0x8095ad8 "hello, world",
      slen = 12, sref = 1, idx = -1}, hash = {next = 0x8095598, name = 0x0,
      length = 134830808, value = 0xc, ref = 1}}, type = Node_val, flags = 29}
(gdb) print flags2str(t[i]->flags)                      Print flag value
$5 = 0x80918a0 "MALLOC|PERM|STRING|STRCUR"
```

We hope you'll agree that the current general-purpose mechanism is considerably more elegant than the original one, and easier to use.

Careful design and use of arrays of `structs` can often replace or consolidate repetitive code.

15.4.1.5 Avoid Unions When Possible

> "There's no such thing as a free lunch."
> —**Lazarus Long**—

The C union is a relatively esoteric facility. It allows you to save memory by storing different items within the same physical space; how the program treats it depends on how it's accessed:

```
/* ch15-union.c --- brief demo of union usage. */

#include <stdio.h>

int main(void)
{
    union i_f {
        int i;
        float f;
    } u;

    u.f = 12.34;    /* Assign a floating point value */
    printf("%f also looks like %#x\n", u.f, u.i);
    exit(0);
}
```

Here is what happens when the program is run on an Intel x86 GNU/Linux system:

```
$ ch15-union
12.340000 also looks like 0x414570a4
```

The program prints the bit pattern that represents a floating-point number as a hexadecimal integer. The storage for the two fields occupies the same memory; the difference is in how the memory is treated: u.f acts like a floating-point number, whereas the same bits in u.i act like an integer.

Unions are particularly useful in compilers and interpreters, which often create a tree structure representing the structure of a source code file (called a *parse tree*). This models the way programming languages are formally described: if statements, while statements, assignment statements, and so on are all instances of the more generic "statement" type. Thus, a compiler might have something like this:

```
struct if_stmt { ... };              Structure for IF statement
struct while_stmt { ... };           Structure for WHILE statement
struct for_stmt { ... };             Structure for FOR statement
... structures for other statement types ...

typedef enum stmt_type {
    IF, WHILE, FOR, ...
} TYPE;                              What we actually have
```

```
/* This contains the type and unions of the individual kinds of statements. */
struct statement {
    TYPE type;
    union stmt {
        struct if_stmt if_st;
        struct while_stmt while_st;
        struct for_stmt for_st;
        ...
    } u;
};
```

Along with the `union`, it is conventional to use macros to make the components of the `union` look like they were fields in a `struct`. For example:

```
#define if_s      u.if_st
#define while_s   u.while_st
#define for_s     u.for_st
...
```
So can use `s->if_s` *instead of* `s->u.if_st`
And so on ...

At the level just presented, this seems reasonable and looks manageable. The real world, however, is a more complicated place, and practical compilers and interpreters often have several levels of *nested* `struct`s and `union`s. This includes `gawk`, in which the definition of the `NODE`, its flag values, and macros for accessing `union` components takes over 120 lines![10] Here is enough of that definition to give you a feel for what's happening:

```
typedef struct exp_node {
    union {
        struct {
            union {
                struct exp_node *lptr;
                char *param_name;
                long ll;
            } l;
            union {
                ...
            } r;
            union {
                ...
            } x;
            char *name;
            short number;
            unsigned long reflags;
            ...
        } nodep;
```

---

[10] We inherited this design. In general it works, but it does have its problems. The point of this section is to pass on the experience we've acquired working with `union`s.

```
            struct {
                AWKNUM fltnum;
                char *sp;
                size_t slen;
                long sref;
                int idx;
            } val;
            struct {
                struct exp_node *next;
                char *name;
                size_t length;
                struct exp_node *value;
                long ref;
            } hash;
#define hnext    sub.hash.next
#define hname    sub.hash.name
#define hlength sub.hash.length
#define hvalue   sub.hash.value
...
        } sub;
        NODETYPE type;
        unsigned short flags;
...
} NODE;

#define vname sub.nodep.name
#define exec_count sub.nodep.reflags

#define lnode     sub.nodep.l.lptr
#define nextp     sub.nodep.l.lptr
#define source_file sub.nodep.name
#define source_line sub.nodep.number
#define param_cnt    sub.nodep.number
#define param    sub.nodep.l.param_name

#define stptr    sub.val.sp
#define stlen    sub.val.slen
#define stref    sub.val.sref
#define stfmt    sub.val.idx

#define var_value lnode
...
```

The NODE has a union inside a struct inside a union inside a struct! (Ouch.) On top of that, multiple macro "fields" map to the same struct/union components, depending on what is actually stored in the NODE! (Ouch, again.)

The benefit of this complexity is that the C code is relatively clear. Something like 'NF_node->var_value->slen' is straightforward to read.

There is, of course, a price to pay for the flexibility that `unions` provide. When your debugger is deep down in the guts of your code, you can't use the nice macros that appear in the source. You *must* use the real expansion.[11] (And for that, you have to find the definition in the header file.)

For example, compare `NF_node->var_value->slen` to what it expands to: `NF_node->sub.nodep.l.lptr->sub.val.slen`! You must type the latter into GDB to look at your data value. Look again at this excerpt from the earlier GDB debugging session:

```
(gdb) print *tree                                       Print NODE
$1 = {sub = {nodep = {l = {lptr = 0x8095598, param_name = 0x8095598 "xU\t\b",
        ll = 134829464}, r = {rptr = 0x0, pptr = 0, preg = 0x0, hd = 0x0,
        av = 0x0, r_ent = 0}, x = {extra = 0x0, xl = 0, param_list = 0x0},
     name = 0x0, number = 1, reflags = 0}, val = {
     fltnum = 6.6614606209589101e-316, sp = 0x0, slen = 0, sref = 1,
     idx = 0}, hash = {next = 0x8095598, name = 0x0, length = 0, value = 0x0,
     ref = 1}}, type = Node_K_print, flags = 1}
```

That's a lot of goop. However, GDB does make this a little easier to handle. You can use expressions like `($1).sub.val.slen` to step through the tree and list data structures.

There are other reasons to avoid `unions`. First of all, `unions` are *unchecked*. Nothing but programmer attention ensures that when you access one part of a `union`, you are accessing the same part that was last stored. We saw this in `ch15-union.c`, which accessed both of the `union`'s "identities" simultaneously.

A second reason, related to the first, is to be careful of *overlays* in complicated nested `struct`/`union` combinations. For example, an earlier version of `gawk`[12] had this code:

```
/* n->lnode overlays the array size, don't unref it if array */
if (n->type != Node_var_array && n->type != Node_array_ref)
   unref(n->lnode);
```

---

[11] Again, GCC 3.1 or newer and GDB 5 can let you use macros directly, but only if you're using them together, with specific options. This was described earlier, in Section 15.4.1.2, "Avoid Expression Macros If Possible," page 580.

[12] This part of the code has since been revised, and the example lines are no longer there.

Originally, there was no `if`, just a call to `unref()`, which frees the `NODE` pointed to by `n->lnode`. However, it was possible to crash `gawk` at this point. You can imagine how long it took, in a debugger, to track down the fact that what was being treated as a pointer was in reality an array size!

As an aside, `unions` are considerably less useful in C++. Inheritance and object-oriented features make data structure management a different ball game, one that is considerably safer.

Recommendation: Avoid `unions` if possible. If not, design and code them carefully!

15.4.2 Runtime Debugging Code

Besides things you add to your code at compile time, you can also add extra code to enable debugging features at runtime. This is particularly useful for applications that are installed in the field, where a customer's system won't have the source code installed (and maybe not even a compiler!).

This section presents some runtime debugging techniques that we have used over the years, ranging from simple to more complex. Note that our treatment is by no means exhaustive. This is an area where it pays to have some imagination and to use it!

15.4.2.1 Add Debugging Options and Variables

The simplest technique is to have a command-line option that enables debugging. Such an option can be conditionally compiled in when you are debugging. But it's more flexible to leave the option in the *production* version of the program. (You may or may not also wish to leave the option *undocumented* as well. This has various tradeoffs: Documenting it can allow your customers or clients to learn more about the internals of your system, which you may not want. On the other hand, not documenting it seems rather sneaky. If you're writing Open Source or Free Software, it's better to document the option.)

If your program is large, you may wish your debugging option to take an argument indicating what subsystem should be debugged. Based on the argument, you can set different flag variables or possibly different bit flags in a single debugging variable. Here is an outline of this technique:

```
struct option options[] = {
    ...
    { "debug", required_argument, NULL, 'D' },
    ...
}

int main(int argc, char **argv)
{
    int c;

    while ((c = getopt_long(argc, argv, "...D:")) != -1) {
        switch (c) {
        ...
        case 'D':
            parse_debug(optarg);
            break;
        ...
        }
    }
    ...
}
```

The `parse_debug()` function reads through the argument string. For example, it could be a comma- or space-separated string of subsystems, like `"file,memory,ipc"`. For each valid subsystem name, the function would set a bit in a debugging variable:

```
extern int debugging;

void parse_debug(const char *subsystems)
{
    char *sp;

    for (sp = subsystems; *sp != '\0';) {
        if (strncmp(sp, "file", 4) == 0) {
            debugging |= DEBUG_FILE;
            sp += 4;
        } else if (strncmp(sp, "memory", 6) == 0) {
            debugging |= DEBUG_MEM;
            sp += 6;
        } else if (strncmp(sp, "ipc", 3) == 0) {
            debugging |= DEBUG_IPC;
            sp += 3;
        ...
        }
        while (*sp == ' ' || *sp == ',')
            sp++;
    }
}
```

Finally, application code can then test the flags:

```
if ((debugging & DEBUG_FILE) != 0) ...          In the I/O part of the program

if ((debugging & DEBUG_MEM) != 0) ...           In the memory manager
```

It is up to you whether to use a single variable with flag bits, separate variables, or even a `debugging` array, indexed by symbolic constants (preferably from an `enum`).

The cost of leaving the debugging code in your production executable is that the program will be larger. Depending on the placement of your debugging code, it may also be slower since the tests are always performed, but are always false until debugging is turned on. And, as mentioned, it may be possible for someone to learn about your program, which you may not want. Or worse, a malevolent user could enable so much debugging that the program slows to an unusable state! (This is called a *denial of service attack*.)

The benefit, which can be great, is that your already installed program can be reinvoked with debugging turned on, without requiring you to build, and then download, a special version to your customer site. When the software is installed in remote places that may not have people around and *all* you can do is access the system remotely through the Internet (or worse, a slow telephone dial-in!), such a feature can be a lifesaver.

Finally, you may wish to mix and match: use conditionally compiled debugging code for fine-grained, high-detail debugging, and save the always-present code for a coarser level of output.

15.4.2.2 Use Special Environment Variables

Another useful trick is to have your application pay attention to special environment variables (documented or otherwise). This can be particularly useful for testing. Here's another example from our experience with `gawk`, but first, some background.

`gawk` uses a function named `optimal_bufsize()` to obtain the optimal buffer size for I/O. For small files, the function returns the file size. Otherwise, if the filesystem defines a size to use for I/O, it returns that (the `st_blksize` member in the `struct stat`, see Section 5.4.2, "Retrieving File Information," page 141). If that member isn't available, `optimal_bufsize()` returns the `BUFSIZ` constant from `<stdio.h>`. The original function (in `posix/gawkmisc.c`) looked like this:

```
 1   /* optimal_bufsize --- determine optimal buffer size */
 2
 3   int
 4   optimal_bufsize(fd, stb)              int optimal_bufsize(int fd, struct stat *stb);
 5   int fd;
 6   struct stat *stb;
 7   {
 8       /* force all members to zero in case OS doesn't use all of them. */
 9       memset(stb, '\0', sizeof(struct stat));
10
11       /*
12        * System V.n, n < 4, doesn't have the file system block size in the
13        * stat structure. So we have to make some sort of reasonable
14        * guess. We use stdio's BUFSIZ, since that is what it was
15        * meant for in the first place.
16        */
17   #ifdef HAVE_ST_BLKSIZE
18   #define DEFBLKSIZE  (stb->st_blksize ? stb->st_blksize : BUFSIZ)
19   #else
20   #define DEFBLKSIZE  BUFSIZ
21   #endif
22
23       if (isatty(fd))
24           return BUFSIZ;
25       if (fstat(fd, stb) == -1)
26           fatal("can't stat fd %d (%s)", fd, strerror(errno));
27       if (lseek(fd, (off_t)0, 0) == -1)   /* not a regular file */
28           return DEFBLKSIZE;
29       if (stb->st_size > 0 && stb->st_size < DEFBLKSIZE) /* small file */
30           return stb->st_size;
31       return DEFBLKSIZE;
32   }
```

The constant DEFBLKSIZE is the "default block size"; that is, the value from the struct stat, or BUFSIZ. For terminals (line 23) or for files that aren't regular files (lseek() fails, line 27), the return value is also BUFSIZ. For regular files that are small, the file size is used. In all other cases, DEFBLKSIZE is returned. Knowing the "optimal" buffer size is particularly useful on filesystems in which the block size is *larger* than BUFSIZ.

We had a problem whereby one of our test cases worked perfectly on our development GNU/Linux system and every other Unix system we had access to. However, this test would fail consistently on certain other systems.

For a long time, we could not get direct access to a failing system in order to run GDB. Eventually, however, we did manage to reproduce the problem; it turned out to be related to the size of the buffer gawk was using for reading data files: On the failing systems, the buffer size was larger than for our development system.

We wanted a way to be able to reproduce the problem on our development machine: The failing system was nine time zones away, and running GDB interactively across the Atlantic Ocean is painful. We reproduced the problem by having optimal_bufsize() look at a special environment variable, AWKBUFSIZE. When the value is "exact", optimal_bufsize() always returns the size of the file, whatever that may be. If the value of AWKBUFSIZE is some integer number, the function returns that number. Otherwise, the function falls back to the previous algorithm. This allows us to run tests without having to constantly recompile gawk. For example,

```
$ AWKBUFSIZE=42 make check
```

This runs the gawk test suite, using a buffer size of 42 bytes. (The test suite passes.) Here is the modified version of optimal_bufsize():

```
1   /* optimal_bufsize --- determine optimal buffer size */
2
3   /*
4    * Enhance this for debugging purposes, as follows:
5    *
6    * Always stat the file, stat buffer is used by higher-level code.
7    *
8    * if (AWKBUFSIZE == "exact")
9    *     return the file size
10   * else if (AWKBUFSIZE == a number)
11   *     always return that number
12   * else
13   *     if the size is < default_blocksize
14   *         return the size
15   *     else
16   *         return default_blocksize
17   *     end if
18   * endif
19   *
20   * Hair comes in an effort to only deal with AWKBUFSIZE
21   * once, the first time this routine is called, instead of
22   * every time.  Performance, dontyaknow.
23   */
24
25  size_t
26  optimal_bufsize(fd, stb)
27  int fd;
```

```
28  struct stat *stb;
29  {
30      char *val;
31      static size_t env_val = 0;
32      static short first = TRUE;
33      static short exact = FALSE;
34
35      /* force all members to zero in case OS doesn't use all of them. */
36      memset(stb, '\0', sizeof(struct stat));
37
38      /* always stat, in case stb is used by higher level code. */
39      if (fstat(fd, stb) == -1)
40          fatal("can't stat fd %d (%s)", fd, strerror(errno));
41
42      if (first) {
43          first = FALSE;
44
45          if ((val = getenv("AWKBUFSIZE")) != NULL) {
46              if (strcmp(val, "exact") == 0)
47                  exact = TRUE;
48              else if (ISDIGIT(*val)) {
49                  for (; *val && ISDIGIT(*val); val++)
50                      env_val = (env_val * 10) + *val - '0';
51
52                  return env_val;
53              }
54          }
55      } else if (! exact && env_val > 0)
56          return env_val;
57      /* else
58          fall through */
59
60      /*
61       * System V.n, n < 4, doesn't have the file system block size in the
62       * stat structure. So we have to make some sort of reasonable
63       * guess. We use stdio's BUFSIZ, since that is what it was
64       * meant for in the first place.
65       */
66  #ifdef HAVE_ST_BLKSIZE
67  #define DEFBLKSIZE  (stb->st_blksize > 0 ? stb->st_blksize : BUFSIZ)
68  #else
69  #define DEFBLKSIZE  BUFSIZ
70  #endif
71
72      if (S_ISREG(stb->st_mode)          /* regular file */
73          && 0 < stb->st_size            /* non-zero size */
74          && (stb->st_size < DEFBLKSIZE  /* small file */
75          || exact))                     /* or debugging */
76          return stb->st_size;           /* use file size */
77
78      return DEFBLKSIZE;
79  }
```

The comment on lines 3–23 explains the algorithm. Since searching the environment can be expensive and it only needs to be done once, the function uses several `static` variables to collect the appropriate information the first time.

Lines 42–54 execute the first time the function is called, and only the first time. Line 43 enforces this condition by setting `first` to false. Lines 45–54 handle the environment variable, looking for either `"exact"` or a number. In the latter case, it converts the string value to decimal, saving it in `env_val`. (We probably should have used `strtoul()` here; it didn't occur to us at the time.)

Line 55 executes every time but the first. If a numeric value was given, the condition will be true and that value is returned (line 56). Otherwise, it falls through to the rest of the function.

Lines 60–70 define `DEFBLKSIZE`; this part has not changed. Finally, lines 72–76 return the file size if appropriate. If not (line 78), `DEFBLKSIZE` is returned.

We did fix the problem,[13] but in the meantime, we left the new version of `optimal_bufsize()` in place, so that we could be sure the problem hasn't reoccurred.

The marginal increase in code size and complexity is more than offset by the increased flexibility we now have for testing. Furthermore, since this is production code, it's easy to have a user in the field use this feature for testing, to determine if a similar problem has occurred. (So far, we haven't had to ask for a test, but it's nice to know that we could handle it if we had to.)

15.4.2.3 Add Logging Code

It is often the case that your application program is running on a system on which you can't use a debugger (such as at a customer site). In that case, your goal is to be able to examine the program's internal state, but from the outside. The only way to do that is to have the program itself produce this information for you.

There are multiple ways to do this:

- Always log information to a specific file. This is simplest: The program always writes logging information. You can then look at the file at your convenience.

---

[13] By rewriting the buffer management code!

The disadvantage is that at some point the log file will consume all available disk space. Therefore, you should have multiple log files, with your program switching to a new one periodically.

Brian Kernighan recommends naming the log files by day of the week: `myapp.log.sun`, `myapp.log.mon`, and so on. The advantage here is that you don't have to manually move old files out of the way; you get a week's worth of log files for free.

- Write to a log file only if it already exists. When your program starts up, if the log file exists, it writes information to the log. Otherwise, it doesn't. To enable logging, first create an empty log file.

- Use a fixed-format for messages, one that can be easily parsed by scripting languages such as `awk` or Perl, for summary and report generation.

- Alternatively, generate some form of XML, which is self-describing, and possibly convertible to other formats. (We're not big fans of XML, but you shouldn't let that stop you.)

- Use `syslog()` to do logging; the final disposition of logging messages can be controlled by the system administrator. (`syslog()` is a fairly advanced interface; see the *syslog*(3) manpage.)

Choosing how to log information is, of course, the easy part. The hard part is choosing *what* to log. As with all parts of program development, it pays to *think before you code*. Log information about critical variables. Check their values to make sure they're in range or are otherwise what you expect. Log exceptional conditions; if something occurs that shouldn't, log it, and if possible, keep going.

The key is to log only the information you need to track down problems, no more and no less.

15.4.2.4 Runtime Debugging Files

In a previous life, we worked for a startup company with binary executables of the product installed at customer sites. It wasn't possible to attach a debugger to a running copy of the program or to run it from a debugger on the customer's system. The main component of the product was not started directly from a command line, but indirectly, through shell scripts that did considerable initial setup.

To make the program start producing logging information, we came up with the idea of special debugging files. When a file of a certain name existed in a certain directory, the program would produce informational messages to a log file that we could then download and analyze. Such code looks like this:

```
struct stat sbuf;
extern int do_logging;      /* initialized to zero */

if (stat("/path/to/magic/.file", &sbuf) == 0)
    do_logging = TRUE;
...
if (do_logging) {
    logging code here: open file, write info, close file, etc.
}
```

The call to `stat()` happened for each job the program processed. Thus, we could dynamically enable and disable logging without having to stop and restart the application!

As with debugging options and variables, there are any number of variations on this theme: different files that enable logging of information about different subsystems, debugging directives added into the debugging file itself, and so on. As with all features, you should plan a design for what you will need and then implement it cleanly instead of hacking out some quick and dirty code at 3:00 A.M. (a not uncommon possibility in startup companies, unfortunately).

> NOTE   All that glitters is not gold. Special debugging files are but one example of techniques known as *back doors*—one or more ways for developers to do undocumented things with a program, usually for nefarious purposes. In our instance, the back door was entirely benign. But an unscrupulous developer could just as easily arrange to generate and download a hidden copy of a customer list, personnel file, or other sensitive data. For this reason alone, you should think extra hard about whether this technique is usable in your application.

15.4.2.5   Add Special Hooks for Breakpoints

Often, a problem may be reproducible, but only after your program has first processed many megabytes of input data. Or, while you may know in which function your program is failing, the failure occurs only after the function has been called many hundreds, or even thousands, of times.

This is a big problem when you're working in a debugger. If you set a breakpoint in the failing routine, you have to type the `continue` command and press ENTER hundreds or thousands of times to get your program into the state where it's about to fail. This is tedious and error prone, to say the least! It may even be so difficult to do that you'll want to give up before starting.

The solution is to add special debugging "hook" functions that your program can call when it is close to the state you're interested in.

For example, suppose that you know that the `check_salary()` function is the one that fails, but only when it's been called 1,427 times. (We kid you not; we've seen some rather strange things in our time.)

To catch `check_salary()` before it fails, create a special dummy function that does nothing but return, and then arrange for `check_salary()` to call it just before the 1,427th time that it itself is called:

```
/* debug_dummy --- debugging hook function */
void debug_dummy(void) { return; }

struct salary *check_salary(void)
{
    ... real variable declarations here ...
    static int count = 0;      /* for debugging */

    if (++count == 1426)
        debug_dummy();

    ... rest of the code here ...
}
```

Now, from within GDB, set a breakpoint in `debug_dummy()`, and then run the program normally:

```
(gdb) break debug_dummy                            Set breakpoint for dummy function
Breakpoint 1 at 0x8055885: file whizprog.c, line 3137.
(gdb) run                                          Start program running
```

Once the breakpoint for `debug_dummy()` is reached, you can set a second breakpoint for `check_salary()` and then continue execution:

```
(gdb) run                                          Start program running
Starting program: /home/arnold/whizprog

Breakpoint 1, debug_dummy () at whizprog.c, line 3137
3137  void debug_dummy(void) { return; }          Breakpoint reached
(gdb) break check_salary                          Set breakpoint for function of interest
Breakpoint 2 at 0x8057913: file whizprog.c, line 3140.
(gdb) cont
```

When the second breakpoint is reached, the program is about to fail and you can single-step through it, doing whatever is necessary to track down the problem.

Instead of using a fixed constant ('++count == 1426'), you may wish to have a global variable that can be set by the debugger to whatever value you need. This avoids the need to recompile the program.

For gawk, we have gone a step further and brought the debugging hook facility into the language, so the hook function can be called from the awk program. When compiled for debugging, a special do-nothing function named stopme() is available. This function in turn calls a C function of the same name. This allows us to put calls to stopme() into a failing awk program right before things go wrong. For example, if gawk is producing bad results for an awk program on the 1,200th input record, we can add a line like this to the awk program:

```
NR == 1198 { stopme() }   # Stop for debugging when Number of Records == 1198
```

... rest of awk program as before ...

Then, from within GDB, we can set a breakpoint on the C function stopme() and run the awk program. Once that breakpoint fires, we can then set breakpoints on the other parts of gawk where we suspect the real problem lies.

The hook-function technique is useful in and of itself. However, the ability to bring it to the application level multiplies its usefulness, and it has saved us untold hours of debugging time when tracking down obscure problems.

15.5 Debugging Tools

Besides GDB and whatever source code hooks you use for general debugging, there are a number of useful packages that can help find different kinds of problems. Because dynamic memory management is such a difficult task in large-scale programs, many tools focus on that area, often acting as drop-in replacements for malloc() and free().

There are commercial tools that do many (or all) of the same things as the programs we describe, but not all of them are available for GNU/Linux, and many are quite expensive. All of the packages discussed in this section are freely available.

15.5.1 The dbug Library — A Sophisticated printf()

The first package we examine is the dbug library. It is based on the idea of conditionally compiled debugging code we presented earlier in this chapter, but carries things much further, providing relatively sophisticated runtime tracing and conditional debug output. It implements many of the tips we described, saving you the trouble of implementing them yourself.

The dbug library, written by Fred Fish in the early 1980s, has seen modest enhancements since then. It is now explicitly in the public domain, so it can be used in both free and proprietary software, without problems. It is available from Fred Fish's FTP archive,[14] as both a compressed tar file, and as a ZIP archive. The documentation summarizes dbug well:

> dbug is an example of an internal debugger. Because it requires internal instrumentation of a program, and its usage does not depend on any special capabilities of the execution environment, it is always available and will execute in any environment that the program itself will execute in. In addition, since it is a complete package with a specific user interface, all programs which use it will be provided with similar debugging capabilities. This is in sharp contrast to other forms of internal instrumentation where each developer has their own, usually less capable, form of internal debugger…

> The dbug package imposes only a slight speed penalty on executing programs, typically much less than 10 percent, and a modest size penalty, typically 10 to 20 percent. By defining a specific C preprocessor symbol both of these can be reduced to zero with no changes required to the source code.

> The following list is a quick summary of the capabilities of the dbug package. Each capability can be individually enabled or disabled at the time a program is invoked by specifying the appropriate command line arguments.

- Execution trace showing function level control flow in a semi-graphical manner using indentation to indicate nesting depth.

- Output the values of all, or any subset of, key internal variables.

---

[14] ftp://ftp.ninemoons.com/pub/dbug/

- Limit actions to a specific set of named functions.

- Limit function trace to a specified nesting depth.

- Label each output line with source file name and line number.

- Label each output line with name of current process.

- Push or pop internal debugging state to allow execution with built-in debugging defaults.

- Redirect the debug output stream to standard output (stdout) or a named file. The default output stream is standard error (stderr). The redirection mechanism is completely independent of normal command line redirection to avoid output conflicts.

The dbug package requires you to use a certain discipline when writing your code. In particular, you have to use its macros when doing a function return or calling setjmp() and longjmp(). You have to add a single macro call as the *first* executable statement of each function and call a few extra macros from main(). Finally, you have to add a debugging command-line option: By convention this is -#, which is rarely, if ever, used as a real option. In return for the extra work, you get all the benefits just outlined. Let's look at the example in the manual:

```
1   #include <stdio.h>
2   #include "dbug.h"
3
4   int
5   main (argc, argv)
6   int argc;
7   char *argv[];
8   {
9       register int result, ix;
10      extern int factorial (), atoi ();
11
12      DBUG_ENTER ("main");
13      DBUG_PROCESS (argv[0]);
14      DBUG_PUSH_ENV ("DBUG");
15      for (ix = 1; ix < argc && argv[ix][0] == '-'; ix++) {
16          switch (argv[ix][1]) {
17          case '#':
18              DBUG_PUSH (&(argv[ix][2]));
19              break;
20          }
21      }
```

```
22      for (; ix < argc; ix++) {
23          DBUG_PRINT ("args", ("argv[%d] = %s", ix, argv[ix]));
24          result = factorial (atoi (argv[ix]));
25          printf ("%d\n", result);
26          fflush (stdout);
27      }
28      DBUG_RETURN (0);
29  }
```

This program illustrates most of the salient points. The DBUG_ENTER() macro (line 12) must be called after any variable declarations and before any other code. (This is because it declares some private variables of its own.[15])

The DBUG_PROCESS() macro (line 13) sets the name of the program, primarily for use in output messages from the library. This macro should be called only once, from main().

The DBUG_PUSH_ENV() macro (line 14) causes the library to look at the named environment variable (DBUG in this case) for control strings. (The dbug control strings are discussed shortly.) The library is capable of saving its current state and using a new one, creating a stack of saved states. Thus, this macro pushes the state obtained from the given environment variable onto the stack of saved states. As used in this example, the macro creates the initial state. If there is no such environment variable, nothing happens. (As an aside, DBUG is rather generic; perhaps something like GAWK_DBUG [for gawk] would be better.)

The DBUG_PUSH() macro (line 18) passes in the control string value obtained from the -# command-line option. (New code should use getopt() or getopt_long() instead of manual argument parsing.) This is normally how debugging is enabled, but using an environment variable as well provides additional flexibility.

The DBUG_PRINT() macro (line 23) is what produces output. The second argument uses the technique we described earlier (see Section 15.4.1.1, "Use Debugging Macros," page 577) of enclosing the entire printf() argument list in parentheses, making it a single argument as far as the C preprocessor is concerned. Note that a terminating newline character is *not* provided in the format string; the dbug library provides the newline for you.

---

[15] C99, which allows variable declarations mixed with executable code, makes this less of a problem, but remember that this package was designed for K&R C.

When printing, by default, the dbug library outputs all DBUG_PRINT() statements. The first argument is a string that can be used to limit the output just to DBUG_PRINT() macros using that string.

Finally, the DBUG_RETURN() macro (line 28) is used instead of a regular return statement to return a value. There is a corresponding DBUG_VOID_RETURN macro for use in void functions.

The rest of the program is completed with the factorial() function:

```
1   #include <stdio.h>
2   #include "dbug.h"
3
4   int factorial (value)
5   register int value;
6   {
7       DBUG_ENTER ("factorial");
8       DBUG_PRINT ("find", ("find %d factorial", value));
9       if (value > 1) {
10          value *= factorial (value - 1);
11      }
12      DBUG_PRINT ("result", ("result is %d", value));
13      DBUG_RETURN (value);
14  }
```

Once the program is compiled and linked with the dbug library, it can be run normally. By default, the program produces no debugging output. With debugging enabled, though, different kinds of output are available:

```
$ factorial 1 2 3                         Regular run, no debugging
1
2
6
$ factorial -#t 1 2 3                      Show function call trace, note nesting
| >factorial
| <factorial
1                                          Regular output is on stdout
| >factorial
| | >factorial
| | <factorial
| <factorial                               Debugging output is on stderr
2
| >factorial
| | >factorial
| | | >factorial
| | | <factorial
| | <factorial
| <factorial
6
```

```
<?func?
$ factorial -#d 1 2                       Show debugging messages from DBUG_PRINT()
?func?: args: argv[2] = 1
factorial: find: find 1 factorial
factorial: result: result is 1
1
?func?: args: argv[3] = 2
factorial: find: find 2 factorial
factorial: find: find 1 factorial
factorial: result: result is 1
factorial: result: result is 2
2
```

The -# option controls the dbug library. It is "special" in the sense that DBUG_PUSH() will accept the entire string, ignoring the leading '-#' characters, although you could use a different option if you wish, passing DBUG_PUSH() just the option argument string (this is optarg if you use getopt()).

The control string consists of a set of options and arguments. Each group of options and arguments is separated from the others by a colon character. Each option is a single letter, and the arguments to that option are separated from it by commas. For example:

```
$ myprog -#d,mem,ipc:f,check_salary,check_start_date -f infile -o outfile
```

The d option enables DBUG_PRINT() output, but only if the first argument string is one of "mem" or "ipc". (With no arguments, all DBUG_PRINT() messages are printed.) Similarly, the f option limits the function call trace to just the named functions: check_salary() and check_start_date().

The following list of options and arguments is reproduced from the dbug library manual. Square brackets enclose optional arguments. We include here only the ones we find useful; see the documentation for the full list.

d[, *keywords*]

> Enable output from macros with specified *keywords*. A null list of keywords implies that all keywords are selected.

F

> Mark each debugger output line with the name of the source file containing the macro causing the output.

`i`

Identify the process emitting each line of debug or trace output with the process ID for that process.

`L`

Mark each debugger output line with the source-file line number of the macro causing the output.

`o[,`*`file`*`]`

Redirect the debugger output stream to the specified file. The default output stream is `stderr`. A null argument list causes output to be redirected to `stdout`.

`t[,`*`N`*`]`

Enable function control flow tracing. The maximum nesting depth is specified by *N*, and defaults to 200.

To round out the discussion, here are the rest of the macros defined by the `dbug` library.

`DBUG_EXECUTE(`*`string, code`*`)`

This macro is similar to `DBUG_PRINT()`: The first argument is a string selected with the `d` option, and the second is code to execute:

```
DBUG_EXECUTE("abort", abort());
```

`DBUG_FILE`

This is a value of type `FILE *`, for use with the `<stdio.h>` routines. It allows you to do your own output to the debugging file stream.

`DBUG_LONGJMP(jmp_buf env, int val)`

This macro wraps a call to `longjmp()`, taking the same arguments, so that the `dbug` library will know when you've made a nonlocal jump.

`DBUG_POP()`

This macro pops one level of saved debugging state, as created by `DBUG_PUSH()`. It is rather esoteric; you probably won't use it.

`DBUG_SETJMP(jmp_buf env)`

This macro wraps a call to `setjmp()`, taking the same argument. It allows the `dbug` library to handle nonlocal jumps.

In a different incarnation, at the first startup company we worked for,[16] we used the dbug library in our product. It was invaluable during development, and by omitting the -DDBUG on the final build, we were able to build a production version, with no other source code changes.

To get the most benefit out of the dbug library, you must use it consistently, throughout your program. This is easier if you use it from the beginning of a project, but as an experiment, we found that with the aid of a simple awk script, we could incorporate the library into a 30,000 line program with a few hours work. If you can afford the overhead, it's best to leave it in the production build of your program so that you can debug with it without first having to recompile.

We find that the dbug library is a nice complement to external debuggers such as GDB; it provides an *organized and consistent* way to apply instrumentation to C code. It also rather nicely combines many of the techniques that we outlined separately, earlier in the chapter. The dynamic function call trace feature is particularly useful, and it proves invaluable for help in *learning* about a program's behavior if you're unfamiliar with it.

15.5.2 Memory Allocation Debuggers

Ignoring issues such as poor program design, for any large-scale, practical application, the C programmer's single biggest challenge is dynamic memory management (by malloc(), realloc(), and free()).

This fact is borne out by the large number of tools that are available for debugging dynamic memory. There is a fair amount of overlap in what these tools provide. For example:

- Memory leak detection: memory that is allocated and then becomes unreachable.

- Unfreed memory detection: memory that is allocated but never freed. Never-freed memory isn't always a bug, but detecting such occurrences allows you to verify that they're indeed OK.

- Detection of bad frees: memory that is freed twice, or pointers passed to free() that didn't come from malloc().

---

[16] Although we should have learned our lesson after the first one, we went to a second one. Since then we've figured it out and generally avoid startup companies. Your mileage may vary, of course.

- Detection of use of already freed memory: memory that is freed is being used through a dangling pointer.

- Memory overrun detection: accessing or storing into memory outside the bounds of what was allocated.

- Warning about the use of uninitialized memory. (Many compilers can warn about this.)

- Dynamic function tracing: When a bad memory access occurs, you get a traceback from where the memory is used to where it was allocated.

- Tool control through the use of environment variables.

- Log files for raw debugging information that can be postprocessed to produce useful reports.

Some tools merely log these events. Others arrange for the application program to die a horrible death (through SIGSEGV) so that the offending code can be pinpointed from within a debugger. Additionally, most are designed to work well with GDB.

Some tools require source code modification, such as calling special functions, or using a special header file, extra #defines, and a static library. Others work by using special Linux/Unix shared library mechanisms to transparently install themselves as replacements for the standard library versions of malloc() and free().

In this section we look at three dynamic memory debuggers, and then we provide pointers to several others.

15.5.2.1 GNU/Linux mtrace

GNU/Linux systems using GLIBC provide two functions for enabling and disabling memory tracing *at runtime*:

```
#include <mcheck.h>                                          GLIBC

void mtrace(void);
void muntrace(void);
```

When mtrace() is called, the library looks at the environment variable MALLOC_TRACE. It is expected that this names a writable file (existing or not). The library opens the file and begins logging information about memory allocations and frees. (No logging is done if the file can't be opened. The file is truncated each time the program runs.) When `muntrace()` is called, the library closes the file and does not log any further allocations or frees.

The use of separate functions makes it possible to do memory tracing for specific parts of the program; it's not necessary to trace everything. (We find it most useful to enable logging at the start of the program and be done, but this design provides flexibility, which is nice to have.)

Once the application program exits, you use the `mtrace` program to analyze the log file. (The log file is ASCII, but the information isn't directly usable.) For example, `gawk` turns on tracing if `TIDYMEM` is defined:

```
$ export TIDYMEM=1 MALLOC_TRACE=mtrace.out        Export environment variables
$ ./gawk 'BEGIN { print "hello, world" }'         Run the program
hello, world
$ mtrace ./gawk mtrace.out                         Generate report

Memory not freed:
-----------------
   Address     Size     Caller
0x08085858     0x20   at /home/arnold/Gnu/gawk/gawk-3.1.3/main.c:1102
0x08085880     0xc80  at /home/arnold/Gnu/gawk/gawk-3.1.3/node.c:398
0x08086508     0x2    at /home/arnold/Gnu/gawk/gawk-3.1.3/node.c:337
0x08086518     0x6    at /home/arnold/Gnu/gawk/gawk-3.1.3/node.c:337
0x08086528     0x10   at /home/arnold/Gnu/gawk/gawk-3.1.3/eval.c:2082
0x08086550     0x3    at /home/arnold/Gnu/gawk/gawk-3.1.3/node.c:337
0x08086560     0x3    at /home/arnold/Gnu/gawk/gawk-3.1.3/node.c:337
0x080865e0     0x4    at /home/arnold/Gnu/gawk/gawk-3.1.3/field.c:76
0x08086670     0x78   at /home/arnold/Gnu/gawk/gawk-3.1.3/awkgram.y:1369
0x08086700     0xe    at /home/arnold/Gnu/gawk/gawk-3.1.3/node.c:337
0x08086718     0x1f   at /home/arnold/Gnu/gawk/gawk-3.1.3/awkgram.y:1259
```

The output is a list of locations at which `gawk` allocates memory that is never freed. Note that permanently hanging onto dynamic memory is fine if it's done on purpose. All the cases shown here are allocations of that sort.

15.5.2.2 Electric Fence

In Section 3.1, "Linux/Unix Address Space," page 52, we described how dynamic memory comes from the heap, which can be made to grow and shrink (with the `brk()` or `sbrk()` calls, described in Section 3.2.3, "System Calls: `brk()` and `sbrk()`," page 75).

Well, the picture we presented there is a simplified version of reality. More advanced system calls (not covered in this volume) make it possible to add additional, not necessarily contiguous, segments of memory into a process's address space. Many `malloc()`

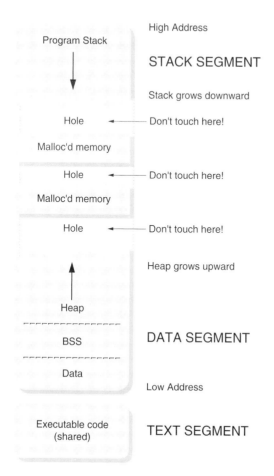

FIGURE 15.1
Linux/Unix process address space, including special areas

debuggers work by using these system calls to add a new piece of address space for *every* allocation. The advantage of this scheme is that the operating system and the computer's memory-protection hardware cooperate to make access to memory outside these discontiguous segments invalid, generating a SIGSEGV signal. The scheme is depicted in Figure 15.1.

The first debugging package to implement this scheme was Electric Fence. Electric Fence is a drop-in replacement for malloc() et al. It works on many Unix systems and GNU/Linux; it is available from its author's FTP archive.[17] Many GNU/Linux distributions supply it, although you may have to choose it explicitly when you install your system.

Once a program is linked with Electric Fence, any access that is out of bounds generates a SIGSEGV. Electric Fence also catches attempts to use memory that has already been freed. Here is a simple program that illustrates both problems:

```
 1   /* ch15-badmem1.c --- do bad things with memory */
 2
 3   #include <stdio.h>
 4   #include <stdlib.h>
 5
 6   int main(int argc, char **argv)
 7   {
 8       char *p;
 9       int i;
10
11       p = malloc(30);
12
13       strcpy(p, "not 30 bytes");
14       printf("p = <%s>\n", p);
15
16       if (argc == 2) {
17           if (strcmp(argv[1], "-b") == 0)
18               p[42] = 'a';      /* touch outside the bounds */
19           else if (strcmp(argv[1], "-f") == 0) {
20               free(p);          /* free memory and then use it */
21               p[0] = 'b';
22           }
23       }
24
25       /* free(p); */
26
27       return 0;
28   }
```

This program does simple command-line option checking to decide how to misbehave: -b touches memory out of bounds, and -f attempts to use freed memory. (Lines 18 and 21 are the dangerous ones, respectively.) Note that with no options, the pointer is never freed (line 25); Electric Fence doesn't catch this case.

One way to use Electric Fence, a way that is guaranteed to work across Unix and GNU/Linux systems, is to statically link your program with it. The program should then be *run from the debugger*. (The Electric Fence documentation is explicit that

---

[17] ftp://ftp.perens.com/pub/ElectricFence

Electric Fence should not be linked with a production binary.) The following session demonstrates this procedure and shows what happens for both command-line options:

```
$ cc -g ch15-badmem1.c -lefence -o ch15-badmem1        Compile; link statically
$ gdb ch15-badmem1                                     Run it from the debugger
GNU gdb 5.3
...
(gdb) run -b                                           Try -b option
Starting program: /home/arnold/progex/code/ch15/ch15-badmem1 -b
[New Thread 8192 (LWP 28021)]

   Electric Fence 2.2.0 Copyright (C) 1987-1999 Bruce Perens <bruce@perens.com>
p = <not 30 bytes>

Program received signal SIGSEGV, Segmentation fault.   SIGSEGV: GDB prints where
[Switching to Thread 8192 (LWP 28021)]
0x080485b6 in main (argc=2, argv=0xbffff8a4) at ch15-badmem1.c:18
18                      p[42] = 'a';     /* touch outside the bounds */
(gdb) run -f                                           Now try the -f option
The program being debugged has been started already.
Start it from the beginning? (y or n) y                Yes, really

Starting program: /home/arnold/progex/code/ch15/ch15-badmem1 -f
[New Thread 8192 (LWP 28024)]

   Electric Fence 2.2.0 Copyright (C) 1987-1999 Bruce Perens <bruce@perens.com>
p = <not 30 bytes>

Program received signal SIGSEGV, Segmentation fault.     SIGSEGV again
[Switching to Thread 8192 (LWP 28024)]
0x080485e8 in main (argc=2, argv=0xbffff8a4) at ch15-badmem1.c:21
21                      p[0] = 'b';
```

On systems that support shared libraries and the LD_PRELOAD environment variable (including GNU/Linux), you don't need to explicitly link in the efence library. Instead, the ef shell script arranges to run the program with the proper setup.

Although we haven't described the mechanisms in detail, GNU/Linux (and other Unix systems) support *shared libraries*, special versions of the library routines that are kept in a single file on disk instead of copied into every single executable program's binary file. Shared libraries save some space on disk and can save system memory, since all programs using a shared library use the same in-memory copy of the library. The cost is that program startup is slower because the program and the shared library have to be hooked together before the program can start running. (This is usually transparent to you, the user.)

The `LD_PRELOAD` environment variable causes the system's program loader (which brings executable files into memory) to link in a special library *before* the standard libraries. The `ef` script uses this feature to link in Electric Fence's version of the `malloc()` suite. Thus, relinking isn't even necessary. This example demonstrates `ef`:

```
$ cc -g ch15-badmem1.c -o ch15-badmem1                    Compile normally
$ ef ch15-badmem1 -b                                      Run using ef, dumps core

  Electric Fence 2.2.0 Copyright (C) 1987-1999 Bruce Perens <bruce@perens.com>
p = <not 30 bytes>
/usr/bin/ef: line 20: 28005 Segmentation fault      (core dumped)
    ( export LD_PRELOAD=libefence.so.0.0; exec $* )
$ ef ch15-badmem1 -f                                      Run using ef, dumps core again

  Electric Fence 2.2.0 Copyright (C) 1987-1999 Bruce Perens <bruce@perens.com>
p = <not 30 bytes>
/usr/bin/ef: line 20: 28007 Segmentation fault      (core dumped)
    ( export LD_PRELOAD=libefence.so.0.0; exec $* )
$ ls -l core*                                             Linux gives us separate core files
-rw-------    1 arnold    devel       217088 Aug 28 15:40 core.28005
-rw-------    1 arnold    devel       212992 Aug 28 15:40 core.28007
```

GNU/Linux creates `core` files that include the process ID number in the file name. In this instance this behavior is useful because we can debug each `core` file separately:

```
$ gdb ch15-badmem1 core.28005                             From the -b option
GNU gdb 5.3
...
Core was generated by `ch15-badmem1 -b'.
Program terminated with signal 11, Segmentation fault.
...
#0  0x08048466 in main (argc=2, argv=0xbffff8c4) at ch15-badmem1.c:18
18                          p[42] = 'a';    /* touch outside the bounds */
(gdb) quit

$ gdb ch15-badmem1 core.28007                             From the -f option
GNU gdb 5.3
...
Core was generated by `ch15-badmem1 -f'.
Program terminated with signal 11, Segmentation fault.
...
#0  0x08048498 in main (argc=2, argv=0xbffff8c4) at ch15-badmem1.c:21
21                          p[0] = 'b';
```

The *efence*(3) manpage describes several environment variables that can be set to tailor Electric Fence's behavior. The following three are the most notable.

EF_PROTECT_BELOW

> Setting this variable to `1` causes Electric Fence to look for *underruns* instead of overruns. An overrun, accessing memory beyond the allocated area, was demon-

strated previously. An underrun is accessing memory located in front of the allocated area.

EF_PROTECT_FREE

Setting this variable to 1 prevents Electric Fence from reusing memory that was correctly freed. This is helpful when you think a program may be accessing freed memory; if the freed memory was subsequently reallocated, access to it from a previously dangling pointer would otherwise go undetected.

EF_ALLOW_MALLOC_0

When given a nonzero value, Electric Fence allows calls of 'malloc(0)'. Such calls are technically valid in Standard C, but likely represent a software bug. Thus, by default, Electric Fence disallows them.

In addition to environment variables, Electric Fence supplies similarly named global variables. You can change their values from within a debugger, so you can dynamically alter the behavior of a program that has already started running. See *efence*(3) for the details.

15.5.2.3 Debugging Malloc: dmalloc

The dmalloc library provides a large number of debugging options. Its author is Gray Watson, and it has its own web site.[18] As with Electric Fence, it may already be installed on your system, or you may have to retrieve it and build it yourself.

The dmalloc library examines the DMALLOC_OPTIONS environment variable for control information. For example, it might look like this:

```
$ echo $DMALLOC_OPTIONS
debug=0x4e40503,inter=100,log=dm-log
```

The 'debug' part of this variable is a set of OR'd bit flags which is nearly impossible for most people to manage directly. Therefore, the documentation describes a two-stage process for making things easier to use.

The first step is to define a shell function named dmalloc that calls the dmalloc driver program:

---

[18] http://www.dmalloc.com

```
$ dmalloc () {
> eval `command dmalloc -b $*`        The 'command' command bypasses shell functions
> }
```

Once that's done, you can pass options to the function to set the log file (-l), specify the number of iterations after which `dmalloc` should verify its internal data structures (-i), and specify a debugging level or other tag ('low'):

```
$ dmalloc -l dm-log -i 100 low
```

Like Electric Fence, the `dmalloc` library can be statically linked into the application or dynamically linked with `LD_PRELOAD`. The following example demonstrates the latter:

```
$ LD_PRELOAD=libdmalloc.so ch15-badmem1 -b        Run with checking on
p = <not 30 bytes>                                Normal output shown
```

> **NOTE** Do *not* use 'export `LD_PRELOAD=libdmalloc.so`'! If you do, *every* program you run, such as `ls`, will run with `malloc()` checking turned on. Your system will become unusable, quickly. If you do this by accident, you can use 'unset `LD_PRELOAD`' to restore normal behavior.

The results go into the `dm-log` file, as specified:

```
$ cat dm-log
1062078174: 1: Dmalloc version '4.8.1' from 'http://dmalloc.com/'
1062078174: 1: flags = 0x4e40503, logfile 'dm-log'
1062078174: 1: interval = 100, addr = 0, seen # = 0
1062078174: 1: starting time = 1062078174
1062078174: 1: free bucket count/bits:  63/6
1062078174: 1: basic-block 4096 bytes, alignment 8 bytes, heap grows up
1062078174: 1: heap: 0x804a000 to 0x804d000, size 12288 bytes (3 blocks)
1062078174: 1: heap checked 0
1062078174: 1: alloc calls: malloc 1, calloc 0, realloc 0, free 0
1062078174: 1: alloc calls: recalloc 0, memalign 0, valloc 0
1062078174: 1:  total memory allocated: 30 bytes (1 pnts)
1062078174: 1:  max in use at one time: 30 bytes (1 pnts)
1062078174: 1: max alloced with 1 call: 30 bytes
1062078174: 1: max alloc rounding loss: 34 bytes (53%)
1062078174: 1: max memory space wasted: 3998 bytes (98%)
1062078174: 1: final user memory space: basic 0, divided 1, 4062 bytes
1062078174: 1:  final admin overhead: basic 1, divided 1, 8192 bytes (66%)
1062078174: 1:  final external space: 0 bytes (0 blocks)
1062078174: 1: top 10 allocations:
1062078174: 1:  total-size  count in-use-size  count  source
1062078174: 1:          30      1           30      1  ra=0x8048412
1062078174: 1:          30      1           30      1  Total of 1
```

```
1062078174: 1: dumping not-freed pointers changed since 0:
1062078174: 1:  not freed: '0x804c008|s1' (30 bytes) from 'ra=0x8048412'
1062078174: 1:  total-size  count  source
1062078174: 1:          30      1  ra=0x8048412        Allocation is here
1062078174: 1:          30      1  Total of 1
1062078174: 1:  unknown memory: 1 pointer, 30 bytes
1062078174: 1: ending time = 1062078174, elapsed since start = 0:00:00
```

The output includes many statistics, which we're not interested in at the moment. The line that is interesting is the one indicating memory that wasn't freed, with a return address indicating the function that allocated the memory ('ra=0x8048412'). The dmalloc documentation explains how to get the source code location for this address, using GDB:

```
$ gdb ch15-badmem1                          Start GDB
GNU gdb 5.3
...
(gdb) x 0x8048412                           Examine address
0x8048412 <main+26>:       0x8910c483
(gdb) info line *(0x8048412)                Get line information
Line 11 of "ch15-badmem1.c" starts at address 0x8048408 <main+16>
   and ends at 0x8048418 <main+32>.
```

This is painful, but workable if you have no other choice. However, if you include the "dmalloc.h" header file in your program (*after* all other #include statements), you can get source code information directly in the report:

```
...
1062080258: 1: top 10 allocations:
1062080258: 1:  total-size  count in-use-size  count  source
1062080258: 1:          30      1          30      1  ch15-badmem2.c:13
1062080258: 1:          30      1          30      1  Total of 1
1062080258: 1: dumping not-freed pointers changed since 0:
1062080258: 1:  not freed: '0x804c008|s1' (30 bytes) from 'ch15-badmem2.c:13'
1062080258: 1:  total-size  count  source
1062080258: 1:          30      1  ch15-badmem2.c:13
1062080258: 1:          30      1  Total of 1
...
```

(The ch15-badmem2.c file is the same as ch15-badmem1.c, except that it includes "dmalloc.h", so we haven't bothered to show it.)

Individual debugging features are enabled or disabled by the use of *tokens*—specially recognized identifiers—and the -p option to add a token (feature) or -m option to remove one. There are predefined combinations, 'low', 'med', and 'high'. You can see what these combinations are with 'dmalloc -Lv':

```
$ dmalloc low                                              Set things to low
$ dmalloc -Lv                                              Show settings
Debug Malloc Utility: http://dmalloc.com/
  For a list of the command-line options enter: dmalloc --usage
Debug-Flags 0x4e40503 (82052355) (low)                     Current tokens
   log-stats, log-non-free, log-bad-space, log-elapsed-time, check-fence,
   free-blank, error-abort, alloc-blank, catch-null
Address      not-set
Interval     100
Lock-On      not-set
Logpath      'log2'
Start-File   not-set
```

The full set of tokens, along with a brief explanation and each token's corresponding numeric value, is available from 'dmalloc -DV':

```
$ dmalloc -DV
Debug Tokens:
none (nil) -- no functionality (0)
log-stats (lst) -- log general statistics (0x1)
log-non-free (lnf) -- log non-freed pointers (0x2)
log-known (lkn) -- log only known non-freed (0x4)
log-trans (ltr) -- log memory transactions (0x8)
log-admin (lad) -- log administrative info (0x20)
log-blocks (lbl) -- log blocks when heap-map (0x40)
log-bad-space (lbs) -- dump space from bad pnt (0x100)
log-nonfree-space (lns) -- dump space from non-freed pointers (0x200)
log-elapsed-time (let) -- log elapsed-time for allocated pointer (0x40000)
log-current-time (lct) -- log current-time for allocated pointer (0x80000)
check-fence (cfe) -- check fence-post errors (0x400)
check-heap (che) -- check heap adm structs (0x800)
check-lists (cli) -- check free lists (0x1000)
check-blank (cbl) -- check mem overwritten by alloc-blank, free-blank (0x2000)
check-funcs (cfu) -- check functions (0x4000)
force-linear (fli) -- force heap space to be linear (0x10000)
catch-signals (csi) -- shutdown program on SIGHUP, SIGINT, SIGTERM (0x20000)
realloc-copy (rco) -- copy all re-allocations (0x100000)
free-blank (fbl) -- overwrite freed memory space with BLANK_CHAR (0x200000)
error-abort (eab) -- abort immediately on error (0x400000)
alloc-blank (abl) -- overwrite newly alloced memory with BLANK_CHAR (0x800000)
heap-check-map (hcm) -- log heap-map on heap-check (0x1000000)
print-messages (pme) -- write messages to stderr (0x2000000)
catch-null (cnu) -- abort if no memory available (0x4000000)
never-reuse (nre) -- never re-use freed memory (0x8000000)
allow-free-null (afn) -- allow the frees of NULL pointers (0x20000000)
error-dump (edu) -- dump core on error and then continue (0x40000000)
```

By now you should have a feel for how to use dmalloc and its flexibility. dmalloc is overkill for our simple demonstration program, but it is invaluable for a larger scale, real-world application.

15.5.2.4 Valgrind: A Versatile Tool

The tools described in the previous section all focus on dynamic memory debugging, and indeed this is a significant problem area for many programs. However, dynamic memory problems aren't the only kind. The GPL-licensed Valgrind program catches a large variety of problems, including those that arise from dynamic memory.

The Valgrind manual describes the program as well or better than we can, so we'll quote (and abbreviate) it as we go along.

> Valgrind is a flexible tool for debugging and profiling Linux-x86 executables. The tool consists of a core, which provides a synthetic x86 CPU in software, and a series of "skins", each of which is a debugging or profiling tool. The architecture is modular, so that new skins can be created easily and without disturbing the existing structure.

The most useful "skin" is `memcheck`:

> The `memcheck` skin detects memory-management problems in your programs.
>
> All reads and writes of memory are checked, and calls to `malloc/new/ free/delete` are intercepted. As a result, `memcheck` can detect the following problems:
>
> * Use of uninitialized memory.
> * Reading/writing memory after it has been `free`'d.
> * Reading/writing off the end of `malloc`'d blocks.
> * Reading/writing inappropriate areas on the stack.
> * Memory leaks—where pointers to `malloc`'d blocks are lost forever.
> * Mismatched use of `malloc/new/new []` vs `free/delete/delete []`.
> * Some misuses of the POSIX pthreads API.
>
> Problems like these can be difficult to find by other means, often lying undetected for long periods, then causing occasional, difficult-to-diagnose crashes.

Other skins are more specialized:

> * `cachegrind` performs detailed simulation of the I1, D1, and L2 caches in your CPU and so can accurately pinpoint the sources of cache misses in your code.

- The `addrcheck` [skin] is identical to `memcheck` except for the single detail that it does not do any uninitialized-value checks. All of the other checks—primarily the fine-grained address checking—are still done. The downside of this is that you don't catch the uninitialized-value errors that `memcheck` can find.

  But the upside is significant: Programs run about twice as fast as they do on `memcheck`, and a lot less memory is used. It still finds reads/writes of freed memory, memory off the end of blocks and in other invalid places, bugs which you really want to find before release!

- `helgrind` is a debugging skin designed to find data races in multithreaded programs.

Finally, the manual notes:

Valgrind is closely tied to details of the CPU, operating system and to a lesser extent, compiler and basic C libraries. This makes it difficult to make it portable, so we have chosen at the outset to concentrate on what we believe to be a widely used platform: Linux on x86s. Valgrind uses the standard Unix '`./configure`', '`make`', '`make install`' mechanism, and we have attempted to ensure that it works on machines with kernel 2.2 or 2.4 and glibc 2.1.X, 2.2.X or 2.3.1. This should cover the vast majority of modern Linux installations. Note that glibc-2.3.2+, with the NPTL (Native POSIX Thread Library) package won't work. We hope to be able to fix this, but it won't be easy.

If you're using GNU/Linux on a different platform or if you're using a commercial Unix system, then Valgrind won't be of much help to you. However, as x86 GNU/Linux systems are quite common (and affordable), it's likely you can acquire one on a moderate budget, or at least find one to borrow! What's more, once Valgrind has found a problem for you, it's fixed for *whatever* platform your program is compiled to run on. Thus, it's reasonable to use an x86 GNU/Linux system for development, and some other commercial Unix system for deployment of a high-end product.[19]

---

[19] Increasingly, GNU/Linux is being used for high-end product deployment, too!

Although the Valgrind manual might lead you to expect that there are separate commands named `memcheck`, `addrcheck`, and so on, this isn't the case. Instead, a driver shell program named `valgrind` runs the debugging core, with the appropriate "skin" as specified by the `--skin=` option. The default skin is `memcheck`; thus, running a plain `valgrind` is the same as '`valgrind --skin=memcheck`'. (This provides compatibility with earlier versions of Valgrind that only did memory checking, and it also makes the most sense, since the `memcheck` skin provides the most information.)

Valgrind provides a number of options. We refer you to its documentation for the full details. The options are split into groups; of those that apply to the core (that is, work for all skins), these are likely to be most useful:

`--gdb-attach=no|yes`
> Start up with a GDB attached to the process, for interactive debugging. The default is `no`.

`--help`
> List the options.

`--logfile=file`
> Log messages to `file.pid`.

`--num-callers=number`
> Show `num` callers in stack traces. The default is 4.

`--skin=skin`
> Use the skin named `skin`. Default is `memcheck`.

`--trace-children=no|yes`
> Also run the trace on child processes. The default is `no`.

`-v, --verbose`
> Be more verbose. This includes listing the libraries that are loaded, as well as the counts of all the different kinds of errors.

Of the options for the `memcheck` skin, these are the ones we think are most useful:

`--leak-check=no|yes`
> Find memory leaks once the program is finished. The default is 'no'.

`--show-reachable=no|yes`

> Show reachable blocks when the program is finished. If `--show-reachable=yes` is used, Valgrind looks for dynamically allocated memory that still has a pointer pointing to it. Such memory is not a memory leak, but it may be useful to know about anyway. The default is 'no'.

Let's take a look at Valgrind in action. Remember `ch15-badmem.c`? (See Section 15.5.2.2, "Electric Fence," page 614.) The `-b` option writes into memory that is beyond the area allocated with `malloc()`. Here's what Valgrind reports:

```
$ valgrind ch15-badmem1 -b
1   ==8716== Memcheck, a.k.a. Valgrind, a memory error detector for x86-linux.
2   ==8716== Copyright (C) 2002-2003, and GNU GPL'd, by Julian Seward.
3   ==8716== Using valgrind-20030725, a program supervision framework for x86-linux.
4   ==8716== Copyright (C) 2000-2003, and GNU GPL'd, by Julian Seward.
5   ==8716== Estimated CPU clock rate is 2400 MHz
6   ==8716== For more details, rerun with: -v
7   ==8716==
8   p = <not 30 bytes>
9   ==8716== Invalid write of size 1
10  ==8716==    at 0x8048466: main (ch15-badmem1.c:18)
11  ==8716==    by 0x420158D3: __libc_start_main (in /lib/i686/libc-2.2.93.so)
12  ==8716==    by 0x8048368: (within /home/arnold/progex/code/ch15/ch15-badmem1)
13  ==8716==    Address 0x4104804E is 12 bytes after a block of size 30 alloc'd
14  ==8716==    at 0x40025488: malloc (vg_replace_malloc.c:153)
15  ==8716==    by 0x8048411: main (ch15-badmem1.c:11)
16  ==8716==    by 0x420158D3: __libc_start_main (in /lib/i686/libc-2.2.93.so)
17  ==8716==    by 0x8048368: (within /home/arnold/progex/code/ch15/ch15-badmem1)
18  ==8716==
19  ==8716== ERROR SUMMARY: 1 errors from 1 contexts (suppressed: 0 from 0)
20  ==8716== malloc/free: in use at exit: 30 bytes in 1 blocks.
21  ==8716== malloc/free: 1 allocs, 0 frees, 30 bytes allocated.
22  ==8716== For a detailed leak analysis,  rerun with: --leak-check=yes
23  ==8716== For counts of detected errors, rerun with: -v
```

(Line numbers in the output were added to aid in the discussion.) Line 8 is the output from the program; the others are all from Valgrind, on standard error. The error report is on lines 9–17. It indicates how many bytes were incorrectly written (line 9), where this happened (line 10), and a stack trace. Lines 13–17 describe where the memory was allocated from. Lines 19–23 provide a summary.

The `-f` option to `ch15-badmem1` frees the allocated memory and then writes into it through a dangling pointer. Here is what Valgrind reports for this case:

```
$ valgrind ch15-badmem1 -f
==8719== Memcheck, a.k.a. Valgrind, a memory error detector for x86-linux.
...
p = <not 30 bytes>
==8719== Invalid write of size 1
==8719==    at 0x8048498: main (ch15-badmem1.c:21)
==8719==    by 0x420158D3: __libc_start_main (in /lib/i686/libc-2.2.93.so)
==8719==    by 0x8048368: (within /home/arnold/progex/code/ch15/ch15-badmem1)
==8719==    Address 0x41048024 is 0 bytes inside a block of size 30 free'd
==8719==    at 0x40025722: free (vg_replace_malloc.c:220)
==8719==    by 0x8048491: main (ch15-badmem1.c:20)
==8719==    by 0x420158D3: __libc_start_main (in /lib/i686/libc-2.2.93.so)
==8719==    by 0x8048368: (within /home/arnold/progex/code/ch15/ch15-badmem1)
...
```

This time the report indicates that the write was to freed memory and that the call to free() is on line 20 of ch15-badmem1.c.

When called with no options, ch15-badmem1.c allocates memory and uses it but does not release it. The --leak-check=yes option reports this case:

```
 $ valgrind --leak-check=yes ch15-badmem1
 1  ==8720== Memcheck, a.k.a. Valgrind, a memory error detector for x86-linux.
    ...
 8  p = <not 30 bytes>
 9  ==8720==
10  ==8720== ERROR SUMMARY: 0 errors from 0 contexts (suppressed: 0 from 0)
11  ==8720== malloc/free: in use at exit: 30 bytes in 1 blocks.
12  ==8720== malloc/free: 1 allocs, 0 frees, 30 bytes allocated.
    ...
16  ==8720==
17  ==8720== 30 bytes in 1 blocks are definitely lost in loss record 1 of 1
18  ==8720==    at 0x40025488: malloc (vg_replace_malloc.c:153)
19  ==8720==    by 0x8048411: main (ch15-badmem1.c:11)
20  ==8720==    by 0x420158D3: __libc_start_main (in /lib/i686/libc-2.2.93.so)
21  ==8720==    by 0x8048368: (within /home/arnold/progex/code/ch15/ch15-badmem1)
22  ==8720==
23  ==8720== LEAK SUMMARY:
24  ==8720==    definitely lost: 30 bytes in 1 blocks.
25  ==8720==    possibly lost:   0 bytes in 0 blocks.
26  ==8720==    still reachable: 0 bytes in 0 blocks.
27  ==8720==         suppressed: 0 bytes in 0 blocks.
28  ==8720== Reachable blocks (those to which a pointer was found) are not shown.
29  ==8720== To see them, rerun with: --show-reachable=yes
```

Lines 17–29 provide the leak report; the leaked memory was allocated on line 11 of ch15-badmem1.c.

Besides giving reports on misuses of dynamic memory, Valgrind can diagnose uses of *uninitialized* memory. Consider the following program, ch15-badmem3.c:

```
1   /* ch15-badmem3.c --- do bad things with nondynamic memory */
2
3   #include <stdio.h>
4   #include <stdlib.h>
5
6   int main(int argc, char **argv)
7   {
8       int a_var;  /* Both of these are uninitialized */
9       int b_var;
10
11      /* Valgrind won't flag this; see text. */
12      a_var = b_var;
13
14      /* Use uninitialized memory; this is flagged. */
15      printf("a_var = %d\n", a_var);
16
17      return 0;
18  }
```

When run, Valgrind produces this (abbreviated) report:

```
==29650== Memcheck, a.k.a. Valgrind, a memory error detector for x86-linux.
...
==29650== Use of uninitialised value of size 4
==29650==    at 0x42049D2A: _IO_vfprintf_internal (in /lib/i686/libc-2.2.93.so)
==29650==    by 0x420523C1: _IO_printf (in /lib/i686/libc-2.2.93.so)
==29650==    by 0x804834D: main (ch15-badmem3.c:15)
==29650==    by 0x420158D3: __libc_start_main (in /lib/i686/libc-2.2.93.so)
==29650==
==29650== Conditional jump or move depends on uninitialised value(s)
==29650==    at 0x42049D32: _IO_vfprintf_internal (in /lib/i686/libc-2.2.93.so)
==29650==    by 0x420523C1: _IO_printf (in /lib/i686/libc-2.2.93.so)
==29650==    by 0x804834D: main (ch15-badmem3.c:15)
==29650==    by 0x420158D3: __libc_start_main (in /lib/i686/libc-2.2.93.so)
...
a_var = 1107341000
==29650==
==29650== ERROR SUMMARY: 25 errors from 7 contexts (suppressed: 0 from 0)
==29650== malloc/free: in use at exit: 0 bytes in 0 blocks.
==29650== malloc/free: 0 allocs, 0 frees, 0 bytes allocated.
==29650== For a detailed leak analysis,  rerun with: --leak-check=yes
==29650== For counts of detected errors, rerun with: -v
```

The Valgrind documentation explains that copying of uninitialized data doesn't produce any reports. The memcheck skin notes the status of the data (uninitialized) and keeps track of it as data are moved around. Thus, a_var is considered uninitialized, since its value came from b_var, which started out uninitialized.

It is only when an uninitialized value is *used* that memcheck reports a problem. Here, the use occurs down in the C library (_IO_vfprintf_internal()), which has to convert the value to a string; to do so it does a computation with it.

Unfortunately, although Valgrind can detect the use of uninitialized memory, all the way down to the bit level, it cannot do array bounds checking for local and global variables. (Valgrind can do bounds checking for dynamic memory since it handles such memory itself and therefore knows the start and end of each region.)

In conclusion, Valgrind is a powerful memory debugging tool. It has been used on large-scale, multithreaded production programs such as KDE 3, OpenOffice, and the Konquerer web browser. It rivals several commercial offerings, and a variant version has even been used (together with the WINE Emulator[20]) to debug programs written for Microsoft Windows, using Visual C++! You can get Valgrind from its web site.[21]

15.5.2.5 Other Malloc Debuggers

Two articles by Cal Erickson in *Linux Journal* describe `mtrace` and `dmalloc`, as well as most of the other tools listed below. These articles are *Memory Leak Detection in Embedded Systems*, Issue 101,[22] September 2002, and *Memory Leak Detection in C++*, Issue 110,[23] June 2003. Both articles are available on the *Linux Journal* web site.

The other tools are similar in nature to those described earlier.

`ccmalloc`
> A `malloc()` replacement library that does not need special compilation and that can be used with C++. See `http://www.inf.ethz.ch/personal/biere/projects/ccmalloc`.

Mark Moraes's `malloc`
> An early but full-featured `malloc()` replacement library that provides profiling, tracing, and debugging features. You can get it from `ftp://ftp.cs.toronto.edu/pub/moraes/malloc-1.18.tar.gz`.

`mpatrol`
> A highly configurable memory debugging and testing package. See `http://www.cbmamiga.demon.co.uk/mpatrol`.

---

[20] `http://www.winehq.com`

[21] `http://valgrind.kde.org`

[22] `http://www.linuxjournal.com/article.php?sid=6059`

[23] `http://www.linuxjournal.com/article.php?sid=6556`

memwatch

> A package that requires the use of a special header file and compile-time options. See http://www.linkdata.se/sourcecode.html.

njamd

> Not Just Another Malloc Debugger. This library doesn't require special linking of the application; instead, it uses LD_PRELOAD to replace standard routines. See http://sourceforge.net/projects/njamd.

yamd

> Similar to Electric Fence, but with many more options. See http://www3.hmc.edu/~neldredge/yamd.

Almost all of these packages use environment variables to tune their behavior. Based on the *Linux Journal* articles, Table 15.1 summarizes the features of the different packages.

TABLE 15.1
Memory tool features summary

Tool	OS	Header	Module/Program	Thread safe
ccmalloc	Multivendor	No	Program	No
dmalloc	Multivendor	Optional	Program	Yes
efence	Multivendor	No	Program	No
memwatch	Multivendor	Yes	Program	No
Moraes	Multivendor	Optional	Program	No
mpatrol	Multivendor	No	Program	Yes
mtrace	Linux (GLIBC)	Yes	Module	No
njamd	Multivendor	No	Program	No
valgrind	Linux (GLIBC)	No	Program	Yes
yamd	Linux, DJGPP	No	Program	No

As is clear, a range of choices is available for debugging dynamic memory problems. On GNU/Linux and BSD systems, one or more of these tools are likely to already be installed, saving you the trouble of downloading and building them.

It is also useful to use multiple tools in succession on your program. For example, `mtrace` to catch unfreed memory, and Electric Fence to catch invalid memory accesses.

15.5.3 A Modern `lint`

In Original C, the compiler couldn't check whether the parameters passed in a function call matched the parameter list in the function's definition; there were no prototypes. This often led to subtle bugs since a bad function call might produce only mildly erroneous results, which went unnoticed during testing, or might not even get called at all during testing. For example:

```
if (argc < 2)
    fprintf("usage: %s [ options ] files\n", argv[0]);      stderr is missing
```

If a program containing this fragment is never invoked with the wrong number of arguments, the `fprintf()`, which is missing the initial `FILE *` argument, is never called.

The V7 `lint` program was designed to solve such problems. It made two passes over all the files in a program, first collecting information about function arguments and then comparing function calls to the gathered information. Special "`lint` library" files provided information about the standard library functions so that they could be checked as well. `lint` also checked other questionable constructs.

With prototypes in Standard C, the need for `lint` is decreased, but not eliminated, since C89 still allows old-style function declarations:

```
extern int some_func();            Argument list unknown
```

Additionally, many other aspects of a program can be checked *statically*, that is, by analysis of the source code text.

The `splint` program (Secure Programming Lint[24]), is a modern `lint` replacement. It provides too many options and facilities to list here, but is worth investigating.

One thing to be aware of is that `lint`-like programs can produce a flood of warning messages. Many of the reported warnings are really harmless. In such cases, the tools allow you to provide special comments that indicate "yes, I know about this, it's not a problem." `splint` works best when you provide lots of such annotations in your code.

`splint` is a powerful but complicated tool; spending some time learning how to use it and then using it frequently will help you keep your code clean.

----

[24] http://www.splint.org

15.6 Software Testing

Software development contains elements of both art and science; this is one aspect of what makes it such a fascinating and challenging profession. This section introduces the topic of software testing, which also involves both art and science; thus, it is somewhat more general and higher level (read: "handwavy") than the rest of this chapter.

Software testing is an integral part of the software development process. It is very unusual for a program to work 100 percent correctly the first time it compiles. The program isn't responsible for being correct; the *author* of the program is. One of the most important ways to verify that a program functions the way it's supposed to is to test it.

One way to break down the different kinds of testing is as follows:

Unit tests

These are tests you write for each separate unit or functional component of your program. As part of this effort, you may also need to write *scaffolding*—code designed to provide enough supporting framework to run the unit as a standalone program.

It is important to design the tests for each functional component *when you design the component*. Doing so helps you clarify the feature design; knowing how you'll test it helps you define what it should and shouldn't do in the first place.

Integration tests

These are tests you apply when all the functional components have been written, tested, and debugged individually. The idea is that everything is then hooked into place in the overall framework and the whole thing is tested to make sure that the interactions between the components are working.

Regression tests

Inevitably, you (or your users!) will discover problems. These may be real bugs, or design limitations, or failures in weird "corner cases." Once you've been able to reproduce and fix the problem, keep the original failing case as a regression test.

A regression test lets you make sure that when you make changes, you haven't reintroduced an old problem. (This can happen easily.) By running a program through its test suite after making a change, you can be (more) confident that everything is working the way it's supposed to.

Testing should be automated as much as possible. This is particularly easy to do for non-GUI programs written in the style of the Linux/Unix tools: programs that read standard input or named files, and write to standard output and standard error. At the very least, testing can be done with simple shell scripts. More involved testing is usually done with a separate `test` subdirectory and the `make` program.

Software testing is a whole subfield in itself, and we don't expect to do it justice here; rather our point is to make you aware that testing is an integral part of development and often the motivating factor for using your debugging skills! Here is a *very* brief summary list:

- Design the test along with the feature.

- Test boundary conditions: Make sure the feature works both inside and at valid boundaries and that it fails correctly outside them. (For example, the `sqrt()` function has to fail when given a negative argument.)

- Use assertions in your code (see Section 12.1, "Assertion Statements: `assert()`," page 428), and run your tests with the assertions enabled.

- Create and reuse test scaffolding.

- Save failure cases for regression testing.

- Automate testing as much as possible.

- Print a count of failed tests so that success or failure, and the degree of failure, can be determined easily.

- Use code coverage tools such as `gcov` to verify that your test suite exercises all of your code.

- Test early and test often.

- Study software-testing literature to improve your ability to develop and test software.

15.7 Debugging Rules

Debugging isn't a "black art." Its principles and techniques can be learned, and consistently applied, by anyone. To this end, we highly recommend the book *Debugging* by David J. Agans (ISBN: 0-8144-7168-4). The book has a web site[25] that summarizes the rules and provides a downloadable poster for you to print and place on your office wall.

To round off our discussion, we present the following material. It was adapted by David Agans, by permission, from *Debugging*, Copyright © 2002 David J. Agans, published by AMACOM,[26] a division of American Management Association, New York, New York. We thank him.

1. **Understand the system.** When all else fails, read the manual. You have to know what the troubled system and all of its parts are supposed to do, if you want to figure out why they don't. So read any and all documentation you can get your hands (or browser) on.

   Knowing where functional blocks and data paths are, and how they interact, gives you a roadmap for failure isolation. Of course, you also have to know your domain (language, operating system, application) and your tools (compiler, source code debugger).

2. **Make it fail.** In order to see the bug, you have to be able to make the failure occur consistently. Document your procedures and start from a known state, so that you can always make it fail again. Look at the bug on the system that fails, don't try to simulate the problem on another system. Don't trust statistics on intermittent problems; they will hide the bug more than they will expose it. Rather, try to make it consistent by varying inputs, and initial conditions, and timing.

   If it's still intermittent, you have to make it look like it's not. Capture in a log every bit of information you can, during every run; then when you have some bad runs and some good runs, compare them to each other. If you've captured enough data you'll be able to home in on the problem as if you could make it fail every time. Being able to make it fail every time also means you'll be able to tell when you've fixed it.

3. **Quit thinking and look.** There are more ways for something to fail than you can possibly imagine. So don't imagine what could be happening, look at

---

[25] http://www.debuggingrules.com

[26] http://www.amacombooks.org

it—put instrumentation on the system so you can actually see the failure mechanism. Use whatever instrumentation you can—debuggers, `printf()`s, `assert()`s, logic analyzers, and even LEDs and beepers. Look at it deeply enough until the bug is obvious to the eye, not just to the brain.

If you do guess, use the guess only to focus the search—don't try to fix it until you can see it. If you have to add instrumentation code, do it, but be sure to start with the same code base as the failing system, and make sure it still fails with your added code running. Often, adding the debugger makes it stop failing (that's why they call it a debugger).

4. **Divide and conquer.** Everybody knows this one. You do a successive approximation—start at one end, jump halfway, see which way the error is from there, and jump half again in that direction. Binary search, you're there in a few jumps. The hard part is knowing whether you're past the bug or not. One helpful trick is to put known, simple data into the system, so that trashed data is easier to spot. Also, start at the bad end and work back toward the good: there are too many good paths to explore if you start at the good end. Fix the bugs you know about right away, since sometimes two bugs interact (though you'd swear they can't), and successive approximation doesn't work with two target values.

5. **Change one thing at a time.** If you're trying to improve a stream-handling module and you simultaneously upgrade to the next version of the operating system, it doesn't matter whether you see improvement, degradation, or no change—you will have no idea what effect your individual changes had. The interaction of multiple changes can be unpredictable and confusing. Don't do it. Change one thing at a time, so you can bet that any difference you see as a result came from that change.

If you make a change and it seems to have no effect, back it out immediately. It may have had some effects that you didn't see, and those may show up in combination with other changes. This goes for changes in testing as well as in coding.

6. **Keep an audit trail.** Much of the effectiveness of the above rules depends on keeping good records. In all aspects of testing and debugging, write down what you did, when you did it, how you did it, and what happened as a result. Do

it electronically if possible, so that the record can be emailed and attached to the bug database. Many a clue is found in a pattern of events that would not be noticed if it wasn't recorded for all to see and compare. And the clue is likely to be in the details that you didn't think were important, so write it all down.

7. **Check the plug.** Everyone has a story about some problem that turned out to be "it wasn't plugged in." Sometimes it's literally unplugged, but in software, "unplugged" can mean a missing driver or an old version of code you thought you replaced. Or bad hardware when you swear it's a software problem. One story had the hardware and software engineers pointing fingers at each other, and it was neither: The test device they were using was not up to spec. The bottom line is that sometimes you're looking for a problem inside a system, when in fact the problem is outside the system, or underlying the system, or in the initialization of the system, or you're not looking at the right system.

Don't necessarily trust your tools, either. The tool vendors are engineers, too; they have bugs, and you may be the one to find them.

8. **Get a fresh view.** There are three reasons to ask for help while debugging.

The first reason is to get fresh insight—another person will often see something just because they aren't caught up in it like you are. The second reason is to tap expertise—they know more about the system than you do. The third reason is to get experience—they've seen this one before.

When you describe the situation to someone, report the symptoms you've seen, not your theories about why it's acting that way. You went to them because your theories aren't getting you anywhere—don't pull them down into the same rut you're stuck in.

9. **If you didn't fix it, it ain't fixed.** So you think it's fixed? Prove it. Since you were able to make it fail consistently, set up the same situation and make sure it doesn't fail. Don't assume that just because the problem was obvious, it's all fixed now. Maybe it wasn't so obvious. Maybe your fix wasn't done right. Maybe your fix isn't even in the new release! Test it! Make it not fail.

Are you sure your code is what fixed it? Or did the test change, or did some other code get in there? Once you see that your fix works, take the fix out and make it fail again. Then put the fix back in and see that it doesn't fail. This step assures you that it was really your fix that solved the problem.

More information about the book *Debugging* and a free downloadable debugging rules poster can be found at `http://www.debuggingrules.com`.

15.8 Suggested Reading

The following books are excellent, with much to say about both testing and debugging. All but the first relate to programming in general. They're all worth reading.

1. *Debugging*, David J. Agans. AMACOM, New York, New York, USA 2003. ISBN: 0-8144-7168-4.

    We highly recommend this book. Its tone is light, and amazing as it sounds, it's fun reading!

2. *Programming Pearls*, 2nd edition, by Jon Louis Bentley. Addison-Wesley, Reading, Massachusetts, USA, 2000. ISBN: 0-201-65788-0. See also this book's web site.[27]

    Chapter 5 of this book gives a good discussion of unit testing and building test scaffolding.

3. *Literate Programming*, by Donald E. Knuth. Center for the Study of Language and Information (CSLI), Stanford University, USA, 1992. ISBN: 0-9370-7380-6.

    This fascinating book contains a number of articles by Donald Knuth on *literate programming*—a programming technique he invented, and used for the creation of TEX and Metafont. Of particular interest is the article entitled "The Errors of TEX," which describes how he developed and debugged TEX, including his log of all the problems found and fixed.

4. *Writing Solid Code*, by Steve Maguire. Microsoft Press, Redmond, Washington, USA, 1993. ISBN: 1-55615-551-4.

---

[27] `http://www.cs.bell-labs.com/cm/cs/pearls/`

5. *Code Complete: A Practical Handbook of Software Construction*, by Steve McConnell. Microsoft Press, Redmond, Washington, USA, 1994. ISBN: 1-55615-484-4.

6. *The Practice of Programming*, by Brian W. Kernighan and Rob Pike. Addison-Wesley, Reading, Massachusetts, USA, 1999. ISBN: 0-201-61585-X.

15.9 Summary

- Debugging is an important part of software development. Good design and development practices should be used to minimize the introduction of bugs, but debugging will always be with us.

- Programs should be compiled without optimization and with debugging symbols included to make debugging under a debugger more straightforward. On many systems, compiling with optimization and compiling with debugging symbols are mutually exclusive. This is not true of GCC, which is why the GNU/Linux developer needs to be aware of the issue.

- The GNU debugger GDB is standard on GNU/Linux systems and can be used on just about any commercial Unix system as well. (Graphical debuggers based on GDB are also available and easily portable.) Breakpoints, watchpoints, and single-stepping with `next`, `step`, and `cont` provide basic control over a program as it's running. GDB also lets you examine data and call functions within the debuggee.

- There are many things you can do when writing your program to make it easier when you inevitably have to debug it. We covered the following topics:
  - Debugging macros for printing state.
  - Avoiding expression macros.
  - Reordering code to make single-stepping easier.
  - Writing helper functions for use from a debugger.
  - Avoiding `unions`.
  - Having runtime debugging code in the production version of a program and having different ways to enable that code's output.

- Adding dummy functions to make breakpoints easier to set.

- A number of tools and libraries besides just general-purpose debuggers exist to help with debugging. The dbug library provides a nice internal debugger that uses many of the techniques we described, in a consistent, coherent way.

- Multiple dynamic memory debugging libraries exist, with many similar features. We looked at three of them (mtrace, Electric Fence, and dmalloc), and provided pointers to several others. The Valgrind program goes further, finding problems related to uninitialized memory, not just dynamic memory.

- splint is a modern alternative to the venerable V7 lint program. It is available on at least one vendor's GNU/Linux system and can be easily downloaded and built from source.

- Besides debugging tools, software testing is also an integral part of the software development process. It should be understood, planned for, and managed from the beginning of any software development project, even personal ones.

- Debugging is a skill that can be learned. We recommend reading the book *Debugging* by David J. Agans and learning to apply his rules.

Exercises

1. Compile one of your programs with GCC, using both -g and -O. Run it under GDB, setting a breakpoint in main(). Single-step through the program, and see how closely execution relates (or doesn't relate) to the original source code. This is particularly good to do with code using a while or for loop.

2. Read up on GDB's *conditional breakpoint* feature. How does that simplify dealing with problems that occur only after a certain number of operations have been done?

3. Rewrite the parse_debug() function from Section 15.4.2.1, "Add Debugging Options and Variables," page 595, to use a table of debugging option strings, flag values, and string lengths.

4. (Hard.) Study the gawk source code; in particular the NODE structure in awk.h. Write a debugging helper function that prints the contents of a NODE based on the value in the type field.

5. Take one of your programs and modify it to use the dbug library. Compile it first without -DDBUG, to make sure it compiles and works OK. (Do you have a regression test suite for it? Did your program pass all the tests?)

    Once you're sure that adding the dbug library has not broken your program, recompile it with -DDBUG. Does your program still pass all its tests? What is the performance difference with the library enabled and disabled?

    Run your test suite with the -#t option to see the function-call trace. Do you think this will help you in the future when you have to do debugging? Why or why not?

6. Run one of your programs that uses dynamic memory with Electric Fence or one of the other dynamic memory testers. Describe the problems, if any, that you found.

7. Rerun the same program, using Valgrind with leak checking enabled. Describe the problems, if any, that you found.

8. Design a set of tests for the mv program. (Read *mv*(1): make sure you cover all its options.)

9. Search on the Internet for software testing resources. What interesting things did you find?

Chapter 16

A Project That Ties Everything Together

In this chapter

For the first half of this book, we tied together everything that had been presented, rather neatly, by looking at the V7 `ls.c`. However, as much as we would like to have it, there is no single program, small enough to present here, for tying together the concepts and APIs presented starting with Chapter 8, "Filesystems and Directory Walks," page 227.

16.1 Project Description

In day-to-day use, the one program that does use just about everything in the book is the shell. And indeed, there are Unix programming books that write a small but working shell to illustrate the principles involved.

Real shells are large and messy creatures. They must deal with many portability issues, such as we've outlined throughout the book, and above and beyond that, they often have to work around bugs in different versions of Unix. Furthermore, to be useful, shells do many things that don't involve the system call API, such as maintaining shell variables, a history of saved commands, and so on. Providing a complete tour of a full-featured shell such as Bash, `ksh93`, or `zsh` would take a separate volume.

Instead, we suggest the following list of steps for writing your own shell, either as a (large) exercise to cement your understanding or perhaps as a cooperative project if you're in school.

1. Design your command "language" so that it will be easy to interpret with simple code. While compiler and interpreter technology is valuable when writing a production shell, it's likely to be overkill for you at this stage.

   Consider the following points:

   - Are you going to use i18n facilities?

   - What commands must be built in to the shell?

   - To be useful, your shell will need a command search path mechanism, analogous to $PATH of the regular shell. How will you set it?

   - What I/O redirections do you wish to support? Files only? Pipes too? Do you wish to be able to redirect more than file descriptors 0, 1, and 2?

   - Decide how quoting will work: single and double quotes? Or only one kind? How do you quote a quote? How does quoting interact with I/O redirections?

- How will you handle putting commands in the background? What about waiting for a command in the background to finish?

- Decide whether you will have shell variables.

- What kind of wildcarding or other expansions will you support? How do they interact with quoting? With shell variables?

- You should plan for at least an `if` and a `while` statement. Design a syntax. We will call these *block statements*.

- Decide whether or not you wish to allow I/O redirection for a block statement. If yes, what will the syntax look like?

- Decide how, if at all, your shell language should handle signals.

- Design a testing and debugging framework *before* you start to code.

2. If you're going to use i18n facilities, do so from the outset. Retrofitting them in is painful.

3. For the real work, start simply. The initial version should read one line at a time and break it into words to use as separate arguments. Don't do any quoting, I/O redirection, or anything else. Don't even try to create a new process to run the entered program. How are you going to test what you have so far?

4. Add quoting so that individual "words" can contain whitespace. Does the quoting code implement your design?

5. Make your built-in commands work. (See Section 4.6, "Creating Files," page 106, and Section 8.4.1, "Changing Directory: `chdir()` and `fchdir()`," page 256, for at least two necessary built-in commands.) How are you going to test them?

6. Initially, use a fixed search path, such as `"/bin:/usr/bin:/usr/local/bin"`. Add process creation with `fork()` and execution with `exec()` (see Chapter 9, "Process Management and Pipes," page 283). Starting out, the shell should wait for each new program to finish.

7. Add backgrounding and, as a separate command, waiting for process completion (see Chapter 9, "Process Management and Pipes," page 283).

8. Add a user-settable search path (see Section 2.4, "The Environment," page 40).

9. Add I/O redirection for files (see Section 9.4, "File Descriptor Management," page 320).

10. Add shell variables. Test their interaction with quoting.

11. Add wildcard and any other expansions (see Section 12.7, "Metacharacter Expansions," page 461). Test their interaction with shell variables. Test their interaction with quoting.

12. Add pipelines (see Section 9.3, "Basic Interprocess Communication: Pipes and FIFOs," page 315). At this point, real complexity starts to settle in. You may need to take a hard look at how you're managing data that represents commands to be run.

    You could stop here with a legitimate feeling of accomplishment if you get a working shell that can do everything mentioned so far.

13. If you're up for a further challenge, add `if` and/or `while` statements.

14. Add signal handling (see Chapter 10, "Signals," page 347).

15. If you'd like to use your shell for real work, explore the GNU Readline library (type '`info readline`' on a GNU/Linux system or see the source for the Bash shell). This library lets you add either Emacs-style or `vi`-style command-line editing to interactive programs.

Keep two things constantly in mind: always be able to test what you're doing; and "no arbitrary limits!"

Once it's done, do a post-mortem analysis of the project. How would you do it differently the second time?

Good luck!

16.2 Suggested Reading

1. *The UNIX Programming Environment*, by Brian W. Kernighan and Rob Pike. Prentice-Hall, Englewood Cliffs, New Jersey, USA, 1984. ISBN: 0-13-937699-2.

   This is the classic book on Unix programming, describing the entire gestalt of the Unix environment, from interactive use, to shell programming, to programming with the `<stdio.h>` functions and the lower-level system calls, to program development with `make`, `yacc`, and `lex`, and documentation with `nroff` and `troff`.

Although the book shows its age, it is still eminently worth reading, and we highly recommend it.

2. *The Art of UNIX Programming*, by Eric S. Raymond. Addison-Wesley, Reading, Massachusetts, USA, 2004. ISBN: 0-13-142901-9.

    This is a higher-level book that focuses on the design issues in Unix programming: how Unix programs work and how to design your own programs to fit comfortably into a Linux/Unix environment.

    While we don't always agree with much of what the author has to say, the book does have considerable important material and is worth reading.

Part — IV

Appendixes

647

Teach Yourself Programming in Ten Years

"Experience, n: Something you don't get until just after you
need it."
—Olivier—

This chapter is written by and Copyright © 2001 by Peter Norvig. Reprinted by permission. The original article, including hyperlinks, is at `http://www.norvig.com/21-days.html`. We have included it because we believe that it conveys an important message. The above quote is one of our long-time favorites, and as it applies to the point of this appendix, we've included it too.

Why Is Everyone in Such a Rush?

Walk into any bookstore, and you'll see how to *Teach Yourself Java in 7 Days* alongside endless variations offering to teach Visual Basic, Windows, the Internet, and so on in a few days or hours. I did the following power search at Amazon.com:

```
pubdate: after 1992 and title: days and
(title: learn or title: teach yourself)
```

and got back 248 hits. The first 78 were computer books (number 79 was *Learn Bengali in 30 days*). I replaced "days" with "hours" and got remarkably similar results: 253 more books, with 77 computer books followed by *Teach Yourself Grammar and Style in 24 Hours* at number 78. Out of the top 200 total, 96% were computer books.

The conclusion is that either people are in a big rush to learn about computers, or that computers are somehow fabulously easier to learn than anything else. There are no books on how to learn Beethoven, or Quantum Physics, or even Dog Grooming in a few days.

Let's analyze what a title like *Learn Pascal in Three Days* could mean:

- **Learn:** In 3 days you won't have time to write several significant programs, and learn from your successes and failures with them. You won't have time to work with an experienced programmer and understand what it is like to live in that environment. In short, you won't have time to learn much. So they can only be talking about a superficial familiarity, not a deep understanding. As Alexander Pope said, a little learning is a dangerous thing.

- **Pascal:** In 3 days you might be able to learn the syntax of Pascal (if you already knew a similar language), but you couldn't learn much about how to use the syntax. In short, if you were, say, a Basic programmer, you could learn to write programs in the style of Basic using Pascal syntax, but you couldn't learn what Pascal is actually good (and bad) for. So what's the point? Alan Perlis once said: "A language that doesn't affect the way you think about programming, is not worth knowing." One possible point is that you have to learn a tiny bit of Pascal (or more likely, something like Visual Basic or JavaScript) because you need to interface with an existing tool to accomplish a specific task. But then you're not learning how to program; you're learning to accomplish that task.

- **in Three Days:** Unfortunately, this is not enough, as the next section shows.

Teach Yourself Programming in Ten Years

Researchers (Hayes, Bloom) have shown it takes about ten years to develop expertise in any of a wide variety of areas, including chess playing, music composition, painting, piano playing, swimming, tennis, and research in neuropsychology and topology. There appear to be no real shortcuts: even Mozart, who was a musical prodigy at age 4, took 13 more years before he began to produce world-class music. In another genre, the Beatles seemed to burst onto the scene, appearing on the Ed Sullivan show in 1964. But they had been playing since 1957, and while they had mass appeal early on, their first great critical success, *Sgt. Peppers*, was released in 1967. Samuel Johnson thought it took longer than ten years: "Excellence in any department can be attained only by the labor of a lifetime; it is not to be purchased at a lesser price." And Chaucer complained "the lyf so short, the craft so long to lerne."

Here's my recipe for programming success:

- Get interested in programming, and do some because it is fun. Make sure that it keeps being enough fun so that you will be willing to put in ten years.

- Talk to other programmers; read other programs. This is more important than any book or training course.

- Program. The best kind of learning is learning by doing. To put it more technically, "the maximal level of performance for individuals in a given domain is not attained automatically as a function of extended experience, but the level of performance can be increased even by highly experienced individuals as a result of deliberate efforts to improve" (p. 366) and "the most effective learning requires a well-defined task with an appropriate difficulty level for the particular individual, informative feedback, and opportunities for repetition and corrections of errors." (p. 20–21) The book *Cognition in Practice: Mind, Mathematics, and Culture in Everyday Life* is an interesting reference for this viewpoint.

- If you want, put in four years at a college (or more at a graduate school). This will give you access to some jobs that require credentials, and it will give you a deeper understanding of the field, but if you don't enjoy school, you can (with some dedication) get similar experience on the job. In any case, book learning alone won't be enough. "Computer science education cannot make anybody an expert programmer any more than studying brushes and pigment can make somebody an expert painter" says Eric Raymond, author of *The New Hacker's Dictionary*. One of the best programmers I ever hired had only a High School degree; he's produced a lot of great software, has his own news group, and through stock options is no doubt much richer than I'll ever be.

- Work on projects with other programmers. Be the best programmer on some projects; be the worst on some others. When you're the best, you get to test your abilities to lead a project, and to inspire others with your vision. When you're the worst, you learn what the masters do, and you learn what they don't like to do (because they make you do it for them).

- Work on projects *after* other programmers. Be involved in understanding a program written by someone else. See what it takes to understand and fix it when the original programmers are not around. Think about how to design your programs to make it easier for those who will maintain it after you.

- Learn at least a half dozen programming languages. Include one language that supports class abstractions (like Java or C++), one that supports functional abstraction (like Lisp or ML), one that supports syntactic abstraction (like Lisp), one that supports declarative specifications (like Prolog or C++ templates), one that supports coroutines (like Icon or Scheme), and one that supports parallelism (like Sisal).

- Remember that there is a "computer" in "computer science." Know how long it takes your computer to execute an instruction, fetch a word from memory (with and without a cache miss), read consecutive words from disk, and seek to a new location on disk. (Answers below.)

- Get involved in a language standardization effort. It could be the ANSI C++ committee, or it could be deciding if your local coding style will have 2 or 4 space indentation levels. Either way, you learn about what other people like in a language, how deeply they feel so, and perhaps even a little about why they feel so.

- Have the good sense to get off the language standardization effort as quickly as possible.

With all that in mind, its questionable how far you can get just by book learning. Before my first child was born, I read all the *How To* books, and still felt like a clueless novice. 30 months later, when my second child was due, did I go back to the books for a refresher? No. Instead, I relied on my personal experience, which turned out to be far more useful and reassuring to me than the thousands of pages written by experts.

Fred Brooks, in his essay *No Silver Bullets* identified a three-part plan for finding great software designers:

1. Systematically identify top designers as early as possible.

2. Assign a career mentor to be responsible for the development of the prospect and carefully keep a career file.

3. Provide opportunities for growing designers to interact and stimulate each other.

This assumes that some people already have the qualities necessary for being a great designer; the job is to properly coax them along. Alan Perlis put it more succinctly: "Everyone can be taught to sculpt: Michelangelo would have had to be taught how not to. So it is with the great programmers."

So go ahead and buy that Java book; you'll probably get some use out of it. But you won't change your life, or your real overall expertise as a programmer in 24 hours, days, or even months.

References

Bloom, Benjamin (ed.) *Developing Talent in Young People*, Ballantine, 1985.

Brooks, Fred, *No Silver Bullets*, IEEE Computer, vol. 20, no. 4, 1987, p. 10–19.

Hayes, John R., *Complete Problem Solver*, Lawrence Erlbaum, 1989.

Lave, Jean, *Cognition in Practice: Mind, Mathematics, and Culture in Everyday Life*, Cambridge University Press, 1988.

Answers

Timing for various operations on a typical 1GHz PC in summer 2001:

execute single instruction	1 nsec = (1/1,000,000,000) sec
fetch word from L1 cache memory	2 nsec
fetch word from main memory	10 nsec
fetch word from consecutive disk location	200 nsec
fetch word from new disk location (seek)	8,000,000nsec = 8msec

Footnotes

This page[1] also available in Japanese translation[2] thanks to Yasushi Murakawa and in Spanish translation[3] thanks to Carlos Rueda.

T. Capey points out that the *Complete Problem Solver* page on Amazon now has the *Teach Yourself Bengali in 21 days* and *Teach Yourself Grammar and Style* books under the "Customers who shopped for this item also shopped for these items" section. I guess that a large portion of the people who look at that book are coming from this page.

---

[1]   This appendix is quoted verbatim from the web page cited at its beginning.

[2]   http://www1.neweb.ne.jp/wa/yamdas/column/technique/21-daysj.html

[3]   http://loro.sf.net/notes/21-dias.html

B

Caldera Ancient UNIX License

CALDERA

240 West Center Street
Orem, Utah 84057
801-765-4999 Fax 801-765-4481

January 23, 2002

Dear UNIX® enthusiasts,

Caldera International, Inc. hereby grants a fee free license that includes the rights use, modify and distribute this named source code, including creating derived binary products created from the source code. The source code for which Caldera International, Inc. grants rights are limited to the following UNIX Operating Systems that operate on the 16-Bit PDP-11 CPU and early versions of the 32-Bit UNIX Operating System, with specific exclusion of UNIX System III and UNIX System V and successor operating systems:

    32-bit 32V UNIX
    16 bit UNIX Versions 1, 2, 3, 4, 5, 6, 7

Caldera International, Inc. makes no guarantees or commitments that any source code is available from Caldera International, Inc.

The following copyright notice applies to the source code files for which this license is granted.

Copyright(C) Caldera International Inc. 2001-2002. All rights reserved.

Redistribution and use in source and binary forms, with or without modification, are permitted provided that the following conditions are met:

Redistributions of source code and documentation must retain the above copyright notice, this list of conditions and the following disclaimer. Redistributions in binary form must reproduce the above copyright notice, this list of conditions and the following disclaimer in the documentation and/or other materials provided with the distribution.

All advertising materials mentioning features or use of this software must display the following acknowledgement:

This product includes software developed or owned by Caldera International, Inc.

Neither the name of Caldera International, Inc. nor the names of other contributors may be used to endorse or promote products derived from this software without specific prior written permission.

USE OF THE SOFTWARE PROVIDED FOR UNDER THIS LICENSE BY CALDERA INTERNATIONAL, INC. AND CONTRIBUTORS "AS IS" AND ANY EXPRESS OR IMPLIED WARRANTIES, INCLUDING, BUT NOT LIMITED TO, THE IMPLIED WARRANTIES OF MERCHANTABILITY AND FITNESS FOR A PARTICULAR PURPOSE ARE DISCLAIMED. IN NO EVENT SHALL CALDERA INTERNATIONAL, INC. BE LIABLE FOR ANY DIRECT, INDIRECT INCIDENTAL, SPECIAL, EXEMPLARY, OR CONSEQUENTIAL DAMAGES (INCLUDING, BUT NOT LIMITED TO, PROCUREMENT OF SUBSTITUTE GOODS OR SERVICES; LOSS OF USE, DATA, OR PROFITS; OR BUSINESS INTERRUPTION) HOWEVER CAUSED AND ON ANY THEORY OF LIABILITY, WHETHER IN CONTRACT, STRICT LIABILITY, OR TORT (INCLUDING NEGLIGENCE OR OTHERWISE) ARISING IN ANY WAY OUT OF THE USE OF THIS SOFTWARE, EVEN IF ADVISED OF THE POSSIBILITY OF SUCH DAMAGE.

Very truly yours,

/signed/ Bill Broderick

Bill Broderick
Director, Licensing Services

* UNIX is a registered trademark of The Open Group in the US and other countries.

C

GNU
General Public
License

Version 2, June 1991

Preamble

The licenses for most software are designed to take away your freedom to share and change it. By contrast, the GNU General Public License is intended to guarantee your freedom to share and change free software—to make sure the software is free for all its users. This General Public License applies to most of the Free Software Foundation's software and to any other program whose authors commit to using it. (Some other Free

Software Foundation software is covered by the GNU Library General Public License instead.) You can apply it to your programs, too.

When we speak of free software, we are referring to freedom, not price. Our General Public Licenses are designed to make sure that you have the freedom to distribute copies of free software (and charge for this service if you wish), that you receive source code or can get it if you want it, that you can change the software or use pieces of it in new free programs; and that you know you can do these things.

To protect your rights, we need to make restrictions that forbid anyone to deny you these rights or to ask you to surrender the rights. These restrictions translate to certain responsibilities for you if you distribute copies of the software, or if you modify it.

For example, if you distribute copies of such a program, whether gratis or for a fee, you must give the recipients all the rights that you have. You must make sure that they, too, receive or can get the source code. And you must show them these terms so they know their rights.

We protect your rights with two steps: (1) copyright the software, and (2) offer you this license which gives you legal permission to copy, distribute and/or modify the software.

Also, for each author's protection and ours, we want to make certain that everyone understands that there is no warranty for this free software. If the software is modified by someone else and passed on, we want its recipients to know that what they have is not the original, so that any problems introduced by others will not reflect on the original authors' reputations.

Finally, any free program is threatened constantly by software patents. We wish to avoid the danger that redistributors of a free program will individually obtain patent licenses, in effect making the program proprietary. To prevent this, we have made it clear that any patent must be licensed for everyone's free use or not licensed at all.

The precise terms and conditions for copying, distribution and modification follow.

Terms and Conditions for Copying, Distribution and Modification

   0.   This License applies to any program or other work which contains a notice placed by the copyright holder saying it may be distributed under the terms of this General Public License. The "Program", below, refers to any such program

or work, and a "work based on the Program" means either the Program or any derivative work under copyright law: that is to say, a work containing the Program or a portion of it, either verbatim or with modifications and/or translated into another language. (Hereinafter, translation is included without limitation in the term "modification".) Each licensee is addressed as "you".

Activities other than copying, distribution and modification are not covered by this License; they are outside its scope. The act of running the Program is not restricted, and the output from the Program is covered only if its contents constitute a work based on the Program (independent of having been made by running the Program). Whether that is true depends on what the Program does.

1. You may copy and distribute verbatim copies of the Program's source code as you receive it, in any medium, provided that you conspicuously and appropriately publish on each copy an appropriate copyright notice and disclaimer of warranty; keep intact all the notices that refer to this License and to the absence of any warranty; and give any other recipients of the Program a copy of this License along with the Program.

   You may charge a fee for the physical act of transferring a copy, and you may at your option offer warranty protection in exchange for a fee.

2. You may modify your copy or copies of the Program or any portion of it, thus forming a work based on the Program, and copy and distribute such modifications or work under the terms of Section 1 above, provided that you also meet all of these conditions:

   a. You must cause the modified files to carry prominent notices stating that you changed the files and the date of any change.

   b. You must cause any work that you distribute or publish, that in whole or in part contains or is derived from the Program or any part thereof, to be licensed as a whole at no charge to all third parties under the terms of this License.

   c. If the modified program normally reads commands interactively when run, you must cause it, when started running for such interactive use in the most ordinary way, to print or display an announcement including an appropriate copyright notice and a notice that there is no warranty (or else, saying that you provide a warranty) and that users may redistribute the program under these conditions, and telling the user how to view a copy of this License. (Exception: if the Program itself is interactive but does not normally print such an announcement, your work based on the Program is not required to print an announcement.)

These requirements apply to the modified work as a whole. If identifiable sections of that work are not derived from the Program, and can be reasonably considered independent and separate works in themselves, then this License, and its terms, do not apply to those sections when you distribute them as separate works. But when you distribute the same sections as part of a whole which is a work based on the Program, the distribution of the whole must be on the terms of this License, whose permissions for other licensees extend to the entire whole, and thus to each and every part regardless of who wrote it.

Thus, it is not the intent of this section to claim rights or contest your rights to work written entirely by you; rather, the intent is to exercise the right to control the distribution of derivative or collective works based on the Program.

In addition, mere aggregation of another work not based on the Program with the Program (or with a work based on the Program) on a volume of a storage or distribution medium does not bring the other work under the scope of this License.

3. You may copy and distribute the Program (or a work based on it, under Section 2) in object code or executable form under the terms of Sections 1 and 2 above provided that you also do one of the following:

   a. Accompany it with the complete corresponding machine-readable source code, which must be distributed under the terms of Sections 1 and 2 above on a medium customarily used for software interchange; or,

   b. Accompany it with a written offer, valid for at least three years, to give any third party, for a charge no more than your cost of physically performing source distribution, a complete machine-readable copy of the corresponding source code, to be distributed under the terms of Sections 1 and 2 above on a medium customarily used for software interchange; or,

   c. Accompany it with the information you received as to the offer to distribute corresponding source code. (This alternative is allowed only for noncommercial distribution and only if you received the program in object code or executable form with such an offer, in accord with Subsection b above.)

The source code for a work means the preferred form of the work for making modifications to it. For an executable work, complete source code means all the source code for all modules it contains, plus any associated interface definition files, plus the scripts used to control compilation and installation of the executable. However, as a special exception, the source code distributed need not include anything that is normally distributed (in either source or binary form) with the major components (compiler, kernel, and so on) of the operating system on which the executable runs, unless that component itself accompanies the executable.

If distribution of executable or object code is made by offering access to copy from a designated place, then offering equivalent access to copy the source code from the same place counts as distribution of the source code, even though third parties are not compelled to copy the source along with the object code.

4. You may not copy, modify, sublicense, or distribute the Program except as expressly provided under this License. Any attempt otherwise to copy, modify, sublicense or distribute the Program is void, and will automatically terminate your rights under this License. However, parties who have received copies, or rights, from you under this License will not have their licenses terminated so long as such parties remain in full compliance.

5. You are not required to accept this License, since you have not signed it. However, nothing else grants you permission to modify or distribute the Program or its derivative works. These actions are prohibited by law if you do not accept this License. Therefore, by modifying or distributing the Program (or any work based on the Program), you indicate your acceptance of this License to do so, and all its terms and conditions for copying, distributing or modifying the Program or works based on it.

6. Each time you redistribute the Program (or any work based on the Program), the recipient automatically receives a license from the original licensor to copy, distribute or modify the Program subject to these terms and conditions. You may not impose any further restrictions on the recipients' exercise of the rights

granted herein. You are not responsible for enforcing compliance by third parties to this License.

7. If, as a consequence of a court judgment or allegation of patent infringement or for any other reason (not limited to patent issues), conditions are imposed on you (whether by court order, agreement or otherwise) that contradict the conditions of this License, they do not excuse you from the conditions of this License. If you cannot distribute so as to satisfy simultaneously your obligations under this License and any other pertinent obligations, then as a consequence you may not distribute the Program at all. For example, if a patent license would not permit royalty-free redistribution of the Program by all those who receive copies directly or indirectly through you, then the only way you could satisfy both it and this License would be to refrain entirely from distribution of the Program.

    If any portion of this section is held invalid or unenforceable under any particular circumstance, the balance of the section is intended to apply and the section as a whole is intended to apply in other circumstances.

    It is not the purpose of this section to induce you to infringe any patents or other property right claims or to contest validity of any such claims; this section has the sole purpose of protecting the integrity of the free software distribution system, which is implemented by public license practices. Many people have made generous contributions to the wide range of software distributed through that system in reliance on consistent application of that system; it is up to the author/donor to decide if he or she is willing to distribute software through any other system and a licensee cannot impose that choice.

    This section is intended to make thoroughly clear what is believed to be a consequence of the rest of this License.

8. If the distribution and/or use of the Program is restricted in certain countries either by patents or by copyrighted interfaces, the original copyright holder who places the Program under this License may add an explicit geographical distribution limitation excluding those countries, so that distribution is permitted only in or among countries not thus excluded. In such case, this License incorporates the limitation as if written in the body of this License.

9. The Free Software Foundation may publish revised and/or new versions of the General Public License from time to time. Such new versions will be similar in spirit to the present version, but may differ in detail to address new problems or concerns.

   Each version is given a distinguishing version number. If the Program specifies a version number of this License which applies to it and "any later version", you have the option of following the terms and conditions either of that version or of any later version published by the Free Software Foundation. If the Program does not specify a version number of this License, you may choose any version ever published by the Free Software Foundation.

10. If you wish to incorporate parts of the Program into other free programs whose distribution conditions are different, write to the author to ask for permission. For software which is copyrighted by the Free Software Foundation, write to the Free Software Foundation; we sometimes make exceptions for this. Our decision will be guided by the two goals of preserving the free status of all derivatives of our free software and of promoting the sharing and reuse of software generally.

NO WARRANTY

11. BECAUSE THE PROGRAM IS LICENSED FREE OF CHARGE, THERE IS NO WARRANTY FOR THE PROGRAM, TO THE EXTENT PERMITTED BY APPLICABLE LAW. EXCEPT WHEN OTHERWISE STATED IN WRITING THE COPYRIGHT HOLDERS AND/OR OTHER PARTIES PROVIDE THE PROGRAM "AS IS" WITHOUT WARRANTY OF ANY KIND, EITHER EXPRESSED OR IMPLIED, INCLUDING, BUT NOT LIMITED TO, THE IMPLIED WARRANTIES OF MERCHANTABILITY AND FITNESS FOR A PARTICULAR PURPOSE. THE ENTIRE RISK AS TO THE QUALITY AND PERFORMANCE OF THE PROGRAM IS WITH YOU. SHOULD THE PROGRAM PROVE DEFECTIVE, YOU ASSUME THE COST OF ALL NECESSARY SERVICING, REPAIR OR CORRECTION.

12. IN NO EVENT UNLESS REQUIRED BY APPLICABLE LAW OR AGREED TO IN WRITING WILL ANY COPYRIGHT HOLDER, OR

ANY OTHER PARTY WHO MAY MODIFY AND/OR REDISTRIBUTE
THE PROGRAM AS PERMITTED ABOVE, BE LIABLE TO YOU FOR
DAMAGES, INCLUDING ANY GENERAL, SPECIAL, INCIDENTAL
OR CONSEQUENTIAL DAMAGES ARISING OUT OF THE USE OR
INABILITY TO USE THE PROGRAM (INCLUDING BUT NOT LIMIT-
ED TO LOSS OF DATA OR DATA BEING RENDERED INACCURATE
OR LOSSES SUSTAINED BY YOU OR THIRD PARTIES OR A FAILURE
OF THE PROGRAM TO OPERATE WITH ANY OTHER PROGRAMS),
EVEN IF SUCH HOLDER OR OTHER PARTY HAS BEEN ADVISED
OF THE POSSIBILITY OF SUCH DAMAGES.

END OF TERMS AND CONDITIONS

How to Apply These Terms to Your New Programs

If you develop a new program, and you want it to be of the greatest possible use to
the public, the best way to achieve this is to make it free software which everyone can
redistribute and change under these terms.

To do so, attach the following notices to the program. It is safest to attach them to
the start of each source file to most effectively convey the exclusion of warranty; and
each file should have at least the "copyright" line and a pointer to where the full notice
is found.

```
one line to give the program's name and an idea of what it does.
Copyright (C) year  name of author

This program is free software; you can redistribute it and/or
modify it under the terms of the GNU General Public License
as published by the Free Software Foundation; either version 2
of the License, or (at your option) any later version.

This program is distributed in the hope that it will be useful,
but WITHOUT ANY WARRANTY; without even the implied warranty of
MERCHANTABILITY or FITNESS FOR A PARTICULAR PURPOSE.  See the
GNU General Public License for more details.

You should have received a copy of the GNU General Public License
along with this program; if not, write to the Free Software
Foundation, Inc., 59 Temple Place, Suite 330, Boston, MA 02111, USA.
```

Also add information on how to contact you by electronic and paper mail.

If the program is interactive, make it output a short notice like this when it starts in an interactive mode:

```
Gnomovision version 69, Copyright (C) year name of author
Gnomovision comes with ABSOLUTELY NO WARRANTY; for details
type `show w'.  This is free software, and you are welcome
to redistribute it under certain conditions; type `show c'
for details.
```

The hypothetical commands 'show w' and 'show c' should show the appropriate parts of the General Public License. Of course, the commands you use may be called something other than 'show w' and 'show c'; they could even be mouse-clicks or menu items—whatever suits your program.

You should also get your employer (if you work as a programmer) or your school, if any, to sign a "copyright disclaimer" for the program, if necessary. Here is a sample; alter the names:

```
Yoyodyne, Inc., hereby disclaims all copyright
interest in the program `Gnomovision'
(which makes passes at compilers) written
by James Hacker.

signature of Ty Coon, 1 April 1989
Ty Coon, President of Vice
```

This General Public License does not permit incorporating your program into proprietary programs. If your program is a subroutine library, you may consider it more useful to permit linking proprietary applications with the library. If this is what you want to do, use the GNU Lesser General Public License instead of this License.

Example Use

This section is *not* part of the GPL. Here we show the copyright comment from the GNU env program:

```
/* env - run a program in a modified environment
   Copyright (C) 1986, 1991-2002 Free Software Foundation, Inc.

   This program is free software; you can redistribute it and/or modify
   it under the terms of the GNU General Public License as published by
   the Free Software Foundation; either version 2, or (at your option)
   any later version.

   This program is distributed in the hope that it will be useful,
```

```
but WITHOUT ANY WARRANTY; without even the implied warranty of
MERCHANTABILITY or FITNESS FOR A PARTICULAR PURPOSE.  See the
GNU General Public License for more details.

You should have received a copy of the GNU General Public License
along with this program; if not, write to the Free Software Foundation,
Inc., 59 Temple Place - Suite 330, Boston, MA 02111-1307, USA.  */
```

This is typical usage. It contains the following, essentially boilerplate items:

- A one-line comment naming and describing the program. In a larger program, it would name and describe the purpose of the file within the proram.

- A copyright statement.

- Two paragraphs of explanation and disclaimer.

- Where to get a copy of the GPL.

Index

Symbols

- (dash)
  as filename, 85, 97, 476, 478
  in `nl_langinfo()`, 506
  in options, 24–25, 28, 34
  in permissions, 5, 139
  in regular expressions, 493
-- (dash-dash)
  in long options, 27
  as special argument, 26
`_()` macro, **512–513**, 516, 518, 527
, (comma)
  as decimal point, 496
  in option arguments, 26
; (semicolon)
  in `getopt_long()`, 37
  in `nl_langinfo()`, 504
: (colon)
  in `getopt()`, 31–33
  in `nl_langinfo()`, 504
  in `optstring`, 30
  in `PATH` variable, 296
  in regular expressions, 493, 524–525
? (question mark), in `getopt()`, 31–33
/ (forward slash), as root directory, 10, 162, 229–231, 276
. (dot)
  as current working directory, 10, 125, 130, 132, 136, 162, 208, 463, 515
  as decimal point, 489, 496
  in filenames, 463
  in format specifiers, 500
  in `nl_langinfo()`, 506
  in regular expressions, 473
. . (dot-dot), parent directory, 125, 130, 132, 136, 162, 208, 277, 463
  in the root of a mounted filesystem, 229
^ (hat), in regular expressions, 473–474

' (single quote), in format specifiers, 500–502, 516
() (parentheses), in regular expressions, 474–475
[] (square brackets), in regular expressions, 475, 493
{} (braces), in regular expressions, 475
$ (dollar sign)
  as currency sign, 488, 496, 499
  in format specifiers, 514–515
  as prompt, xxvi
  in regular expressions, 473–474
\ (backslash), for continuation lines, 68, 71
(hash)
  as comment specifier, 238
  in format specifiers, 500
  as prompt, 236
#!, in scripts, 8, 294
% (per cent sign), in format specifiers, 499
+ (plus sign)
  in format specifiers, 499
  in `nl_langinfo()`, 506
= (equal sign), in option arguments, 27
> (greater-than)
  as operator, 110
  as prompt, xxvi
>> operator, 110
| (vertical bar)
  as flag separator, 586–589
  as pipe construct, 12
|&, in `gawk`, 337

A

`a.out` (Assembler OUTput) format, 8
`abort()`, 363, 373, 429, **445–446**, 481, 572
`accept()`, 364
access time, 143–144, 208, 247
  changing, 157–161, 163
  formatting, 176
  retrieving, 545, 562
`access()`, 364, **410–412**, 425
Acorn Advanced Disc Filing System, 233

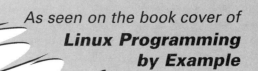